Weizmann at 73 (1947)

THE
LETTERS AND
PAPERS OF
CHAIM
WEIZMANN

The Letters and
Papers of
Chaim Weizmann

ENGLISH EDITION

SERIES A · LETTERS

VOLUME I
Summer 1885 – 29 October 1902

Edited by
LEONARD STEIN
in collaboration with
GEDALIA YOGEV

LONDON
OXFORD UNIVERSITY PRESS
1968

Oxford University Press, Ely House, London W.1

GLASGOW NEW YORK TORONTO MELBOURNE WELLINGTON
CAPE TOWN SALISBURY IBADAN NAIROBI LUSAKA ADDIS ABABA
BOMBAY CALCUTTA MADRAS KARACHI LAHORE DACCA
KUALA LUMPUR HONG KONG TOKYO

PRINTED IN GREAT BRITAIN

CONTENTS

THE LETTERS AND PAPERS OF CHAIM WEIZMANN

General Foreword by Meyer Weisgal	ix
General Introduction	xix
Appendices to General Introduction	
I Note on transliteration of Russian	xxx
II The Zionist Organization and associated institutions	xxxi
III Chaim Weizmann—concise table of dates	xxxvi
IV Acknowledgements	xxxviii

SERIES A. LETTERS

VOLUME I

Summer 1885—29 October 1902

List of letters	3
List of illustrations	11
Introduction by Leonard Stein	13
Letters	33
Biographical Index	408
Index	429

GENERAL FOREWORD

THE Weizmann Archives in their present form were inaugurated at Rehovoth in 1950 under Dr. Weizmann's direct inspiration. The undertaking grew out of a letter which he wrote to me on 20 February 1949 from Weizmann House, his Rehovoth home, in the following terms:

Dear Meyer,

Now that 'Trial and Error' is published and is in process of being translated into 'shivim leshonot',[1] I have been thinking about the many unpublished documents and letters of the past forty years and more that might be of some public interest. These letters and documents are scattered all over the world and in many hands. The main sources, however, are London, Jerusalem, Rehovot and New York. I should very much like to see them collected in one place and prepared for proper editing and publication. Would you be willing to undertake this task? I know it is quite a job and will involve a great deal of collaboration and probably several years of work.

I cannot think of anyone other than yourself to whom I would entrust this work with the feeling that it will be done with responsibility and fidelity. Will you undertake it? If so, let this be your authority to begin gathering the material and to approach any and all persons and organisations in whose possession these letters and documents may be.

I shall appreciate greatly if you will let me know what your views are and how you propose to proceed in the matter.

Affectionately,
Chaim Weizmann.

Although I had then no conception of the scope and size of the difficulties ahead nor of the time the project would necessarily take, I accepted the task willingly and began to organize the initial procedures. It will be seen from what follows how much preliminary work had to be done before the assembling of the material and its orderly arrangement had been completed and a start could be made with preparing it for publication. The editing of some 15,000 letters, with all the laborious research that this involves, must of necessity be a lengthy process, no matter how diligently pursued, but the complete set of volumes will, I believe, present an impressive picture of one man's endeavour for the regeneration of his people.

[1] Hebrew: 'seventy tongues'.

Seen from that standpoint, the Weizmann Papers are unique in contemporary Jewish history.

It was not until 1950 that the building up of the Archives on their present scale was taken in hand, but their beginnings date back to the time, very early in Dr. Weizmann's career, when he started systematically to accumulate documentary material relating to or connected with his Zionist activities. His copies of some outgoing letters written between November 1902 and February 1904 and some fragments of his incoming correspondence are all that have survived from his files for the years up to 1913, but for the years from 1914 onwards those responsible for the organization of the Archives had as their starting-point a mass of material from his personal and office records on a scale reflecting the contrast between the comparatively restricted activities of his earlier years and their vastly extended range from the time when he assumed the responsibilities of leadership. These collections formed the basis of the Weizmann Archives, to be supplemented, as time went on, by extensive acquisitions from other sources, including a number of original letters presented to the Archives by the recipients or their successors.

Long before the Archives as they now exist began to take shape Dr. Weizmann was thinking about the preservation of the records of his life and work. In June 1940, when England was awaiting a German attempt at invasion, he addressed the following memorandum to his friends, Arthur Lourie, (the late Sir) Lewis Namier, (the late) Moshe Shertok (Sharett), and Leonard Stein:

In case I do not survive the present emergency, I would ask of my friends who do to try and collect the material regarding my forty years' work. The material is to be found partly in Canada[1] and partly in Palestine, and on that basis, as well as on the attached note,[2] I think it might be possible to produce a connected record. I am sending copies of this note to the following people, and trust that some or all of them may be able to meet when peace is ultimately achieved.

Chaim Weizmann.

The material which Dr. Weizmann had in mind covered a broad area and was spread over a variety of sources. There were the files of the Geneva and Manchester periods up to the end of 1915 and the considerable volume of correspondence after he and Mrs. Weizmann took up residence in London in the middle of the First

---

[1] Some Zionist records had early in the war been sent for safe-keeping to Canada.
[2] The note referred to the contents of the files sent to Canada.

World War. It was from that time onwards that Zionist political activity grew in extent as efforts became more intensive to secure a declaration in favour of a Jewish National Home in Palestine from the British Government. This and each succeeding chapter of Zionist history up to 1940 had contributed its quota to the material referred to in Dr. Weizmann's memorandum. To this were to be added, after 1940, many important papers belonging to the twelve years which still remained to him.

During this period of half a century he wrote many thousands of letters (a large number of them in his own hand) in Hebrew, Yiddish, Russian, German, English, and French. Not only could he express himself freely in each of these languages but he was widely read in all of them. His familiarity with so many diverse literatures, to which was added a more than superficial interest in the arts, especially in music, helped to make him the humanist of wide sympathies and cultivated tastes that he can be seen to be in the letters, and most clearly in those of his later years.

In addition to official correspondence and formal documents of the nature of State Papers, the hitherto unpublished material comprised in the Archives includes some thousands of private letters in which Dr. Weizmann unburdens himself without inhibitions to his intimates. Of these an outstanding example is provided by the group of some 1,250 letters—the largest number addressed to one person—written to his wife, who faithfully preserved them, from the time of their first meeting in 1900 until their marriage in 1906, and thereafter up to 1940, when the flow of correspondence ceased because thenceforth she was constantly by his side and was his inseparable companion in his world-wide travels on Zionist missions. Many of these letters deal with purely personal matters, but, looked at as a whole, they turn out to be a lively running commentary on men and affairs—the evolving history of their times. They are replete with vivid detail not to be found in the official reports of the Congresses, conferences, and other meetings in which Dr. Weizmann took part and provide illuminating foot-notes to the formal records of his public activities.

His correspondence, whether public or private, does not tell the full story of his patient diplomacy in the service of the Zionist cause. The two thousand interviews which, as he told a Zionist meeting in 1919, helped to pave the way to the Balfour Declaration were only a part—though doubtless the most important and rewarding part—of his innumerable conversations with Ministers, high officials, and other influential persons over a period of some forty years. Of most of these no formal record can be traced, but of some of them a faint reflection, if no more, can be found in notes made at the time by Dr. Weizmann or on his behalf and preserved in the Archives. Though these cannot convey the full flavour of what passed on these occasions, they help in some measure to fill the gap.

An important stage in the systematic collection and arrangement of the Weizmann papers was reached in 1930, when Dr. Weizmann first began to consider writing his memoirs. He undertook a careful examination of the papers then at his disposal, annotating them and assigning dates to undated letters. He made arrangements for the collection of material which he considered to be needed to complete the picture, and about the same time he began to write his own autobiographical notes.

In the summer of 1931, after his relinquishment of the presidency of the World Zionist Organization as a result of an adverse vote at the Seventeenth Zionist Congress, his private papers were separated from the archives of the London Zionist Executive. He remained out of office until again elected President in 1935, but copies of certain official documents still found their way into his files. During this period collections were made of the papers relating to the foundation of the Daniel Sieff Research Institute at Rehovoth, of material accumulated by Dr. Weizmann during his visits to Palestine, and of much of his correspondence relating to the rescue and rehabilitation of German Jewry after Hitler's rise to power. A little later Dr. Josef Cohn, having been entrusted with the assembling of material for the autobiography, made a careful search of the Central Zionist Archives, which had in 1933 been removed from Berlin to Jerusalem, with a view to completing the collection of papers concerning the initial steps towards the establishment of a University in Jerusalem (1913–14), the Balfour Declaration (1914–17), the early activities in Palestine of the Zionist Commission (1918), and the Paris Peace Conference (1919).

Further additions to the Weizmann papers in 1935–7 included material relating to the presentation of the Zionist case before the Royal Commission on Palestine appointed in 1936. A collection was made of Dr. Weizmann's speeches and writings up to 1937. From 1937 onwards he deposited in the Archives the correspondence conducted by him from his new home at Rehovoth and from his office at the Daniel Sieff Research Institute.

In 1937 that part of the material collected by or on behalf of Dr. Weizmann which consisted of papers of the Geneva, Manchester, London, and Rehovoth periods up to 1935 was moved to the basement of the house he had had built for him at Rehovoth. Papers which had in 1940 been sent for safe-keeping to Canada were returned to London at the end of the war and from there brought to Palestine and added to the collection at Weizmann House. The Archives were further enriched by large numbers of important documents collected or brought into existence in London, New York, and Jerusalem during the war years.

Then came the final period of Dr. Weizmann's life, when he served as President of the Israel Provisional State Council in 1948–9 and as President of the State of Israel in 1949–52. More papers—many of them of historical importance—were gathered in the President's bureau at Hakirya (Tel Aviv), then the seat of the Israel Government, and at his home in Rehovoth.

Early in 1950 Mr. Boris Guriel was appointed Curator of the Weizmann Archives, at that time still housed in the basement of Dr. Weizmann's Rehovoth home. He had the benefit of Dr. Weizmann's personal guidance in the arrangement of the papers then comprised in the collection and was able to turn to him for explanations of doubtful points or obscure allusions, especially as to matters relating to his earlier years. Drawing on their personal recollections, Dr. Weizmann during his lifetime and, both then and later, Mrs. Weizmann were able to provide important information not available from any other source, thus materially facilitating the task of those who were to become responsible for preparing the papers for publication.

After Dr. Weizmann's death in November 1952 the Government of Israel and the Jewish Agency established Yad Chaim Weizmann (the Chaim Weizmann National Memorial), with myself as Chairman, and the Weizmann Archives became part of its statutory responsibilities. In 1957 Mrs. Weizmann, to whom the ownership of the Weizmann papers had passed on her husband's death, formally transferred them to Yad Chaim Weizmann, with the stipulation that any dealings with the papers should be subject to the approval of a Board of Trustees consisting of (the late) Mrs. Weizmann, Sir Isaiah Berlin, (the late) Dr. Josef Blumenfeld,

Mr. Guriel, Mr. Abraham Levin, (the late) Lord Nathan, and myself. Mr. Yigal Allon and Lord (then Mr. Israel) Sieff were appointed, with Mrs. Weizmann's approval, to fill the vacancies caused by the death of Dr. Blumenfeld and of Lord Nathan. In April 1967, after the death of Mrs. Weizmann, I appointed Mr. Julian Meltzer, with the approval of the other Trustees, as the seventh member of the Board.

In October 1958, thanks to the generosity of Mr. and Mrs. Abraham Wix, of London, the Archives were transferred to their present home as part of the Central Library in the grounds of the Weizmann Institute of Science at Rehovoth.

The papers now comprised in the Archives consist partly of original documents, partly of photostatic copies of originals retained by their recipients or forming part of other archives, and partly of Dr. Weizmann's own copies of outgoing letters or other documents emanating from him of which the originals have not been traced. Also included in the Archives are collections of photographs, press cuttings, diaries and other biographical material, and of Dr. Weizmann's scientific lectures, writings, and patents. With the help of an elaborate card-index system any particular document in the Archives can be promptly identified and produced for inspection.

Recognizing that the time had come for the editorial work to be taken in hand, I proceeded in 1957 to confer with leading scholars and friends of the late President in England and Israel, notably Sir Isaiah Berlin, Mr. Leonard Stein, and the late Sir Lewis Namier and Sir Charles Webster, and organized an Editorial Board which came into being in the spring of 1957. Its members consisted, in addition to myself, of Mrs. Weizmann, Sir Isaiah Berlin, Mr. Aubrey Eban, Mr. Eliahu Elath, Dr. Nahum Goldmann, Mr. Boris Guriel, Mr. Berl Locker, Mr. Julian Meltzer, Sir Lewis Namier, Mr. Maurice Samuel, Mr. Zalman Shazar (now President of Israel), Mr. Leonard Stein, and Professor Yigael Yadin. Professors Jacob Katz, Joshua Prawer, J. L. Talmon, and Nathan Rotenstreich, all of the Hebrew University of Jerusalem, and Lord Sieff were appointed later. I became Chairman of the Editorial Board and General Editor of the Weizmann Papers.

The first meeting of the Editorial Board was held in Rehovoth, under my chairmanship, on 31 March 1958. Those present were Mrs. Weizmann, Sir Isaiah Berlin, Mr. Guriel, Mr. Meltzer, Sir

Lewis Namier, Mr. Shazar, and Professor Yadin, together with Dr. Alexander Bein, Mr. Joseph Brainin, Professor Ritchie Calder, Dr. Georg Herlitz, Mr. Samuel Shihor, Professor Talmon, Dr. Mayir Verete, and Mr. David Wahl as guests. It was decided that, subject to the general supervision of the Editorial Board, the papers should be prepared for publication under the direction of a small committee (to be known as 'the Implementation Committee') consisting of Sir Isaiah Berlin, Mr. Leonard Stein, Sir Lewis Namier, and Sir Charles Webster. Dr. Mayir Verete was appointed Editor. His appointment terminated in the spring of 1960.

In June 1961 the London Implementation Committee was replaced, at its own suggestion, by an Editorial Committee in Israel consisting of Professors Katz, Prawer, Rotenstreich, and Talmon. The Editorial Committee met informally at Rehovoth on 19 October 1961 for a preliminary exchange of views. This was followed by a formal meeting in the spring of 1962, when a point had been reached at which the Committee felt it possible to frame a reasonably realistic programme of work, though without seeking to prescribe a rigid time-table for a project which, involving as it did the editing of some thousands of letters, must of necessity extend over a considerable period of years.

In the interval between the two meetings, Dr. Gedalia Yogev, who had been working on the papers after the termination of Dr. Verete's appointment in 1960, was at the end of 1961 appointed Research Editor. In March 1963 Mr. Leonard Stein accepted membership of the Editorial Committee and agreed to serve as Consulting Editor. The Editorial Committee has met regularly, and an important conference to review current progress was held in the summer of 1963, when Mr. Stein spent some time in Rehovoth and undertook, at the request of the Committee, to be responsible for certain volumes of the English edition.

In addition to Dr. Yogev as Research Editor, the research staff consisted of Miss Dvorah Barzilay, Mr. Evyatar Friesel, Miss Shifra Kolatt, Dr. Moshe Mishkinsky, Mr. Yaakov Rau, and Mr. Joseph Schatzmiller. In view of the growing pressure of administrative matters, and in order to improve the organization and co-ordination of the editorial work, I appointed Mr. Julian Meltzer to be the Managing Editor, one of his functions being to assist in the preparation and publication of the English edition.

To sum up, the activities of the Weizmann Archives may be grouped into time-divisions as follows:

Organization and Preparatory Work   1950–8
Initial Research   1958–62
Research and Editing for Volume I   1962–6

It is with deep regret that I have to record the death, on 24 September 1966, of Mrs. Weizmann, who had from the inception of the Archives been a never-failing support to those responsible for the management and editing of the Weizmann Papers. She was always at their disposal, and from her personal recollection of many of the events touched upon in the letters she was able to give them invaluable assistance in closing gaps and clearing up obscurities.

I gratefully acknowledge the devoted efforts of others who have been associated with the Weizmann Archives from the beginning or from a later stage.

Words would be insufficient to record my debt to Sir Isaiah Berlin and Mr. Leonard Stein. Mr. Stein, in particular, is discharging a key function in the whole undertaking. I have been fortunate in being able to turn for guidance and advice to the distinguished scholars who, as members of the Editorial Committee, have been available at every stage for consultation. To Mr. Joseph Brainin, of New York, I am grateful for his rôle in supervising the collection of Weizmann material in the United States of America, and to Mr. Julian Meltzer for his continual assistance and service at my side.

All those associated with Dr. Yogev in preparing the Weizmann Papers for publication have benefited greatly by the skill and devotion with which he has performed his exacting task. Mr. Guriel, the Curator of the Archives from 1950 to his retirement in the summer of 1966, enjoys the distinction of being the chronicler of the Weizmann family in all its ramifications and has an encyclopaedic knowledge of Dr. Weizmann's life and work. I should like to express my warm appreciation of his most valuable services, together with those of the Assistant Curator, Mrs. Louisa Calef.

Thanks are also due to the members, named above, of Dr. Yogev's research team, to the principal members of the secretarial staff at the Jerusalem Office of the Weizmann Archives, Mrs. Ruth Adler, Mrs. Hanna Avihai, and Miss Shlomit Harburger, and also, for their work in connexion with the English edition, to Miss Doris

May and Mr. S. J. Goldsmith. Nothing could have been achieved without the whole-hearted co-operation of the translators and linguistic experts, Dr. Georgette Donchin, Miss Bernadette Folliot, and Dr. Geoffrey Butler, whose indispensable contribution is gratefully recognized.

Generous assistance in financing the project has been received from various foundations and bequests as well as from the Government of Israel and the Jewish Agency, which have provided part of the budgetary income of Yad Chaim Weizmann. The Weizmann Archives have benefited greatly by valuable gifts of documentary material from many quarters, and notably from the Central Zionist Archives in Jerusalem. In this connexion a special tribute is due to Dr. Georg Herlitz and Dr. Alexander Bein, and likewise to Dr. Michael Heymann, who has most kindly allowed his special knowledge to be freely drawn upon. The numerous correspondents who have so readily responded to enquiries addressed to them have provided valuable material for the annotation of the Weizmann Papers. To all of these I offer my most sincere thanks. To many other institutions and individuals throughout the world my colleagues and I are deeply indebted for their co-operation. A complete list will be found later in this volume at the end of the General Introduction.

It is my earnest hope that the years immediately ahead will be a period of fruitful production, and that a complete collection of the Weizmann Papers may, as early as the nature and scale of the project permit, become available as a guide for scholars, students, and the general public who seek an understanding of the mainsprings and inner significance of contemporary Zionist and general Jewish history.

MEYER W. WEISGAL

Rehovoth, Israel
April 1967

GENERAL INTRODUCTION

THE purpose of the work commencing with this volume is to make available, in Hebrew and English, a comprehensive collection, with explanatory notes, of the letters and papers, speeches and writings, other than scientific writings, of Chaim Weizmann. The exclusion of his scientific writings does not rule out the possibility of their being separately published at some future time.

It is proposed to divide the work into two distinct series of volumes—Series A, letters, including communications which, though not strictly letters, can conveniently be classified under that head, and Series B, papers not within the category of letters, speeches, and writings. The speeches to be published in Series B will, with a few possible exceptions, be limited to those of which the full text is available from a reliable source; speeches of which there are only condensed press reports will not normally be included.

In preparing the material for publication priority will be given to the letters, so that there will usually be some delay before the period covered by a volume in Series A is reached in Series B. The notes to the letters will include summaries of any relevant speeches or documentary material due to be published in full in Series B but not yet available in that Series.

The introductory explanations which follow relate primarily to Series A, though they may in part be relevant also to Series B.

I. *Contents of Series A*

For the purposes of Series A, a letter signed by Weizmann will be treated as his whether drafted by him or not, and, in the case of a handwritten letter, even though only the signature is his, the text being in another hand. This is subject to the exception that it is not proposed to include certain letters written by another person on blank sheets signed by Weizmann in advance and dispatched without having been seen by him. A letter of which only a press copy or carbon copy has survived will be included if, in the case of a press copy, the signature is Weizmann's, and, in the case of a carbon copy, it is clear beyond reasonable doubt that the top copy was signed by him. It is recognized that there can be no absolute certainty that a carbon copy is an exact reproduction of the letter actually sent. Where both the top copy and the carbon of a typed letter have been preserved, there are a number of cases in which a hand-written postscript has been added by Weizmann to the top copy without being carried on to the carbon.

Taking together letters of which the originals have been found and those which have survived only in press copies or carbon copies, the total number of Weizmann letters known to be in existence and, with the exception about to be mentioned, available for publication is approximately 23,000.

The exception just referred to consists of a collection of some 230 letters, belonging mainly to the years 1897–1902, from Weizmann to his first fiancée, Sophia Getzova. These are under the control of a private person (not connected with the Weizmann family) resident in the United States. Efforts to make them available for publication having failed, they will have to be omitted. In number they are relatively insignificant, but they would have helped to fill some of the gaps which will be perceptible to the reader in the letters belonging to the period, ending in October 1902, to be covered by Volume I. Other gaps in that volume are explained by the disappearance of all the letters which Weizmann must certainly have written home to members of his family while at school in Pinsk (1885–92) and during his student days in Germany and Switzerland (1892–8). Certain deficiencies in some others of the earlier volumes reflect the loss of nearly the whole of Weizmann's private papers, including any copies he may have kept of his outgoing correspondence, for the period of almost nine years from his arrival in England in July 1904 to March 1913. Even after March 1913, though the gaps are less serious, it still remains obvious that the collection is incomplete. Not all the losses are necessarily irretrievable. Experience has shown that the Weizmann Archives may still expect to hear from time to time of fresh discoveries. Any letters brought to light too late for inclusion in the volume to which they properly belong will be published in a later volume.

Of the Weizmann letters available for publication a considerable number will be omitted from Series A for one or other of the following reasons:

(i) It is not proposed to include letters concerned solely with technical matters relating to Weizmann's scientific interests, with the possible exception of a group of letters belonging to the period of the First World War and relating to his scientific work for the British Government.

(ii) Where there are two or more letters to different persons in identical terms, or with only trifling verbal variations, the letter to one only of these persons will be published in full, with a note giving the name of each other recipient of a similar letter and the date on which it was sent to him.

(iii) Letters of a merely routine or formal character, such as acknowledgements of congratulations or the like, will normally be omitted.

(iv) The same applies to letters of a trivial nature, such as instructions to a secretary to book a seat on a train or to lay in a stock of stationery.

This will result in the letters to be included in Series A being reduced in number to some 15,000. They will be published in strict chronological order.

The Weizmann Archives possess photostats of nearly the whole of the letters to be published in Series A, but with some notable exceptions, including in particular Weizmann's letters to his wife, they do not possess the originals. Certain letters of which the originals have been lost have survived in press or carbon copies, and in these cases those copies are in the possession of the Archives. The heading to each letter will show where the original, or, as the case may be, the press or carbon copy, is to be found—see below, under III.

With the permission of the Weizmann Archives, representing Yad Chaim Weizmann as copyright owner, certain Weizmann letters, or extracts from them, have been quoted by various writers, but these constitute only a negligible proportion of those to be included in Series A, which will consist almost entirely of letters hitherto unpublished.

ii. *Translations*

General Observations. The originals of the letters to be published in Series A are, up to about 1914, mainly in Russian or German, and thereafter in Russian, German, or English. Other languages occasionally used are Hebrew, Yiddish, and French.

For the purposes of this work, all the letters have had to be translated either into Hebrew or into English and the majority of them into both. The reader will be informed in every case of the language of the original.

The photostats referred to above under I will be available at the Weizmann Archives for comparison with the translations. Should it be desired to inspect the originals, the headings to the letters will show where these are to be found. With a view to making the originals more readily accessible to scholars, consideration will be given to the possibility of arranging for complete sets of microfilms to be deposited at a limited number of Central Libraries in various parts of the world.

The translations will in every case represent the unexpurgated text of the original, subject to the remote contingency of its being thought necessary to expunge words which might be considered defamatory of, or which would cause distress to, some person living at the date of publication. No such case is foreseen, but should any such omission be unavoidable, it will be indicated thus: [(number) words omitted].

The principle on which the translations have been made is that in a work of this type accuracy must be the first consideration. The translators have, therefore, adhered as closely as possible to the original, even though this means that their renderings do not always read as smoothly as they could have been made to do by resort to paraphrases. In exceptional cases in which a literal translation would clearly not do justice to the original some latitude has been thought permissible, the literal meaning of the expression being explained in a footnote.

As regards the Russian letters, it must be borne in mind that Weizmann's native language was not Russian but Yiddish. The well-known difficulties attending translations from the Russian are all the greater where, as sometimes happens in Weizmann's earlier letters in that language, there are passages reading somewhat awkwardly even in the original.

Punctuation. It has not been thought obligatory to adhere rigidly to Weizmann's punctuation where, in the translated version of a letter, this would be confusing or stylistically unacceptable.

Transliteration of Russian words. Russian words, including proper names, have, in the English edition, been transliterated in accordance with the principles set out below in Appendix I, except where the existence of a well-established English equivalent would make their application pedantic.

In the Hebrew edition transliteration will be effected in accordance with the principles set out in the corresponding part of the General Introduction to that edition.

'Foreign' words and phrases. Weizmann's Russian letters are often liberally interspersed with Hebrew, Yiddish, German, or other 'foreign' words or phrases. The same applies, *mutatis mutandis*, though in a smaller degree, to his letters in other languages.

In order to preserve, as far as possible, the flavour of the original, 'foreign' expressions, other than those written in cyrillic characters, will be reproduced in the translations exactly as they appear in the originals. Any necessary explanations will be provided in footnotes. Though for many readers notes on German words or phrases will be unnecessary, these have usually been provided, but it has been assumed that in the English edition notes on familiar French expressions would be superfluous. Hebrew and Yiddish expressions will be reproduced as written, whether they are or are not in conformity with present-day usage.

III. *Description of documents and guides to location*

The symbols and abbreviations set out below, to appear immediately under the heading to each letter, will be used in Series A to indicate, in the undermentioned order:

(1) For documents other than letters strictly so-called, the nature of the document (postcard, visiting-card,[1] telegram).

(2) The mode of writing employed (handwritten, handwritten by amanuensis, typed).

(3) The location, if known, of the original. Where the undermentioned symbols are not applicable, the location, if known, of the original will be specified.

[1] Writing in small script on both sides of a fairly large visiting-card, Weizmann succeeded in packing surprisingly long communications into such cards.

(4) Where the location of the original is unknown, the nature (e.g. press copy or carbon copy) and location of the best available text.

As already stated, the Weizmann Archives have an almost complete set of photostats, and, in the absence of an indication to the contrary, it can be assumed that a photostat of each document is in the possession of the Archives.

The symbols and abbreviations to be used are as follows:

Pcd.   = Postcard
T.   = Telegram
Vcd.   = Visiting-card[1]

H.W.   = Handwritten
H.W.A. = Handwritten by amanuensis
Typ.   = Typed

C.C.   = Carbon copy
P.C.   = Press copy
Ph.   = Photostat

C.Z.A.   = The Central Zionist Archives, Jerusalem
N.L.   = The Jewish National and University Library, Jerusalem
U.C.L.   = University College Library, London
W.A.   = The Weizmann Archives, Rehovoth, Israel
Y.I.V.O. = The Yivo Institute for Jewish Research, New York

Where the information thus provided needs to be expanded or explained this will be done in a head-note.

IV. *Ascription of Dates and Places of Origin*

The translated text of every letter bearing a date will include a reproduction of the date as it appears in the original. The heading to each letter will show the date editorially ascribed to it. Where, as will sometimes happen, this is not identical with Weizmann's dating, or where the letter is undated, the following symbols or abbreviations will be used:

Pmk.   = Postmark
[ ]   = Date established beyond reasonable doubt
[?]   = Conjectural date
*   = N.S. (New Style, i.e. Gregorian) date substituted for O.S. (Old Style, i.e. Julian) date.

---

[1] See p. xxiii.

The last point calls for some explanation. The Julian calendar in use in Russia up to February 1918 ran, until 12 March 1900 (N.S.) twelve days, and thereafter thirteen days, behind the Gregorian calendar. Thus, for example, 31 December in the Gregorian calendar would be 19 December, or, after the change in 1900, 18 December, in the Julian calendar. All Weizmann's letters from Russia were written while the Julian calendar was in force, and it has been assumed, save in any exceptional case in which there is clear evidence to the contrary, that Weizmann's dates are Julian (O.S.) dates. The substitution, in the headings, of the corresponding N.S. dates has been thought necessary in order to avoid confusion in the chronological order of the letters.

Except where it is indicated by an asterisk that a N.S. has been substituted for an O.S. date, the reasons for the editorial dating of a letter, where this departs from Weizmann's dating, or where the letter is undated, will be explained in a head-note.

Where a letter from Russia mentioned in a note bears one date only, being a date which can be assumed to be an O.S. date, the corresponding N.S. date will be indicated thus: 'A to B, 8 (21) Nov. 1902'.

The heading to each letter will include the place of origin. Where this is not mentioned in Weizmann's dating, it will be enclosed in square brackets—[ ]—if beyond reasonable doubt and, if conjectural, in square brackets preceded by a question-mark—[?]. The heading will also include the location of the addressee where, as will usually be the case, this is not in doubt, whether or not specifically mentioned in the letter.

v. *Omissions, Mutilations, Illegible Words*

Words accidentally omitted, incomplete or illegible words, mutilated sheets, blurred or faded press copies or carbon copies, and contractions or abbreviations will be dealt with as follows:

(1) Where there is considered to be no reasonable doubt as to how the gap should be filled or the contraction or abbreviation expanded, the missing words or parts of words will be supplied in square brackets—[ ].

(2) Where there is considered to be room for a conjectural insertion, this will be denoted by square brackets preceded by a question-mark—[?].

(3) In all other cases, a lacuna will be represented by a series of dashes in square brackets—[- - - - -]—related in length to the presumed number of missing words or letters.

Except where there is a mere expansion of a contraction or abbreviation, the cause and extent, or estimated extent, of the gap will be explained in a note.

VI. *Annotation*

Mode of Annotation. The annotation in Series A will in the main take the form of footnotes appended to the texts of the letters and linked to some particular word or sentence.

Where there occur, in quick succession, a number of letters dealing with the same topic, the earliest of them will usually be preceded by an introductory head-note. Head-notes will also be used from time to time to explain the background to a letter or to provide other information concerning the letter as a whole, or to draw attention to the earliest reference to some topic which is thereafter to figure prominently in Weizmann's correspondence.

In addition to head-notes, concise bridge-notes of a narrative character will occasionally be provided where, because of a gap in the letters, it is thought that the reader might otherwise have difficulty in following the course of events.

Guiding Principles. The notes to the letters will aim at dealing as concisely as possible with matters directly relevant to the explanation or interpretation of the letters to which they relate.

Though the notes will usually be concerned with specific questions arising on the letter under notice, the first mention of a particular subject may sometimes be made the occasion for a fuller note than is strictly necessary at that point, where this will help to prepare the reader for later references to the same or a related subject.

In the annotation of the English edition it has been borne in mind that to anyone not versed in Jewish affairs various expressions and allusions may be incomprehensible without explanations which for readers of the Hebrew edition can be assumed to be superfluous. At a later stage of the work the position may be reversed, but in the early volumes, at all events, it will at times be necessary to provide the English edition with notes with which the Hebrew edition can dispense.

Citation of Sources. In determining the scale on which sources should be cited in the notes, the guiding principles will be, first, that, while the indispensable minimum must be provided, there must be no multiplying of citations for the sake of a display of learning, and, secondly, that there must be some sense of proportion. Thus, for example, notes on obscure points of minor importance in early Zionist history will not necessarily contain exhaustive references to the source-material. There will be cases of other types in which a fuller citation of sources will be appropriate and will be provided. In all cases full information about the material assembled by the researchers will be obtainable from their working-notes, which will be preserved in the Weizmann Archives.

Information about persons. The General Index to each volume of Series A will contain the name of every person mentioned in a letter comprised in that volume, together with references to the place or places at which the name appears and, where thought necessary, a brief indication of the context.

Persons are frequently referred to in the letters by forenames or nicknames. A footnote to the earliest letter in which any such forename or nickname is used will explain who is meant, and all such names will appear in the General Index with the appropriate cross-references.

A separate Biographical Index to be included in each volume of Series A will provide concise biographical data, with special reference to matters of Jewish interest, about those persons mentioned for the first time in letters comprised in that volume who can, on a reasonably liberal view, be regarded as part of the *dramatis personae.* Information about any person not considered to be within that category, whether important or unimportant in himself, will be relegated to a footnote, usually at the place where the name first appears.

The Biographical Index will not be cumulative. A name appearing in the Biographical Index to any volume will not, unless there is supplementary information to be added, reappear in the corresponding Index to any later volume. It is hoped, however, that, when Series A is complete, it may be found possible to bring together the contents of each successive Biographical Index in a comprehensive biographical supplement.

The General Index to each volume will provide a guide to the biographical data by means of a bold-type entry under each name directing the reader to the relevant Biographical Index, whether belonging to that or to an earlier volume, or, as the case may require, to the relevant footnote.

It is recognized that, especially as regards the earlier part of the period to be covered by Series A, there are in some cases serious gaps in the biographical data provided. The difficulty of excavating reliable material will be better understood if it is borne in mind that there exist few works on Zionist history based on thoroughgoing research and hardly any authentic biographies of Zionist personalities.

Information about institutions and organizations. Any necessary information about an institution or organization referred to in the letters will, with the exception to be mentioned in the next paragraph, be provided in a footnote—usually at the place at which the name first appears. All such names appearing in any volume of Series A will be included in the General Index to that volume, with an indication, in bold type, of the place, whether in that or in an earlier volume, at which an explanatory footnote will be found.

This is subject to the qualification that the explanation of technical terms in use in the Zionist Movement will be found in the note on the Zionist Organization and associated institutions annexed to this Introduction as Appendix II. Where in any volume of Series A there is a reference to, for example, 'the Actions Committee', 'the Annual Conference', 'the shekel', these expressions will appear in their alphabetical place in the General Index to that volume, followed by a reference to Appendix II to the General Introduction.

Though the expression 'Actions Committee' reads somewhat awkwardly in English, it has been thought best to retain it in the English edition, at least until the point is reached, some considerable time after the establishment of the Zionist Organization, at which 'Executive' (or 'Zionist Executive') and 'General Council' came to be accepted as the English equivalents of 'Engeres Aktions-Komitee' and 'Grosses Aktions-Komitee' respectively.

VII. *Biographical and Chronological Aids*

A full-scale biography of Dr. Weizmann has yet to be written, but for a general view of the biographical background to the Weizmann

Papers the reader may be referred to Weizmann's autobiography, *Trial and Error* (London, 1949), and to *Chaim Weizmann—A Biography by Several Hands* edited by Meyer Weisgal and Joel Carmichael (London, 1962). A condensed biography will be included in the 1951–60 Supplement to the *Dictionary of National Biography*, due to be published in 1969. As regards *Trial and Error*, it should be borne in mind that the material at Weizmann's disposal when he wrote his autobiography was incomplete and that he had to rely to some extent on his memory, with the result that the narrative, illuminating as it is, is not always entirely accurate, especially as to dates.

Since all these works are or will shortly be readily accessible, it is thought that there would be little point in rounding off this Introduction with a biographical sketch. What will, it is believed, be of more practical service to the reader, will be to preface each volume of letters in Series A with an Introduction surveying and analysing its contents, drawing attention to their salient features, and adding such comment and background material as may help to clarify the picture thus presented.

The reader may find it useful to have before him the skeleton table of salient dates printed below as Appendix III. The date of Weizmann's birth cannot be established with certainty, but the date given in Appendix III, 27 November 1874, being that now generally accepted in Israel, will be assumed to be correct for the purposes of any reference, in the page-headings or elsewhere in this work, to Weizmann's age at a given point of time.

VIII. *Additional Abbreviations*

(see also Sections III, IV)

Bein, *Herzl*	= Alex Bein, *Theodor Herzl* (Philadelphia, 1945)
D.N.B.	= *Dictionary of National Biography*
Herzl Diaries	= *The Complete Diaries of Theodor Herzl*, ed. R. Patai (New York and London, 1960)
J.C.	= *The Jewish Chronicle* (London weekly)
T. and E.	= Chaim Weizmann, *Trial and Error* (London, 1949)
'V.W. Memoirs'	= Vera Weizmann, *The Impossible Takes Longer* (London, 1967)

Z.C. Prot.   = Protocol (stenographic report) of Zionist Congress—(I Z.C. Prot. = Protocol of First Zionist Congress)

APPENDIX I

NOTE BY DR. GEORGETTE DONCHIN ON TRANSLITERATION OF RUSSIAN

In latinizing the Cyrillic alphabet, a choice had to be made between two parallel systems of transliteration widely in use today, namely the Czech-style transliteration known as the International system, and the British system. The first of these, fairly popular in the United States, creates certain typographical problems, and its use in Great Britain is strictly confined to linguistics, the British system being invariably preferred in non-linguistic writing. The British system, being the more practical of the two, has been adopted for transliteration purposes in this work.

In its less consistent manifestations, the British method gives way to the pressure of tradition and discriminates in transliteration between certain proper names and the rest of the vocabulary. Moreover, it permits itself certain liberties for the sake of simpler spelling, as for instance the occasional omission of intervocalic *y* and the palatalization mark.

As far as proper names are concerned, it has been necessary to compromise further. In many instances, usage has had to be adhered to. Many of Weizmann's Russian-Jewish friends wrote in several languages, settled outside Russia, and adopted their own methods of spelling their names either in Latin or Hebrew characters. Many of them became internationally known in this form. A case in point is Chaim Weizmann himself, who, according to strict transliteration rules, would have to be rendered as Khaim Veytsman. In particular, an important group of people mentioned in Weizmann's letters either had adopted, voluntarily or under compulsion, German names (this applies especially to Jews living in the Austro-Hungarian Empire), or had Yiddish names which, when written in Latin characters, were spelt as if they were German. In all such cases the rules governing transliteration of Russian names are inapplicable, and the German names, or German equivalents of Yiddish names, have been retained.

Finally, Russian names written in Latin characters are reproduced throughout as given in the original Russian or non-Russian text. Russian names appearing in the letters both in their Latin and Cyrillic form are, therefore, rendered accordingly: in the former case as in the original, and in the latter following the above-mentioned rules of transliteration, but with the qualification that where there are variations in Weizmann's spelling, in cyrillic characters, of the same proper name, a uniform standard transliteration has been adopted throughout.

APPENDIX II

THE ZIONIST ORGANIZATION AND ASSOCIATED INSTITUTIONS

THE purpose of this note is to describe in broad outline, and without going closely into details, the structure and constitutional machinery of the Zionist Organization from its establishment in 1897 to 1929, when it had to adapt itself to the new situation created by the coming into existence of the enlarged Jewish Agency for Palestine. The adjustments then required will be explained when that point is reached. During the period covered by this note various innovations were introduced, but none of outstanding importance except those connected with the emergence within the Movement of organized parties. At the end of this note will be found a brief account of certain institutions closely associated with the Zionist Organization.

1. *The Basle Programme.* Meeting at Basle in August 1897, the First Zionist Congress set up an organization (the name 'Zionist Organization' was not formally adopted until 1899) for the purpose of giving effect to a statement of aims (commonly known as 'The Basle Programme'), which, in the official translation of the original German, reads as follows:

Zionism strives to create for the Jewish people a Home in Palestine secured by public law.

The Congress contemplates the following means to the attainment of this end:

1. The promotion, on suitable lines, of the colonization of Palestine by Jewish agricultural and industrial workers.
2. The organization and binding together of the whole of Jewry by means of appropriate institutions, local and international, in accordance with the laws of each country.
3. The strengthening and fostering of Jewish national sentiment and consciousness.
4. Preparatory steps toward obtaining Government consent, where necessary, to the attainment of the aim of Zionism.

2. *The Shekel.* Membership of the Organization was open to any Jew or Jewess who signified assent to the Basle Programme by paying the shekel—a small annual registration-fee, originally fixed at one German mark or its equivalent in other currencies.

3. *The Zionist Congress.* The supreme governing body of the Organization was the Zionist Congress.

Every adult shekel-payer was entitled to take part in the election of delegates. For electoral purposes, the adult shekel-payers in each country were formed into one or more electoral groups (*Wahlgruppen*) entitled to return delegates in the ratio of one to every 100 voters up to 1903, thereafter, until 1921, one to every 200, and from 1921, one to every 2,500.

In the earlier years of the period under notice, the delegates from each country, known collectively as a *Landsmannschaft*, were accustomed to work together as a group. It was the practice for the various *Landsmannschaften* to meet separately on the eve of a Congress, and, if necessary, while the Congress was in session, with a view to agreeing on a concerted approach to the main questions on the agenda.

More elaborate electoral arrangements than those devised for a Congress in which party politics were unknown came to be needed when adherents of various schools of thought within the Zionist Movement began to organize themselves into parties. The 'Democratic Fraction', founded at the end of 1901, soon flickered out, but before long other parties, better disciplined and more efficiently organized, appeared on the scene—in 1902 the *Mizrahi* (upholders of Orthodox Judaism), and, soon afterwards, the left-wing *Poale Zion* ('Zionist Workers'). To these were subsequently added other compact groups with distinctive ideologies. Competition between rival parties became an accepted feature of the Congress and led to the development of a complicated electoral system designed to ensure that the composition of the Congress should reflect as accurately as possible the relative strength of the parties.

The Congress met annually until 1901, and thereafter biennially until 1913 and, after an interruption during the war years, from 1921 onwards.

The main business of the Congress, in its opening sessions, was normally to receive and discuss the reports of the Smaller Actions Committee or Executive Committee (see below) and of representative leaders in the main centres of Zionist activity, and also, on some occasions, to hear addresses of a more academic nature by invited speakers. After a general debate, the Congress would proceed to set up Political, Organization, Finance and, where thought necessary, other Committees, which, after discussion—usually prolonged—behind closed doors, would eventually produce their recommendations. Special importance was attached to the composition of the *Permanenz Ausschuss* ('Standing Committee'), which, besides acting as a Steering Committee, was responsible for the submission of nominations for office. At its closing plenary sessions the Congress would consider and vote upon resolutions drafted by the various Committees and any proposals put forward by individual delegates. It was at this stage that a final decision had to be reached—more often than not after complicated negotiations behind the scenes—about the composition of the incoming Smaller Actions Committee (Executive) and Greater Actions Committee (General Council), as to which see paras. 5 and 6, below.

4. *The Annual Conference* (JAHRESKONFERENZ). From the time when it was decided at the Fifth Congress in 1901 to substitute biennial for annual Congresses, there was held in each non-Congress year an 'Annual Conference' (sometimes known as 'The Small Congress') consisting of the members of the Smaller and Greater Actions Committees, together

with the holders of certain offices in, or connected with, the Organization. An Annual Conference had only a limited measure of authority and could not exercise the full powers of Congress.

5. *The Greater Actions Committee* (GROSSES AKTIONS-KOMITEE). This body (sometimes referred to simply as 'The Actions Committee', and later represented in English by the name 'General Council') was the authority to which the working Executive, the Smaller Actions Committee, was directly responsible, with an obligation to furnish the members of the G.A.C. with periodical reports and to consult them on all matters of importance. In electing the G.A.C. it was usual for the Congress to provide for the representation of all countries in which there were organized bodies of Zionists, and of all recognized parties within the Movement.

6. *The Smaller Actions Committee* (ENGERES AKTIONS-KOMITEE). Likewise elected by the Congress, the Smaller Actions Committee (in 1921, by a decision of the Twelfth Congress, re-named 'The Executive') constituted a directorate charged with the day-to-day conduct of Zionist affairs and, in practice, taking the lead in the shaping of policy. The 1921 Congress divided the Executive into two sections, assigning some members to London and the remainder to Jerusalem.

7. *The President.* Though until his death in 1904 Herzl was designated by successive Congresses as Chairman of the Smaller Actions Committee, and was, in that capacity, the acknowledged head of the Organization, he was never formally given the title of President. During the period in which David Wolffsohn was Chairman of the S.A.C. in succession to Herzl, the Congress adopted, in 1907, a revised Constitution expressly providing for the election of a President of the Organization *eo nomine* and in 1909 rejected a proposal to delete this provision, but it is not clear that either at the 1907 or the 1909 Congress Wolffsohn was, in fact, formally elected President. After Wolffsohn's retirement from office in 1911, Otto Warburg was elected by the S.A.C. as its Chairman and thus became the *de facto* head of the Organization, but there was no question of his being, or claiming to be, entitled to be described as President. In 1920 the London Zionist Conference conferred the title of President of the Zionist Organization on Weizmann, and in 1921 the Twelfth Congress, having resolved that Congress should have power to elect a President of the Zionist Organization and (as a separate office) a President of the Zionist Executive, exercised that power in favour of Weizmann and Sokolow respectively. During the remainder of the period under notice, ending in 1929, successive Congresses re-elected Weizmann as President of the Organization and Sokolow as President of the Executive.[1]

8. *The Central Office.* A Central Office was maintained by the Organization at the seat of the Smaller Actions Committee—until 1905 in Vienna, thereafter until 1911 in Cologne, and from 1911 in Berlin until the end

---

[1] Thanks are due to Mr. Josef Fraenkel and to Dr. Michael Heymann for their assistance in clarifying the question of the presidency.

of the First World War. In 1920 a Zionist Office which had been opened in London in 1917 became the Central Office of the Organization. In 1921, when the Zionist Executive was divided between London and Jerusalem (see para. 6, above), there was a corresponding division of the work of the Central Office.

9. *Zionist Federations.* Zionist societies in every country in which they existed were normally federated in territorial organizations, each such federation being responsible, through its own elected governing body, for propaganda, fund-raising, and other Zionist activities in the country concerned.

In Russia, where, under the Czarist régime, a full-scale Zionist Federation could not lawfully function on the same lines as elsewhere, the country was divided, for Zionist purposes, into a number of regions, each with a regional leader elected by the local Zionists—usually a member of the Greater Actions Committee. These regional leaders met from time to time for consultation and were, in effect, collectively responsible for the direction of Zionist activities in Russia. Some measure of administrative centralization was secured by the maintenance of a Finance Office at Kiev and, in the early stages, of a 'Correspondence Centre' at Kishinev, replaced in 1901 by an Information Bureau at Simferopol, whose functions were subsequently taken over by a small directorate (*Landeskomitee*) of four members unostentatiously formed in 1903 and reconstituted in 1905 and again in 1906, for the purpose (never, in fact, effectively achieved) of centralizing the direction of Russian Zionist affairs.

After the March Revolution in 1917, an All-Russian Zionist Organization was able to come into the open and to function freely, but only for a few months, the Bolshevik régime being implacably hostile to Zionism, so that before long it became impossible for Zionist activities to be continued in any organized form.

10. *Separate Unions* (SONDERVERBÄNDE). From 1909 onwards a status equivalent to that of the territorial federations mentioned in the preceding paragraph was enjoyed by certain Separate Unions (*Sonderverbände*) consisting of the adherents, wherever resident, of certain recognized parties within the Movement. At the close of the period under notice, ending in 1929, there existed, side by side with the federations and cutting across the territorial organizations represented by them, four such Separate Unions—the *Mizrahi*, the *Poale Zion*, another left-wing party, the *Hitahdut* ('Union'), being an amalgamation of two socialist groups, and (rather anomalously) an organization functioning only in England and having no distinctive ideology, the Order of Ancient Maccabaeans.

Associated Institutions

11. *The Jewish Colonial Trust.* The Jewish Colonial Trust (*Jüdische Kolonialbank*), incorporated as an English company in 1899, was designed to serve as the financial instrument of the Zionist Organization and to

satisfy the need for a legally constituted body corporate capable of accepting the Charter which it was hoped to secure from the Turkish Government. Founders' shares issued to the persons who, at the date of the incorporation of the company, constituted the Smaller Actions Committee, and also to certain of the then members of the Greater Actions Committee, carried an aggregate voting-power equal to the combined voting-power of all other shareholders, thus giving the holders effective ultimate control over the conduct of the company's affairs. The holders of the founders' shares were also entitled to be represented on the Board of Directors by governors entitled to veto any resolution coming before the Board. The exercise of the powers attaching to the founders' shares was controlled by a council (known in German as the *Aufsichtsrat*) consisting of the holders for the time being of the founders' shares, with power to co-opt a certain number of additional members drawn from the Greater Actions Committee. The council set up, in 1899, a small executive committee consisting of members of the Smaller Actions Committee.

A subsidiary of the J.C.T., the Anglo-Palestine Company (later re-named 'The Anglo-Palestine Bank'), designed to carry on banking business in Palestine and Syria, with its head office at Jaffa, was incorporated as an English company in 1903.

12. *The Jewish National Fund*. The object of the Jewish National Fund (*Keren Kayemeth le-Israel*) was to raise by voluntary donations a fund to be used for the acquisition of land in Palestine and Syria, all land so acquired to be held in perpetuity as the property of the Jewish people and to be leased only to Jews. The J.N.F. was incorporated in 1907 as an English company with a membership consisting of the holders of founders' shares in the Jewish Colonial Trust. Though it had its own directorate, its constitution gave a large measure of control to the members for the time being of the Smaller Actions Committee.

13. *The Palestine Foundation Fund*. To meet the needs of the new situation created by the Balfour Declaration, the Palestine Foundation Fund (*Keren Hayesod*), incorporated as an English company in 1921, was established to serve as the principal fund-raising agency of the Zionist Organization for all purposes, except to the extent to which the acquisition and improvement of land remained the responsibility of the Jewish National Fund. The main object of the Foundation Fund, as set out in its Memorandum of Association, was 'to do all such acts and things as shall appear necessary or expedient for the purpose of carrying out the declaration of His Majesty's Government . . . as to the establishment of a Jewish National Home in Palestine'. When plans were being made in 1920–1 for the setting up of the Fund, controversies arose as to its management and as to the principles to govern the use of its resources. The nature of these controversies and the manner in which they were settled will be explained in the notes to the relevant letters when that point is reached.

APPENDIX III

CHAIM WEIZMANN

Concise Table of Dates

1874, 27 Nov.	Born at Motol (White Russia).[1]
1885	Enters secondary school, Pinsk.
1892–9	Student (with about a year's break in 1895–6) at Darmstadt Polytechnic, Charlottenburg (Berlin) Polytechnic, and Swiss University of Fribourg.
1899	Ph.D., Fribourg. Appointed lecturer in chemistry and assistant to Professor of Chemistry, Geneva University.
1901	Takes leading part in organization of Zionist Youth Conference and of Democratic Fraction.
1904	Settles in England. Accepted as research student in Chemical Department of Manchester University (later promoted to research fellow, 1905, and senior lecturer, 1907).
1905	Member of Greater Actions Committee.
1906	Marries Vera Khatzman. Meets Arthur Balfour.
1907	Becomes widely known by impressive intervention at Eighth Zionist Congress.
1910	Becomes naturalized British subject.
1913	Appointed Reader in Biochemistry, Manchester University. Chairman, Standing Committee, Eleventh Zionist Congress.
1914	Meets C. P. Scott and Herbert Samuel.
1915	Meets Lloyd George. Appointed chemical adviser on acetone supplies, Admiralty and Ministry of Munitions.
1916	Director of Admiralty laboratories.
1917	President, English Zionist Federation. First meeting with Mark Sykes. Mission to Gibraltar on behalf of Foreign Office. The Balfour Declaration.
1918	Received by King George V. Heads Zionist Commission to Palestine. Lays foundation stone of Hebrew University of Jerusalem.
1919	Weizmann-Feisal Agreement. Addresses Council of Ten at Paris Peace Conference. Co-opted to Zionist Executive.
1920	Elected President, World Zionist Organization.

---

[1] As to date of birth see General Introduction, Section VII, last paragraph.

1921	First visit to U.S.A.—Conflict with Brandeis Group.
	Contract with Commercial Solvents Corporation (U.S.A.) concerning commercial application of patented inventions opens the way to financial independence.
1925	Present with Balfour at inauguration of Hebrew University.
1929	Opens inaugural session of Council of enlarged Jewish Agency for Palestine and elected President of enlarged Agency.
1931	As sequel to Passfield White Paper (1930), Seventeenth Zionist Congress passes vote of no confidence, signifying that Weizmann no longer acceptable as President.
1931–4	Resumes chemical work.
	Launches Daniel Sieff Research Institute, Rehovoth.
	Chairman of Jewish Agency Central Bureau for Settlement of German Jews.
	Undertakes Zionist Missions to U.S.A. and South Africa.
1935	Re-elected President of World Zionist Organization and of Jewish Agency for Palestine.
1936	Heads representation of Jewish Agency at sittings of Royal Commission on Palestine.
1939	Heads Jewish Agency delegation at St. James's Palace Conference on Palestine.
	At Twenty-first Zionist Congress denounces 1939 Palestine White Paper.
1942	Attends the New York 'Biltmore Conference', at which it is resolved to work for a Jewish Commonwealth in Palestine.
1946	Gives evidence in Jerusalem before Anglo-American Committee of Enquiry.
	Lays corner-stone of Weizmann Institute of Science at Rehovoth.
	As sequel to adoption of resolution implying no confidence, withdraws from Twenty-second Zionist Congress, which leaves office of President vacant.
1947	Gives evidence in Jerusalem before United Nations Special Committee on Palestine, and in New York before United Nations *ad hoc* Committee on Palestine.
1948	While in U.S.A., intervenes with President Truman in interests of effective implementation of partition scheme.
	Advises Zionist leaders in Palestine to proclaim Jewish State.
	Elected President, Israel Provisional Council of State.
1949	Elected and sworn in as President of the State of Israel.
	Presides at formal dedication of Weizmann Institute of Science.
1952, 9 Nov.	Died at Rehovoth.

APPENDIX IV

ACKNOWLEDGEMENTS

The list mentioned in the Foreword of the institutions and individuals whose co-operation it is desired gratefully to acknowledge is as follows:

*Aaronsohn House, Zikhron Yaakov
†*Elhanan Aberson, Geneva
 Mrs. Zahara Aberson, Geneva
 Yaakov David Abramsky, Jerusalem
*Arthur Adler, Liverpool
 A. Aharoni, Tel Aviv
 Shneour Aharonov, Tel Aviv
*Yigal Allon, Ginossar
 David Aloni, Tel Aviv
 Michael Alroi, Binyamina
*Dr. Abraham Alsberg, Jerusalem
*Dr. M. Altbauer, Tel Aviv
 Heinz Altschul, Ennetbaden
†*Leopold Amery, London
*Yehuda Araten, Haifa
*Archives:
  American Jewish, Cincinnati
  Bund, New York
  Central Zionist, Jerusalem
  History of Haganah, Tel Aviv
  Jabotinsky Institute, Tel Aviv
  Jewish Historical General, Jerusalem
  Public Record Office, London
  State of Israel, Jerusalem
  Truman, Independence, Mo., U.S.A.
  Felix Warburg, Cincinnati
  Workers', Tel Aviv
*Sima (Mrs. Chaim) Arlosoroff, Tel Aviv
*M. Arnon, Tel Aviv
 Gregor Aronson, New York
 Dr. Eliyahu Auerbach, Haifa
*Dr. Y. Aviad (Wolfsberg), Jerusalem
*David Ayerst, London

*Richard Baer, Zurich
*Walter Baer, Zurich
*Mrs. Walter Baer, Zurich
 Dr. Marianne Basch, Paris
*Mrs. Bass (Kind), Paris
*Dr. Yehuda Bauer, Jerusalem
 Mrs. Anka Becker, Geneva
*Dr. Alexander Bein, Jerusalem
 Mrs. Leah Ben-Dor, Jerusalem
*Jacob Ben-Dov, Jerusalem

*Ram Ben-Efraim, Tel Aviv
 Dr. Reuven Ben-Shem, B'nei Brak
*Professor Norman Bentwich, London
*Mrs. Rahel Yanait Ben-Zwi, Jerusalem
*Shlomo Ben-Zvi, Rehovoth
*Mrs. D. Berenblum, Rehovoth
 Professor Shmuel Hugo Bergman, Jerusalem
 Professor Ernst D. Bergman, Tel Aviv
 Yitzhak Dov Berkowitz, Tel Aviv
*Sir Isaiah Berlin, Oxford
 Theodore M. Berman, Dallington
 Rabbi Yaakov Berman, Rehovoth
 Miriam Bernstein-Kohan, Tel Aviv
*Bialik House, Tel Aviv
†*Rabbi Biegun, Yifath
*Pierre Bigar, Geneva
 Birkbeck College, London
*Maurice Bisgyer, New York
†*Dr. Benjamin Bloch, Rehovoth
 J. Blum, Nahariya
†*Dr. Josef Blumenfeld, Paris
*Mrs. Rahel Blumenfeld, Paris
†*Dr. Chaim Boger, Tel Aviv
*Lord Boothby, London
*Joseph Brainin, New York
 J. Bramson, Montreuil
*Lazar Braudo, Gan-Binyamin
*Lord Brockway, London
†*Professor Selig Brodetsky, London
*Yaakov Bromberg, Tel Aviv
†*Professor Martin Buber, Jerusalem
*Stanley Burton, Harrogate
*Professor J. R. M. Butler, Cambridge

 Dr. Jean Cahana, Paris
 Moni Calef, Geneva
 Bernard Chapira, Jerusalem
*A. L. Chissick, Herzlia
 D. Cnaani, Merhavia
 Barukh Cohen, Ramat-Gan
*Judge Benjamin V. Cohen, Washington
*Gabriel Cohen, M.K., Jerusalem
†*Israel Cohen, London

* denotes a contributor of documentary material.
† denotes a person who has died before the compilation of this list (April 1968).

*Dr. Josef Cohn, Zurich
*Gaalyahu Cornfeld, Tel Aviv
*Richard Crossman, London

Darmstadt Polytechnikum
*Samuel Davies, Manchester
*Shmuel Dayan, Nahalal
*J. de Leon, Tel Aviv
Michael Deouell, Tel Aviv
Dr. Anna Descoudres, Corcelles
Mrs. Gita Dounie, Haifa
*Mordecai Drapkin, Kiryath-Chaim, Haifa
Emil Dreifuss, Berne
*Michael Dugdale, London
*Helen Dukas, Princeton

*Abba Eban, Jerusalem
*Yoram Efrati, Zichron Yaakov
*Daniel Efron, Jerusalem
†*Professor Albert Einstein, Princeton
Professor Shmuel Eisenstadt, Tel Aviv
*Eliahu Elath, Jerusalem
†*Aaron Eliasberg, Jerusalem
†*Lydia Eliasberg, Jerusalem
†*Yaakov Eliasberg, Jerusalem
*Mrs. Janet Ellison (Lieberman), Kfar Shmaryahu
Nahum Epstein, Haifa
*Peretz Epstein, Jerusalem
*Rose Ettinger, Jerusalem

Dr. Yosef Farber, Petah Tikva
*Zwi Fein, Nahalal
*Abraham Feinberg, New York
†*Dr. Esther Feiwel, London
S. Fischer Verlag, Frankfurt a. M.
Dr. Yosef Fodiman, Tel Aviv
*L. Fordsham, London
*Foreign Ministry, Jerusalem
*Foreign Office, London
†*Professor Abraham Fraenkel, Jerusalem
*Josef Fraenkel, London
*Mrs. Leonie Frank, Tel Aviv
Mrs. Lilly Freidenberg, Tel Aviv
*Shalheveth Freier, Rehovoth
Professor Arthur Freud, Jerusalem
*Fribourg University, Switzerland
*Dr. Isaiah Friedman, London
†*Justice Gad Frumkin, Jerusalem
*Tosca R. Fyvel, London

Abraham Gabay, Merhavia
†*Dr. Nathan M. Gelber, Jerusalem
*Geneva University
Shlomo Gepstein, London

†*Sigmund Gestetner, London
*Gershon Gideoni, Rehovoth
*Abraham Gilboa, Jerusalem
B. C. Gillinson, Leeds
Mrs. Shoshana Ginis, Beer Yaakov
Dr. B. Ginsbourg, Paris
Mark Ginsburg, Tel Aviv
*Dr. Sally Ginsburg, Istanbul
Moshe Glikin, Haifa
*Dr. Nelson Glueck, Cincinnati
*Gnazim Writers' Association, Tel Aviv
†*Rabbi J. K. Goldbloom, London
*Harold Goldenberg, Minneapolis
*Dr. Joseph Goldin, Jerusalem
*Dr. Frieda Goldschmidt, Rehovoth
*Dr. Israel Goldstein, Jerusalem
Moshe Gordon, Jerusalem
Dr. A. Gourvitz, Haifa
*Government Press Office, Jerusalem
*Eliezer Gravitsky, Givat Brenner
*Judge Leopold Greenberg, Johannesburg
Yitzhak Grinbaum, Gan Shmuel
*Paul Guiness, London and Geneva
*Frances Gunther, Jerusalem
*Boris Guriel, Tel Aviv
*M. J. Gutman, Jerusalem

Professor Yitzhak Haber-Schaim, Rehovoth
*Habimah Theatre, Tel Aviv
†*Mordechai Ben-Hillel Hacohen, (estate) Jerusalem
Mrs. Yvonne Halbwachs-Basch, Paris
Professor Hayim Halperin, Tel Aviv
†*Dr. Georg Halpern, Jerusalem
*Mrs. Yehudit Harari, Tel Aviv
*Josef Harel, Tel Aviv
*Jehoshua Harlap, Rehovoth
*Mrs. Alice Ivy Hay (Paterson), Edinburgh
*Mrs. Ethel Hayman, London
*Hebrew University, Jerusalem
*Dr. Esther Hellinger, London
†*Dr. Georg Herlitz, Jerusalem
Mrs. Shlomit Hermoni, Tel Aviv
G. Hermoni, Paris
*Mrs. Benjamin Hertzberg, New York
I. S. Herz, New York
Dr. Max Herzberg, Manchester
*Dr. Jacob Herzog, Jerusalem
Professor G. Heymann, Frankfurt
*Dr. Paul Hirsch, Tel Aviv
*Professor Yehuda Hirschberg, Rehovoth
†M. Hodes
†*Jacob Hodess, Jerusalem
Nahum Hurvitz, Kfar Giladi

*Marie (Mrs. Albert) Hyamson, London

Dr. Gertrude Ickelheimer, Tel Aviv
Mrs. Rahel Israel-Shriro
Rabbi J. Israelstamm, London
*Leo Istorik, London
Dr. I. Itzkovich, Haifa
*Mrs. Leah Itzkovich, Haifa

*Edward Jacobson, Kansas City
*A. Jaffe, Manchester
Benjamin Jaffe, Jerusalem
*Marc Jarblum, Tel Aviv
*Jewish National and University Library, Jerusalem
*Jewish Theological Seminary, New York
*Dr. Ernst Joel, Rehovoth
*Colonel Pierce Joyce, Crowthorne, Berks.

†*Sir Elly Kadoorie, London
*Dr. Helena Kagan, Jerusalem
*Dr. Menachem Kahany, Geneva
*Dr. Walter Kahn, Tel Aviv
*Moshe Kalchheim, Tel Aviv
*Abraham Kamini, Tel Aviv
*Dr. Dvorah Kaplan, Jerusalem
Mrs. Yehudit Katinka-Zweig, Jerusalem
*Dr. Abraham Kaufman, Ramat Gan
Paul Kaufman, Jerusalem
*Yehuda Kaufman (Ibn-Shmuel), Jerusalem
*Dr. Kelly, Jerusalem
*Yigal Kimchi, Tel Aviv
Eliyahu Kino, Ramat Gan
*Eli Kirschner, Tel Aviv
*Ruth (Mrs. Frederick) Kisch, London
Dr. Miriam Kisselova-Smilansky, Tel Aviv
*Dr. Israel Klausner, Jerusalem
†Jacob Klebanoff, Haifa
Dr. Lionel Kochan, Norwich
*Israel Kolatt, Jerusalem
*Dr. M. Kopissarov, Manchester
Dr. Nathan Korn, Jerusalem
*Aba Kovner, Tel Aviv
*Siegfried Kramarsky, New York
Getzel Kressel, Tel Aviv
Yaffa Krinkin, Tel Aviv
†Dr. Yosef Kruk, former address, Jerusalem
*Edith Kruss, Ashkelon

*Neville Laski, London
*Dr. Leo Lauterbach, Jerusalem

Professor David Lavi, Rehovoth
*Professor Samuel Lepkovsky, Berkeley, Cal.
*Moshe Leshem, Jerusalem
†Yaakov Lestschinsky,
Michael Levin, Rehovoth
*Moses Levin, Rehovoth
Mrs. Naomi Levin-Richter, Haifa
Dr. Vera Levin, Tel Aviv
*Harry Levine, Cambridge, Mass.
Isaac Don Levine, Waldorf, Maryland
*Judge Louis Levinthal, Philadelphia
Aryeh Levite, Ain Harod
Dr. Salomea Levite, Tel Aviv
†*Mrs. Chaya Lichtenstein, Tel Aviv
*Ivor Joseph Linton, London
*Berl Locker, Jerusalem
*Arthur Lourie, Jerusalem
*Saul Lourie, Santa Monica, Cal.
Leo Lubin, Tel Aviv
†Michael Naamani Lubin, London
Samuel Lubin, Tel Aviv
Zalman Lundin, Ramat Gan

*James G. Macdonald, New York
Professor Yonathan Magnes, Jerusalem
Itzhak Mamlock, Givatayim
*Nahum Man, Tel Aviv
*'Manchester Guardian', London and Manchester
*Manchester University
*Manchester Zionist Council
*Professor Jacob Marcus, Cincinnati
*Jacob Marcus, Rehovoth
*Dr. A. Margalit, Tel Aviv
*Mrs. Israela Margalith, Tel Aviv
*Lazar Margulies, Montreal
*Estelle Mark, New York
†Lord Marks, London
*Doris May, Lancing, Sussex
Daniel Mayer, Paris
†Dr. Eugen Mayer, Jerusalem
Nachman Mayzel, New York
Moshe Medzini, Jerusalem
†*Colonel Richard Meinertzhagen, London
*Julian Meltzer, Rehovoth
Dr. M. Merlub-Sobel, Haifa
Yisrael Merom, Tel Aviv
Dr. Eugen Messinger, Berne
Dr. Berthold Meyer, Basle
Uriel Meyer, Jerusalem
Mrs. M. Meyerstein, Haifa
*Sarah Gertrude Millin, Johannesburg
*Ministry of Interior, Jerusalem
J. Minor, Vanves, France
*Kibbutz Mishmar Ha-Emek

xl

*Eli Mizrachi, Jerusalem
*Emanuel N. Mohl, Nathanya
Montreux Municipality
Dr. Hedwig Moses, Tel Aviv
*Motele Landsmannschaft, New York
Marius Moutet, Paris

*Dr. Mordecai Nadav, Jerusalem
Dr. A. Naftali, Jerusalem
Mrs. Jeanne Naiditsch-Bienstock, Basle
*Lady Namier, London
†*Sir Lewis Namier, London
M. Namir, Tel Aviv
†*Lord Nathan, London
*Yehuda Nedivi, Tel Aviv
*Kibbutz Negbah
Dr. Ludwig Nelken, Jerusalem
*Dr. Chaim Neufeld, Tel Hashomer
*Rabbi A. A. Newman, Philadelphia
*New York City Council
Dr. Norah Nicholls, London
Dr. Nahum Nir, Ramat Gan
†*M. A. Novomeysky, Jerusalem
Mordekhay Noy, Jerusalem

Yosef Okrainitz, Hadera
Mrs. Sophia Olinsky, Holon
*Dr. Emanuel Olswanger, Jerusalem
†*Professor J. Robert Oppenheimer, Princeton, N.J.

†Dr. Josef Paamoni
*Pierre van Paassen, New York
Zvi (Herman) Parnass, Holon
Isidore David Passov, New York
N. R. Passovsky, Tel Aviv
Yaakov Pevsner, Tel Aviv
Pinhas Pick, Jerusalem
F. Pinczower, Tel Aviv
Theodore Pinkus, Zurich
*W. P. Polack, Tel Aviv
Edward Poznanski, Jerusalem
*President of Israel's Office, Jerusalem
Dr. Emanuel Propper, Jerusalem
*Judge Joseph Proskauer, New York

*Dr. Oscar K. Rabinowicz, New York
Yitzhak Rabinowitch, Jerusalem
*Dr. Ze'ev Rabinowitz, Haifa
Aryeh Rafaeli (Zenzipper), Tel Aviv
*M. Rahav, Rehovoth
†*Professor William Rappard, Geneva
*Eva, Marchioness of Reading, London
*Rehovoth Municipality
Ajzyk Remba, Tel Aviv
*Aharon Remez, Tel Aviv
*Shlomo Reznik, Haifa

*Bernard G. Richards, New York
*S. Richardson, Pretoria
Mrs. Naomi Ritcher-Levin
Yisrael Ritov, Tel Aviv
*Adolph J. Robison, New York
Louis Rosen, Mulhouse
*Pinhas Rosen (Felix Rosenblueth), M.K., Jerusalem
*Dr. A. S. W. Rosenbach, New York
Dr. Leah Rosenberg, Haifa
Bernard Rosenblatt, New York
*Judge Samuel Rosenman, New York
*Rabbi Shlomo Rosenson, Ashkelon
†*David Rosolio, Jerusalem
*Professor Nathan Rotenstreich, Jerusalem
*Professor Cecil Roth, Jerusalem
*Morris Rothenberg (Estate), New York
†*James de Rothschild, London
*Mrs. James de Rothschild, London
*Dr. Paul Rothschild, London
*Lord Rothschild, Cambridge
*Mme. Hanna Rovina, Tel Aviv

*Harry Sacher, London
Professor Dov Sadan, Jerusalem
Professor Arye Sadowsky, Jerusalem
*Yeheskel Sahar, Herzliya
*Viscount Samuel, London
Dr. Raphael Sandler, Tel Aviv
Leo Savir, Jerusalem
Professor L. B. Schapiro, London
*Mrs. Eliahu Schein, Bucharest
*Milton L. Scheingarten, New York
I. Schneerson, Paris
*Schocken Library, Jerusalem
*Aryeh Schur, Tel Aviv
†*Lady Schuster, Manchester
†*A. Schwadron, Jerusalem
*Carl Schwartz, Tel Aviv
*Rabbi Jesse Schwartz, Montreal
†*Dr. Ignaz Schwartzbart, New York
Mrs. Anni Schwerin, Zurich
Ludwig Schwerin, Ramat Gan
Dr. Richard Seligmann, London
*Mrs. Ada Sereni, Givath Brenner
Chaim Shalev, Merhavia
Mrs. Lilly Shalit, Savion
Georges Shapiro, Paris
*Ze'ev Sharef, Jerusalem
†*Moshe Sharett (Shertok), Jerusalem
*Yehuda Sharett, Tel Aviv
*President Zalman Shazar, Jerusalem
*Mordechai Shenhabi, Mishmar Ha-Emek
*Dr. Moshe Sherman, Tel Aviv
Shmuel Shihor, Tel Aviv
Tzvi Shner, Kibbutz Lohmei Hagetaot

Mrs. Tsila Shoham, Haifa
Dr. Azriel Shohat, Jerusalem
Miriam Shriro, Ramat Gan
*Lord Sieff, London
†*Rebecca (Mrs. Israel) Sieff, Tel Aviv
*Professor Ernst Simon, Rehovoth
Professor Ernst Akiva Simon, Jerusalem
*Julius Simon, New York
†*Sir Leon Simon, London
Dr. Adam Simonson, Tel Aviv
†Professor Nahum Slouschz
Yaakov Smilansky, Tel Aviv
*A. Snowman, London
Mrs. Esther Spanien, Geneva
Rafael Spanien, Geneva
*Dr. Spiegel, Washington, D.C.
*Dr. Manka Spiegel, Jerusalem
*Claude M. Spiers, London
*Lord Stafford, London
*'The Star', Johannesburg
*Sarah (Mrs. Leonard) Stein, London
*Leonard Stein, London
*F. G. Steiner, New York
*Professor H. Stephen, Oxford
*Dewey Stone, Brockton, Mass.
W. Strang, Paris
William Straus, Marshall, Cal.
M. Sturman, Jerusalem
*Gershon Swet, New York
*Christopher Sykes, London

*Baruch Tal, Tel Aviv
*Professor Jacob Talmon, Jerusalem
*Dorothy Thompson, New York
†*Samuel Tolkowsky, Ramat Gan
Professor Jacques Trefouël, Paris
*Abraham Tulin, New York

*Siegfried Ullman, New York
*M. Ungerfeld (Bialik House), Tel Aviv
*University College Library, London
*Yaakov Ury, Nahalal
*Rabbi B. Z. Uziel, Jerusalem

*J. Vardi, Buenos Aires
Mark Vishniak, New York

†*Professor Yitzhak Volcani, Rehovoth

*Mrs. Lola Hahn-Warburg, London
*Gisella Warburg-Wyzanski, Cambridge, Mass.
*Professor Selman Waxman, New Brunswick
*Dr. Israel Wechsler, New York
A. David Weisgal, New York
*Meyer W. Weisgal, New York
*Aharon Weiss, Tel Aviv
†*David Weissman, Tel Aviv
†*Dr. Anna Weizmann, Rehovoth
*Benjamin Weizmann, Limerick, Eire
*General Ezer Weizmann, Ramat Hasharon
Dr. Helena Weizmann, Tel Aviv
Herzl Weizmann, Geneva
*Mrs. Ida Weizmann, Tel Aviv
*Weizmann Institute of Science, Rehovoth
Dr. Masha Weizmann, Rehovoth
†*Professor Moshe Weizmann, Haifa
†*Vera (Mrs. Chaim) Weizmann, Rehovoth
†*Yehiel Weizmann, Haifa
*Dr. Robert Weltsch, London
Dr. T. A. Werner, London
Israel Wilfrid, (estate), London
*Chaim Winocur, Tel Aviv
*Abraham Wix, London
Professor Ernest Wolf, Basle
*J. Wolfson, Manchester
Georges Wormser, Paris

*YIVO, New York
Mrs. Gerda Yuval, Jerusalem

David Zakay, Tel Aviv
*Sh. Zemach, Jerusalem
*Samuel Zemurray, New Orleans
*Jacob Zerubabel, Tel Aviv
*I. Zuckerman, La Chaux de Fonds, Switzerland
*Dr. Leon Zuckerman, La Chaux de Fonds, Switzerland.

Weizmann at 27 (1901)

SERIES A
THE LETTERS OF CHAIM WEIZMANN

———

VOLUME I

Summer 1885—29 October 1902

List of letters   3

List of illustrations   11

Introduction by Leonard Stein   13

Letters   33

Biographical Index   408

Index   429

LIST OF LETTERS

[Translations from the Russian by Dr. Georgette Donchin, School of Slavonic and East European Studies, University of London, from the German by Dr. Geoffrey Butler, Department of German, University College, London, subject, in each case, to some editorial emendations of a stylistic nature.]

Letter no.	Date[1]	Addressee	Page
	1885		
1.	[Summer]	Shlomo Tsvi Sokolovsky	35
	? 1886 or 1887		
2.	..	Shlomo Tsvi Sokolovsky	38
	1890		
3.	4 September	Ovsey Lurie	38
4.	5 October	Ovsey Lurie	40
5.	23 November	Ovsey Lurie	41
6.	[December]	Ovsey Lurie	43
	1891		
7.	5 January	Ovsey Lurie	44
	1892		
8.	3 March	Ovsey Lurie	45
	1894		
9.	26 April	Leo Motzkin	47
10.	18 December	Heinrich Loewe	47
	1895		
11.	20 June	Leo Motzkin	48
12.	3 September	Leo Motzkin	50
13.	10 September	Leo Motzkin	50
14.	25 September	Leo Motzkin	53
15.	25 September	Leo Motzkin	54
16.	26–27 September	Leo Motzkin	54
17.	29 November	Leo Motzkin	55

[1] Dates in square brackets are conjectural.

Letter no.	Date	Addressee	Page
	1896		
18.	23 January	Leo Motzkin	57
19.	11 February	Leo Motzkin	58
20.	[February or March]	Leo Motzkin	59
21.	[19 March]	Leo Motzkin	60
22.	20 September	Leo Motzkin and Israel Motzkin	61
	1897		
23.	[Late May or early June]	Leo Motzkin	63
24.	4 June	Leo Motzkin	63
25.	29 June	Leo Motzkin	64
26.	[July]	Leo Motzkin	64
27.	31 July	Leo Motzkin	65
	1898		
28.	[24 September]	Leo Motzkin and Paula Rosenblum	65
	1899		
29.	28 January	Theodor Herzl	67
30.	4 February	Leo Motzkin and Paula Rosenblum	68
31.	20 February	Arieh Reich	68
32.	11 March	Arieh Reich	69
33.	28 April	Max Bodenheimer	69
34.	11 May	Leo Motzkin	70
35.	27 July	Sigmund Veit	71
36.	5 August	Paula Rosenblum	72
37.	12 August	Rebecca Getzova	74
38.	19 August	Theodor Herzl	74
39.	3 September	Moses Gaster	75
40.	11 September	Leo Motzkin	75
41.	17 October	Die Welt	77
42.	12 November	Die Welt	78
	1900		
43.	10 January	Leo Motzkin	78
44.	9 June	Leo Motzkin	79
45.	21 June	Leo Motzkin	81
46.	5 August	Paula Motzkin	82
47.	12 August	Sophia Getzova	82
48.	16 August	Paula Motzkin	83
49.	1 November	Arieh Reich	83
50.	20 November	Arieh Reich	84
51.	[Late 1900 or early 1901]	Vera Khatzman	84
52.	[Late 1900 or early 1901]	Vera Khatzman	84
53.	[Late 1900 or early 1901]	Vera Khatzman	85

Letter no.	Date	Addressee	Page
	1901		
54.	[Early 1901]	Catherine Dorfman	85
55.	3 February	Leo Motzkin	86
56.	12 February	Moses Gaster	89
57.	13 February	Leo Motzkin	89
58.	22 February	Leo Motzkin	89
59.	[23 February]	Leo Motzkin	90
60.	3 March	Leo Motzkin	90
61.	11 March	Leo Motzkin	93
62.	[13] March	Vera Khatzman	93
63.	[14] March	Vera Khatzman	94
64.	[15] March	Vera Khatzman	96
65.	19 March	Vera Khatzman	98
66.	22 March	Leo Motzkin	100
67.	26 March	Leo Motzkin	102
68.	30 March	Vera Khatzman	102
69.	30 March	Vera Khatzman	103
70.	30 March	Leo Motzkin	103
71.	31 March	Vera Khatzman, Esther Weinberg, and Anna Ratnovskaya	104
72.	1 April	Vera Khatzman	104
73.	1–2 April	Vera Khatzman	105
74.	2 April	Vera Khatzman	107
75.	2 April	Vera Khatzman	108
76.	3 April	Vera Khatzman	109
77.	[3 April]	Leo Motzkin	110
78.	15 April	Vera Khatzman	110
79.	15 April	Vera Khatzman	111
80.	20 April	Ahad Ha'am	112
81.	24 April	Leo Motzkin	114
82.	11 May	Vera Khatzman	115
83.	25 May	Leo Motzkin	116
84.	3 June	Vera Khatzman	119
85.	8 June	Vera Khatzman	121
86.	9 June	Ahad Ha'am	123
87.	12 June	Aaron Eliasberg	126
88.	14 June	Vera Khatzman	127
89.	15 June	Vera Khatzman	129
90.	21 June	Vera Khatzman	130
91.	23 June	Ahad Ha'am	132
92.	23 June	Leo Motzkin	133
93.	25 June	Vera Khatzman	135
94.	26 June	Leo Motzkin	138
95.	28 June	Vera Khatzman	139
96.	29 June	Catherine Dorfman	142
97.	30 June	Vera Khatzman	142
98.	1 July	Vera Khatzman	144
99.	1 July	Vera Khatzman	144
100.	4–5 July	Vera Khatzman	145

LIST OF LETTERS

Letter no.	*Date*	*Addressee*	*Page*
	1901		
101.	5 July	Theodor Herzl	148
102.	5 July	Theodor Herzl	149
103.	5 July	Catherine Dorfman	149
104.	6–7 July	Vera Khatzman	152
105.	17 July	Vera Khatzman	154
106.	19 July	Vera Khatzman	155
107.	22 July	Theodor Herzl	156
108.	22 July	Catherine Dorfman	159
109.	23 July	Vera Khatzman	160
110.	26 July	Catherine Dorfman	160
111.	4 August	Catherine Dorfman	162
112.	7 August	Vera Khatzman	164
113.	[11 August]	Catherine Dorfman	165
114.	12 August	Vera Khatzman	168
115.	18 August	Vera Khatzman	169
116.	[20 August]	Catherine Dorfman	171
117.	[20 August]	Leo Motzkin	172
118.	22 August	Catherine Dorfman	172
119–20.	30 August	Catherine Dorfman	173
121.	31 August	Catherine Dorfman	174
122.	31 August	Leo Motzkin	174
123.	1 September	Catherine Dorfman	175
124.	2 September	Catherine Dorfman	175
125.	4 September	Catherine Dorfman	177
126.	7 September	Vera Khatzman	178
127.	8 September	Vera Khatzman	178
128.	12 September	Catherine Dorfman	180
129.	16 September	Catherine Dorfman	181
130.	19 September	Vera Khatzman	183
131.	[20 September]	Catherine Dorfman	186
132.	30 September	Catherine Dorfman	187
133.	3 October	Catherine Dorfman	188
134.	12 October	Catherine Dorfman	189
135.	27 October	Leo Motzkin	191
136.	31 October	Ahad Ha'am	194
137.	31 October	Theodor Herzl	197
138.	7 November	Leo Motzkin	198
139.	9 November	Catherine Dorfman	198
140.	16 November	Leo Motzkin	199
141.	21 November	Leo Motzkin	203
142.	21 November	Leo Motzkin	204
143.	21 November	Zionist Congress Bureau	204
144.	23 November	Leo Motzkin	205
145.	28 November	Aaron Eliasberg	210
146.	30 November	Leo Motzkin	211
147.	9 December	Leo Motzkin	212
148.	9 December	Leo Motzkin	213

Letter no.	Date	Addressee	Page
	1902		
149.	2 January	Vera Khatzman	215
150.	14 January	Leo Motzkin	215
151.	20 January	Leo Motzkin	219
152.	31 January	Leo Motzkin	220
153.	1 February	Leo Motzkin	225
154.	2 February	Theodor Herzl	225
155.	3 February	Theodor Herzl	225
156.	5 February	Ahad Ha'am	227
157.	15 February	Vera Khatzman	231
158.	16 February	Catherine Dorfman	231
159.	16 February	Vera Khatzman	231
160.	17 February	Vera Khatzman	232
161.	2 March	Leo Motzkin	233
162.	10 March	Berlin Group of Democratic Fraction	234
163.	14 March	Leo Motzkin	235
164.	16 March	Leo Motzkin	236
165.	16 March	Leo Motzkin	237
166.	20 March	Vera Khatzman	238
167.	21 March	Vera Khatzman	238
168.	21 March	Leo Motzkin	239
169.	22 March	Vera Khatzman	239
170.	23 March	Vera Khatzman	240
171.	23 March	Vera Khatzman	240
172.	25 March	Vera Khatzman and Esther Weinberg	241
173.	26 March	Vera Khatzman	243
174.	27 March	Vera Khatzman	243
175.	27 March	Vera Khatzman	244
176	28 March	Leo Motzkin	244
177.	28–29 March	Vera Khatzman	244
178.	30 March	Vera Khatzman	246
179.	31 March	Vera Khatzman	247
180.	1 April	Vera Khatzman	247
181.	1 April	Vera Khatzman	248
182.	2 April	Catherine Dorfman and Anne Koenigsberg	249
183.	2 April	Vera Khatzman	249
184.	[3] April	Catherine Dorfman and Anne Koenigsberg	250
185.	[3] April	Vera Khatzman	250
186.	4 April	Esther Weinberg and Anna Ratnovskaya	251
187.	4 April	Vera Khatzman	251
188.	4 April	Vera Khatzman	252
189.	4 April	Vera Khatzman	253
190.	5 April	Catherine Dorfman	253
191.	5 April	Vera Khatzman	254
192.	[8 April]	Leo Motzkin	254

Letter no.	*Date*	*Addressee*	*Page*
	1902		
193.	13 April	Leo Motzkin	254
194.	20 April	Ahad Ha'am	256
195.	[20 April]	Catherine Dorfman	257
196.	22 April	Vera Khatzman	257
197.	24 April	Aaron Eliasberg	257
197A.	24 April	Vera Khatzman	258
198.	25 April	Leo Motzkin	258
199.	26 April	Aaron Eliasberg	259
200.	3 May	Leo Motzkin	260
201.	7 May	Aaron Eliasberg	260
202.	7 May	Theodor Herzl	261
203.	16 May	Leo Motzkin	262
204.	21 May	Theodor Herzl	263
205.	21 May	Theodor Herzl	265
206.	2 June	Leo Motzkin	265
207.	4 June	Theodor Herzl	266
208.	12 June	Theodor Herzl	267
209.	25 June	Theodor Herzl	268
210.	26 June	Vera Khatzman	269
211.	[27] June	Vera Khatzman	270
212.	[28] June	Vera Khatzman	272
213.	30 June	Catherine Dorfman	273
214.	30 June	Vera Khatzman	274
215.	[late June]	Leo Motzkin	275
216.	1 July	Vera Khatzman	275
217.	1 July	Leo Motzkin	276
218.	2 July	Catherine Dorfman	277
219.	2 July	Vera Khatzman	277
220.	2 July	Vera Khatzman	279
221.	3 July	Vera Khatzman	279
222.	4 July	Vera Khatzman	280
223.	[5 July]	Catherine Dorfman and Anne Koenigsberg	282
224.	5 July	Catherine Dorfman	283
225.	5 July	Vera Khatzman	285
226.	[6] July	Vera Khatzman	287
227.	7 July	Catherine Dorfman	287
228.	7 July	Vera Khatzman	288
229.	[8] July	Vera Khatzman	288
230.	9 July	Aaron Eliasberg	290
231.	9 July	Vera Khatzman	291
232.	[9 July]	Vera Khatzman	292
233.	10 July	Vera Khatzman	293
234.	11 July	Vera Khatzman	293
235.	11/23 July	Vera Khatzman	295
236.	12 July	Vera Khatzman	296
237.	13 July	Vera Khatzman	296
238.	14 July	Catherine Dorfman	297

Letter no.	*Date*	*Addressee*	*Page*
239.	[14 July]	Vera Khatzman	300
240.	15–16 July	Vera Khatzman	302
241.	16 July	Theodor Herzl	304
242.	17 July	Catherine Dorfman	305
243.	17 July	Vera Khatzman	306
244.	17 July	Leo Motzkin	307
245.	18 July	Vera Khatzman	308
246.	20 July	Vera Khatzman	309
247.	21 July	Vera Khatzman	311
248.	[23] July	Vera Khatzman	313
249.	23 July	Vera Khatzman	315
250.	24 July	Aaron Eliasberg	316
251.	24 July	Vera Khatzman	318
252.	24 July	Catherine Dorfman	320
253.	24 July	Vera Khatzman	320
254.	25 July	Vera Khatzman	321
255.	26 July	Catherine Dorfman	322
256.	26 July	Vera Khatzman	323
257.	28 July	Vera Khatzman	326
258.	28 July	Leo Motzkin	328
259.	29 July	Vera Khatzman	329
260.	30 July	Vera Khatzman	331
261.	31 July	Catherine Dorfman	333
262.	31 July	Vera Khatzman	335
263.	31 July	Leo Motzkin	337
264.	1 August	Vera Khatzman	337
265.	2 August	Vera Khatzman	338
266.	3 August	Vera Khatzman	340
267.	4 August	Vera Khatzman	341
268.	4 August	Vera Khatzman	343
269.	5 August	Vera Khatzman	343
270.	5 August	Leo Motzkin	345
271.	6 August	Vera Khatzman	346
272.	[7] August	Vera Khatzman	347
273.	8 August	Vera Khatzman	349
274.	8–9 August	Vera Khatzman	350
275.	9 August	Vera Khatzman	354
276.	10 August	Vera Khatzman	354
277.	11 August	Vera Khatzman	357
278.	11 August	Leo Motzkin	358
279.	11 August	Vera Khatzman	361
280.	12 August	Vera Khatzman	363
281.	13 August	Vera Khatzman	365
282.	13 August	Vera Khatzman	366
283.	13 August	Catherine Dorfman	367
284.	14 August	Vera Khatzman	368
285.	14 August	Vera Khatzman	368
286.	15 August	Vera Khatzman	370
287.	16 August	Vera Khatzman	370

LIST OF LETTERS

Letter no.	Date	Addressee	Page
	1902		
288.	17 August	Vera Khatzman	371
289.	17 August	Vera Khatzman	373
290.	17 August	Vera Khatzman	373
291.	18 August	Vera Khatzman	374
292.	20 August	Vera Khatzman	375
293.	20 August	Vera Khatzman	375
294.	20 August	Regina Schimmer	376
295.	21 August	Vera Khatzman	377
296.	23 August	Vera Khatzman	378
297.	25 August	Vera Khatzman	379
298.	26 August	Moshe Glikin	381
299.	26 August	Vera Khatzman	382
300.	27 August	Catherine Dorfman	384
301.	27 August	Vera Khatzman	385
302.	29 August	Vera Khatzman	386
303.	[31 August]	Moshe Glikin	389
304.	31 August	Vera Khatzman	390
305.	[1 September]	Vera Khatzman	392
306.	2 September	Vera Khatzman	393
307.	3 September	Vera Khatzman	394
308.	3 September	Vera Khatzman	394
309.	4 September	Catherine Dorfman	395
310.	4 September	Vera Khatzman	396
311.	4 September	Vera Khatzman	396
312.	5 September	Vera Khatzman	397
313.	[6 September]	Vera Khatzman	397
314.	14 September	Menahem Ussishkin	398
315.	14 September	Moshe Glikin	399
316.	15 September	Theodore Herzl	399
317.	16 September	Vera Khatzman	401
318.	13 October	Vera Khatzman	402
319.	15 October	Vera Khatzman	404
320.	29 October	Vera Khatzman	406

ILLUSTRATIONS

facing page

Frontispiece Weizmann at 73 (1947)   iii

Frontispiece to Vol. I Weizmann at 27 (1901)   1

1. Weizmann at 11 (1885)   64

2. Letter to Shlomo Sokolovsky (1885)   65

3. Letter to Paula Motzkin (1900)   80

4. Vera Khatzman (1900)   81

5. Letter to Ahad Ha'am (1902)   256

6. Letter to Herzl (1902)   257

7. Weizmann and Feiwel (1902)   272

8. Chaim Weizmann with his brothers Moshe and Samuel
   (1902)   273

INTRODUCTION TO VOLUME I

LEONARD STEIN

THE letters contained in this volume range in date from the summer of 1885 to the autumn of 1902. We first meet Weizmann as a boy of just under eleven, about to start his secondary education at the High School in Pinsk, the nearest place of any size to his home in the White Russian townlet of Motol. We leave him seventeen years later, a few weeks before his twenty-eighth birthday, teaching chemistry at the University of Geneva, busily engaged in research, feeling his way as an inventor, and struggling to reconcile the demands of his scientific interests with intense activity in the Zionist Movement, in which, though still only a minor figure, he is already beginning to make his mark as a spirited young man with gifts of leadership and a mind of his own.

Of this period of seventeen years, the last twenty-two months— January 1901 to October 1902—account for 269 letters out of a total of 322. This leaves only fifty-three letters for the years before 1901, and of these only eight are earlier than April 1894, when Weizmann was nineteen. Reference has already been made in the General Introduction (page xx) to the disappearance of all the letters that Weizmann must have written to his family during his schooldays in Pinsk and his student years in Germany and Switzerland between 1885 and 1898, and to the unavoidable omission of his letters, starting in 1897, to Sophia Getzova. This helps to explain why the years before 1901 are so poorly represented. Even when we come to 1901–2, the position is that, of the 269 letters belonging to those years, 232 are to one or other of three persons— Vera Khatzman (145), Leo Motzkin (48), and Catherine Dorfman (39). It is obvious that many letters to other persons have been lost. No help can be got from Weizmann's copies of his outgoing correspondence, for no such copies are available for any part of the period covered by this volume.

Zionism and Weizmann's Zionist activities are throughout the predominant theme, but his frequent references to his scientific work are a reminder of the important part it played in his life, not

13

only because it provided him with a living, but because he was deeply interested in it for its own sake.

At his school in Pinsk he attracted attention by his aptitude for science and was encouraged to specialize in chemistry. Though the admission of Jews to Russian universities was severely limited, his exceptional abilities might have gained him a place. But even after surmounting the barrier of the *numerus clausus* he would still, as a Jew, have been subject to humiliations which he was not prepared to contemplate. Accordingly, on leaving school in 1892 he turned westward, continuing his studies, first at the Darmstadt Polytechnic (1892–3), then in Berlin at the Charlottenburg Polytechnic (1893–7, with a break of about a year in 1895–6), and finally at the Swiss University of Fribourg, which in 1899 awarded him his Ph.D. *magnâ cum laude*. In the summer of that year he began teaching chemistry as an accredited lecturer (*privat-docent*) under the auspices of the University of Geneva, with some additional duties in the University laboratories.

Except for some glimpses of his life in Berlin, the few letters of this period which have survived tell us little about Weizmann's student days on his way to his doctorate. It is when we come to his Geneva years, commencing in 1899, that we begin to realize how much his scientific work meant to him. The importance he attached to it can be seen from the letters in which he speaks of hopeful chemical experiments, of the technical treatise he is preparing to write, and of the beginning of a promising association with the Bayer chemical works at Elberfeld. Writing to Vera Khatzman in September 1901 while on a visit to his parents in Pinsk, now the family home, he tells her that he is in a hurry to get back to Geneva, where he means, that winter, to concentrate on his scientific interests, abjuring all social distractions: 'I feel as though I am not keeping abreast of science, which is bad for me in every respect.' Early in 1902 he writes that he is working up to the eyes in his laboratory, and a little later he announces jubilantly that he sees himself on the brink of an important discovery in the field of dyestuffs chemistry.

No. 130
(19 Sept.
1901)

Weizmann speaks in his autobiography of 'the tug-of-war between my scientific inclinations and my absorption in the Zionist Movement. My scientific labours and my Zionist interests ultimately coalesced, but'—he goes on—'it was not so in Geneva—at least it did not seem to be so, and during the 1900–1904 period

I suffered much because of the seeming division of my impulses.'
'I must', he tells Vera Khatzman in July 1902, 'regulate my
activities in such a way that Zionism does not interfere with
chemistry. I shall then be healthier and more creative', and again,
a fortnight later, 'You know how it has always tormented me to
be unable to devote as much time as I wished to chemistry. I am
going to fill in those gaps now.' There was a moment in that summer
when, absorbed in his Jewish University project (more will be said
of this later), he felt that he might have to give up his chemistry—
'the laboratory, with all its joys and sorrows'—because his Zionist
duty might require that painful sacrifice.

As is not surprising, the strain told on his health. The letters of
1901 are full of complaints about the drain on his energies—'How
I have aged!'—'my head is splitting'—'I am neglecting all my
work, do not go out and stay in bed part of the time'—'All this
work is too much for me.' In January 1902 he writes: 'I was at the
doctor's yesterday. He diagnosed neurasthenia and weakness of
the respiratory organs—over-fatigue and over-excitement.' Some
months later his doctor told him that he was suffering from general
weakness and exhaustion.

Before passing to the correspondence concerned mainly with
Weizmann's Zionist activities, there is one other group of letters
which may be mentioned at this point because the emotional crisis
reflected in them may well have contributed to the nervous tension
which was in 1901 undermining his health. At some time towards
the end of 1900 he met Vera Khatzman, the young Geneva medical
student (she was just nineteen) from Rostov-on-Don who was
some six years later to become his wife. He was engaged to be
married to Sophia Getzova, a Berne student of his own age from
Minsk. His correspondence with Vera Khatzman in 1901 shows
how strong was their mutual attraction, how quickly he realized
that he was in honour bound to put an end to an impossible
situation by breaking off his engagement, and what agony he
endured in steeling himself to tell his fiancée the truth. This he did
in the summer of 1901. That painful duty once performed, he
could breathe more freely. How much Vera Khatzman had come
to mean to him can be seen from the letters, full of ardent expressions of devotion, in which he plans their future together—a future
in which he pictures her, coming from a very different milieu from
his own, aroused by him to a consciousness of her duty as a Jewess

No. 225
(5 July
1902)

No. 247
(21 July
1902)

No. 260
(30 July
1902)

No. 128
(12 Sept.
1901)

No. 139
(9 Nov.
1901)

No. 140
(16 Nov.
1901)

No. 152
(31 Jan.
1902)

No. 185
(3 Apr.
1902) and standing by his side as a servant of the Jewish people. 'I had never loved', he tells her, 'and now I am in love.' He was happy now, but he was still living on his nerves—still tormenting himself at times about the past, and abandoning himself to nameless fears and fits of depression bordering on melancholia when he and Vera were separated—she in Rostov and he in Geneva—and a few days passed without his having heard from her.

His health might suffer, his prospects of a distinguished scientific career might be prejudiced, he might be distracted by the problems of his personal life, but nothing could be allowed to stand in the way of his service to the cause which had already fired his imagination when as a boy of eleven he sent his Motol teacher, Shlomo Sokolovsky, his essay on 'The *Hovevei Zion* Society and Jerusalem, which is in our Land'. Though inspired, no doubt, by what he had heard about the *Hovevei Zion* from his teacher or his father, he seems clearly to be expressing his own response to what they had told him when he speaks with fervent admiration of the founders of No. 1
(Summer
1885) the Society and of the 'lofty and elevated idea' for which they stood.

This essay was written a few months after a Conference at Kattowitz, in Upper Silesia, had fused into an organized movement (the precursor of the Zionist Movement to be founded thirteen years later by Theodor Herzl) the *Hovevei Zion* ('Lovers of Zion') societies which had begun to spring up in Russia in 1882 against the background of the pogroms following the assassination of the Czar Alexander II. Their purpose, broadly stated, was to promote the regeneration of the Jewish people and the revival of its national consciousness by propagating the idea of *Shivat Zion* ('Return to Zion') and, in particular, by encouraging the settlement of Jews in Palestine as workers on the land. Weizmann recalls in his autobiography that he began to be drawn into Zionist work (meaning at this stage work for *Hibbath Zion*) at the age of fifteen, and that, while still at High School in Pinsk, he did what a schoolboy could for the *Hovevei Zion*, collecting funds and distributing literature. The letters which have been preserved throw no light on his early Zionist activities until we reach his student days in Berlin. There, between 1894 and 1897, we see him in his early twenties drawn into the self-contained world in which the Jewish student colony carried on its busy social and intellectual life, and identifying himself enthusiastically with that section of it to which he naturally gravitated—the group of ardent Jewish nationalists represented by the Russian-Jewish Academic Society (commonly known as the *Verein*), for which he claims in his autobiography that it can justly be regarded as 'the cradle of the modern Zionist Movement'. Zionism was to owe much to the ferment of ideas generated by the endless debates in which these young men engaged among themselves and in set battles with their socialist or assimilationist antagonists.

Prominent among the leaders of the *Verein* was Leo Motzkin, who was later to become well known to the Jewish public as an important figure at Zionist Congresses and as Secretary-General of the Committee of Jewish Delegations at the Paris Peace Conference in 1919. When Weizmann entered the Charlottenburg Polytechnic in 1893, Motzkin, though seven years his senior, was still studying in Berlin. They saw much of each other, and it is to Motzkin that most of the letters surviving from Weizmann's Berlin period are addressed. Though there was even in the Berlin days some friction between them, Weizmann became a warm admirer of Motzkin and in 1901, four years after leaving Berlin, is to be found still speaking of him with marked respect—'the best brain among our young people', 'a teacher to whom to a considerable extent I owe my ability to work'. 'I', he writes to Motzkin in November 1901, 'may be a good recording-machine . . . but you, my dear friend, are the brains.' But between Motzkin, brilliantly gifted but rather vague, erratic, and disorganized, and the brisk, quick-moving Weizmann, knowing exactly where he was going, determined to get things done and impatient of inefficiency, there were temperamental differences which were in the end to drive them apart. The year 1902 opened with each of them nursing grievances against the other, and by the autumn they were barely on speaking terms. Weizmann's letters present only one side of the story. It is not necessarily to be assumed that the fault was all Motzkin's, but the fact is that in the letters of 1902 we see their relations gradually deteriorating and Weizmann's growing irritation turning into something like positive antagonism.

No. 65 (19 Mar. 1901)

No. 135 (27 Oct. 1901)

No. 146 (30 Nov. 1901)

Motzkin had, nevertheless, played an important part in Weizmann's Zionist education, and, in spite of the estrangement just mentioned, there are only friendly references to him in *Trial and Error*. But much more profound and more lasting was the impression made upon Weizmann by the teachings of Asher Ginzberg (1856–1927), the most distinguished Hebrew writer of his day, commonly known by his pen-name of *Ahad Ha'am* ('One of the people').

The essence of those teachings was that *Hibbath Zion* meant, or ought to mean, much more than the settlement of Jews in Palestine. This was to be encouraged, but the Lovers of Zion must on no account allow themselves to forget that it was not an end in itself and, as Weizmann puts it, 'had meaning only as an organic part of the re-education of the Jewish people'. Its value would lie in its contribution to the revival of the Jewish national consciousness and to the re-awakening of Jewry as a whole to a pride in its spiritual heritage. The key to Ahad Ha'am's approach to Zionism, whether in the inchoate form represented by the *Hovevei Zion* or in the more sophisticated form represented by the Basle Programme, is to be found in what his biographer, Leon Simon, describes as his conception of a 'national spiritual centre in which the secular and religious aspects of Jewish nationalism are subtly blended'.[1]

By the time Weizmann began his studies at the Charlottenburg Polytechnic in 1893, Ahad Ha'am's writings, with their penetrating analysis of the true nature of the Jewish problem and of its Zionist solution, had already made a deep impression on the more thoughtful minds among the *Hovevei Zion*, and especially on those of the generation to which Weizmann belonged. Though Ahad Ha'am's home was in Odessa, he lived for a time in Berlin, where Weizmann met him in 1896, having already gained admission to the *Bnei Moshe* ('Sons of Moses')—a group of ardent Jewish nationalists founded under the leadership of Ahad Ha'am in 1899 and dedicated as a *corps d'élite* to the service of *Hibbath Zion*. Ahad Ha'am's uncompromising intellectual honesty made him remorseless in his exposure of what he conceived to be fallacies or illusions in the conventional exposition of the ideas of the *Hovevei Zion*. The youthful Weizmann, with his dynamic energy and his eager, thrusting temperament, might have been expected to be somewhat chilled by the critical probings of the older man's analytical mind. But for Weizmann these only cleared the way for a deeper understanding of the true significance of *Hibbath Zion* and of what was, or ought to be, its purpose. Behind what might look like negations he perceived and was captivated by the constructive aspect of Ahad Ha'am's teachings, which were to continue throughout his life to colour his thinking about Zionism.

[1] Leon Simon, *Ahad Ha'am*, Philadelphia, 1960, p. 287.

Not that he blindly followed Ahad Ha'am; it was not in his nature blindly to follow anyone. He did not, for example, stand aloof, as Ahad Ha'am did, when Herzl's appearance on the scene with the publication in 1896 of his tract *Der Judenstaat* led, a year later, to the establishment of the Zionist Organization as the instrument of a movement designed to achieve by political means the main object of a programme much more ambitious than that of the *Hovevei Zion*—'the establishment in Palestine of a home for the Jewish people secured by public law'. We have no letters throwing light on Weizmann's response to these events, but we know that it was the opposite of Ahad Ha'am's. He immediately accepted Herzl's leadership, identified himself with the new movement and actively assisted in the preparations for the First Zionist Congress (Basle, 1897), which he would have attended as the delegate from what had by then become his home town, Pinsk, had he not at the last moment been unavoidably prevented from doing so. Ahad Ha'am, on the other hand, would have nothing to do with the Congress, disdainfully brushing aside the pretensions of the new Organization, castigating the irresponsible propaganda which had brought to Basle 'a rabble of youngsters—in years or knowledge', and declaring that 'the salvation of Israel will be achieved by prophets and not by diplomats'.[1] After the Third Congress (Basle, 1899) Weizmann wrote to Leo Motzkin: 'The distrustful nervous attitude to political Zionism may be expected to disappear, and a true understanding of its aims and tasks to take root.' The distrustful, nervous attitude in which a good number of the *Hovevei Zion* still persisted was in part a reflection of the misgivings so strongly felt by Ahad Ha'am.

No. 40 (11 Sept. 1899)

But if Weizmann was not prepared to be guided on all points by Ahad Ha'am, neither was he prepared to give unquestioning allegiance to Herzl. As the Zionist Movement developed, he became critical of certain aspects of Herzl's leadership. Though he never dreamed of seceding from the Zionist Organization, he became convinced that the health of the Movement was being endangered by Herzl's failure, as it seemed to him, to realize that a political success, even if attainable, could take the Zionists only part of the way—that what was at least equally essential was a sustained and

[1] The quotations are from a note in *Hashiloah* on the First Congress reprinted, in Leon Simon's English translation, in *Ten Essays on Zionism and Judaism* (London, 1922).

19

determined effort to rouse the Jewish masses from their torpor, to make them conscious of themselves as a people with a heritage worth preserving, and to demonstrate to the Jewish intelligentsia that in Zionism it could find the reassurance and inspiration for which it was hungering. The ideas which he began to press with growing impatience bore the mark of his response to the teachings of Ahad Ha'am the *'cher maître'* whom he implored, but without success, to appear as the leading figure at a Conference called to voice the demand of the younger Zionists for a more satisfying diet than was being offered to them by the conventional Zionist propaganda.

No. 136
(31 Oct.
1901)

To this part of the story of Weizmann's Geneva years we shall return when we come to look more closely at his relations with Herzl. Another part of that story is his trial of strength with the Bundists and other Jewish left-wingers. The Bund was a proletarian Jewish organization at this time closely linked to the Russian Social Democratic movement, and represented in Geneva by a considerable proportion of the large Russian-Jewish student colony. The Bundists' Marxist ideology made them implacable opponents of Zionism, in which they saw a bourgeois nationalist movement having nothing to offer the Jewish masses and calculated, if not indeed designed, to divert them from the revolutionary struggle and the class war. Outside the Bund but as strongly anti-Zionist and, unlike the Bundists, not interested in identifying themselves as Jews, were the students—apparently a majority—who had cut loose from their Jewish moorings and had swallowed whole the doctrines of the Russian revolutionary movement in their most uncompromising form. Behind them stood a number of Russian revolutionary émigrés then resident in Switzerland, among them the formidable George Plekhanov. Writing to Motzkin from Geneva in June 1900, Weizmann speaks of the pernicious influence of 'the General of the Russian Revolution, Plekhanov', on the Jewish students 'poorly assimilated as regards Judaism, degenerate, rotten, lacking in any moral fibre'. He threw himself vigorously into what he describes in his autobiography as an episode in 'the struggle for the possession of the soul of that generation of Russian Jews in the West'. His Geneva letters tell us of at least two set battles in this campaign—the first, in February 1901, a debate with a renegade Zionist turned Bundist, and the second, in the following November, an encounter with no less a person than

No. 44
(9 June
1900)

Plekhanov, who was, he writes triumphantly, 'debunked and routed'. No. 144 (23 Nov. 1901)

Both the Bundists and the Jewish Social-Democrats outside the Bund were irreconcilable enemies of Zionism, but there were also Jews who, while accepting the Zionist ideology, were at the same time strongly attracted by the idea that only in a socialist society would it be possible to establish a régime of social justice. Among these a representative figure was a member of Weizmann's Berlin circle, Nahman Syrkin, who in the summer of 1901 came out with a call for the formation of a group of Zionist Socialists. Weizmann was violently indignant, as can be seen from a letter to Vera Khatzman in which he speaks contemptuously of 'a red cap with a blue-and-white ribbon—a national group hailing internationalism with childish yells. . . .' 'Thank God,' he goes on, 'the Jewish movement has until now been free of socialist megalomania.' As a matter of No. 93 (25 June 1901) self-preservation it was important, if the Zionists were to keep clear of the Russian secret police, that they should not appear to be mixed up with socialism, but quite apart from this Weizmann had comprehensible reasons for being disturbed by Syrkin's activities. From other references to the subject in his 1901 correspondence it would appear that he suspected Syrkin of being a socialist first and a Zionist afterwards. To him it was clear that Zionists must keep their eyes firmly fixed on their goal, that the Movement could not afford any divided allegiance, and that there must, accordingly, be firm resistance from the start to what might become a dangerous deviation. How much Weizmann disliked and distrusted the Zionist Socialists is shown by the suspicion with which he viewed their attempts to insert themselves into the Zionist Youth Conference of 1901.

The enthusiasm with which Weizmann threw himself into the organization of the Youth Conference showed how firmly he was convinced that it had become imperative, in the long-term interests of the Movement, for the dissatisfied elements among the younger Zionists to assert themselves. His feeling that there was something lacking in Herzl's leadership seems to have come to a head about 1900. Unavoidably prevented from attending the First Zionist Congress, he was present at the Second Congress in 1898, but we have no letters throwing light on his impressions. At the end of the Third Congress in August 1899 he joined with two of his friends in sending Herzl a postcard bearing his likeness and inscribed: 'This

No. 38
(19 Aug.
1899)

No. 40
(11 Sept.
1899)

No. 44
(9 June
1900)

No. 48
(16 Aug.
1900)

is a picture which is ever in our mind's eye and which we always carry and shall carry in our hearts.' All the same, some discordant voices were now beginning to be heard. Writing from Russia a few weeks later to Leo Motzkin, Weizmann tells him that 'the Congress Opposition evokes great sympathy among the people; they appreciate it and are beginning to see it in its true light'. It was not a question of objecting to Herzl's conception of Zionism as a political movement; on the contrary, earlier in the same letter Weizmann speaks, in a passage already quoted, of his hope that those who still mistrust political Zionism will overcome their nervous fears. What did disturb the group of Russian delegates (himself among them) described by Weizmann as 'the Congress Opposition' was a tendency, as they saw it, to neglect what he calls in one of his letters 'the prophetic aspect of Zionism', to place all the emphasis on Zionist activities in the political and diplomatic field, to delude and confuse the masses by suggesting that a spectacular success might before long open the way to the realization of the Basle Programme, and to pay too little attention to the cultural activities—the patient educational work—without which the Movement could have no sure foundation. A year later, Weizmann left the Fourth Congress (London, 1900) in a mood of utter dejection. 'Exhausted and weary', he wrote to Motzkin's wife, Paula, 'broken morally and physically, I send you greetings, hoping that we may in the future see at our national assemblies more life, strength and courage in thought and deed.' For what he regarded as the failure of the London Congress the main responsibility seemed to him to rest with Herzl, who, he writes in his autobiography, 'was interested more in the impression he might produce on English publicists and statesmen than in the internal strength of the Movement. . . . I was forced to say that the striving after external effect was leading to neglect of internal construction.'

This was typical of the questionings among some of the younger men, and especially among the Russian intellectuals, which were to lead to a movement for the organization of a Zionist Youth Conference. The idea of a Youth Conference (originally conceived as a students' conference) began to crystallize towards the end of 1900. It did not originate with Weizmann, but with a group of Russian-Jewish students in Munich. Weizmann promptly identified himself with the project and in close association with the Munich group worked energetically from Geneva on the organization of a

Preparatory Conference, which, meeting at Munich under his chairmanship in April 1901, put him in charge of a Conference Office set up in Geneva to complete the arrangements.

A circular letter distributed by the Geneva Office soon after the Munich meeting explained that the object of the Youth Conference was to bring together people 'who are already Zionists but for whom the framework of the old Organization had become too narrow and uncomfortable'. This was how it was put in this formal communication, but Weizmann's real feelings about the meaning and underlying purpose of the Conference come out more clearly in his personal letters to various sympathizers. 'If we only knew that there was already a group of responsible men of action', then, he tells Catherine Dorfman, 'we could declare war on Herzl with a light heart'. In a letter to Vera Khatzman he recognizes that 'to convene the Conference means to declare war on Herzlism as a whole', but 'not to hold the Conference is quite impossible'. In another letter to Catherine Dorfman he writes: 'Dr. Herzl has no idea of Russian Zionism and of Russian Zionists. Dr. Herzl is being misled by various creatures, flatterers, "friends of the cause".'

No. 80
(20 Apr. 1901)

No. 103
(5 July 1901)

No. 104
(6–7 July 1901)

No. 124
(2 Sept. 1901)

For all this rebellious language, it would be wrong to suppose that Weizmann had lost interest in political Zionism or that he would not have been as jubilant as any other Zionist if a political success had been achieved. Only two months after the Youth Conference he wrote to Vera Khatzman: 'Great things are happening in Zionism now. Our dear untiring leader is in Constantinople, and yesterday I received a telegram from Buber in Vienna: "Wide concessions expected".' What he wanted was forcibly to demonstrate to Herzl that, if he was concerned for the future of the Movement, he could not afford to disregard the views of those younger men who were convinced that it must broaden its foundations and were insisting on being heard.

No. 160
(17 Feb. 1902)

After several postponements the Youth Conference met at Basle at the end of 1901, but not without its organizers having had to fight hard against opposition from various quarters—from those who saw in it a threat to the unity of the Zionist Movement, from those who suspected that its purpose was to declare war on religion, and, above all, from Herzl himself, who, when the project was brought to his notice, told Weizmann that it must be abandoned, since any indiscretions might prejudice delicate negotiations in which he was then engaged, meaning his discussions with certain

Turkish Ministers and officials following on his reception, in May 1901, by the Sultan. A little later, in a letter to one of Weizmann's associates, Bernstein-Kohan, Herzl expressed anxiety about factious activities calculated to split the Movement. What he particularly wanted to avoid was anything which could be construed as a provocation by the religious wing of the Movement—the Zionists who, faithful to Orthodox Judaism, saw in cultural work not directly related to religion, and generally in the ideas underlying the promotion of the Youth Conference, a challenge which must be firmly resisted. Weizmann, for his part, did not shrink from a collision with the religious Zionists. 'Our group', he wrote to Motzkin on the eve of the Conference, 'will always be critical and in opposition whenever dealings with the clericals . . . are concerned.' In deference to the 'clericals' Herzl had caused a resolution in favour of cultural work to be side-tracked at the Fourth Congress in 1900. Though he does not seem expressly to have said so, the same anxiety to prevent differences of opinion within the Movement from being embittered by the injection of a religious issue was, without doubt, one of his reasons for discouraging the holding of the Youth Conference.

No. 144
(23 Nov.
1901)

'I am appalled', Weizmann wrote to Catherine Dorfman, 'by the behaviour of the "leader" and fear that the time has come to open fire.' At the end of July he sent Herzl an indignant letter protesting against the attempt to suppress the Conference, which 'has not been brought about artificially but is the natural outcome of an emerging need'. In the end Herzl relented and, after an interview with Weizmann in Vienna, not only agreed to countenance the Conference but promised the active support of the Zionist Organization, being satisfied that the promoters had no sinister motives and that their efforts might, indeed, serve a useful purpose.

No. 103
(5 July
1901)

No. 107
(22 July
1901)

The six days' Conference—18–23 December 1901—did not result, as originally contemplated, in the establishment of a Zionist Youth Organization with limited objects designed to appeal to the younger intellectuals. The proceedings of the Conference are not described or commented upon in any of the Weizmann letters which have survived, but from the (incomplete) minutes, supplemented by information from other sources, it appears that, while some delegates insisted that the Conference should not go beyond its avowed purpose, Motzkin, supported—it would seem—by Weizmann, successfully argued that a loosely knit Youth Organization would not be enough; the progressive elements must be welded into an organized *Fraktion* (in effect, a synonym for Party) within the Movement, free to express its views and, where necessary, to oppose the leadership on any questions which might arise, including political questions, and to press for reforms in the structure of the Organization.

In the end the Conference resolved to perpetuate itself in the form of a 'Democratic Fraction' within the Zionist Movement. It was decided to provide the Fraction with an Information Bureau, to be directed by Weizmann, at Geneva. The programme of the Democratic Fraction was left to be worked out by a committee appointed for the purpose, but the committee was to be guided by a 'Protocol', the main features of which can be summarized as follows: First, the structure of the Zionist Organization must be reformed in conformity with democratic principles—the Organization must not revolve round a personality. Secondly, the Fraction must undertake cultural work on its own account independently of anything that might be done in that sphere under other auspices. Thirdly, the Fraction must devote itself to 'the study of the physical, political and social conditions of Palestine'. Lastly, it was affirmed that any group of Zionists having distinctive views in common ought to form itself into a Fraction, and that such groupings were essential to the healthy development of the Zionist Movement, subject to the acceptance by all Fractions of the Basle Programme.

The Democratic Fraction had an initial success. The Conference ended on the eve of the Fifth Zionist Congress, which opened at Basle on 26 December 1901. At the Congress the concerted efforts of the thirty-seven delegates belonging to the Fraction were largely instrumental in bringing about the adoption of a resolution, in which Herzl concurred, declaring that 'the education of the Jewish people in a national spirit is an essential part of the Zionist programme', and the election of a Cultural Commission with a membership including Weizmann and Ahad Ha'am.

Cultural Commissions had been set up by earlier Congresses but had never achieved anything. This time the Commission had not only an impressive membership but the backing of a strong resolution, endorsed by Herzl, in favour of cultural work. Nevertheless, it was as unproductive as its predecessors. The Commission, or sections of it, met once or twice, but with no perceptible results. Nor did the Democratic Fraction live up to the hopes of its founders.

After its auspicious start at the Fifth Congress it began almost at once to run into trouble as a result of serious dissensions between its Berlin adherents, headed by Motzkin, and Weizmann, backed by his colleagues at the Geneva office. Weizmann refused to be discouraged. 'This', he told Ahad Ha'am in February 1902, 'is the first time this year that I have felt that we are fulfilling our Jewish civic duty. Our group has infused a new purifying spirit into the Organization as a whole and the cause as a whole.' The quarrels between Berlin and Geneva might, indeed, have been no more than teething-troubles. But they were, in fact, only the prelude to a long period of tension between two of the Fraction's leading figures, Weizmann and Motzkin. Motzkin had been entrusted with the final revision of the programme of the Fraction. During the months which passed before this had been finished Weizmann grew more and more exasperated, and, discouraged by what seemed to him to be the apathy of other members of the Fraction, he began to despair of it. 'Motzkin', he wrote to Vera Khatzman in July 1902, 'is outrageously lazy. I am not writing to him any more and, generally, shall cease to take any further interest in the fate of the Fraction. I am fed up with playing the rôle of an *enfant terrible*, who, by the way, is paying out more than anyone else.' It was not until well into August that the programme was at last ready for publication. From the summary of this rather verbose document in the bridge-note following letter No. 298 it will be seen that it was in general conformity with the principles set out in the 'Protocol' approved by the Youth Conference. But the Democratic Fraction never really got on its feet. It was still alive in a semi-animate condition in 1903, but, in spite of attempts to revive it, it faded out in 1904.

The establishment of the Democratic Fraction represented the first deliberate move in the direction of the party-system which was to play an increasingly influential and, in the end, a dominant part in the internal politics of the Movement. This gives the Fraction, short-lived though it was, a significant place in Zionist history, but its only visible achievement had been its successful pressure, almost immediately after coming into existence, for a Congress resolution recognizing cultural work as an important part of the Zionist programme. Even this had turned out to be a dead letter, and apart from this the Fraction's direct impact on Zionist policies had been negligible. But this is not to say that it died without

No. 156
(5 Feb.
1902)

No. 222
(4 July
1902)

leaving any mark on Zionist thinking. Thus, for example, its programme—on this point going rather further than the 'Protocol' of
December 1901—demanded that an immediate start should be
made with the acquisition of land in Palestine for future settlement
by Jews. The view still tenaciously held by the straiter sect of
Political Zionists was that no activity should be undertaken in
Palestine until mass immigration had been authorized by the
Charter on which they staked their hopes. In its open challenge to
what was then the orthodox creed the Fraction can be regarded as
having contributed to the eventual victory of the Practical Zionists,
who were to come into the ascendant a few years later. Ideas which
were to fructify later were implicit also in the further demand that
Jewish colonies to be established in Palestine under Zionist auspices
should be organized on collectivist lines.

It should, moreover, be remembered that, unimpressive as were
the achievements of the Democratic Fraction itself, some important
new developments, especially in the field of cultural work, were
due to the initiative of certain of the younger Zionists prominently
associated with the Fraction. Of this one example is the establishment in Berlin of a Jewish publishing-house, the *Jüdischer Verlag*,
with Martin Buber and Berthold Feiwel among its founders.
Another is the Jewish University project, to which, in close co-
operation with Feiwel, Weizmann was devoting much of his energies
in 1902.

The idea was not new. At the First Zionist Congress in 1897 one
of the delegates, Professor Shapira, had spoken vaguely about the
establishment of a Hebrew University in Palestine. But this was
only a distant dream; no practical steps towards the foundation of
such a University were taken or discussed. At the Fifth Congress
(1901) Weizmann set the ball in motion with a speech in which he
urged the Congress to recognize that the time had come to treat the
question of a Jewish University as a matter of immediate practical
importance. He spoke in general terms of a Jewish University, not
of a Hebrew University in Palestine. He made no proposal about the
seat of the University and expressed no opinion on the question
whether it must necessarily be in Palestine.

He had already given the subject some thought, and so had some
of the other Zionists associated with the Youth Conference, though
they had still to clear their minds as to exactly what they wanted.
Was the University to be in Palestine or in Europe? Was it to be

a genuine University concerned with the advancement of learning, or was there a still more pressing need for a high-grade technical institute of the type of the Charlottenburg Polytechnic? Writing in August 1901 to Catherine Dorfman, Weizmann pointed out that the whole question had now become urgent because of the fresh restrictions recently imposed on the admission of Jews to Russian universities and other institutions of higher learning, and because, even in Germany, where so many Jewish students had found openings denied to them in Russia, there was intensive propaganda in favour of discrimination against Russian Jews. Weizmann's conclusion was that the proper course would be to begin with plans for the establishment of two or three technical colleges in the Jewish Pale of Settlement in Russia, 'and afterwards we should develop the Jewish University project'—whether in Europe or Palestine is not made clear. These ideas reappear, though in a somewhat altered form in a letter of 5 February 1902 to Ahad Ha'am: 'At our insistence, the Congress spoke about a Jewish institute of higher education. I must admit that I only joined the Cultural Commission to tackle this task . . . I think there must be two institutions from the start, one in Palestine devoted especially to Jewish learning, and another in Europe—a general University with a technical faculty and, of course, a Chair of Jewish Studies. . . . What an important European Jewish intellectual centre could be created at a Jewish University; it would be a synthesis of Yavneh and Europe!'

No. 113
(11 Aug.
1901)

No. 156
(5 Feb.
1902)

Working closely with Feiwel, Weizmann now began to press the Jewish University project on Herzl, whose response was sympathetic, and in May 1902 he sent Herzl a 'Preliminary plan for a Jewish University'. As to the character of the institution, his proposal was that it should be a combination of a University properly so-called and a Polytechnic. As to where it should be established, he said that it ought, if possible, to be in Palestine; should this be impracticable, the only alternative worth considering was Switzerland. Switzerland had evidently been already mentioned to Herzl as a possible second best, for he had earlier in the month told Feiwel that he was prepared to take the matter up with the Sultan (to whom he did, in fact, submit the project, but without receiving any encouragement) or with the Swiss Government.

The case for the establishment, as a matter of urgency, of a Jewish University was set out at some length in a brochure, *Eine jüdische Hochschule*, the joint work of Weizmann and Feiwel, not published until the latter part of 1902 but completed in July. As to the seat of the University, the view expressed was that it should, if possible, be established in Palestine, but that if this should be for the time being impracticable, then—since the need was pressing —in some other country, which might be England or Switzerland, but only as a temporary expedient and on the understanding that it was intended eventually to move the institution to Palestine. This implies that Weizmann was no longer pressing the view that it was essential that facilities for higher education should be provided in Europe as well as in Palestine. In appearance at least, he moved still further away from his original position when the University question came before the Zionist Annual Conference in October 1902. Though in the debate he made it clear that, like Martin Buber, he did not regard it as axiomatic that in no circumstances could any alternative to Palestine be considered, this did not prevent him from submitting, jointly with Buber, a resolution in favour of the establishment of a Jewish University in Palestine. Recognizing the emotional appeal of Palestine, Weizmann and Buber had framed their proposal in terms which could reasonably be expected to make it acceptable to the Conference. In this they were mistaken. The strength of that appeal was demonstrated when, to make assurance doubly sure, the Conference rejected the Buber–Weizmann resolution and substituted another calling upon the leadership to work for the establishment of a Jewish University, 'but only in Palestine'.

The truth seems to be that Weizmann was too much of a realist not to doubt whether, under the conditions prevailing in 1902, it would be practicable to set up a University in Palestine and rapidly to develop it to a point at which it would satisfy the needs of some of the mass of frustrated Jewish students or would-be students in Eastern Europe—this even assuming that such students would be able to make their way to Palestine, and that the Turks in their then mood would be willing to admit such an influx of Jews. This does not mean that there was any question in Weizmann's mind as to the ideal objective. What it does mean is that he had still to be convinced that the University must from the start be 'only in Palestine'.

With what intense application he worked for the Jewish University project can be seen from his letters of 1902 and from those which will become available in the next volume. For the time being, it all came to nothing. The Kishinev pogroms of 1903, the death of Herzl in 1904, and the controversy then raging about the 'Uganda' scheme, pushed the University question into the background and caused Weizmann's campaign to be suspended. We shall see, as this work progresses, how out of these early gropings there was to emerge a credible plan for the establishment of a Hebrew University in Jerusalem, and with what ardour Weizmann worked for its realization.

In Weizmann's handling of the University project, as illustrated by the letters in this volume, can be seen, even at this early stage of his career, a characteristic combination of burning enthusiasm for an idea which had fired his imagination with the commonsense of a realist preferring to bide his time and feel his way rather than rush forward before the ground had been properly prepared. In his efforts to win support for the project he spent himself to the point of exhaustion. In the interests of his campaign there was no sacrifice he was not prepared to make—even, if need be, the sacrifice of the distinguished career he could foresee for himself in chemistry. At the same time, his scientific training made him suspicious of short cuts and snap decisions. On no account would he agree to a half-baked scheme being given premature publicity for the benefit of Zionist propaganda. It will be noticed that one of his favourite words is *wissenschaftlich* and that there was no one for whom he had less respect than the dilettante. He would have nothing to do with slipshod improvisations. It was, he insisted, incumbent upon him and his associates to study the problems which had had to be tackled in the foundation of other universities, to dig deep into the literature on the subject, not to shrink from the dull task of compiling relevant statistics, and, in general, to make sure that before any scheme was launched the foundations had been solidly laid.

At the close of the period covered by this volume Weizmann was just under twenty-eight, with nearly two years still to go before he left Geneva for England, and twelve before he started on the road which was to lead to the Balfour Declaration. Thinking of the historical figure he was destined to become, we could easily form an exaggerated view of his standing, in those early years, in the Zionist Movement and give a disproportionate place in Zionist history to the events which loom so large in the letters here surveyed. At the age at which we leave him at the close of this volume Weizmann was still only a minor figure in the Movement, admired by a small group of kindred spirits—the ardent young men and women who come to life in his correspondence (though sometimes quarrelling even with these), acquiring a growing reputation among the Russian Zionists, less favourably known to the leaders as a gadfly, but occupying as yet nothing like a commanding position in the Zionist world. In the voluminous diaries kept by Herzl from 1895 to his death in 1904 Weizmann is never mentioned, Yet, though he had still to rise to his full stature, these letters reflect the self-confidence of a man who knows exactly where he is going, refusing to swim with the tide and expressing his views with an emotional intensity and, at times, with an almost startling vehemence which speak of the passionate conviction behind them. Not that we do not sometimes find a touching note of humility. 'A great moral rebirth', he declares, 'influenced by great spirits, people of eagle vision, like our Prophets—that is what Israel needs today. We, the pygmies, will not save "the wandering Jew"—we are the "mortal little Jews".' 'We are nervy', he writes a few days later, 'unstrung, flabby, and we are unfit for the Jewish cause. . . . I can see before me the faces of our best people. They are all helpless now—yet they are giants in comparison with me.' So he could write when overwhelmed by a sense of inadequacy in face of the immensity of the task with which but a feeble beginning had been made. What sustained him, as it was to sustain him throughout his life, was his unshakable conviction that it must be and would be accomplished. His deepest feelings are movingly expressed in his letter to Vera Khatzman at the turn of the Jewish year in the autumn of 1901:

No. 97
(30 June 1901)

No. 104
(6–7 July 1901)

May Israel rise, poor, oppressed, abused Israel, forgotten by its own sons. . . . May its sons and daughters return and apply their strength to healing the sores that have appeared in the body of an ancient people which yet harbours so much youthful fervour. . . . May the young generation now being born understand at last that it is their duty to save their honour, their integrity, to liberate themselves and their nation from Exile, from centuries-old chains. Israel is awaiting its children—and they are coming, they are returning, and may the coming years be a festival of reunion, a festival of the return of him who has been lost.

No. 127
(8 Sept. 1901)

THE LETTERS

C 5177

[Where information about a person mentioned in a letter is not provided in a footnote to that letter, the Biographical Index should be consulted. If the name does not appear there, a heavy type entry in the General Index will indicate the place at which the relevant information will be found.

The same applies where a footnote is confined to identifying a person mentioned in a letter without providing any further information about him: e.g., in letter No. 1, where W. mentions 'Rothschild', the object of the footnote is merely to make it clear that he means Baron Edmond de Rothschild.

An identification will be provided in a footnote to the earliest letter in which a person is referred to by a forename, nickname, or the like, and a person so referred to can, in any case, be identified by reference to the General Index.

As regards proper names other than names of persons:

1. In the case of institutions associated with the Zionist Organization (e.g. Actions Committee, Jewish Colonial Trust), a heavy-type entry in the General Index will indicate the relevant page in Appendix II to the General Introduction.

2. In all other cases (e.g. Russian-Jewish Academic Society, Jewish Colonization Association), the necessary information will be provided in a footnote to the letter in which the name first occurs, the position of such a footnote being indicated by a heavy type entry in the General Index.

An asterisk attached to a date in the heading to a letter signifies that the corresponding N.S. (Gregorian) date has been substituted for an O.S. (Julian) date in the original—see General Introduction, III.]

1. To Shlomo Tsvi Sokolovsky. *Motol* [*Summer, 1885*] Aet. 10¾

Hebrew: H.W.: W.A. (phot.)

[A transcription of this letter in Sokolovsky's hand was sent by him to W. under cover of a letter dated Lodz, 2 July 1919 (W.A.). The text, taken from this transcription, was published in the Tel Aviv weekly *Hapoel-Hazair* on 26 July 1922. A photograph of the letter, without any indication of its origin, was found in W.'s London files when they were incorporated in the Weizmann Archives. This is clearly the photograph referred to by W. in his letter of 11 Nov. 1920 to an American friend, Abraham Tulin (W.A.), in which he writes: 'I am sending you . . . a letter which I've written in 1885 from Motole, when I was 11, to my Hebrew teacher, which this teacher kept all this time and has now presented me with a photograph.' Sokolovsky died in Poland in 1925, and what happened to the original is unknown.—In his letter to Tulin, W. refers to Sokolovsky as 'my Hebrew teacher', and this is what the opening sentences of the letter would suggest. On the other hand, W.'s mother, Rachel Weizmann, in reminiscences published in the New York Yiddish newspaper *Der Tog* on 25 April 1938, speaks of Sokolovsky as 'his [W.'s] first teacher of Russian', and there is in W.A. a record of an interview, in 1955, with W.'s brother Moshe, in which he said that he remembered Sokolovsky's having tutored W. in Russian and prepared him for admission to the Pinsk secondary school. For admission to the school, which he entered in August 1885, it was essential for W. to know Russian, which, coming from a Yiddish-speaking home, he had to learn as a foreign language. It seems certain that Sokolovsky did teach W. Russian, though it is probable that he also gave him lessons in Hebrew.—The letter is written on the office stationery of W.'s father, Ozer Weizmann. It is headed '1885', below which is Sokolovsky's name in Russian characters. From the contents of the letter it seems clear that it was written at Motol in the summer of 1885, shortly before W. left home to start his secondary education in Pinsk. From the reference to Sir Moses Montefiore it may be inferred that W. was writing before the news had reached Motol of Montefiore's death on 28 July 1885.]

My teacher and guide, R.[1] Shlomo Sokolovsky,

How very glad I was to receive the precious letter which came to me from you, and how very pleased to have your greetings to me in that letter.[2] In answer to your letter, which is more precious to me than any wealth, I would reply that I shall observe your command not to throw away behind me our sacred tongue and the teachings of our sages of blessed memory because I am bound to study the Hebrew language. And please, my dear teacher, do not imagine that when I attend the Gymnasium[3] I shall throw off the

---

1. [1] 'R' ('Reb') is merely a deferential form of address appropriate to a learned person but with no implication that Sokolovsky was, in the generally accepted sense, a Rabbi.

[2] The letter referred to has not been found.

[3] i.e. the Pinsk Secondary School.

garb of Judaism. No! On no account. I have determined in my
heart to observe Judaism and I shall oppose the opinion of those
who say that one becomes a doctor because he casts off his faith.
This is contrary to culture and to civilisation. Can such a one be
called 'aristo-crat'?[4] to cast his faith behind his back. If that be so,
woe to you, 'aristo',[5] that they who follow your opinion should act
in this way!—My brother Feivel[6] is now at home and is not doing
any work and is also not studying at all.

From me, your pupil, Chaim Weizmann

I am sending you one of my ideas for you to see, AND THAT CON-
CERNS HEVRAT HOVEVEI ZION[7] AND JERUSALEM WHICH IS IN OUR
LAND. How lofty and elevated the idea which inspired our brethren
the sons of Israel to establish the Hovevei Zion Society. Because
by this we can rescue our exiled, oppressed brethren who are
scattered in all corners of the world and have no place where to put
up their tents, and all will attack us and the Jew is a burden on all
the nations and on all the Kings of Europe in general and on the
King of Russia in particular, and this may become the 'BEGINNING
OF REDEMPTION'. Therefore we must support this esteemed society
and we must also thank all the supporters of this society such as
Dr. Yasinovsky[8] and Dr. PINSKER[9] and all who have rallied

[4] In orig. the word 'aristo-crat' is represented by the same word (hyphenated as
shown in the translation) in Hebr. transliteration.

[5] 'aristo' (written without a capital A, there being no capitals in Hebrew script) is
the accepted Hebrew equivalent of 'Aristotle'. W., of course, knew no Greek, but he
tells us in *T. and E.* (p. 25) that his father was a student of Maimonides, and without
really knowing anything about Aristotle or his 'opinion', he may well have heard
the name in this connexion. He seems to have had a vague idea that there was some
link between 'aristocrat' and 'Aristotle' and to be attempting the kind of play on
words then in fashion.

[6] Feivel (b.? 1872) was about two years older than W., and the eldest of his four
brothers.

[7] 'The Society of Lovers of Zion.' The *Hibbath Zion* ('Love of Zion') movement,
whose members were known as *Hovevei Zion* ('Lovers of Zion'), the precursor of the
Zionist Movement founded in 1897 by Herzl, sprang up in Russia in 1882 and assumed
an organized form as a result of a conference of *Hovevei Zion* societies held at Kattowitz (now Katowice), Upper Silesia, in 1884, its objects, broadly stated, being to
promote the regeneration of the Jewish people and the revival of its national
consciousness by propagating the idea of *Shivat Zion* (Return to Zion) and, in particular, by encouraging the settlement of Jews on the land in Palestine.

[8] Dr. Israel Yasinovsky was the head of the Warsaw office of the *Hovevei Zion*.

[9] Leo Pinsker, of Odessa (1821–91), the author of *Autoemanzipation* (1882), which in
large measure anticipated the argument of Herzl's *Der Judenstaat* and was to become
a Zionist classic, stood, at the time of this letter, at the head of the *Hovevei Zion*
organization and was generally regarded as the leading figure in the movement.

beneath the flag of this society. We must also thank the two patriots who are MOSHE MONTEFIORE[10] AND ROTHSCHILD.[11] In conclusion we must support this society which understands what lies before it and sees the evil threatening us, therefore the obligation rests upon us to establish a place to which we can flee for help. Since in America, where enlightenment prevails, we will be beaten.[12] And in all the countries of Africa in general and the State of Morocco in particular we will be beaten and we will not be pitied.[13]—Let us carry our banner TO ZION AND RETURN TO OUR FIRST MOTHER UPON WHOSE KNEES WE WERE BORN.—For why should we look to the Kings of Europe for compassion that they should take pity upon us and give us a resting-place? In vain! All have decided: THE JEW MUST DIE, but England will nevertheless have mercy upon us.[14] In conclusion to Zion!—Jews—to Zion! let us go.

Chaim Weizmann

[10] Sir Moses Montefiore (1794–1885), honourably known for his exertions on behalf of persecuted or poverty-stricken Jewish communities in various parts of the world, had paid seven visits to Palestine, the last in 1875, and had there done his best to promote the welfare of the Jewish population, then mainly concentrated in Jerusalem and the other centres of Jewish piety and traditional learning. The Federation of *Hovevei Zion* societies established at the Kattowitz Conference (see n. 7 above) was designated, in his honour, *Mazkeret Moshe* (A remembrance of Moses). In *T. and E. W.* speaks (p. 16) of the impression made upon him as a child by what he was told by his grandfather about Montefiore's visit to Russia in 1846.

[11] Baron Edmond de Rothschild.

[12] An exodus of Jews from Eastern Europe to the United States had begun in the early 1880s and was, by 1885, rapidly gaining momentum. What W. is trying to say might, it would seem, be paraphrased somewhat as follows: Do not let us delude ourselves with the idea that there is a sure haven for Jews in the United States. Even enlightened America will, in the end, turn against us. Only in Palestine can we be at rest in a home of our own.

[13] The Jewish press of the period was full of reports about the unhappy position of the Jews in North Africa, and especially in Morocco. At the beginning of 1885, as a result of a serious anti-Jewish outbreak at Demnat, grave anxiety was being expressed about the safety of the Jewish population in the interior of Morocco.

[14] The Jews of Eastern Europe had long been accustomed to cherish the picture of England as a humane and liberal Power which had on a number of occasions during the nineteenth century shown a benevolent interest in the welfare of the Jews. They were particularly impressed by the honoured position accorded in England to Moses Montefiore and by the British Government's manifest sympathy with his exertions on behalf of his fellow-Jews in the East and elsewhere. In the Russian Jewish literature of the day the strength of anglophile sentiment is reflected in such widely read writings as Mendele Mokher Sforim's novel *The Journeys of Benjamin the Third* (1878) and Yehudah-Leib Gordon's contributions to *Hamelitz* in the early 1880s.— W.'s reference to England has sometimes been interpreted as a prediction that England would help the Jews to find their way to Palestine. What he is really saying seems to be, in effect: Even though all others turn against us, England will befriend us. Even so, our true hope is in a return to Palestine; there alone can we find salvation.

Motole[15]

If God be willing when I write you another letter I shall send several ideas which I have written.

From me, the above

[Translated by J. L. Meltzer, in consultation with members of the Editorial Board. The translation conforms to the Hebrew as regards paragraphing, punctuation, capital letters, and asterisking.]

2. To Shlomo Tsvi Sokolovsky. [? *Pinsk, c. 1886–7*]

Yiddish: H.W.: C.Z.A.—Z4/305/12

[Date and place of origin uncertain, but probably written from Pinsk during W.'s school years there (1885–92). By contrast with the letter of 4 Sept. 1890 (No. 3), the juvenile style suggests a considerably earlier date.]

Dear Teacher Shlomo Hirsch,[1]

Thank you for sending your regards. I am very happy with them. I beg you to make the effort to write to me. I beg you to write if you are in good health and if all is well with you, for I think of you as though you were my own brother.

That is all I have to write to you. Keep well and happy. This is the desire of your pupil, who sends you his best wishes.

Chaim Weizmann

3. To Ovsey Lurie, Mitava. *Pinsk, 4 September 1890**

Russian: H.W.: W.A.

[In or about 1888, Idel (Samuel) Lurie, of Pinsk, a well-to-do Jewish industrialist, engaged W. to supervise the homework of his son Saul, who was several forms below W. at the Pinsk Secondary School. Lurie was a banker and a member of the family described in W.'s autobiography (*T. and E.*, p. 40) as 'the great clan of industrialists with branches in Warsaw, Libau and Danzig, who owned the match factory in Pinsk'. The Luries were interested in the timber trade and, from information for which acknowledgment is due to Mr. Boris Guriel, it would seem (though it cannot be conclusively established) that they had business connexions with W.'s father, Ozer W., as a contractor for the transportation of timber. W. became a member of the Lurie household and lived with the family until the end of his Pinsk schooldays in 1892: see *T. and E.*, p. 32. This and the five following letters were written to Saul's brother, Ovsey (Hosea) Lurie, who was at school in Mitava (Courland). The letters from Ovsey referred to by W. have not been preserved.]

[15] In orig., 'Motole' in Latin characters. The Russian name of the town was 'Motol', but it was commonly known among Jews by its Yiddish name, 'Motole'.

2. [1] As to Sokolovsky see head-note to No. 1. 'Hirsch' is the Yidd. equivalent of the Hebr. 'Tsvi'.

Pinsk, 23 August 90

My dear friend O.L.,

Please forgive me for not writing to you for such a long time in spite of my promises: while in Pinsk I was busy with my vacation work; from Motol, however, I did send you a postcard which you probably received. I shall be writing to you regularly from now on, as promised.

From our dirty Pinsk, but from my clean heart, I am sending you, my young friend, congratulations on getting through to the next form. May you study well in this and all the other forms, so that you easily reach the goal you are aiming at. Remember, you will attain this only by diligence and a conscientious attitude to your work. But let's drop moralising; you may well get angry with me and refuse to read my letter. So I shall change my tone.

I am going to tell you in detail what I have been doing since you left. Two hours after your departure I could still be seen at that station of our peerless Polesie Railways which is named 'Pinsk'. Of course, the train was late as usual and, you may remember, it was pouring with rain. At last the train arrived, and I finally got into the carriage. I ought also to tell you that I bought a ticket; from Pinsk there is a through connection to Yukhnovichi. The tickets were a shade of bluish-grey. The train pulled out and before long I got to Yukhnovichi, and from Yukhnov[ichi]—straight home. It would be far too long to tell you everything I did at home. All I can remember is that a fortnight later I found myself at a steam-mill, also in the God-forsaken town of Pinsk.

To tell the truth, I have nothing to write to you about; I am simply beating the air or milling the wind and—if one looks closely —there is neither air nor wind.

Do write to me in detail in what order you were re-examined, and what questions you were asked, but do leave Mr. Tirumoprutkevich[1] in peace, as Derzhimorda, Svistunov, Bobchinsky and Dobchinsky,[2] and especially Shel'menko[3] (a crafty man), are people who easily take offence.

Please write to me often, as we have agreed, about the things you are learning at school, and I shall be answering you from here and shall explain everything by letter. This time I am cutting my letter short, for sleep—that idler—makes me close my eyes.

Ever yours affectionately,
Chaim Weizmann

3. [1] This seems to be a fanciful invented name.
  [2] These four are characters in Gogol's *Inspector-General*.
  [3] Another invented name, with an allusion to the Russian word for 'rascal'.

P.S. You have probably received grandmother's letter; Sheyka[4] also wrote to you in the same letter.

Good-night; you too must go to bed when the time comes, but first prepare your lessons, as it behoves you. This was penned by me—the same gentleman.

Ch. W.

P.P.S. Imagine Bobchinsky with a bleeding nose, lying on a broken-down door. Shel'menko comes up to him and gives him a flick on the bleeding nose, while Pan Shpak[5] stands by and laughs: 'Oh, my sides are splitting: I am struck by horror and fear.' That's enough chatter, isn't it?

4. To Ovsey Lurie, Mitava. *Pinsk, 5 October 1890**

Russian: H.W.: W.A.

Pinsk, 23 September 1890

My very dear Ovsey,

I was truly pleased to read your letter in which you inform your parents of your progress at school. If your work is satisfactory, try to improve it; if it is good—make it even better, for this is the main purpose of the happy years of your youth. I trust that you have already taken to heart everything your father has been saying about education in general and about reading in particular. I should like to know, indeed I should be most interested to learn from you— if this is not too difficult—what are you reading just now? What author did you begin with? By the way, I would suggest starting with Gogol, and then on to Turgenev, Grigorovich,[1] Dostoevsky, Pisemsky,[2] etc.; in general all the writers of the new school, that is all those coming after Gogol. I myself am now reading Weber— 'The History of the Reformation',[3] and as fiction Machtet.[4] As a friend of yours, I consider it my duty to remind you that reading

---

[4] Saul Lurie.

[5] 'Pan'—Polish equivalent of 'Mr.', but having, in this Russian letter, a slightly derisive connotation—someone who thinks himself important.

4. [1] D. V. Grigorovich (1822–99), writer on peasant life.

[2] A. F. Pisemsky (1821–81), novelist and playwright.

[3] Georg Weber, *Geschichte des Reformations-Zeitalters* (Leipzig, 1874). It is not to be inferred that W. had already a sufficient mastery of German to be able to read this work in the original. A Russian translation by Chernyshevsky was published in 1888.

[4] G. O. Machtet (1852–1901), one of whose works, written under the impact of the pogroms of the 1880s, was a novel entitled *Zhid* ('The Jew') dealing sympathetically with a Jewish subject.

is very, very important for you, and that unless you have done a lot of reading you will find it hard to face the terrible ordeal[5] in a few years' time.

My own studies are going well, thank God. I have a great deal to do, and this is the real reason why I so seldom write to you. But you, my dear friend, should not reproach me for my silence.

Farewell. I wish you success in your studies. May you attain an understanding of that great and beneficial truth that with iron will and industry man can overcome all obstacles. As the adage goes, 'where there's a will, there's a way'. May this guide you through life.

Ever yours affectionately,
Ch. Weizmann

5. To Ovsey Lurie, Mitava. *Pinsk, 23 November 1890*

Russian: H.W.: W.A.

Pinsk, 11 November 1890

Dear Ovsey,

Forgive me, please, for not answering your letter. I am somewhat to blame but can partly justify myself by lack of time. Your last letter, in which you tell me how industrious you are and how well you are studying, has made me very happy. I was surprised, however, by your grumbling and tears. As you will understand, you alone are to blame for the reproaches with which your father has censured you. Your parents saw how far you were lagging behind your friends and relations. It is but natural that this made a bad impression on them, and they—loving you as they do, and also wanting to reform you quickly (which in fact did happen), wishing to give you a certain push in the right direction—had to use just that tone. 'Spare the rod and spoil the child', as the saying goes. Your father might even not have written to you at all, but that would have been much worse. And now your parents are very glad that their words have had the necessary effect and have inspired you with industry, willingness, and love for work. Of course, if you will continue to study in the same way, if you read a lot and generally strive to improve yourself, you will soon fill the gap which still remains. Your diligence will then help you to overcome any obstacle which may appear in your path, and you will firmly march towards your goal and certainly reach it. Laziness, on the other hand, is the basest of human failings; it brings in its wake a complete confusion in the human being, both in the moral and the

---

[5] Presumably his matriculation examinations.

physical sense, a complete demoralisation. May the Almighty be praised for having delivered you from this state, for having woken you out of the somnolent inertia into which you let yourself sink for some years. You have come to your senses now, you have come to understand all that is all-important to any respectable man, and especially to us, the sons of Jacob, poor wanderers, martyrs for our sacred and pure faith. We need incessant toil, constant labour; we need quick intellectual development; we must learn everything that is noble and useful and as yet unknown to us. If you engage in this worthy task you will be happy all your life. Boileau, the famous French writer, said: 'A noble mind without shame or blame derives a lawful profit from its labour.' All great men have worked hard; they were active throughout their lives; they worked for the benefit of all mankind; and how many now proclaim their fame! Does not the whole of civilised Europe bow before their great geniuses? The names of Socrates, Plato, Descartes and Locke are still alive to-day in philosophy; those of Homer, Virgil, Dante and Shakespeare in poetry; Aristotle, Galileo, Newton and Lavoisier live on in the field of science; whilst the contemporary rulers, consuls, presidents etc., who took no interest in noble causes but only in relatively petty intrigues, have been long ago forgotten. All the scholars mentioned above worked and toiled, ignoring all the obstacles. Our famous sage, Rabbi Akiva, was a shepherd in his youth. He was so poor that he could not even pay the small entrance-fee to the synagogue to hear the famous Jewish Tannaim.[1] He had to lie in the loft of the synagogue to listen to the teaching of the Rabbis. But his noble enthusiasm was so great that he was once found on the roof, covered with snow.[2] That is why he achieved so much; he became a leading authority and acquired up to 2,400 pupils. This is an example of steadfastness and industry; and one can think of many, many noble and diligent figures!

And so don't give in, and take courage! Go on working and toiling! Believe me, the joy of your parents is very great indeed; you have given them great, great pleasure. Your parents, who would like to see you and have always wished you to be first a truly well-behaved and fine youth, and then an educated and well-developed man and a good exemplary Jew, will certainly not cover you with reproaches for your apparent laziness. My heart rejoices, and I thank the Creator for having inspired you. Please write to

5. [1] Hebr., lit. 'Teachers'—the Jewish sages associated with the development of the *Mishnah* (Oral Law).

[2] In the *Talmud*, from which this story comes (Yoma, 35b), it is told about Hillel., but it is Akiva who is said (Yevamoth, 62b) to have claimed 24,000 (not 2,400) disciples.

me about the progress of your studies, especially in languages and mathematics. Read Dostoevsky, Pisemsky,[3] and then Turgenev. All is well with me, thank God; Saul's[4] studies are not too bad either {but not as good as I expected}.[5]

Farewell! Your affectionate friend,

Ch. Weizmann

These brackets were put in by Saul.[6]

6. To Ovsey Lurie, Mitava. [*Pinsk*], [*mid-December 1890*]

Russian: H.W.: W.A.

[Undated, but approximate date can be deduced from some lines added to the letter by Lurie's mother, who writes that her husband is in Minsk and will remain there until Sunday, 9 Dec. (= 21 Dec. N.S.). The 9 (21) Dec. fell on a Sunday in 1890.]

Dear Ovsey,

Thank you very much for your letter which reached me the other day. I have no special news that might interest you. The only thing to say is that my studies are not going too badly, and Saul's too; it looks as if this school-term too he might get by without any particularly bad marks. I should very much like to know how things are with you, what marks you get this term and, most important, whether you are still working with that zeal and industry you were telling us about previously. I hope that you have taken note of all that I wrote to you in my first letter. Take care not to forget it, keep it constantly in mind, and you will invariably be successful in your studies, acquiring the reputation of an assiduous man who will always be a shining example to all and sundry. The holidays are already approaching, and you ought to devote this free time to learning your history, a subject with which, as far as I remember, you are not very familiar as yet and which is essential to you, and to revising all you have learned up to now, in order that you may assimilate your subjects better in future. And remember mathematics and general reading, for the latter is essential too. When it comes to writing an essay, you must have the facts and ideas already well marshalled in your mind and not try to crib them from some book, for this is sheer waste of time and can never lead to anything sensible. In the upper forms, you should know, many pupils frequently come across this sort of trouble. They always find

---

[3] See n. 2 to No. 4.   [4] Saul Lurie.
[5] Lines through brackets are in the original.
[6] In orig., written in W.'s hand in the margin.

it a strain to write anything. This is because they have never read much. The human mind must strive to grasp as much as possible, and only while trying to do so and endeavouring to take things in do we comprehend the essence of things. If, however, we don't apply our own will, we shall be beaten like the Swedes at Poltava.[1] I fear I have bored you with these remarks.[2] I must stop pouring oil on the blazing fire of your scholastic zeal. May God grant that this flame will never die within you and that, with your skilful tending, it may gradually fan out, and that nothing may extinguish its devouring force—to the joy of your parents and your affectionate friend,

Ch. Weizmann

[Postscripts by Saul Lurie and Bella Lurie (mother of Saul and Ovsey).]

7. To Ovsey Lurie, Mitava. *Pinsk, 5 January 1891**

Russian: H.W.: W.A.

Pinsk, 24 December 1890

Dear Ovsey,

I am very surprised that I have not heard from you for so long. You must have had your term's marks by now, and it is strange that you should be silent about them. Surely you do realise that everyone is looking forward to hearing of your achievements, because—to judge from your previous letters, the number of which has recently diminished—your marks should be good. Therefore I don't think there is any point in postponing news of them until some other, perhaps more convenient, time. Most likely something quite incidental is really the main reason for your prolonged silence. Please, Ovsey, do write to me about everything—how did your term end, and what are you doing now? How do you feel? Have your intellectual powers matured? Are those good, happy beginnings, up to now somewhat concealed, about to bear fruit which it is my hope to see very soon? When, please God, we meet again, I trust that you will confide in me all the spiritual or, more precisely, all the emotional stirrings and feelings that you experienced when overcoming your former apathy. As I understand it, Ovsey, you must have been undergoing a spiritual regeneration during this time, and I am very, very glad of it. However, your late display of

---

6. [1] At the Battle of Poltava (1709) the Swedes were defeated by the Russians under Peter the Great.   [2] Lit. 'these sounds'.

indifference really worries me. You must understand that I am very interested in all your activities in the scholastic field.

Your mother is most distressed that you don't write, so do try as soon as possible to atone for your blunder and write about everything. Our second term is over, and we are now free from school. On Thursday I shall be going home[1] for a few days. Saul's work this term may be described as good in one respect, and not so good in another. He got two very bad marks for drawing and calligraphy; this alas is his congenital failing! And you know how distressing it is when one can't help it, however much one tries. My studies this term, as well as last, have gone well; it would be sinful to complain.

Adieu! Your affectionate friend,

Ch. Weizmann

[Postscript by Bella Lurie.]

8. To Ovsey Lurie, Mitava. *Pinsk, 3 March 1892**

Russian: H.W.: W.A.

Pinsk, 20/II/92

Dear Ovsey,

Forgive me for not having written to you for such a long time. Honestly, I haven't had the time. You know that until I get around to it, seven times seven nights go by. But now I have set about it and am writing to you. What I am to write I really don't know— there isn't anything special and, behold, I can finish this miserable epistle already. Now comes a pause: I am thinking what to write to you. Wait, I haven't enough supplies. By the way, it is Shrove-tide, and we are on holiday, except that the fatal Monday already looms in front of us when, books under arm, we must be off to school. You must be working up to your ears just now, my friend; all the same, do try to write to me about your studies. Don't count your letters, brother, as the aristocrats generally like to do. I am a simple fellow; when I have no time, I don't write, and when I do, I go and spin a long yarn—and if there is no sense in such a letter, that is not my business: take a deep breath and read it if you want to, and if you don't—throw it under the bench or use it for another purpose . . . if the paper is soft and doesn't hurt. Well, you ought to know our sort; we are plain chaps, we don't think a lot, just get down to it and patch up a letter. Here you are, here is a blot on the paper; pity, but on the other hand, doesn't it add to the effect? Wait, let me

7. [1] To Motol.

add another blot for good measure.[1] Look how elegant: two most respectable blots hand in hand against a white background. This often happens, it's true; but it even happens that a sausage explodes like a gun, and so on. See, I am writing to you in a purely aristocratic manner, leaving margins, etc. I am doing it for a very simple reason, so that the letter should appear longer: 'the bigger, the better', האט אמאל איינער געזאגט.[2]

Indeed I have written a great deal; there will be a lot to read and a lot to laugh at: ha, ha, ha—don't grieve, brother. I am in a very good temper now, and frisky as a calf. Given half a chance, I would take off for Algiers posthaste, and would pluck out that lump which for some sixty years now has been dangling under the nose of the infidel Dey.[3] An excellent idea, isn't it? And you too would join me in such an expedition. Funny: off we go, not to Algiers but to Berlin to enter the University, and not now but in August.[4] As to the books, I thank you most humbly, but my finances are low, brother, actually non-existent, and anyhow what are books? Let them go to hell, I am thoroughly fed up with them. Write to me, brother, don't be mean, and buy an extra stamp for a letter to me; I shall be most, most grateful.

No news from your home, everything as usual: it's terribly cold, the cold is beastly, etc., etc., etc. We live, suffer from cold, and vegetate. We have no other communication to make. Spring will soon be with us—I expect you know that yourself. Haman wanted to come to Pinsk for Purim,[5] but he was told that there are enough of his kind here without him—a whole legion. I hope you will enjoy the poppy-seed Purim cakes, if Mme Neuberg[6] gives you any. No more paper.

Farewell,

Affectionately yours,

Ch. Weizmann

Please write to me separately, under separate cover. Don't begrudge me a stamp.

8. [1] Lit. 'for greater show'.

[2] Yidd. 'as someone once said'.

[3] '. . . dangling under the nose . . .'—An echo of a passage in Gogol's *Memoirs of a Madman*.

[4] W. entered the Berlin (Charlottenburg) Polytechnic (not Berlin University) in the autumn of 1893—see bridge-note following this letter.

[5] Haman, would-be persecutor of the Jews, the villain of the Book of Esther, whose downfall, and the triumph of the Jews over their enemies, are commemorated in the merry-making Festival of Purim, falling in February or March.

[6] Ovsey Lurie's landlady.

[After seven years at the Pinsk Secondary School, W. left in the summer of 1892 and in the autumn of that year went to Germany to study chemistry. He attended the Darmstadt Polytechnic for two semesters, first as a *Hospitant* (a student not taking a full course) and then as an *ausserordentlicher Studierender* (a student taking a full course but not qualified by a High School certificate for admission as an *ordentlicher Studierender*). In the autumn of 1893 he was enrolled as a regular student at the Berlin (Charlottenburg) Polytechnic: see Pinsk Secondary School Matriculation Certificate, dated 1893, and Darmstadt and Berlin (Charlottenburg) Polytechnic Leaving Certificates, dated respectively 1893 and 1897, all in W.A.

In Berlin, W. came into contact with Leo Motzkin, seven years his senior, as a fellow member of the Russian-Jewish student colony.]

9. To Leo Motzkin, Berlin. [*Berlin*], *26 April 1894*

Russian: H.W.: Pod.: C.Z.A.—A126/16/2

[In this and all succeeding letters to Motzkin up to and including that of 11 Sept. 1899 (No. 40) W. uses the formal 'you' (plur.). In 1900 Motzkin moved from Berlin proper to Charlottenburg, which had at that time the status of a separate municipality. In the headings to letters to Motzkin any technical distinction between Berlin and Charlottenburg has been disregarded, and 'Berlin' means Greater Berlin, including Charlottenburg.]

Dear Mr. Motzkin,

I shall be able to come for a lesson on Saturday. If you are free then, please let me know. Be so kind as to have the 20 Marks ready for me by Saturday. I desperately need the money.[1] I am sorry that I was unable to come on Tuesday: I had a lecture until 4 o'clock.

Yours very truly,
Ch. Weizmann

26/IV/94

Perhaps you could lend me some money as well; you would be doing me a great favour. I shall repay you on the first.

10. To Heinrich Loewe, Berlin. *Berlin*, [*17*] *December 1894*

German: H.W.: Pod.: C.Z.A.—A146/24
[Dated by W. 18 Dec., but pmk 17 Dec.]

Berlin, NW. 18/XII. 94

Dear Mr. [Loewe],

Unfortunately I was unable to get hold of the necessary newspapers. Davidsohn had some, so had Motzkin, and this will explain

---

9. [1] W. was evidently supplementing his income by giving lessons to Motzkin, who was reading for his Ph.D. In what subject he was coaching M. is not known. The twenty marks probably represent fees due to W. For W.'s straitened circumstances at this time see *T. and E.*, p. 55: 'During all the years of my sojourn in Berlin I did not eat a single solid meal except as somebody's guest.'

what I have said. I am really sorry, but hope that you will be so kind as to forgive me. Next week I shall let you have a fuller report than has been possible hitherto.[1]

My regards to you and to Dr. Soskin.[2]

Ch. Weizmann

11. To Leo Motzkin, Berlin. *Pinsk, 20 June 1895*

Russian: H.W.: C.Z.A.—A126/16/2

[In the spring of 1895, after completing his third semester at the Charlottenburg Polytechnic, W. returned home to Pinsk, to which his family had moved from Motol in 1894 or 1895. He went back to Berlin in the spring or early summer of 1896 (the exact date is uncertain) and resumed his studies at the Polytechnic in the winter semester of 1896–7.]

Pinsk, 8.20 June 95

Dear Motzkin,

Despite my promise to write to you immediately upon my arrival in the God-forsaken town of Pinsk, I have not done so. I have no special reasons to put forward, so I cannot justify myself. The trouble is that after Berlin, Pinsk has made such a vile, repulsive impression on me that I find it unpleasant, even distasteful, to share it, dear friend, with you. There is nothing here and no-one: instead of a town—just an enormous rubbish-heap; instead of people, one comes across creatures devoid of all personality, with no interests, no desires, no demands, who are pleased or displeased for some reason or other known to no-one, not even to themselves. Hundreds of Jews push on and hurry about the streets of our town, with anxious faces marked by great suffering, but they seem to do it unconsciously, as if they were in a daze. As in any other well-organised society, there is a so-called intelligentsia here too; this is the name they have given themselves, as being the most commonly used and the most euphonious. In point of fact, the male

---

10. [1] Motzkin was president, Eliahu Davidson (here spelt 'Davidsohn') was vice-president, and both Loewe (though he was a German—not a Russian—Jew) and W. were members of the Russian-Jewish Academic Society. The newspapers were evidently required for the compilation of a weekly report (presumably on current events) which W. was expected to send to Loewe, but for what purpose is not clear, except that it can be assumed to have been connected with the activities of the R.-J.A.S. From a notice in the *Juedische Volkszeitung* of 19 Dec. 1894 it appears that on the 22nd there was to be a meeting of the Society at which W. was to survey the events of the week, but this does not explain why he should be sending a report to Loewe, unless, indeed, the 'report' was a draft of his survey.

[2] Selig Soskin was at this time active in Jewish nationalist circles in the Berlin student colony.

'intellectuals' are busy paying court to intellectual damsels, while the married men and[1] women spend their time playing cards, gossiping and indulging in other similar, avowedly innocent, amusements. All this is quite natural and understandable if one bears in mind how much free time these ladies and gentlemen dispose of, and how few higher or even average interests they have. From all this you will understand that I am incredibly bored here. I have, of course, a host of acquaintances who would gladly spend their time with me—a student from Berlin (they are very fastidious as to their acquaintances!), but I don't go anywhere and have not taken up at all with the *jeunesse dorée* of Pinsk. I have antagonised a few people in this way (though very few!), but no harm done! I am busy the whole day long, either at the factory[2] or giving lessons, and this saves me from out-and-out boredom. Of course, I earn a little אפותיקי,[3] I read, I study, and that is all.

What good news have you? What's happening in the *Verein*?[4] Have there been any good papers? Have you written your paper on anti-semitism? What about *Hilfe*?[5] What about the reading-room?[6] What about the techn[ical] *Verein*?[7] Please don't begrudge the time and write to me about everything. It is in your power to pull me out of this slough, at least for a time, and give me the chance to transport myself—at least in thought—into your circle and to live your life. I shall not write much, for there isn't much to write about, but I promise you *hoch und heilig*[8] to reply every time. Regards to all our dear comrades, Davidson, Eliashev, Syrkin, Kunin, Makhlin, etc.[9] Give Eliashev regards from his two sisters,

11. [1] Orig., 'respektiv'—'or as the case may be'.
   [2] The chemical products factory belonging to Gregory Lurie, a member of the same family as Idel. Lurie (see head-note to No. 3), where W. worked during his year in Pinsk.
   [3] Yidd., 'property'—i.e. 'I made a little money'.
   [4] In orig. in cyrillic characters. The *Russisch-Juedischer Wissenschaftlicher Verein* (Russian-Jewish Academic Society), founded in Berlin in 1889 by Motzkin and some other Jewish students in sympathy with Jewish nationalism, and later described by W. (*T. and E.*, p. 52) as 'the cradle of the modern Zionist movement', the members including, in addition to Motzkin and W., Shmarya Levin, Victor Jacobson, and other future Zionist leaders. W. served on the Committee in 1894–5—see *Juedische Volks-zeitung*, 19 Dec. 1894. The Verein was later reconstituted under the name of *Kadimah* ('Forward').
   [5] '*Hilfe*' ('Help') was a mutual aid society founded in 1889 by Jewish students at the Charlottenburg Polytechnic.
   [6] The Jewish Reading-Room (*Juedische Lesehalle*), a joint enterprise of the Verein and other Jewish organizations, including in particular students' societies, founded in Berlin in 1894, with Motzkin as one of the two joint secretaries. Students in sympathy with Jewish nationalism were well represented on the Committee.
   [7] It is not certain what *Verein* is meant, but W. is probably referring to a students' society at the Charlottenburg Polytechnic.   [8] 'by all that is holy'.
   [9] All Berlin students and members of the Russian-Jewish Academic Society.

also to Shmarya:[10] they are now at the *dacha*[11] near Pinsk, and yesterday I spent the evening there. How is Davidson? All the best. Until my next letter,

Your friend,
Ch. Weizmann

Address: Weizmann,

    c/c Ch. Lubzhinsky, Pinsk.

12. To Leo Motzkin, Berlin.[1] *Pinsk, 3 September 1895**

Russian: H.W.: Pcd.: C.Z.A.—A126/16/2

Pinsk, 22/VIII. 95

My good friend,

I wrote you one letter[2] but have had no reply. Perhaps you did not receive it. Please write at least a brief note about yourself and other friends. I shall be coming after the Holy Days.[3] Write to me at once, even a few words: where are you, what you are doing, how, why, and wherefore.

Yours,
Weizmann

Addr[ess]:

    Ch. Weizmann, Pinsk.

13. To Leo Motzkin. *Pinsk, 10 September 1895*

Russian: H.W.: C.Z.A—A126/16/2

[The last paragraph of the letter shows that it was written *before* the Jewish New Year ('It will soon be *Rosh Hashanah*'). Since the O.S. date of the New Year in 1895 was 7 September it would seem to follow that W.'s '10 September' cannot mean 10 September O.S. but must mean 10 September N.S. corresponding to 29 August O.S.]

---

[10] Shmarya Friedman, one of W.'s Pinsk friends, at this time studying in Berlin.
[11] Country rest-house.

12. [1] Addressed to Berlin but forwarded to Friedenau (Brandenburg), where M. was staying at the time.

   [2] Presumably his letter of 20 June 1895 (No. 11).

   [3] The series of Jewish Holy Days (the New Year, the Day of Atonement and the Festival of Tabernacles) ending in 1895, according to the civil calendar, on 11 Oct. (N.S.). W. did not, in fact, return to Berlin until, at the earliest, the spring of 1896— the exact date is uncertain. His return was delayed, in the first instance, because of his impending call-up for military service (see No. 17), and subsequently, it would appear from *T. and E.* (p. 49), because of his father's financial difficulties.

13. *To Leo Motzkin*

Pinsk, 10 September 1895[1]

Dear Motzkin,

Your letter[2] made me so happy that I cannot thank you enough. Reading your lines I felt transported into quite a different world; they aroused in me a burning wish to see you and all our friends as soon as possible. Unfortunately I cannot comply with your request today, but it will be done within 3–4 [or] say 5 days. I shall send you about 50 r[oubles] per *Anweisung* Meyer and Co.[3] in Berlin. Now let me tell you about myself. I have been vegetating in Pinsk all this time. The first half of the day I work at Lurie's factory;[4] apart from this I have got a few fairly good lessons. I am pretty fed up with all this by now, and I am only waiting for the happy day that will free me פֿון דיא גוישע העענט[5] and take me to Berlin. If it weren't for the work I am doing, I could die of boredom and no-one would even notice it, for there is very little intelligentsia here. This consists of the chemist, the doctors, the accountants, etc.; it is only a gambling intelligentsia which, without any twinge of conscience, incessantly plays cards and doesn't care a hoot about any other interests; not that there is anything to care about! With the exception of my family and a few friends who assemble for the vacations, I have no-one here, although I am acquainted with 10/9 of the whole town.[6] There is a whole legion of Palestinians[7] here: the most prominent are Berger,[8] Strick,[9] and Hiller.[10] I am not being biased when I say that they are the only decent and educated people in our bog of a town;[11] they are very keen on the Palestine movement. Berger is devoted body and soul to the cause and stops short of nothing that may further its development among our masses. By the way, his methods are of the purest, and as a man

13. [1] 'Pinsk . . . 189–' printed; '10 September' and '5' written in by W.

[2] Not found. No letter from Motzkin to W. before 1901 has come to light.

[3] By draft on Meyer and Co. The nature of the payment is not known. It may represent repayment of a loan (see W.'s request for a loan in No. 9), or W. may himself be making a loan to Motzkin—see No. 24, where W. presses him for repayment of a debt.
[4] See n. 2 to No. 11.

[5] Yidd., 'from the hands of the gentiles'—i.e. from the uncongenial people of Pinsk, ironically described as 'gentiles'.

[6] So in orig. The great majority of Pinsk's 30,000 inhabitants were Jews.

[7] Jews associated with the *Hibbath Zion* (Love of Zion) movement, the precursor of the Zionist movement founded by Herzl in 1897—see n. 7 to No. 1, and Introduction to this volume, p. 16.
[8] Juda Leib Berger.

[9] Mordekhai Strick (1860–?), a bank clerk, was secretary of the Pinsk *Hovevei Zion* Society and a member of the Pinsk Lodge of the *Bnei Moshe* (Sons of Moses), as to whom see n. 2 to No. 16.

[10] Hirsch (Tsvi) Hiller, a clerk, was one of the early leaders of the Pinsk *Hovevei Zion* and, after 1897, of the Pinsk Zionists, and was later (1902–3) associated with W. in the movement for a Jewish University.

[11] Pinsk, built on marshy soil, was in a double sense a 'bog'.

of action he often has to suffer and endure the stupid sarcasms of our asinine betters in their fashionable frock-coats. Thanks to these three men and some fellow-students, we have managed to found a literary circle which has been joined by the best people in Pinsk; the circle is national in character, but our members do not really understand nationalism. I spoke at the circle about the dissemination of Peretz's books[12] among the masses, but this was received with distrust somehow. As it is, these books are hardly to be seen in Pinsk; the reason is very simple: the masses do not read anything and have no spiritual interests. Moreover, it must be noted that most of the Palestinians lay stress on the three roubles that have to be sent to the Odessa Committee[13] and worry less about stimulating [national] consciousness. I have been unable to observe any particular trends among the Jews, although I try to come into close contact with all sorts of people. There is a depressed dull state of mind everywhere; people expect something, some sort of miracle and look vacantly into the future. After all this it will be clear to you how deadly boring it is here! The monotony is only broken occasionally when one indulges in indignation at the emptiness and nastiness of our leading Jews, their slavishness and servility. It seems to me that on no one did the Golus[14] have such a noxious influence as on the Jews of Pinsk. They tremble and crawl before the goy,[15] they are ready to disregard everything just to please him; and this is true of all of them, big and small alike. But you have had enough of my boring jeremiad. What is happening in Berlin? Probably more than in Pinsk and Motol together, און אפילו מיט דער גאנצען סביבה.[16] Believe me, even in Jargon[17] I have not made much progress; I haven't enriched my vocabulary with any strong expressions, except perhaps with a few select קללות[18] which one picks up walking along our streets.

Never mind, it will be merrier soon, and it will be Berlin, too! Everybody will assemble there, and we shall start a good life again. I shall be on my way around mid-October, immediately after the call-up.[19] I have a request to make of you: whether you are willing

---

[12] The Hebrew and Yiddish litterateur J. L. Peretz (1851–1915). The reference here is to his Yiddish writings.

[13] The *Hibbath Zion* movement was directed by a Central Committee, with its seat in Odessa. Three roubles (then roughly equivalent to six shillings) was at this time the minimum annual subscription.

[14] In orig. in cyrillic characters. Hebr. *Galuth* ('Exile') in Ashkenazic pronunciation.

[15] Yidd., 'gentile'.

[16] Yidd., 'and the whole area put together'—lit., 'even including the whole area'.

[17] Synonym (not necessarily derogatory) for Yiddish.   [18] Hebr., 'curses'.

[19] W. was soon afterwards passed fit for military service but never served: see *T. and E.*, pp. 49–50 for his account of the interview at which 'I managed to talk my way out

or unwilling is immaterial to me—you have to agree. You will absolutely have to initiate me into the mysteries of mathematical science;[20] this is indispensable to me for my further improvement on the path of progress. Why?—I shall tell you when I come. I am going to take these studies very seriously, remember that. Enough for now. You will, of course, write, as soon as possible I hope, so that I get the letter this year (an obvious joke, even if common, for it will soon be ראש השנה).[21] I fully share your view that Kunin will recover—עֶר וֶועט וֶוערן רייט וֹויא אַ עפעלע.[22]

Regards to Lurie,[23] Eliashev and the others (to those who deserve it!)

Goodbye,

Yours,

Ch. Weizmann

14. To Leo Motzkin, Warsaw.[1] *Pinsk, 25 September 1895*

Russian: H.W.: C.Z.A.—A126/16/2

Pinsk, 13/25 Sept. 1895

Dear Motzkin,

I received your telegram[2] last night and hoped to have a letter to-day. This did not, however, materialise. The other day I sent you 25 roubles and I think I shall be able to send you as much again within the next few days.[3] As to our meeting in Brest-Lit[ovsk],[4] I am burning with impatience in expectation of that day. The best thing would be for you to leave Warsaw on Saturday night, and I would [start] from Pinsk at the same time. At 6. a.m. we shall meet in the 2nd cl[ass] [? waiting-room or restaurant] at the Brest railway-station. On Saturday you will get a telegram from me. You can still write to me until Saturday, i.e. if you post the letter by

---

of the army', securing exemption on the ground that his education ought not to be interrupted. As to the delay in his return to Berlin see below, No. 17.

[20] Mathematics were Motzkin's speciality.

[21] Hebr., *Rosh Hashanah* (New Year).

[22] Yidd., 'He will become as ruddy as an apple'.   [23] Joseph Lurie.

14. [1] Warsaw would have been on Motzkin's route on his way from Berlin to his home at Brovari, near Kiev.

[2] Not found.   [3] See n. 3 to No. 13.

[4] No earlier reference to such a meeting has been found, and it looks as though it must have been proposed in Motzkin's telegram. W. returns to the subject in No. 15 and again in No. 16.

half-past one on Friday, I shall get it in Pinsk on Saturday morning. And so I ask and beg you to do this. On Saturday you will receive a telegram, and I shall expect your letter on Saturday morning.

Au revoir,
Yours,
Ch. Weizmann

P.S. While I was writing this, I received 25 roubles. This will be sent to you by to-morrow's post, as it's already too late to-day. Letters containing money are only accepted here until 2 p.m., and it's already 4 o'clock.

Le même

15. To Leo Motzkin, Warsaw. *Pinsk, 25 September 1895**

Russian: H.W.: C.Z.A.—A126/16/2

Pinsk, 13 Sept. 95

Dear Motzkin,

Having dropped the letter in the box to-day, I realised that I had written about our meeting on Sunday morning.[1] I have just worked out that it would be more convenient for us to meet on Monday morning, and thus you and I would leave Warsaw and Pinsk resp[ectively] on Sunday night.

I should like to invite you to come to Pinsk itself, but we'll discuss this when we meet. In any case, it is essential that we should meet. I hope to receive another letter from you, and then I'll still have time to answer. So you will be leaving on Sunday evening, about 11 o'clock, and you will get to Brest on Mond[ay] morning. By that time I shall be there. I shall telegraph to you on Sun[day], or perhaps on Saturday. I'll send the money to-morrow.[2]

Awaiting your letter,
Yours,
Ch. Weizmann

16. To Leo Motzkin, Warsaw. *Pinsk, 26–27 September 1895**

Russian: H.W.: C.Z.A.—A126/16/2

Pinsk, 14/26 Sept. 1895

Dear Motzkin,

I am surprised at your silence. You should have received the

---

15. [1] See No. 14.   [2] See postscript to No. 14.

25 roubles.¹ I am sending you the same amount to-day. Do write something about your stay in Warsaw. I sent you two letters yesterday, and I hope you will fulfil the heartfelt request I expressed in them, and which I now repeat. I should like to write more, but there really is nothing to say. I am postponing everything till our meeting.²

Yours,
Ch. Weizmann

15/27

As yesterday was a holiday,³ I am sending the money to-day. I am surprised there is no letter!

17. To Leo Motzkin, Berlin. *Pinsk, 29 November 1895*

Russian: H.W.: C.Z.A.—A126/16/2

Pinsk, 17/29 Nov. 95

Dear Motzkin,

Fate has willed that I should remain stuck here for another few months. The fact is they wanted to conscript me, and I only managed to get off thanks to long-drawn-out trials.¹ You can imagine that this whole ordeal, which cost me a great deal of worry, was not to my liking. I shall probably stay here until March and then be on my way. I anticipate intolerable boredom, all the more since it will probably be interesting in Berlin this winter. But what can I do? One has to reconcile oneself to all this, even though it is exceedingly unpleasant! What's the latest news? What's going on in our crowd? Which of our acquaintances has returned to B[erlin]? What is happening to the R.E.N.F. ?² What news in *Nauka i zhizn* ?³

16. ¹ See No. 14—'The other day I sent you 25 roubles'.

² No description of the meeting has come to light, but that it took place is shown by W.'s reference to it in his letter to Motzkin of 23 Jan. 1896 (No. 18): 'I told you in Brest . . .'. From the sources cited below it appears that one result of the meeting was that, at Motzkin's instance, W. applied for and was admitted to membership of the *Bnei Moshe* (Sons of Moses), a select group formed in 1889 under the leadership of Ahad Ha'am and dedicated, as a *corps d'élite*, to the service of *Hibbath Zion*: Minkovich, leader of *Bnei Moshe* Pinsk Lodge to Central Lodge, 6 Heshvan, 5656 (= 24 Oct. 1895); Minutes of Pinsk Lodge, 1st intermediate day of Passover, 5656 (= 31 March 1896)—C.Z.A.—A. 35/22/11.

³ The Orthodox Feast of the Exaltation of the Holy Cross (Holy Cross Day).

17. ¹ See n. 19 to No. 13.

² Initials representing the Russian name of the Russian-Jewish Academic Society.

³ 'Science and Life', the name of a Russian-Jewish students' socialist society in Berlin, an opponent of the nationalist R.-J.A.S.—see A. Bein in *Sefer Motzkin* ('The Motzkin Book'), Jerusalem, 5699 (1938–9), p. 42.

What's new in the technical circle?[4] Does it still exist? What are they doing there, and who is in command? Have any new <u>Jewish</u> students arrived? Where is your brother[5] now? I wrote him two long letters but received no reply. Since then I haven't written to him any more. Our Levin[6] has got a fairly well-paid job: he is getting 70 roubles a month for four lessons in some small town, within the Pale, of course. You have probably written to your brother about the factory project,[7] and I hope you had a reply. What does he say? Write about anything.

I have told you about the progressive *heder*.[8] Everything is going splendidly. The children are making excellent progress. By this summer, the number of pupils will be up to 40, and the character of the *heder* is that of a model Jew[ish] school. We are now busy organising popular lectures on Jew[ish] history. And, do you know, we shall have the synagogue at our disposal. Do send me some of the papers recently read in B[erlin].[9] At least their titles, if it is impossible to obtain the pap[ers]. I shall also ask you, dear friend, to send me some copies of 'Zion'[10] if it's possible. What is the price of Geiger's *Das Judenthum und seine Geschichte*?[11] Enough for now. Do write at once to

Yours,

Ch. Weizmann

Pinsk (Gov[ernment][12] of Minsk)

[4] This may well be the same society as that referred to in No. 11 as 'the technical *Verein*', which, as suggested in n. 7 to that letter, was probably a students' society at the Charlottenburg Polytechnic.

[5] Israel Motzkin, of whom little is known except that he was a chemist and that he was secretary of the Russian-Jewish Academic Society in 1894.

[6] Probably N. Levin, of Odessa, a chemistry student at Charlottenburg, where he was a contemporary of W. and associated with his research.

[7] The nature of the project can be inferred from the fact that Israel Motzkin was a chemist, but nothing further is known of it.

[8] A *heder* (Hebr., lit., 'room') was an elementary school of the type normally attended by Jewish children, with the emphasis on religious instruction. Attempts were being made in Russia at this time to modernize the traditional curriculum and old-fashioned pedagogical methods of the *heder*.

[9] W. probably means papers read at meetings of the R.-J.A.S.

[10] The monthly organ, published in Berlin, of the pre-Herzlian Jewish national movement in Germany and Austria.

[11] *Das Judenthum und seine Geschichte* ('Judaism and its History'), Breslau, 1865–71, was a collection of lectures by Abraham Geiger (1810–74), a pioneer of the nineteenth-century Jewish Reform movement in Germany and an advocate of the elimination from the Jewish religion of (as he said) obsolete 'national' elements.

[12] i.e. province.

18. To Leo Motzkin, Berlin. *Pinsk, 23 January, 1896**

Russian: H.W.: C.Z.A.—A126/16/2

Pinsk, 11 Jan. 96

Dear Friend,

I wrote you a long epistle some weeks ago,[1] in which I informed you of the reason for my stay in Pinsk, of my discharge from military service, etc.

To my regret, I have still had no reply from you! Is it possible that you did not receive my letter? This seems hardly credible, for it has not been returned to me. Why don't you write? What has been happening at your end this winter? Has it been a very interesting one? Have any new people joined our side?

What's the latest in the Palestine circles[2] in Berlin? What about your personal affairs? What about your studies?

I shall come in March without fail for a long stay and shall not be returning to Russia so soon.

Hardly anything happens over here. Our Jewish society is marking time. There is something in the air, and people are expecting great changes for the better! What do you know at your end? Have you heard anything about the memorial that the Jews intend to submit at the time of the Coronation?[3] You remember I told you in Brest[4] about the model *heder* established in Pinsk;[5] it is a great success and is creating an upheaval in all local educational affairs. Like every upheaval, it is accompanied by revolutionary outbursts and abusive protests on the part of the *melamdim*.[6] Altogether, a violent struggle! It looks as if the *Talmud Torah*[7] and the other Jewish institutions will fall into our hands. All this is not [achieved] without a violent struggle, and as you see, in actual fact I have already succeeded in accomplishing something practical along our lines! You know, I am very, very glad that I stayed here for the winter. For in spite of everything, I have managed to accomplish something! How is Eliashev? Please let me know

---

18. [1] See No. 17.

[2] i.e., Jews interested in the Palestine (*Hibbath Zion*) movement.

[3] A Jewish deputation was received by the Czar Nicholas II on the occasion of his Coronation in May 1896 but nothing is known of the submission of a memorial.

[4] As to their meeting in Brest-Litovsk, see Nos. 14, 15.

[5] See n. 8 to No. 17.

[6] Hebr. (in orig. in cyrillic characters), 'teachers', denoting teachers of the old-fashioned type concerned mainly with religious instruction.

[7] Hebr. (in orig. in cyrillic characters), lit. 'Study of the Law'—a school at which education of substantially the same type as was given at the *heder* was provided, at the expense of the local Jewish community, for orphans or children whose parents could not afford to pay fees.

whether there is any truth in Wintz's report about the expulsion of Russian-Jew[ish] students from Berlin;[8] who exactly was expelled?

Write at once, without delay.

Ever yours,

Ch. Weizmann

I sent two letters to Israel at Brovari[9] and have had no reply. Where is he now?

Regards to all the colleagues.

19. To Leo Motzkin, Berlin. *Pinsk, 11 February 1896**

Russian: H.W.: C.Z.A.—A126/16/2

Pinsk, 30 Jan. 96

Dear Motzkin,

I received a letter from Makhlin to-day, informing me of the meeting [of the society] for the dissemination of education with the aid of books in Yiddish.[1] I am becoming increasingly convinced that you are to blame for not letting me know about the programme and exact aims of this society. I am certain that it would have been possible to do a great deal in Pinsk[2] with my help.

I did not wait for your letters, however, and, it seems, have done rightly. Without any noise or meetings, I took it upon myself to start this work in Pinsk, and I think it will prove successful.

Be that as it may, I feel deeply offended at being ignored like this, all the more because it is you who are doing it. How often have you yourself spoken about organisation, frequent contact between members, unanimity, etc., etc.? In practice, the exact opposite happens. In spite of my frequent appeals and requests, you do not

---

[8] The Warsaw Hebrew journal *Hatzefirah*, 2/14 Jan. 1896, published a report from Berlin by J. L. Wintz about expulsion orders served by the Prussian Government on a number of Russian Jews, including some students, who had failed to satisfy the authorities that they could support themselves. The report went on to say that the Prussian Minister of the Interior had acted in the matter without consulting the Chancellor, and that the orders had been cancelled before they had been fully executed.

[9] The Motzkin family home, near Kiev.

19. [1] A meeting of Russian-Jewish students in Berlin early in Feb. 1896, under the auspices of the Russian-Jewish Academic Society, resulted in the formation of a society for the distribution of reading-matter for the masses in Yiddish (later known as *Bildung*: *Verein zu Foerderung der Literatur in Juedisch-deutscher Mundart*— Society for the promotion of literature in the Yiddish tongue). The society made ambitious plans but achieved little: for material on *Bildung* see C.Z.A.—A126/17.

[2] See No. 13.

give a single sign of life. Everything simply disappeared without trace. Perhaps you did this deliberately, in which case I dare not protest. But if it was all simply for some insignificant reason, I protest with every fibre of my soul. I intended to approach the committee of the circle with an official enquiry, but <u>obviously and naturally</u> both its address and its composition are unknown to me. In future, I shall refuse to understand why so much noise is made about practical activity. If the members do not wish to arrange matters among themselves, how is regular activity conceivable?

Believe me, at first I was concerned about your health and was terribly worried. But Makhlin's letter has assured me that everything is all right. It follows that you simply did not want to write. This would drive anybody wild.

Yours,
Weizmann

20. To Leo Motzkin, Berlin. [*Pinsk*], [*between mid-February and mid-March 1896*]

Russian: H.W.: C.Z.A.—A126/16/2

[Undated but apparently written after No. 19 (11 Feb. 1896 N.S.) and before No. 21 (19 March 1896 N.S.).]

Dear Motzkin,

I am very worried at not having yet received an answer to my three letters to you,[1] for I really cannot imagine that you did not want to reply to me for some reason or other, or that you haven't yet got down to it. Something must have happened to compel you to keep silent. If, on the other hand, everything is going on as usual, then I have every right to jump on you, for, if I may say so, it is by no means comradely not to write at a time when I need news of you and all our friends.[2] Even assuming that you have no time (?)[3] to show any interest in me, Pinsk itself is in some respects of interest to us, and were I to receive proper instructions from Berlin, I could do a great deal for the Jews of Pinsk, for the ground here has already been prepared. Even when I get some scanty news about Berlin, it is always cursory, second-hand! Makhlin, by the way, writes about some meeting [? of the society] for the dissemination of Yiddish literature.[4] I do not know what it is all about. Meanwhile

20. [1] 'Two' altered by W. to 'three', the three letters in question being, presumably, Nos. 17, 18, 19.   [2] Lit., 'ours'.
[3] Note of interrogation in orig.   [4] See n. 1 to No. 19.

I badly need the <u>most detailed</u> information of activities of this nature. And so, even if you do not want to write to me, Weizmann, it is still your duty to initiate me into the affairs of the R.E.N.F.,[5] as a member in full sympathy with its activities. I repeat, I ought to consider myself well and truly insulted, but זאל מיינס איבערגעהען[6] In the name of all that is dear to us, the undersigned demands to hear from you.

Yours,

Ch. Weizmann

Pinsk (Gov[ernment] of Minsk)

Regards to all the comrades. I impatiently await an immediate reply with detailed news of everything that I <u>must know</u>.

21. To Leo Motzkin, Berlin. *Pinsk, 19 [? March] 1896*

Russian: H.W.: C.Z.A.—A126/16/2

[The month omitted from W.'s date is probably March.]

Pinsk, 7/19 [. . .] 96

Dear Motzkin,

אנסה נא עוד הפעם לדבר[1]

I have to write for the sixth time,[2] and beg you for the reply I need so much. I can imagine very vividly how fed up with my letters you must be by now. On the other hand, I hasten to assure you that were it not for the absolute necessity of finding out about the detailed programme of the latest student meetings in Berlin, as well as the decisions taken there concerning the dissemination of Yiddish books (which ones, exactly??)—I would certainly not impose myself upon you who consider it quite superfluous to answer my frequent appeals. In all probability you have your own weighty reasons, which entirely elude me. Believe me, your behaviour has made me reflect more than once, but save for the purest comradely feelings, I do not feel guilty of anything. But enough of this! I shall make the following suggestion: do answer me in the name of the circle,[3] or alternatively—if you really do not want or find it

---

[5] The Russian-Jewish Academic Society.   [6] Yidd., 'I will not insist'.

21. [1] Hebr., 'I shall try once more to speak'.

[2] In No. 20 W. complains of Motzkin's not having answered 'my three letters', meaning, presumably, Nos. 17, 18, and 19. No. 20 makes a fourth unanswered letter, but it is not possible to account for W.'s 'for the sixth time'. Either a letter has been lost or W.'s 'for the sixth time' is a slip for 'for the fifth time'.

[3] It is not clear whether 'the circle' means the society for the dissemination of Yiddish literature or the Russian-Jewish Academic Society.

impossible to write—instruct one of the colleagues to let me know what I have asked.

All I need is information! Any other details I do not dare to hope for even in my dreams. May I wish you all the best.

At your service,
Ch. Weizmann

22. To (i) Leo and (ii) Israel Motzkin, Brovari. *Berlin, 20 September 1896*

Russian: H.W.: C.Z.A.—A126/16/2

[W. had in the spring or summer of 1896 returned from Pinsk to Berlin to resume his studies at the Charlottenburg Polytechnic.]

Berlin, N.W., 20.ix. 96
Calvinstr. 27 Hof links I.

Dear Motzkin,

I promised you to write more from Berlin, and we[1] have decided to share this task between the two [of us]. But there isn't much to share. Everything here is as quiet as before, there are no new faces, and some of the old ones are missing too. The most awful shortage of money. If anybody is unlucky enough to fall into our clutches, he is fleeced without any further discuss[ion] until he becomes like us; such was the fate of Mr. Mirkin.[2] Eliashev presumably wrote to you about him, moreover you have seen him yourself. In my view he has many characteristics of the half-baked Palestinian[3] whose first impulse is to shove this disorderly mass of Jews off to Palestine merely so that they should be there. The three of us[4] visited Ahad Ha'am today. The conversation turned on various rather unimportant questions; we did not touch upon anything fundamental as this first visit was of an official character[5] and we had to take into account the duration of his stay. He is leaving here in a week's time and [? is going] to Cracow, where in many respects

---

22. [1] The person with whom W. had agreed to share the task of keeping Motzkin informed about events in Berlin appears from the context to have been Eliashev, with whom W. is known to have shared a room for a time when they were both studying in Berlin.

[2] Nahum Mirkin, of Kiev, at this time studying in Berlin; later one of the Zionist leaders in Kiev.

[3] i.e., interested in the Palestine movement, but for the wrong reasons.

[4] W., Eliashev, and Mirkin.

[5] 'Official' perhaps in the sense that they went as representatives of the Russian-Jewish Academic Society, or 'official' may mean merely 'formal'.

it will be easier for him to work.[6] On the whole Ahad H[a'am]
makes a very pleasant impression as a European.[7] He spoke about
the Palestine cause with restraint, not too much, without heat and,
or perhaps it only seemed so to me, with a little pinch of scepticism.

We intend to pay a visit to Birnbaum soon. Davidson, Syrkin,
Esterman are all well. The first[8] is working very hard and will
probably earn quite well. Kunina[9] will soon be moving to our part
of the world. She is very bored, poor soul, and her brother will
most likely not arrive for another month. Well, that is all there is
to say about the Berlin crowd. What news at your end? What is
the miscellany you mentioned in your postcard?[10] Is its publication
merely a conjecture or is it already a fact? Do write about it. You
needn't be afraid of our keeping silent; we shall conscientiously
do our best to reply. The first session of the *Frauenkongress*[11] took
place today. The entrance-fee was 5 marks. You can understand
what an enormous obstacle this is for us, and moreover tickets are
difficult to get hold of. The Town Hall was crowded. The attendance
was greater than expected: there were 600 women. All the same, we
hope to get in tomorrow. We shall scrape the money together
somehow. Write about your health and whether the baths have
already had an effect.

Keep well,

Yours,
Ch. Weizmann

My dear Israel,

You still remain silent. Where after all is the promised letter?
What are you doing and what do you intend to do? I really don't
understand why you keep silent. I hope that your tongue will

---

[6] Ahad Ha'am was in Berlin in connexion with his plans for the publication of
his Hebrew monthly, *Hashiloah*. As permission to publish in Russia was not forthcoming, he had been thinking of Berlin or Cracow as possible alternatives. He
eventually decided on Berlin, where *Hashiloah* was published until 1903, though,
except for the first few months, it was edited by A. H. from his home in Odessa, to
which he returned, after a short stay in Berlin, in 1897: see Leon Simon, 'Ahad
Ha'am', pp. 130 ff.

[7] 'as a European'—i.e. like someone belonging to the Western world.

[8] By 'the first' W. means Birnbaum, who had recently arrived from Vienna in
Berlin, where he hoped to get some help from the Zionists and was, soon after his
arrival, appointed editor to *Zion*, as to which see n. 10 to No. 17.

[9] Sister of Lazare Kunin.

[10] From a letter of the same date, 20 Sept. 1896, from Eliashev to Motzkin (C.Z.A.—
A126/16/4) it appears that Motzkin was contemplating the publication of what
Eliashev describes as 'a collection of writings'—presumably on Jewish subjects. So
far as is known, nothing came of the project.

[11] An International Congress of Women opened in Berlin on 19 Sept. 1896.

loosen at last. I have been asking you for this for such a long time. Tomorrow I shall start work at the laboratory. Until now haven't done a thing.

Do write to

Yours
Ch. Weizmann

Please bring cigarettes and tobacco: we are all smoking some kind of rubbish, Eliashev—the Herzegovina brand, and I—something like mahorka.[12] Davidson collects stubs. Save our lungs!

23. To Leo Motzkin, Berlin. *Berlin,* [*late May or early June 1897*]

Russian: H.W.: C.Z.A.—A126/16/2

[Undated, but written before W.'s final departure from Berlin in the summer of 1897 and, apparently, shortly before his letter of 4 June 1897 (No. 24).]

My dear Mr. Motzkin,

I am forwarding a letter received at my address; you will probably be going to this meeting. It is in connection with the ball.[1]

Unfortunately I cannot go as I am very unwell. If you can, please send me 3 marks[2]—I shall be very grateful.

I am in bed without a pfennig, and I am in dire need.

Yours,
Ch. Weizmann

24. To Leo Motzkin, Berlin. *Berlin, 4 June 1897*

Russian: H.W.: C.Z.A—A126/16/2

N.W., 4.6.97

Mr. Motzkin,

I am still without a reply to my letter.[1] My need for money increases every day, and I urgently <u>insist</u> on some kind of an answer.

---

[12] Shag.

23. [1] Possibly the annual charity ball given by the Russian-Jewish students in Berlin—see *T. and E.*, p. 58.

[2] '3 marks' looks like a slip for '30 marks', the sum mentioned in W.'s letter of 29 June (No. 25). The words 'the rest of the amount owing to me' in his letter of 31 July (No. 27) show that W. was pressing for the payment of money owing to him by Motzkin.

24. [1] See No. 23.

I consider your attitude towards me quite incomprehensible. Am awaiting a reply.

Yours faithfully,
Ch. Weizmann

If I get no reply by <u>Tuesday</u>, I shall consider the debt <u>lost</u>.

25. To Leo Motzkin, Berlin. [*Berlin*], *29 June* [*1897*]

Russian: H.W.: C.Z.A.—A126/16/2

[Year omitted by W. but obviously 1897.]

My dear Mr. Motzkin,

Unfortunately I cannot come to you and am forced to contact you in writing. I am terribly hard-up; I positively haven't a single pfennig to my name. The first is approaching, and I am unable to pay the landlady; I owe money to several persons who are causing me unbearable unpleasantness. I therefore beg you to let me have at least 30 marks, without fail. This is the only source on which I can count. If you refuse, I shall find myself in a positively desperate situation. If I were able to find any other solution, I would have left you in peace, but I am in terrible straits and in fact depend entirely on you. I have nothing to pawn. My compasses have long been in the appointed place,[1] and they are my only wealth.

Forgive me for appealing to you.

Yours,
Weizmann

29/vi

26. To Leo Motzkin, Berlin. *Berlin*, [*July 1897*]

Russian: Vcd.: H.W.: C.Z.A.—A126/16/2

[No signature; written on visiting-card in W.'s handwriting.]

Have been waiting for your reply till now. Nothing has come. You have thus driven me to extremes—a thing I really did not expect. I expect the money to-morrow morning at eight. If you do not let me have it by then, I shall be forced to seek another solution, which may result in serious unpleasantness. To avoid this, I am warning you for the fourth or fifth time.

---

25. [1] Presumably the pawnbroker's.

1. Weizmann at 11 (1885)

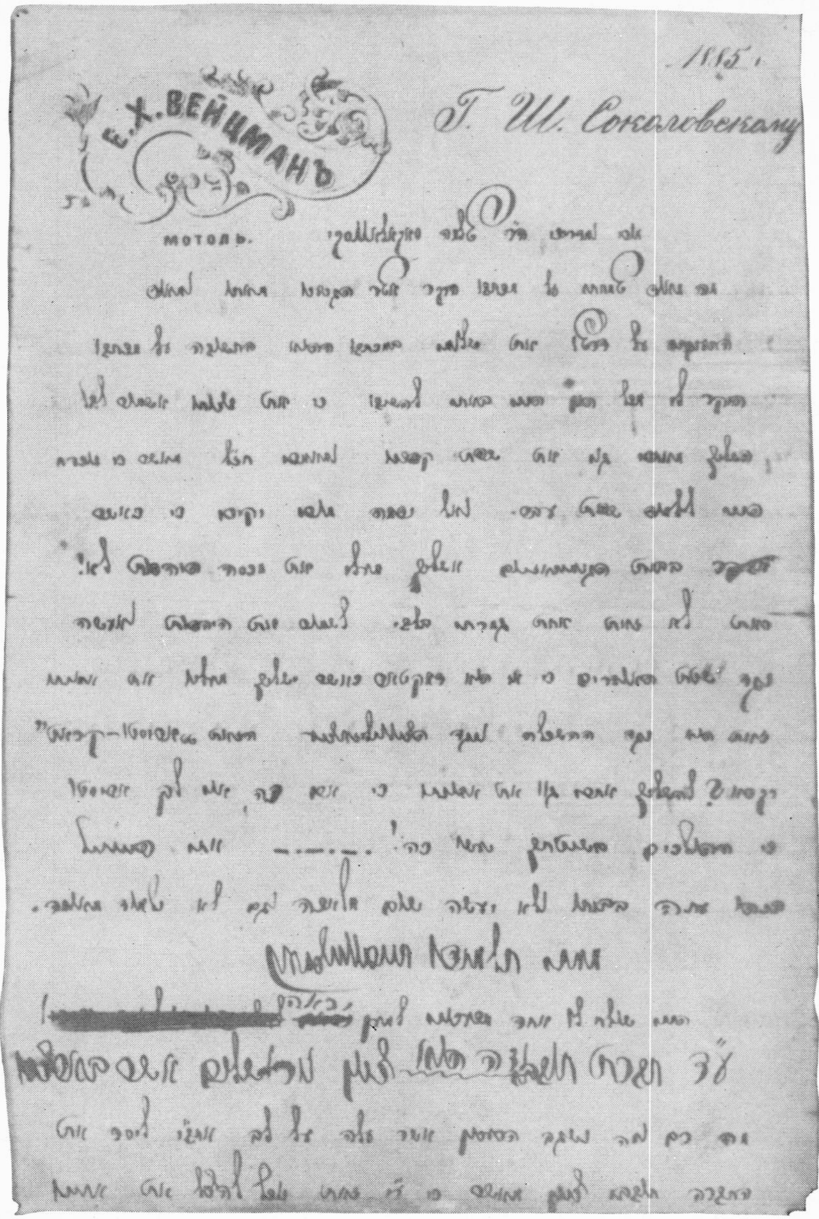

1885

Е. Х. ВЕЙЦМАНЪ

МОТОЛЬ

Г. Ш. Соколовскому

2. Letter to Shlomo Sokolovsky (1885) [Letter 1]

27. To Leo Motzkin, Berlin. *Berlin, 31 July 1897*

Russian: H.W.: C.Z.A.—A126/16/2

N.W., 31.VII. 97
Calvinstr. 27

Mr. Motzkin,

I am leaving Berlin on Monday, and do not intend to return here any more.[1] Were it not for my dire need, the existence of which you don't admit in this instance (as I have succeeded in discovering), I would not approach you at all, of course. I need **30 marks**[2] before my departure, which I count upon and which I ask you to let me have without fail. I hope that you will not refuse me this last time, despite the wrathful persecution and the crusade you started against me.[3] I am awaiting an immediate satisfactory reply and would point out that this is my last appeal to you. You can give Mr. Esterman the rest of the amount owing to me.

Yours faithfully,
Ch. Weizmann

[Apart from certain letters from W. to his first fiancée, Sophia Getzova, which, as explained in the General Introduction (see Section I. p. xx), are in private hands and have not been made available for publication, the only W. letter belonging to his Fribourg period (autumn 1897–early 1899) which has been found is that printed below, written while he was on a visit to his home at Pinsk after attending the Second Zionist Congress (Basle, Aug. 1898), the first Congress in which he took part—he missed the First Congress (Basle, Aug. 1897), notwithstanding his election as a delegate, for the reasons explained in *T. and E.*, pp. 65–68.]

28. To Leo Motzkin and Paula Rosenblum,[1] Berlin.
*[Pinsk], [? 24 September] 1898**

Russian: H.W.: C.Z.A.—A126/16/2

[Written (undated) on the reverse side of a letter from Sophia Getzova to Leo Motzkin and Paula Rosenblum dated 12/24.10.98. The last sentence of

27. [1] W. left Berlin for good that summer, returning to his home in Pinsk. In the autumn of 1897 he became a student at the Swiss University of Fribourg, where, after the submission of a thesis in January 1899, he was awarded his doctorate (Ph.D.) *magnâ cum laude.*
[2] See No. 25.   [3] It is not known what W. is alluding to.

28. [1] Paula (Polya) Rosenblum, Motzkin's future wife; they were married in Oct. 1899.

W.'s letter shows, however, that he was writing before *Hol Hamoed Sukkot* (the middle days of the Festival of Tabernacles), and these, in 1898, ended, according to the civil calendar, on 25 Sept./7 Oct. A conjectural explanation of the discrepancy is that Sophia Getzova's '12/24.10' was a slip for '12/24.9'.]

My dear friends,

And so once again you are in our good Berlin! Back at your daily chores after the portentous days of the Congress.[2] Over here there's a lot of pleasant news. Sonechka[3] has arrived! This means holiday-time down our way. Everybody is feeling splendid. We shall be very pleased to hear your news as soon as possible. Here there is much talk about Zionism and very little action for the time being. The collection of shekels[4] is only just being organised. As yet no instructions from Kishinev.[5] Propaganda is not yet being conducted as it should. A great shortage of speakers is felt. One ought to take advantage of these fiery times and of the holidays[6] but opportunities are being missed. Moreover, interest in the Dreyfus affair[7] is so great that Zionism falls into the background. In my opinion a conference of regional leaders is essential; they were unable to arrange things at Basle.[8] In Pinsk things are going very well! Propaganda is being conducted seriously and very successfully. During חוהמ״ס[9] I shall tour the neighbourhood and shall inform

[2] The Second Zionist Congress.

[3] Sophia (Sonia) Getzova.

[4] The annual registration-fee payable by members of the Zionist Organization—see General Introduction, Appendix II, para. 2.

[5] The Russian Zionists had, since 1897, maintained at Kishinev, under the direction of Jacob Bernstein-Kohan (usually referred to by W. as Kohan-Bernstein), a 'Correspondence Centre' whose duties included the receipt of reports from Zionist societies and regional leaders and the circulation of information and directives. As to its closure in 1901 see n. 12 to No. 144.

[6] The autumn series of Jewish Holy Days, ending with the Festival of Tabernacles.

[7] Captain Alfred Dreyfus, a Jewish officer in the French Army serving on the General Staff, had in Dec. 1894 been found guilty by a court-martial of treason. Jews throughout the world, and not least those of Eastern Europe, were, for obvious reasons, emotionally involved in the controversy raging in France at the time of this letter between Dreyfusards convinced that Dreyfus had been convicted on fabricated evidence and pressing for his rehabilitation, and anti-semitic right-wing elements violently opposed to the reopening of the case. If the date suggested for the letter in the headnote, 24 September 1898, is correct, it was written during the period of suspense between the setting up by the French Government, on 17 September, of a committee to consider whether the Dreyfus case should be reopened, and the Government's decision, on 26 September, to remit the question of revision to the Court of Cassation.

[8] Each of the areas into which Russia was divided for Zionist purposes had its 'regional leader'—usually one of the Russian members of the Greater Actions Committee. What W. seems to be saying is that meetings of regional leaders during the recent Congress had left various problems relating to their activities unresolved.

[9] Hebr., *Hol Hamoed Sukkot*—see head-note.

[you] afterwards what effect the Congress has had on these *Gottver-lassene*[10] towns.

Keep well,

Yours,
Chaim

After the Holy Days I shall go via Berlin to Paris.[11]

29. To Theodor Herzl, Vienna. *Berne, 28 January 1899*

German: H.W.: C.Z.A.—Z1/291

[Though signed also by Abraham Lichtenstein, the letter is in W.'s handwriting.—Early in 1899, after leaving Fribourg, W. appears to have lived for a short time in Berne before moving, in March, to Clarens-Baugy (Lake Geneva), and then, in April, to Geneva, where soon afterwards, at a date not precisely ascertainable but not later than August (see his letter of 5 Aug. 1899 —No. 36), he qualified as a *privat-docent* (accredited lecturer, unsalaried and paid by pupils' fees) under the auspices of the University and was also appointed Assistant to the Professor of Chemistry, Dr. Graebe.]

Berne, 28 January 1899

Dear Dr. [Herzl],

We should like, with your permission, to bring to your notice something which, in our opinion, may be of great value to the Zionist cause. On the occasion of a propaganda meeting one evening,[1] during which we succeeded in establishing closer contact with the local community here, we met a man whose association with the Zionist Organisation could be of far-reaching importance to our cause throughout Switzerland and even beyond.

We refer to Mr. Jacob Dreyfuss,[2] *Chef de Bureau* in the Swiss Political Department, Berne, Hirschengraben 4. We were struck by the way in which he tried to state the case against Zionism. However, he was only expressing his doubts as to the feasibility of the Zionist ideal; both the national idea and the necessity of Zionism, its ethical and cultural value, he acknowledged unreservedly.

In private conversation he proved to be an enthusiastic Jewish nationalist and to have a thorough knowledge of Jewish studies, especially Jewish history. He has intimated that, regardless of his position, he would be a spirited champion of Zionism once his

[10] Godforsaken.

[11] The purpose of W.'s projected visit to Paris is not known, nor is it known whether he did, in fact, go there.

29. [1] There is a report of the meeting, including W.'s opening speech, in *Die Welt* (the official organ of the Zionist Organization—see n. 7 to No. 35), 10 Feb. 1899.

[2] 'Dreyfuss' is a mis-spelling for 'Dreyfus'. Jacob Dreyfus (1846–1917) was the Head of the Emigration Department in the Swiss Foreign Office.

doubts have been dispelled. We therefore think it desirable that you should exert your influence to win his further support for Zionism in its practical aspect. A fighter will then have joined our ranks who, by reason of his highly respected position, his integrity, culture and eloquence, will have a decisive influence on all sections of the Jewish population in Switzerland.

May we ask you, Sir, if you would give us your views on this delicate question?[3]

With Zion's greetings,

Yours truly,
Dr. Ch. Weizmann
A. Lichstenstein[4]
(Schwarzthorstr. 59. I)

30. To Leo Motzkin and Paula Rosenblum, Berlin.
[Berne], 4 February 1899

Russian: Pcd.: H.W.: C.Z.A.—A126/16/2

4. II. 99

Dear Leo and Paula,

Why do you not write? And we think of you so often. Write to yours,

Chaim

[Also signed, with short messages, by Sonia (Sophia) and Rebecca Getzova, Chaim Khissin, Abraham Lichtenstein, Saul Stupnitzky, and two other persons.]

31. To Arieh Reich,[1] Basle. *Berne, 20 February 1899*

German: H.W.: C.Z.A.—Z1/156

Berne, 20. II. 99
Drosselweg 25.

Dear Fellow-Zionist,[2]

I take the liberty of sending you an invitation to our ball.[3] We wish to combine this ball with a certain amount of propaganda,

---

[3] Herzl's reply, if any, has not been found. So far as is known, nothing came of this contact with Dreyfus.

[4] Abraham Lichtenstein, who later married W.'s sister Haya, was president of the Berne Academic Zionist Society.

31. [1] At this time director of the Congress Office maintained by the Zionist Organization at Basle.

[2] Here, and in all succeeding letters, *Gesinnungsgenosse* has been translated 'fellow-Zionist'.

[3] Probably a ball to be given by the Berne Academic Zionist Society, of which W. was one of the founders.

and should be delighted if you were able to join us that evening. You will then also have an opportunity of addressing those present.

Would you, my dear Mr. Reich, be so kind as to let me know whether you intend coming to Berne on Thursday, March 2nd?

With Zion's greetings,

Yours truly,
Dr. Ch. Weizmann

32. To Arieh Reich, Basle. *Clarens-Baugy, 11 March 1899*

German: H.W.: C.Z.A.—Za/156

Clarens-Baugy, 11. III. 99
Maison Martin.

Dear Fellow-Zionist,

I've now left Berne for good and shall be spending the vacation on the shores of Lake Geneva. It would be a good idea to hold a propaganda meeting here.

With your help and that of friends in Berne it will be possible to make the necessary contacts with the local Jews and to work on them during this month. I'd therefore like to have your reactions soon. What news is there? I have already been cut off from all Zionist activities for a week. I should be very pleased to hear from you. Do drop me a line.

With best wishes,

Yours very truly,
Ch. Weizmann

33. To Max Bodenheimer, Cologne. *Geneva, 28 April 1899*

German: Pcd.: H.W.: C.Z.A.—A15/203

[Addressed to 'The Zionist Organization of Germany, c/o Dr. Bodenheimer'. Bodenheimer was the Chairman.]

Geneva, 28.IV. 99
Rue de l'Ecole de Chimie, 2.

Dear Dr. [Bodenheimer],

On behalf of our local Zionist Society I should like to ask if you would send me your various pamphlets, which I badly need for propaganda purposes.

With Zion's greetings,

Yours truly,
Dr. Ch. Weizmann
President.[1]

33. [1] W. had on 23 April been elected president of the Geneva Zionist Society:—see Veit to A.C., 30 Apr. 1899: C.Z.A.—Z1/295.

34. To Leo Motzkin, Berlin. *Geneva, 11 May 1899*

Russian: H.W.: C.Z.A.—A126/16/2

[This is the earliest extant letter in which W. addresses Motzkin as "Leo".]

Geneva, 11. v. 99

My dear Leo,   Rue de l'Ecole de Chimie, 2.

This is about the tenth time[1] that I've had to start my letter to you with a reproach. This time I am seriously worried. I am quite unable to find a more or less satisfactory explanation of the complete absence of any news from you. Now I even have all sorts of most unpleasant visions, and they are rapidly followed by still more gloomy ones. And both you and Polya persist in your silence.

Of course, I could begin this with a whole series of questions about your present life in Berlin, or I could ask you about Zionist affairs, but I know in advance that I shan't get a detailed reply and consequently won't be satisfied, while all my questions will seem to you just a banal flow of words. So I refrain. At the same time I think this attitude of yours is unfair. If a complete stranger turned to you for information about the progress of a cause that interested him, and with which you happened to be concerned, you would have to reply for the sake of the cause. Whereas I have asked you dozens of times already to give me at least some idea about the state of Zionism in Berlin, both among the Russian Jewish students and in other circles, and all I get in reply is stubborn silence!

As you see, my letter has taken on the tone of an indictment, but surely you do realise that all this is a true expression of my state of mind. There is little of interest that I can relate about myself: I live here, engrossed in my laboratory work, which is advancing very successfully. There is Zionist work here too, but about this—some other time. How were Ber[nard] Lazare's resignation and his last article in *Flambeau*[2] received in Berlin?

---

34. [1] W.'s letter of 4 Feb. 1899 (No. 30) to Motzkin and Paula Rosenblum complains of his not having heard from them, but, apart from this, the letters here referred to have not been found.

[2] Writing to Herzl on 24 March 1899 (C.Z.A.—H. VIII. 479/12) Bernard-Lazare tendered his resignation from the Greater Actions Committee, complaining of that body's autocratic behaviour and the secrecy of its proceedings, and expressing anxiety about the danger of its abusing the power placed at its disposal by the establishment of the Jewish Colonial Trust (see General Introduction, Appendix II). This letter was published in the April 1899 issue of the Paris Zionist monthly, *Flambeau*, together with the text of a letter from the Editor, Jacques Bahar, to the Greater Actions Committee tendering his resignation, and an article in which he explained why he and Bernard-Lazare were withdrawing from the G.A.C. *Flambeau*, which began publication in 1899, had, up to the time of this letter, published only one article signed by Bernard-Lazare—'The Jewish Proletariat and Anti-semitism'. In speaking of 'his [B.L.'s] last article in *Flambeau*' W. is probably referring to what had appeared there about B.L.'s resignation.

My best regards to Polya. I am waiting, my dear friends, for detailed news from you. If you cannot or do not want to write a detailed letter, at least write a few lines to let me know whether all is well with you.

Yours,
Chaim

35. To Sigmund Veit, Basle. *En route to Nieder-Ingelheim-on-Rhine,* [*27*] *July 1899*

German: Pcd.: H.W.: C.Z.A.—Z1/297

[Railway pmk. Cologne–Frankfurt train, 27.7.99, though dated by W. July 28.]

At[1] Nieder-Ingelheim-on-Rhine,
28.VII.99
c/o Dr. Chr. Deichler[2]

Dear Fellow-Zionist,

I have just had news from Geneva that they have not yet received the electoral lists.[3] It is to be feared that there will be some delay. Mr. Reich[4] told me when I visited him that the electoral districts could not possibly be changed.[4] This would have to be authorised by the Central Committee.[5] I by no means share this view. Each country's organisation is surely entitled to divide up the districts as may be appropriate, and our amendment[6] does not constitute an infringement of the instructions received. Do please drop me a line, my dear Mr. Veit, and tell me how the whole thing goes. Who is standing in Berne? I'm staying here till the 7th and then going

---

35. [1] In orig., *z. Zeit* ('temporarily').

[2] This visit to Christian Deichler's home at Nieder-Ingelheim is the earliest indication, in the letters which have been preserved, of W.'s association with Deichler during his Geneva years, in research in the field of dye-stuffs chemistry, as to which see n. 15 to No. 55 and n. 10 to No. 92.

[3] Lists of voters entitled to take part in the election of delegates to the impending Third Zionist Congress.

[4] In connexion with the preparatory stages of the election, there was a difference of opinion between Veit, the Swiss member of the Greater Actions Committee, and Reich as to the delimitation of electoral districts in Switzerland, Veit taking the view that the arrangement favoured by Reich could open the door to the election of unsuitable candidates—see their respective letters to the Smaller Actions Committee in C.Z.A.—Z1/197. What Veit wanted—and W.'s reference to 'our amendment' shows that he wanted the same—was to have the Geneva Zionist group incorporated, for electoral purposes, in one of the Berne groups.

[5] i.e., the Smaller Actions Committee, the central authority, in contradiction to the committee of the territorial organization in the country concerned.

[6] See above, n. 4.

on to Basle. Could you perhaps send me copies of the last few issues of the '*Welt*'?[7] I'd be extremely grateful. Au revoir.

Yours sincerely,
Ch. Weizmann

36. To Paula Rosenblum, Heringsdorf.[1] *Darmstadt, 5 August 1899*

Russian: H.W.: C.Z.A.—A126/16/2

At[2] Darmstadt, 5.VIII.99

Thanks for your news![3] It's not good, not good at all, that you've taken it into your head to be ill, but I do hope that you will be better soon. Why didn't you come to Switzerland? Last year it did you so much good, and we expected you again without fail. In any case, you must look after yourself seriously [and] take a thoroughgoing course of treatment to make sure that this sort of thing shall not happen again, and besides, you should not work so hard. You see how good I am at giving advice! Sonechka left for home[4] some ten days ago and arrived safely. She is going to work at the clinic of one of the Pinsk doctors.[5] Her address is: Weizmann, Pinsk. Rivochka[6] is in Berne. She is coming to Basle in four days' time, and we shall stay there till after the Congress.[7]

We are all living under a terrible nervous strain. What will our 3rd Assembly bring us? As you know, much in Zionism depends on it—almost everything.[8] There are so many enemies on all sides,

[7] German weekly, the official organ of the Zionist Organization, founded in Vienna, 1897.

36. [1] A Baltic seaside resort.

[2] In orig., '*z[ur] Z[ei]t*' ('temporarily').

[3] The letter referred to has not been found.

[4] By 'home' W. means, apparently, his own home in Pinsk—see, a few lines further down, 'Her address is: Weizmann, Pinsk'.

[5] Sophia (Sonia) Getzova was a medical student at Berne.

[6] Rebecca (Rivochka) was Sophia's sister and, like her, a student at Berne.

[7] The Third Zionist Congress opened at Basle on 15 Aug. 1899.

[8] Within the Zionist Movement there had developed serious strains and stresses arising from controversies in which both sides held strong views vehemently expressed—notably the differences between 'political' Zionists, who insisted that no practical work should be undertaken in Palestine until, by negotiation with the Sultan and the Powers, a Charter should have been secured authorizing immigration *en masse*, and *Hovevei Zion*, who disliked and distrusted the shifting of the emphasis to action on the political plane, and again between advocates and opponents of the recognition of 'cultural work' (see n. 8 to No. 40) as an integral part of the Zionist programme—a proposal in which both the 'political' Zionists and the religious wing of the Movement, though for different reasons, scented danger. There were also serious disputes about the control of the Jewish Colonial Trust and the use to be made of its resources, and there were the grievances of the members—especially the Russian

so many attacks, and all this has to be fought off in a straight-forward, open struggle. Will our delegates have enough energy and courage to rise to the height of the task they have been called to fulfil? Shall we succeed in attaining peace in Zionism and doing away with *Bruderkrieg*?[9] Shall we be able to make the delegates understand the true rôle they have to play? Will our assembly be able to devote itself soberly to sensible criticism without being carried away by appearances and external circumstances?[10] I am going to Basle now with *Schweren Herzens*:[11] shall I find relief there? Oh, how I longed to talk things over with you, with Leo: perhaps everything is clearer to you, more understandable, perhaps you are closer to the things that matter—but alas, there has been no response from you to my letters. This has tormented me terribly! I am impatiently looking forward to the day when I shall see our cheerful Leo, Leo the optimist, and shall be able to talk to him. I hope he will already be in Basle on Monday.

In my private life, as you already know, many pleasant things have happened. I managed to complete a successful *Habilitations-arbeit*[12] (an investigation into the field of *Naphthasarin-Farbstoffe*;[13] passed an examination, though not a very important one (*Collo-quium über neuere chemische Literatur*[14]); and have been appointed *privat-docent*. Furthermore, I am to be in charge of part of Professor Graebe's organic chemistry laboratory; I shall have 15 students, 5 of whom are working for a doctorate. I have every opportunity of continuing my work, of which, naturally, I want to take full advantage. I am very pleased by the turn of events. On the 20th I too am going to Pinsk,[15] where Sonia and I will remain until October. I shall come to Berlin. I don't think Heringsdorf is far from Berlin, and I shall drop in to see you for a few hours; it

members—of the Greater Actions Committee, who complained of dictatorial behaviour on the part of the Smaller Actions Committee in Vienna. Marred by some violent altercations, the Second Congress (Aug. 1898), though not entirely unfruitful, had been, on the whole, a disappointment. It is no wonder that W. was anxious about what was going to happen at the approaching Third Congress.

[9] In speaking emotionally of *Bruderkrieg* ('fraternal strife') it is impossible to be certain whether W. is referring to some particular controversial issue or to the cumulative effect of all the various causes of dissension within the Movement.

[10] What W. seems to be saying is that the delegates must be on their guard against allowing themselves to be dazzled by talk of prospective diplomatic successes or distracted by concentration on 'political' activity from a serious examination of the internal state of the Movement. [11] 'with a heavy heart'.

[12] The dissertation required to be submitted in order to qualify for appointment as a *privat-docent* (see head-note to No. 29).

[13] Naphthazarin dyes.

[14] Oral examination on recent chemical literature.

[15] Sophia Getzova was already in Pinsk (see opening para. of this letter), and W. intends to join her there.

would be nice to find you quite well by then. Sonia and Rivochka have probably written to you too.

From here I am going to Heidelberg, and tomorrow evening to Basle. My address in Basle: *postlagernd.*[16] Do write and tell me how you feel, Polya, how you spend your days, and how long you are staying at the *Kurort.*[17]

Keep in good health. See you soon.

Ch. Weizmann

37. To Rebecca Getzova, Berne. *Basle,* [*12 August 1899*]

Russian: Pcd.: H.W.: C.Z.A.—A88

[Date from pmk.]

My dear,

I am staying at 22.1 Kebgasse, which is behind the bridge, but do write to me always c/o *Zionisten-Kongress.* Leo[1] is not coming before Monday, nor need you be here any earlier, for neither of you will be admitted to the *Vorkonferenzen.*[2] Let me know exactly at what time you will arrive.

Yours
Chaim

Regards to Stupnitzky and Auerbach.[3] The cards[4] have been ordered.

38. To Theodor Herzl, Basle. *Basle,* [*19 August*] *1899*

German: Pcd.: H.W.: C.Z.A.—H.vii: 915

[Postcard, with Herzl's picture, in W.'s handwriting. Date from pmk.]

Town-Casino 5 hours after close of
the third splendid Congress[1]

This is the picture which is ever in our mind's eye and which we always carry and shall carry in our hearts.

Dr. Bruck
Dr. J. Lury
Dr. Ch. Weizmann

Hurrah!!![2]

---

[16] Poste restante.   [17] Spa.

37. [1] Motzkin.

[2] 'preliminary conferences'. Before the opening of a Congress it was customary for the delegates from each of the countries represented to meet separately—usually behind closed doors.

[3] It is not certain who is meant by 'Auerbach'. Among the Berne Jewish students at the time there were three persons of this name.

[4] Probably Congress visitors' admission cards.

38. [1] In orig., *des dritten glaenzenden Kongresses.* As to the outcome of the Congress see below, n. 3 to No. 40.   [2] In orig., *Hoch!*

39. To Moses Gaster, London. *Pinsk, 3 September 1899* *

German: Pcd.: H.W.: Gaster Papers, U.C.L.

[Written on Zionist Congress postcard with printed heading: '3 Zionist Congress, 15–19 August, Basle'.]

~~Basle~~[1]

Pinsk, 22.VIII. 99

Third Zionist Congress
9–13 Ellul 5659[1]

My very sincere good wishes for the New Year.[2] Long may you be spared to us, to the glory of Jewry and Zionism.

לשנה טובה תכתב ותחתם[3]

Dr. Ch. Weizmann

40. To Leo Motzkin, Berlin. *Homel, 11 September 1899* *

Russian: H.W.: C.Z.A.—A126/16/2

[After attending the Third Zionist Congress, which closed on 19 Aug. 1899, W. did some propagandist work in Russia.]

At[1] Homel, 20. VIII. 99

Dear Leo,

Thanks for your letter. I am most concerned about the vague way you write. Has there been a change in your plans? And we expected you in Russia and intended to come to see you. Where is Polya now? Gregory Lurie passed on her regards to me; he saw her at Druskienniki.[2]

Work is beginning here, and it promises to be very fruitful. Satisfaction with the outcome of the Congress[3] will now be reflected

---

39. [1] W. was using a Third Zionist Congress postcard with printed heading (in Hebrew), as here shown in English, above the text of the message. For the printed word 'Basle' he substituted 'Pinsk'.

[2] The Jewish New Year came in, in 1899, on the evening of 5 September.

[3] Hebr.: 'May you be inscribed and sealed for a good year', the traditional New Year greeting.

40. [1] In orig., *z. Zt* ('temporarily').

[2] A holiday resort on the border between White Russia and Lithuania.

[3] Bein, *Herzl*, p. 324: 'The Third Congress . . . differed from the first two in one important respect, namely that the ideological opponents of political Zionism took no part in it. The result was a mitigation of the internal strains. . . .' On some of the points mentioned in n. 8 to No. 36 there were still sharp differences of opinion, but the impression left by the Third Congress, as compared with the Second, was that its debates had been conducted in a better atmosphere, in a more realistic spirit, and with a greater sense of responsibility.

in [? increased] activity. The distrustful, nervous attitude to political Zionism may be expected to disappear and a true understanding of its aims and tasks to take root.[4] Lectures on Zionism and the 3rd Congr(ess) have begun in every town; the Holy Days[5] give us an opportunity of carrying out propaganda among the broad masses of the people.

People are amazingly receptive in their response to lectures and as soon as they leave the synagogue[6] would at once like to do something. It's a pity, however, that we have not enough active workers to keep that flame alight. The need for an organisation dealing exclusively with accurate, serious propaganda is all the more pressing now. This propaganda must not play on the passions and emotions of the masses; unfortunately many propagandists often consider it incumbent upon them to copy Herzl's London speech.[7] The opposition at the Congress[8] evokes great sympathy among the people; they appreciate it and are beginning to see it in its true light.

As you see, this is my third day with Bruck.[9] Things are going well in his area, thanks to his personality and his warm, straightforward attitude to his lofty and difficult task. Spirits are high everywhere; there is initiative, indeed a boundless love for the cause and its representative.

[4] As to the Herzlian Zionists' insistence that the Movement must concentrate its efforts on the securing of a Charter authorizing the settlement of Jews in Palestine *en masse* see n. 8 to No. 36. Among the *Hovevei Zion* there had at first been many who were opposed to, or at least suspicious of, Herzl's political Zionism, foreseeing that this would lead to loss of interest in the gradual building up of Jewish agricultural colonies in Palestine—the main practical objective of the *Hibbath Zion* movement,— and fearing that, by antagonizing the Turks, it would endanger the Jewish colonists and put an end to further infiltration.

[5] The period commencing with the approaching Jewish New Year and finishing, some three weeks later, with the end of the Festival of Tabernacles.

[6] Zionist meetings in Russia were often held in synagogues in order to circumvent the legal restrictions on public assemblies.

[7] At a Zionist meeting in London on 3 Oct. 1898 Herzl had confidently predicted that the time would soon come for a mass exodus of Jews to Palestine—see report in 'J.C.', 7 Oct. 1898. At the Third Zionist Congress (1899) Motzkin criticized this speech for arousing false hopes and thus creating difficulties for Zionist propagandists: III. Z.C. Prot., p. 69.

[8] There was no organized 'Opposition' at the Third Congress, but a number of Russian delegates (W. among them) criticized the Zionist leadership on various counts, including its preparations for the establishment of the Jewish Colonial Trust, its cold-shouldering of the members of the Greater Actions Committee, and its lack of interest in the encouragement of activities, commonly known as 'cultural work', designed to strengthen the national consciousness of the Jewish people and its attachment to its cultural heritage.

[9] Gregory Bruck was, as 'regional leader', in charge of Zionist activities in the area (known as the Vitebsk region) comprising the provinces of Vitebsk, Mohilev, and Minsk.

We have had two meetings here in the synagogue; of the intelligentsia and of the masses. Both were splendid, especially the latter.[10] We spoke to a huge crowd (perhaps over three thousand). The speakers were Bruck, Khissin, and *meine Wenigkeit*.[11] It was a staggering success. I have given a lecture in Pinsk and shall speak there once more, and now I am going to Mozyr.[12] During חוה״מ[13] I shall be going to Slonim, and after the Festival I shall probably be leaving: if there is the slightest opportunity I shall go south. I'll stay in Russia until the 1st Oct[ober], o[ld] st[yle].[14]

Please write to Pinsk and give me your news. Sonechka feels well, does a lot of both theoretical and practical work in the Jew[ish] hospital and has won the reputation of a Mumche[15] throughout Pinsk. Write at once, my dear Leo, to your faithful

Chaim

[Postscript by Gregory Bruck]

41. To the Editor of <u>Die Welt</u>, Vienna. *Berlin, 17 October 1899*

German: H.W.: Pcd.: N.L. (Schwadron collection)

At[1] Berlin, 17/x. 99

Please be so kind as to send 5 copies of the stenographic record of the proceedings of the Third Zionist Congress (C.O.D.).

Yours faithfully,
Dr. Ch. Weizmann

Geneva,
Rue de l'Ecole de Chimie, 2.

---

[10] A description by an eye-witness of the enthusiasm aroused by W.'s speeches at Homel is to be found in Yehuda Kahanovich's *Me Homel ad Tel Aviv* ('From Homel to Tel Aviv'), Tel Aviv, 5712 (1951–2), p. 29.

[11] 'your humble servant'.

[12] Mozyr and Slonim—small towns in White Russia.

[13] Abbreviation of Hebr. name, *Hol Hamoed*, for the middle days of the Festival of Tabernacles.

[14] —13 Oct., N.S.

[15] Hebr., in orig. in cyrillic characters, 'expert'.

41. [1] In orig., z. *Zt* ('temporarily'): W. was passing through Berlin *en route* from Pinsk to Geneva.

42. To the Editor of Die Welt, Vienna. *Geneva, 12 November 1899*

German: Pcd.: H.W.: N.L. (Schwadron collection)

Geneva, 12. XI. 99
Rue de l'Ecole de Chimie, 2.

Kindly send 10 copies of the record of the proceedings of the Third Congr[ess] and also 5 copies of both the Second and First Congr[esses], which I need for propaganda purposes.

Yours faithfully
Dr. Ch. Weizmann
Member of the Zionist Organisa-
tion of Switzerland

Kind regards to Mr. Reich.[1]

Could I, perhaps, also have Birnbaum's[2] writings and *'Auto-emanzipation'*?[3]

43. To Leo Motzkin, Berlin. *Geneva, 10 January 1900*

Russian: Pcd.: H.W.: C.Z.A.—A126/16/2

Geneva, 10. I. 1900

Dear Leo,

I am writing under the terrible impact of Kohan-Bernstein's letter in which he speaks of the crusade started against him.[1]

Let me know your views on all this at once. I shall write at length soon,[2] but do not wait for my detailed letter and reply without delay.

Best wishes to you and Polya,

Yours,
Chaim

42. [1] Arieh Reich (see n. 1 to No. 31) had been transferred from Basle to the Zionist Central Office in Vienna.

[2] Nathan Birnbaum ranked at this time as the leading theoretician of the Zionist Movement in Germany and Austria.

[3] As to Leo Pinsker's *Autoemanzipation*, see n. 9 to No. 1.

43. [1] Kohan-Bernstein to W., 26 Dec. 1899 (7 Jan. 1900), W.A., describing a campaign launched against him by the Zionist regional leaders in Russia, who accused him of wrongfully using circulars distributed by him in his capacity as Director of the Kishinev Zionist Correspondence Centre as a medium for the dissemination of his personal views, which were on a number of points at variance with the official line. As to the final phase of this controversy, ending with the closing down of the Kishinev Centre, see below, n. 12 to W.'s letter to Motzkin of 23 Nov. 1901 (No. 144).

[2] No such letter has been found.

44· To Leo Motzkin, Berlin. *Geneva, 9 June 1900*

Russian: H.W.: C.Z.A.—A126/16/2

Geneva, 9. vi. 1900
Rue de l'Ecole de Chimie, 2.

Dear Leo,

You must surely have given up all hope of receiving any letters from me. I am very much in the wrong as regards you and Polya, and 'ירָאתי בפצותי שיח להשחיל'.[1] My only excuse is that all this time I have been busy beyond endurance. There has been so much work of all kinds in the most unrelated fields that I now feel worn out and am in a hurry to go home[2] in order to rest for a couple of weeks. You will, of course, ask what we have achieved here. It is difficult to give a positive answer to this. Such an expenditure of strength and energy would have made it possible to move mountains among our masses in Russia, but here among the Swiss students, quasi-socialist, poorly assimilated as regards Judaism, degenerate, rotten, lacking in *moralischer Halt*,[3] the atmosphere spread by Plekhanov,[4] the General of the Russian revolution and *tutti quanti* has a pernicious effect upon them.[5] I have seen socialists here unable to utter two words without swearing, spitting or slandering someone three times, and I confess, my dear friends,[6] that I am not filled with respect for these representatives of social conscience and social justice. All the socialism of most of the local people, even of the most outstanding of them, is merely an *Ausfluss*[7] of their own insignificance and individual weakness: they need the crowd to hide behind it, not to educate it. They flock to the crowd because they are frightened of themselves. Only bitterness and similar negative motives drive our semi-Jewish youth here into the socialist camp, and on the whole they bring to socialism the elements of corruption and ferment. In this sense they are the true sons of their own people, agents of decomposition![8] The general picture is dreadful: *Kein Hirt und eine Heerde!*[9]

44. [1] Hebr., 'I tremble when I open my mouth to utter my words'—quoted from a passage in the Jewish New Year liturgy.

[2] To Pinsk.   [3] 'moral fibre'.

[4] The Russian revolutionary leader George Plekhanov was at this time and had been for many years resident as a political *émigré* in Switzerland.

[5] Cf. W.'s description in *T. and E.* (pp. 69–73) of 'the struggle . . . for the possession of the soul of that generation of young Russian Jews in the West'.

[6] 'friends'—thus in orig., meaning the two Motzkins.   [7] 'result'.

[8] Lit., 'fermenting fungi'. By the rather obscure words 'they are the true sons of their own people' (the Russian orig. does not admit of any other rendering) W. seems to mean that in this respect they correspond to the conventional picture of the rootless diaspora Jew.

[9] 'Sheep (lit., "flock") without a shepherd'. W.'s *Heerde* is a slip for *Herde*.

This is why they cannot be Zionists. They are lackeys, and lackeys in socialism cannot understand the boldness and the great cultural and ethical significance of the idea of the liberation of Jewry. They can understand Zionism only by analogy with other nationalist currents of this century: they can assess it only *relativ*,[10] by comparison with the Polish or Armenian movements. Not being Jews, they cannot see the purely Jewish side of the picture. They would like to free the Jews in accordance with a plan, to confine Zionism to the little frames which fit into their little heads, and being materialists (sic!)[11] they can never understand the prophetic aspect of Zionism.

In such circumstances, work here is exceedingly difficult. The lack of a Jewish *Weltanschauung*[12] on the one hand and the rottenness of our own times on the other! The Diaspora is dreadful. We have managed to be treated with respect here, to be considered a force and accorded some sympathy, *et c'est tout*! If you like, this could be called a foundation, but it meant cleaning out the whole *Augiasstall*.[13] O Lord, what a way to be using my energy! But enough of this.

I myself am very busy with chemistry. I have done three good pieces of work: one on my own, the other two with my postgraduate students. I have been reading a lot, delivered several papers, etc., etc. I have been travelling around for propaganda purposes, joining in all kinds of circles, in a word—I have tried to do something.

In a fortnight, at most in three weeks, I shall come to Berlin. Write and tell me your news, dear Leo, and under what *Insignien*[14] the Fourth Congress will meet?[15] Will you be in Ber(lin)? Where is Polya? How is she? What about your studies? How are things with you? Will I be able to stay with you? Please answer all my questions immediately.

I shall stay in Berlin 5 or 6 days, and then home. I still want to tour the district before the Congress.

What were the reasons for changing the place of the Congress: just because of the Trust?[16] What, in general, may be expected of

---

[10] 'relatively'.   [11] Thus in orig.

[12] The word used by W. in orig. is not *Weltanschauung* but its Russian equivalent, which is considered to be best represented here by *Weltanschauung* in the absence of any exactly corresponding English expression.

[13] 'Augean stables'.   [14] 'under what star' (lit., 'insignia').

[15] The Fourth Zionist Congress, originally intended to be held at Basle, opened in London on 13 Aug. 1900.

[16] The main purpose of holding the Congress in London was to secure greater publicity for its proceedings and, more particularly, to enable the Movement, as Herzl put it (Bein, *Herzl*, p. 341), 'to present itself to the English world and to solicit its support'. W. is here conjecturing (mistakenly, it would seem) that the change of

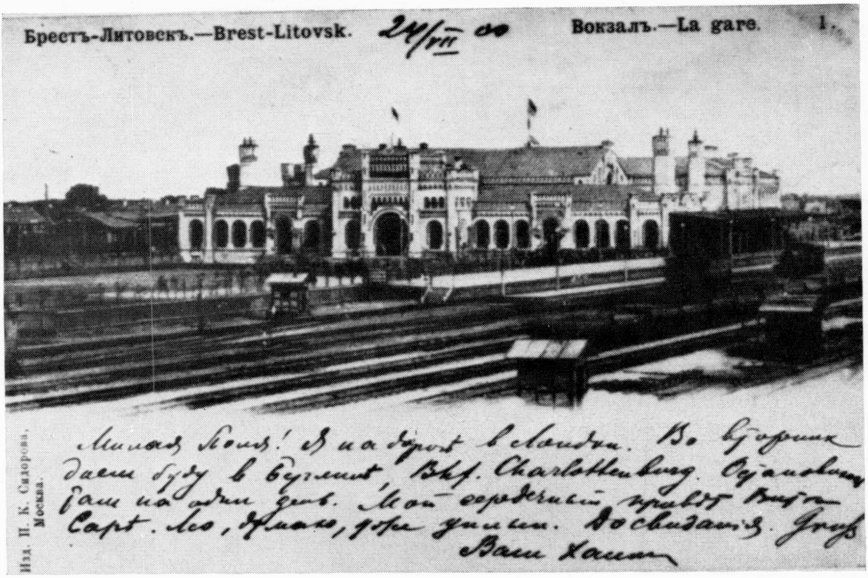

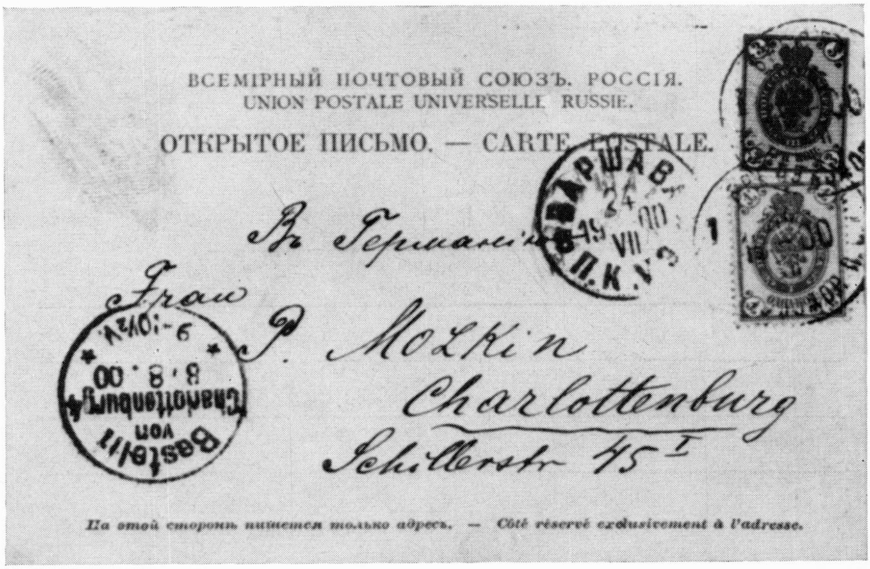

3. Letter to Paula Motzkin (1900) [Letter 46]

4. Vera Khatzman (1900)

the Fourth Congress? Oh, I am afraid of it. Leo, I implore you to write to me here at once about everything. I need it all before I leave. I require all the information for proceeding further, as I am still going to tour Berne, Lausanne and perhaps Zurich. Write *post-wendend.*[17]

Tomorrow I am off to Sonechka in Berne: we haven't seen each other for a long time. I am going to tear her and Rivochka away from their books, and we'll go up to the mountains for three days. On my return, I shall find a letter from you, shan't I?

How is Kunin? Has he passed his examination yet?[18] Or are his *Geburtswehen*[19] still continuing?

Once again my best wishes to you and Polya. My dear friends, how I should like to see you now, to have a chat about everything. I should feel refreshed and start living again. As it is, I am afraid I have already become provincial.

Please write, Leo, and you too, Polya, write at least a line and tell me how things are with you. I'd be so happy to get your news.

See you soon,

Yours ever,
Chaim

45. To Leo Motzkin, Berlin. *Geneva, 21 June 1900*

Russian: H.W.: C.Z.A.—A126/16/2

Geneva, 21/vi. 1900
Rue de l'Ecole de Chimie, 2.

Dear Leo,

Why don't you write? Are you really so busy that you cannot spare me a moment? I ask you to tell me immediately whether I shall find you in Berlin and whether you will be able to meet me. I am leaving on Tuesday and shall be in Berlin on Wednesday or Thursday morning. I am not sure whether Grolmanstr. is your correct address. I therefore ask you to write at least a few words, but *postwendend,*[1] and I shall wait for your reply. Some letters are

venue from Basle to London, which had been decided upon in May, shortly before the date of this letter, had something to do with the fact that the recently established Jewish Colonial Trust had its seat in London.

[17] 'by return of post'.
[18] Lazare Kunin was one of W.'s Berlin student friends. What examination he was preparing for is unknown.
[19] 'birth-pangs'.

45. [1] 'by return of post'.

probably already waiting for me at your place. Please write at
once. Best regards to Polya.

See you soon,

Yours,
Chaim

46. To Paula Motzkin, Berlin. [? *Brest-Litovsk*], 6 *August 1900**

Russian: Pcd.: H.W.: C.Z.A.—A126/16/2

[Written on a Brest-Litovsk picture postcard. Under 'Brest-Litovsk' (printed)
appears the date '24.7.00' written by W. Though there is a Warsaw as well as
a Brest-Litovsk pmk. (both dated 24.7.00), the card was evidently posted in
Brest-Litovsk.]

Brest-Litovsk, 24/VII. 00

My dear Polya,

I am on my way to London.[1] I shall be in Berlin on Tuesday,
Bhf. Charlottenburg.[2] I shall stop for a day. My best regards to
Vitya and Sarah.[3] Leo, I presume, has already sailed.

See you soon. *Gruss.*[4]

Yours,
Chaim

47. To Sophia Getzova, Berne. *London,* [12] *August 1900*

Russian: Pcd.: H.W.: C.Z.A.—A88

[Written on souvenir postcard of Fourth Zionist Congress. Berne pmk.
14 Aug. 1900; London pmk. missing. Undated, but date—12 Aug.—can be
inferred from the reference to the 'big meeting yesterday'—see n. 1.]

Darling,

I send you greetings. As yet I cannot be very pleased with the
way things have developed. A large bunch of unsuitable individuals
has arrived here. Sonechka, please write to Paris, *Poste restante.*
There was a big meeting yesterday attended by 7,000 people.[1] Am
feeling fine.

Keep well,

Yours,
Chaim

46. [1] As a delegate to the Fourth Zionist Congress, W. was travelling from Pinsk to
London for the opening of the Congress on 13 Aug.

   [2] The Charlottenburg railway station.

   [3] Not identified.   [4] 'Greetings'.

47. [1] On 11 Aug. 1900 there was a crowded public meeting at the Great Assembly
Hall, in the East End of London, to welcome the Congress delegates.

48. To Paula Motzkin, Berlin. *London* [? *16*] *August 1900*

Russian: Pcd.: H.W.: C.Z.A.—A126/16/2

[Undated. London pmk. missing; Charlottenburg (Berlin) pmk. 18 Aug. 1900. The Fourth Congress closed on 16 Aug.]

Exhausted and weary, broken morally and physically, I send you greetings, my good Polya, hoping that we may in the future see at our national assemblies more life, strength and courage in thought and deed.[1]

Yours,
Chaim

[Greetings added by Israel and Leo Motzkin.]

49. To Arieh Reich, Vienna. *Geneva, 1 November 1900*

German: Pcd.: H.W.: C.Z.A.—Z1/314

Geneva, 1 November 1900

Dear Mr. Reich,[1]

If minutes of the Fourth Congress are already available, would you be so kind as to send me a few copies? I could certainly do with them now that we are starting our propaganda campaign here. Only arrived here yesterday.[2]

Kind regards,

Yours,
Ch. Weizmann

Rue de l'Ecole de Chimie, 2.

48. [1] Writing in the Russian-Jewish weekly *Voskhod*, 15 (28) April and 3 (16) May 1901, W. expresses his regret that the proceedings of the Fourth Congress were directed mainly to making an impression on the outside world, to the neglect of any serious and realistic consideration of the Movement's own problems, adding that the Congress was all the more disappointing because of the low calibre of many of the delegates. In his recollections of the Fourth Congress in *T. and E.* (pp. 78–79), W. speaks of the disheartening contrast between 'the grandiose talk of a Jewish State' and 'the pitiful eleemosynary gesture' represented by an impromptu appeal for stranded refugees from Rumania who staged a demonstration at the doors of the Congress. Anxious for tangible evidence of progress, he was not impressed by 'big talk of Charters and international negotiations'. W. may also have been discouraged by the failure of the renewed attempt (see n. 8 to No. 40) to secure recognition of the importance of cultural work.

49. [1] See n. 1 to No. 42.
[2] No information is available as to W.'s movements between the end of the Fourth Congress in August and his return to Geneva on 31 Oct.

50. **To Arieh Reich, Vienna.** *Geneva, 20 November 1900*

German: Pcd.: H.W.: C.Z.A.—Z1/314
[Undated. Date from pmk.]

Geneva,
Rue de l'Ecole de Chimie.

Should the stenographic record of the IVth Congress have appeared, I should be grateful if you would send 5 cop[ies] c.o.d.; also 1 cop[y] of Hess, 'Rome and Jerusalem'.[1]

Yours sincerely,
Dr. Ch. Weizmann

51. **To Vera Khatzman, Geneva.** *Geneva, [? late 1900 or early 1901]*

Russian: H.W.: W.A.

[Written on a card (not a visiting-card). Undated, but the use of the formal 'you' (plur.) in this and the next following letters (Nos. 52 and 53) shows that all three are earlier than the letter of 30 March 1901 (No. 68), in which W. uses the more intimate form of address.—Vera Khatzman (b. 1881), whose home was at Rostov-on-Don, came to Geneva as a medical student in the early autumn of 1900, when she was just under nineteen, and there met W., whom she was to marry in 1906. For her own account of her first meeting with W. see her memoirs, *The Impossible Takes Longer*, London, 1967, p. 17.]

I came to see you at 8.30. Will call again at 10. I have a meeting of the Jargon Committee.[1]

Ch. W.

52. **To Vera Khatzman, Geneva.** *Geneva, [? late 1900 or early 1901]*

Russian: H.W.: W.A.

[Written on two separate sheets of paper. Undated.]

My dear friend,

You are bored, and I have a frantic desire to settle down with you in some corner and tell you a lot of things, but there are

50. [1] In *Rom und Jerusalem: die letzte Nationalitaetsfrage* (Leipzig, 1862) Moses Hess (1812–71), writing more than thirty years before the coming of Herzl, joined battle with the assimilationists and propounded the view that only by the establishment of a Jewish State in Palestine could the Jews hope to regularize their position and secure their rightful place in the world.

51. [1] 'Jargon'—a synonym, with no disparaging connotation, for Yiddish. A *Bildung* Society was founded in Geneva in Nov. 1900 for the same purpose—the encouragement and dissemination of Yiddish writings—as the society of the same name founded in Berlin in 1896—see n. 1 to No. 19.

unwanted eyes. I am not afraid of them, but they profane both of us, or rather—the relationship between us. This gets me down, I am insulted, but I feel better when I look at you, so calm and pure and a 'human being'.

Your friend

Nietzsche's[1] only characterisation of Goethe was: Goethe was a human being.

53. To Vera Khatzman, Geneva. *Geneva,* [? *late 1900 or early 1901*]

Russian: H.W.: W.A.
[Written on a card (not a visiting-card). Undated.]

Dear Vera Issayevna,

If you can, do please come to me at 1.30 or 1.45. I shall be waiting for you at home.

Yours,[1]
Ch. Weiz[mann]

54. To Catherine Dorfman, Geneva. *Geneva,* [? *early in 1901*]

Russian: Vcd.: H.W.: W.A.
[This undated note, unsigned but in W.'s handwriting, must have been written at some date between Catherine Dorfman's arrival in Geneva in the autumn of 1900 and Esther Shneerson's departure in the summer of 1901. The reference to Wasserman's book (as to which see n. 1) suggests a date early in 1901.]

I should be very grateful to you, Dorfman, if you would get Wasserman's [book][1] for me from Koenigsberg[2] and my Nietzsche

52. [1] This is the earliest of numerous references to Nietzsche in the letters of the period. At the turn of the century there was a considerable vogue for Nietzsche among the Russian-Jewish intelligentsia. How strong was the impression he made on W. can be seen, for example, from No. 266 (to V.K., 3 Aug. 1902): 'I am sending you Nietzsche. . . . This is the best and the finest thing I can send you.' W. nowhere explains precisely what it was in Nietzsche that so strongly attracted him, but, paradoxical as his youthful enthusiasm may appear in so fervent an admirer of the strongly contrasting teachings of Ahad Ha'am, it may well be seen as a reflection of his contempt for Jews who 'tremble and crawl before the goy' (see his letter to Motzkin, No. 13), and of his passionate desire to see the Jewish people liberating itself from its servile inhibitions and by its own efforts shaking off the chains of the Galuth.

53. [1] Lit., 'shaking your hand'.

54. [1] A writer in the Jerusalem Hebrew journal *Doar Hayom,* 19 Jan. 1934, recalls a lecture delivered by W. at Berne early in 1901, in which he discussed Jacob Wasserman's *Die Juden von Zirndorf*.
[2] Anne Koenigsberg, of Nikolayev, at this time studying medicine at Geneva,

from Shneerson. I need both books for my paper. I am so busy all day today that I shall be unable to go to them, but you will be seeing them anyhow at the club.[3]

I am leaving tomorrow morning. Please, dear Dorfman, do this, and give my regards to all our friends.

Yours[4]

55. To Leo Motzkin, Berlin. *Geneva, 3 February 1901*

Russian: H.W.: C.Z.A.—A126/24/7/2/2

[Lower part of last page missing—see below n. 12—This is the earliest of the W. letters which have been preserved in which reference is made to the idea of a Zionist students' conference (later usually spoken of as a Zionist Youth Conference, with the implication that it was not necessarily restricted to students)—a project which, as will be seen, was to absorb much of W.'s thoughts and energies until it fructified in a Zionist Youth Conference ('*Conferenz der Zionistischen Jugend*') at Basle in Dec. 1901.]

Geneva, 3/II. 1901
Rue de l'Ecole de Chimie, 2.

Dear Leo,

Thank you for such an interesting letter.[1] Here the story of the Berlin meetings[2] was related in a somewhat different tone. I knew at once, however, that the accounts were very biased. All the same, it is just as well that I know it all. It is most unlikely that there will be a further clash with the Bund[3] now, as

worked with W. in 1901 in the preparations for the Zionist Youth Conference and in 1902 in the Information Bureau of the Democratic Fraction. Later, practised medicine at Nikolayev.

   [3] Tatare's Club, the Geneva Zionist students' meeting-place.   [4] Unsigned.

55. [1] Not found.

   [2] What, or from whom, W. had heard about the Berlin meetings is unknown, but from a letter of 15 Jan. 1901 from Aaron Gourland to the Chairman of the Berlin *Kadimah* Society (see n. 9 below), C.Z.A.—A 126/14, it appears that at meetings organized by *Kadimah* there had been clashes between Zionists and supporters of the anti-Zionist Bund, among the matters most hotly debated being the affair mentioned in n. 11 below.

   [3] Founded in 1897, the Bund (*Allgemeiner Jiddischer Arbeiterbund in Lite, Poiln un Russland*—Yidd. 'General Confederation of Jewish Workers in Lithuania, Poland, and Russia') was affiliated to the Russian Social Democratic Party. Accepting its ideology, the Bund was implacably opposed to the Zionist Movement, with its Jewish nationalism and its appeal to the Jewish people to focus its aspirations on Palestine, insisting that the paramount duty of the Jewish masses in Russia was to stand shoulder to shoulder with their fellow-workers in the class-war and the revolutionary struggle against the Czarist autocracy. As to the future of the Jews in Russia, the Bund was in the embarrassing position of being conscious of its distinctive identity as a Jewish organization but at the same time aware that any claim to a separate 'national' status for the Jews, as distinct from the [recognition of their right, as individuals, to equal citizenship, might appear to cut across the principle of class

Davidson[4] intends to keep silent. All the others have had their rebuff. It will be some time before the next אידישער ארבייטער[5] appears. I have read the articles you mentioned. I am terribly pleased to hear from you that you intend to go through with the examination.[6] I have no doubts about your success. Though you are greatly needed, indeed indispensable just now, on the other hand it will be good if you snatch some time to settle this matter. *Wohlauf!*[7]

A pity you didn't give any answer about the student conference.[8] It seems to me (perhaps I am mistaken) that you do not entirely sympathise with this venture. Why is it? Was the question discussed in *Kadimah*?[9] I attach enormous importance to the cultural value and binding power of a lively youth organisation.[10] That is why I ask you to let me have your opinion. I understand that you yourself will not now be able to play an active part in arranging the conference, but other Berliners can replace you in this. Would it not be possible for a few people to gather together at Easter to join in a discussion of the matter? I should very much like *Kadimah* to express their view, and I think that this might better be done now.

Once again, I ask you for an immediate reply about this.

A preliminary conference is being proposed in one of the following

solidarity. After some wavering, the Bund was, at the time of this letter, moving towards a demand for 'cultural autonomy' for the Russian Jews. This is relevant to W.'s reference, later in this letter, to the Bund's 'so-called national programme'.

[4] Eliahu Davidson, described by W. in his letter of 20 June 1895 (No. 11) as one of his 'dear comrades', had, at or about the beginning of 1899, changed sides and aligned himself with the Bundists.

[5] Yidd., *Yiddisher Arbeiter* ('The Jewish Worker'), the Bund's Yiddish organ, at this time published in Geneva. The Bund had at its Third Convention (Dec. 1899) resolved that the *Yiddisher Arbeiter* should find space for a full discussion of Jewish nationalism, but the issue giving effect to that decision did not, in fact, appear until some months after the date of this letter.

[6] For a Ph.D. (Economics).   [7] 'Cheer up!'

[8] The letter to which Motzkin had failed to reply has not been found.—After a false start in the summer of 1900, the idea of a Zionist students' conference had been revived later in that year by a group of Jewish students in Munich. W. had associated himself with that group, and at the time of this letter work in preparation for the projected conference had already been started by W. in Geneva in conjunction with Alexander Nemser and Gregory Abramovich in Munich: see their letter to W. of 18 Dec. 1900 (C.Z.A.—A 126/16) and Nemser's letter to Motzkin of 12 Feb. 1901 (W.A.).

[9] The Berlin Russian-Jewish Academic Society had in December 1898 been reconstituted under the name of *Kadimah* (a transliteration of a Hebrew word meaning 'Forward'), with objects substantially unchanged but with a membership not limited by its constitution to Jewish students from Russia. W. was one of the founders of the Berlin *Kadimah* Society and served at the start as one of the two joint secretaries: see material on *Kadimah* in C.Z.A.—A 126/14.

[10] Lit., 'I attach an enormous cultural significance to a young, lively organisation, and a gathering one [*sic*], too.'

three towns: Munich, Berne, Heidelberg. Which do you all prefer?

It seems to me that you attach too much significance to the Bund and its behaviour at the Congress.[11] This is no doubt a nasty case, but manifestations of this kind are no part of its real *raison d'être*. That's why I did not feel like raising this charge against them in the discussions here. Another Zionist did it. As a matter of fact, the public over here has not yet grown up sufficiently to understand the significance of such cowardly behaviour. And the centre of gravity of our debates lay just in the so-called 'national programme'.[12] How sad is the duality, the lack of unity of this section of the Jewish intelligentsia. I suffered for them, I suffered greatly. And in this internal life of the Bund we witness the eternal and fateful struggle between two principles, a struggle which has had such an exhausting effect on Jewry and made it so nervous.

The Bund have no programme. They drift with the Russian *Fahrwasser*.[13] This is not what they want, at least some of them.

In our attitude towards them we must be more sensitive and look deeper. I sinned against the Bund, I spoke terribly flippantly about them when I came to see you last time, do you remember? This was only an excess of fervour, and it was wrong.

They can become a productive, creative element in the Jewish sense, but they need some fresh blood. A youth fraction in Zionism —this again is what this [- - - - - - - - - - - -][14] signifies for me for the time being.

I have received the contract from the factory [- - - - - - - - - - - -] today.[15]

[Signature missing.]

[11] The International Socialist Congress, Paris, Sept. 1900, at which the Bund was represented, adopted a resolution expressing sympathy with various oppressed peoples, but without mentioning the Jews. In Feb. 1901 *Kadimah* passed a vote of censure on the Bund's delegates for 'not having raised their voices on behalf of their people': text in *Die Welt*, 8 March 1901.

[12] See n. 3.

[13] 'current'—i.e. in the wake of the Russian Social Democrats.

[14] Lower part of last page of orig. torn off, leaving the gaps indicated in the printed text.

[15] The sentence commencing 'I have received the contract . . .' is written in the margin of the letter. Though it cannot be identified, this was probably a contract received from the Bayer Works, Elberfeld (later incorporated in *I.G. Farbenindustrie*), with which W. came to be closely associated, for the exploitation of a discovery, the joint work of W. and Christian Deichler, of Berlin, concerning the production of dye-stuffs. During his Geneva period (1899–1904) W. was engaged, in co-operation with Deichler, in a number of projects in the field of dye-stuffs chemistry: see details of patents registered in their joint names in P. Friedlander, *Fortschritte der Teerfarbenfabrikation*, 1900–2, p. 426; 1902–4, pp. 129, 240–2.

56. To Moses Gaster, London. *Geneva, 12 February 1901*

German: H.W.: Gaster Papers, U.C.L.

Geneva, 12. II. 1901
Rue de l'Ecole de Chimie, 2.

Dear Dr. Gaster,

The bearer of this message,[1] a compatriot[2] from Kiev, has suffered a severe misfortune through no fault whatever of his own and has been compelled to leave everything behind and escape to London.

He comes to this metropolis a complete stranger, almost a broken man and with scanty means. He is an honourable and respectable person, the father of a large family of intelligent children.

It is with a heavy heart that I address these lines to you; I know very well how many are the claims upon you.

We have here, however, a quite exceptional case, and I hope that you will not deny this gentleman the benefit of your advice.

With the greatest respect and Zion's greetings,

Dr. Ch. Weizmann

57. To Leo Motzkin, Berlin. *Geneva, [13 February 1901]*

Russian: Pcd.: H.W.: C.Z.A.—A126/24/7/2/2
[Undated. Date from pmk.]

Dear Leo,

We send you our heartfelt greetings from the meeting at which Davidson read a paper.[1] Things are going well.

Yours,
Ch. Weizmann

[Also signed by Catherine Dorfman, Anne Koenigsberg and three other persons.]

58. To Leo Motzkin, Berlin. *Geneva, [22 February 1901]*

Russian: Pcd.: H.W.: C.Z.A.—A126/24/7/2/2
[Undated. Date from pmk.]

Dr. Leo,

I am waiting for a letter from you as for manna from heaven.

56. [1] Not identified.   [2] *ein Stammesgenosse.*
57. [1] The meeting described in No. 60. In orig., 'is reading' corrected to 'read'.

Shall be in Berlin about March 20th. With best regards to you and
Polya.

Yours,
Chaim

Greetings from my friends.

59. To Leo Motzkin, Berlin. *Berne,* [? *23 February*] *1901*

Russian: H.W.: C.Z.A.—A126/16/2

[Undated, but the words 'from a Zionist ball at Berne' probably refer to a
party given by the Berne Academic Zionist Society on 23 February 1901
(mentioned in *Die Welt,* 22 Feb. 1901) in aid of the Zionist Reading Room
and the Jewish students' canteen—a date which fits in with W.'s repetition
of his request (see No. 55) for *Kadimah*'s views on the projected Conference.]

Dear Leo,

From the Zionist ball at Berne[1] I send warmest greetings to you
and Polya.

Am impatiently awaiting your letter and communications about
Kadimah's decisions concerning the conference.[2]

Yours,
Chaim

[Postscript by Sophia Getzova.]

60. To Leo Motzkin, Berlin. *Geneva, 3 March 1901*

Russian: H.W.: C.Z.A.—A126/24/7/2/2

Geneva, 3/III. 1901
Rue de l'Ecole de Chimie, 2.

Dear Leo,

Why don't you write ? I am simply in despair at not having heard
from you; your reply would have encouraged and heartened me.
You know that perfectly well yourself, so why don't you do it ?
I have made up my mind to leave between the 15th and 20th.[1]
I cannot possibly manage any earlier. Will you still be at home by
then ? But this I must know straight away. If you will be away
I shall not, of course, go to Berlin. On the way I shall be visiting
several University towns, and I want to make arrangements

---

59. [1] See head-note.
　　[2] As to the proposed Students (or Youth) Conference see n. 8 to No. 55.

60. [1] See No. 58: 'Shall be in Berlin about March 20th'.

everywhere about the Conference.[2] On the way back from Berlin I shall visit Leipzig and Munich.

However, so far I still do not know whether your *Kadimah* people want a student conference, whether this question was discussed among you, and in what form, and what proposals were made. My God, how difficult it is to do anything! One comes up either against silence or against meaningless phrases.

Well, I do not want to get more worked up. I hope I shall be getting a proper letter from you—you know what I mean—without delay.

Davidson has been propounding his critique of Zionism here. Khissin and I replied.[3] It is true that he speaks in a patronising way, and do you know he strikes one as a *meshumed*[4]—וואס ווערט א פרומער ‎גוי.[5]

He argued that Zionism leads to slavery, to the attachment of Jews to capitalism, and he denied the very existence of Jewish cultural creative power. In his opinion, the revival of Jewry is both impossible and not worth while from the material[6] as well as from the spiritual point of view.

A smell of corpses and of death pervaded his whole speech. It was a dirge sung out of tune.

The Bund applauded him strongly, very strongly.

I must admit that I didn't expect to hear this from Davidson. *Jargon Judenthum*[7] is still his sheet-anchor, but all this seems strange to me. You know there is so much incongruity in it that Davidson himself comes out as a truly tragic figure.

He is a vanquished, subdued Jew. *Resigniert!*[8] I cannot even feel angry, though Mr. Davidson doesn't hesitate to use cheap, journalistic methods of polemics; he has unpacked his *Kleinkram*[9]

---

[2] The projected Students' Conference.

[3] The debate here referred to, part of the polemics between the Zionists and the Bundists, appears from No. 57 to have taken place on 13 Feb. 1901. As to Davidson's defection to the Bundists see n. 4 to No. 55.

[4] Hebr., in orig. in Latin characters, 'a convert [to Christianity]'.

[5] Yidd., 'who becomes a devout gentile'.

[6] In orig., 'economic' corrected to 'material'.

[7] 'Jargon [Yiddish]-speaking Jewry'. Davidson had taken an active part in the movement for the popularization of Yiddish writing. W. was not antagonistic to Yiddish; in 1896 he had interested himself in the *Bildung* movement started in Berlin (see n. 1 to No. 19), and in Geneva he had joined the Committee of a Society with similar objects (see n. 1 to No. 51). The mistake with which W. seems to be charging Davidson is that of clinging to the conception of Russian Jewry as a self-contained Yiddish-speaking society rooted in its present home, rather than as a part of the Jewish people—a people with national aspirations centred on Palestine and with Hebrew—not Yiddish—as the national language.   [8] 'resigned'.

[9] 'petty wares'.

culture, Gaster's speech at the 2nd Congress[10] and above all the Bank, the Bank, the Bank![11]

By way of introduction he read a historical essay on the development of Zionism—copied from Arndt's article in *Mir Bozhyi*.[12]

Alles klang hohl.[13]

The Bund, of course, are pleased. They thrive on such things, it lulls their conscience to sleep. Zhitlovsky is going to speak here one of these days on Jewish culture (in a positive sense!). Mr. Davidson will, of course, perform again.

Not that he is here on Bund business; he has come to marry Ettinger.[14] *C'est tout!*

Dear Leo, please do write at once. You people must be very anxious on account of the Karpovich case.[15]

On what lines is the anthology you are editing being done?[16]

I urgently ask you to let me know your views on the Youth Conference—but without fail and at once.

My very best wishes to Polya.

Yours,
Chaim

Regards to Mirkin.[17]

[10] At the Second Zionist Congress (Basle, 1898) Gaster contended that there was no future for a Zionism stripped of traditional Jewish values and religious faith: II. Z.C. Prot., pp. 202–7.

[11] The Jewish Colonial Trust was denounced by the Bundists as an instrument of capitalist exploitation.

[12] In an article published in the Russian monthly *Mir Bozhyi* ('God's World'), 1901, No. 1, B. Arndt (pseud. for Barukh Brandt) surveyed the history of the Zionist Movement. While not opposing Jewish national aspirations, he contended that the Jews had no need to look outside Europe for a solution to their problems, since, with growing enlightenment, anti-semitism would dwindle and eventually disappear.

[13] 'It all rang hollow'.

[14] Yevgeny Ettinger, a Jewish Social Democrat from Kiev.

[15] On 27 Feb. 1901, in St. Petersburg, a student named Peter Karpovich had shot and mortally wounded the Russian Minister of Education, Bogolepov. Karpovich had been studying in Berlin. He was not a Jew, but from a reference to him in the reminiscences of Franz Kursky, a Bundist, who was in 1901 a student in Berlin, he appears to have had contacts there with Bundist circles: F. Kursky, *Gesammelte Schriften*, New York, 1952, p. 174. W. may have known of Karpovich's Jewish associations and, in any case, would naturally assume that 'you people' (Motzkin and his circle), as Russian students in Berlin, would be 'very anxious on account of the Karpovich case'.

[16] The Kiev *Kadimah* Society was making plans for the production of a series of miscellanies (W.'s reference to an 'anthology' is inaccurate) designed to provide a platform for the group of younger Zionists (W. was one of them) associated with the 'Opposition' views first openly aired at the Third Zionist Congress in 1899—see n. 8 to No. 40. The editorship had been accepted by Motzkin, who, however, later changed his mind and proposed that it should be offered to W. In the end nothing came of the project.   [17] See n. 2 to No. 22.

61. To Leo Motzkin, Berlin. *Geneva, 11 March 1901*

Russian: Pcd.: H.W.: C.Z.A.—A126/24/7/2/2

Geneva, 11/III. 1901

Leo, Leo,

How much longer do you intend to keep silent? You must realise that the whole itinerary of my journey[1] depends on your reply. You are an odd person, my friend. Let me have at least some news of you. Best wishes to you and Polya. I am waiting!

Yours,
Chaim

62. To Vera Khatzman, Clarens-Baugy. *Geneva, [? 13 March] 1901*

Russian: H.W.: W.A.

[Undated. 'March 1901', not in W.'s handwriting, appears to have been written in later. That the letter was probably written on 13 March 1901 can be inferred from (1) the announcement in the Geneva newspapers of a concert to be given on the evening of that day; (2) the words 'now I am rushing to a concert'; (3) the reference to 'yesterday's concert' in the undated letter (No. 63) later marked by W. as having been written on 14 March 1901.]

My dear friend,

I am in a terrible hurry. I worked right through the day and then letters came which had to be answered at once, and now I am rushing to a concert. All I have time for is to send you my <u>warmest</u> greetings, over there in that beautiful natural setting of yours.

I want you, my dear, to have a good rest, both in body and soul, from all that has been upsetting you so much, my sweet.[1] You have my ardent wishes for complete spiritual fulfilment: you do deserve it, my dearest.

I shall write more tomorrow. Nothing new has happened during the day. I have not seen anyone and do not want to. I have been terribly busy today, but tomorrow, I am afraid, I shall be moping. Sunday is not far away.

61. [1] See No. 60.

62. [1] 'All that has been upsetting you so much'—It is not known to what W. is alluding.

Sun and a sunny mood—these are my wishes for you.

Yours,

Ch.W.

My cordial [greetings ?] and warm regards to Esfir Gr.[2] *Wohlauf!*[3]

63. To Vera Khatzman, Clarens-Baugy. *Geneva,* [? *14 March*] *1901*

Russian: H.W.: W.A.

[Undated. '14 March 1901', in W.'s handwriting, appears to have been written in later. This dating is supported by the reference to 'yesterday's concert' (see head-note to No. 62) and fits in with the words 'bowling along on Saturday', 16 March 1901 being a Saturday.]

Dear Verochka,

You have probably already received the postcard from Nyon with the winter-sports picture.[1] On my return from there, I started duplicating,[2] and this got me down so much that I want to cheer myself up by writing to you. It looks as if you are lucky: the weather here is good. How glad I'd be if you really felt well in beautiful Montreux or, to be more exact, in less beautiful Baugy. I imagine the whole Pale of Settlement[3] is there: *und Junker und Jud, und Halunke und Heiliger, und jeglich Vieh aus der Arche Noach.*[4] But I trust you will be able to protect yourself from intrusion by Russian Jewish students (?).[5]

All that is needed is for someone to come there to deliver a lecture on the immortality of cockchafers and on the influence of Marxism on sojourns in Swiss health resorts, and then arrange a party for the benefit of the Russian idiots, at which Khanevskaya[6] would sing and be a success—and that's that.

[2] Esfir Grigoryevna, i.e. Esther (Esfir) Weinberg, a Rostov friend of Vera Khatzman, at this time studying medicine and allied subjects at Geneva; later married the Benjamin Herzfeld mentioned in No. 220.   [3] 'Cheer up!'

63. [1] Not found. Both this and the preceding letter (No. 61) were certainly written from Geneva, so that if—as is probable—the dates here attributed to them are correct, W. can have made only a day-trip to Nyon.

[2] W. is probably referring to the duplicating of the circular mentioned in his letter of 26 March 1901 (No. 67) concerning preparations for the Youth Conference.

[3] i.e. all Russian Jewry, the Pale of Settlement being that part of the Russian Empire (the ten Polish and the fifteen contiguous Russian provinces) to which Jews not having special permission to reside elsewhere were restricted.

[4] 'Junker and Jew, rascal and saint, and every animal from Noah's Ark'—source of quotation not traced.

[5] The significance of the question-mark is not clear, but it may represent an ironica commentary on 'students'.

[6] Identified by Mrs. Weizmann, from her personal recollection, as a Geneva woman student from Rostov with a reputation as a singer.

But I have let my tongue run loose. *Punktum!*[7] There is nothing new here, and besides I don't see anyone. By 'anyone' I am referring to people able to talk scandal.

Bilit[8] and I gossiped a bit today, just for the fun of it, and not going deep. I have not seen Nyusechka;[9] I shall visit her tomorrow.

As to yesterday's concert, I can report that it did not justify expectations. We were yawning in the dress circle, and Lichtenberger's paper on Nietzsche was not good at all.[10] The French are incapable of understanding Nietzsche. They are too superficial for a revaluation of all values. Moreover, this fellow Lichtenberger seems to have strong nerves, and this is a handicap when studying Nietzsche.[11]

I meant to write you a serious letter, but it has turned out to be a silly one. It's always like that. However, why not write nonsense? I am fed up with all the brainy, serious propositions, such as that two and two make four, or that the whole world is divided into two classes, or that a man's head is the humble servant of his stomach or of the stomach of another, stronger man, or that science is a good thing and that it is a pity that the surplus value theory cannot be applied to Darwinism, and so on and so forth. I like gay nonsense. Long live the merry fools, down with the gloomy sages!

You will most certainly decide that I am not in my right mind or that I am tipsy, but you can judge from my handwriting that

[7] 'Enough of that' (lit., 'Full stop').

[8] A chemist, at this time resident at Geneva, where he associated himself with the Russian Social Democrats, from whom, however, he went over, in 1902, to the Social Revolutionaries.

[9] Anna (Nyusechka) Ratnovskaya, a Rostov friend of Vera Khatzman, at this time a medical student at Geneva.

[10] Henri Lichtenberger (1864–1941) taught German Literature at French Universities. Among his published works was *La Philosophie de Nietzsche* (Paris, 1898). *Le Genevois*, 13 and 15 March 1901, contains announcements of two lectures by Lichtenberger—one, on 13 March, on 'Wagner at Bayreuth' and the other, on 15 March, on 'Wagner and Nietzsche'. There is no reason to doubt that the attribution of this letter to 14 March (see head-note) is correct. If so, it is difficult to understand W.'s condemnation of Lichtenberger's 'paper on Nietzsche', since, according to the advertised programme, this was not due until 15 March. Even if the order of the two lectures had been reversed, this would not dispose of the difficulty, since W.'s reference to 'yesterday's concert' ('we were yawning in the dress circle') makes it clear that he actually attended it, and if so, he could not also have attended Lichtenberger's lecture on the same date, for the concert was at the Victoria Hall, whereas the lecture was advertised for the same hour at the University. A possible explanation of the puzzle may be that W. is merely reporting what he had been told about Lichtenberger's lecture by someone who had heard it, mistakenly supposing it to have been the 'Wagner and Nietzsche' lecture, and commenting on the lecturer's inadequacy on the strength of his writings on Nietzsche.—W.'s disdain for Lichtenberger did not prevent him from deciding to attend the lecture on 15 March (see No. 64).

[11] This is what W. writes. What he means is not clear.

I am in perfect order—except that something came over me. Well, a 'something'.

Verusya, my little girl, we shall soon be coming over to you, my dear, and then we shall really have fun. And do you know, it is possible we shall be bowling along on Saturday, towards the evening. Yes, indeed. This has been decided in the Cyclists' Council. Everything, of course, depends on the weather which is, alas, changeable. But have we not been accustomed to changeability of another sort? Don't you find me witty? (And now comes your little smile).

Verochka, get better, do you hear? Be meticulous about all the dressings, etc., please. You should listen to Esfir, the sensible Esfir, to whom I send herewith my very very best regards.

What I am going to do tonight I don't exactly know. It would be nice to have a toothache—that would be something to occupy my mind.

And why no word from you?

Shall be seeing you soon.

With all the very best wishes,

Your humble slave,
Reb[12] Chaim

64. To Vera Khatzman, Clarens-Baugy. *Geneva,* [? *15 March 1901*]

Russian: H.W.: W.A.

[Undated. '15 March 1901', not in W.'s handwriting, appears to have been written in later. The reference to 'my silly letter of yesterday', obviously meaning No. 63, shows that this dating is correct, if, as is probable, No. 63 can safely be taken to have been written on 14 March. The dating 15 March fits in well with 'I am going to hear Lichtenberger today' since L. does appear to have lectured on 15 March—see n. 10 to No. 63. Since 16 March 1901 was a Saturday, the attribution of this letter to 15 March is further substantiated by W.'s promise to V.K. to try to cycle over to her 'tomorrow', read together with what he says in No. 63 about visiting her on 'Saturday'.]

Dear Verochka,

Once again I am writing to you. I miss you. I'd love to see you, but—as if out of spite—it is drizzling today. It will be terrible if tomorrow's the same, for I am already looking forward to the pleasures of tomorrow's outing.

---

[12] See n. 1 to No. 1.

You may not yet have recovered from my silly letter of yester-day,[1] and here you are already getting another one. Have you not tired of me yet? Do tell me. There is nothing new, of course, except that having shut down my little shop today I ran into two boys on my bicycle, or rather they ran into me.

Should the weather be good tomorrow, we shall leave here at one o'clock or half-past, and will be at your place by six [or] six-thirty. I should like to ask you to come and meet us at the Castle of Chillon and not in Vevey, as we have decided to go along the French side and not by way of Lausanne. I saw Ratnovskaya yesterday. She is leaving tomorrow. She is quite cheerful, though she does not like staying at home. I am going to hear Lichtenberger today.[2]

And you, my dear girl, you are enjoying nature. Well done! Excellent, the way things have turned out. Long live M. Biske![3] May God grant him a long life!

Verochka, how good that the whole wicked nightmare is over and gone, and that we have got rid of these horrid feelings. *Dem Reinen ist alles rein, dem Schweine ist alles Schwein*,[4] and let this *Schwein*[5] abide where it belongs.[6]

(Some hours later)[7]

I interrupted this epistle to you as the Cyclists' Council decided to go out to reconnoitre the road. The way out was wonderful, but, oh horrors, on the way back we were caught in the most disgusting rain. The whole Council got wet to the skin. We have now changed, made ourselves respectable, and all is well. It is doubtful whether it will be possible to go tomorrow; the road has probably got worse. But I have decided the following. Should it not be possible to cycle, I shall come by train tomorrow, late in the day. I shall let you know by telegram.

How glad I am, Verochka, that for you it is all a thing of the past.[8] My dear girl, what respect I feel for you! If you only knew how much I think of you. Such good, straightforward people are truly rare. I do not doubt that you are not just smoothing the way [for yourself] for the future. There will be nothing insincere about you—no question of that. It would be ridiculous for either of us—even in our thoughts—to start making comparisons. That would be sheer blasphemy.

64. [1] See No. 63.   [2] See n. 10 to No. 63.   [3] Not identified.

   [4] 'To the pure all is pure, to the swine all is swinish'—an echo of the Epistle to Titus i. 15.   [5] In orig. in cyrillic characters.

   [6] This paragraph obviously refers to some episode in W.'s personal life but beyond this does not admit of any confident explanation.

   [7] These words are written in W.'s hand in the margin.   [8] See above, n. 6.

Today I received a most delightful and comforting letter from
Father. All is well at home. I wrote back today to say that I shall
not be coming for Passover. Brailovskaya[9] has just been to see me.
She sends you her best wishes.

Keep well, dear Verochka, au revoir,

Yours,
Ch.

Many greetings to Esfir Grigoryevna.
You're cramming for all you're worth, aren't you?[10]

65. To Vera Khatzman, Clarens-Baugy. *Geneva, 19 March 1901*

Russian: H.W.: W.A.

Geneva, 19/III. 1901

Dear Verochka,

Forgive me, my sweet, for not writing until now. Last night it
was quite impossible. We only got to the flat at half-past six. After
supper I had to go to a meeting from which I didn't return till
half-past twelve. Nothing new has happened here during [my]
absence.[1] The meeting[2] was stupid and boring, as was to be expected. A 'new' committee was elected from among old members,
and instead of Fuchs[3] a worthy successor was elected in the person
of Miss Doktor,[4] and, to replace Salomon,[5] Comrade Rabinovich,[6]
a newly arrived student from Berne. Apparently very pleasant,
though a most provincial man. I saw Brailovskaya today.[7] She is
proposing to set out tomorrow, together with Livshina.[8] Idelevich
met me at the meeting yesterday with the following question:
'Have you nothing to pass on to me?' This was followed by my
very curt 'Nothing', accompanied by a very civil bow, and that

[9] Agnes (Zina) Brailovsky, a Geneva student from Rostov.
[10] She was in her first year as a medical student.

65. [1] See No. 64 as to his plans for meeting Vera Khatzman at Chillon. He was
evidently away from Geneva for a short time between 16 and 18 March.

[2] Probably a meeting of the 'Cercle Israélite' (according to a writer in the Hebrew
weekly *Hatzofe* 2/15 July 1904, founded by W.), which served the needs of Zionist
students until superseded by the establishment of a Geneva Zionist students' society,
under the name of *Hashahar* ('The Dawn'), in Feb. 1902.

[3] Probably Sylvia Fuchs, a Geneva medical student who is known to have been in
1902 a member of *Hashahar*.

[4] There was at the time a Geneva woman student named Doktor. Nothing more is
known of her.

[5] Not identified.

[6] 'Rabinovich' must be Jacob Rabinovich, at this time studying in Switzerland.

[7] See n. 9 to No. 64.   [8] Not identified.

was the end of the matter.[9] This is, generally speaking, all the news. As you can see, very little of interest. And what news from you, my dear? I hope you are not depressed and are continuing with the task, so brilliantly started, of mending your health which is so dear to us.

I am already in a travelling mood. The room is in disorder, suitcases are lying about, and I am packing. Only the money is lacking, but this will be here tonight, I hope. Among the letters I found here was one from Berlin from Leo, and just imagine, my dear, a very disconcerting one.[10] He has such a lot of worries and troubles that he will not be going to Munich.[11] It is also possible that I may not find him in Berlin,[12] and therefore shall not go there but shall go straight on from Frankfurt to Munich. What a fateful turn all this is taking! Our dear good Leo; even he is not spared by fate all kinds of petty worries that prevent him from giving himself up completely to our precious cause.

I am very upset by the thought that I may not see him this time. We need him so much—his is the best brain among our young people, and how young he is![13]

We have such small forces, and it is frightening to think that such power as Leo's is being spent on paltry chores. *Tant pis!* But this does not mean a thing.

I found yesterday's meeting[14] so stupid, so insignificant, and on summing up [our] activities during the past term, I felt so ashamed of myself that I could not look straight, and throughout the evening I confined myself to a couple of caustic remarks addressed to some fools.

I am hoping a great deal from this journey of mine,[15] and to think, O God, that I am undertaking such a trip already tired—and what has made me tired, what has worn me out? How shameful all this

---

[9] Idelevich cannot be identified, nor is anything known as to the background to this incident.

[10] W. is referring to Motzkin's letter of 15 March 1901 (W.A.), in which, after explaining that various personal problems had left him little time for letter-writing, he told W. that he had his doubts about the projected Youth Conference, though he might be prepared to take a somewhat less sceptical view of it if satisfied that it would be composed of 'more or less homogeneous elements'. It would in any case, he said, be impossible for him to take an active part in the project because (among other reasons) he was preoccupied with a Miscellany which the Kiev *Kadimah* Society had invited him to edit, and to which he asked W. to contribute: see, as to the Miscellany, n. 16 to No. 60.

[11] For the preparatory conference, opening in Munich on 1 April, to discuss arrangements for the proposed Youth Conference.

[12] From No. 70 it appears that by 30 March Motzkin had left Berlin.

[13] What W. had in mind is not clear; Motzkin was now in his early thirties. The word used is 'young', but possibly this should be taken to mean 'youthful'.

[14] See above, n. 2.   [15] To Munich—see above, n. 11.

is—how vulgar and nasty. How could I have been unable to lift my head above all this farce, all this nastiness in which I nearly got bogged down ?[16]

Were it not for you, my radiant, pure, pure girl! How bright is the image of you that appears before me,[17] my darling Verochka! I am not going to put into words what is now so very close to me. To put it on paper would be to profane it.

I still hope, Verusya, to receive a message from you today. I shall be leaving probably at 10.30 tomorrow, and if I decide not to go to Berlin, then from Lausanne I shall go on for a day to Montreux, to you. However, all this is still doubtful. By tonight everything will be decided.

Keep well, dear Verochka, my sweet, good girl. Write to me at once. After having received this letter, Verusya, please write to Heidelberg and also to Darmstadt, as follows: Herrn Saul Lurie für Dr. Weizmann, Darmstadt, Georgenstr. 9 pt.[18]

It would make me feel so good to get a line from you in every town.

Keep well, my little one,

Yours,
Chaim

My best regards to Esfir Grigoryevna and Anna Salomonova.[19] See to it, ladies, that you get a proper rest, and do protect yourselves from being visited by all sorts of people who would only spoil the scenery. *Salut!*

W.

66. To Leo Motzkin, Berlin. *Clarens-Baugy, 22 March 1901*

Russian: H.W.: C.Z.A.—A126/16/2

[Before going to Munich for the Conference in preparation for the Youth Conference W. spent a few days at Clarens-Baugy, where Vera Khatzman was staying, and then continued his journey via Berne and Zurich, reaching Munich on 30 March.]

Clarens, 22/III. 1901

Dear Leo,

Your last letter[1] left me completely at a loss. There is so much anguish in it that it seems to me that my journey to you all may

---

[16] See n. 6 to No. 64.

[17] Here W. breaks for a moment from the formal plur. into the intimate sing.; lit. rendering would be: '... the image of you, of thee ...'.   [18] parterre.

[19] Anna Ratnovskaya. Her father's name was Zelik-Solomon.

66. [1] Motzkin's letter of 15 March 1901 (W.A.), as to which see nn. 10 and 12 to No. 65.

prove useless, the more so because there is the risk of not finding you in Berlin.[2] In any case, I could not have stopped for any length of time at your place, four or five days at the most, as I want to be in Munich by the first of the month. I have settled down here for this week before leaving for Munich.

Naturally, I cannot say anything at all about the Conference for the time being. I do not know where those homogeneous elements are to be found;[3] we must look for them, and the first conference is of a tentative nature and, like everything else with us, it has not yet emerged from the experimental stage. How can one extract the homogeneous elements without first knowing them?

From my correspondence with the groups[4] I have gained the impression that in each of them there are two or three interesting people, and it is with these that contact should be established.

As to the Miscellany, I shall be able to contribute two articles— on the 4th Congress and on the Student Conference.[5] But I should like to know about the form and policy of the Miscellany.

My dear friend, why such anxiety? What has happened? Why do both of you have to leave Berlin? Are you thinking of staying long at Goettingen?[6] I should like to know all this as I am very worried.

I might, after all, snatch a day or so after Munich to call on you. At least a few words, please, about how you have arranged things. When will you need these articles by?

In Geneva there is a certain **Dr. Pasmanik** who would like to contribute an article to the Miscellany,[7] but he, too, wants to know more about it.

Write, if only briefly, to

Yours,

Ch. Weizmann

Best wishes to Polya.

[2] Motzkin had said in his letter that he and his wife would be leaving Berlin. He went to Russia (see No. 73) but was back in Berlin by the end of May (see n. 1 to No. 83).

[3] A reference to the passage in which Motzkin spoke of his misgivings about the Youth Conference in the absence of an assurance that it would be composed of 'more or less homogeneous elements'.

[4] By 'the groups' W. probably means bodies of Zionist students at various Universities. There are preserved in W.A. assurances of sympathetic interest in the Conference project received by W., before the date of this letter, from the Cologne and Heidelberg *Kadimah* Societies and from the Leipzig Ziona Society.

[5] See n. 10 to No. 65.

[6] Goettingen is not mentioned in Motzkin's letter of 15 March 1901, and the allusion cannot be explained except on the hypothesis that W. is referring to something he had been told about Motzkin's plans by someone else.

[7] See n. 16 to No. 60.

67. To Leo Motzkin, Berlin. *Clarens-Baugy, 26 March 1901*

Russian: H.W.: C.Z.A.—A126/16/2

z. Zt. Clarens-Baugy, 26/III. 1901

Dear Leo,

You have probably already received my circular letter sent to *Kadimah*.[1] Whatever your attitude may be, I assume that you will not offend us and will send your delegate.

I hope that all the groups will be represented, and it would be bad indeed if Berlin did not send its representative.

I am counting on you, dear Leo. It may be that I will go to Berlin from Munich, if only time allows. Please, Leo, write to Munich [telling me] how things are with you and what has been arranged. I am very worried. I am looking forward impatiently to your news.

Keep well,

Yours,
Chaim

Cordial greetings to Polya.

Address: G. Abramovich, Technische Hochschule, Munich.

68. To Vera Khatzman, Clarens-Baugy. *Berne, 30 March 1901*

Russian: H.W.: W.A.

[Except for a momentary deviation in the letter of 19 March 1901 (see n. 17 to No. 65), the intimate form of address (second person singular instead of the formal plural) is here used by W. for the first time in his letters to V.K.]

Berne, 30/III. 1901

Dear Verochka,

I wanted to write to you, my darling, even last night, but couldn't manage it. Khissin was at my place and we talked endlessly. I am writing to you now at 8 a.m. In two hours' time I shall be leaving and tonight at 10 will be in Munich. The Berne delegate[1]

---

67. [1] A circular dated 15 March 1901 and signed by Gregory Abramovich, Alexander Nemser and W. (copy in W.A.) invites Zionist Youth groups to send delegates to a meeting at Munich on 1 April for the purpose of considering plans for the convening of a Zionist Youth Conference.

68. [1] There were, in fact, two Berne representatives at the Munich meeting—Chaim Khissin, the Chairman of the Berne Academic Zionist Society, and Aaron Borukhov, but as in this letter W. mentions Khissin by name, the person referred to as 'the Berne delegate' seems clearly to be Borukhov.

has already left. I shall meet the Basle colleagues on the way.
I feel in excellent form. I am cheerful. At times there are sad spells,
but I drive these thoughts away because, after all, it's childish.
Isn't it, my dear? Forgive me for so many smears in this letter;
I am in such a hurry.

Verochka, my darling, my love. I am sure you are not pining, but
happy. I am also in good spirits and cheerful. I am very confident
of the success of our dear cause because your warm, pure feelings
are with me.

My beloved, I think I shall be able to write again from Zurich.
We are in everything together, Verochka; all those little stings we
have experienced up to now have gone and will not re-appear. We
love, love, love each other! I am happy when I think of it, and you
should be happy too.

I kiss you many many times, my sweetest Verochka, and hold
you closely in my arms.

Till we meet again. Be well.

Yours, your own,
Chaim

69. To Vera Khatzman, Clarens-Baugy. *Zurich,* [30] *March 1901*

Russian: Pcd.: H.W.: W.A.
[Undated. Date from Zurich pmk.]

Dear Verochka,

Best wishes to you.
Am going on to Munich in an hour.

Ch. W.

70. To Leo Motzkin, [*see head-note*]. *Munich, 30 March 1901*

German: T.: C.Z.A.—A126/24/7/2/2

[The telegram, handed in at Munich at 10.30 p.m. on 30 March 1901, is
addressed: 'Motzkin, Schillerstr. 45, Charlottenburg', W. having not yet been
informed of Motzkin's departure for Russia (see No. 73). On the back of the
telegram is a note reading (in translation); 'House closed. No bell'. How the
telegram eventually found its way into the Motzkin papers in C.Z.A. is not
clear, but the probable explanation is that it was dropped into the letter-box
and found by Motzkin on his return.]

Cannot do without you. Telegraph arrival.

Chaim

71. To Vera Khatzman, Esther Weinberg, Anna Ratnovskaya, Clarens-Baugy. *Munich, 31 March 1901*

Russian: Pcd.: H.W.: W.A.

31/III

I am sending you, my dear ones, my best wishes. Khissin has just arrived. In an hour's time the comrades from Leipzig, Berne and Paris[1] will be here. Everything will be fine. Greetings.

Ch.W.

[Signed also by Isaac Sherman,
    Aaron Perelman,
    Aaron Borukhov,
    Chaim Khissin,
    Alexander Nemser,
    Gregory Abramovich,
    and two other persons.]

[The Munich Preparatory Conference opened on 1 April 1901 and closed the following night. Described in a resolution setting out its conclusions as a meeting of 'representatives of Zionist student groups', it was attended by delegates from Geneva (represented by W.), Berne, Berlin, Cologne, Karlsruhe, Leipzig, and Munich, with W. in the chair throughout. A record of its proceedings is in C.Z.A.—A139/5, For the outcome of the Conference see bridge-note following No. 75.]

72. To Vera Khatzman, Clarens-Baugy. *Munich, [1] April 1901*

Russian: Pcd.: H.W.: W.A.

[Undated, but the first sentence shows that W. was writing on 1 April. Munich pmk. not clearly legible but probable reading is 1 April 1901.]

Dear Verochka,

The first session was held today.

It was most interesting. Shall write in detail tomorrow. I have started already, but haven't yet finished.[1] My paper went down well.[2] So far, I am very, very satisfied. Verochka, my sweet darling,

71. [1] There was, in fact, no Paris delegate at the Munich meeting.
72. [1] See No. 73.

[2] The burden of W.'s opening address was that the rôle of the projected Youth Organization would be to serve as a dynamic force in the Zionist Movement generally, and to concern itself, in particular, with (a) cultural work and propaganda; (b) the investigation of conditions in Palestine; (c) the organization of Jewish economic life; (d) the creation of a Zionist press.—What W. meant by the organization of Jewish economic life is not altogether clear. He said in his address: 'Zionists must devote themselves to the economic organization of Jewry', giving as a reason the importance of fighting the 'anti-national groups' (meaning the Bundists and other Jewish left-wingers—see Introduction to Vol. I, pp. 20, 21) for the support of 'the youthful productive forces among the Jewish masses. . . . Besides its positive aspect and intrinsic interest, economic organization has a purely tactical interest for us, since in this manner we can strengthen our position'.

I send you all my best wishes. Many regards to Esfir and Nyusya.[3]

Chaim

73. To Vera Khatzman, Clarens-Baugy. *Munich, 1–2 April 1901*

Russian: H.W.: W.A.

[This letter, which commences 'The Conference starts in a few minutes' time', was evidently begun before No. 72, which commences 'The first session was held today', but was left uncompleted and finished on 2 April, after No. 72 had been posted.]

Munich, 1/iv. 1901

Dear Verochka,

The Conference starts in a few minutes' time. Leo did not come from Berlin, but those who have assembled here are very serious and likeable fellows. Leo has gone off to Russia[1] where, following our example, a similar conference is taking place in Kiev.[2] Our undertaking is being received very sympathetically everywhere. Many messages of greeting have arrived. I am in excellent spirits, although I have a slight cold; my nose is running, etc.

My dearest darling, this is such a solemn occasion, and all signs are that it will lead to great consequences, and I begin to wonder at this stage whether we have matured sufficiently for such a venture.

Interval

Verochka, I am continuing my letter. I have delivered the opening speech. It went off well. The debate on it is about to start; in fact it has already begun: intense, serious and thorough. The colleagues from Berlin are suggesting that we should restrict the aims of the Conference.[3] Others insist on a broad programme. The

---

[3] Esther ('Esfir') Weinberg and Anna ('Nyusya') Ratnovskaya were at Clarens-Baugy with V.K.—see No. 71.

73. [1] According to the biographical sketch of Motzkin by A. Bein cited in n. 3 to No. 17, M.'s parents lived at Brovari, near Kiev, so long as their children were in need of a Jewish education. (This was unobtainable in Kiev, which was out of bounds for all but a limited category of Jews.) In the latter part of this letter W. writes 'Leo has left for Kiev', from which it may be inferred that the family home was now in Kiev.

[2] Nothing is known of any such conference in Kiev.

[3] A Berlin delegate, Chaim (Boris) Gurevich, contended, on behalf of his group, that the projected Youth Conference should not lose itself in the discussion of practical problems with which it was not equipped to deal, but should address itself, as its primary task, to what he described as 'the theoretical substantiation of Zionism', by which he seems to have meant an attempt to explore the nature, and establish the validity, of the reasoning underlying the Zionist Movement.

Jewish disease—doubt in one's own strength—is again coming to the fore. This is terrible, my sweet.

One of our colleagues is speaking now, and his speech is making a very unpleasant impression on me. He is pounding on my nerves and he is talking paradoxes.[4]

How sorry I am, my darling, that you are not here. It is most instructive and interesting. When I come I shall tell you everything in detail. But do you know, my little one, my sweet darling, it is possible that I shall have to go from here to Leipzig? The colleagues from Berlin, Dresden and Leipzig have been insisting on this. Although I have neither the strength nor the time, I shall have to do it. Tonight after the session I shall let you know all the details. I am writing now as the meeting is in progress.

2 [April], morning, before
the session (8 a.m.)

All through yesterday the debate centred on my report.[5] Apparently my resolution[6] will be carried. We shall be sitting all day today.

I shall try my utmost not to go to Leipzig. In any event, I shall let you know by telegram tomorrow afternoon. Should I go to Leipzig, I shall not be arriving at Clarens till Monday. Please, my dear, tell the landlord. In this case, send all letters to Munich, care of Schapiro[7] at 96 Augustenstrasse.

Leo has left for Kiev.[8] I think I have already written to you about it.[9] I shall bring detailed minutes of the meeting. The Minutes of yesterday's meeting take up thirty pages. I am already pretty tired. I shall probably still have to give a lecture here to the local colony.[10]

My darling, I am sorry I am writing so much about the meeting and about myself, and have not even thanked you for your marvellous warm letter. My good Verusya. The leading lung specialist happens to be away, and at Berne I shall see Professor Sahli[11] who

---

[4] It is not known who is referred to.   [5] i.e., his opening address.

[6] The contents of W.'s resolution are not to be found in the record of proceedings and are unknown. The final text of the main resolution adopted by the Conference (see bridge-note following No. 75) was framed by a drafting committee not including W., but the resolution was in general accord with the ideas propounded by W. in his opening address.

[7] Presumably the Munich student of that name who is known to have been active in Jewish nationalist circles in 1901–3.

[8] See above, n. 1.

[9] Motzkin's departure for Russia is mentioned in the first paragraph of this letter but not in any earlier letter to V.K. which has been preserved.

[10] The Jewish student colony.

[11] Professor Hermann Sahli (1856–1933) was a specialist in internal diseases.

has already examined me several times and treated me when I was ill.[12]

Why are you pining so much? Verusya, it has been difficult for me to leave. But the cause is so great. And you should not be sad. How sweet our meeting will be! Verusya, I love and adore you, my little girl. I keep on thinking all the time how good it is to be together. Forgive me for this letter being so incoherent. I am in a hurry. In a matter of minutes I have to go to the meeting. Many, many kisses.

Yours, all yours,
Chaim

You have probably received all my postcards.[13] My warmest greetings to Esfir and Nyusya. Hello, my good friends! For the time being, things are going well.

74. To Vera Khatzman, Clarens-Baugy. *Munich, 2 April 1901*

Russian: Pcd.: H.W.: W.A.

Munich, Hotel Elite,
2/iv. 1901

Dear Verochka,

I am not going to Leipzig.[1] But I have to read a paper here[2] the day after tomorrow. The Conference ends tomorrow night.[3]

I am leaving on Thursday, and on Friday, some time during the day, shall be at Clarens.

Things are going well. I am very tired and am writing little. Verochka, my sweetest, best regards. Greetings to Esfir and Nyusya.

Ch. W.

[12] There is in W.A. a letter to W. from his sister Haya, dated Pinsk, 7 (20) Dec. 1900, in which she writes: 'Your health worries all of us more than it worries you, and for the sake of our love for you take care of yourself. . . .' A lung haemorrhage suffered by W. many years later was traced by his doctor to the privations of his first eight months in Germany (1892)—see *T. and E.*, p. 49.

[13] See Nos. 71 and 72. Any other postcards which W. may have sent from Munich or on his way there have been lost.

74. [1] See No. 73 as to the pressure on him to go to Leipzig.

[2] Presumably to the Jewish student colony—see n. 10. to No. 73.

[3] The Conference did not, in fact, end 'tomorrow night', 3 Apr., but on the night of 2 Apr. The next night, 3 Apr., was the Eve of Passover, and the participants remained in Munich to take part together in the *Seder* service (the traditional domestic service inaugurating the Festival).

75. To Vera Khatzman, Clarens-Baugy. *Munich, 2 April 1901*

Russian: H.W.: W.A.

Munich, 2/IV. 1901 (9.30 p.m.)

Dear Verochka,

I am taking advantage of a break in the proceedings to write to you a few words, my dearest girl. All the difficult part has already been disposed of and went off exceedingly well. Today we were sitting for about nine hours and I hope that the *ordre du jour* will be covered by midnight. The speeches were clear and to the point and all the resolutions were carried intelligently. There is still editorial work to be done tomorrow, and this is dull but not difficult. I have been in the chair all the time. All that remains is the election of the Bureau and the technical part; that concerned with essentials has now been completed.

Verusya, all this is much more interesting, significant, and important than I could even have imagined. I believe we have coped with our task well, and this will encourage us to proceed with our work.

Our night session starts at 10 p.m., and tomorrow I shall be free. I shall only deliver my paper,[1] and then start post-haste to you, my dear friend, to you, my beloved.

You will find me tired. But, my little girl, this does not matter, all this will pass. And I am so happy now.

My sweet one, how do you spend your days? You should not be sad, my darling. Much of my present work, much of what I said, I have dedicated to you. I am impatiently looking forward to our meeting. How much there will be to tell. . . . It is only a pity that I shall not be able to be with you for Passover.[2] But then we shall have a feast when I arrive. I hope you will come to Lausanne without fail, my darling. I shall send you a telegram. I expect to get to Lausanne on Friday at 6 p.m.—at least I shall try. You will get the telegram on Friday, in the morning.

Verochka, I must finish. I am tired and the people are gathering already and starting to talk all round me. Keep well, au revoir.

Many, many kisses.

For ever yours,
Chaim

A good *Yom Tov*.[3] My best wishes to dear Esfir and Nyusya. Happy holidays.

75. [1] See n. 10 to No. 73.   [2] See n. 3 to No. 74.
[3] Hebr., 'Festival' (lit., 'good day').

[The main decisions of the Munich Preparatory Conference are set out in a resolution embodied in the record of its proceedings preserved in C.Z.A.— A139/5 and also stencilled as a separate document, copies of which are in W.A. (Circulars, 1901.) The resolution, briefly summarized, was to the effect that the time had come for the setting up of a Zionist Youth Organization (not, it should be noted, merely a Zionist Students' Organization as originally contemplated), in which the younger members of the Zionist intelligentsia would have an opportunity of making their distinctive contribution to the realization of the Zionist ideal, the new Organization, while remaining faithful to the Basle Programme, to single out for itself the following tasks, viz. (1) to explore the ideological foundations of Zionism and the relations between the Zionist Movement and 'various social trends' (probably meaning, in particular, socialism); (2) to improve the cultural standards and living conditions of the Jewish masses; (3) to inspire the Jewish intellectuals with nationalist ideas and attract them to the Zionist Movement; (4) to engage in a study of Palestine and of the conditions under which Jews could be settled there. Agreement was reached on an agenda for a Zionist Youth Conference, copies of which, stencilled as a separate document, are in W.A. (Circulars, 1902 Box.)

It was further decided to set up a Zionist Youth Conference Bureau (sometimes later referred to as 'The Organization Bureau') with headquarters, under W.'s direction, at Geneva, and a 'Correspondence Bureau', under the direction of Alexander Nemser and Gregory Abramovich, in Munich. In addition to these three, Jacob Kohan-Bernstein, Leo Motzkin, and Daniel Pasmanik were elected members of the Conference Bureau.]

76. To Vera Khatzman, Clarens-Baugy. [*Munich*], *3 April 1901*

Russian: Pcd.: H.W.: W.A.
[Written on a Munich picture postcard. Pmk. cut out with stamp.]

3/IV. 1901

Verochka,

I am leaving tomorrow and shall be in Berne late in the evening. On Friday morning I shall leave Berne, and that means that during the day I shall get to Clarens. I am very tired, Verochka, and would be happy to have a rest at last. I have been elected head of the Bureau which is to organise the Conference;[1] You can imagine how much work will be involved. From Berne I shall cable my Verochka. I expect to be in Lausanne about 2 o'clock.

Regards to Esfir and Nyusya.

Verochka, my dearest, dearest, good-bye.

Ch. W.

76. [1] See preceding bridge-note.

77. To Leo Motzkin, [? Kiev]. [*Munich*], [? *3 April*] *1901*

Russian: H.W.: C.Z.A.—A126/24/7/2/2

[Undated. Appended by W. to letter to Motzkin from Chaim (Boris) Gurevich, one of the Berlin representatives at the Munich Conference, dated 3 April 1901. M. had by this time gone to Russia—see No. 73. It is not possible to say whether Gurevich's letter, with W.'s note appended to it, was sent, either by Gurevich or by W., to Motzkin's home address in Kiev, or whether it was posted to his Charlottenburg address and found there by him on his return from Russia.]

Dear Leo,

Comrade Gurevich has already informed you in general terms about the work of our Conference.[1] I am leaving today or tomorrow morning and shall write you a detailed account of everything as soon as I get home.[2] I must admit that I am very pleased with the work of the Conference; my only regret is that more delegates didn't come. We are receiving good-will greetings from everywhere, and we may count upon a success. As soon as I get home I shall settle down to editing circular letters and the relevant [. . . . .],[3] and you will receive the most detailed information about everything. I am very tired and therefore do not write much.

Many, many regards to you and Polya and all your family. Best wishes for the holiday.

Yours,
Chaim

78. To Vera Khatzman, Clarens-Baugy. [*En route to Geneva*], *15 April 1901*

Russian: Pcd.: H.W.: W.A.

In railway-carriage, 15/IV. 1901

Dear Verochka,

I did not even manage to say good-bye properly. Please send on my luggage and post the receipt or bring it along yourself.

My very best wishes, dearest.

Au revoir. Regards to Nyusya.

Chaim

It would be better if you posted the receipt. I have nothing to wear tomorrow in the Labor[atory].

---

77. [1] Gurevich's letter contains a lengthy description of the Munich Conference.
    [2] i.e. when he is back in Geneva. W. later apologized to Motzkin for having failed to send him the promised fuller report.
    [3] Word missing in orig.

79. To Vera Khatzman, Clarens-Baugy. *Geneva, 15 April 1901*

Russian: H.W.: W.A.

Geneva, 15/IV. 1901

Dear Verochka,

I am writing in haste at Esfir's; she has no decent writing paper. I have been running round a lot today, have seen everything and everyone, and arranged everything. I did not find Nyusya's landlady at home, and so I don't know whether the money has arrived. I went there three times, but she, wretched woman, had gone out visiting. In any case, the things will be pawned tomorrow, and between ten and eleven I shall telegraph 100 francs. I already have 40, and I am bound to get 60 for the things. I sent you 35 francs today, just in case. Nyusya's money may arrive after you have left. I sent 35 because Shereshevskaya[1] did not send the 10 francs and presumably spent 5 francs on my ticket and on sending the luggage. Enough about accounts. Tomorrow, my dear, you will be here and how happy I am that I shall be able to embrace you and give you such ardent kisses. I have managed to learn some of the local news, but am far from having a clear idea. For the time being, Ruthstein, Levinson (worker), Karmin, Skorchev, Levinsky, Arkhiniantz, and Bernstein (worker) are under arrest.[2] I do not know the others. Tomorrow it will be known what will be done with them. It isn't as terrible as people say. The only terrible thing is that the students are behaving like a wild horde, and that no one, not even Plekhanov,[3] can make them see reason. I have already been to the laboratory. It hasn't been burnt down,[4] and all is well. I am starting work tomorrow.

My room has been tidied up, though not the way I wanted it. I shall keep on fighting with the landlady. I have not yet seen Bilit. Esfir is feeling fine. She sends lots of love and awaits you impatiently. At this moment, we are having strong tea with lemon.

79. [1] A Geneva woman student of this name was in 1901 secretary of the Geneva *Bildung* society for the dissemination of Yiddish literature. In the absence of any letters throwing light on these tangled transactions, they must be left to speak for themselves.

[2] The *Journal de Genève*, 11 and 13 April 1901, gives the names of a number of foreign students and other foreigners, including some Jews, detained by the Geneva police as a result of their having been implicated in a disorderly demonstration, on 5 Apr., against the Czarist régime in Russia. Among them can be identified all the persons mentioned by W. except Levinsky. 'Bernstein' is Leon (Leib) Bernstein of Vilna, a Bundist and at this time manager of the Social-Democratic press in Geneva.

[3] As to Plekhanov's influence on the Jewish students see No. 44.

[4] Apparently a sarcastic allusion to the activities of the 'wild horde'.

I have found a letter here from Koh[an]-Bernst[ein][5] in which he assures me that we are going to meet.

I travelled with Iza[6] and it was very boring. She kept asking whether Zionism will soon become a reality. I am afraid she may be thinking of going to Palestine. I have not yet seen a number of friends, nor do I intend to. There is little gossip. Everybody is busy, not with studies but with politics. One day there is going to be a revolution in Russia.

Best regards to Nyusya. Esfir, of course, also joins in these greetings. Children,[7] do come tomorrow and leave your headaches at Baugy; you can pass them on to one of your friends.

With best regards and love,

Chaim

8o. To Ahad Ha'am (Asher Ginzberg), Odessa. *Geneva, 20 April 1901*

Russian: H.W.A. and H.W. (see head-note): Ahad Ha'am Papers N.L.

[The personal letter commencing 'As you may remember . . .' is in W.'s hand. In the formal letter to which it is appended, only the words 'Mit Zionsgruss' and 'On behalf of the Organization Bureau of the Conference' and the signature are in W.'s hand, the whole of the remainder being in the handwriting of Esther Shneerson, one of W.'s assistants at the Youth Conference Bureau.]

Geneva, 20/IV. 1901

Dear Comrade,

We beg to inform you that the Preliminary Conference of representatives of Jewish students' groups abroad has taken place, and in sending you the resolutions and plans adopted by that body[1] we ask for your participation and support in the proposed general conference of all intellectual and democratic elements in the Zionist Party.

As you know, the aim of the Conference will be the setting up of a new organisation to be composed of those who are already Zionists but for whom the framework of the old Organization[2] has become too narrow and uncomfortable. We consider the present moment fully ripe for such an undertaking. We hope that you will agree

[5] Letter dated 27 March (9 Apr.) 1901, W.A.

[6] Full name not ascertained but mentioned in several of W.'s 1905 letters and known to have completed her studies at Geneva in that year.

[7] i.e., V.K. and Nyusya.

8o. [1] The word 'resolutions' in the plural, probably refers to the decisions embodied in the main resolution of the Munich Conference as set out in the stencilled document mentioned in the bridge-note following No. 75, where those decisions are summarized, and the word 'plans' to the proposed agenda of the Youth Conference as set out in that document.   [2] i.e., the existing Zionist Organization.

with our view and will not refuse to prepare a paper for the Conference on one of the subjects suggested;[3] in particular, we would be interested to receive a paper from you on Hebrew literature and language.

Should it be more convenient for you to present a paper on any other of the subjects mentioned, we shall, of course, gratefully accept it.

We are hoping for your valuable assistance at this important stage in the implementation of that difficult task ahead which we consider necessary for our national movement.

Mit Zionsgruss,[4]

On behalf of the Organization Bureau of the Conference,

Dr. Ch. Weizmann
2, Rue de l'Ecole de Chimie, Geneva.

Dear Comrade,

As you may remember, we have already discussed in Warsaw the creation of an organisation for real work and not just for 'speeches'.[5] All this is, of course, still at an embryonic stage. Your valued advice, your support, your sympathy, will be a great contribution. There are young people everywhere who are prepared to work and make sacrifices; they must be gathered and guided. This, in my view, is a matter of great importance.

I am sending you (in two envelopes) the first circular issued by the Bureau[6] and impatiently await your reply.[7]

Yours sincerely,
Ch. Weizmann

[3] The proposed agenda provided (*inter alia*) for the reading of papers on Zionism, on the tasks of the projected Youth Organization, and on the position of the Jews. The agenda did not include a paper on the subject here specifically mentioned by W. —Hebrew literature and language—but did provide for a debate on 'Educational activity' under two main heads, one of which was 'Dissemination of Hebrew language and literature'. [4] 'With Zion's greetings'.

[5] The only known meeting between them in Warsaw before the date of this letter was at the Russian Zionist Conference held there in Aug. 1898. Both W. and Ahad Ha'am took part in the Conference, at which one of the subjects discussed was a proposal by Nahum Mirkin for the formation of a Zionist Youth Organization—see Mirkin to Motzkin, 16 (28) Sept. 1899: C.Z.A.—A126/30/3.

[6] A circular issued by the Bureau (copy in W.A., Circulars, 1901), undated, but from its contents clearly the Bureau's first circular, called upon Zionist students' societies and other Young Zionist groups to discuss the questions raised in the main resolution of the Munich Conference and invited them to put forward suggestions for the projected Youth Conference. Attached to the circular were the texts of the resolution and of the proposed agenda for the Youth Conference, together with an appeal to the younger Zionists outlining the tasks confronting them.

[7] There was no reply from Ahad Ha'am, the letter having arrived after he had left Odessa for Paris, where he met W. early in May—see No. 83.

81. To Leo Motzkin, [? Kiev]. *Geneva, 24 April 1901*

Russian: H.W.: C.Z.A.—A126/24/7/2/2

Geneva, 24/IV. 1901
2, rue de l'Ecole de Chimie

Dear Leo,

As a matter of fact, I don't know where to send this letter to you. I do not know your address.[1] I didn't manage to write to you immediately after the Munich Conference because I was over-whelmed with work. Gurevich has already written to you at some length about everything.[2] And now there is such a lot of corre-spondence both with individuals and with groups that there is no time to think of anything else. I am not going to ask you questions, my dear friend, about how things are with you, what you are doing, etc., etc. For you realise how anxious I am to know all about it, and every piece of news about you and your life is of great interest to me. I am sure that because of this you will write. The Munich Conference proposes that you should read a paper on the economic problem—more precisely on the working out of a programme of economic activity.[3]

At the same time you were elected, subject to your consent, to the Bureau which is to organize the Conference. All routine work is taken off your shoulders in advance; all you will have to do is *von Zeit zu Zeit*[4] to give your advice and opinion.

Dear Leo, I would ask you to let me have at once all your com-ments on this matter. I expect a great deal from it. There is strength enough, and it will be possible to form homogeneous groups[5] and to split up the work, so that there is no danger of *Konglomerat*.[6] The whole enterprise now depends on how seriously and energetically it is dealt with by the Zionist groups.

I pin my hopes on Berlin and count upon it. On May 7th I am going to Paris, where I shall meet the delegation[7] and talk to

81. [1] W. knew that Motzkin had gone to Russia (see No. 73). He had assumed in that letter that M. had gone to Kiev but was evidently now uncertain of his Russian address.   [2] See No. 77.

[3] 'Economic Organization' (as to which see n. 2 to No. 72) was one of the subjects for discussion included in the agenda approved by the Munich Conference.

[4] 'from time to time'.

[5] As to the importance attached by Motzkin to 'homogeneous elements' see the summary of his letter of 15 March 1901 in n. 10 to No. 65.

[6] i.e., of its all being massed together indiscriminately.

[7] A delegation organized by the Odessa Committee of the *Hovevei Zion*, acting on a suggestion by Ahad Ha'am, went to Paris early in May 1901 to make representations to Baron Edmond de Rothschild and to the Jewish Colonization Association, which had undertaken the administration of the Jewish agricultural settlements in Palestine

K[ohan]-B[ernstein], Bernard-Lazare, Ahad Ha'am. I consider the journey useful.

Can you give me any instructions?

Write at once. Regards to Polya.

Yours ever,
Chaim

I am sending you the definitive text of the resolution.[8] What is the mood of the comrades in Kiev?[9]

82. To Vera Khatzman, Geneva. *Paris, 11 May 1901*

Russian: H.W.: W.A.

[Written on stationery of Hotel de Cologne, Paris.]

11/v. 1901

My darling,

My head is splitting from endless talk and negotiations and I am terribly tired. I found all the colleagues in a dreadful mood. My God, what humiliation! It is doubtful whether the delegation[1] will achieve a thing, and it is not yet clear what steps will be taken afterwards. The delegation did not come with any definite plan of action.

On Tuesday there will be an audience with Baron Rothschild.[2] For the present, negotiations are being conducted with others. The Tuesday meeting will have a decisive influence. I have already met and spoken to Ahad Ha'am and Kohan-Bernstein. As far as the conference[3] is concerned, things are not bad. I am seeing Nordau and Bernard-Lazare tomorrow and, of course, shall write at once.

---

supported by him, in favour of the settlers' demands for more attention to their needs and for less paternalistic methods of management. The delegation, led by Yehiel Tschlenov, included Ahad Ha'am, Ussishkin, and Bernstein-Kohan. It was given a hearing but achieved nothing: see n. 2 to No. 82. Its failure is described in Tschlenov's report in *Die Welt*, 23 May 1901.

[8] i.e., the main resolution of the Munich Conference—see bridge-note following No. 75.

[9] This sentence was added by W. at the back of the letter. As to the enquiry about the 'Kiev comrades' see the opening paragraph of No. 73.

82. [1] See n. 7 to No. 81.

[2] The delegation saw Baron Edmond on 15 May, but the results of the interview were disappointing.

[3] The projected Zionist Youth Conference.

Verochka, my sweet, write to me. I have a terrible headache. It's really awful.

I understand now why there are indignant Zionists.

With very very many kisses, darling,

Yours,
Chaim

83. To Leo Motzkin, Berlin.[1] *Geneva, 25 May 1901*

Russian: H.W.: C.Z.A.—A126/24/7/2/2

Geneva, 25/v. 1901
2, rue de l'Ecole de Chimie

Dear Leo,

I received your letter yesterday[2] and it cheered me up like manna from heaven. I was waiting for your news with great impatience, and have been looking out for you at Halle and Goettingen,[3] but without avail. I am very pleased, for your sake, that in spite of everything you have found time to get down to your examination. When do you expect to sit for it? What are your plans in general? Will Polya be staying long in Russia? As far as I am concerned there is nothing new. I am swamped with work for the Conference, which might have made good progress but for its being somewhat impeded. I was in Paris ten days ago to see Bernard-Lazare, Kohan-Bernstein, Ahad Ha'am and others.[4] Everybody responded with exceptional warmth and understanding to the idea of setting up the youth organization. B.-L. has undertaken to prepare a report on the economic question.[5] I hope he does it well. The organization

---

83. [1] Motzkin's letter of 23 May 1901, summarized in n. 2 below, shows that he was now back in Berlin, though from the letter under notice it appears that his wife, Polya, was still in Russia.

[2] Writing to W. from his Charlottenburg (Berlin) address on 23 May 1901 (W.A.), Motzkin explained that he was getting ready for his examinations [for a Berlin Ph.D.] and was about to write his thesis, and had, therefore, no time to take part in the preparations for the Youth Conference. With regard to the proposed Miscellany (see n. 16 to No. 60), he said that he had decided that he could not, after all, undertake the editorship and suggested that W. should take it over. Referring, apparently, to proposals made some months earlier by some Russian Jewish students at Kiev, Berlin, and Heidelberg for the formation of a Radical [i.e. Leftist] Group (*Fraktion*) within the Zionist Organization, Motzkin asked W. whether he had been approached and whether he had joined the *Fraktion*.—The proposed formation of such a Radical group is mentioned in a letter to Motzkin from Abraham Kasteliansky, dated 21 Jan. 1901: C.Z.A.—A126/7/2/3.   [3] See n. 6 to No. 66.

[4] See n. 7 to No. 81.   [5] See n. 3 to No. 81.

plan will be worked out by K.-B. together with colleagues from some Russian University towns.[6] Up to now there have been replies from Kiev, Kharkov, Moscow, Grodno, Odessa, Homel, Pinsk, Zhitomir, and from all the foreign universities with the exception of Berlin. From the last I have had no reply because I do not know whom to approach. I am sending you, for *Kadimah,* Circular No. 2,[7] and I urgently implore you, my dear friend, to pass it on immediately. Let me also know at once, please, the address of Dr. Gurevich who was at Munich.[8] I cannot tell you how much work there is. For the time being, the three of us[9] are managing quite well. I should, of course, be doing everything with even more joy if I were getting replies from those colleagues on whom one should be able to count most. The 2nd circular will convey to you my frame of mind and my ideas about the Conference. I have also written a notice for *Voskhod,* No. 29; the resolution appears there too. Nos. 25 and 30 contain my article on the 4th Congress, which is not yet completed and which has, incidentally, been outrageously

[6] In the context of the words 'setting up the youth organization' it looks as if, in speaking of 'the Organization plan', W. is referring, not to the planning of the Conference, but to the planning of the organization to be launched by the Conference, though it is still not clear whether what is meant is a programme of work for the organization or a draft constitution. References in this and later letters to the framing of a 'plan of organization' are difficult to reconcile with one another and do not admit of any wholly satisfactory explanation. In the letter under notice, W. speaks of an 'organization plan' to be worked out by Kohan-Bernstein and others not named, but later in the letter he tells Motzkin that he himself has 'the plan of organization' and will send it on within the next ten days. On 9 June (No. 86) he writes: 'The main task . . . will be to work out a programme for the Organization', adding that 'the plans' are now being worked out. On 21 June (No. 90) he writes 'I am now working out an organization plan', but on 23 June (No. 92) he says that 'Kohan-Bernstein, Gourland, Aberson and some others are working out the organization plan'. Draft statutes for the Youth Organization were sent on 1 June to W. by Aaron Gourland of Heidelberg (W.A.), and this suggests that, in No. 92, the words 'the organization plan' refer to the drafting of a constitution. But no document answering to the description of an 'organization plan' in this sense was submitted to the Youth Conference when it met in Dec. 1901 or was mentioned by Kohan-Bernstein in addressing the Conference, and from his speech, which was concerned with the functions, and not with the constitutional structure, of the projected Youth Organization, it can be inferred that the definition of those functions was the object primarily in view in the preparation of a 'plan'.

[7] The Organization Bureau's second circular (undated)—W.A. (May 1901 Box)— reports on the progress of the preparations for the Youth Conference, explains its purpose, speaks of the urgent need for a Zionist Youth Organization through which new forces may be attracted to the Movement, and invites the recipients of the circular to make their views known. The circular also announces that Bernard-Lazare, Kohan-Bernstein, and Joshua Bukhmil have agreed to read papers at the Youth Conference.

[8] Gurevich, who had taken part in the Munich Conference, had shortly after the Conference been elected Chairman of the Berlin *Kadimah* Society.

[9] W.'s two principal assistants at the Organization Bureau were Esther Shneerson and Anne Koenigsberg.

abridged by the editors.[10] I am very sorry to trouble you, dear Leo, but you know how I value your attitude to this venture, and also your directives and your criticisms, and so I ask you to express your views. From the Munich resolution, the notice in *Voskhod*, and finally from the circular now being distributed you should be able to form *ein Bild*[11] of the situation. I also have an organization plan[12] which I shall be sending you within the next ten days. Once again, I ask you urgently to comment on everything I touch upon in the above-mentioned articles. K[ohan]-B[ernstein] passed on to me[13] the information that you regard all this coolly, even with disapproval. Presumably you have your reasons, and one would like to know them. I think the whole venture will be a success if everyone takes part in working out the programme and in the distribution of work. Maybe it will be possible to create a workers' 'League', and then all Zionist youth groups[14] would take up appropriate positions.

As to the Fraction about which you write,[15] I personally do not know a thing about it, except from our brief talk. How many times already have I asked for a programme to be sent to me—I still haven't got it and meanwhile need it badly. Here and in Berne there are people who are following all the vital developments in Zionism with a burning and genuine interest, but for some reason they are being ignored. Gourland promised to send [it], but I failed to get anything out of him.

I am making every effort to examine thoroughly a number of problems that are pre-occupying me at present, and when the *Hochflut*[16] of work lets up a bit, I shall let you know at once whether I will join or not. In principle, I am for such a Fraction.

I shall take upon myself the editing of the Kiev Miscellany,[17] and have already written about it to Kiev today. But it is desirable that I should have all their material and know what ideas have been worked out so far. You must forgive me for this letter being so disjointed. I did not want to leave you long without a reply, and therefore I am merely giving an outline of the main points, while

---

[10] A note by W. on the Munich Conference in the periodical *Voskhod* ('Sundries'), No. 30 (not No. 29), 29 Apr. (12 May) 1901, explains the reasons for convening a Youth Conference and sets out the Munich resolution (see bridge-note following No. 75). W.'s article in *Voskhod*, Nos. 26 and 31 (not Nos. 25 and 30), 15 (28) Apr. and 3 (16) May 1901, is concerned mainly with the shortcomings of the Fourth Congress, with special reference to the inadequacy of the Actions Committee's report and the failure of the Congress to deal with the weaknesses of the Movement.

[11] 'a picture'.   [12] See n. 6 above.

[13] Probably when they met in Paris earlier in the month—see n. 7 to No. 81.

[14] In orig., *Fraktions*.   [15] See n. 2, above.

[16] 'flood'.   [17] See n. 2, above.

reserving the right to return to all this in greater detail in the near future. For the time being, I ask you at once

(1) to pass the circular on to *Kadimah* and point out to them that their speedy reply is essential;
(2) to let me have the address of Dr. Gurevich or of the official *Kadimah* representatives;
(3) to state your attitude to the whole matter.

I trust that you will be precise. Bearing in mind that there is very little time, I am working like a donkey, and every delay muddles me up completely.

Sonya and Rivochka are now hard at work. Sonya's examinations are due very soon. She now has a lot of clinical work and worries. Do write everything about yourself.

I am expecting news from you.

Yours,
Chaim

I know that there exists a draft of the Fraction's programme. Couldn't you send it on to me?

The circular is under separate cover.

84. To Vera Khatzman, Rostov. *Geneva, 3 June 1901*

Russian: H.W.: W.A.

Geneva, 3/vi. 1901
2 rue de l'Ecole de Chimie

Dear Verochka,

I did not write to you yesterday because I was waiting for news from home. This came today, but apparently nothing has happened there. I assume that the report of the first fire[1] got delayed in the newspapers.

You are home already, my dearest;[2] and are probably feeling wonderful in the warm home atmosphere, far away from cold and remote strangers.

Although I am no longer capable of experiencing such feelings, to some extent I can still understand you.

I hope you found everything and everyone in the best order, and all those who are dear to you the same good people as when you left them.[3] They must all be very good people.

84. [1] As a result of outbreaks of fire in Pinsk in the spring of 1901, some 750 Jewish families were left homeless and many Jewish workers were thrown out of employment.
[2] She had gone home to Rostov for the summer vacation.
[3] Lit., 'as good as when you left them'.

My letter is a day late, but do you know, Verusya, I am too depressed, so depressed that I can't lift my hand to write. I don't want to make you gloomy. It is all the more needless because this frame of mind, although rather agonising, will soon pass. There will be work up to the neck, and it is <u>imperative</u> that private life should not interfere with the fulfilment of public duty. Yes, that is essential. How fateful indeed, Verochka, is this problem for people like me. No, today is a terrible day, my fingers are all thumbs, nothing hangs together, and this is a very bad letter too.

Do you know, during these days right after your departure I have been engaged in a terrible self-analysis and have discovered many, very many, shortcomings. So many, Verochka, that I am getting frightened. Your letters from Buchs[4] have just been delivered. I can imagine, my darling, how worried you were. Just as well that it all ended in this way.[4] My little girl, I too have been thinking a lot about our time together. Those were good days, full and wonderful. They were days of deliverance from the nasty things belonging to the time before we got to know each other.[5] How quickly it all passed! I hope these days will be repeated and that it will be even better for both of us together. You most certainly deserve pure unclouded happiness. As for me, I do not know. I haven't yet settled accounts with myself. Verochka, there is one thing I will tell you—human beings are nasty animals. . . .

Do not let my epistle startle you. It is so disjointed, bad and bitter. I feel such a weight in my heart, and this is the consequence of actions for which I am punishing myself, but committed I do not know why, I do not know what for. I used to take a better view of people and of life, but I have erred—I make mistakes myself.

My little girl, my little Verusya. As it happens, in these last two days there has been nothing interesting. The groups[6] keep silent. Only from Munich—a most stupid silly postcard.[7] A great part of my joy of living has departed together with you, Verochka, and this is not good. It should not be so. I have no right to let this happen at all.

My 'correspondence' with b., as you call it, has yielded no results

---

[4] Vera Khatzman's 'letters from Buchs' have not been preserved, and in their absence it is not possible to say what W. is referring to.

[5] See n. 6 to W.'s letter to V.K. of 15 March 1901 (No. 64) on the words 'that whole wicked nightmare'.

[6] The Zionist students groups.

[7] Probably a reference to a postcard dated 28 May 1901 (W.A.) in which Alexander Nemser, one of the joint directors of the Munich 'Correspondence Bureau' concerned with preparations for the Conference, pressed for amendments to the Geneva Bureau's second circular, as to which see n. 7 to No. 83.

so far.[8] I have had no reply from that set of people so beloved by me and who love me no less. It will presumably be negative. And so nothing has happened here.

I am getting very much confused about the question of fixing the date of the conference. I am afraid it will be towards the autumn. The Munich crowd irresponsibly insists on July. I doubt whether we should manage to cope with the work, which has only just started.[9] If that is how it turns out, I shall be leaving for home on July 10th, as Haya's wedding has been arranged for the 15th.[10]

Verochka, my darling, you will, I hope, give me a description of everything and everyone. How did you find your sisters?[11] Give them my warm greetings, the very warmest.

I shall try to write to you often. But in no case must you worry if a letter from me is a day or two late, for you know how many letters I have to turn out at times.

Give your brothers[11] and Yema[12] the regards of a stranger who holds them in high esteem. They are good people, aren't they?

For some reason I recall the phrase you typed: 'You have good impulses, etc.'

Well, that's enough complaining. *Il y a toujours un mais.*

Verochka, Verochka, be happy, gay and well.

Lots of love.

Yours,
Chaim

You will be seeing Nyusya, of course. Please give her my friendly greetings, sincerely meant. Tell her that she is a nice person, and that I want her always to remain so. Tell her that.

85. To Vera Khatzman, Rostov. *Geneva, 8 June 1901*

Russian: H.W.: W.A.

Geneva, 8/VI. 1901
2 rue de l'Ecole de Chimie

My dearest darling,

I have not written to you for several days now. Worries, anxiety,

---

[8] 'b' means the Bund, as can be seen from No. 85, from which it appears that W. had been trying to extract money from the Bund for some purpose which cannot be identified, no trace of the correspondence having been found.

[9] In the end, the Youth Conference met in December.

[10] The marriage of W.'s sister Haya to his friend Abraham Lichtenstein: the wedding was postponed from 15 to 30 July—see No. 108.

[11] V.K. had two brothers, both older than herself, Lev (Levchik, Lyolya) and Michael (Misha). She had also three elder sisters, Liubov (Liuba), Sophia (Sofochka) and Anna (Nyunechka), and one younger sister, Rachel (Raya, Rayechka).

[12] Pet-name of Benjamin Hasudovsky, a Rostov friend of V.K.

accumulation of work, and, chiefly, low spirits—these were the reasons for my silence. I have not yet had a single peaceful day since you went away, and I am miserable, Verochka, very miserable. There is nowhere to go in the evenings, nobody one could go to to relax. I have not even been to see Esfir all this time; this is bad, but I simply can't bring myself to do so. Koenigsberg occasionally comes to see me—she does help a little. But enough about myself. I'd be so happy to receive a note from you to say that you have reached home safely at last and are already having a rest.

How happy you must be, my dear. I am terribly glad for you, my darling. Only see that you settle down well, so that you can rest and study.

My affairs are not going too badly. In all probability the conference will not take place until October;[1] it cannot be done otherwise. And so I shall leave in July, when term ends, and after I have settled all my money matters. I'd love a break even now; I want so much to breathe freely after all the excitement, but everything still seems so distant, there is still so much to be done before I can leave, that it's no use poisoning my life with thoughts. You wanted very much to know, Verusya, how the correspondence with the Bund ended. In nothing, my child. Naturally they did not give a penny, and I am just waiting for an opportunity to give them a piece of my mind. I hope there will be such an opportunity. They are just nasty, very nasty.[2]

As to news in town—nothing outstanding. On Wednesday night there will be a Jewish party at the Ariana.[3] We hope it will be a success. The Trachtenbergs[4] and Brailovskaya are working very hard, and good results are expected. We shall see.

Yes, my little Verusya, this commotion too will soon pass. We shall soon have to draw up the balance-sheet of this academic year too. I hope it will be better than last year's.

Nevertheless, something has been achieved. Were any other nation to spend so much energy in a similar cause there would no doubt be more to show, but here lies the whole horror of the Jewish problem—one has to work in such terrible conditions, where one doesn't know who is friend or foe, when the stench of decay hits one at every step. And years will pass, and many will still fall victims to these terrible conditions before creative, constructive work starts. Are we going to see all that? No, I doubt it. Our fate, the fate of people who live in a time of transition, is to be given activities of a purely negative character. To understand and ponder

85. [1] See n. 9 to No. 84.   [2] See n. 8 to No. 84.
[3] For a description of the party see No. 88.   [4] Not identified.

over old Jewish values, to understand only to discard them perhaps, or to reappraise them at a later stage—my God, this is agonising labour, agonising work, and we, the feeble and the weak, have to bear it on our shoulders.

On Monday Mlle Axelrod,[5] from Berne, is giving a lecture here on Nietzsche and soc(ialism). Poor, poor Nietzsche, what ugly lips will be uttering his words,[6] and these Messrs. Soc[ialists] are trying to pull their little red cap on that giant genius's head.[7] It seems clear enough that no one liked that fraternity less than Nietzsche. They might have left him in peace, they might have let him lie peacefully in his grave instead of bandying his name about, and to what purpose? Mlle. A. will presumably prove that Nietzsche was wrong, that had he known her, he would have been much wiser. Pack, Pack, Pack![8]

And so, Verusya, my dearest, dearest darling, little by little you are getting some idea of the very rich life here. A bog!

I hope to finish some work soon, then I shall do a little cycle tour. That will be good.

From you, my little one, I am awaiting the most detailed news about absolutely everything. What are you doing, how did you find things at home, in a word—everything, all your impressions and thoughts.

Verochka, I find it hard to be without you. I wish I could see you for at least a single moment. But you are so far, so far away.

Keep well, my darling little Verusya, my good girl.

I kiss you again and again—many many kisses.

Yours,
Chaim

86. To Ahad Ha'am (Asher Ginsberg), Odessa. *Geneva, 9 June 1901*

Russian: H.W.: Ahad Ha'am papers, N.L.

Geneva, 9. VI. 01
2 rue de l'Ecole de Chimie

Esteemed and dear comrade,

It is only now, when the matter of the conference is beginning to assume a somewhat more tangible shape, that I am writing to

---

[5] Of the two Axelrod sisters, Liubov and Ida, both members of the Social Democratic Party and prominent figures in the Russian *émigré* colony in Berne, W. is probably referring to Liubov (1868–1946), who was a philosopher and sociologist.

[6] Lit., 'what ugly lips he has fallen upon'.

[7] See n. 1 to No. 52.   [8] 'What a rabble!'

you with reference to our discussion in Paris.[1] I hope you were able to have at least some rest (if it is at all possible to speak of rest) after the Paris trip with all its delights, and that you will now devote some of your time to our cause. We have approached various groups and individuals whom we thought most suitable for the proposed organization, and we have received satisfactory replies from almost every quarter. The conclusion to be drawn from all this is that the venture on which we are embarking is not something *gekünsteltes*,[2] but a necessity, a need which has come to a head. Weariness reigns everywhere, this being the outcome of the meaninglessness of recent Zionist work, but there is no denying this gratifying development, that among the younger men there are enough—I would not say too many—good people who need a push, a guiding idea, to make them work fruitfully. Such are my general impressions, based of course on letters received from all sides. I don't think, therefore, that it is possible at such a time not to respond to the enquiries coming in all sincerity from the healthier part of our intelligentsia, especially at a time when there are so many unhealthy spots in the general Zionist organism,[3] and when everything is so hopeless.

If the shape which the youth organisation will assume is not yet altogether clear, if it is still impossible to get one's bearings amid so many practical and theoretical questions, this must be explained precisely by the fact that until now—with a very few fortunate exceptions—there has been no inclination to concentrate on solving them. The main task, of course, will be to work out a programme for the organization[4] which could really be brought to life. Even at this point I have no doubt that its basic principle will indeed be complete independence of the general Zionist Organization, and that there will be no concessions in this respect. As soon as I have the plans in my possession (these are now being worked out) I will forward them to you immediately.

As to the date of the Conference, it is now safe to say that it will take place in October.[5] There is too much work to be done to be ready by mid-July. This is why I return now to my request that you should read a paper on the cultural question or a general theoretical paper on Zionism. There is no need to tell you, Osher Isayevich, how important for our cause would be your active participation, not just your full sympathy. We shall benefit enormously from your directives. I am sure that you will now have

---

86. [1] In the middle of May—see No. 83.   [2] 'artificial'.
[3] 'organism'—thus in orig. (not. 'organization').
[4] See n. 6 to No. 83.   [5] It was, in fact, postponed to December.

more time for the preparation of the paper, and you must not refuse.

Under separate cover we are sending you our 2nd circular letter,[6] and we earnestly beg you to reply as soon as possible.[7]

I don't know whether you are already aware that the 'cultural question' has been included in the *Tagesordnung*[8] of the 5th Congr[ess]. From the choice of speakers one can form in advance some idea of the content of the addresses to be delivered.[9] It is no use expecting a prophet from that quarter; as I see it, this was incorporated in the *Tagesordnung* merely to fill one or two days, as an embellishment, or perhaps under the influence of the complaints which arose last year after the notorious cultural debates.[10] It is all the more necessary for a sound and truthful word to be spoken, and this can be said by you. It is your duty now to emerge from your reserve, and, believe me, I am expressing the opinion of a considerable section of the younger people. Your literary work is, unfortunately, beyond the grasp of many, and this is one more reason why your paper will be well-timed and absolutely necessary.

There is much more that I could add in support of my request, but I do hope that you will write to me and raise all the questions which you wanted to raise in P[aris], and thus give us an opportunity of expressing ourselves more fully and perhaps also more clearly.

Please accept now my sincere greetings and best wishes,

Yours,
Ch. Weizmann

May I remind you about your photograph?

[6] See n. 7 to No. 83.

[7] For Ahad Ha'am's refusal of the invitation, and his reasons, see n. 20 to No. 100.

[8] 'agenda'.

[9] As to the 'cultural question' see n. 8 to No. 40.—The provisional agenda, as agreed upon by the Greater Actions Committee on 17 May 1901, included addresses by Berthold Feiwel ('Amelioration of the physical, spiritual and economic condition of Jewry'); Leopold Kahn ('Jewish history, literature and language'); Martin Buber ('Jewish art'); Simon Rosenbaum ('Jewish science'); Alfred Nossig and Shmarya Levin ('Popular education').

[10] At the Fourth Congress (London 1900) advocates of cultural work had been given a hearing, but a resolution proposed by them had been side-tracked by Herzl and not put to the vote: see IV Z.C. Prot., pp. 221–116.—Objections to the recognition of cultural work as an integral part of the Zionist programme came from two distinct quarters—first from the religious wing of the Movement, jealous custodians of traditional Jewish beliefs and observances, who saw in educational or cultural activities not directly related to religion a threat to the values they prized, and, secondly, also from political Zionists, who held that nothing must be allowed to deflect the Movement from the efforts in the political and diplomatic field on which they believed that all its energies ought, at this stage, to be concentrated.

87. To Aaron Eliasberg, St. Blasien.[1] *Geneva, 12 June 1901*

Russian: H.W.: W.A. Jerusalem.

Geneva, 12. vi. 1901
2 rue de l'Ecole de Chimie

Dear Aaron,

Thank you for giving a sign of life.[2] Hard as I tried to find your address, I could not discover a thing. I knew more or less everything that had happened to you and am very happy that you have managed to recuperate. Take care of yourself, Aaron; people like you are so badly needed now. Your letter has arrived just when work is in full swing, and I haven't a moment to spare; you'll forgive me if I only give you a brief account of the situation, without going into details.

A prelim[inary] conference was held in Munich on April 1st and 2nd, at which was decided to convene a Youth Congress. I was entrusted with the *Centralleitung*[3] of all this preliminary work. So far, I am very pleased with the way things are going. All the foreign groups, and, among the Russians, the St. Petersburg, Odessa, Kiev, Warsaw, Grodno, Yekaterinoslav, Berdyansk, Vilna, Melitopol, Kharkov, and Moscow groups, have responded to our call. Many have already nominated their delegates, some have put forward speakers on a number of issues. It is evident that the venture has fully matured. This will be a conference not only of students, but of progressive youth in general.[4] From the circular letters[5] enclosed with this letter you will be able to form an idea of the aim and significance of the congress.

A most lively correspondence with the groups is going on. The problems raised at the Munich conference are being debated everywhere. The place of the Conference: Geneva, or a town in centr[al] Germany. Time: mid-July or mid-October.[6]

It is beyond all doubt that the Conference will take place. So much is already being said and written about it and against it. Moreover, all the speakers are already getting ready. Preparations are going on everywhere, so success in this respect is no longer in

---

87. [1] In the Black Forest, Germany.

[2] No earlier letter from either to the other has come to light.

[3] 'central direction'.

[4] It had at one time been proposed that the Conference should be confined strictly to students.

[5] As to the Organization Bureau's first and second circular letters see n. 6 to No. 80 and n. 7 to No. 83.

[6] What actually happened was that the Youth Conference met at Basle in Dec. 1901.

doubt. All the threads of the venture are in my hands, since everything converges here. So you can imagine how much work there is. Moreover, it is still necessary to fight the *Indolenz* to which our Zionists are such a prey. I have four assistants[7] here, but we can hardly cope with all the work. We have to write letters and answer them, to abuse and be abused, to hectograph, and similar joys.

Add to this that it is impossible to get a thing from our groups, that there isn't a penny available, and that everything has to be managed like all other Jewish affairs, and you will have the full picture.

But all in all, I am pleased and cheerful.

My personal affairs are going well. I have done a piece of work, sold it to a factory,[8] and am getting a very decent salary.

If the Conference doesn't take place in July, I shall go home at the end of July and undertake a journey through the Pale.[9] My people were spared by the fire.[10]

Do write, dear friend, about everything, about your health, how you feel, where are you going to spend the summer, where the spa is, in what part of the country[11] (*Geographie ungenügend!*).[12] Write, of course, about your attitude to everything and, if you can, please translate the enclosed second circular letter into German. You will thus save me some trouble.

And, if you can, send a little money; we shall accept it with gratitude. Write at once to yours,

Chaim

Until the next letter!
All the documents are going in a separate packet.

88. To Vera Khatzman, Rostov. *Geneva, 14 June 1901*

Russian: H.W.: W.A.

Geneva, 14. VI. 01

My dear little girl,

Today I am already getting worried, Verochka, because I have had no word from you; I have been looking forward so much to a

---

[7] In addition to the two women students referred to in earlier letters, Esther Shneerson and Anne Koenigsberg, W.'s assistants appear to have included also Rosa Grinblatt and Catherine Dorfman.

[8] Almost certainly the Bayer Works at Elberfeld—see n. 15 to No. 55.

[9] The Pale of Settlement—see n. 3 to No. 63.

[10] As to the Pinsk fires see n. 1 to No. 84.

[11] Lit., 'in what area'.   [12] '[my] geography [is] inadequate'.

nice letter with a full description of everything. It is already a week since you reached home, my darling. You must have had a lot of impressions, my dearest, and you must hurry to share them with me. Here there has been nothing special. My state of acute malaise has to some extent gone, though I cannot boast of particularly good spirits, especially in the evenings. But what can one do? There is plenty of work, and in spite of my best intentions to find some diversion and relaxation, to go away somewhere, I simply cannot afford it. Letters keep on arriving all the time, and all have to be answered. We are now conducting a particularly lively correspondence with St. Petersburg, Moscow, Kiev, Paris and Berlin. Everywhere there is great interest in the conference.[1] The provincial areas, too, are responding little by little. You can imagine, therefore, my child, how much there is to do.

The Jewish party[2] has now taken place. It went off indifferently. The proceeds were small, some hundred francs in all. There was an interesting incident. The tickets stated that part of the proceeds would go to those who lost everything in the fire.[3] The police had granted the permit only on condition that the party would be for the benefit of the victims of the fire, and Trachtenberg got scared and crossed out the word 'part', but when we were selling the tickets we kept on saying that in spite of the deletion (only for the sake of the police), a part of the proceeds would be used for the benefit of Zionism. Comr[ade] Granovsky[4] appeared at the party, and in the presence of a number of people made the following pointed remark: 'You say that you are arranging the party for the benefit of the victims of the fire, but you are taking money for Zionism. This is a swindle, and your chief organiser is a swindler.' I was not present at the time. Just think, my dear, how disgusting! But he was properly humiliated.

This is all the news. You have much more news, and I implore you, do write at once.

The conference will not take place in July, and I am leaving on the 10th. By then everything will be settled.

I shall certainly be in the south, and will, of course, come to Rostov. Write and write. I am brief today, my dearest, because there is still heaps of work.

Even now we[5] are meeting three or four times a week.

88. [1] The Zionist Youth Conference.

[2] Evidently the party mentioned in No. 85.

[3] The reference is, presumably, to the victims of the outbreaks of fire in Pinsk a few weeks earlier, as to which see n. 1 to No. 84.

[4] Not identified.

[5] W. and his assistants at the Youth Conference Organization Bureau.

Lots of kisses, my little Verusya; I love you, I love you and I miss you greatly.

Yours,
Chaim

Best regards to Nyusechka. What is her address? I want to write to her. Give her warmest greetings from me.

89. To Vera Khatzman, Rostov. *Geneva, 15 June 1901*

Russian: H.W.: W.A.

Geneva, 15/vi. 01

My dear sweet girl,

I received your letter[1] today. Do you know, I had a premonition of something bad, and how awful—it came true. I can imagine how you felt, my darling, when you found someone dear to you in such a state.[2] Write, Verusya, how everything is at home, how you found your sisters, and how you are spending your days. I am afraid that you will have no rest at all, that you will not go for walks, and that you will be as gloomy as before. Verochka, I implore you, take care of yourself.

I am surprised, my darling, that you have not received my letters. This is my fourth. One should have been awaiting you at Rostov on arrival, the second you should have got this week, the third was posted yesterday,[3] and this is the fourth.

From my last letter you will learn everything that is of interest to you, my dear.

Guterman's whole attitude was expressed by four roubles[4]— That is what he is worth.

There is nothing fresh since yesterday. An interesting letter from Berlin and Paris.[5]

89. [1] Not found.

[2] The passage in No. 90 commencing 'What is the matter with your sister?' supports the conjecture that W. is here referring to the matrimonial troubles, ending in divorce, of V.K.'s eldest sister, Liubov (Liuba).

[3] See Nos. 84, 85, 88.

[4] On behalf of the Rostov *Dorshei Zion* ('Seekers of Zion'), Hillel (Ilya) Guterman, a lawyer and a leading Rostov Zionist, had sent W. four roubles (the equivalent of about 8*s.*) for the Youth Conference Organization Bureau, with a covering letter dated 27 May (9 June) 1901 (W.A.) conveying his Society's view that action should be taken only within the framework of the Zionist Organization and with the consent of the Zionist Congress.

[5] 'an interesting letter'—presumably a slip for 'interesting letters'. The letters in question cannot be identified with certainty, but W. may be referring to (1) a letter dated Berlin, 8 June 1901 from Chaim (Boris) Gurevich, Chairman of the Berlin

It is sheer misery, Verusya, and I shall try to get away as soon as possible. If I do manage, not later than the 10th.

I shall come to see you without fail.[6] I do so much want to see you. I am very worried. Verusya, why do you write: 'Don't forget me'? Why, my sweet?

If my letters are late, you know, my darling, how much work I have.

There can be no other reason. If something interesting occurs I will let you know at once. I shall keep you *au courant*.

Kissing you affectionately, my darling Verochka,

Yours,
Chaim

90. To Vera Khatzman, Rostov. *Geneva, 21 June 1901*

Russian: H.W.: W.A.

Geneva, 21. VI. 01
Rue de l'Ecole de Chimie, 2

My dear little girl,

I have today received your letter[1] which I have been awaiting so impatiently. It is strange that the longer it is since we parted the more I long for you. I don't know how I shall be able to stand it till we meet again. How strange of you, my dearest, to thank me for not forgetting you. My funny little Verochka. How can you thank me like that? It is wrong, you know. At my end, darling, there is nothing special. I am up to my eyes in work. Though the flood of letters has somewhat subsided this week, there is still enough to keep me busy in connection with the Conference. I am now working out an organization plan[2]—quite a complicated matter. We shall soon issue the third circular[3]—and this, too, means work.

Kadimah, assuring W. that, in spite of misgivings felt by many members about the lack of a definite programme of work, the Society would not decline to take part in the Youth Conference, and (2) a letter dated Paris, 13 June 1901 from a Dr. Klugman (of whom nothing is known except that he was in some way associated with Bernard-Lazare), telling W. that B.-L. ought not to have been included in the list of persons who had consented to read papers at the Youth Conference—see n. 7 to No. 83 and n. 2 to No. 93.   [6] He did not, in fact, go to Rostov.

90. [1] Not found.   [2] See n. 6 to No. 83.
[3] There is in W.A. (Circulars 1901) a draft of a Youth Conference Bureau communication headed 'with the third circular', but there is no evidence of any such 'third circular' having ever been distributed and it seems clearly to have been dropped. Apart from this, after the first two circulars (see n. 6 to No. 80 and n. 7 to No. 83) there is no trace of any follow-up until Sept. 1901, when a circular announcing the date of the Conference was distributed on behalf of the Geneva Organization Bureau by the Zionist Correspondence Centre in Kishinev—see below, n. 12 to No. 129.

Furthermore, there are so many interesting things in the laboratory that I am now working intensively there. I want to work until the 5th and then, before my departure, spend a few days cycling. I have not yet managed a tour, and I propose to go out next Sunday for a day or two for a change of air. On the whole, I am tired and shall be glad to rest for a couple of days. About local news—of which there is none—I have told you in my previous letters. The Conference will take place in October, most likely in Germany.[4]

I still do not know anything definite. There has been a stirring in the bog, and propaganda against the Conference is already in full swing. Underground intrigues are going on in Paris and St. Petersburg.[5] These petty little people like Guterman,[6] who see no further than their noses, how pitiful they are! (The Jewish nose, however, can cast a shadow over the whole world!)

Do you know, my dearest darling, that I have not had any letters from home for a very long time indeed, and I am getting worried. I shall be sending a telegram if there is nothing by tomorrow. Funny people, they seem to have forgotten me completely. The financial crisis is almost over;[7] in this respect I feel a sense of relief. But I have more worries than hairs on my head (not that I have so many!).

Do forgive me, my dearest, for keeping on chattering about myself. You do not seem to be in a happy mood at all. How I should like to embrace you and kiss you, my sweet, and share confidences with you. For you are a bit lonely. You cannot tell everything to everyone. Verusya, what is the matter with your sister? Why does she feel so bad? Has she been suffering physically as well? Of course, she was dealt a cruel blow.[8] Poor woman, you should comfort her, Verusya. When are you planning to go to the Caucasus? In July I shall be able to tell you exactly when I am coming to you. But I shall be completely incognito. I shall have nothing to do with your Zionists. Guterman is a 'Shabes-Zionist'.[9] May God forgive him his stupidity and his boundless obtuseness. A letter has arrived from him which I did not think even worth answering—a specimen of the court-room eloquence of a provincial

[4] See n. 6 to No. 87.

[5] No explanation can be offered of the reference to St. Petersburg. As regards Paris, W. may be thinking of the news which had reached him in the letter mentioned in n. 5 to No. 89 suggesting a cooling-off in Bernard-Lazare's attitude towards the Youth Conference. [6] See n. 4 to No. 89.

[7] In his letter of 14 June (No. 88) he had told V.K. that he wanted to get away for a rest, but 'I simply cannot afford it'.

[8] See n. 2 to No. 89.

[9] *Shabes* (in orig. in cyrillic characters), Ashkenazic pronunciation of Hebr. *Shabbat* (Sabbath)—i.e. he is a Zionist once a week.

fool. God alone may forgive him. Let the sum of four roubles (4 silver roubles)[10] go to other institutions to Guterman's taste.

The members of the Bureau will soon be leaving, and I shall remain alone. Shneerson has to cram very hard now. But I shall manage.

Verochka, write to me twice, three times, a week. Please do. I get news from you so seldom. Do write, write.

Esfir[11] has probably arrived already. How do you like her sudden departure? What a trick to play! It is true that she did not feel very well here. Give her my regards, and especially give my regards to Nyusya. I shall soon get round to writing her a real missive: let her know.

Keep well, my darling. Lots and lots of love.

Yours,
Chaim

91. To Ahad Ha'am (Asher Ginzberg), Odessa. *Geneva, [23] June 1901*

Russian: Pcd. H.W.: Ahad Ha'am Papers, N.L.
[Dated by W. 24 June 1901, but Geneva pmk. 23 June 1901.]

Geneva, 24/vi. 01

Esteemed Comrade,

I wrote to you two weeks ago[1] and am most impatiently awaiting your reply. I know that you are very busy and it is with *schweren Herzens*[2] that I trouble you, but you will agree that your reply is of importance and interest to us and to the whole cause. I beg you, therefore, to spare us some of your time. By the end of the week I shall inform you of the progress of the prepar[atory] work.[3]

Best wishes,

Yours,
Ch. Weizmann

---

[10] See n. 4 to No. 89.
[11] Esther Weinberg.

91. [1] See No. 86.
    [2] 'with a heavy heart'.
    [3] No further letter from W. to Ahad Ha'am earlier than 31 Oct. 1901 (No. 136) has been found.

92. To Leo Motzkin, Berlin. *Geneva, 23 June 1901*

Russian: H.W.: C.Z.A.—A126/24/7/2/2

Geneva, 23. VI. 1901
Rue de l'Ecole de Chimie, 2

Dear Leo,

I have left you in peace all this time, bearing in mind that you are very busy. I admit that in the depths of my heart I kept thinking that you would לפנים משורת הדין[1] and write all the same.

Nor would I disturb you now were I not forced to do so by our affairs. The other day we received a pamphlet issued by the Zionist Socialists—London 1901—entitled 'An appeal to the Zion[ist] Jewish Youth'.[2] We are accustomed here to all kinds of pamphlets, and we are not particularly spoiled in this respect, but I have never read a pamphlet like this before. If the new Fraction wants to be recognised within a community of very exacting young people (I mean intelligent people), then their *profession de foi* should not be set out in the form of a biting magazine article or a short *feuilleton*, but in the form of serious reasoned criticism of the present with a closely defined future programme. The points set out at page 16[3] *setzen dem Werke die Krone auf*[4] [with their immodesty].[5] I do not imagine for a single moment that you would approve anything of the sort, and I should like very much to know at once what you think and your attitude to all this.

This is sheer madness, and a number of phrases remind me of Syrkin's paper.[6] It makes me indignant that people think it possible to feed 'youth' on such things.

---

92. [1] Hebr., 'not [insist] on strict justice'.

[2] 'Manifesto to Jewish Youth', London, 1901, published by 'a group of Zionist Socialists' and containing a condensed version of a lecture given by Nahman Syrkin to the Russian Jewish colony in Berlin. Printed in Berlin but published in London to avoid possible trouble with the German police.

[3] At p. 16 of the Manifesto the basic conditions for the Jews' solution of their problems were set out, in substance, as follows: (1) The Jewish masses must be organized on social-democratic lines in the countries in which they reside. (2) A Jewish socialist State must be established in Palestine and the neighbouring territories. (3) 'Practical religion' [*sic*]—meaning, presumably, the practice of religion—must be fought and the socialist-nationalist creed adopted in its place.

[4] 'crown the work'.

[5] In orig. words in brackets not clearly legible.

[6] W. had not heard the lecture on which the pamphlet was based but may possibly be recalling a lecture by Syrkin which he had heard at a meeting of the Berne Zionist Students Society in Dec. 1898 (see *Die Welt*, 20 Jan. and 10 Feb. 1899). On that occasion, Syrkin, speaking as a Zionist-Socialist, had severely criticized the Zionist Organization and the Second Zionist Congress and had incurred much resentment by his rebellious attitude and his vehement expression of left-wing views. See further as to this lecture, No. 146 and n. 2 to that letter.

As to the affairs of the Conference, I am in correspondence with the *Kadimah* colleagues, and you probably know what is going on there.

Preparatory work is considerably advanced, and I hope that before long all those on whom we should be able to count will respond to our call.

Replies have arrived recently from Dr. Lurie—Warsaw, Idelson —Moscow, Portug[alov]—St. Petersburg, and from Ahad Ha'am.[7] Hickel, Zweig (Olmütz) and Feiwel have also responded.[8] I am now in correspondence with Eliashev, Jacobson and Dr. Bendersky. The Russian provinces are reacting feebly, although the places that did reply by sending the minutes of their meetings have shown an exceptionally serious attitude to the venture. When I come to Berlin (not later than the 15th–16th July) I shall bring the correspondence with me. It is interesting in some respects. Meanwhile, until my departure, definite answers will presumably arrive from a number of people. K[ohan]-B[ernstein], Gourland, Aberson, and some others are working out the organization plan.[9] I hope it will soon be possible to publish it as material for debate both in the groups and at the Conference.

I have a very great deal to talk over with you seriously and thoroughly, and I doubt whether it can all be done by letter. I insist now on the requests made in my previous letter to you that you should declare your attitude. Only after receiving a letter from you shall I be able to expound all that has matured in my mind.

I have, of course, a lot to do, but I am in such an elated state of mind that I could easily cope with an even greater volume of work.

About myself I have little new to report. In general I am quite satisfied, except for the worries we shall always have in our life and work.

Things are going well in the laboratory and I shall soon publish an enormous work[10] which is in part my *Habilitations-*

---

[7] There are in W.A. letters showing interest in the Youth Conference from Joseph Lurie and Portugalov, dated respectively 24 May (6 June) and 30 May (12 June) 1901. The letter here referred to from Ahad Ha'am has not been found. His letter of 18 June (1 July) 1901 declining the invitation to address the Youth Conference did not reach W. until early in July—see n. 20 to No. 100.

[8] A letter in W.A., dated 13 June 1901, from M. Schmidt, of Odessa, at this time studying in Vienna and in active correspondence with W. on matters concerning the Youth Conference, reports favourable replies from Hickel, Zweig, and Feiwel, all of whom had been invited to read papers at the Conference.

[9] See n. 6 to No. 83.

[10] As to W.'s 1899 dissertation on naphthazarin dyes see nn. 12 and 13 to No. 36. The 'enormous work' soon to be published has not been traced; either it has been lost

schrift;[11] until now I have been unable to do so because of *Patentschutz*.[12]

How are your studies progressing ? When are the examinations ?[13] Where is Polya ?

Do write about everything. Are you going to read a paper at the 5th Congress ?[14]

Write at once.

Yours,
Chaim

93. To Vera Khatzman, Rostov. *Geneva, 25 June 1901*

Russian: H.W.: W.A.

Geneva, 25. VI. 1901
The Chemical Laboratory

Dear Verochka,

I am taking advantage of a bit of free time—we are filtering a hundred grammes of a substance which filters poorly—to send you, my darling girl, just a few words. Your letter[1] came yesterday and I am very grateful to you, my child, for having started to write more often.

But you are still not telling me in detail how you pass the time, how things are at home, how is father's health, etc. If I have not asked about this, my darling, it is because I do not like to set out such a list of obvious commonplace questions, assuming that you are fully aware that all this interests me.

Are you studying a lot with Nyusya ? Why do you meet so rarely ? I think that Nyusya is your best friend and at the same time the worthiest.

Except for worries, there has been nothing at my end for the past few days. As for the worries, these have been brought about by

or, as is not unlikely, it was, in fact, never published. It seems clearly to be distinct from the 'monograph' mentioned by W. in his letter to V.K. of 28 June 1901 (see No. 95 and n. 17 to that letter), since the words 'I shall soon publish' suggest that W. is the sole author, whereas the monograph is to be the joint work of W. and Deichler, and (*b*) the 'enormous work' is described by W. in June as almost ready for publication, whereas he writes in No. 95 that he will not be able to apply himself seriously to the monograph until October.

[11] See n. 12 to No. 36.

[12] 'patent protection'; as to patents registered in the joint names of W. and Deichler see n. 15 to No. 55.

[13] Motzkin was working for a Berlin Ph.D. He never got it, and from what is known of his University career it is doubtful whether he ever took the examinations.

[14] The Fifth Zionist Congress opened at Basle on 26 Dec. 1901 but at the time of this letter the date had not been finally fixed.

93. [1] Not found.

the changes and surprises that fate has in store for us, just to pamper us somewhat. Bernard-Lazare has refused to take part in the Conference.[2] You will realise how unpleasant this is for me. The reason is one of principle—he does not adhere to the Basle Programme[3]—but behind this issue of principle there is some underhand plotting, and I am beginning to discern the threads.[4] I shall let you know when the time is ripe.

Furthermore, for a long time I had no news at all from my brother-in-law[5] and my sister Mariya in Warsaw. It turns out that my brother-in-law went to Odessa on business and fell ill there. He developed a malignant tumour (*Karbunkel*). An operation saved his life. You can imagine how pleasant all this was. Add to this the petty day-to-day worries, and the picture is complete. But do you know, Verochka, I am beginning to learn to bear everything and to get used to everything, like a beast of burden which after a short time gets reconciled to the load placed on its back. What is most annoying of all is that energy is being wasted on things that do not deserve attention and without which the equilibrium of the universe would in no way be upset. I am not a fatalist, and I do not believe that everything has to be like that.

The result of these worries has been a certain weariness and a desire to leave quickly, to see comrades everywhere, to talk to them, to arrange everything. The responsibility is enormous, and at times one feels that a whole shower of reproaches will come down on you and you will not be able to provide an answer. If other speakers follow B[ernard]-L[azare]'s example there will be a terrible mess, which it will be up to me alone to disentangle. If plots and intrigues are being hatched in secret I have absolutely no strength to fight them. While ready to enter an open struggle, I am powerless against underhand tactics. It is, of course, extremely easy to disrupt everything, and the half-finished edifice we have erected may collapse if the forces of darkness become active.

I am having another article in *Voskhod*.[6] This time it will be

---

[2] Writing to W. on 24 June 1901 (W.A.) Bernard-Lazare protested against the inclusion of his name, without his consent, in the list of speakers at the Youth Conference (see n. 7 to No. 83), and declined to take part in the Conference, since he could not associate himself with the acceptance of the Basle Programme, holding that before aspiring to a land of their own, the Jewish people must first liberate themselves from outworn traditions and be educated to think on rationalist lines.

[3] See General Introduction, App. II, p. xxxi.

[4] It has not been found possible to throw any light on the nature of W.'s suspicions or the reasons for them.

[5] Chaim Lubzhinsky, the husband of W.'s eldest sister, Miriam (Marya).

[6] This article cannot be traced unless (as is highly improbable) it can be identified with an article by W. on the Youth Conference published in *Voskhod* (weekly series), 12 Dec. 1901.

a challenge to the Jewish intelligentsia, and a reproach to the gentlemen representing official Zionism.

This article will lead to replies, and *la lutte est engagée.*

You have read the review of *Werther der Jude.*[7] It does not go very deep, though some of the ideas are not bad. The critic is a young fellow, very pleased with himself and with his Zionism. Everything is clear to him, and he thinks that the Jewish ship has already sailed into calm waters. My God, if only one could knock off some of their self-satisfaction from those people, some of their *Selbstberäucherung*[8]—they would be better people.

Geneva was recently shaken by the appearance of a new pamphlet published by the Socialist Zionists (the double 'ist's').[9] In all my life I have never seen such a pamphlet nor such an insolent and outrageously irresponsible article. A red cap with a blue-and-white ribbon, a national group hailing internationalism with childish yells, dancing around great names; self-worship and Jewish impudence. What an outrageous mixture of meaningless phrases and sheer stupidity!

A terrible confusion has come about in people's ideas. Vestiges of the past are being polished up afresh, refurbished, and sold as something new.

Thank God, the Jewish movement has until now been free of socialist megalomania. Now this too has appeared. I live in the hope that this filth will not spread beyond this pamphlet.

However, all kinds of pestilence start from very little.

You are fed up with my incoherent epistle, my darling Verochka. Do admit it. I shall stop this raving now.

I will try to leave as soon as possible. It will, no doubt, be better for me. I shall put in some hard work these last few days in order to be entirely free by the beginning of July.

Verochka, I am longing—how I am longing—for you. At times my heart is so heavy that I feel like boxing my own ears, just for the fun of it.

Do write more often. Write to

Yours,

Chaim

Very many thanks for the photographs. They are good, very good indeed, Verunchik. If you can, please send half a pound of tob[acco].

[7] Joseph Melnik (1880–?), a young journalist from Bialystok, who had studied at Heidelberg, had reviewed in *Voskhod* (monthly series), Apr. 1901, a German novel by the Jewish writer Ludwig Jacubovsky (1868–1901), the theme of the book being the tragedy of an assimilated young Jew who finds himself rejected by Gentile society. The review reflects a Zionist point of view, but Melnik's ideas about Zionism struck W. as superficial and over-simplified: cf. his rather contemptuous reference to Melnik in No. 97. [8] 'self-intoxication'. [9] See n. 2 to No. 92.

94. To Leo Motzkin, Berlin. *Geneva, 26 June 1901*

Russian: H.W.: C.Z.A.—A126/24/7/2/2

Geneva, 26. vi. 01
2 rue de l'Ecole de Chimie

Dear Leo,

I wrote to you on Monday,[1] but now, without waiting for your reply, I have to write again. Bernard-Lazare has declined to read the paper.[2] In a very detailed letter he gives the reasons for his refusal. He does not recognise the Basle programme nor any other programme. (I shall duplicate a few copies of his letter today and will let you have a copy.) As you see, he has caused me a whole lot of additional worries.

How sad it all is, how pitiable, in my view, the reasons for his refusal. You will see for yourself when you read the letter.

And so for the most important issue we have no speaker. Admittedly, Hickel of Brno is reading a paper on *gewerkschaftliche Organisation*,[3] but this cannot be one of the addresses on the programme.[4] יראתי בפצותי שיח להתחיל.[5] You cannot decline now, and you must take on the theoretical paper.

The Conference will take place in October before the General Congress,[6] and you cannot thus desert the cause of the young, all the more since it is gradually assuming greater importance and will—in my opinion—have a really profound significance which will only become obvious after the Conference, when the whole organization is built up.

To my deep regret, you have not even once uttered a single word concerning your attitude to the Youth Conference question, and it is fatal that the best of friends and comrades should stand aloof from this venture. Believe me, had I not such faith in the decisive importance of a progressive youth organization I should not spend so much strength and energy on this cause.

94. [1] 'Monday' would have been 24 June. No letter to Motzkin of this date has been found. The reference must almost certainly be to W.'s letter of 23 June (No. 92).

[2] See n. 2 to No. 93. Bernard-Lazare's subject was to have been 'The economic position of the Jewish people'.

[3] 'Trade Union Organization'.

[4] i.e., one of the addresses concerning the programme of the projected Youth Organization. The first item on the provisional agenda of the Youth Conference consisted of two addresses described as 'Programmatic papers'—one on Zionism and the other on the tasks of the Youth Organization.

[5] Hebr., 'I tremble when I open my mouth to utter my words'—quoted from a passage in the Jewish New Year liturgy.

[6] At the date of this letter, the Fifth Zionist Congress was expected to meet early in October 1901. In the event, it met at Basle in December, and the Youth Conference met there immediately before the Congress.

I shall soon be in Berlin and am planning to have several meetings with *Kadimah*. I shall read a paper there entitled 'The Youth Organization and its rôle in Jewry'. When I know the exact date of my arrival I shall tell Gurevich and you. I also have to go to Heidelberg and Munich.[7] We shall discuss everything personally, but this must not keep you from writing to me at once.

I am waiting.

Yours ever,
Chaim

95. To Vera Khatzman, Rostov. *Geneva, 28 June 1901*

Russian: H.W.: W.A.

Geneva, 28. VI. 01
2 rue de l'Ecole de Chimie

My darling, dear Verochka,

I received your precious letter[1] today. Thank you, Verunchik, for having started to write often. Why am I moping? My child, I never thought it would be so dreary, but that's how it is. The amount of work has decreased considerably, as we have contacted everybody. There will be more work, however, immediately before my departure.[2] I shall issue a 3rd circular letter.[3] Dorfman left yesterday and Shneerson is very busy with her examinations, so that I am practically on my own.[4] It's a good thing that this will not last long and I shall soon be on my way. The journey too will presumably be hard, with stops in Munich, Heidelberg and Berlin, and perhaps in Vienna.[5] I shall be just in time for Chaya's wedding,[6] i.e. for the 25th, new style.

[7] In connexion with the arrangements for the Youth Conference, W. was being strongly urged by Abramovich to come to Munich, where the Munich Conference had set up a 'Correspondence Centre', and he had also been invited by Gourland to visit him in Heidelberg: see letters from Abramovich of 8 June and from Gourland of 18 June 1901 (W.A.).

95. [1] Not found.

[2] He left for Berlin *en route* for Russia at the end of July.

[3] It seems clear that no such circular was, in fact, issued at this time—see n. 3 to No. 90.

[4] i.e. in the Youth Conference Organization Bureau, where Catherine Dorfman and Esther Shneerson had been working with him. Another of his assistants, Anne Koenigsberg, who left Geneva later that summer (see No. 106), was still there at the date of this letter but was no longer giving him much help—see his letter of 8 June 1901 (No. 85). Shneerson soon after the date of this letter left Geneva for good and, after spending some time in Russia, went to Berlin, but both Dorfman and Koenigsberg returned to Geneva after the summer vacation—see No. 139.

[5] As to Munich and Heidelberg see n. 7 to No. 94. Vienna was at this time the seat of the Zionist Central Office.

[6] The marriage of W.'s sister Haya to Dr. Abraham Lichtenstein.

I am very glad, my darling, that things are somewhat better at home.[7] Let us hope that all will be well. I have not yet heard a thing from my brother-in-law in Odessa[8] although they send me reassuring news from home.

You are indignant about the G[ranovsky] affair.[9] It is true. As I told you, I was not present. Mr. Kaufman[10] told me about it. Afterwards, Malomian[11] talked it over with him, i.e. with Gr[anovsky], at some length. I repeat once more that there was no shadow of deception, since everyone was told, including him, that part of the proceeds would go to the benefit of Zion[ism]. Some of the money— 25 francs—I have sent for the victims of the fire. *C'est tout.* He just behaved vilely. He was supported by a comrade who, nevertheless, found it possible to stand and sell at the buffet and to make up to everyone. But let us drop the subject, since it isn't interesting even from a psychological point of view.

In the last few days some very interesting letters have arrived: from one of my colleagues, Eliashev[12] (he is in the photograph of our Berlin group, on the extreme left), from Aberson,[13] and a splendid circular, devoted to the Conference, from Koh[an]-Bernst[ein].[14] This compensated me for the Bernard-Laz[are] letter.[15] I shall have his letter duplicated and will send you a copy. Motzkin will take Bernard-Lazare's place,[16] so from this point of view also the problem is settled. Reports show that there is much interest in Russia in the Conference question. God grant that it be so, Verochka; I shall soon be able to see for myself.

The laboratory work is going well. I have been working very hard and shall soon finish. Verochka, let me tell you about a new project on which I have already started work. I want to write a monograph on the chemistry of high molecular compounds with three, four or more benzene nuclei, a field in which I have been working for some time, and with which I am very familiar.

---

[7] See n. 2 to No. 89.   [8] See n. 5 to No. 93.

[9] See No. 88.   [10] Not identified.

[11] A person of this name was at this time contributing articles on the Armenian question to the *Journal de Genève*.

[12] Eliashev to W., Kovno, 13/26 June 1901 (W.A.), offering to contribute a paper to be read at the Youth Conference, and warning W. against relying on the Zionist youth groups in Russia, which—he said—consisted of immature youngsters.

[13] Aberson to W., 19 June 1901 (W.A.), reporting that the Paris Zionist students' society had decided to take part in the Youth Conference.

[14] A circular dated 12/25 June 1901, distributed to Zionist study-groups (known as 'theoretical groups') in Russia by Kohan-Bernstein, the director of the Zionist Correspondence Centre at Kishinev (C.Z.A.—Z1/379), pointed out the importance of the impending Youth Conference and described its aims.   [15] See n. 2 to No. 93.

[16] Motzkin had been pressed by W. to replace Bernard-Lazare (see No. 94) but had not yet replied and, in the end, refused (see Nos. 110, 111).

I am going to work on this with a very good man and very good chemist who is also employed at Elberfeld.[17] In general, this field is exceptionally interesting and has a great scientific and technical future. For me it is doubly interesting, since a small chapter in this field belongs to me. Do wish me success, my little one.

We shall start compiling the work in October, and until then we will be busy collecting material and, as far as possible, arranging it. For the moment, of course, I shall not be able to do very much, but in October I shall devote all my free time to this work. It will in all respects be of the utmost importance for me.

There, my sweet little girl, you have all that has happened in the last few days. And now I have a request to make. Send me your picture, but straight away, darling. I badly want to look at you, at least in a photograph. Verusya, my darling Verochka, my sweet adorable one, my own.

You can still reply to this letter here. The next letter should be sent to Berlin, to Dr. Ch. Weizmann, N.W. *Postlagernd*,[18] *Postamt*[19] 7. I shall let you know the Pinsk address in due course.

Tomorrow I am going with *chéri*[20] to Chamonix and Aix-les-Bains for three whole days. By now you have certainly seen Esfir. Give her my best regards, and also to Nyusya, and especially to your sisters, my darling.

I think that I shall be in your part of the world in August, and then we shall see each other.[21] That will really be a festive occasion! God, how happy I shall be. How I long to look at you, even for one little moment. Verunya, write often.

I send you many kisses. I love you, I am deeply in love with my dear lovely Verusya.

Chaim

---

[17] The 'very good chemist who is also employed at Elberfeld' is Christian Deichler, as to whose association with W. in his chosen field of dyestuffs chemistry see n. 15 to No. 55. No trace of the 'monograph' has been found unless, indeed, it can be identified with a series of papers published in 1903 under the joint names of Deichler and W. in the Bulletins of the German Chemical Society (*Berichte der Deutschen Chemischen Gesellschaft*), vol. 36—*Studien und Synthesen in der Reihe der Naphthacenicons*— setting out the results of their joint work in dyestuffs chemistry. An alternative possibility is that the work done on the projected monograph had something to do with the discovery mentioned in No. 165 (16 March 1902) as about to be offered to Elberfeld and shown by subsequent correspondence on the subject—see, e.g. No. 185 (3 Apr. 1902)—to have been the result of work done jointly by W. and Deichler.

[18] Poste restante.

[19] Post Office.

[20] He did not, in fact, leave until 1 July (see No. 98). 'Chéri' is, presumably, the 'M. Batschevanov' (of whom nothing further is known) referred to by W. as *chéri* in No. 133.

[21] W. did not, in fact, go to Rostov that year.

96. To Catherine Dorfman, Kherson. *Geneva, 29 June 1901*

Russian: H.W.: W.A.

Geneva, 29/vi. 01

Dear Friend,

I am forwarding a postcard which arrived for you.[1]

Rather a pessimistic letter came from Eliashev this morning.[2] He offers to write a paper on 'The Character of the Jewish Press' (Hebrew, Russian, Yiddish). I think this is acceptable.

We all felt rather melancholy yesterday, and this kind of mood— Heaven knows what it is—still persists. I'll be leaving tomorrow.[3] The weather is good, that's a blessing. I shall await news from you impatiently.

Please send your next letter from Kherson to Berlin, at the following address: Dr. Ch. Weizmann, Berlin NW, *Poste Restante, Postamt* 7.

Koenigsberg and Shneerson send you their sincere regards, and I send you my warm greetings and best wishes. *Bon voyage!*[4]

Ch.W.

97. To Vera Khatzman, Rostov. *Geneva, 30 June 1901*

Russian: H.W.: W.A.

Geneva, 30. vi. 01
2 rue de l'Ecole de Chimie

My darling,

I sent you a letter yesterday. Our trip to Chamonix has been put off for a few hours, and I am taking advantage of some free moments to drop you a line. My adorable one, I have a piece of good news for you. I went to see Professor Graebe today and discussed all sorts of things with him, including future plans and work. I also told him about the book project of which I wrote to you yesterday,[1] and he approved it fully. I thought that G[raebe] was rather angry, and that is why I decided to go and see him. All is well.

And now, in case I forget, one more small matter. I walked past Stapelmohr's[2] yesterday. He gave me back the money I gave him

96. [1] She had left Geneva for her home in Kherson on 27 June—see No. 95.

[2] See n. 12 to No. 95.

[3] On 1 July (see No. 98) he left for Chamonix, returning to Geneva after a few days' holiday (see No. 100).   [4] In orig., in Russian, 'Happy journey'.

97. [1] 'Yesterday' would be 29 June. No letter of that date to V.K. has been traced, but on 28 June (No. 95) he wrote to her about his projected monograph.

[2] Stapelmohr's scientific bookshop in Geneva.

on your behalf, for, on checking the accounts, it turned out that he owes you 1 fr. 25 cts. in silver. Perhaps you have forgotten, my dear, that you gave him back the Troost chemistry textbook.[3]

Verusenka, I so much long to look at you for one little moment, to see you smile and to kiss you. Verochka, send the picture[4] without fail.

Graebe said today that the laboratory is closing down on the 15th, but I shall be leaving earlier as I want to have time to visit several places.

My darling, why don't you go out? Why don't you visit anyone, why do you feel so lonely? Don't let these feelings get you down. It is not right, my child. After all, your sisters are at home. How is Rayka?[5] Still so merry and full of life? Is she going abroad this year? Write, my darling, and give my best regards to your sisters. Do they know about me, have you told them?

Ruthstein,[6] poor devil, had a fight in jest with some character and broke his leg in earnest. He is in hospital but on the mend already. He is like the unlucky man who was drowned in a tea-cup.

Verusya, my good little girl, keep an eye on that boys' circle.[7] Maybe there is something in it. In England, you know, there are lots of boys' groups where they play at Parliament, and eminent political figures have already emerged from there. But there in England such activity is conducted in an orderly manner, and under the guidance, and very good guidance, of older people. This is an interesting phenomenon. If Guterman stands at the head of Zionism, it leaves me cold.[7]

There is no Russian translation of *Werther*. The article in *Voskhod* is not a very good one, I heartily agree. Mr. Melnik is still a very young man and, as it seems to me, not very bright.[8] I had a glimpse of him at Congress[9] and saw him on one occasion in Berlin. He is somewhat affected. Such things should never be written tendentiously—he shows off his Zionism 'like a fool with his mortar', as

---

[3] L. Troost, *Traité élémentaire de chimie*, 12th edition, Paris, 1899.

[4] The picture asked for in his letter of 28 June (No. 95).

[5] V.K.'s youngest sister, Rachel.

[6] Probably the Ruthstein who was one of those arrested in connexion with the anti-Czarist demonstrations in Geneva on 5 Apr. 1901: see No. 79.

[7] Nothing is known of this, but it may be inferred that, in a letter not found, V.K. has told W. about an attempt being made in Rostov, under Zionist auspices, to form some kind of debating society for Jewish boys. As to Guterman and W.'s opinion of him, see Nos. 89, 90.

[8] As to Joseph Melnik's review in *Voskhod* of *Werther der Jude* see n. 7 to No. 93.

[9] The only Zionist Congress known as a fact to have been attended by Melnik was the First (Basle, 1897), at which W. was not present, but W. may well have seen him at some later Congress.

they say in our part of the world.[10] Why, Zionism is still helpless to heal the wounds of the Jewish soul, wounds inflicted over 2,000 years of suffering and wandering. A great moral rebirth influenced by great spirits, people of eagle vision—like our Prophets—that is what Israel needs today. We, the pygmies, will not save the 'Wandering Jew'; we are the 'mortal little Jews'.[11]

I am finishing now so as not to lapse into an elegiac—and still worse—a pathetic tone.

To you, my beloved Verochka, I send every good wish.

Yours ever,
Chaim

98. To Vera Khatzman, Rostov. *Vevey, 1 July 1901*

Russian: Pcd.: H.W.: W.A.

Vevey, 1/VII. 01

We[1] did set out for Chamonix but rain overtook us here and we are waiting to see how the wind blows. We shall continue our journey in the evening. These parts are full of memories.[2] Best regards to Nyusya.

Ch.W.

As I have no stamp, I am sending this without one.

99. To Vera Khatzman, Rostov. [*Martigny*], *1 July 1901*

Russian: Pcd.: H.W.: W.A.

1/VII

My warm greetings. The journey is excellent. Am now on my way up to Chamonix. I am not far from the St. Bernard Pass. *Gruss.*[1]

Ch.W.

[10] i.e., with the clumsy ostentation with which a fool handles a heavy vessel. The phrase quoted by W. has a Byelo-Russian flavour—hence 'as they say in our part of the world'.

[11] In orig. 'Eternal Jew' (the Russian equivalent of 'Wandering Jew') in quotation marks, and likewise 'mortal little Jews', 'mortal' [i.e. not eternal] being contrasted with 'Eternal'.

98. [1] i.e., W. and the travelling-companion referred to in No. 95 as '*chéri*', as to whom see n. 20 to that letter.

[2] i.e., memories of her stay at Clarens-Baugy, and of his visit to her there, in the spring of 1901—see head-note to No. 66.

99. [1] 'Greetings'.

100. To Vera Khatzman, Rostov. *Geneva, 4–5 July 1901*

Russian: H.W.: W.A.

Geneva, 4/VII. 1901
2 rue de l'Ecole de Chimie

Verochka, my little darling,

I received your letter today, in which you justly grumble that I don't write very much;[1] but in fact before it arrived I did send you a whole lot of letters and postcards, postcards from various places we stopped at.[2] Our trip went off splendidly. It's Thursday today—a pile of work is in front of me—and I am completely on my own, Verusya, as Shneerson is sitting for her exams[3] in three or four days' time.

These are my last few days here. I am finishing off what still remains to be done and shall soon be on my way.[4] I already feel very much like leaving—changing my surroundings—for more interesting work than this is awaiting me everywhere.

The business of the Conference is going ahead: letters, both sensible and foolish, keep on coming and have to be answered. You ask, my darling, about the results of Herzl's audience of the Sultan.[5] Nothing is known about it, absolutely nothing. I had an argument with Koh[an]-Bernst[ein] on the subject, and almost quarrelled with him, but did not get any further.[6] We shall not find out anything about it until the coming 5th Congress,[7] and it is doubtful whether we shall learn anything even then. Anyhow, I haven't the slightest wish to meet the Rostov Zionists. Not much will come out

100. [1] Not found.

[2] As to postcards sent to V.K. during the trip to Chamonix see Nos. 98, 99. No letters have been found.

[3] She was reading economics at the University.

[4] To Russia via Berlin.

[5] Herzl was received in Constantinople by the Sultan Abdul Hamid on 17 May 1901. This was reported in *Die Welt* on 23 and 31 May 1901, and in other papers, but without any details of the conversation. Herzl suggested that, given a public pronouncement by the Sultan of a nature to appeal to the Jewish world, he might be able to influence financial circles in a scheme for extricating Turkey from the embarrassment of the Ottoman Public Debt: see Bein, *Herzl*, pp. 354 ff.

[6] What W. is referring to appears to be a controversy with Kohan-Bernstein in an exchange of letters ending with one from K.-B. dated 14 (27) June 1901 (W.A.), the only part of it which has been preserved. K.-B. there refers to certain letters he has had from W. and deplores their irritated tone. Exactly what they were corresponding about is not clear, but K.-B. does mention specifically 'your [W.'s] dissatisfaction with Herzl's policy and your amazement at the behaviour of the regional leaders, the members of the Actions Committee' [? in supporting Herzl], as to which he tells W.: 'I answered you on this point and now once more you are displeased.'

[7] The Fifth Zionist Congress, at this time expected to take place in London in October but eventually postponed to December, when it met in Basle. Both the date and the venue having been changed, W. did, in fact, attend the Congress.

of them.[8] Verochka, make me have some faith in these people and I shall work quite differently. As it is, I often look round and see nothing but ruins, and instead of human heads—just cattle. All these people are nasty and venal. They contribute nothing, absolutely nothing; they will not even sacrifice their peace of mind for the cause. We don't need such people; they're just a nuisance and only fit for cannon-fodder.

How much longer shall we have to wait for the right people? A very very long time, until the day Israel gets stronger and we have assembled a group of united, honest fighters. Look round, look closely at the Jews of Russia, at their servile faces, at those insipid, indolent idlers, and you can see what has become of this once highly-cultured nation with such rich potentialities. I have no faith in the present Zionist masses; they are lifeless people who have had their day. All things being equal, I shall be with you in August, Verochka.[9] I'll know more definitely in a few weeks' time and will write accordingly.

Shall I be going to the big Congress?[10] Probably not. I shall simply not have the strength, I can see that, and anyhow, what do they need me for? The date is most inconvenient, too, the end of October[11]—and by the 10th I have to start at the laboratory. There, too, I have a lot of work.

My darling Verunchik, my lovely little girl. Plans, duties, work and worries are weighing heavily upon me, and I am alone, all alone. I have never felt so lonely as now, even—I am afraid— rather helpless. All these terrible evil people around me, for whom nothing is sacred, who think only of profit and material gain and want to make capital out of public affairs.

My little one, I strongly advise you to read Koh[an]-B[ernstein]'s circular letter to the study groups.[12] You can get it at Guterman's.[13] K[ohan]-B[ernstein] is an excellent and wonderful man, though childish in many ways.

But I'd better stop whining; I know this is cowardly.

My article will soon appear in *Voskhod.*[14] I have said all I want

---

[8] For W.'s disdainful comments on Guterman's letter to him on behalf of the Rostov *Dorshei Zion*, see Nos. 89, 90: see also, as to his opinion of Guterman, Nos. 97, 115.

[9] In the event, he did not go to Rostov that year.

[10] i.e. the Zionist Congress, as distinct from the Youth Conference.

[11] See above, n. 7.

[12] i.e. the circular mentioned in n. 14 to No. 95.

[13] Presumably the Guterman mentioned in n. 8 above.

[14] No article by W. can be found in *Voskhod* at or about this time, and, as explained in n. 6 to No. 93, the article here referred to does not seem ever to have been published.

to say there and have communicated all my feelings to the reading public.[15] Perhaps that, too, is superfluous.

I am not quite clear yet about my programme of work for the vacation. In any case, it's going to be very full. Whether I shall manage to get through it all is another question.

I shall be leaving here not later than the 12th; I shall go on to Munich and Berlin and hope to get home between the 20th and the 25th. Berlin and Munich will probably take up much of my time. I have almost settled my financial affairs, though I still haven't enough for the journey. But this will probably be all right, too.

My darling Verusya, my lovely girl, you know how I love you, how I adore you, my dear girl. They have written to me from home to say that Moiseychik has managed to pass and has now begun his second academic year.[16] From him, the scoundrel, I have received no letters at all. He will probably come to the Congress as a delegate. Samuil is getting ready for the journey abroad,[17] and as for my sister Hanele, I don't know whether she enrolled or not.[18] My brother-in-law[19] is better now and has already left Odessa.

I have ordered a whole lot of books and shall take them home. I shall try to study in between my other activities. This is my firm intention.

My most sincere good wishes to Nyusechka. Regards to Esfir.

Good-bye, my darling. Send your reply to this letter to the following address: Dr. Ch. Weizmann, Berlin N.W., *Poste Restante, Postamt* 7.

At Munich, write c/o A. Nemser, for Weizmann, Munich, Goerrestr. 16.

I shall be writing to you, my darling, from everywhere. Keep well and cheerful.

Lots of love,
Your loving Chaim

5/VII

My little one, I didn't manage to send off this letter yesterday. The post brought new surprises this morning. First, a letter from

---

[15] Lit., 'the reading multitude'.

[16] Moshe, a younger brother of W. (b. 1879), was studying chemistry at the Kiev Polytechnic.

[17] Shmuil (Samuel), another of W.'s younger brothers (b. 1882). '. . . getting ready for the journey abroad', i.e. if he should fail to qualify for admission to the Kiev Polytechnic (see No. 114). He did fail at the first attempt (see No. 130) but tried again (see No. 305) and was eventually admitted, as shown by his letter to W. of 21 Apr. (4 May) 1903 (W.A.).

[18] W.'s sister Hana (Anna), b. 1886. What enrolment is referred to is unknown.

[19] Chaim Lubzhinsky: as to his illness see No. 93.

Ahad Ha'am, and such a sad one. You can't imagine how worn out he is after his trip to Paris.[20] But most interesting of all, Dr. Herzl has given signs of life and asks me not to hold the Congress.[21] We are now having a diplomatic exchange of telegrams and letters.[22] Unfortunately, I may not tell you Herzl's motives for the time being but shall let you know as soon as possible. I will only say that the next step may well prove to be a turning-point for our cause. Verochka, my dear, if I only knew that we could rely on real people, I should not be afraid of a struggle, but the deeper I go into the forest, the less do I see the wood for the trees. Responsibility keeps on growing and growing. One must hold firmly on to the tiller.

A big kiss, Verunechka dear,

Ch. W.

101. To Theodor Herzl, Vienna. *Geneva,* [*5 July 1901*]

German: T.: C.Z.A.—Z1/323

[Date as recorded on telegram.]

Wire whether agree my telling other Bureau members contents of letter[1] impossible decide alone.[2]

Weizmann

[20] Writing from Odessa on 18 June (1 July) 1901 (W.A.), Ahad Ha'am, while assuring W. of his sympathetic interest in the Youth Conference, declines to take part in it, explaining that he is so disheartened by the feeble performance in Paris of the delegation organized by the Odessa Committee (see n. 7 to No. 81 and n. 2 to No. 82) that he has decided to withdraw, at least for a time, from all public activity. He advises W. to look for new people and not to trouble with 'the old ones'.

[21] Herzl to W., Vienna, 2 July 1901 (W.A.), urging that the Youth Conference should not take place, since its proceedings might embarrass the political negotiations he has in hand, and appealing to W., as a loyal and disciplined Zionist, to see that it is abandoned. Herzl enjoins W. to treat what he has said about the political situation as strictly confidential, and asks him simply to inform those concerned, without giving the reason, that the Conference has been cancelled.—The negotiations referred to by Herzl are certain discussions with Turkish Ministers and officials following on his audience of the Sultan (see above, n. 5).

[22] See n. 21 above, and W.'s telegram and letter to Herzl of 5 July (Nos. 101, 102).

101. [1] Herzl's letter of 2 July 1901—see n. 21 to No. 100.

[2] The telegram elicited a reply dated 6 July 1901 and signed by two members of the Smaller Actions Committee, Kokesch and Marmorek (W.A.), who, writing 'on the instructions of the Chairman', authorized W. to show Herzl's letter of 2 July 'to two of your colleagues, who will, however, undertake in writing, together with you, not to divulge its contents to other persons'.

102. To Theodor Herzl, Vienna. *Geneva, 5 July 1901*

German: H.W.: C.Z.A.—Z1/322

Geneva, 5. VII. 1901
2 rue de l'Ecole de Chimie

The Chairman,
Zionist Actions Committee for the
personal attention of
Dr. Th. Herzl.

Vienna.

Dear Fellow-Zionist,

I confirm the receipt of your letter of the 2nd inst.[1] and also my telegram,[2] 'Wire whether agree my telling other Bureau members contents of letter. Impossible decide alone.'

I shall not be in a position to return to the contents of your letter until there has been a reply to my telegram and until, subject to that reply,[3] the other members of the Bureau elected by the Munich Conference have been consulted.

With Zion's greetings,

Yours truly,
Dr. Ch. Weizmann

103. To Catherine Dorfman, Kherson. *Geneva, 5 July 1901*

Russian: H.W.: W.A.

Geneva, 5/VII. 1901
2, rue de l'Ecole de Chimie

Dear Dorfman,

Thanks for your two letters.[1] I am impatiently awaiting your detailed letter from home. I hope you found your whole family all right and that you are pleased to be under your own roof. What was the journey like?

I was not mistaken when I told you that a whole mass of correspondence was about to arrive. Every post brings something, so much that my head begins to whirl.

---

102. [1] See n. 21 to No. 100. [2] No. 101.
    [3] 'subject to that reply'—in orig. '*sowie nach ev. Beratung* . . .'. As to the Bureau, see bridge-note following No. 75. For Herzl's reply see n. 2 to No. 101.

103. [1] Not found.

(i) A letter came from a student called Tyomkin from Kiev, in which he says that in spite of the ardent desire of the Kiev people to go to the Conference, none of them will be able to do so for lack of funds. I wrote Tyomkin a suitable reply.[2] He also says that he, together with Zolotarev from Kiev and the Odessa comrades, has decided to publish a pre-Conference pamphlet in which they intend to explain in detail the aims, ideology[3] and significance of the Conference. I advised Tyomkin to get into touch with you at once and said I thought you would willingly assist with the publication. Between ourselves, I should have no faith in the venture unless you did. Tyomkin is at present in Yelizavetgrad. His address is: V. L. Tyomkin, student, c/o Kanevsky, dentist. I advise you to get into touch with him at once and try to find out who these Odessa comrades are: as far as I know, they are nothing but a myth.

(ii) Letters have also arrived from young Zionist intellectuals in Plotsk and Ismail. The intellectual stalwarts of these towns are in full agreement with us.

(iii) But I have left the most interesting thing to the end. A reply came today from Ahad Ha'am.[4] His letter, my dear Dorfman, is the height of tragedy. Complete disenchantment with life, with everything. A.H. has left the Palestine Committee.[5] This is enough to explain his state of mind. I am ashamed to write this, but tears came to my eyes when I was reading his words and saw how the vulgarity of contemporary Zionism and the nonentities who are in it have managed to break the spirit of such a man. A.H. has decided to 'retire from the world' (his own expression) and devote himself to self-analysis. He warmly sympathises with our cause but assures us (and I fully believe him) that at present he cannot take an active part in it. This is how Paris has affected him; he describes the behaviour of the delegation[6] as a 'shameful, disgraceful, cowardly flight, the bankruptcy of our "best people". . .'. O Lord, how worthless all these people are to us!

(iv) Berthold Feiwel is taking the lectures upon himself:[7] he

[2] Tyomkin was a member of the Kiev Zionist students society, *Kadimah*. His letter, dated 14 (27) June 1901, is in W.A. W.'s reply has not been found.

[3] Lit., 'tendencies'.   [4] See n. 20 to No. 100.

[5] i.e. the Odessa Committee of the *Hovevei Zion*. Ahad Ha'am had not, in fact, left the Committee but had only asked to be excused, till further notice, from taking part in its work.

[6] As to the Paris delegation, of which Ahad Ha'am was a member, and its failure, see n. 7 to No. 81.

[7] Feiwel to W., 1 July 1901 (W.A.), undertaking to prepare papers for the Youth

replied to my cold letter[8] very warmly and expressed his entire readiness to work, placing the (yellow!) *Welt*[9] completely at our disposal. There have been no replies from the others yet.

(v) And now the most interesting thing of all. Naturally, I am telling you this under the seal of the utmost secrecy. I received a letter from Dr. Herzl today.[10] He asks us (don't you know the tone of his requests?!?) not to convene the Conference for reasons and considerations of high policy. He appeals to our *Parteidisciplin*,[11] especially my own; and what is most interesting, he has tied my hands, addressing the letter to me personally, thus depriving me of the possibility of communicating its contents to the other members of the Bureau. I sent him a telegram today: *Drahtantwort ob einverstanden Briefinhalt anderen Bureaumitgliedern mitzutheilen unmöglich allein Beschluss fassen.*[12] There has been no reply so far. I am appalled by the behaviour of the 'leader' and fear that the time has come to open fire. As soon as I have Herzl's reply I shall send you a copy of his letter.

All this has happened during this short time. My loneliness grows day by day. I don't like to bother Sh[neerson] and K[oenigsberg]. They are working too hard now, poor devils, and I should not like to upset them. Incidentally, I have also received a few lines from Portug[alov]: our last letter has reached him.[13]

As you see, then, the most important moment is now approaching. But we must not lose our heads. If only we knew that there was already a group of responsible men of action, we could declare war on H[erzl] with a light heart.[14] As it is, we ourselves have not yet carried out the necessary survey. I am not frightened of remaining alone on the field of battle, but there is a danger that everything that has already been achieved with such effort may crumble. Bukhmil is quite right when he says that the young people are entirely Herzlised, and you can count on your fingers those who

Conference on (*a*) The Jewish communities in Austria and the attitude of the Zionists towards them, and (*b*) the history of Zionism in Austria.   [8] Not found.

[9] Feiwel was at this time editing *Die Welt*. The paper had a yellow cover, symbolizing the yellow badge which Jews were compelled to wear in some parts of medieval Europe. W. is lightheartedly suggesting that it belonged, in a double sense, to the yellow press.   [10] See n. 21 to No. 100.   [11] 'party discipline'.

[12] Quoted by W. in the orig. German; for translation see No. 101.

[13] W.'s letter has not been found, nor has the letter from Portugalov. It had been suggested that Portugalov, representing the Zionist study-group in St. Petersburg, should read a paper on these groups (known as 'theoretical circles') at the Conference. In a letter dated 30 May (12 June) 1901 (W.A.), Portugalov told W. that he had found someone else to deal with this subject, but that he was willing to prepare a paper on the Jewish students in Russia. No trace has been found of any later letter from P. which could have reached W. before the date of the letter under notice.

[14] See Introduction to vol. i, p. 23.

would consent to sacrifice their peace of mind and their smug attitudes of 'contemplative men of action' to go on the warpath. Phrase-making has eaten too deeply into our colleagues.

I shall be leaving very soon. Any day now the article for *Voskhod*[15] and the third circular[16] will be ready. I shall wait only for the conclusion of my correspondence with H[erzl]. Do write to me about absolutely everything, to Berlin, N.W.,* *Poste Restante, Postamt* 7.

I am not feeling too well and have already forgotten my wonderful mood at the time of our very successful excursion and the day after.[17] What will be the result of it all? Will things come right in the end or shall we have nothing but trouble? You are probably your usual self—an incorrigible optimist who sees a lot of good in all this. May you be right!

Do write and write, Dorfman. A very warm handshake from
Ch. Weizmann

* N.W. means a quarter in B[erlin]—North-West. This is useful to know.

104. To Vera Khatzman, Rostov. *Geneva, 6–7 July 1901*

Russian: H.W.: W.A.

Geneva, 6/VII. 01

My dear Verochka, my sweet,

Nothing much has happened today, and the post brought nothing. I wrote to you yesterday to say that a letter had arrived from Herzl.[1]

Do you know, he demands that there should be no Conference, and the reason he gives is that political negotiations are pending and that a Conference would prejudice them. So you see, my dear, that the situation is, to say the least, precarious. He ties our hands, or at any rate wants to. His reasons are neither clear nor intelligible to me. I assume that he simply does not want the Conference to take place. For a variety of reasons it is undesirable for him. To convene the Conference means to declare war on Herzlism as a whole,[2] and not to hold it—is quite impossible. You can only wage war successfully if you know who supports you; can we say confidently that such-and-such forces are backing us? No, certainly

---

[15] See n. 6 to No. 93 and n. 14 to No. 100.
[16] See n. 3 to No. 90.   [17] It is not known what this refers to.

104. [1] See postscript to No. 100.   [2] See Introduction to vol. I, p. 23.

not. There is such a confusion of ideas now, and the last thing I want is for us to be taken for Soc[ialist] Zionists[3] or any other 'ists trying to find safety behind a common label.

I cabled Herzl to say that his letter alone is not enough for me; that I should like a precise explanation of his demand and a thorough debate within the Bureau.[4] No answer to this has come yet. I don't know how to explain his silence. A letter will probably come from him tomorrow, and then we shall know something definite.

Verunechka, my darling, I so much want you to be here, to be able to talk to you. I feel so wretched; something is stifling me, choking me, and I cannot get rid of a nightmare that torments me: I feel that something extraordinary is going to happen, that a prophet will appear in Israel, otherwise we are doomed. Everywhere, among all those dear to us, there prevails such a feeling of disappointment, such a terrible mood, that this will have to bring matters to a head.

And you, my dearest, are so infinitely far away (geographically speaking) at this difficult moment. The letter I received yesterday from Ahad Ha'am gave me a bad jolt.[5] This steadfast man suddenly speaks in a broken voice: he is disillusioned with everything, everything seems to him so utterly hopeless.

Bukhmil, a colleague from Montpellier, came to see me today; he is the one who will read the main paper on Zionism at the Conference. He, too, is in a pessimistic mood. O Lord, everywhere I see only ruin and destruction.

Where are the youthfulness, the freshness that are needed now? Though I was bright and cheerful until now, I too am beginning to weaken, to feel that my deep faith in the forces of Jewry is disappearing, and I am in despair. My angel, my Verochka, give me, do give me, this faith, and you will save me. Verusya, I love you so very, very much, and I am ready to weep now, my heart is so heavy. The captain weeps. The man setting out to war weeps. We are nervy, unstrung, flabby, and we are unfit for the Jewish cause. All our lives we have been serving many gods, and now we cannot concentrate on the ideal of freedom, of our own freedom. How will it all end?

I can see before me the faces of our best people. They are all helpless now, yet they are giants in comparison with me. Verusya, my dearest, all this is terrifying. Our sensitiveness has made us

[3] See n. 2 to No. 92.
[4] See No. 101. W.'s paraphrase of his telegram is not, however, quite accurate.
[5] See n. 20 to No. 100.

vacillating creatures, it has killed all initiative in us, it has paralysed everything within us.

Don't be surprised by the tone of this letter, my little one. The things that have been smouldering inside me have broken out into words.

7/VII

I had a very long talk with Bukhmil and finished by saying that for me Zionism is only an experiment. This isn't true, but I was in such a nasty vicious mood yesterday, and I am sorry now that I expressed myself so bitterly to Bukhmil. I feel deeply that for me, outside this enterprise which is bound up with my honour and my life, with my best desires and dreams—outside this there exists absolutely nothing. Verochka, my mood was such that I was capable of talking myself into sheer absurdity. We had a good evening with Bukhmil yesterday. Shn[eerson], Grinblatt, Koenigsb[erg] and Tarle[6] were with us. I am waiting for the post now, and then shall go cycling. I don't want to stay at home today, I shall go out for the whole day. One more week left.[7] I am afraid to re-read this letter, I should certainly tear it up. I shouldn't write all these things to you. You will only worry, my dearest. On the other hand, my feeling of boundless confidence in you and your attitude tells me that I should write to you about everything, everything, without leaving anything out.

And so, goodbye, my dearest. Every good wish.

A huge kiss from the man who loves you so dearly and who has such deep <u>respect</u> for you.

Chaim

105. To Vera Khatzman, Rostov. *Geneva, 17 July 1901*

Russian: H.W.: W.A.

Geneva, 17/VII. 1901
2 rue de l'Ecole de Chimie

Dear Verochka,

You are no doubt very much surprised at my not having written to you all this time. But, my darling, there have been a lot of reasons, one more important than another. I have just gone through the most difficult time of my life, the most difficult, my dear

---

[6] M. Tarle (full forename unknown) was a Geneva woman student from Nikolayev.

[7] He intended leaving for Russia via Berlin in about a week's time.

Verunya. Emotion and worry have kept me here, so that I shall not be leaving for home until tomorrow. Leaving everything else aside for the moment, let me say briefly that I have told my fiancée[1] the whole truth. You can imagine, my dear heart, that this was not an easy thing to do, but it had to happen and it did happen. The days preceding this and the time that followed were one long[2] torment, torture, anxiety, and upset of all kinds for me.

I couldn't and I didn't want to write to you, Verochka: you will understand and forgive. Had you been here then I could have borne it better, but you were far away and I was on my own, terribly lonely all this time, I was so that I only took the firm decision to go home yesterday. I could not bring myself to do this before. I am not going to describe in detail how it all happened. *C'est un fait accompli*, and the chapter is closed. I know that now comes the time for self-analysis, self-reproach, etc., etc. O God, I have been through all this game before, but that just makes it the more painful now. I am still pondering over one basic problem.[3] It is a problem which it is terribly difficult for me to solve, but after going through agonies I shall cope with that too, and then I shall write to you at once. My desire to see you has grown to painful proportions, has made me melancholy and causes me burning pain. I feel an irresistible need to see you, to hold you, but you are far away, so infinitely far.

I hope to find a very detailed letter from you in my dearly beloved Berlin. That would be wonderful.

Verochka, my dear, do not condemn me, do not blame me. I so very much long to see you, you, my dearest one.

Such ardent, such long, such endless kisses, my Verusya.

Yours,
Chaim

I shall write from Berlin.

106. To Vera Khatzman, Rostov. *Geneva, 19 July 1901*

Russian: H.W.: W.A.

Geneva, 19/vii. 01

My dear Verunchik,

If ever you saw a man in a foolish predicament, it's me! My luggage is packed, there is fantastic disorder in the room, and here

---

105. [1] Sophia Getzova, to whom he had become engaged, exactly when is uncertain, but probably in 1897 or 1898.   [2] Lit., 'a sequence of'.

[3] The context suggests that he was at a loss to know how to tell his parents about the breaking off of his engagement.

I am sitting excitedly waiting for the money-order telegram which is due any minute now. What an idiotic situation!

I doubt whether I shall be able to leave tonight, as it is already half-past nine, but I hope the money will arrive by tomorrow morning. I feel intolerably depressed, and I want so terribly to be in different surroundings, to get at least partly rid of all these terrible associations. There isn't a living soul around, and I am fed up with everything.

All this time not a word from you, my dear child; you probably addressed all your letters to Berlin. How I'd love to be there already, but I feel as though I shall never get there. What nonsense all this is really!

Verunya, Verunya, my lovely darling. I want you dreadfully, and I am already burning with longing to read your letters. Immediately after getting these foolish lines, please write to me, dearest, to Pinsk: To Dr. Ch. Weizmann (personal), Pinsk, Government[1] of Minsk. I should be there not later than the 26th if no new *embête-ments* crop up.

Nothing new has happened. I spent the last few days wastefully, woolgathering, waiting, and frittering away my time on this and that. Koenigsberg is leaving today.[2] I didn't write to anyone and haven't received any letters as everybody thinks that I am already on the move. *Enfin*, maybe I shall leave tomorrow.

Verusya, as soon as I am on the way I shall write, and I hope it will be a more cheerful letter. You aren't cross, are you, my little one, at my not having written these last few days? You do understand why, my dearest, don't you? Forgive me, please.

Goodbye, my darling, my little one, I kiss you endlessly.

Yours,
Chaim

107. To Theodor Herzl, Vienna. *Geneva–Munich, 22 July 1901*

German: H.W.: C.Z.A.—Z1/323

[The letter is signed jointly by W. and Esther Shneerson, one of his principal assistants at the Youth Conference Organization Bureau at Geneva. It was intended to be signed also by Alexander Nemser, on behalf of the Munich Office; hence the heading 'Geneva–Munich'. In No. 108 W. tells Catherine Dorfman that the letter was 'signed by Shneerson, myself and Nemser', but it does not, in fact, bear Nemser's signature.]

106. [1] i.e., province.
    [2] She went home to Russia for the vacation and returned to Geneva in the autumn.

Geneva–Munich, 22 July 1901

Dear Dr. Herzl,

We have not until today been in a position to reply to your letter of the 2nd inst.[1]

First, we cannot help expressing our surprise that only now, for the first time, has the Actions Committee deemed it necessary to make known its position in regard to the Young Zionists' Congress.[2] On April 2nd there was a preliminary conference in Munich,[3] at which the question of the Congress was gone into, and the editor of the *Welt* was informed by telegram. Shortly afterwards the resolution adopted by the Munich preliminary conference was published, and also an account of the Munich discussions.

Certain of the Russian members of the A.C. are taking this matter up with some vigour. Dr. Bernstein-Kohan[4] has sent out several circulars about it to the so-called 'theoretical' groups in Russia,[5] and a grant of 100 roubles has been made to us from the Russian funds.[6] This should satisfy you that there is no question of concealment or of any breach of discipline.

Apart, however, from these purely formal points, we regret that we must disagree with you, since we cannot see at all how our proceedings, being wholly outside the realm of Zionist diplomacy, can be to its detriment. At the Congress we shall be concerned primarily with internal Zionist questions; discussions relating to diplomacy or politics will, of course, be ruled out.

We intended, in any case, to exclude the public as far as possible, and we shall adhere strictly to this in regard to all questions of a delicate nature. As Russian citizens, we know, unfortunately, too well how necessary it is to exercise the utmost care in this respect. Moreover, as the Congress will not be large, and as it is not designed to be in any way of the nature of a demonstration, we believe that we have made sufficient allowance for all contingencies.

Further, we cannot agree that societies and individuals of whose intention to take part in the Congress we were advised as long as two months ago should be told by us, without any explanation, that

---

107. [1] See n. 21 to No. 100.

[2] *Jung-Zionisten-Congresse.* The word used throughout this letter for the Youth Conference is 'Congress'.

[3] See bridge-notes following Nos. 71 and 75.

[4] Here correctly called 'Bernstein-Kohan', though usually referred to in W.'s letters as 'Kohan-Bernstein'.

[5] As to the circular distributed to the Russian Zionist study groups ('theoretical circles') under date 12 (25) June 1901 see n. 14 to No. 95. W. speaks of 'several circulars'. It is not known what other circulars are referred to, but it looks as though there must have been at least one other which has not been traced.

[6] i.e., from the Russian Zionists' financial centre at Kiev.

it will not take place. At the Second Basle Congress, when an attempt to organize a student conference was defeated, there was room for the consoling thought that the project did not yet seem fully ripe.[7] But now the situation is quite different; the Youth Congress has become a live question. The convening of the Congress has not been brought about artificially but is the natural outcome of an emerging need.

There was a significant number of fellow-Zionists who are not happy about the Zionists' dilatory and meditative approach to the solution even of domestic problems, or about the stagnation which has set in among the societies. The decline of the societies, the lack of initiative on the part of the vast majority of Zionists, the negative attitude of most intellectuals (in Russia) towards our Movement— these, as numerous letters have shown us well enough, are factors which could be of fatal significance for the Movement. The internal conflicts which have arisen are so numerous, and there is so much discontent, that it is very much to be feared that many valuable forces will be drained away into the non-Zionist camp.

If, after having with great difficulty achieved a measure of success in rallying our young forces, we now proceed to destroy that achievement, the despondency and disillusionment will be so intense that we shall be unable in the foreseeable future to rely any further on a sympathetic response on the part of the Jewish intelligentsia. We cannot and must not dismiss our fellow-Zionists, who are impatiently looking forward to the Congress, with a meaningless answer, and we regard this as incompatible with our conception of the responsibility we have incurred, as well as with the democratic principles of Zionism.

With Zion's greetings,

Yours truly,
Dr. Ch. Weizmann
E. Shneerson

Dr. Ch. Weizmann
Pinsk (Government[8] of Minsk), Russia.

---

[7] In connexion with the Second Zionist Congress (Basle, Aug. 1898), proposals with which W. was associated were put forward by the Berne Academic Zionist Society, in which W. was a prominent figure, and by a similar group of Jewish students at Zurich, for the holding, immediately after the Congress, of a Students' Conference, with a view to the setting up of an Association of Students' Zionist Societies. The idea was not followed up, and nothing came of it: see A. Weintraub and Nahman Syrkin to Actions Committee, 19 and 21 June 1898, and manifesto concerning the proposed Conference and suggested agendas—all in C.Z.A.—Z1/286, 287.   [8] I.e. province.

108. To Catherine Dorfman, Kherson. *Geneva, 22 July 1901*

Russian: H.W.: W.A.

Geneva, 22/vii. 1901

Dear Friend and comrade,

You are probably greatly surprised by my silence, and also by the fact that I am still here.[1] But it so happened that I had to postpone my departure from day to day and am finally a whole week late. Since the wedding[2] is on the 30th, I am leaving today. I am not going to Munich,[3] as I shall arrange everything by letter. As for Berlin, I shall stop there for three days. In this way I shall lose nothing.

Nothing has been happening out here all this time: no letters could have come anyhow, as I told everyone to write to Berlin and Pinsk. I am looking forward to Berlin: a lot of news must have been piling up there. I shall write to you from there about everything without fail. As for Herzl, the question has not yet been clarified, and I sent him a sharp reply to the effect that under no circumstance could I agree to the Conference being postponed; the letter was signed by Shneerson, myself and Nemser.[4] He, i.e. H., no doubt will be fuming, but this doesn't worry me. I'll get his reply in Berlin.

And so you are devoting yourself to your studies at home. Is Kherson interesting? Are there any people? What are our Kherson correspondents like, that is to say that single correspondent who did not reply to our letter?[5] What about the pre-Conference pamphlet?[6] No doubt I shall find your letters and the answers to some of my questions in Berlin. Did you see Tarle? She was to pass on to you lots of good wishes from all of us, and *beaucoup d'amitié.*

I shall be seeing you soon, Dorfman, and I shall have a lot to tell you. The days since you left have been miserable. I was depressed, and apart from this a great many personal things poisoned my life.[7] I have partly *überwunden*[8] these, but only partly. I am glad that I am leaving today. The journey will be interesting.

One more thing. I managed to get funds for the journey to

108. [1] He had written to her on 29 June (No. 96) that he expected shortly to be in Berlin.

[2] The wedding in Pinsk of his sister Haya, originally fixed for 15 July—see n. 10 to No. 84.

[3] See n. 7 to No. 94.   [4] See No. 107 and head-note thereto.

[5] It is not known what this refers to.   [6] See No. 103 under (i).

[7] See No. 105.   [8] 'overcome'.

Palestine.[9] Perhaps I shall go myself if we can't find anyone more suitable. In any case, I shall be seeing you.

Forgive this letter turning out to be so silly. It's *Reisestimmung*.[10] One hurries and rushes about without stopping to ask why. I shall write more from Berlin, and more sensibly too. A warm, comradely handshake.

Yours,

Ch. Weizmann

Shneerson and Grinblatt send their warmest greetings. My address in Pinsk is: Mr. Ch. Weizmann, the Jew, Pinsk, Government[11] of Minsk.

109. To Vera Khatzman, Rostov. *Berne, 23 July 1901*

Russian: Pcd.: H.W.: W.A.

Berne, 23/vII. 1901

I am on my way. I shall be in Frankfurt this evening and in Berlin tomorrow, where I am dying to be as a whole pile of letters is waiting for me there. I didn't believe that I should ever leave, but the day has come.

Best wishes

Ch.W.

110. To Catherine Dorfman, Kherson. *Berlin, 26 July 1901*

Russian: H.W.: W.A.

[On stationery of Hôtel Reich.]

Berlin, N.W. 26/vII. 01

Dear Dorfman,

You already know why I am so late in replying to your most welcome[1] Berlin letter—I only arrived here yesterday.

I have already answered some of your questions. I saw Motzkin yesterday and we had a long talk. He will not be able to produce a paper,[2] though he will take part in the Conference. Apparently a

---

[9] It had been suggested at the Munich Conference that someone should go to Palestine with a view to giving a report to the Youth Conference. For a further reference to this see No. 111.

[10] 'the travel-bug'—lit., 'the mood for travel'.   [11] i.e., province.

110. [1] Lit., 'much-cherished'.

[2] See No. 94 as to W.'s attempt to induce Motzkin, in view of Bernard-Lazare's withdrawal, to read a paper on 'The Economic Position of the Jewish People'.

good deal of energy has been wasted here on a struggle with Syrkin and Co.,[3] though in my opinion this was quite unnecessary. I gave a lecture here last night on the Conference, and we and the Berliners seemed to understand each other. There is a rather interesting crowd here. Some of them—who were quite immature when I was here last year—have grown up since and gained in strength and will be good Zionists.

There are high hopes of the Conference, and I am fortified again and again in my conviction that we should push forward with redoubled energy.

I shall find out at home in a few days' time how the controversy with Herzl[4] is going to be settled.

I shall only stay a fortnight at home, and will then be on my way.[5] That's how it has to be.

Oh, God, how much work is waiting for me, how much labour— I should face it with joy, however, if only trifles didn't stand in my way. Abramov[ich] is coming to Pinsk, and some of our Kiev people are going to be there for the wedding;[6] Eliasberg is coming too—i.e. there will be a group whom we shall be able to use. I hope to find out about the pamphlet[7] in Pinsk.

Why don't you write anything about yourself? How did you find all and sundry at home? How do you spend your days? In brief, you do realise, don't you, that everything in the life of one of the best comrades is of interest to me? I am not writing a great deal from here because I haven't had time to see everybody yet, and besides I am so tired that I can hardly stand. And how much running about there is to do still, how much talk, endless talk. I am besieged here as befits a *guten Yudin*[8] and apart from that I still have to visit some of the mighty of this chemical world, etc., p.p.[9] I shall write again from Pinsk. Keep well. With a warm handshake,

Yours,

Ch.W.

If you see Tarle, give her my regards.

[3] As to Syrkin's 'Zionist Socialists' see No. 92. The reference is probably to polemics between the Zionist students' society *Kadimah* and the Zionist-Socialist society '*Hessiana*' founded by Syrkin, as to which see below, n. 12 to No. 135.

[4] See Nos. 101, 102, 107.

[5] He was making plans for visiting various Russian centres for propaganda purposes—see the group of letters commencing with No. 117.

[6] See n. 2 to No. 108.

[7] Probably the 'pre-Conference pamphlet' mentioned in No. 108: see also No. 103, under (i).

[8] Thus, in latin characters, in orig.—an echo of the Yidd. expression '*guter yid*' (lit. 'good Jew'), denoting, in the Hassidic vocabulary, a 'wonder-Rabbi', i.e. a miracle-working holy man, though it can mean simply a Hassidic Rabbi.

[9] 'praemissis praemittendis'.

111. **To Catherine Dorfman, Kherson.** *Pinsk, 4 August 1901**

Russian: H.W.: W.A.

Pinsk, 22/vii. 1901

My dear friend,

The wedding upheaval[1] has prevented me from replying promptly to your last letter. By now, the Lord be praised, the whole thing is over, and here I am writing. I am not going to tell you about my journey or my arrival—all that is of surprisingly little interest. Our towns, and especially Pinsk, which will take a long time to get over the catastrophe that befell it,[2] are one big ruin in every respect. The people are lifeless, ignorant, inert. A few letters arrived recently, among them one from Dr. Herzl.[3] In a lengthy epistle adorned with the words *streng vertraulich*,[4] he attempts to justify the attitude of the Actions Committee to the Youth Conference, and in the end agrees with the arguments I laid before him. Thus, in this respect, the matter is settled. Of course, the letter is not without its quota of threats: I am said to be taking a tremendous responsibility upon myself in convening the Conference, and there follow some unflattering references to the Russian members of the Actions Committee who are sympathetic to the project.[5] But all this is unimportant. At the moment, I don't know how to do more to put the affairs of the Bureau[6] in order. I shall, of course, answer all letters from here without fail—but we ought also to start a correspondence with new people.

Eliasberg is coming here, my brother[7] is here, we shall be able to cope with this work.

111. [1] See n. 2 to No. 108.

[2] See n. 1 to No. 84.

[3] In a letter to W. dated Vienna, 28 July 1901 (W.A.) Herzl repeated his warning [see n. 21 to No. 100] against the danger of his being embarrassed in his political negotiations by the proceedings of the Youth Conference, but, taking note of the assurances contained in W.'s letter of 22 July [No. 107], intimated that he would not object to a Conference meeting behind closed doors, and would, indeed, welcome any contribution it might make, if only it would concentrate on that object, towards the revival of waning enthusiasm, while at the same time reminding W. that he was assuming a heavy responsibility. Herzl's letter included some critical comments on the inconsistent behaviour of Russian members of the Actions Committee who had favoured the Youth Conference but had rejected his own proposal that the Zionist Congress should be convened for July, thus supporting (he said) the holding of a 'junior Congress' (i.e. the Youth Conference) involving the same dangers as a full-scale Congress without offering the same advantages.

[4] 'strictly confidential'.   [5] See above, n. 3.

[6] The Youth Conference Organization Bureau at Geneva.

[7] It is not certain which of W.'s brothers is meant, but most probably Moshe, who was a Zionist and who is mentioned in W.'s letter of 18 Aug. (N.S.) (No. 115) as being then in Pinsk.

I have known Dr. Krinkin a long time; I discovered his address only recently: Kazan, Sobachiy Pereulok.[8] He is a former member of the Berlin *Kadimah*, but he came to Berlin after I had already left. He is a very good Zionist, but an even better man, with a very varied and honourable past and with enormous knowledge. My Berlin friends told me a lot about him. I intend to write to him. Do write to him too, my dear Dorfman.

Jaffe[9]—a Leipzig student (formerly of Heidelberg)—is a rather gifted young man, with a very good heart but a very youthful one indeed. In any case, a devoted and honest Zionist; he is now doing propaganda work in the Volga region.

As far as we are concerned *kommt er wenig in Betracht*:[10] budding poets are the last thing we need just now. That's why I have lost sight of him.

I am thinking of leaving for your part of the world soon (in about ten days).[11] I am only waiting for Shneerson's arrival in Russia and for the meeting with her at Ahad Ha'am's—he now lives not far from us.[12] As far as the visit to P[alestine] is concerned,[13] I still haven't found the right person, and it is doubtful whether I shall be able to go myself as my presence here is absolutely necessary—not being on the spot may result in all plans being thrown into confusion. We shall talk it over when we meet; meantime I shall go on looking. Perhaps one of the Kiev people would go.

As for the affairs of the Bureau, I shall be answering all letters for the time being; when all three of us (you, Shneerson and myself) meet, we shall edit the 3rd circ[ular][14] and arrange for its distribution. We shall there definitely inform our comrades of the time and place of the Conference. It seems that Germany is not quite suitable after all. There would be too much trouble with *polizeiliche Ueberwachung*.[15] The Berliners themselves are not in favour of Germany. We shall probably settle on Switzerland.[16]

Is Motzkin going to read a paper? No. It proved impossible to talk him into it,[17] and as far as the economic question is concerned, things stand pretty badly, and the matter is very urgent. I shall still get in touch with Farbstein. But I doubt whether I'll succeed.

---

[8] 'Sobachi Lane'. [9] Leib Jaffe.
[10] 'he hardly comes into the picture'—lit., 'he comes little into consideration'.
[11] '(in about ten days)', written by W. above the line.
[12] Ahad Ha'am was at this time staying with his friend Mordecai Ben-Hillel Hacohen at Ryezhitsa, near Homel. It is not known whether the meeting took place.
[13] See n. 9 to No. 108.   [14] See n. 3 to No. 90.   [15] 'police supervision'.
[16] The Youth Conference met in Dec. 1901 at Basle.   [17] See n. 2 to No. 110.

Still no word from Tyomkin ?[18]—How nice. The Kiev boys are a very smart lot, judging by some of my brother's descriptions, and by one example who arrived at the wedding, but Russian incapacity for organization ruins the finest people, turning most of them into minor Hamlets. Do pester him again, please.

How are you spending your time in Kherson ? Do you often meet Zionists there ? Are they the same in Kherson as our Zionists here ? Yes, one does not often come across anything to be pleased with.

I shall bring the entire correspondence with me.

I don't feel too bad, though I am more bored than in past years. The transition from intensive work to my present state hasn't had too good an effect, but this will pass, the more so as I shall soon start working and will be leaving even sooner. Keep well.

A handshake from

Yours,
Ch.W.

112. To Vera Khatzman, Rostov. *Pinsk, 7 August 1901**

Russian: H.W.: W.A.

Pinsk, 25/VII. 1901

Verochka, my sweet, my darling.

I am now at a loss. I hope you have calmed down since you had my postcards from Frankfurt, Freiburg, Berlin (a letter) and Warsaw.[1] I found your letter at Pinsk, but I did not send you a telegram as my letter from Geneva[2] should have explained everything to you. I do not understand your silence, Verusya. Did my letters surprise you so much that you prefer to be silent, Verochka ? You do understand, don't you, how all this worries me, and I should very much like to get a line from you, to say nothing of the fact that I want to know everything, everything: how you pass your time, how you feel, what you are doing with yourself, etc., etc.

I have been at home the whole week. The wedding upheaval[3] took up four or five days; now everything has settled down. I didn't feel very well all this while, at times even frankly rotten. I am suppressing too much to be able to laugh and rejoice. Oh, Verochka, how very difficult it all is, is it good or bad, who can disentangle it ?

---

[18] See No. 103.

112. [1] None of these have been found, nor has the letter from V.K. mentioned in the next sentence.

[2] Presumably, his letter of 17 July (No. 105).

[3] See n. 2 to No. 108.

I found everything and everybody at home in very good shape. My brother-in-law[4] is all right, except that he still has a scar on his face. I am not very pleased, however, with my eldest brother and his wife. He is not much of a success.[5] In the local Zionist circles there is absolutely nothing of interest. I shall assemble all the groups tomorrow, and on Saturday I am going to speak at the Synagogue.[6] The affairs of the Conference are moving forward: little by little everything is being settled. A satisfactory letter arrived from Herzl.[7]

My dear Verochka, I am writing to you about everything so concisely and briefly because I am at a loss and your silence disturbs me greatly. As soon as I get a word from you I shall write more, a great deal, about everything that I have been through, about all my experiences.

I shall stay here for another ten days and then go south. I'll let you know my exact itinerary in my next letter. Write to me at this address; the letters will be sent on. Write about everything, Verusya, and above all explain your silence. Forgive me, my darling, if I have caused you any uneasy days. My little one, the tormented state I have been in and am still in ought to justify me in your eyes, Verusya.

You will forgive

Your loving Chaim

Verusya, I kiss you again and again. Please do write everything, the whole truth—in a word, do not hold anything back.

113. To Catherine Dorfman, Kherson. *Pinsk, (? 11 August) 1901**

Russian: H.W.: W.A.

[There seems clearly to be something wrong with W.'s dating of this letter—'Pinsk, 29 Aug. 1901'. From the group of letters from Odessa commencing with that dated by W. 9 Aug. (No. 118) and ending with that dated by him 19 Aug. (No. 123) it can be seen that 29 Aug. would be well after the date of his departure from Pinsk and arrival in Odessa. All the letters in question

---

[4] See n. 5 to No. 93.

[5] Feivel, about two years older than W., and the eldest of his four brothers, was the only one who did not have a higher education and entered his father's timber business. A disparaging mention of him in W.'s 1885 letter (No. 1) suggests a certain dislike, but there is a passage in *T. and E.* in which W. speaks of him rather sympathetically (pp. 31–32). W.'s reason for disapproving of Feivel's wife Fanya, a sister of W.'s brother-in-law, Chaim Lubzhinsky, is not known.

[6] As to the use of synagogues for Zionist propaganda see n. 6 to No. 40.

[7] See n. 3 to No. 111.

having been written from Russia to addressees in Russia, it can safely be assumed that W.'s datings are, in each case, O.S., but nothing turns on the point, since, even if this assumption were incorrect, the dating 29 Aug. could still not be made to fit. It seems a fair conjecture that '29 Aug.' is a slip for 29 July, and that the correct date of this letter is 29 July, O.S., corresponding to 11 Aug., N.S.

Though W. refers in this letter to the idea of a Jewish University as if it was already in the air (it had, in fact, at his instance, been proposed by the Munich Conference in Apr. 1901 as a subject for discussion at the projected Youth Conference), this is the earliest known W. letter in which it is mentioned.—In later years what is here spoken of as a 'Jewish University' is frequently referred to as a Jewish Institution of Higher Learning (*Jüdische Hochschule*). As can be seen from n. 2 to No. 204, the *Hochschule*, as conceived by W., would not be limited to a University strictly so-called but would include a Technological Institute. Nevertheless, it has been thought best to avoid the constant repetition of 'Institute of Higher Education' by translating the expression *Jüdische Hochschule*, wherever it appears, as 'Jewish University'.]

Pinsk, 29 Aug. 1901

Dear friend,

For the time being there is nothing new. I expect your letter will bring some news about the proposed pre-Conference pamphlet.[1] In two or three days I shall know when I am going to leave, and I admit I can hardly wait. It's more useful to be anywhere rather than Pinsk. Here one merely lets the grass grow under one's feet, *et c'est tout*. Of course I shall let you know at once about my departure and will telegraph the day of my arrival. If I had money I'd leave at once. I am also waiting for news from Shneerson,[2] though I am not sure whether she is in Russia yet. In the local Zionist circles there are many worth-while people; the masses are not bad here, much better than the intelligentsia. I have already spoken several times in Synagogues, and yesterday I gave my first lecture on Jew[ish] history; we have now organised a regular course here.

Now about something else far more important. You know, of course, about the new restrictions on the admission of Jews to universities and secondary schools.[3] I am certain that Jewry will

---

113. [1] See No. 103, under (i).

[2] She had left Geneva for Russia at some date before 4 Aug.—see No. 111.

[3] In 1900–1 there were student disturbances in St. Petersburg, and in Feb. 1901 a student, Peter Karpovich, shot and mortally wounded the Russian Minister of Education, Bogolepov—see n. 15 to No. 60. Though Karpovich was not a Jew, Bogolepov's successor, General Vannovsky, issued a statement putting the blame for the disturbances on the Jews and proceeded to tighten up the restrictions on the educational facilities available in Russia to Jews.—With regard to Universities, the rule had been that each University must limit the number of Jews to be admitted as students to a specified proportion of the total number of admissions. By a circular dated 26 May (8 June) 1901 the Minister directed that the Jewish quota should be separately calculated for each Faculty, the object being to keep down the number

now adopt a different attitude to the question of establishing a Jew[ish] University, since it is no longer a luxury but a necessity, all the more so since in all German academic circles, high and low, a strong 'anti-Russian' (anti-Jewish) propaganda is now being conducted with great success.[4] It is therefore necessary to conduct the propaganda on behalf of a Jew[ish] Univ[ersity] in a different way, to make preparations even before our Conference,[5] to collect material. Here, in my opinion, is a possible plan of action: projects for two or three technical schools must be worked out on the lines of the Swiss *Technikum* (Winterthur) or of the German one (at Mittweide);[6] they ought to be set up in two or three main centres of the Pale—Warsaw, Vilna, Odessa; and afterwards we should develop the Jewish University project.[7]

These projects, together with a detailed memorandum on the importance and significance of this problem, backed by the signatures of Jewish students and young people who want to study (there will be quite a lot of these), should be presented to Jewish public opinion in Russia, Rumania, Germany, Austria and America, etc.; at the same time a 'representative' delegation should approach ICA,[8] and propaganda should be launched in America, and I think it would then be possible to rouse Jewry as a whole.

of Jews in Faculties (e.g. Law and Medicine) specially favoured by Jews: text in C. V. Pozner's *Evrei Obschei Shkole* ('The Jews in General [= non-Jewish] Schools'), St. Petersburg, 1914, Supplement No. 12. A limited measure of temporary relief from the strict application of these instructions was provided by a supplementary circular dated 22 July (4 Aug.) 1901: ibid. Suppl. No. 13.—As to Schools, a circular dated 1 (14) June provided that, in addition to the existing *numerus clausus* for the admission of Jews to the lower secondary schools, the *numerus clausus* should thenceforth—contrary to the former practice—apply also to the passage of Jews from the lower to the higher secondary schools: ibid. Suppl. No. 50. This note incorporates information for which the Editor is indebted to Professor L. B. Schapiro.

[4] This campaign is surveyed in the brochure *Eine Juedische Hochschule* by Buber, Feiwel, and Weizmann, Berlin, 1902 (copy in W.A.), as to which see n. 3 to No. 240.

[5] The Youth Conference.

[6] In Saxony, near Chemnitz.   [7] See head-note.

[8] The Jewish Colonization Association (I.C.A.) was established in 1891 for the purpose of administering a fund of £2 m. (later increased to a considerably larger sum) provided by the Austrian Jewish millionaire philanthropist, Baron Maurice de Hirsch, the main object of the Association, which was incorporated as an English company, being stated in its Memorandum of Association to be 'to assist and promote the emigration of Jews from any parts of Europe and Asia, and principally from countries in which they may for the time being be subjected to . . . disabilities, to any other parts of the world, and to establish colonies in various parts of North and South America and other countries . . .'. The Association devoted a substantial part of its resources to the settlement of Jews on the land in South America, and more particularly in Argentina. By the early 1900s it had begun to do some work in Palestine, both as the administrator, from 1900, of the Rothschild agricultural colonies and also on its own account, though only on a small scale as compared with its activities in South America.

We must make the first move, call together such representatives of the Russian Universities as are ready to approve our plan and elect a committee to put it into practice, and then enlist the support of the student communities in the West.

I think that this matter will elicit the support of all sections of Jewish students. I submit the plan to your judgment and await an immediate reply. If there are any people in your town with whom you can discuss such a question, especially students, then have a word with them about it. It's an important matter, and we must take advantage of the moment! *Realpolitik!* I believe the initiative should come from the Zionist students—lucky youngsters to be still able to study!

I may be with you before your reply comes, but it doesn't matter: write immediately on receipt of this. You understand, don't you, how excited I am at the prospect of leaving. I hope it will be possible soon.

Perhaps we should also arrange a conference in Kiev[9] in September to deal with this problem specifically.

How are you, how is life, are you working a lot, are you very bored? Write about everything. A warm handshake, dear Dorfman.

Ch.W.

114. To Vera Khatzman, Rostov. *Pinsk, 12 August 1901**

Russian: H.W.: W.A.

Pinsk. 30. VII. 1901

I have received your letter,[1] dear Verochka, and now I am reassured. For I really didn't know what to think. Of course, my darling, a very great deal has happened, but there is still more to come. The cup of sorrow is not yet drained, and in life we have to pay for the big and little sins of our youth. That's why I am so miserable. Verochka, I didn't at all want to draw you into this— you have enough worries of your own as it is.[2] Even here, among my family, I am not satisfied. I am not at peace, I cannot stay in one place, I want to go away, to work, to be among strangers, and not to sit down with my arms folded even for a minute. And indeed I shall be leaving soon. I would leave at once if I had the money, but I haven't. So I have to wait.

[9] No such conference was held.

114. [1] Not found but probably, from the context, a reply to W.'s letter of 17 July (No. 105) about the breaking-off of his engagement to Sophia Getzova.
[2] See n. 2 to No. 89.

This week I shall know definitely whether I am leaving, and if I do go I'll let you know at once. I have a lot on my plate just now. I have to see lots of people, I still have a great deal to do. I pin great hopes on my journey;[3] perhaps I shall manage to achieve something. You see, Verochka, the new restrictions[4] are going to alarm our young people even more, and the idea of a Jewish University will not now seem such a heresy as it did. We must take advantage of this and prepare the ground before the Conference. I have a definite plan of action in connection with this;[5] whether I shall be able to carry it through is another question.

Here, of course, there is nothing new. At home everything is the same. There are still all the petty daily worries which, it is true, are fewer every year, but nevertheless are still there, and it will be some time yet before the outlook for the family brightens up. Father still has to work very hard, and the children, too, have to tax their strength to a great extent. Of course, it's better now than it was last year, but it's still very difficult.

The mood in town is dreadful. It is affected by the general crisis[6] and by the disaster that happened to Pinsk.[7]

My little one, if I am not very cheerful there are many reasons for it. It doesn't seem any use telling you why; we shall soon see each other and then we will talk to our hearts' content.

Samuil will go abroad only if he fails his exams in Kiev.[8]

Verochka, my darling, write to this address. I shall write again soon. Keep well, my dearest, my darling.

Many kisses, Verunchik.

Yours,
Chaim

115. To Vera Khatzman, Rostov. *Pinsk, 18 August 1901**

Russian: H.W.: W.A.

Pinsk, 5 Aug. 1901

Verochka, I hope you are not worried any longer. You see, my dear friend, a spell in Russia always affects me rather badly. The transition is too drastic, and things seen from a distance look different when one comes face to face with the reality. The calamities

---

[3] See n. 5 to No. 110.   [4] See n. 3 to No. 113.   [5] See No. 113.
[6] Meaning, presumably, the crisis in Zionist affairs described in No. 107.
[7] The Pinsk fires—see n. 1 to No. 84.   [8] See n. 17 to No. 100.

that are befalling our co-religionists[1] are enough to make anyone stop and think. Why am I going away? Verochka, my dearest darling, how can one sit back with arms folded and 'take it easy'[2] when one knows that work has to be done, that there is plenty of it, that one is needed here there and everywhere?

My dear Mother is also very much displeased about my journey, but you know, my child, nothing can influence me. My things are packed, and the fast train will soon take me to Odessa, where I shall remain for about a week, and then on to Kishinev. Only there shall I be able to decide when I shall be with you.[3]

Verusya, my little one, I haven't been insincere. It is only that severe trouble leaves its mark and sometimes strikes a wrong note which brings discord where there shouldn't be any. My dear, I have gone through a great deal lately; I shall relax by working, and through work alone I shall find peace of mind. It is difficult to remain alone with one's thoughts.

I shall get away, see friends, talk things over with them; I hope this journey will be useful. And then, my child, the meeting with you—that is a wonderful prospect, and later—Geneva and work. Everything will go better than it used to. We shall meet and talk everything over. As for the Conference,[4] the final decision will be taken in Odessa. From there I shall let you have definite news. In all probability, my child, it will take place in Geneva[4] so that you, my dear, will [? be able to] attend it. The correspondence with Herzl is closed.[5] I have already written to you about it. I will show you the letters when we meet.

My dearest, my article[6] will appear only when the agenda of the V. Congr[ess] is published and its date definitely known. Here I have already managed to quarrel with all the Zionists of whom I made mincemeat at three meetings.[7] I spoke at the Synagogue, I gave several lectures on Jewish history; in short, not a day passes without my having a chance to make a noise. The local comrades have taken full advantage of me.

115. [1] W. seems to be referring generally to the tragic plight of Russian Jewry. Nothing is known of any particular event which he may have had in mind, unless it be the coming into force of the new educational restrictions mentioned in n. 3 to No. 113.

[2] In quotation-marks in orig., perhaps referring to something in a lost letter from V.K.

[3] In the event, he found it impossible to get to Rostov.

[4] The Youth Conference. In view of the decision to hold the Fifth Zionist Congress at Basle, this, and not Geneva, was the venue eventually chosen for the Conference.

[5] See n. 3 to No. 111.

[6] Presumably the *Voskhod* article mentioned in No. 93—see n. 6 to that letter.

[7] What the 'quarrel' was about is unknown, but it may well have had something to do with W.'s ideas about 'war on Herzlism' (see No. 104, second para.).

Our family as a whole is not doing too badly. My brother Samuil hopes to enter Kiev. If not, he will either do military service[8] for a year or else go abroad, but I hope he gets in at Kiev, as he is very well prepared.[9] Moisey is now here, he has developed splendidly this year; he will do well in public work. The others are doing well. My sister has settled down quite nicely,[10] and is very satisfied. Her husband is a fine man. They live modestly but comfortably. Father is going abroad on business and will be away right through the Festivals,[11] so Mother is rather sad. Verochka, my sweet, my little one, the only thing still on the agenda in our family is the education of the youngsters. Once this is settled, Father will be able to relax; it's high time he did.

My little darling, write to me at Odessa c/o Gr. Abramovich, Odessa, Troitskaya 5. Then to Kishinev c/o Dr. Y. M. Bernstein-Kohan, Kishinev.

Write about everything, my sweet. Regards to Sofochka. I shall come.[12]

By the way, a group of Rost[ov] Zionists has come out in favour of the Conference, but very clumsily. Guterman signed this letter, too, Dreadful! Regards to Nyuska.[13] What is Esfir doing?

Lots of love and kisses, Verunya,

Yours ever,
Chaim

116. To Catherine Dorfman, Kherson. *Pinsk*, [? 20] *August 1901*

Russian: Pcd.: H.W.: W.A.

[In relation to 9 Aug., O.S., 'tomorrow' would not be a Wednesday but a Friday, so that W.'s dating is, on the face of it, incorrect. The explanation that 'Wednesday' is a slip for 'Friday' is ruled out by the fact that it appears from No. 118 that by Thursday, 9 Aug. W. was already in Odessa. It would seem, therefore, that '9 Aug.' must be a slip for '7 Aug.'. The point cannot be settled by reference to the Pinsk pmk., since this, together with the stamp, has been torn off the postcard. Kherson pmk. date is 11 Aug. which would, in itself, be consistent with W.'s '9 Aug.', but, for the reason given above, the correct date of the letter is probably 7 Aug.]

[8] The expression used by W. can mean either 'do military service' or 'do a job'. The former meaning is the more likely here.

[9] See n. 17 to No. 100. What Samuel actually decided to do after his initial failure to secure admission to the Kiev Polytechnic is unknown.

[10] After her marriage at the end of July to Abraham Lichtenstein—see n. 2 to No. 108.

[11] The impending autumn series of Jewish Holy Days and Festivals commencing with the New Year, which came in that year, according to the civil calendar, on 31 Aug./13 Sept.—The business carried on by W.'s father, Ozer W.—the transportation of timber—often involved his absence from home for a large part of the year: see *T. and E.*, pp. 16–19.

[12] See above, n. 3.   [13] Nyusechka (Anna Ratnovskaya).

Pinsk, 9/VIII. 01

Shall be in Odessa tomorrow, Wednesday evening.[1] From there will let you know when I am likely to get to Kherson.

Salut!
Ch.W.

Address in Odessa:
Gr. Abramovich, Troitskaya 5.

117. To Leo Motzkin, Berlin. *Pinsk,* [20] *August 1901**

Russian: Pcd.: H.W.: C.Z.A.—A126/16/2

[As in the case of No. 116, W.'s dating, 10 Aug., seems clearly to be incorrect, the Pinsk pmk. date being 7 Aug. 1901.]

Pinsk, 10/VIII. 01

Dear Leo,

I am going to Odessa today, and from there on to Kishinev, Kherson, Nikolayev, Yelizavetgrad, Yekat[erinoslav], Kharkov and Kiev. At Odessa I shall let you know what is of interest to you.[1] If you can please write me a few lines to Kishinev, c/o K[ohan]-B[ernstein]. How are things? Has Israel[2] arrived? Where is Polya now? Please write to

Yours,
Chaim

Regards to the comrades.

118. To Catherine Dorfman, Kherson. *Odessa, 22 August 1901**

Russian: Pcd.: H.W.: W.A.

[This letter marks the opening of W.'s propaganda campaign in Russia. That the campaign was financed, at least in part, from Zionist funds can be inferred from a letter dated 17 (30) Apr. 1902 (C.Z.A.—A157/2) in which the writer (signature illegible) reminds Tyomkin, the director of Zionist activities in the Yelizavetgrad region, that contributions towards the cost of W.'s tour had been made by Zionist societies in the towns included in his itinerary.]

116. [1] In orig., 'Thursday' crossed out and 'Wednesday' substituted.

117. [1] A certain ambiguity in the orig. makes it impossible to be sure whether the meaning is 'anything that is of interest to you' or 'that which interests you'. The rendering adopted has been preferred because nothing is known of any particular matter concerning Odessa in which Motzkin would have been specially interested.
  [2] Leo Motzkin's brother.

Odessa, 9/VIII

Chère camarade,

In Kherson on Saturday morning.[1] Please let everyone know. Tell Tarle too.

Besten Gruss,[2]
Ch. Weizmann

119–20. To Catherine Dorfman, Kherson. *Odessa, 30 August 1901**

Russian: Pcd.: H.W.: W.A.

Odessa, 17/VIII. 01

My dear,

Naturally, my mood has been spoiled. I knew in advance this would happen.[1] I am only staying here till Sun[day],[2] and will then go to Kishinev, Poltava and Kharkov, where I am expected already.

Write to me with all your news. Best regards to your people.

Yours
Ch.W.

[Postscripts by Gregory Abramovich, Aaron Perelman, and an unidentified person signing himself 'D.Z.'.]

---

118. [1] 11/24 Aug.   [2] 'Best regards'.

119–20. [1] W. is referring to an incident described as follows in a postcard (undated— Odessa pmk. dated 17 Aug. 1901 [30 Aug. N.S.]) from Moses Sherman to Catherine Dorfman (W.A.):

> I feel like telling you in a few words about our visit to Nikolayev. On the first evening, despite the presence of our critics, the Zionist meeting was extremely uninteresting. Due to extreme fatigue, Weizmann himself was much feebler than in Kherson. The second meeting took place in the Synagogue. Numerous informers in Nikolayev saw to it that the police put in an appearance. After Weizmann had left with the Chief of Police for the police-station, your Geneva friends and I, as well as the rest of the audience, were terribly worried. In an hour, Weizmann returned home. To sum up: 'In Nikolayev (Weizmann's words) the Town Governor is an anti-Zionist, the Chief of Police is going to become a Zionist, while among the Zionists there are a lot of informers.' The prevailing mood is miserable.

The following is appended to Sherman's report:

> 'Am feeling very well. Confirm authenticity.
> Weizmann.'

W. describes the incident (mistakenly attributing it to 1903) in *T. and E.* (pp. 100–2) —The 'Geneva friends' mentioned by Sherman are probably Anne Koenigsberg and M. Tarle, both Geneva students from Nikolayev.

[2] 19 Aug., O.S. (1 Sept. N.S.).

121. To Catherine Dorfman, Kherson. *Odessa, 31 August 1901**

Russian: Pcd.: H.W.: W.A.

Odessa, 18/VIII. 01

Dear comrade and friend,

I really feel like writing you a long letter. It's true, isn't it, that there was still a lot we wanted to talk about;[1] this was my dream, but it proved impossible, just as it is now impossible to snatch a free moment to have a heart-to-heart talk with you, my dear friend. Koen[igsberg][2] has probably written to you about Nikolayev. Everything is dead and dull here.[3] Am going to Kishinev tomorrow, and then on to Kharkov; my address in Kh[arkov]: Nemirovsky, Solicitor, Rymarskaya 28. Shall await your dear words impatiently. A warm handshake and friendly greetings.

Regards to all your family.

Yours,
Ch.W.

122. To Leo Motzkin, Berlin. *Odessa, 31 August 1901**

Russian: Pcd.: H.W.: C.Z.A.—A126/24/7/2/2

Odessa, 18/VIII. 01

Dear Leo,

I haven't a free minute to describe everything in detail. In general things are going quite well at the moment, with the exception of Odessa, where everything is awful. I have already been to Kherson, Nikolayev and smaller places in the area. Am going tomorrow to Kishinev, from there on to Poltava, Kharkov, perhaps Kiev. Shall write about everything in detail. For the moment I send my best wishes.

Please do write to Pinsk.

Yours,
Ch.

---

121. [1] As to W.'s visit to Kherson see No. 118.

[2] Anne Koenigsberg was staying with her parents in Nikolayev. As to the Nikolayev incident see n. 1 to Nos. 119–20.

[3] For further references to the situation in Odessa see Nos. 122, 123, and 124, and W.'s full description of what he found there in No. 135.

123. To Catherine Dorfman, Kherson. *Odessa, 1 September 1901**

Russian: Pcd.: H.W.: W.A.

Odessa,[1] 19/VIII

My dear,

I am leaving Odessa. Am in the worst of moods. Am off to Kishinev and thence to Kharkov. I am impatiently awaiting your letter. There is such nastiness at Odessa that it's simply not even worth writing [about]. If one believes in the Zionist cause, one must believe that other people will come forward. Best regards to Finkelstein,[2] the Brombergs,[3] your entire family. Do write, write, I beg of you.

Yours,
Ch.W.

124. To Catherine Dorfman, Kherson. *Kishinev, 2 September 1901**

Russian: Pcd.: H.W.: W.A.

Kishinev, 20/VIII. 01

My dear good friend,

I have been here only a few hours, and you realise, of course, that the transition from the corruption of Odessa to the pure atmosphere that surrounds our dear K[ohan]-B[ernstein] can have nothing but a salutary effect. I suffered a great deal in Odessa; I was agitated and upset and there were times when I felt like summoning you there by telegram; I had a feeling that something dreadful would happen, and I badly needed the presence of a friend. The cause is in ruins and the wretched people have debased and defiled Zionism, and—my God, all this in Zionism—slander and spy in its name and for its benefit.

I attended one meeting at which I told the Zionists the whole truth, showing them that they have turned Zionism into a game, into filth, but my three hours' speech, after which there wasn't a single live cell left in my body, obviously couldn't have exerted any effect, since there is nothing solid there. Everything is hollow, hollow and futile.

I have learned many interesting things here, among them about

123. [1] Printed.
  [2] Nothing is known of Finkelstein (forename unknown) except that he was a Kherson Zionist.
  [3] Fyodor Bromberg and his wife Anastasya, Catherine Dorfman's sister.

K[ohan]-B[ernstein]'s exchange of letters with Herzl on the subject of the Conference.[1] To sum up: the whole thing is feeble. Dr. Herzl has no idea of Russian Zionism and of Russian Zionists. Dr. H. is being misled by various creatures, flatterers, 'friends of the cause'. At the 5th Congress, which to my greatest joy will be held in December and at Basle, it will be our task to talk about all this and raise all these points.

K[ohan]-B[ernstein] and the local Zionist comrades are pinning their hopes on the Conference.[2]

Rumours are being spread in Odessa that we want to preach Socialism under the banner of Zionism. How ironic![3] How can people be so lacking in understanding? Cowardice[4] has completely blinded them. My years of work are apparently not enough for them; one must lay bare one's soul to them and only then will these liars realise that they are lying. But this isn't worth doing.

To hell with them all!

I shall be staying here about two days, and then on to Kharkov— my last stop. I am terribly tired. Odessa finished me off. A feeling of total impotence in the struggle against a sea of evil and adversity.

What news in Kherson? Has any effect remained?[5] Will it be

---

124. [1] There is in C.Z.A. (Z1/233) a letter dated 19 July (1 Aug.) 1901 from K.-B. to Herzl in reply to a letter (not found) in which Herzl had taken him to task for associating himself with the projected Youth Conference. The contents of H.'s letter can be inferred from K.-B.'s reply, in which he (*a*) argues that it is imperatively necessary to organize the few really active elements among the Zionists; (*b*) repudiates the suggestion that he had worked behind H.'s back; (*c*) contends that, having been entrusted with the central direction of the 'theoretical circles' (study-circles), he occupies an independent position *vis-à-vis* the Greater Actions Committee. To this H. replied on 6 Aug. (C.Z.A. Z1/180) with a warning against factious' activities calculated to create dissensions among Zionists, and a suggestion that K.-B.'s association with the Youth Conference was not in keeping with his position as a member of the Greater Actions Committee.—H. had been warned by Daniel Pasmanik that the idea behind the Youth Conference was the setting up of an organized opposition to the Zionist leadership—see Herzl to Pasmanik, 28 July 1901: C.Z.A.—HB112, replying to Pasmanik's letter of 25 July, the contents of which were later published in *Die Stimme der Wahrheit*, Würzburg, 1905.

[2] It had originally been proposed that the Fifth Zionist Congress should meet in October, and if Herzl had had his way, it would have met, like the preceding Congress, in London. W.'s reasons for welcoming the decision now announced were obviously that Basle was within easy reach of Geneva, and that, because of his University duties, December (the date actually fixed for the opening of the Congress was 26 Dec., during the Christmas vacation) would suit him much better than October; as to the latter point see No. 100 (4–5 July 1901)—'The date is most inconvenient, too, the end of October, and by the 10th I have to start at the laboratory.'

[3] As to W.'s feelings about the 'Zionist Socialists' see Nos. 92, 93, 104.

[4] Meaning, presumably, that believing the Young Zionists to be tinged with left-wing views, the Odessa Zionists were nervously afraid of having anything to do with them for fear of getting into trouble with the Russian authorities.

[5] i.e., from his visit to Kherson towards the end of August.

easier to work now? How happy I'd be if only it were. Koenigsberg has probably written to you about Nikolayev.[6] Incidentally, she herself was in a kind of daze there. God, doesn't she suffer for the sake of her Zionism? The surroundings in which this woman lives differ radically from yours and make her sufferings more intense.[7] How I should like us to meet at last in Geneva. That would be a real celebration.

My dear, kind Dorfman, please write to me at once in great detail to Kharkov. Best regards to Finkelstein; dear friend, please write too! I shall be writing from here once more before I leave. Best wishes to all your family. Thank you again for those wonderful moments that you and all your people have given me.

Till we meet again,
Ch.W.

125. To Catherine Dorfman, Kherson. *On the way to Yelizavetgrad, 4 September 1901**

Russian: Pcd.: H.W.: W.A.

On the way to Yelizavetgrad
22/viii/01

Dear friend,

I haven't anything special to tell you. As you see, I am on the move again. I shall be in Kharkov on Saturday morning, shall remain there for about four days, and shall not be going to Kiev. There isn't anyone there at the moment. Write to me about everything to Pinsk, dear Dorfman. My best regards to Bromberg and Finkelstein. With best wishes for the New Year to all your family,

לשנה טובה תכתבו[1]

All good wishes,
Ch.W.

---

[6] See Nos. 119–20.

[7] W. is evidently referring to the unfriendly atmosphere in Nikolayev, where she was now staying with her parents, as compared with Kherson; cf. the reference in Sherman's report from Nikolayev (Nos. 119–20) to 'numerous informers'.

125. [1] Hebr. 'May you be inscribed for a good year'—the traditional greeting for the Jewish New Year. The Jewish year 5662 came in, according to the civil calendar, on the evening of 31 Aug./13 Sept. 1901.

126. To Vera Khatzman, Rostov. *Poltava, 7 September 1901**

Russian: Pcd.: H.W.: W.A.

Poltava, 25/VIII. 01

Dear V.I.[1]

We[2] are on the move. By tonight we[2] shall reach Kharkov, where I'll stay until Wednesday. From there I shall be going either to Rostov or to Pinsk. I don't know what has been happening at home as I haven't had any letters all this time. Your dear letter[3] found me in Yelizavetgrad. I have still been unable to reply to it in detail but shall do so from Kharkov. I am terribly tired; it's time for a rest, although I had a great deal of moral satisfaction.

Just in case, write to Pinsk now. A happy New Year. My very best best wishes for you.

Keep well,
Ch.W.

127. To Vera Khatzman, Rostov. *Kharkov, 8 September 1901**

Russian: H.W.: W.A.

Kharkov, 26/VIII. 1901

My dearly beloved darling, my dear friend,

Fate willed that we should not meet here,[1] and I can't wait to see you in G[eneva], where I am impatiently longing to be. I am tired, my dear, very tired. I have spent so much energy and strength during the journey that I now need a complete rest if I am to tackle the enormous amount of work in front of me. The Conference will take place in G[eneva] on December 18th,[2] and the Congress at Basle on December 26th. You will be able to be at both, my darling. I am full of new ideas. On the whole, Zionism does now exist: in spite of everything, it has got some good honest supporters. Our opponents will be wiped out in a few years' time. This will be brought about through life itself, and our movement is on

126. [1] Vera Issayevna—Her father's name was Issay (Isaiah).
   [2] Nothing is known of anyone having accompanied W. on his visits to Poltava and Kharkov, and, though in the third sentence he passes from 'we' to 'I', it seems clear that in the first two sentences 'we' simply means W. himself. A similar point arises in No. 129—see n. 2 to that letter.
   [3] Not found.

127. [1] i.e., in Russia.
   [2] The Youth Conference met on 18 Dec. (N.S.), but at Basle, not Geneva.

the crest of the wave. The forthcoming meetings will be of enormous importance this year.[3] My little one, don't be angry with me for not coming to Rostov. You do understand, don't you, that it isn't because I don't want to but simply because it's a sheer impossibility. I am being nagged from home to make this journey, and I should cause my parents very great grief if I were not at home for *Rosh Hashonah.*[4]

I shall probably stay at home till after the Holy Days.[5] For the second half of *Sukkot*[6] I shall go to Warsaw, to my sister Mariya, and after that I shall be travelling abroad—this time through Vienna. Verochka, let me know the exact date of your departure so that we can meet somewhere on the way.

And so, my darling, please do not be angry with me. It would hurt me very much if you took it any other way.

And now, for the coming year, I send you my sincere good wishes. I wish you strength and courage to continue the studies you have begun; I wish that you may become a true and inspired worker in your native land; I wish that you may become a representative of the new generation which will come to take the place of the shattered company of Jewish workers of today. May your pure bright soul be filled with love for your people, a suffering people, an enslaved people unjustly persecuted, a people brutally rejected by its own sons, and yet a giant people concealing in itself a divine strength, great and wonderful creative power, wisdom, character, and the germ of [a] world conscience. May Israel rise— poor, oppressed, abused[7] Israel, forgotten by its own sons. May the young shoots now appearing on the old time-worn trunk grow into a mighty tree in the shade of which the Wandering Jew may seek repose. May its sons and daughters return and apply their strength to healing the sores that have appeared in the body of an ancient people which yet harbours so much youthful fervour. May those who have sinned against the Jews appreciate the full cruelty of their actions; may the young generation now being born understand at last that it is their duty to save their honour, their integrity,

---

[3] Thus in orig., but the words 'this year' seem, by some slip, to have been misplaced; he obviously means 'the forthcoming meetings this year', referring to the Zionist Congress and the Youth Conference.

[4] Hebr., (according to the Ashkenazic pronunciation) in orig. in latin characters. 'New Year'—see n. 1 to No. 125.

[5] The autumn series of Holy Days and Festivals ended that year, according to the civil calendar, on 23 Sept./6 Oct.

[6] Hebr., in orig. in cyrillic characters, 'Tabernacles'. The eight-day Festival began that year, according to the civil calendar, on the evening of 15/28 Sept.

[7] The word translated 'abused' is not clearly legible in orig. A possible alternative reading would be 'abandoned'.

to liberate themselves and their nation from the Golus,[8] from centuries-old chains.

Israel is awaiting its children—and they are coming, they are returning, and may the coming years be a festival of reunion, a festival of the return of him who has been lost.

Warmest greetings to all your family.

Lots of love and kisses, my Verochka, my dear little love.

Yours,
Ch.

128. To Catherine Dorfman, Kherson. *Homel (en route to Pinsk), 12 September 1901**

Russian (with addendum in Hebrew): H.W.: W.A.

[Written in the train, *en route* from Kharkov to Pinsk.]

30/VIII. 01, Homel
Rail[way] carr[iage]

My dear,

As you can see, I shall soon reach my goal. I'll be home tonight. My journey is over and tomorrow I shall have to take stock of it and of the whole year too. I went through so much, I suffered so much during that time, and how I have aged. There have been moments, indeed, when it seemed to me that we were on the verge of bankruptcy. But all that is past. I am travelling from Kharkov. The success there was unparalleled; even I am satisfied. I spoke in the Synagogue twice there (the debates were in Yiddish, with the rabbinates taking part). The crowd was terrific. The clericals[1] were ignominiously defeated to the utmost delight of the <u>entire public</u>. Never before has culture had such a victory.

The whole Kharkov aristocracy deigned to come to the third meeting (in Russian)—a great p[art] of the students, bankers, the bourgeoisie, even converted Jews, and battle broke out on two fronts: with the confirmed assimilationists and with the Marxists. I felt weak before the meeting but was in excellent form while it was going on. And how this lot was smashed! A real pleasure: sparks flew all the time. They <u>admitted de facto</u> that they were in

---

[8] Hebr., in orig. in cyrillic characters (transliterated into those characters according to the Ashkenazic pronunciation of the Hebr. word), 'Exile'.

128. [1] It is not quite clear whether by 'the clericals' W. means Orthodox Jews of the type hostile to Zionism or (as is much more probable) representatives of the religious wing of the Zionist Movement. As to the objections of 'religious' Zionists to the views of W. and his associates on the 'cultural question' see n. 10 to No. 86.

the wrong. A triumph, wasn't it? The students started coming over to us in huge numbers. I had a special talk on Zionism with them. The Zionists there are a good crowd: the mass of the people is intelligent. I also spoke about a Jewish University and met with a lot of sympathy. A committee of very good capable people was set up.[2] In short, a success. The great propagandist! O God, how little truth there is in this world! Just because you talk to them in a human language, and apparently there are not many who talk and think at the same time. *Enfin soit!* My dear, dear friend, I am writing little to you because the train is jolting abominably, and moreover I am tired, but I wanted to share this joy with you. I wanted to, and I have done so. Once again, on the threshold of another year, I send you, dear comrade, all my sincere good wishes. I wish you all the best, a good, bright future, as you deserve. Regards to your family. Best regards to Mr. Bromberg and your sisters, to Finkelstein, to everybody, and all the best for the New Year.

Yours,
Ch.W.

Dear Sir,[3]

From the bottom of my heart I send you and all yours my best wishes. May the Lord grant you a good year,[4] crowned with happiness, and all those dependent on you. With Zion's greetings.

Chaim Weizmann

129. To Catherine Dorfman, Kherson. *Pinsk, 16 September 1901**

Russian: H.W.: W.A.

Pinsk, 3 Sept. 1901

Dear friend,

To start with, just a few words on the question which you merely mentioned in passing in your letter,[1] i.e. your journey abroad. Is it

---

[2] The Chairman of a committee formed in Kharkov after W.'s departure to propagate the idea of a Jewish University subsequently explained to him that it was felt that the time was not opportune, since the Kharkov Jewish students were pre-occupied with their struggle against the growing strength of anti-Jewish feeling in Russian student circles: L. Vassilevsky to W., 18 Sept. (1 Oct.) and 15 (28) Nov. 1901, W.A.

[3] The note commencing 'Dear Sir' is in Hebrew. It is uncertain to whom it is addressed, but probably to Catherine Dorfman's father.

[4] See n. 1 to No. 125.

129. [1] Not found.

possible that the difficulties you spoke of have grown into obstacles ? I am very worried about this, especially because perhaps you are exaggerating; therefore I implore you, in the name of our friendship, please write exactly how things stand. I shall not mention this subject again until I receive a letter from you in reply to this epistle.

As you see, we[2] are back in Pinsk. I celebrated the New Year[3] in a dignified manner, and am now preparing myself for the Fast.[4] Now I want to summarise the results of my journey, and do it in the form of a memorandum to Dr. Herzl on the theme: The position of Zionism in Russia and the practical measures for organising the cause on a proper basis.[5] Whether this will have any effect—*c'est une question*. Our Generals are so convinced of their own infallibility that they are prejudiced against ideas and heresies coming from such *shkotsim*[6] as Motzkin, Koh[an]-Bern[stein], myself and the rest. Even so, I consider it imperative to do this. I shall get rid of some correspondence first and will then carry out this task. A copy of the report will be sent on to you in due course. I wrote to you briefly in the train, my dear friend, about my impressions of Kh[arkov] and Ye[lizavetgrad].[7] Things are good there. One doesn't even feel there aren't enough people. Do you know what this entire journey has given me ?—One very important thing: the certainty that our opponents are insignificant, and that we can finally dislodge them from their positions with one skilful word.

Zionism is already meeting with a response in those circles which seem totally inaccessible to us abroad. I have gathered some information about the life of our Jewish students here and the relations between them. This material enables us to reduce to nothing the trite arguments of the Günzburgs[8] *et tutti*[9] *quanti*

---

[2] Though in the next sentence W. passes from 'we' to 'I', it seems clear that by 'we' W. means simply himself, as in the opening sentences of No. 126, where 'we' is likewise followed by 'I'—see n. 2 to that letter.

[3] See n. 1 to No. 125.

[4] The Day of Atonement, commencing that year, according to the civil calendar, on the evening of 10/24 Sept.

[5] In No. 130 W. writes that he is composing a memorandum on the subject for Herzl, but nothing more is known of such a memorandum and it is doubtful whether it ever went to Herzl, if, indeed, it was ever completed. No such memorandum has been found among the Herzl papers, nor is there any copy or draft in W.A.

[6] Hebr., in orig. in cyrillic characters, 'rascals'.

[7] The reference is evidently to No. 128, though in that letter, while W. writes about Kharkov, he does not, in fact, say anything about Yelizavetgrad.

[8] Baron Horace de Günzburg, of St. Petersburg (1833–1909), one of the recognized leaders of Russian Jewry, was well-known as a philanthropist and a prominent supporter of Jewish education, but he was not in sympathy with Jewish nationalist ideas as to the type of education to be provided and was strongly opposed to Zionism.

[9] Thus in orig.

against us. This direct contact with Jewish youth has a fortifying effect on our half-shattered nerves. *Enfin*, I must say that I am terribly pleased with my trip. It has yielded a lot.

I shall be staying here till all the Festivals are over.[10] In between, I shall still visit Warsaw and afterwards go via Vienna to G[eneva]. In Vienna I shall be seeing 'him'[11] and his retinue. The Congress has been announced for the 5th;[12] an article will be sent today to *Die Welt*.[13] Berthold Feiwel has left the editorial staff and has been replaced by Martin Buber.[14]

Write to me more often, please, write without waiting for my letters. Sometimes, in spite of my genuine desire to write, I can't because I am overloaded with work. I am getting letters from Shneerson, Grinblatt, Aberson, Schmidt,[15] Idelson, Lurie, and from some people abroad. Every letter has to be answered at once.

Has Koenigsberg been to see you?

All my very, very best wishes. Warmest regards to all your family.

Yours,
Ch.W.

Best wishes to Finkelstein and Bromberg.

130. To Vera Khatzman, Rostov. *Pinsk, 19 September 1901**

Russian: H.W.: W.A.

Pinsk, 6 Sept. 1901

I have just received your letter,[1] in which I could read a string of reproaches for not having kept my promise.[2] My little one, if you only knew how impossible it was to fulfil this wish, you would not, dear Verochka, reproach me. True, it isn't far from Kharkov to Rostov, but I had to come home for the Holy Days,[3] especially as Father went abroad at the end of the New Year[3] and I shall not

---

[10] See n. 5 to No. 127.   [11] Herzl.

[12] A circular issued by the Zionist Correspondence Centre at Kishinev, undated but probably distributed about this time, announced that the Youth Conference (here referred to by W. as 'the Congress') would open on 5 (18) Dec.: C.Z.A.—A.24, vol. 15. The Conference did, in fact, meet on that date.

[13] The article cannot be identified. No article on the Conference appeared at or near this time in *Die Welt*.

[14] Feiwel, who had been editor (not merely a member of the editorial staff) of *Die Welt*, had resigned on a question of policy, and the editorship had been taken over by Buber.   [15] As to Schmidt see n. 8 to No. 92.

130. [1] Not found.

[2] As to his promise to come to Rostov see No. 114 ('We shall soon see each other') and No. 115 ('only there (at Kishinev) shall I be able to decide when I shall be with you').   [3] See n. 11 to No. 115.

see him again for a whole year, to say nothing of the fact that my
family complain that they do not see me at all, that I don't come
to visit them, to say nothing also of the fact that I needed a rest
and could hardly stand after spending about a month in railway-
carriages, in the atmosphere of meetings etc. Finally, I had intended
to arrange my itinerary differently, and it turned out otherwise.
I had to leave Yekaterinoslav and Rostov for next year. Surely
you don't suspect any other reasons than these? Furthermore, I
wrote to you, Verochka, as often as I could. Not four days passed
without my giving you a sign of life. Day after day, I was in the
public eye, surrounded by people, by crowds of Zionists who
exploited me in every possible way, my evenings were filled with
meetings, and only in the railway-carriage or late at night was I
able to snatch even a short time for letter-writing. You know what
my correspondence is like. A packet of letters awaited me in every
town, and I am now spending whole days answering them. All
these circumstances should help to clear me in your eyes. There is
no reason to be indignant, my dear child. I also want to take up a
remark in your previous letter where you speak of insincerity[4] and
a lack of warmth in my recent letters. What made you say that,
my little one? I hope you no longer maintain such a deeply serious
accusation. If my letters reflected a rather nervous state, that
didn't mean insincerity in my feelings to you. However, you will
pay for all this in Geneva, Verunya. I'll deal with you so that
you scream, just you wait and see. I'll smother you. Why has it
suddenly become indifferent to you whether you go to G[eneva]
or remain at home? I refuse to interpret this, Verochka, although it
invites various interpretations. So it makes no difference to you
whether you remain in Rostov and whimper, or go to a place full
of life, to a University, and study, really study? I don't want to
criticise you because I look upon this as a mood of the moment
which has to pass, to disappear, to be obliterated, but I confess it
hurts me to hear this. Dear Lord, how unfair you are: how many
young Jewish boys and girls long to go into the world because they
are choking in the stifling atmosphere of the Pale, how many
sacrifice their homes and their peace for the sake of the University,
and leave of their own free will for privations, suffering, hunger;
there are so many of these people! The University is comparatively
accessible for you, and you are not, I hope, going to G[eneva] as
to an entirely alien town; and this makes no difference to you?
C'est étrange! My only consolation is the thought that this must

---

[4] Cf. No. 115—'Verusya, my little one, I haven't been insincere ...'

have been a slip of the pen, that you yourself have already cast off these feelings and words; I do not at all want to analyse this any further.

Yes, my child, I'll be travelling later than you. The Holy Days end on October 6th, New Style, and I shall probably leave on Tuesday, the 8th. On the 11th I shall leave Warsaw, on the 14th, Vienna, and on the 15th I shall be in G[eneva]. The only difficulty is that I may have to go to the factory in Elberfeld,[5] from which I have had no news for a long time, which worries me and disturbs me a good deal. My salary hasn't come all this time either.

I am already longing to be in Geneva with all my heart. I want terribly to get down to work. I shall devote this winter exclusively to myself. I shall not undertake any social activities, with the exception of the Conference, which will be at Christmas. I feel as though I am not keeping abreast of science, which is bad for me in every respect.

God, what a dreadful thing to happen to the poor Weinbergs![6] Verochka, convey my warmest sympathy to Esfir in the misfortune that has struck her and tell her how I share her sorrow as a friend. Words of comfort are, of course, futile in such cases. Time is the dread physician who heals all wounds.

Everything is all right at home. My brother, of course, did not get in, but there is hope.[7] Not that this makes any difference to me. He will go abroad. Naturally, the whole business is extremely uncomfortable for him, he is worn out, he has lost weight, and his nose has grown to gigantic proportions. He is now living in Kiev (as a tramp); he has no residence permit, of course, but such things don't worry him. If he is caught he will be deported.[8] Father is in Danzig[9] and will remain there throughout the Festivals. My eldest sister[10] has gone to Wars[aw], Gita[11] too. There aren't many people left at home now, and Mother is rather sad. I spend my time sleeping and writing letters and am also composing a memorandum for Herzl on the state of Zionism in Russia;[12] in short, I've

[5] The Bayer works.

[6] A brother of Esther (Esfir) Weinberg had died.

[7] See n. 17 to No. 100. W.'s 'of course' means, presumably, that it could be taken for granted that Samuel's failure was due to the operation of the *numerus clausus* for Jewish students.

[8] Even within the Pale of Settlement there were some towns, of which Kiev was one, in which only Jews of certain categories were authorized to reside. Not having been accepted as a student, Samuel was living in Kiev illegally.

[9] Ozer Weizmann's journeys by river and canal in charge of Russian timber for delivery in Germany ended at Danzig—see *T. and E.*, pp. 18–19.

[10] Mariya.

[11] Gita (Rebecca) was one of W.'s younger sisters; m. Tuvia Dounie.

[12] See n. 5 to No. 129.

become a writer. In the meantime, I'm sure to be summoned somewhere.

Verunchik, my sweet, write at once about everything, absolutely everything. If it comes to that, how often do you write yourself? Heartfelt greetings to Sofochka. Lots and lots of kisses.

Yours,
Chaim

131. To Catherine Dorfman, Kherson. *Pinsk, 20 [September] 1901**

Russian: H.W.: W.A.

[Month omitted in W.'s dating, but clearly September.]

Pinsk, 7/20. 1901

My dear,

Naturally nothing new could have happened during my stay here, and it's a good thing nothing does happen. It doesn't do any harm to get plenty of sleep.

Thank you for the letter.[1] In the meantime you must also have had my letter sent while travelling.[2] The trouble is that letters to Kherson take *eine halbe Ewigkeit*.[3] You were asking about my general impression of the students in Russia. It is a very good impression. The student crowd is more intelligent and united and, what is especially interesting, much more responsible and sincere. True, they have no political training, but then our students,[4] if I may be permitted to say so, certainly have none either. After all, among ourselves, *mon ami Maximov*[5] etc. is an example of good political education.

With them (the Russians) Zionism is less profound than in certain groups abroad, and less militant. This is because conditions for Zionist development here are more peaceful, and they are not as isolated as we are. In Russia you will not find people like Grinblatt, Shneerson or Motzkin, but on the other hand, you certainly will

---

131. [1] Not found.   [2] The reference is, presumably, to No. 128.

[3] 'Half an eternity'.

[4] i.e., the Geneva students. In orig. in feminine form. Most of the Geneva Jewish students were women.

[5] Nicolai Maximov (b. 1876), a medical student from Bulgaria, was among the demonstrators against the Czarist régime in Russia who were arrested in Geneva in Apr. 1901—see n. 2 to No. 79. He was, in his student days, in contact with the emigré Russian Social Democrats and was later active in the Communist movement in Bulgaria.

not find men like Krinkin[6] abroad. I tell you, our opponents can now say what they like, but they are wrong. Our numbers are growing, and they are not the worst kind of people.

Everything that the Bund and people like them say is just funny.

Practically everybody's attitude to the Conference[7] is more or less the same.

The letters[8] will be despatched from Kishinev. I'll let you know about this as soon as I receive exact information. I am only going to stay here till October 6th, New Style,[9] and then to work; and what a lot of work is awaiting me, stacks of it! In a few days I am going to send you my photograph; I have had my photograph taken. Do not refuse to accept it, and follow my example. My dear, don't you dare not go to G[eneva]!

Forgive this incoherent letter. I simply felt like having a little chat with you.

Best regards to the Brombergs and congratulations on the birth of Samson *in spe*, the 'Samsonchik' of today. I wish your sister a speedy recovery and generally *beaucoup de bonnes choses*.

What pleasant memories of Kherson remain on the whole!

Why doesn't F[inkelstein] write? Is he so very busy?

I send him my regards and ask for a few words. Has there been any news from Dr. Kr[inkin]?

Regards to all your people,

Yours,
Ch. W.

132. To Catherine Dorfman, Kherson. *Pinsk, 30 September 1901*

Russian: H.W.: W.A.

Pinsk, 17/Sept. 1901

My dear,

It is wrong of you to have written so little. Do you know, I can only scribble a few lines to you too. I don't feel very well. And my eyes are hurting too.

---

[6] As to W.'s high regard for Krinkin see No. 111.

[7] The Youth Conference.

[8] The reference is probably to the Kishinev Correspondence Centre circular mentioned in n. 12 to No. 129. Though there is no direct evidence on the point, it seems probable that the circular had been drafted by W., jointly with Catherine Dorfman, during his visit to Kherson in August.

[9] i.e., the end of the Holy Day and Festival season, see n. 5 to No. 127.

I am sending you my photograph, my dear. I think it has come out pretty well.

Please address your next letters to Vienna, M. Schmidt, Wien IX, Eisengasse 5 (for me).

There will be a meeting of the Act[ions] Com[mittee] about the time I reach Vienna.[1] I shall be seeing everybody.

Shall await news from you impatiently.

Yours,
Ch. W.

Regards to all your people.

133. To Catherine Dorfman, Geneva. *Pinsk, 3 October 1901**

Russian: H.W.: W.A.

Pinsk, 20 Sept. 1901[1]

My dear,

You yourself will know what joy your postcard[2] has given me! Once again I greet you in your Alma Mater.[3] I too am waiting with great impatience for the day when we meet again. I want to find myself once more in the surroundings in which we felt so happy last term. We are losing one member, namely Shneerson, who is not going abroad this year. She will probably spend the winter here.[4] Thanks to the speed with which mails move, you have apparently failed to get my letter with the enclosed snap which I sent to your home.[5]

I hope it will be sent on to you. I have only six more days here, and then on to Warsaw, Vienna, etc.

I'll be arriving not later than the 15th. Please, dear Dorfman, drop in at my flat on the 14th or 15th; the exact date of my arrival will be known there.

My address is rue Lombard 4, third floor;[6] there you will meet *chéri* (in other words, M. Batschevanoff); he will know in any case.

Meanwhile, you will probably have had a good look at the locusts who have swarmed in during the summer. I shall most likely see Koenigsberg in Vienna, since we are leaving here at the

---

132. [1] The Greater Actions Committee met in Vienna on 9–12 Oct. 1901.

133. [1] 'Pinsk . . . 190 . . .' printed. Blanks filled in by W.   [2] Not found.
    [3] She was back in Geneva after the summer vacation.
    [4] Esther Shneerson did not, in fact, remain in Russia; she went to Berlin to continue her studies in the autumn of 1901.   [5] No. 132.
    [6] W. lived at this new address from the autumn of 1901 until his final departure from Geneva for England in the summer of 1904.

same time. I wrote to her and gave her my address in Vienna. Am writing little because my eyes hurt. Au revoir.[7] All good wishes.

Yours,
Ch.W.

134. To Catherine Dorfman, Geneva. *Vienna, 12 October 1901*

Russian: H.W.: W.A.

['Vienna' printed on note-paper.]

October 12, 1901

Dear friend and comrade,

I arrived here last night and spent the whole of today wandering round Vienna, but haven't yet managed to see anyone except Kohan-B[ernstein] who is now here. Tomorrow at 9 a.m. I am going to see 'him',[1] and tomorrow, too, I shall leave for Geneva, where I long to be at last, as I haven't got a single healthy cell in my body. So much excitement, anxiety, and, my Lord, what dirt! In the evening there is going to be a students' meeting, and at 5 o'clock I shall attend the Actions Committee;[2] all this is repugnant to me in the extreme after discovering by what means not only the Avinovitzkys,[3] but even people whom I considered far superior are trying to fight the Conference and especially myself. Of course,

[7] In orig. a corresponding Russian phrase is used.

134. [1] No W. letter describing his meeting with Herzl has been found, but from his letters of 31 Oct. 1901 to Herzl and Ahad Ha'am respectively (Nos. 136, 137) it can be inferred that the meeting took place as arranged and resulted in Herzl's being persuaded to take a favourable view of the Youth Conference, to promise that any suspicion of its being disapproved by the Zionist leadership should be dispelled by an official statement in *Die Welt*, and to agree that arrangements should be made, with the active co-operation of the leadership, for the Conference to meet in Basle immediately before the opening of the Fifth Zionist Congress.—According to a letter dated 1 Nov. 1901 from Pasmanik to Herzl (C.Z.A.—Z1/320), W. said, on his return to Geneva, that Herzl had offered him financial assistance for the Conference, but he had declined it.—According to Adolf Pollak, who was at the time on the staff of the Zionist Office in Vienna, Buber was present, together with W. at the interview with Herzl: A. Pollak, *Zionistische Chronologie*, pp. 168–9 (copy in C.Z.A.).

[2] 12 Oct., the date of this letter, was the last day of the Greater Actions Committee meeting mentioned in n. 1 to No. 132, but the minutes of the meetings do not include any record of the proceedings on that day, and nothing is known of W.'s participation.

[3] Feibush Avinovitzky (b. Nesizh, Byelorussia, 1870, d. 1919), one of the most fervent exponents of political Zionism in Odessa and Southern Russia, was an uncompromising opponent of the inclusion in the Zionist programme of cultural work or any other activities not of a strictly political nature.

I shall not mince words tomorrow, and I will tell Herzl the unvarnished truth. Remarkable espionage methods have been instituted within Zionism, or, to be more precise, within the Organization as it now exists. Dr. D. Pasmanik, the *privat-docent*,[4] has been doing the dirty on me, and had I not considered it beneath my dignity, I would have kicked up the devil of a row. Do you know, he is in secret correspondence with Vienna and has been behaving treacherously while we were away.[5] Of course you have read his statement in the latest issue of *Voskhod*.[6] I am sorry for the language, but what a dirty swine! And to back him up there is a gang of *Yeshiva* students from Berne[7] [and] Russian informers headed by Zubatov,[8] who (and this is a fact) has demanded the names of the leaders of the Youth Organization. I imagine they are probably known to him already. Such a mess, you simply can't imagine. Just as well that we are on the other side of the border; otherwise while the matter was being clarified we should be under lock and key. Well, well, Pack.[9]

The A[ctions] C[ommittee] meeting was a very stormy one, but K[ohan]-B[ernstein] rubbed the noses of the local Olympians in the dirt.[10]

[4] He was a *privat-docent* in medicine at Geneva.

[5] As to Pasmanik's letter to Herzl of 25 July 1901, warning him against the subversive intentions of the organizers of the Youth Conference, see n. 1 to No. 124. Pasmanik had been elected a member of the Youth Conference Preparatory Bureau—see bridge-note following No. 75. In addition to his warning to Herzl, he had made an unsuccessful approach to the Smaller Actions Committee, which had on 1 Oct. 1901 considered and rejected a proposal emanating from him that it should come out publicly against the Youth Conference (C.Z.A.—Z1/174), and W. may well have got wind of this.

[6] In a letter published in *Voskhod*, 20 Sept./3 Oct. 1901, Pasmanik denied a report that the Youth Conference programme included a discussion of 'the struggle against the religious trend in Zionism' and declared that, should this issue be raised, most of the delegates would leave the Conference. He represented himself as writing as one of those associated with the preparations for the Conference (see n. 5 above) and on behalf of many of the appointed delegates.

[7] *Yeshiva*—A school of Jewish learning in which the traditional Talmudic and cognate studies were pursued in a strictly Orthodox atmosphere. In speaking of 'Yeshiva students from Berne', W. may be referring particularly to Meyer Pines and Jacob Salkind, both of whom had been *Yeshiva* students before coming to Switzerland. In an article published in the Hebrew journal *Hamelitz*, 19 Sept./2 Oct. 1901, Pines had castigated the organizers of the Conference for their alleged intention (see n. 6 above) of launching an attack on the religious Zionists. As to Salkind's later quarrel with W. on other grounds see n. 1 to No. 140.

[8] S. V. Zubatov (1863–1917), the then head of the Moscow secret police (*Okhrana*).

[9] Lit., 'rabble'—'What a gang!'

[10] The minutes of the Greater Actions Committee meetings on 9–10 Oct. 1901 show that there were sharp exchanges between Herzl and Kohan-Bernstein, both on the subject of the latter's conduct of the Kishinev 'Correspondence Centre', and also concerning the aims of the organizers of the Youth Conference, these being objected to by Herzl and stoutly defended by Kohan-Bernstein, who reminded him that the

Am writing scrappily because I am terribly excited and tired. I'd give half a kingdom to see any one of our friends now. Somehow I am worried by the thought that there is a lot of unpleasantness in store for me in Geneva too. I shall not be there before Monday, and therefore ask you, my dear, when you get this, please call at my flat, where there will probably be a telegram giving the time of my arrival.

Please let all our friends know; I send them my best wishes. I shall report about everything *persönlich*.[11]

Keep well. I feel as if a whole eternity still stands between us, but that's just nerves.

Yours,
Ch.W.

135. To Leo Motzkin, Berlin. *Geneva, 27 October 1901*

Russian: H.W.: C.Z.A.—A126/24/7/2/2

Geneva, 27/x. 1901
Rue Lombard 4

My dear Leo, my friend,

I have been intending to write to you for ages, but I spent the whole summer in such a daze that I didn't feel like writing, and kept putting off the letter to you until my impressions had sorted themselves out and I should be able to give you an overall picture instead of mere fragments. These excuses may appear rather flimsy, and in your heart, or possibly even aloud, you may have cursed me a long time ago, but you can be sure of one thing, my dear Leo, that I haven't for a moment forgotten my sacred duty to write to you not only as to a friend—one doesn't write to a friend out of duty— but as to a teacher to whom, to a considerable extent, I owe my ability to work. If you have cursed me, you have cursed me, and now let's have a heart-to-heart talk. I have no idea how you are now. How are you getting on with your work? How are the pre- parations for your exams[1] progressing? They aren't very far off, of course. How are things with you? How is Polya? Where is she now?

As for myself, there is nothing new. Everything, everything is as before. I have started work in the laboratory again, haven't yet got into the routine.

younger men represented the future of the Movement and should not, therefore, be slighted or discouraged: C.Z.A.—Z1/191. As to the effect on Herzl of his interview with W. on 13 Oct. see n. 1 above. [11] 'in person'.

135. [1] For his Ph.D.—see n. 13 to No. 92.

The vacations were interesting enough. I visited seven centres, including Warsaw, i.e. Odessa, Kherson, Nikolayev, Yelizavetgrad, Kishinev, Kharkov, and Warsaw, besides several smaller places in our district. I must say that during my journey I failed to see much that would give comfort. The existing Zionist organisations suffer from a lack of people with a profound understanding of their task and capable[2] of filling the positions in which circumstances have placed them; as a result, a terrible lack of vitality is evident in all the groups.

On the completion of a year's routine work, consisting of collecting dues and holding a few propaganda meetings, whining and complaints about inactivity and lack of work started everywhere. The results of all this are obvious: the body begins to weaken and disintegrate. What terrible poverty of intellect. In this respect, the famous and noisy Odessa עיר ואם בישראל[3] takes the first place. Zionism there has degenerated into a paper kingdom of circulars, shekel receipts, and not fully paid-up shares of the J[ewish] C[olonial] T[rust].[4]

The trite form which Zionism has acquired there, thanks to the fact that the Avinovitzkys[5] and their like are masters of the situation, has antagonised the better elements among the youth and the bourgeoisie. As far as Odessa is concerned, the Organization's ideal is to imitate the red-tape of the Odessa city authorities. Propaganda among the masses is carried on just as hopelessly, using old, debased clichés, devoid of all meaning.

The local Zionist 'rulers' are vigilantly on the lookout in case anyone should invade their kingdom, and they didn't give me a chance, because they thought that I had deliberately come to undermine their authority. The means with which they fight are dreadful. It is my profound conviction that Odessa Zionism is a shameful blot on the entire cause. I wrote about it to the regional head,[6] and expounded the same thing to Herzl, too.[7] In Lodz you find the same thing as in Odessa. A great deal depends, of course, on the character of the Jewish population in those parts, *ein zusammengewürfeltes Gesindel*.[8] Not for nothing do the Litvaks[9] say that

[2] In orig., by what is obviously a slip of the pen, W. wrote 'not capable'.

[3] Hebr., 'a city and mother in Israel' (see 2 Samuel, xx. 19).

[4] One of the main practical tasks of Zionist societies was to obtain subscriptions for shares in the Jewish Colonial Trust.

[5] See n. 3 to No. 134.

[6] The regional director of Zionist activities, Vladimir Tyomkin.

[7] Presumably at his meeting with Herzl on 13 Oct.—see n. 1 to No. 134.

[8] Lit., 'a rabble fortuitously thrown together'—'a fortuitous concourse of atoms'.

[9] The Jews of Lithuania and White Russia.

hell burns for seven miles round Odessa.[10] I felt it extremely. I spent a week in O[dessa], but consider it time lost. Of course I did see Tepper and his colleagues.[11] Among Social-Democrats, T[epper] is a Zionist. Among Zionists he is a Soc[ial] Dem[ocrat]. He preaches the participation of Jewish youth in the Russian revolutionary movement as the Zionists' principal task. His sermons enjoy success. He is liked in Odessa even though he isn't taken very seriously. Everything about him is immature. People regard Syrkin's letters and his pamphlet[12] with derision, although, as is usual among the Russians, 'it is an interesting phenomenon'. In my next letter I shall describe my impressions of the young people.

The Jewish workers in Odessa are fairly open to Zionist propaganda, but I must tell you that in no event will the local Zionist organizations be able to win them over. In Odessa, as throughout the South, there is no Bund. The Jew[ish] workers are either grouped in Zionist organizations which drag out an indifferent existence, or else fall under the influence of Christian propagandists and form mixed Soc[ial] Dem[ocratic] organizations. Were it not for anti-semitism among the workers, the assimilation of the Jew[ish] workers would make great strides in the south, as all the conditions are there: lack of knowledge about Judaism, a hostile attitude to reactionary Zionist groups, etc. The formation of artels,[13] therefore, seemed to me exceptionally useful, and, from the propaganda and organizational point of view, extremely important; these artels are developing in the south, thanks to Levitsky,[13] who is supported by the Zionists. There are artels in Odessa, Nikolayev, Kishinev, Yelizavetgrad, and Kharkov. Zionists are the patrons of these institutions and hence are able to educate such groups in the spirit of Zionism. At first the Jews do not settle well in the artels, and it usually takes six months before *Reibereien*[14] are overcome, but in the long run they manage to settle down together. There have been no instances as yet of an artel disintegrating because of internal dissensions.

[10] W. is quoting, a Yiddish proverb, the more usual version of which speaks of ten (not seven) miles round Odessa.

[11] Kalman Tepper, of Odessa (1879–?), a prominent figure among the younger Odessa Zionists, had at first been attracted, like W., by the teachings of Ahad Ha'am but had by this time identified himself with the Zionist-Socialist group in Odessa.

[12] As to Syrkin and his pamphlet see n. 2 to No. 92. In two 'programmatic letters' published in the second half of 1901 he advocated the setting up of a Zionist-Socialist organization.

[13] Artels were artisans' co-operatives. Of the numerous artels which came into existence at the turn of the century, many were established on the initiative of a lawyer named N. V. Levitzky (1859–?). Levitzky was not a Jew, but the membership of many of the artels was wholly Jewish, and Zionists took an active part in encouraging and guiding the movement.   [14] 'frictions'.

The general mood of the Jewish public is turning towards Zionism. Scepticism and poverty of spirit in the Zionist organizations themselves—these are the enemies of Zionism in Odessa. The position of the Jews in the south is the same as in Lithuania, although they have more life in them and are more complete human beings. As Jews they are less receptive and also more obtuse than the Litvaks. The intelligentsia to be found in the Zionist ranks is almost entirely assimilated, and you will rarely come across a person who knows the Jewish language and Jewish literature. There are very many who have gone over to Zionism from the Russian Populist movement,[15] and are applying the same patterns to the Jewish cause.

Most of these intellectuals do not understand Yiddish nor do they consider it at all necessary to understand Yiddish, and in consequence they are unable to agitate among the wider masses. In the eyes of the masses they will always be *Goyim*.[16] Contact between the educated leaders and the rank-and-file is almost non-existent.

The presence in an organization of even one person capable of doing something has a vitalizing effect, since the responsiveness of the masses is fairly strong.

In my next letter I shall dwell on other problems. I shall not wait for your answer. Please do send me my *Briefordner*[17] which you have and which I badly need.

What is happening in *Kadimah* these days? Who is the chairman? I must have the address of somebody with whom I can exchange letters. Where is Kunin? If he is in B[erlin] send him my best wishes.

Write to me about yourself. If Polya is in Berlin give her my best regards.

Yours,
Chaim

136. To Ahad Ha'am (Asher Ginzberg), Odessa. *Geneva, 31 October 1901*

Russian: H.W. (partly H.W.A.): Ahad Ha'am Papers, N.L.

[Except for the words 'with friendly greetings' and the signature, the first letter is in the handwriting of Anne Koenigsberg. The whole of the letter appended to it is in W.'s handwriting.]

[15] The Narodniki or Populists (*narod*—'people') advocated sweeping agrarian reforms, including the distribution of land among the peasants and the organization of the village community (*Mir*) as a peasants' co-operative. They believed in 'going to the people' and trying to educate them.

[16] Hebr., in orig. in cyrillic characters—'gentiles'.

[17] 'letter-file', probably meaning the file of the Youth Conference Organization Bureau at Geneva.

Geneva, 31/x. 1901
Rue Lombard 4

Dear comrade,

A letter was forwarded to our Bureau[1] the other day from a certain Mr. Weissman of Maryapol,[2] proposing to write a paper for our Conference on the following question. In view of the fact that Jews have no purely Jewish school where Jewish youth can be educated, thus causing the alienation of healthy Jewish manpower, Weissman proposes the establishment in Palestine of a University cum factory. The combination of four hours of physical labour with intellectual work would, on the one hand, ensure an all-round development both of physical and mental powers, while, on the other hand, this project could be implemented at relatively small cost.

This gentleman mentions that at some point he submitted this plan to you and that you have approved of it. We should be very interested to know your views on this and on Mr. Weissman's project in particular,[3] since the question of establishing a University in Europe has been entered on the agenda of our Conference, and several speakers will deliver papers on the subject.[4]

One of the latest news items concerning the Conference is that it will not take place in Geneva, as was expected, but at Basle, a week before the big Congress.[5] The reason for this change is that the Act[ions] Com[mittee], having agreed with our arguments on the

---

136. [1] The Youth Conference Organization Bureau.

[2] David Weissman, Maryapol, to Bernstein-Kohan 2/15 Oct. 1901, W.A. W.'s reply has not been found, but from a letter (undated, but almost certainly attributable to Feb. 1902) from Weissman to Ahad Ha'am (Ahad Ha'am Papers, N.L.) it can be inferred that W. told him that, while in general agreement with the plan, he thought that it should be carried out in Europe rather than in Palestine.

[3] In a letter dated 26 Oct./8 Nov. 1901, W.A., Ahad Ha'am told W. that he had informed Weissman that he approved the plan in principle but saw no prospect of its early implementation.

[4] From the record of the proceedings of the Munich Preparatory Conference (Apr. 1901) in C.Z.A.—A139/5 it appears that it was decided to insert in the programme of the Youth Conference a proposal for the launching of a fund 'for the establishment of a Jewish University in Palestine'; that a reference to the University project had been suggested by W., who had, however, expressed the view that the University might have to be established in Europe; and that the words 'in Palestine' were inserted at the instance of the Chairman of the Berne Academic Zionist Society, Chaim Khissin. Though in the agenda circulated after the Preparatory Conference the above-mentioned proposal, including the words 'in Palestine', duly appears, neither in the (incomplete) record of the proceedings of the Youth Conference in C.Z.A.—A126/24/5/2 nor in the press reports is there anything to show that this subject was, in fact, discussed.

[5] 'the big Congress'—the Fifth Zionist Congress opening at Basle on 26 Dec.

necessity of holding the Conference, have taken upon themselves the job of organizing it, which can, of course, be more conveniently done at the same time as the big Congress.[6] Besides the purely practical aspect, this has the added advantage for us that the Berlin Socialist-Zionists[7] have arranged their Conference in Geneva for the same time—people with whom we might easily be confused.[8] Do you intend to come to the Conference?[9]

We hope to receive an immediate reply from you to the above question.

With friendly greetings,
Ch. Weizmann

Dear, dear comrade,

I have such a lot of work on my hands that I cannot write much, yet I should very much have liked to unburden my heart. True, I cannot boast of a particularly cheerful state of mind, which indeed is hardly possible if one looks attentively at everything that is going on within Jewry in general, and Zionism in particular; so much is bad that whatever little good there is becomes almost completely lost. In spite of all the meanness and the attempts to trip us up, the matter of the Conference will succeed. How happy we should be if you were to support us by taking part in it and giving us your advice. *Cher maître*, can we count on your coming? Do write frankly. Let us know whether you can [come], what is the state of your health, how you are feeling now. I shall impatiently await a line from you.

With a warm handshake.

Ever yours,
Ch. Weizmann
Rue Lombard 4

[6] See n. 1 to No. 134.

[7] Nahman Syrkin had in the spring of 1901 organized a Jewish-Socialist Society, consisting, at the date of this letter, of a handful of Berlin Jewish students, under the name of *Hessiana*, the name being an allusion to Moses Hess, who, besides being the author of *Rom und Jerusalem* (as to which see n. 1 to No. 50), was a friend and collaborator of Karl Marx. *Hessiana* was described in its constitution as 'an academic group concerned with the theoretical aspect of the question of the establishment of a Jewish community on a collectivist basis in Palestine and the adjacent lands under British protection'.

[8] As to W.'s resentment of any suggestion of a link with the Zionist-Socialists see No. 124.

[9] Ahad Ha'am told W. in reply that for personal reasons he would probably be unable to attend the Conference—26 Oct./8 Nov. 1901, W.A.

137. To Theodor Herzl, Vienna. *Geneva, 31 October 1901*

German: H.W.: C.Z.A.—Z1/326

Geneva, rue Lombard 4
31/x. 1901

The Chairman,
Zionist Actions Committee,
Vienna.

Dear Dr. [Herzl],

With reference to our conversation in Vienna,[1] and the promise you gave me, I take the liberty of sending you the enclosed text of a *démenti*[2] which should put an end to the rumours that have been circulated about our Conference.

At the same time, I take the liberty of drawing your attention to an article published in No. 224 of *Hamelitz* demanding vigorous action forthwith on the part of the A.C.[3]

I have always considered it unnecessary to reply to all insinuations, but this goes beyond all limits. The dangers to which all of us are exposed by articles such as that just mentioned are obvious to anyone having even a superficial knowledge of conditions in Russia. What is also deplorable is that the writer of the article— a Mr. Salzmann, a student from Lausanne—is indirectly using the A.C. to cover himself.

I do not insist on adhering to the exact words of the

---

137. [1] On 13 Oct. 1901—see No. 134.

[2] The following is a translation of a statement published in the official information column of *Die Welt*, 8 Nov. 1901 (p. 16):

> The Conference of Young University Zionists [lit., 'The Conference of Academic Zionist Youth'] will be held at Basle on December 18th. With a view to disposing of the reports about this Conference which have been circulated in the press, we feel that it should be made clear that, having been informed by the Organizing Committee of the nature of the Conference, we can only say that we are satisfied that they are loyal and sincere Zionists.

From W.'s draft, which has not been found, a sentence, the contents of which are not known, was deleted as too polemical: see S.A.C. Minutes, 5 November 1901, C.Z.A.— Z1/174; Herzl and Kokesch to W., 6 Nov., W.A.; *Die Welt*, 8 Nov. p. 15.

[3] Writing in the Hebrew journal *Hamelitz*, 12/25 Oct. 1901, A Salzmann (described later in this letter as a student from Lausanne—nothing further is known about him) alleged that the Young Zionists intended to defy the Zionist leadership, to set up an Opposition, and to split the Movement, and that Herzl was against the holding of the Youth Conference. He hinted that Syrkin's Zionist-Socialist group might be expected to take part in the Conference.

enclosed statement, but I should like the sense to remain[4] the same.

Looking forward to your reply, I am,

With Zion's greetings,

Yours truly,

Dr. Ch. Weizmann

138. To Leo Motzkin, Berlin. *Geneva, 7 November 1901*

Russian: Pcd.: H.W. (mainly H.W.A.): C.Z.A.—A1/26/24/7/2/2

[Except for 'Rue Lombard 4', the signature and the words below it, all of which are in W.'s hand, the handwriting is that of Anne Koenigsberg.]

Geneva, 7/xi. 01

Rue Lombard 4

Dear Comrade,

We are extremely surprised at not having had a reply to our last letter[1] and to our request that the papers[2] be sent at once. At a time when there is an accumulation of work here, every day's delay means an obstacle to the common task. This is the second week in which for some reason you have not thought it necessary to carry out such an apparently easy and simple task. We hope that you will reply and despatch the requested papers immediately on receipt of this letter.

Mit Zionsgruss[3]

Dr. Ch. Weizmann

Forgive the official tone.

I am angry!

139. To Catherine Dorfman, Geneva. [*En route from Geneva to Berne, 9 November 1901*]

Russian: Pcd.: H.W.: W.A.

[Picture postcard inscribed *Souvenir de Lausanne* but with Fribourg pmk. 9 Nov. 1901. Presumably bought by W. while travelling by train from Geneva to Berne and posted during stop at Fribourg.]

Best wishes. My head is splitting, but it will pass, I hope. Today at 4 there is a meeting in Berne, and in the evening a lecture.[1] My regards to dear Koenigsberg.

Ch.W.

[4] In orig., only 'b . . . bt' (obviously *bleibt*) is legible.

138. [1] See No. 135.

[2] Presumably the contents of the Geneva Bureau's letter-file—see n. 17 to No. 135.

[3] 'With Zion's greetings.'

139. [1] Nothing is known of the meeting or the lecture.

140. To Leo Motzkin, Berlin. *Geneva, 16 November 1901*

Russian: H.W.: C.Z.A.—A126/24/7/2/2

16/11. 1901, Geneva

My dear good Leo,

A very simple reason, my dear Leo, has made me forgo the pleasure of writing to you as I had started to do. I haven't been at all well for a whole week now; I am neglecting all my work, do not go out, and stay in bed part of the time. A mountain of all kinds of filth, intrigues, dirt, a campaign against the Conference linked with a foul campaign against me personally, pamphlets, lampoons[1] —all this has broken me and shattered me completely. In the whole town there are only two people[2] who are co-operating with me in the Bureau; and we have had to *auskosten*[3] all this. On the one hand I was glad that you didn't know anything about it, yet on the other I wanted so badly to see you, if only for a moment, to share with you everything that has been filling my heart. I think we have now managed to stop this loathsome campaign, admittedly at a high cost[4]—but let us drop this and go over to business.[5]

Up to the present day I have received no letter from Berger. Neither have I received the report which you wrote you were sending.[6] If you have not sent it yet, please do post it at once.

---

140. [1] No such 'pamphlets' as are here mentioned have come to light, but, in addition to Salzmann's animadversions on the Youth Conference in *Hamelitz*, 12/25 Oct. 1901 [see n. 3 to No. 137], there had appeared in the same journal the article mentioned in n. 7 to No. 134, in which Meyer Pines inveighed against the organizers of the Youth Conference for what he believed to be their intention of launching an anti-religious campaign. W. may have heard of a letter raising the same point from Jacob Rabinovich, secretary of the Geneva Zionist Society, to the Smaller Actions Committee, 4 Nov. 1901:—C.Z.A.—Z1/326. Further, Rabinovich, together with Jacob Salkind Chairman of the Berne 'Zion' Society, and Vice-Chairman of the Berne Academic Zionist Society (as to whom see n. 7 to No. 134), had written to W. on 6 Nov. (W.A.) severely criticizing him for having actively interested himself in the setting up at Geneva of an Aid Fund for Jewish students generally, without regard to party affiliations, complaining that by so doing he was undermining the attempts then being made to unify Zionist Aid Funds in Switzerland, and pressing him to withdraw. As to W.'s interest in a non-party Aid Fund see also below, n. 20.

[2] Probably Catherine Dorfman and Anne Koenigsberg.

[3] 'enjoy to the full'—i.e. (ironically) to have all the fun of doing everything ourselves.

[4] What W. means would seem to be that his understanding with Herzl about the Youth Conference [see n. 1 to No. 134] had the effect of restricting the freedom of the 'Young Zionists' to criticize the leadership and its policies.

[5] Most of what follows is concerned with questions arising on a letter from Motzkin to W. dated 10 Nov. 1901 (W.A.).

[6] In his above-mentioned letter Motzkin referred (*inter alia*) to a letter he had had from Isaac Berger, on behalf of the Minsk *Poale Zion* group (as to which see below), together with a circular (here referred to by W. as 'the report') which, he said, he was forwarding to W.—After the Munich Conference (Apr. 1901) in preparation for the

The Zionist Soc[ialists], i.e. the *Hessiana* group, have sent us a notification that they have elected three delegates for the forthcoming Conference: Mirkin, Syrkin and Karolik.[7] They sent their rules as well. I replied that the rules gave no indication of their attitude to the Basle Programme and to the Zionist Organization, and I asked them to express their views on these subjects.[8] I must tell you, my dear Leo, that the Russians have behaved disgracefully in connection with the Conference. Previously, when the Conference was due to be held in Geneva, they sent out circulars with an invitation to their conference to be held in G[eneva] on December 18th, i.e. on the same day as ours.[9] When we fixed the Conference in Basle they invited the Kiev people, as I am informed from there, to a conference at B[asle] on the 18th. All this time they haven't written a word to us about all this. What childish behaviour!

There will be some Austrians at the Conference. There cannot be a great muddle because of this, as those gentlemen know that Russian is to be the main language. I know absolutely nothing of the Odessa scandal.[10]

Those who have definitely promised to come[11] are: Petersburg, Moscow, Kharkov, Warsaw, Odessa, Eliashev from Kovno, Grodno,

Youth Conference, Berger had written to the Geneva Organization Bureau expressing interest in the Conference but had had no reply. On 25 Oct. 1901 he wrote to Motzkin (C.Z.A.—A126/24) enclosing a *Poale Zion* circular (ibid.—Z1/325) for transmission to the Geneva Bureau, with which, he said, he was anxious to be in contact, because the P.Z. and the 'Young Zionists' had a common purpose—the consolidation of the democratic elements in Zionism, plainly hinting that he would like the P.Z. to be represented at the Youth Conference. The gist of the circular, which included a proposal for a *Poale Zion* Conference in Minsk, was that there could be no future for the Movement unless it succeeded in attracting both the intelligentsia and the masses. —The establishment in 1899 (or, according to some authorities, in 1897) of the Minsk *Poale Zion* ('Zionist workers') group, headed at the date of this letter by Isaac Berger, was followed by the organization of P.Z. groups in a number of other Jewish centres in White Russia and Lithuania. In the early stages, the objects of the movement represented by the Minsk P.Z. were to voice the views of working-class Jews with Zionist sympathies; to satisfy the Jewish masses that adherence to Zionism was fully consistent with the pursuit of the workers' struggle for the improvement of their lot; by these means to blunt the edge of Bundist propaganda; and, finally, to press for the 'democratization' of the Zionist Movement. Despite the identity of names, the Minsk P.Z. cannot properly be regarded as the precursor of the powerful *Poale Zion* Movement, which, founded in 1906, was before long to establish itself as a militant left-wing party within the Zionist Organization, combining acceptance of the Basle Programme with an ideology tinged with Marxism.

[7] As to W.'s anxiety that the Youth Conference should not be suspected of any link with the Zionist-Socialists see No. 136. As to *Hessiana* see n. 7 to that letter.

[8] W.'s letter has not been found, but there is a summary of its contents in No. 141, together with a summary of *Hessiana's* reply.   [9] See No. 136.

[10] In his a/m letter of 10 Nov. 1901 Motzkin asked: 'Don't you know of the scandal in Odessa? Terrible things are told here but one must know whether they are not slanders.' Nothing is known about these rumours.

[11] To the Youth Conference.

Vilna, Kishinev, and the University towns outside Russia. As far
as one can judge from letters and personal discussions, these are
democratic elements. I used to correspond with Gourland; he is
now in Russia and gives no news of himself. He isn't doing anything
there, and I am disappointed in him. He stayed at Vilna, not taking
the slightest trouble to examine the state of affairs, but merely
criticising, or, to be more exact, cursing everything and everyone,
and that in private and not in the open. Gourland is not a man of
action. Nor will he on any account join 'Syrkin's' Fraction.[12] There
is no need even to mention Aberson, who is now working with me
whole-heartedly in connection with the Conference. He is against
S[yrkin], against their venture.[13] This is also Bukhmil's opinion.

Evidently Syrkin has some people in Russia, in Kiev and Odessa.
Even Farbstein[14] is against him. Incidentally, F[arbstein] is now
actually working very hard for the Bank, distributing shares in
Zurich. He arranges discussions there both among the students
and among the bourgeoisie; in short, he has completely changed
his attitude.[15] Why? I cannot say. When he was asked why he is
now in favour of the Bank, he replied that he was faced with a *fait
accompli* and considers it his duty to support such a cause. In
Palestine, of course, everything has to be on a socialist basis.[16] I
was also invited to the Zurich debates,[17] but my health does not
allow me to travel and become excited. My nerves are completely
shattered.

Shneerson and Aberson[18] have nothing in common in their attitude to Zionism. Shneerson is a philosopher, a terrible *Grübler-
geist*,[19] punctilious in her attitude to herself and everything about
her. Self-examination, a very profound, honest self-examination,
makes her incapable of adhering to the cause whole-heartedly even

[12] The Zionist-Socialists. Motzkin having asked in his a/m letter of 10 Nov. 1901
whether Aaron Gourland had joined 'the Syrkin Fraction', the point of W.'s reference
to 'Syrkin's' Fraction, with Syrkin in quotation-marks, is merely to remind Motzkin
that the name of the Fraction headed by Syrkin was not, in fact, 'the Syrkin Fraction'.
[13] Before becoming a Zionist, Aberson had had Bundist sympathies, and Motzkin
had enquired how he stood in relation to the Zionist-Socialists.
[14] David Farbstein was a member of the Swiss Social-Democratic Party.
[15] At the Second Zionist Congress (1898) Farbstein had objected to certain features
of the scheme for the establishment of the Jewish Colonial Trust ('the Bank') and had
proposed that the whole project should be shelved for the time being. By 'distributing
shares' W. means soliciting subscriptions for shares.
[16] 'In Palestine, of course. . . .'—i.e. according to Farbstein.
[17] Public debates between Zionists and anti-Zionists were held in Zurich on 26 Oct.
and 16 Nov. 1901: see *Die Welt*, 1 Nov. 1901.
[18] In enquiring about Aberson's attitude Motzkin had mentioned the case of
Esther Shneerson, who had moved from Geneva to Berlin and had there, he understood, been associating with members of Syrkin's *Hessiana*.
[19] 'brooder'.

for a moment. She struggles with herself at every practical step. As far as I know, neither *Kadimah* nor *Hessiana* is to her liking.

If there were some vital, exciting enterprise in Zionism now, she would work, and work excellently; as long as there is none she goes on reasoning with herself.

Aberson is the exact opposite; he is a perfect fighter, but of course he hasn't yet won his spurs. He will win them, for he is growing and gaining in strength.

I ought to continue my letter, but it is difficult for me to write much, and to my great regret I must postpone it. There is a very great deal I should like to write, but at present I can't.

As for you, please write; you know very well that the day your letter arrives is a holiday for me; in view of my present condition, you will write to me. I may have to leave G[eneva] for a week to have a break, but I don't know whether I'll manage it. It is an extremely awkward time.

I should like you, Leo, to let me have an immediate answer to the following: how has the Mutual Assistance Fund been arranged, and the group about which we talked with Blank?[20] Have they started work?

Here, owing to the opposition of the Zionist group, the whole affair has hung fire for the time being.[21] Let me have all the information about this, as well as Blank's address.

I was in Berne last week. Sonia and Rebecca complain of the lack of letters from you, especially from Polya.[22] Sonia will soon be sitting for her exams. They, too, are not feeling very well. I shall probably be there again next week.

How are you getting on? When are your exams? How are things? Write about everything; for God's sake don't be stingy with words. As for Polya, why does she never write a single word?

With brotherly greetings,

Yours,
Chaim

---

[20] A committee for the establishment of an Aid Fund for Russian Jewish students, without distinction of party, had been set up in Berlin, with Reuben Blank as secretary. In orig. it is not quite clear whether W. writes 'I talked' or 'we [Motzkin and himself] talked'. The interview with Blank probably took place during W.'s visit to Berlin in July 1901.

[21] See above, n. 1.

[22] W.'s reference to an apparently friendly meeting with Sonia (Sophia) Getzova is interesting in view of the breaking-off of his engagement in July of that year—see No. 105.

141. To Leo Motzkin, Berlin. *Geneva, 21 November 1901*

Russian: H.W.A.: C.Z.A.—A126/24/7/22

[Signed by W. in his own hand; remainder in handwriting of Anne Koenigs-berg.—From the letter from Kohan-Bernstein mentioned in n. 6 below it can be inferred that a similar communication was addressed to him and probably also to other members of the Youth Conference Bureau, as to which see bridge-note following No. 75.]

Geneva, 21/xi. 01
Rue Lombard 4.

Dear comrade,

Some time ago, a letter arrived from the Berlin group *Hessiana*, who up till then had not given any sign of life. They also sent the society's statutes. The contents of this letter are as follows: In view of the fact that they wish to take part in the Youth Conference and have chosen three delegates,[1] they request us to send them the letters published by the Bureau.[2]

The main item on their programme is the scientific study of the problem of colonising Palestine on collectivist lines.[3] Whether they base themselves on the Basle Programme could not be inferred from this programme; we therefore replied that only people who had joined the general Zionist Organization could be delegates to the Conference, and we asked them to explain their attitude to the Basle Programme. To our great astonishment, we received the following reply: The Group adheres to the Basle Programme. The Basle Programme does not favour any specific form of colonisation, and advocacy of the collectivist principle cannot, therefore, clash with adherence to that Programme. They disapprove of the act[ivities] of the existing Organization but consider that the Organiza[tion] must be reformed from within. They ask us to enter into relations with them at once. To have relations with people who, when the need arises, accept so lightly what they have recently condemned,[4] and to give them an opportunity to obstruct the cause, which they will certainly do, is, at the very least, inconvenient. For the time being we are informing them (in order to gain time) that their delegates

---

141. [1] Names given in No. 140.
  [2] i.e. the Geneva Organization Bureau's bulletins.
  [3] See n. 7 to No. 136.
  [4] It is not clear what W. is referring to. Syrkin, the founder of *Hessiana*, having been censured by the Berne Zionist Students' Society (see *Die Welt*, 20 Jan. 1899) for his attacks on the Zionist Organization in the lecture mentioned in n. 6 to No. 92, had responded by declaring, in a letter published in *Die Welt*, 10 Feb. 1899, that, as a Zionist-Socialist, he could have nothing to do with the Zionism of the Second Congress. This is not, however, a sufficient explanation of the words 'which they had recently condemned'.

must be approved by the other members of the Bureau.[5] Let us have your opinion at once and your advice as to what we should do.[6]

We desire also to inform you that a telegram has arrived from the Act[ions] C[ommittee] in which they ask us to inform them immediately of the names of the persons desirous of attending the Congress as delegates.[7] We telegraphed the following names: Rosenfeld,[8] Mlle. Getzova (Berne),[9] Aberson (Geneva), Eliasberg (Heidelberg), Nemser (Munich), Portugalov (St. Petersburg).

Yours,
Ch. Weizmann

142. To Leo Motzkin, Berlin. *Geneva, 21 November 1901*

Russian: Pcd.: H.W.: C.Z.A.—A126/24/7/2/2

21/xi. 1901, Geneva.

Dear Leo,

I send you greetings from a meeting at which discussions with Davidson are going on.[1] Our side of things is progressing well. The Bureau has sent you a letter.[2] Keep well. Regards to Polya.

Yours,
Chaim

[Also signed by Anne Koenigsberg, Zvi Aberson, and Catherine Dorfman.]

143. To the Zionist Congress Bureau, Vienna. *Geneva, 21 November 1901*

German: H.W.: C.Z.A.—Z1/327

Geneva, 21. xi. 1901
4 rue Lombard

The Zionist Congress Bureau,[1]
Vienna.

Dear Fellow-Zionists,

I confirm receipt of the telegram you sent yesterday, which ran:

[5] From No. 146 it appears that the Geneva Organization Bureau did write to Hessiana to this effect, but the letter has not been found.

[6] Kohan-Bernstein, 17 (30) Nov., opposed the admission of *Hessiana* delegates to the Youth Conference; Motzkin, 27 Nov. (10 Dec.) objected only to the admission of Syrkin: both letters in W.A. In the event, *Hessiana* was not represented, though Syrkin was present as a guest.   [7] See No. 143.   [8] Samuel Rosenfeld.

[9] This might be either Sophia or Rebecca Getzova. It is uncertain which is meant, but probably Sophia, who was an active Zionist.

142. [1] See No. 144.   [2] See No. 141.

143. [1] The official name of the Zionist Central Office in Vienna was '*Erez-Israel, Bureau des Zionisten-Congresses*'.

'Telegraph names of trusted friends who wish to go to Basle as delegates.'[2]

I took the telegram to mean that you were concerned with delegates to the V [Fifth] Congress, that is to say with persons who would like to come as delegates but cannot do so because they have no mandate.

Today I answered your telegram accordingly, naming a few people whom I consider to be very good and staunch Zionists and who will, moreover, come to the V [Fifth] Congr[ess].[3]

If I have misunderstood, would you please be kind enough to explain.

With Zion's greetings,

Yours faithfully,
Dr. Ch. Weizmann

144. To Leo Motzkin, Berlin. *Geneva, 23 November 1901*

Russian: H.W.: C.Z.A.—A126/24/7/2/2

Geneva, 23/xi/1901
4 rue de Lombard[1]

My dear Leo,

Thank you for your letter[2] and your advice, always so precious to me. Of course you were not mistaken in thinking that I would write to you. I only wish I always knew how to write so as to express everything, leaving nothing obscure. I feel better, though not quite well.[3] It's annoying that I am in poor health at such an inopportune moment. I find it quite impossible to leave my post even for a day, as the last days are the most important. The Congress is near at hand. I have read the letter from the Minsk workers;[4] it is good and sensible. The only thing I don't know is whether they have managed to come to terms with their comrades.[5] I have also had a similar letter from the Grodno פועלי ציון.[6] Apparently the

---

[2] When a Zionist Congress was approaching, groups of voters entitled to send delegates sometimes found it impossible to do so because the travelling expenses would be too much for them. The Congress Bureau would, if requested, try to find suitable persons who desired to attend the Congress as delegates but had not found a constituency and would be available to represent such voters.

[3] W.'s reply has not been found but there is a list of his nominees at the end of No. 141.

144. [1] Thus in orig.   [2] Not found.
[3] See first para. of No. 140.   [4] See n. 6 to No. 140.
[5] W. is thinking, presumably, of the proposed Conference of *Poale Zion* groups mentioned in the circular enclosed with the letter from the Minsk *Poale Zion.*
[6] Hebr., *Poale Zion.*

mood of the Zionist workers is identical everywhere. Of course, one wouldn't expect anything else.

I shall now turn to the exposition of my views on forthcoming work. In passing I shall also touch upon some other problems of a personal nature. I imagine that at the Youth Conference there will come into being a democratic nucleus of intelligent young workers for the cause who will constitute a group agreeing on all problems:

(i) As to the existing Zionist Organization, our attitude must be positive, in the sense of taking part in it and working on behalf of its institutions, such as the Bank,[7] shekalim, *eventuell*[8] the National Fund, and especially propaganda. At the same time, our group will always be critical and in opposition whenever dealings with the clericals and with the bourgeoisie (in the sense of *baal-habatim*)[9] are concerned, whenever we see too much showing-off, too much secret diplomacy. As to the last-mentioned point, it will be necessary to demand some sort of control. Opposition and criticism must be orderly, united, ruthless, and always relevant to the cause and to concrete problems. It will be necessary to oppose with the utmost energy the shameful actions in New York, in England and elsewhere,[10] the conduct of affairs in the Bank,[11] the steps taken in respect of the Correspondence Centre.[12] The Correspondence Centre must be reformed. *Es ist ein unhaltbarer Zustand.*[13] Our rôle

[7] The Jewish Colonial Trust.

[8] 'Possibly'—The setting up of the Jewish National Fund, approved in principle by the Fourth Zionist Congress (1900), had still to be finally authorized by the Fifth Congress, which was due to meet shortly after the date of this letter.

[9] Hebr., in orig. in cyrillic characters, 'heads of households', meaning solid middle-class types.

[10] Disputes between the British and American Zionist Federations on the one hand, and various Zionist groups in those countries—including in particular *Hovevei Zion* Societies—on the other, concerning the claims of those groups to autonomy, the procedure for the sale of shekalim, and other organizational questions had been the subject of debate at the Fourth Congress (1900), and were still simmering so as to come up for further discussion at the Fifth Congress in Dec. 1901. W. seems to be alluding to these disputes, but the strong language of the reference to 'shameful actions' cannot be satisfactorily explained.

[11] In one of his speeches at the Fifth Zionist Congress (1901)—5 Z.C. Prot. p. 376—W. demanded that Congress should exercise effective control over the operations of the Jewish Colonial Trust. For W.'s particular complaint against the Trust see the next paragraph of this letter and n. 12 below.

[12] As can be seen from n. 1 to No. 43, Kohan-Bernstein's independent behaviour in his conduct of the Kishinev Correspondence Centre (as to which see n. 5 to No. 28) had got him into trouble with the Russian Zionist leaders. Attempts to clip his wings were made by his opponents at the Fourth Zionist Congress (1900) and again, by Herzl, in 1901. Though at a meeting of Russian delegates to the Fifth Congress in Dec. 1901 W. defended K.-B., the Kishinev Centre was closed down at the end of that year and was replaced by an Information Bureau at Simferopol under the direction of Victor Jacobson.   [13] 'It is an intolerable state of affairs.'

in the general Zionist Organization must consequently be twofold: to work and to criticize, but all this systematically, according to a strictly determined plan of action. We are going to urge the Congress to deal with all those issues that it so readily shelves; we shall conduct propaganda and help to provide money and men on the largest possible scale for their implementation.

(ii) The Youth Organisation singles out for itself the following tasks: (*a*) educational activities, (*b*) the study of economic life and the collection of material, (*c*) the theoretical study of Palestine. In connection with point (*c*) I venture to make the following observation: I find that, in view of the opening of the Bank, this has now become a problem of the utmost importance. It seems to me that the Bank should start its activity in Palestine, in a loyal and legal manner, forthwith.[14] It now spends all its income by way of interest, to the extent of about 100,000 roubles, to no purpose, which is scandalously irresponsible. Hard-earned money is spent on the maintenance of an unnecessary and useless staff who travel about Europe in sleeping-cars, etc., etc.

Out of these funds the Bank should without delay send to Palestine a delegation of young experts and dedicated Zionists who, while spending a minimum on their private needs, should make a thorough study of the country and draw appropriate practical conclusions. I would be the first (and here is the personal touch!) to go there, and I am ready—with only the bare minimum for subsistence—to devote myself wholly to the study of the country and its conditions. And other such people can be found. They must have one able leader, and they will constitute the Research Committee. I should insist that they be mainly Russian Jews. I am afraid that a furious dance will now start around this issue, like that round the golden calf, and that a whole crowd of *Projektenmacher*[15] will appear. We must keep our eyes very wide open.

(*d*) The problem of propaganda among the intelligentsia, the young people, and the working-class by means of the spoken and the printed word must become the domain of the Youth Organization. The creation of a periodical (not a newspaper!) of an intellectual type is essential. The Organization is entitled to require those of its members whom it considers suitable to go to the various

---

[14] The J.C.T., which had been incorporated as an English company in March 1899, was by its Memorandum of Association empowered to open for business when, and not before, it had a paid-up capital of £250,000. This point was reached in Oct. 1901, but the Directors decided to abstain, for the time being, from undertaking any activity and to keep the Trust's resources safely invested: *Die Welt*, 18 Oct. 1901.

[15] 'persons with paper plans'.

places where Jews reside, to carry on propaganda there and attract the people to the cause; the Organization must send a contingent of propagandists to America.

(*e*) The Organization seeks to obtain a decisive influence on Jewish students by promoting the establishment of mutual aid funds, reading-rooms, clubs, etc., and by agitating in favour of a Jewish University in Europe.

(*f*) In order to implement point (*e*), the Organization tries to join the Alliance Isr. Univ.[16] (as you know, that isn't difficult), and endeavours peacefully or by revolutionary methods to influence ICA.[17]

These, in my view, are the concrete tasks on the broadest lines. It is obvious that gigantic forces are required to effect all this, but I sincerely believe, only believe [?],[18] that only in such work shall we mature. The Youth Organisation must be strong as iron. Those who consider themselves strong will gather round a centre to which the healthiest and boldest will be attracted.

I have forgotten to mention my attitude to the Bund and the Russian Soc(ial) Dem(ocrats). To the latter I am indifferent; to the Bund antagonistic, in so far as it is a Russian revolutionary party. Its *sozialpolitische Bedeutung*[19] within Jewry is still negligible; it will become stronger if it concentrates its energy in that field and not on the struggle against autocracy.

As you see, dear Leo, I attach greater importance to practical work than to the theoretical side of the matter. In my opinion, it is in this spirit that the Conference must meet. Once it becomes per-

---

[16] The *Alliance Israélite Universelle*, founded in Paris in 1860, had, as its name implies, been conceived as an organization drawing its members from all parts of the Jewish world, but it had from the start been under French leadership and had from 1870 had a purely French complexion. It maintained a network of Jewish schools in various parts of the East and North Africa, helped to organize Jewish emigration from Eastern Europe to America, and was active in the defence of persecuted or underprivileged Jewish communities. With a view to encouraging the settlement of Jews on the land in Palestine, it had in 1869 established the Mikveh Israel Agricultural School, near Jaffa. Its leaders were, however, out of sympathy with Zionism, and there was no response to Zionist demands for the conduct of its activities on Jewish nationalist lines. Why W. thinks that 'to join the A.I.U. . . . isn't difficult' is not clear.

[17] The Jewish Colonization Association.

[18] 'I sincerely believe, only believe'—There is some obscurity here, but the best explanation that can be suggested is that it arises from a slip of the pen—i.e., that W. meant to say 'I sincerely believe that only in such work. . . .', etc.; that, carried forward by the flow of his thought, he wrote 'only' too early; and that he then corrected himself, but omitting to cross out the first 'only' and by mistake repeating the word 'believe'.

[19] Lit., 'social-political significance'—i.e. its importance as a social and political force.

suaded that manpower exists, it will occupy itself chiefly with the establishment of an organization.

Kohan-Bernstein will present the programme of the org[anization].[20]

Gourland is not going to lecture. Aberson is reading a paper on Zionist attitudes to exist[ing] trends and institutions in Jewry.

Unfortunately, there is no paper on cultural activities, as Dr. Lurie telegraphed yesterday declining to lecture.[21]

In general, I attach more importance to the debates than to the papers. This is the most important thing of all. Perhaps you, dear Leo, would undertake *die Discussion einzuleiten*?[22] Let me know at once.

The Austrians are going to be represented by Berthold Feiwel. They know that Russian will be the main lang[uage].

As far as I can determine now, the people who have responded to the Conference can be relied on. Of course, one has to be cautious. I believe that by putting forward broad demands to the Conference we shall perhaps get rid of any semi-Zionist elements which may happen to come.

Whoever opens the Conference will have to set out in a brief and condensed form everything I have written to you about.

The circular letter[23] is being copied and printed today. You will get it on Wednesday. Davidson was here; as I believe I have already written to you, he is touring the colonies[24] and fighting Zionism. If I still felt *pietätsvoll*[25] for him, any such feeling has now vanished. I tell you he is behaving like a renegade, like a low coward. His methods of fighting are horrible. I have never before experienced such a battle as this.

Aberson, Grinblatt, Pasmanik and I appeared for the Zionists. When Davidson felt that things were going badly, he asked for assistance, and none other than 'he' himself, Plekhanov, came to his aid. D[avidson] thought that here was the opportunity to finish off Zionism and Zionists then and there. They reckoned that

[20] See n. 6 to No. 83. The Minutes of the Youth Conference show that Kohan-Bernstein did, in fact, deliver an address on the functions of the proposed Youth Organization.

[21] The telegram has not been found, but on 2 (15) Dec. 1901 Joseph Lurie wrote to W. (W.A.) regretting his inability to lecture and expressing sympathy with the aims of the Youth Conference.

[22] 'to introduce the discussion'.

[23] The reference is probably to an undated circular (copy in W.A.) prepared by the Geneva Organization Bureau and containing the agenda of the Youth Conference with the names of the principal speakers, together with an explanation of its purpose.

[24] Unless a letter has been lost, W. is mistaken in thinking that he has already written to Motzkin about Davidson's tour of the [student] colonies.

[25] 'If I still had a feeling of respect for him.'

Plekhanov would have the last word, but nothing of the sort happened. The comrade who had the floor after Plekhanov gave up his turn to me, and Mr. Plekhanov was debunked and routed, and retreated in the most ignominious manner. Davidson did not even have the *Schlusswort*.[26] Terrific excitement. This had never happened in Switzerland before. Just think of it: Plekhanov, the favourite, the idol who is worshipped so, and Davidson, who had betrayed the Bund as well,[27] grovelling before him!

I was in the seventh heaven at having knocked out בלעם.[28] I had been looking for an opportunity to come to grips with Mr. P[lekhanov] for a long time, but as you know I would not set foot on his *terrain,* and here he thrust himself upon us, for the first and last time. I doubt whether I shall ever again be in such spirits as I was that evening. We had an almost sleepless night afterwards. The Zionists are jubilant. *Er hat sich eine Blösse gegeben.*[29]

I have received a letter from Blank about the Fund.[30] I do not like the appeal. Please let me know your attitude to it at once.

Until the next letter! Regards to Polya. Continuation will follow soon.

Yours,
Chaim

Aberson sends you his best regards.

145. To Aaron Eliasberg, Heidelberg. *Geneva, 28 November 1901*

Russian: Pcd.: H.W.A. and H.W.: W.A.

[The first part, in the handwriting of Anne Koenigsberg, is obviously a form letter sent to the various persons nominated by W. as suitable for appointment as delegates to the Fifth Zionist Congress—see Nos. 141, 143. The personal note commencing 'My dear Aaron' is in W.'s handwriting.]

28/xi. 01, Geneva
Rue Lombard 4

Comrade,

In reply to the Act[ions] Com[mittee]'s enquiry as to who pro-

---

[26] 'The last word.'

[27] As to Davidson's desertion of the Zionists for the Bundists see n. 4 to No. 55. After the Bund had, in the spring of 1901, adopted the 'national programme' referred to in n. 3 to that letter, Davidson left the Bund, joined the Russian Social-Democrats and took an active part on the anti-Bundist side in the internal ideological controversy which was eventually to result in a temporary severance of the link between the Bund and the Party.   [28] Hebr., 'Balaam'.

[29] 'He exposed himself'—There is a description of the debate in *Be-ikvot Habiluim* ('In the footsteps of the Biluim'), by A. Hermoni, Jerusalem, 1952, p. 92.

[30] See n. 20 to No. 140.

poses to be at the Congress as a delegate from here, we have listed several names, including yours. Let us know whether you agree to attend the Congress in that capacity, as the Act[ions] Com[mittee] will probably send the mandates.

My dear Aaron,

It's quite impossible to write at the moment. Don't be angry. Write when you intend to come.

I embrace you,

Yours,
Chaim

146. To Leo Motzkin, Berlin. *Geneva, 30 November 1901*

Russian: H.W.: C.Z.A.—A126/24/7/2/2

30/xi. 1901, Geneva
Rue Lombard 4

My dear Leo,

Thanks for the letter.[1] Unfortunately, I cannot write much now either, since there is an endless amount of work. Besides, I am not feeling well.

We have not written anything to *Hessiana* and have given no reasons; we merely informed them that we wished to ask for the opinion of the other members of the Bureau. We shall, of course, reject Syrkin. I myself remember the statement. It was written by him from Berne after his utter failure with the Berne group. At the time, I and Lichtenstein had a hand in the whole business.[2]

Yesterday I sent Kunin an *Eilbrief*[3] at your address with an earnest request to come. All this work is too much for me and if somebody doesn't help me I'll collapse before the Conference and

146. [1] Motzkin to W., 27 Nov. 1901, W.A., agreeing to *Hessiana* delegates taking part in the Youth Conference, but excluding Syrkin, who, he says, had announced in *Die Welt* his withdrawal from the Zionist Organization. Motzkin asked if an explanatory reply had been sent to *Hessiana*.—As to Syrkin's statement in *Die Welt*, 10 Feb. 1899, see n. 4 to No. 141.

[2] See n. 6 to No. 92 as to Syrkin's lecture to the Berne Zionist Students' Society in Dec. 1898, which sparked off the controversy leading to his above-mentioned statement of his position in *Die Welt*. W. and Abraham Lichtenstein had been prominent among those who protested against his animadversions on the Zionist Organization and on the Second Congress.

[3] 'express letter'.

shall not be able to take part. Aberson is not a man for careful work. *Auf ihn ist kein Verlass.*[4] In view of the fact that K[unin] is coming to the Conference in any case, he ought to get here some two weeks earlier.

Dubosarsky[5] told me that you are thinking of not coming. Leo, I don't want to persuade you, but this would be a blow to the whole venture. No reasons can be valid. The case demands it. We cannot manage without our best comrades. You must realise that I am neither paying you compliments nor trying to be modest. I may be a good *Registriermaschine*,[6] I even have my own views on things, but you, my dear friend, you are the brains.[7] I, for one, will feel dreadful if you do not come.[8]

Am awaiting news from you. My regards to Polya. See that Kunin leaves. All the best,

Ever yours,
Chaim

147. To Leo Motzkin, Berlin. *Geneva, 9 December 1901*

German: T.: C.Z.A.—A126/24/7/2/2

[Though there is no doubt as to the general sense of the telegram in the light of its background, its obscure wording does not admit of a confident translation.]

Extremely perturbed distress due to misunderstandings[1] letters on the way Weizmann Kunin[2]

---

[4] 'There is no relying on him.'   [5] Secretary of the Berlin *Kadimah*.
[6] 'recording machine'.
[7] The words here translated 'you are the brains' could equally well mean 'you are the leader' the same Russian word meaning 'head' in either of these senses.
[8] In the event, Motzkin did attend the Conference.

---

147. [1] Motzkin had on 7 Dec. telegraphed to W. (W.A.) demanding that the Geneva Organization Bureau should circulate a statement explaining that, through a mistake on the part of the Bureau, his name had been included among the speakers at the Youth Conference in the agenda contained in the Circular mentioned on n. 23 to No. 144. In a letter to W. of the same date (W.A.) Motzkin, referring to his telegram, had protested against his name having been included without his permission and had told W. that he would not attend the Conference.

[2] See W.'s letter of 9 Dec. (No. 148). In addition, Lazare Kunin, who, as suggested by W. (see No. 146), had come from Berlin to Geneva to assist him in the preparations for the Youth Conference, had written to Motzkin on 7 Dec. and wrote to him again on 9 Dec., appealing to him to attend the Conference and not to insist on such a statement as he had demanded—see above n. 1—being circulated by the Bureau (both letters in C.Z.A.—A126/24/7/2/3).

148. To Leo Motzkin, Berlin. *Geneva, 9 December 1901*

Russian: H.W.: C.Z.A.—A126/24/7/2/2

9/XII. 1901, Geneva
r. Lombard 4

Dear Leo

I have received both your letter[1] and your telegram.[2] My telegram[3] went off today before yours arrived. I cannot possibly describe my agitation, with every moment bringing new alarms, new disappointments. I assure you, I hadn't the slightest desire to 'do you a bad turn'.[4] I could not, cannot, and never will be able to think that you may not attend the Conference.

And since you are going to be present,[5] I imagine that you will take part in the debates, especially on the economic issue, on which, in my view, no comprehensive paper can be or ought to be read this year.

The debates will serve as a directive to the future *rapporteur* who will be able to present a paper in a year's time. When I published an agenda in the *Welt*,[6] I merely wrote: *Einleitung in die Discussion von*[7] *den Herren Feiwel, Farbst[ein], Mozkin, Idelson,* bearing in mind all those who might have a word of their own to say on the problem.

The note appended to the circular letter was added with this in mind, that is to say that you are not bound by it.[8] There is no sense in distributing the circular[9] now, as it will not achieve its object; it could go out tomorrow, but even if it had been sent two days ago, it would have been too late.[10]

148. [1] See n. 1 to No. 147.

[2] The reference appears to be to a second telegram from Motzkin, who, in a letter to Kunin dated 9 Dec. 1901 (W.A.) and written after he had received Kunin's letter of 7 Dec. (see n. 2 to No. 147), said that he had just sent a telegram repeating his demand for the circulation of a statement correcting the reference to himself in the Youth Conference agenda.   [3] No. 147.

[4] The words 'do you a bad turn' are not a quotation from Motzkin's letter; W. puts them in quotation-marks merely—it would seem—because he is using a colloquialism.

[5] i.e., though you say that you will not come, I know you will.

[6] 'When I published the agenda . . .'—W. must mean 'When I sent the agenda for publication . . .' for it was not, in fact, published in *Die Welt* until after the date of this letter, viz. on 13 Dec.

[7] 'Discussion introduced by . . .' Names reproduced as spelt in orig.

[8] In sending a copy of the circular containing the agenda, with list of speakers, Kunin had explained: 'This does not bind you to anything': C.Z.A.—A126/24/7/2/3, undated, but obviously sent shortly before Motzkin's letter of 7 Dec. to W. mentioned in n. 1 to No. 147, in which he wrote: 'I have just received your circular . . .'.

[9] By 'the circular' W. must mean the supplementary circular demanded by Motzkin.

[10] 'too late'—presumably because a correction would not have reached the Russian delegates before their departure for Basle.

The exact formulation of the *Tagesordnung*[11] will be worked out before the Conference. I will do anything, anything—even at the expense of my pride—to see that not the slightest slur is cast on you. I repeat—all the awkwardness is simply imaginary. But I'll do anything. How can you make such an insignificant thing a condition of your coming at this terribly responsible time, when every man is so valuable, when we have to rally all our people? How can you press me so urgently for what seems to me no more than a trifle, at a time when everything that goes wrong falls upon me? How can you suspect me of wanting to place you in an awkward position? I hope to see you and then we shall clear everything up.

I cannot write any more now. I am too tired and edgy.

Best regards to Polya.

Yours,
Chaim

[Postscript by Zina Kunin.]

[The Zionist Youth Conference, at which W. delivered the inaugural address, met at Basle on 18–23 Dec. 1901 on the eve of the Fifth Zionist Congress, which opened there on 26 Dec. No complete record of the proceedings has come to light, but there are incomplete sets of Minutes in W.A. and in C.Z.A.— A126/24/5/2. There is also in C.Z.A. (A137/5 ; A24/16) a 'Protocol' setting out the principles agreed upon by the Conference as 'a guide to the framing of the programme of the Zionist Democratic Fraction'. The contents of the Protocol are summarized in the Introduction to this Volume (p. 25), from which it will be seen that the main results of the Conference were: (i) the formation, under the name of 'The Democratic Fraction', of an organized group of Zionists committed to the principles propounded in the Protocol; (ii) the setting up at Geneva of a Democratic Fraction Information Bureau, to be directed by W. ; (iii) the Fraction's successful advocacy, at the 1901 Congress, of a resolution recognizing cultural work as an indispensable part of the Zionist programme (text in 5 Z.C. Prot. p. 427), the acceptance of this principle being emphasized by the appointment of a strong Cultural Commission.—In the event, the results of the Youth Conference were disappointing. The Cultural Commission made no perceptible contribution to the development of cultural work. The Democratic Fraction never got properly on its feet, and by the summer of 1904 had disintegrated, though not without leaving its mark on Zionist thinking.

There being no exact English equivalent, in this context, of the word '*Fraktion*', meaning more than a group and rather less than a Party, it has been thought best to speak throughout of 'the Democratic Fraction'.

Among the W. letters which have been found there are none describing or commenting upon either the Youth Conference or the 1901 Zionist Congress. This is not as surprising as it might appear when it is remembered that while these meetings were in progress W. was in personal contact at Basle with Motzkin and others of his principal Zionist friends.]

[11] 'agenda'.

149. To Vera Khatzman, Geneva. *Clarens, 2 January* [*1902*]

Russian: Pcd.: H.W.: W.A.

[W.'s '1901' is a slip for '1902': Clarens pmk. 2 Jan. 1902.]

Clarens, 2/I. 1901

Verochka, the weather here is terrible, and we shall be in Geneva tomorrow at 7 p.m. at the latest.

All the best, darling,

Au revoir. There is no need to send money.

Chaim

150. To Leo Motzkin, Berlin. *Geneva, 14 January 1902*

Russian: H.W.: C.Z.A.—A126/24/7/2/2

[While the Fifth Zionist Congress was in session at Basle at the end of Dec. 1901, certain delegates met privately, at the instance of Nahman Syrkin, for a confidential exchange of views on a proposal for organizing in some of the principal Jewish centres, and more particularly in London, demonstrations against the Jewish Colonization Association, with the object of putting pressure on that body to provide financial support for Zionist activities. Syrkin's idea made some appeal to W.—see W.'s letter to Motzkin of 23 Nov. 1901 [No. 144], in which he says that one of the tasks of the Youth Organization must be 'peacefully or by revolutionary methods to influence I.C.A.'. Despite his reservations about Syrkin and his activities (see, for example, Nos. 140, 146), W. joined in the discussions initiated by Syrkin, and so did some other members of the newly-formed Democratic Fraction. Its Berlin members, who had not been consulted, considered that this constituted a serious breach of discipline and in a resolution passed on 9 Jan. 1902 (copy in W.A.) registered their protest against the participation of members of the Fraction, without the knowledge of their fellow-members, in discussions to which Syrkin, an outsider, was a party; they further demanded that their protest should be brought to the notice of the whole membership of the Fraction. It is to this controversy that W. refers in the letter under notice, Motzkin being a leading member of the Berlin group. In the end, the Fraction's Geneva Information Bureau circulated the Berlin protest as a confidential appendix to its news-letter No. 3 (18 Mar. 1902), a rejoinder being subsequently circulated in No. 4 (20 Apr.).]

cop.[1]   Geneva, 14/I. 1902

4 rue Lombard

Confidential

Dear Leo,

'יראתי בפצותי שיח להשחיל'[2] **To** tell you the truth, I really don't

150. [1] 'cop.' (in orig. in latin characters), obviously standing for *copie* or *copieren* is in W.'s handwriting and in the same ink as the text of the letter—i.e. it was not inserted by someone other than W., or by W. at some later date. It may possibly signify that a copy is to be made before the letter is dispatched, but what it is intended to convey is uncertain.

[2] Hebr., 'I tremble when I open my mouth to utter my words'—quoted from a

know in what tone to write; so much remained unsaid after our last meeting, and now this makes itself keenly felt. Kohan-B[ernstein] told me in his last letter from Berlin that you would be writing to me. I was waiting for your letter very impatiently, but what a disappointment. Instead of your letter, there came your protest, which startled me both by its content and by its whole tone. But even after the protest I did not lose hope of getting at least a few words from you. They have not come and so I write; I write not knowing how to speak or to whom. Quite frankly, I am at a loss, I do not understand, I do not understand a thing. Can everything have changed so much? Is everything forgotten, scorned, destroyed?

Has this protest slipped out only on the spur of a moment's indignation, a thing I could well understand, assuming that you have been misinformed? Or is this protest the result of a carefully considered strategy? I don't know and I don't understand. One thing alone is clear to me: it can, and will, have disastrous consequences. I shall, of course, do everything in my power to clear the matter up, for the affairs of the Fraction are dear to my heart. Everything that was created at the Youth Conference is dear to me, if only because I have put the best of myself into this venture and am prepared in the future to give all my strength for the sake of the sacred cause and its success. But there is one thing I must assert. If anything can kill energy in a man, it is a relationship such as has now been established between us who, I should like to think, used to entertain at least friendly feelings for one another. You knew that I was the head of the Information Bureau, yet I have to protest against this 'I'.[3] If you all insist, I shall, of course, make this protest public, but at the same time shall give my own explanation as well. For me personally, this affair cannot and will not have any further consequences: but what the other members of the Fraction involved in this[4] will have to say—I do not know. I imagine them to be of a less peaceable disposition, and that is why I think that your action is fraught with disastrous consequences for our common cause. If you did not mean to 'protest' against us, but to point out, for the sake of the cause, the error we have made— was an 'official' protest really necessary? Could not a simple

passage in the Jewish New Year liturgy. For the use of the same phrase in earlier letters to Motzkin see Nos. 44, 94.

[3] i.e., by publishing the Berlin resolution, W., as head of the Bureau, would be associating himself with a protest against his own conduct.

[4] Others besides W. associated with the D.F. who took part in the Syrkin discussions included Aberson, Abramovich, Bukhmil, Gourland, Nemser, Perelman, and Sheinkin.

friendly exchange of views have preceded this drastic irrevocable step? Could you not have found some way of having it out with me otherwise than through the Information Bureau? Is it possible that you have acted on the spur of the moment? Did you really think that I might refuse you a reply to your enquiry?

In brief, I see in that tone of yours a breach of comradely, friendly relations. God grant I may be wrong.

As to the protest itself, it is essentially devoid of all foundation and meaning. צל הרים ראיתי כהרים[5] You are all fighting something that does not exist. I do not know how and what you have learned from this whole incriminating affair. I declare, however:

(1) You could not lawfully have learned a thing. A number of secret consultative meetings took place in Basle. All those present at the meetings were bound upon their honour not to divulge anything. Whoever talked, broke his oath.

(2) I was invited to this meeting: the initiative was not mine.

(3) When I was told of the entire plan, which seemed to me splendid, not contradicting my own convictions, not contradicting general Zionist tactics, and not running counter to the activities of the Democr[atic] Fraction, but on the contrary directly furthering them, I agreed to take part in the consultative meetings.

(4) There can be no talk of any public action so far, since for the time being the whole matter is in the debating stage.

(5) I declare furthermore *en âme et conscience* that I would not have taken any public step without consulting the Fraction and without asking their specific permission, being fully aware that my action might be interpreted as a step taken on behalf of the Fraction as a whole. But haven't I the right to talk about a matter which is not at variance with my conscience and my convictions and which needs as little publicity as possible; haven't I the right to do so without asking the Fraction?

(6) The discussions with Herzl[6] were not on behalf of the Fraction. He knew that the Fraction had nothing to do with it.

(7) We all took part in these consultations as individuals, as private people who had been invited. Where then is the

[5] Hebr., 'You saw a mountain where there was only the shadow of a mountain'—an adaptation of Judges ix. 36: 'Thou seest the shadow of the mountains as if they were men.'

[6] Syrkin, together with Bukhmil, had tried unsuccessfully to secure Herzl's endorsement of the proposal for anti-I.C.A. demonstrations: see *Herzl Diaries*, iii. 1192.

breach of discipline ? Where then is the harmony of our work broken ? Why all this *Scharfmacherei* ?[7]

(8) In view of the points mentioned above, and also taking into account that it has not yet been decided in principle whether a member of the Fraction—as a private individual—has the right to take part in any <u>honourable</u> matter without asking the permission of the Fraction; bearing in mind that it has not yet been decided in respect of all possible ventures which of these is permissible and which not; in view of the fact that our Fraction has not yet determined the essential questions of tactics; and also bearing in mind that this matter demands caution and, in my view, cannot and must not—at present and for a long time to come—be made public even to all circles of the Fraction, I consider that I have not committed any *Verstoss*[8] either formally or in substance against discipline and comradeship within the Fraction as a political association.

Here are the arguments that I can advance in reply. It may well be that I am wrong, but there is nothing disastrous in that. I can only understand that you might all have been indignant to learn that S[yrkin] is involved in this business: this I do understand. But do tell me, please: if I am invited and shown a plan that I fully approve, must I refuse to discuss it just because it originates from S[yrkin], whom I consider an honest man and a Zionist—a conviction that I have just had the opportunity to strengthen at Basle, having observed him closely ? I repeat, I can understand the indignation of all of you, but surely this is only a momentary indignation; it must give way to sensible reflection. Finally, the whole affair is not a trifling matter. I am really ready to drop everything, to go to New York or London and start Zionist propaganda there. I am ready to do all this without delay, if everything is ripe for it. I have proved by my work that I am able to do anything that seems to me expedient and useful for the cause. Is it really necessary, just like this, to reproach a man for his willingness to do some work, moreover responsible work, where *die ganze Person*[9] is at stake ?

I am going to tell you this too: <u>I am ready to carry out this work even at the risk of my life, for I consider it to be the greatest cause.</u> Only I have to ascertain for myself how this would influence general Zionist affairs. This is why I thought it was essential to

---

[7] 'agitation'.   [8] 'offence'.   [9] 'his whole being'.

consult Herzl;[10] this is why I would not have taken one single step without first consulting a small circle of true comrades in the Fraction. I think I have said everything. You can judge for yourself now, and I am convinced that knowing my attitude to you, knowing that I never conceal my innermost thoughts from you, knowing that it has always hurt me to think that there was something unsaid between us, and that I have now freed myself from it like a nightmare by having told you the most difficult part[11] through K[ohan]-B[ernstein], knowing all the answers, you must not and cannot condemn your already exhausted friend

Chaim

151. To Leo Motzkin, Berlin. *Geneva, 20 January* [1902]

Russian: Vcd.: H.W.: C.Z.A.—A126/24/7/2/2

[It is clear from the contents that W.'s '1901' is a slip for '1902'.]

Geneva, 20/I. 1901

cop.[1]

Dear Leo,

I don't know how to explain your silence. Don't you understand that this worries me so much that it deprives me of any will to work?

We have run off the first news-letter;[2] it is a very miserable affair, as we had not received any information from anywhere. I am sending you a resolution sent here by Jewish students. The incident is not settled yet. It is disgusting.[3] What's new in Berlin as far as we are concerned? I am awaiting your early reply. Please tell Kunin that Koenigsberg is asking for money to be sent[4] out of

---

[10] See above, n. 6.

[11] 'the most difficult part' is, in all probability, the communication of the news of the breaking-off of W.'s engagement to Sophia Getzova. The Motzkins were close friends of hers.

151. [1] See n. 1 to No. 150.

[2] The Democratic Fraction's Geneva Bureau's first newsletter, No. 1, dated 24 Jan. 1902 (copy in W.A.).

[3] A resolution passed at a meeting of Geneva Jewish students on 15 Jan. 1902, condemning those students who had associated themselves with a public protest against a message in complimentary terms telegraphed by Herzl to the Sultan Abdul Hamid on 25 Dec. 1901, immediately before the opening of the Fifth Zionist Congress: for the background to the resolution and its sequel see head-note to No. 155.

[4] For the Geneva Information Bureau. It can be inferred that Lazare Kunin was acting as Treasurer of the Berlin D.F. Group.

funds of the Fraction. Are you writing your article?[5] Write at once

to yours
Chaim

Mr. L. Motzkin
  Berlin.

152. To Leo Motzkin, Berlin. *Geneva, 31 January 1902*

Russian: H.W.: C.Z.A.—A126/24/7/2/2

Geneva, 31/I. 1902
Rue Lombard 4

Dear Leo,

I have received your letter of the 29th,[1] and I was very glad to hear from you, for I prefer a letter full of reproaches, even if very

---

[5] There is nothing in any earlier letter which has been preserved to show what is meant by 'Your article', but M. had apparently undertaken to write an article on some subject connected with the Democratic Fraction. There is in C.Z.A. (A126/24/7/2/2) a draft, dated 28 Jan. 1902, of a letter in which Motzkin tells W. (*inter alia*) that he will shortly be sending him his [M.'s] paper on the Fifth Congress and the Democratic Fraction, probably meaning the text of a lecture given by him at a *Kadimah* meeting in Berlin on 18 Jan.—the lecture, mentioning the date and venue, is referred to in a letter of 30 Jan. from Pevsner and Motzkin to W. (W.A.). The text of the lecture may have been intended by Motzkin as a substitute for the promised article. Though the letter itself, as distinct from the draft, has not been found, it is clear from No. 152 (see n. 1 to that letter) that it was received by W., who may well have been referring to it when he wrote, in his letter of 2 March 1902 (No. 161): 'I have been waiting for your report.' On 12 March Motzkin wrote to W. (W.A.): 'I shall shortly deliver the article on the Democratic Fraction and the press', probably meaning press attacks on the D.F.—see n. 6 to No. 156. There is, however, no evidence of W.'s having ever received either the 'report' or an article based on it. On 13 Apr., some five weeks after hearing from M. that he would 'shortly deliver the article', W. told him (No. 193) that a Democratic Fraction meeting had decided that it was essential to have an article on the Fraction and asked whether he would write it. M. did not, in fact, produce any article on the D.F. at that time, but later in the year he contributed a paper on the subject to the 5563 (1902–3) edition of *Luah Ahiasaf* ('The Ahiasaf Yearbook') published by the Warsaw Hebrew publishing firm of that name.

152. [1] This letter has not been found, but there is in C.Z.A. (A126—24/7/2/2) a draft, dated 28 Jan. 1902, being the draft mentioned, in another context, in n. 5 to No. 151, in which Motzkin, rejecting the arguments and explanations in W.'s letter of 14 Jan. (No. 150), makes the following points: (1) W.'s protestations of loyalty to the Democratic Fraction strike him as ironical, since the 'new Fraction' [i.e. the group centred round Syrkin] is wrecking the D.F.; it has not 'discovered America' [i.e. it has no new ideas]—what it is doing is to disrupt the organization of the democratic elements in the Zionist Movement. (2) The D.F.'s discipline must be submitted to if the Fraction is not to be reduced to a nullity. (3) W. had, therefore, no right to give his word to keep his fellow-members of the D.F. in ignorance of his discussions with Syrkin. (4) Syrkin has informed the Bund that he stands outside the Zionist Organization,

bitter, partly undeserved and cruel, to the silence with which you and Kunin have until now answered my letters and telegrams.[2] I did startle you at Basle; surely you cannot be still thinking of our polemic? Is it really possible that you have not yet forgotten it? Can you believe even for a second that I meant to refer to you personally? Even if some harsh words escaped me, do you really know me so little as to think that they concealed a desire to do you any wrong?

Do you know, I had a feeling at Basle that you were not quite at ease in my presence, that you sensed something hostile in me: God be my witness, this was my very last thought. I pushed away this idea, this feeling, though at times I felt an acute pain which poisoned those joyful moments which the work of Basle gave me. I never considered you otherwise than as a friend and a teacher. I fear these words may make you smile, but I shall say only this: you do not know me, you do not know how I look at things. Indeed, we have hardly seen each other in recent years. I repeat: I was bitterly, bitterly hurt in Basle by a great many small things in your attitude towards me, but I did not want, nor do I wish now, to raise this any more; let it die a natural death.

We have known each other and worked together for nine years. Is one instant sufficient to destroy everything? And finally— Basle. Did you not notice the state I was in? You cannot imagine what I had to go through. Even beforehand there was so much distress, so much excitement, that I only kept going during the Conference because I was so worked up and elated. I repeat again: should twenty or more such polemical skirmishes occur, my attitude to you—as to a human being and friend—will not waver. May all the saints protect me: in debate I always hit hard.

which makes it all the more incomprehensible that W. should have entered into a secret pact with him. (5) As to his (Motzkin's) personal relations with W., this is a subject which he must decline to discuss, so outraged does he feel by W.'s behaviour at Basle.—As to the last point, it is evident that Motzkin bitterly resented W.'s comments on his speech at the Youth Conference (W. himself acknowledges, in the letter under notice, that 'some harsh words escaped me'), the burden of W.'s criticism having been, as appears from the minutes of the Conference, (a) that Motzkin was wrong in suggesting that the Democratic Fraction should undertake cultural work independently of the Zionist Organization—its object, in W.'s view, should be to press for a Congress resolution in favour of cultural activity; (b) that Motzkin's suggestion that the Zionists should take a hand in the organization of Jewish workers on Trade Union lines begged the question whether they should get involved in the domestic politics of the countries concerned.—As to Motzkin's reference to Syrkin's having told the Bund that he (Syrkin) stood outside the Zionist Organization, nothing further is known of this; Motzkin gives no details, nor has any information on the subject come to light from any other source.

[2] See W.'s letters to Motzkin of 14 and 20 Jan. (Nos. 150, 151). No telegram to Motzkin has been found, nor has any letter or telegram to Kunin.

Let us turn now to the ill-starred protest.[3] My claim that the affairs of the Fraction are dear to my heart seems ironical to you. No one could have thought of a more cruel insult than this. And it is you who say this to me, knowing how much work I put into the whole business of the Conference. What did I do this for? Merely to smash it afterwards with one blow? Or for yet another reason perhaps? I am sure, Leo, that you have not considered the whole bitterness of that terrible undeserved reproach hurled at a man who has spent so much energy and time on a cause which he has served, and is ready to serve, with his whole being. You are unfair, and I should like to shout this to everybody—to all those who so lightly hurl reproaches of this kind.

You are right about one thing, and I admit it: I should not have given my word of honour. But in this instance I did not transgress the discipline of the Fraction, but only my relationship with you. In fact, of course, I did not break this either, but I did give others ground to suspect a breach; I say others and not you, for [you] should have known that I would never betray you in the slightest. But let me tell you, and I confirm this by all that is sacred, that I was so preoccupied at the time that I did not even stop to think of this; and what is more important, no Fraction was formed.[4] This is really ridiculous. I repeat, we discussed propaganda against I.C.A., but in such manner that it could [not] *Anstoss erregen*;[5] in brief, we talked of the most peaceful matters. Of course, nobody 'discovered America',[6] and we should not have reached the stage of any public action without the consent of the Fraction. If S[yrkin] stands up and declares that he is placing himself outside the Zion[ist] Organiz[ation], then I can have no dealings with him at all. But I did not know about this. I protest, however, against the phrase 'behind the back' of the Fraction. I am not afraid of what I am doing and am always ready to answer for my actions. The assumption that any one of us wished to by-pass the Fraction, or its individual members, is wrong; this is the last thing we were thinking of. 'My secret alliance with S', as you put it, *das klingt gefährlich*.[7] But surely I don't have to repeat again that you are

---

[3] The Berlin protest mentioned in the head-note to No. 150.

[4] As a result of the discussions set in motion by Syrkin, it was decided that steps should be taken to organize a group to be called *Cheirus* (Hebr., 'Freedom') for the purpose of carrying on the projected anti-I.C.A. campaign. Reports of this decision may have reached Motzkin and may help to account for his complaints, in the letter summarized in n. 1 above, about the formation (here denied by W.) of a 'new Fraction' calculated to undermine the Democratic Fraction.

[5] 'give offence'. It is obvious from the context that W. meant to say 'could not.'

[6] See n. 1 above.   [7] 'that sounds dangerous'.

exaggerating and that you were misinformed by the person who told you about this whole business. All those insulting phrases seem unjustified to me. Once again, you are right: knowing S[yrkin]'s attitude to you all and to you in particular,[8] I had no right to talk to him at all even for reasons of personal friendship. But the mistake has been made, and it did happen because, when I was invited, I was hardly thinking of who was inviting me, but rather for what purpose I was being asked. You did not learn this from me because I was bound to silence and would not have spoken of it until it was actually necessary to act. It is my profound conviction that this plan would in no way have affected the course of Zion[ist] propaganda in general, and of the Fraction in particular, but there was no point in speaking of things that were without firm foundation. I am only profoundly distressed and grieved that I acted rashly in discussing this whole matter with S[yrkin], but God be my witness, *Es war gut gemeint.*[9] I do regret, however, that not only you, but everyone from B[erlin] thought it necessary to turn away from me. They have committed a wrong, and a very serious one—something I should not like to have on my own conscience.

Now one more word—the last—about the protest. You all insist on its being printed: what are you trying to achieve by this? Do you want to have us branded? Do you want the good of the Fraction? Do you want to teach us discipline? 'Many will regret that things are starting with a split.' If, of course, you are talking about a Fraction within the Fraction, then we are dissenters, but if this is not so, and it definitely is not, then we are not dissenters, and I declare that your protest will have lamentable results: it will blow up the Fraction and throw to the winds everything that has started to take shape. You are throwing a bombshell without taking into consideration that it will wreck the entire venture. I shall wait to publish the thing until Monday night.[10] Please send me a telegram saying whether you insist on it or not.[11]

This letter will reach you on Monday morning. I do not know about the other members of the I[nformation] B[ureau], but I am in favour of publishing [the protest] if you do not retract your demands. I think the question itself can be discussed at the next conference.[12] For the time being, of course, no steps should be taken.

[8] Probably a reference to the strained relations between Syrkin's '*Hessiana*' and the Berlin *Kadimah*, of which Motzkin was a leading member.

[9] 'it was well meant'.

[10] The protest was not, in fact, published by the Geneva Information Bureau until 18 Mar. 1902—see head-note to No. 150.

[11] No such telegram has been found, and it appears from No. 161 that none was sent.

[12] The projected Democratic Fraction Conference.

Good-bye. In conclusion, I should like to express my fervent wish to put an end to all this. It hurts.

Yours,
Chaim

And more about my health. *Danke für die Nachfrage.*[13] It's not good. As a matter of fact I went to see the doctor yesterday. He diagnosed neurasthenia and weakness of the respiratory organs. *Uebermüdung u[nd] Ueberreizung.*[14] He told me to go to Nice or Davos. Unfortunately, I am unable to do so at the moment: first, I am short of money, and secondly, there is plenty to do in the laboratory and even more outside. Moreover, there is a great deal of local work with which I did not deal before the Conference and which I want to catch up with. A Zion[ist] stud[ent] circle, *Hashahar*,[15] has been founded here; it celebrates its opening today. I shall read a paper on 'The rôle of stud[ent] Zion[ist] groups and their rôle in the colonies[16] abroad'. There has been a great deal of excitement here because of the telegram.[17] I am unable to feel indifferent about the loathsome thing. In two weeks' time I shall go to Munich and Karlsruhe and lecture there on Zionism. I have already been invited a number of times. I am going to devote the Easter vacation to rest, but shall pay a call at Elberfeld (at my factory—not really mine),[18] and from there, without fail, I shall go on to Berlin, because I want to discuss everything personally. I cannot reconcile myself to the thought that any shadow should come between us.

My lab[oratory] work is going very well. I shall soon publish a whole series of very interesting research papers.[19]

Regards to Polya.

Ch.

[13] 'Thanks for the enquiry.'

[14] 'over-fatigue and over-excitement'.

[15] A Zionist student society formed in Geneva as a sequel to the division of opinion among Jewish students about Herzl's telegram to the Sultan, as to which see n. 3 to No. 151 and head-note to No. 155.

[16] i.e., the student 'colonies'.

[17] the telegram referred to in n. 15 above.

[18] In orig., 'that is to say, not mine' added below the line, the effect being the same as if W. had written ' "my" factory'.

[19] Nothing is known of these research papers, unless, as is not improbable, they can be taken to be the series of papers by W., jointly with Deichler, mentioned in n. 17 to No. 95 as having been published in 1903 in the Bulletins of the German Chemical Society.

153. To Leo Motzkin, Berlin. [*Geneva, 1 February 1902*]

German: T.: C.Z.A.—A126/24/7/2/2

[Date and place of origin as shown on telegram.]

You are cordially invited inaugural celebration Zionist student society *Hashahar*[1]—Weizmann.

154. To Theodor Herzl, Vienna. [*Geneva, 2 February 1902*]

German: T.: C.Z.A.—Z1/330

[Date and place of origin as shown on telegram.]

Festive assembly newly founded Zionist student society *Hashahar*[1] greets the Zionists' honoured leader—

Weizmann President

155. To Theodor Herzl, Vienna. *Geneva, 3 February 1902*

German: H.W.: C.Z.A.—Z1/329

[On the eve of the Fifth Zionist Congress, Herzl telegraphed to the Sultan Abdul Hamid (25 December 1901) an expression of 'the deep devotion and gratitude which all Jews feel for the benevolence always shown to them by His Imperial Majesty the Sultan' (trans. from the orig. French: full text in *Herzl Diaries*, iii. 1189). The fact that Herzl had sent a complimentary message to the Sultan did not become publicly known until 28 December, when, without disclosing the exact terms of his telegram, he communicated to the Congress the text of a telegram, signed by a Turkish Court Official, thanking him for his message and expressing the Sultan's gratification (5 Z.C. Prot. 173). This appeared the next day in the press reports of the Congress. On 30 December students of various nationalities, meeting in Geneva, passed a resolution protesting indignantly against Herzl's deferential gesture towards 'the arch-assassin Abdul Hamid', and expressing contempt for the Zionist Congress. It was resolved to telegraph the text of the resolution to Herzl, and this was done. On returning after the Congress from Basle to Geneva, W. and his friends induced some Russian and Polish students to dissociate themselves publicly from the resolution, and convened a meeting of Jewish students which, on 15 January 1902, recorded its condemnation of those Jews who had joined in the protest against Herzl's telegram, charging them with besmirching the honour of the Jewish people. On 21 January *Le Genevois* published an article by Bernard-Lazare disapproving of Herzl's telegram and describing it as characteristic of the 'ghetto politics' of the Zionist leadership. A further meeting, on 28 January, of students in sympathy with the protest resolution

153. [1] See n. 15 to No. 152.

154. [1] See n. 15 to No. 152.

of 30 December was followed by a counter-demonstration at a meeting of Jewish nationalist students on 12 February.—Copies of all the above resolutions, and of Bernard-Lazare's article, are in C.Z.A.—Z1/94. All the resolutions, except that of 15 January, were published in *La Tribune de Genève*.]

Geneva, 3/II. 1902
4, rue Lombard

Dr. Theodor Herzl,
Vienna.

Dear Dr. [Herzl],

I hope you will forgive me for troubling you with a local Zionist matter.

I refer to the unpleasant business of the protest which was started by the students here and has already gone the rounds of various papers. We were all still in Basle when a meeting took place at which a number of Jewish and non-Jewish students passed a resolution—which you may know of—expressing the contempt of these individuals for the Congress. The preamble to the resolution was, of course, not lacking in distortions of fact and calumnies of every kind. On our return from Basle, we called a meeting of the Jewish nationalist students and passed a resolution in which we came out against the rumours which had been spread during our absence and the attitude of the student colony. We also induced some of the Polish and Russian[1] students to declare in the press that the hostile resolution did not represent the opinion of all the students here.

I enclose a German translation of the resolution passed at the Jewish meeting.[2] We have not had it printed yet, but I shall certainly get it printed in the form of an article for the Jewish newspapers.[3] The resolution will be very warmly welcomed by all Zionist student societies in Germany.

Then came Bernard-Lazare's article, which was first printed in 'Pro-Armenia' and then in our local, very influential, *Genevois*, the organ of the Radical Party. There was again a big meeting and a second resolution was passed—a reply in part to ours. I enclose the French text; it was only published yesterday.

We cannot now, I think, ignore the matter. We are, of course, in a position to make the motives of the meeting abundantly clear: those present were mainly anti-nationalists and anti-semites (Greeks and Rumanians), people who, on principle, consider any and every national movement objectionable; the Jews are out-

---

155. [1] In orig. *echtrussischer*, meaning Russians as distinct from Russian Jews.

[2] Text of the translation in C.Z.A.—Z1/94.

[3] No such article was, in fact, published.

and-out assimilationists; they can also be branded for their flirtation with the anti-semites. But should we answer by giving them the facts of the case? Should we explain that the toadyism we are accused of is based on a malicious distortion of the facts, that the telegram to the Sultan is to be taken as an act of diplomatic courtesy? Frankly, I am afraid of embarking on this sort of thing lest I should make an awkward slip somewhere. If you are in favour of our entering into explanations here, might I ask you if you would be good enough to draft the relevant passage of the resolution for me? We shall then include it in our resol[ution]. Should some reply, perhaps, be made to B.-L.? There is need of one.

In the Jewish press we shall, of course, tell these gentlemen the plain truth, but for non-Jewish public opinion the shortest, sharpest answer possible is enough. This is a responsible step, as I am sure you will agree, and I therefore beg you not to refuse us your support in this matter. These pieces of impertinence cannot be allowed to go entirely unanswered.

I shall await your reply with impatience.[4] We must make haste.

With Zion's greetings, I am,
Yours faithfully,
Dr. Ch. Weizmann

2 Enclosures.

156. To Ahad Ha'am (Asher Ginzberg), Odessa.
Geneva, 5 February 1902
Russian: H.W.: Ahad Ha'am Papers, N.L.

Geneva, 5. II. 1902
Rue Lombard 4

Dear comrade,

I have been intending to write to you for some time. It's terrible to think how much has happened since we last met. The work of arranging the Conference, the Congress, all the preparatory and preliminary work, the alarms and the worries, and on top of it all I am but a עבד כנעני[1] in the laboratory—all this did not give me a chance to sit down quietly and write to you. I didn't feel like writing to you in bits and pieces. There is still a great deal to do, but, thank Heaven, times are more peaceful. First of all, one official

---

[4] No reply from Herzl has been found. The resolution adopted by the Jewish nationalist students at their meeting on 12 February 1902 (see head-note) was on the lines tentatively proposed in W.'s letter.

156. [1] Hebr., 'Canaanite slave'.

message: a Zionist student group, 'השחר'[2] has at last been founded here in Geneva, במקום הרשע.[3] A ceremonial inauguration of the group took place on Saturday, February 2nd.[4] At this meeting it was decided to send you a telegram of greeting, as follows: 'The Geneva *Hashahar* group extends its greetings to the dear and only Ahad Ha'am, and wishes him long and glorious service to the national cause.' At the same time it was decided to inform you of the text of the telegram by letter, and to present the amount saved to the National Fund,[5] which was done. In wholeheartedly associating myself with this greeting, I am at the same time carrying out a pleasant task entrusted to me by our new group.

You have undoubtedly been following the press, and have been able to form some idea of the decisions of the Conference. I am, of course, referring only to the decisions, as these were reported more or less correctly. Everything else was distorted with shocking irresponsibility and cynicism. Those who mourn for the Jewish people, like Kleinman and Slousch, have done their best to poison public opinion and showered abuse and slander upon us.[6] But I have no doubt that reading even these quasi-reports, you were able to discover in them a *Körnchen Salz*,[7] which is important in this case. Moreover, I happen to know that Klausner has written an account for *Hashiloah*, which, incidentally, I am awaiting impatiently. K[lausner] wrote to me to say that it will appear in the January issue.[8] I hope to read your appreciation as well in the near future. My general mood is better now. Do you know, this is the first time this year that I have felt we are fulfilling our Jewish civic duty. Our group has infused a new and purifying spirit into the Organization as a whole and the cause as a whole. It was not yet quite prepared, it still suffered a great deal from having to do a lot of improvisation in its attitude to many questions at the Congress, but

---

[2] *Hashahar*.   [3] Hebr., 'this centre of evil'.
[4] See No. 154 and n. 15 to No. 152.   [5] The Jewish National Fund.
[6] The founders of the Democratic Fraction had been attacked and derided by Nahum Slousch in *Hamelitz*, 21 Jan./3 Feb. 1902, and by Moses Kleinman in two series of articles in the same paper, commencing respectively 11/24 Dec. 1901 and 17/30 Jan. 1902. Referring to the Geneva students' protest against Herzl's telegram to the Sultan (see head-note to No. 155), Slousch taunted the Young Zionists with their failure to convince their gentile friends that Zionism was 'democratic' and described them contemptuously as 'the heroes of claptrap'. Kleinman, while conceding that there was some merit in the Youth Conference, criticized the organizers for having convened it without any indication of their intention of establishing a Fraction.
[7] 'grain of salt'.
[8] Klausner to W., 27 Jan. 1902 (W.A.). In an article on the Fifth Zionist Congress published in the Jan. 1902 issue of *Hashiloah* Klausner made some critical, but on the whole friendly, references to the Youth Conference and the formation of the Democratic Fraction.

the basic points have been clarified. Our draft programme, which, by the way, will be published in its final form only in two months' time,[9] does not represent anything new. What is new and fresh is that it has been implemented and, I hope, will be consistently put into effect. The existence of such a group, quite apart from its autonomous positive work, is of importance for the general Organization, since such disgraceful performances as there have been at past Congresses will no longer be possible. The V Congress has already provided much evidence of this.[10]

But most significant of all are the positive independ(ent) activities of the association which has been formed. These activities, to my mind, will show themselves in the first instance mainly in propaganda, campaigning and cultural work. The creation of an organ, the creation of a statistical bureau, these are, in my view, the two important tasks facing us. At our insistence, the Congress spoke about a Jewish institution for higher education.[11] I must admit that I only joined the Cultural Commission[12] to tackle this task—its theoretical aspect first. I am now studying the problem of the establishment of new Universities among them[13] and shall, perhaps, extract something interesting for us as well. I think there must be two institutions from the start: one in Palestine, devoted especially to Jewish learning, another in Europe—a general University with a technical faculty and, of course, a Chair of Jewish studies. It is my deep conviction that in view of the ever-growing restrictions on admission to foreign Universities as well,[14] this latter

---

[9] It did not, in fact, appear until Aug. 1902.

[10] See bridge-note following No. 148 as to the success of the Democratic Fraction group at the Fifth Congress in their advocacy of an emphatic affirmation of the important place of cultural work in the Zionist programme. Because of its controversial nature the discussion of this subject had been discouraged at the Third Congress (1899)—see Bein, *Herzl*, p. 328, and at the Fourth Congress (1900) a resolution proposed by the enthusiasts for cultural work had been side-tracked and not voted upon—see n. 10 to No. 86, and W.'s reference in that letter to 'the complaints which arose last year [1900] after the notorious cultural debates'.

[11] At the Fifth Congress, a resolution moved by Martin Buber on behalf of the Congress Cultural Commission and supported by W. called upon the Actions Committee to go closely into the question of the establishment of a Jewish University. The resolution was not voted upon, but Herzl gave the Congress an assurance that the question would be examined by the A.C.—5 Z.C. Prot., 390, 392–3, 428.

[12] He had been elected to the Commission as the representative of Switzerland.

[13] The language of the orig. is rather obscure and does not admit of a satisfactory translation. What W. seems to be saying is that he is looking into the way in which gentiles (referred to as 'they', i.e. 'the others') handle the establishment of new Universities.

[14] In orig., the words 'as well' [i.e., as well as to Russian Universities] written above the line. The point that W. is making is that, in addition to the recent tightening of statutory restrictions on the admission of Jews to Russian Universities (as to which see n. 3 to No. 113), Jews were also having difficulty in finding places in other

is no longer a luxury but a necessity. What an important European-Jewish intellectual centre could be created at a Jewish University; it would be a synthesis of *Yavneh*[15] and Europe! I don't deceive myself as to the practical difficulties, but this problem would have to be dealt with at a later date. Much time must still pass until Jewish public opinion becomes interested in this whole issue. Dear comrade, let me have your views on the subject.

Please write to me how you are getting on, how you feel now, how work is going. But do write. I should like to know your views, which I value, about all that has taken place in the past months. You realise, don't you, that this is no mere curiosity.

Kohan-Bernstein proposes to visit you at Odessa to discuss what can be done now by the Cultural Commission.[16] Please let me know, if at all possible, the results of your discussions.

There is more life noticeable now in the groups abroad[17] than in past years. There are already some Zionists. We cannot boast, of course, that we are looked upon with any particular good will. The Jewish assimilationists, who exist here in various guises and who use revolutionary phraseology as a cover, are always ready to calumniate Zionism, but they are being strongly rebuffed. Much effort is wasted on this דור המדבר[18] and, O God, the things that are done by other nations without a word of protest demand the most intense efforts from our entire nervous system. One needs a whole arsenal of logical arguments to make these callous people understand that the death of Jewry is a bad thing. But, to hell with them. . . .

I'll be waiting impatiently for a word from you.

Keep well.

Yours,
Ch. Weizmann

Universities outside Russia. Nothing is known of the existence at the time of any formal *numerus clausus* at such Universities, but in his above-mentioned letter W. speaks of the growing strength of anti-Russian, meaning anti-Jewish, propaganda in academic circles in Germany, and the brochure, *Eine Jüdische Hochschule*, publ. later in 1902 (see n. 3 to No. 240) dwells at some length on the tightening up of conditions for the admission of Jewish students to German and Swiss Universities.

[15] The Jewish academy founded by Johanan b. Zakkai at Yavneh, near Jaffa, became the spiritual and intellectual centre of Palestinian Jewry after the Roman occupation of Jerusalem, and the destruction of the Second Temple, in A.D. 70. The motto chosen by W., Feiwel and Buber for their brochure, *Eine Jüdische Hochschule* (see n. 3 to No. 240) was, 'Give me Yavneh and its sages'.

[16] Both Kohan-Bernstein and Ahad Ha'am were among the members of the Cultural Commission representing Russia.

[17] i.e., the Jewish student groups in the West.

[18] Hebr., 'generation of the desert.'

157. To Vera Khatzman, Geneva. [*Munich*], *15 February 1902*

Russian: Pcd.: H.W.: W.A.

[Shown by pmk. to have been sent from Munich.]

15/II. 1902

My best wishes. The paper went off very well.[1] I am very pleased,

Chaim

[Signed also by Isaac Sherman and five other persons.]

158. To Catherine Dorfman, Geneva. [*Munich*], *16 February 1902*

Russian: Pcd.: H.W.: W.A.

[Pmk. torn off but written on postcard showing a Munich view.]

16/II. 1902

Dear Katyusha,

It was wrong of you to be cross with me and not come to Koenigsberg's. Things are going well. I'm worn out. We shall be in session today for about six hours. The paper went off well.[1] I press dear Katyusha's hand.

Chaim

159. To Vera Khatzman, Geneva. [*Munich*], *16 February 1902*

Russian: Vcd.: H.W.: W.A.

16/II. 1902

My darling Verochka,

The lecture went down excellently.[1] I am terribly tired, as yesterday's session lasted until half-past one and today the debate starts

---

157. [1] W. was the opening speaker at a debate in Munich between Zionists and anti-Zionists commencing 15 Feb. 1902, continued 16 Feb. and ending, on 17 Feb., with what *Die Welt* (14 March 1902) described as a moral victory for the Zionists. W.'s address, as reported in *Die Welt*, was devoted largely to an attack on the Bund, which, in spite of the so-called 'national programme' (see n. 3 to No. 55) did not, he said, concern itself with the Jewish people as a whole, but only with the Jewish proletariat in Russia, whereas the Jewish people did not consist only of members of the proletariat, and only one-half of it was in Russia ; further, the Bund was interested only in the use to be made of the Jews as a means to an end [i.e. the social revolution], and not in the rehabilitation of the Jewish people as an end in itself.

158. [1] See n. 1 to No. 157.

159. [1] See n. 1 to No. 157.

at 2 p.m. In the evening I am reading a paper at the Germans'.[2] The general impression is excellent; the opposition insignificant, the assimilationists with their outworn phrases; the Bund is speaking today. I shall not leave until tomorrow night. I am writing little because the comrades have already arrived. All *amcho*[3] is in my room.

I kiss you, my dear, good, sweet Verochka,

Always yours,
Chaim

160. To Vera Khatzman, Geneva. *Munich, 17 February 1902*

Russian: Vcd.: H.W.: W.A.

Munich, 17/ɪɪ. 1902

My dearest Verochka, my girl,

This is the last day of debate.[1] I am worn out and am physically unable to continue the discussions any further. Things are going well but, O Lord, O Lord, how much energy is being wasted on matters which other nations can understand from a hint. Darling, I can't give you the exact time of arrival but as soon as I come I'll call at your place, that is if it's not at night and if I am unable to send a telegram.

My good girl, great things are happening in Zionism now. Our dear untiring leader is in Constantinople, and yesterday I received a telegram from Buber in Vienna: 'Wide concessions expected'.[2] Keep this secret, my little girl!

I am tired, tired, tired! No propaganda trip has ever exhausted me as much as this one. Verusya, my joy, I am leaving for home[3] today and am already happy because I shall be there.

With many kisses,

Yours,
Chaim

[2] W. may be referring to the local Zionist Society, but in speaking of 'the Germans' he may well mean the Munich Jewish Students' Association (*Verband der Juedischen Studierenden zu München*), which, in contrast to the Russian-Jewish Students' Society *Kadimah*, had a membership consisting mainly of German Jews.

[3] Colloquial Hebr., in orig. in latin characters, for 'the crowd' (lit., 'Your (God's) people').

160. [1] See n. 1 to No. 157.

[2] Herzl was in Constantinople from 14 to 18 Feb. 1902. He was not, on this occasion, received by the Sultan. He had talks with some members of the Sultan's entourage, but in spite of hopes which appear, from Buber's telegram, to have been entertained at Zionist headquarters in Vienna, his efforts to negotiate some arrangement with the Turks came to nothing.   [3] Geneva.

161. To Leo Motzkin, Berlin. *Geneva, 2 March 1902*

Russian: H.W.: C.Z.A.—A126/24/7/2/2

Geneva, 2/III. 1902
Rue Lombard 4

Mr. L. Motzkin,
Berlin.

Dear Leo,

I have decided to try my luck once more. Perhaps this time I shall be favoured with a reply. You and the rest of the colleagues have chosen to meet my last two letters[1] with silence and have thus placed me and the others in a position of utter uncertainty. However that may be, I feel that all this friction has had a bad effect on everything and on everybody. For the present, I must report that a blissful state of inactivity reigns in the Fraction. Nobody has done a thing, nobody has carried out the work he undertook, nobody has fulfilled even such passive duties as sending subscriptions. We are here with no news and no money, awaiting the post from day to day, but this brings nothing except perhaps a reproach about papers that have not been published, about minutes that have not been published, etc., etc.[2] I can't give any reply to anyone. First because I myself am just a letter-box, and can't do a thing, and secondly because I have no idea what has been done by the others and in what way. I have been waiting for your report.[3] It would have served as an answer to all the reproaches and insinuations in the press,[4] but I have received nothing. Bukhmil alone has sent a paper for the minutes;[5] nothing has come from the others yet. Everybody is looking forward to the results of the programme committee's work.[6] As far as I know, nothing has yet been

---

161. [1] One of these must be W.'s letter of 31 Jan. (No. 152). The other is probably a letter of 2 Feb. (signed by Anne Koenigsberg) from the Democratic Fraction's Geneva Information Bureau to the Berlin group of members of the Fraction, raising objections to the publication by the Bureau of the Berlin protest against the participation of W. and certain other members of the D.F. in the discussion of the Syrkin plan mentioned in the head-note to No. 150, and asking to be informed by telegram whether the Berlin group insists on publication. A copy, in W.'s handwriting, of the letter of 2 Feb. is in C.Z.A.—A126/24/7/2/2.

[2] The reference is to the proceedings of the Youth Conference.

[3] See n. 5 to No. 151.   [4] See n. 6 to No. 156.

[5] Bukhmil had addressed the Conference on 'Zionism and the way to its realization'. An incomplete text is in W.A.

[6] The Youth Conference had elected a committee to draft the programme of the D.F., together with a provisional constitution. W. was not a member of the committee, which consisted of Aberson, Bernstein-Kohan, Bukhmil, Feiwel, Klausner, Motzkin and Sheinkin, with Leib Jaffe as an alternate. It did not meet until June 1902.

done by the other members—I don't know how things are with you. It's March already, and the programme must be published by the end of the month.[7]

To all the proposals touched upon in the circular letters[8] there has not yet been a sufficient response for them to be put to the vote and therefore it is impossible to start implementing them. The venture thus lacks all sense of direction. Even passive duties, such as the sending of subscriptions, are performed by absolutely nobody. I have thought it necessary to say all this. For the time being I refrain from further comments which I could make in this context.

On March 15th I am off to Lucerne for the Sw[iss] Zionist Conference,[9] and then on to Germany. I shall be at Heidelberg, Karlsruhe and Darmstadt. I would call at Berlin too, were I sure that one could work there. I shall await your reply.

As far as I myself am concerned, there is nothing good.

Yours,
Chaim

162. To the Berlin Group of the Democratic Fraction.
Geneva, 10 March 1902

Russian: H.W.: C.Z.A.—A126/24/7/2/2

Geneva, 10. III. 1902
Rue Lombard 4

To the Berlin Fraction Group,

With reference to your letter received by us yesterday,[1] the I[nformation] B[ureau] begs to state in reply that the protest will

---

[7] It was not, in fact, published until August.

[8] News-letters Nos. 1 and 2 (24 Jan. and 10 Feb. 1902) of the Geneva Information Bureau—copies of both in W.A.

[9] W. did not, in fact, attend the Lucerne Conference.

162. [1] Letter dated 3 March 1902 from the Berlin group of the D.F. to the Geneva Information Bureau (W.A.) with extracts from minutes of group meeting on 1 March, raising the following points: (*a*) The group reiterated its demand for the publication of its protest (see head-note to No. 150) against the participation of certain members of the D.F. (including W.) in the discussion of Syrkin's proposed anti-I.C.A. campaign. (*b*) The group demanded, further, that W. and Zvi Aberson, who had interested themselves in the action proposed to be taken for giving effect to the Syrkin plan (see n. 4 to No. 152) should dissociate themselves from this project. (*c*) The group also complained that a proposal it had made about the publication of the minutes of the Youth Conference had been inaccurately quoted in the Information Bureau's news-letter No. 2 (10 Feb.). (*d*) There was a further complaint about the I.B.'s failure to publish in full a report provided by the Berlin group of a students' meeting at which Motzkin had been the principal speaker.

be published in the next news-letter, which we shall be issuing probably by the end of the week.[2]

As regards your surprise at the incorrect rendering of your proposal, having compared your letter with the published text in the circular letter, we find that the Berlin com[rades]' proposal was given correctly. Nevertheless it will be published a second time.[3]

The information that 200 peo[ple] attended comr[ade] Motzkin's address has appeared in the circular letter. We omitted only to mention that there was a continuation of the debate, in which comr[ades] Tyomkin and Jaffe took part;[4] of them we wrote that they had delivered addresses at a *Kadimah* meeting. We are unable to report all communications in extenso, and we thought it right to omit certain minor details. In future we shall not do this, so as not to give rise to misunderstandings.

Ch. Weizmann

As to the complaints about the Geneva comr[ades],[5] they will have an opportunity to state their case in the news-letter. I confirm the receipt of 37 Fr[ancs] from comr[ade] Pevsner.[6] I do not know what account to credit.

Ch.W.

163. To Leo Motzkin, Berlin. [*Geneva, 14 March 1902*]

German: T.: C.Z.A.—A126/24/7/2/2
[Date and place of origin as shown on telegram.]

Coming as soon as possible probably 25th[1] details by letter[2] regards

Chaim

[2] In the event, the protest was published as a confidential appendix to news-letter No. 3 (18 March), (W.A.).

[3] It was republished in extenso in news-letter No. 3.

[4] See n. 1, above, under (*d*).

[5] See n. 1, above, under (*b*). A statement by W. and Aberson in reply to the Berlin group's protest was published by the I.B. as an appendix to its news-letter No. 4 (20 Apr.), (W.A.).

[6] Sent on behalf of the D.F. Berlin group: Berlin group to Information Bureau, 3 March 1902, W.A.

163. [1] W.'s reply to a suggestion in Motzkin's letter of 12 March (as to which see further n. 1 to No. 164) that he should come to Berlin to heal the breach between the D.F. Berlin group and the Geneva Information Bureau.

[2] See Nos. 164, 165.

164. To Leo Motzkin, Berlin. *Geneva, 16 March 1902*

Russian: H.W.: C.Z.A.—A126/24/7/2/2

[Written on the notepaper of the D.F.'s Geneva Information Bureau.]

Geneva, 16/III. 1902
Rue Lombard 4

Dear Leo,

Unfortunately, I was unable to do the right thing by replying at once to your *Eilbrief*. Meanwhile, your second letter has arrived,[1] and I am now in a position to reply to both. First, with reference to the news-letter, we [have] already finished[2] it but have not yet had time to distribute it; we are now printing your latest communication in the form of an appendix, and everything will be sent out tomorrow. The protest (without any replies by the I[nformation] B[ureau]) is going to be distributed,[3] together with another confiden[tial] communication received separately from Glikin,[4] if we can manage it, tomorrow; if not, the day after at the latest.

A great deal has become clearer to me now. Your group did not receive one of our letters sent to you [? before][5] the publication of the 2nd news-letter, as you yourself can see from the enclosed copy.

Had we had an answer to this letter, the protest would have appeared in the 2nd news-letter. As to my visit—in a personal letter.[6]

Mit Zionsgruss,[7]

Ch. Weizmann

A copy of the letter of 2/II. 1902[8] enclosed.

---

164. [1] In an express letter (*Eilbrief*) dated 12 March 1902, and in a further letter dated 14 March (both in W.A.) Motzkin (*a*) asked for certain items of news to be published in the Information Bureau's news-letter No. 3; (*b*) asked that the Bureau's reply to the Berlin Group's protest (see head-note to No. 150) should not be published simultaneously with the protest; (*c*) urged W. to come to Berlin to re-establish normal relations between the Berlin Group and the Bureau.

[2] Orig. reads 'already wanted finished it'. 'Wanted finished' does not make sense. W. evidently changed his mind as to what he was going to say and omitted to cross out 'wanted'.

[3] News-letter No. 3, 18 March 1902 (copy in W.A.) included two appendixes containing respectively the news items which Motzkin had asked W. to publish and the Berlin Group's protest, not accompanied by any rejoinder.

[4] Writing to W. from Warsaw on 19 Feb. 1902 [? N.S.], W.A., Glikin told him that in various towns in Russia Bundist meetings were being organized under the guise of Zionist meetings in order to mislead the police. No stencilled copy of this letter has been found, but it is not necessarily to be inferred that it was not, in fact, distributed by the Information Bureau.   [5] In orig. word missing after 'sent to you'.

[6] See No. 165.   [7] 'With Zion's greetings'.

[8] The letter from the Information Bureau to the D.F. Berlin Group mentioned in n. 1 to No. 161. The copy here referred to is, without doubt, the copy in W.'s handwriting preserved in C.Z.A.—126/24/7/2/2, notwithstanding that it does not occupy its proper place immediately after the letter under notice.

165. To Leo Motzkin, Berlin. *Geneva, 16 March 1902*

Russian: H.W.: C.Z.A.—A126/24/7/2/2
[Written on W.'s personal notepaper.]

Geneva, 16/III. 1902

Dear Leo,

I am not going now into details about all our ordeals. There has been much ill-feeling, and—one may ask—whatever for? I hope for a personal meeting, and indeed I shall be happy to have one, if our hopes are justified and everything is cleared up and settled and the *Spleen*[1] passes. What I am still unable to understand is why Kunin thought it possible and fitting to break off all relations. The man did not reply to two letters and a telegram.[2] I shall not forgive him for this and I think he had no justification. I hope that on thinking it over he himself will mark this down on the debit side.

To my very great regret, I cannot come now, as I am being held up by very important matters.

You must understand that in general it is difficult for me to leave Switzerland. I must be able, at short notice, to be in Berne, where everything is very miserable.[3] I shall be going there again tomorrow and shall go on from there after spending a few days at Rivochka's. It is essential for me to visit the factory.[4] I have completed one piece of work which may have enormous results: I have no right to hold it back a single day longer and must pass it on to the management. Moreover, I want to know what they are going to say.[5] Do you know, this should reduce the cost of alazarin[6] by 30–35 per cent? If it proves technically sound, for from the scientific point of view there is no doubt, I shall drop chemistry for two or three years and travel to America to do propagandist work, and throughout Russia also, all of which could easily happen. I'll be free on the 23rd/24th and on the 25th, in the morning, I could be in Berlin. I don't think this delay can do much harm.

My best wishes to you and Polya,

Yours,
Chaim

165. [1] The German word *Spleen*—'madness'.
[2] Neither of the letters has been found, nor has the telegram. Lazare Kunin was a member of the Democratic Fraction Berlin group.
[3] The reference is to the fatal illness of Rebecca (Rivochka) Getzova.
[4] The Bayer Works at Elberfeld.
[5] From W.'s letter of 3 Apr. 1902 to Vera Khatzman (No. 185) it can be inferred that the discovery was the joint work of W. and Deichler. From his letter to her of 11 July 1902 (No. 234) it can be seen that the Bayer Works' evaluation of the discovery turned out to be disappointing.
[6] A basic material in the manufacture of dye-stuffs.

166. To Vera Khatzman, Geneva. *Berne, 20 March [1902]*

Russian: Vcd.: H.W.: W.A.

Berne, 20/III 5 a.m.

My darling Verochka,

Have just arrived in Berne. I am tired and exhausted. I decided to wait a bit at the railway station, as it is too early to call on a sick woman.[1] What am I going to find there? I slept a little during the night but hardly feel rested at all. Am feeling rotten. My dear girl, please write to me at once to Germany at the address shown below. My darling, work hard at your studies so as to finish off your exams.[2] Berne has never appeared to me as lifeless as it does now. One can feel death in the air. Best regards to Nyusya and Esfir. Many kisses from your

Chaim

Address: Weizmann,
　　　c/o Dr. Deichler,
　　　　Nieder-Ingelheim-on-Rhine,
　　　　nr. Mainz.

167. To Vera Khatzman, Geneva. *Berne, 21 March 1902*

Russian: Pcd.: H.W.: W.A.

Berne, 21/III. 02

Dear Verochka,

I am leaving at 2 o'clock. Shall spend the night with Aronchik[1] at Heidelberg. Nothing good here. It is the beginning of the end.[2] The torment is dreadful. Write to me at Deichler's[3] about everything. How are your studies with Bilit?[4]
Many kisses from

Yours,
Chaim

Regards to Esfir and Nyusya.

---

166. [1] Rebecca Getzova: see n. 3 to No. 165.
　[2] The examinations awaiting her as a second-year medical student.

167. [1] Aaron Eliasberg.
　[2] The reference is to Rebecca Getzova's illness, which was to end fatally.
　[3] i.e., at the address given in No. 166.
　[4] W.'s friend, Bilit, a chemist, was evidently giving her some coaching in preparation for the examinations referred to in No. 166.

168. To Leo Motzkin, Berlin. *Berne, 21 March 1902*

Russian: Pcd.: H.W.: C.Z.A.—A126/24/7/2/2

Berne, 21/III. 1902

Dear Leo,

Am going to Elberfeld[1] today. Shall be in Berlin on the 25th. I am making every effort to be with you as soon as possible.

Yours,
Chaim

Postscript by Sophia Getzova.

169. To Vera Khatzman, Geneva. *Heidelberg, 22 March 1902*

Russian: H.W.: W.A.

Heidelberg, 22/III. 1902

Dear Verochka,

As you see, my darling, I am here already. I arrived yesterday. Aaron[1] did not receive my telegr[am] and did not come to meet me, but I still managed to get to his flat.

Abramovich and Perelman[2] are here. I shall remain here the whole of today, and tomorrow shall go on to that German of mine.[3]

The behaviour of the Berliners[4] is arousing indignation everywhere, and if I wished to fight them now, I should have strength on my side. However, my darling, I have decided not to bring about an open rupture until I get to Berlin and find out exactly what is behind the whole story. I still do not know precisely on what day I shall be at the factory.[5]

You have probably written to me, darling. I should like very much to know everything that concerns you. How are your studies? Are you working with Bilit?[6] Examinations are approaching. Keep cheerful, my dear Verochka. I miss you terribly, my sweet. I'd love to see you, to embrace you, to cover you with kisses. I left in such a hurry that we had no chance to say our goodbyes.

168. [1] See No. 165.

169. [1] Aaron Eliasberg.
[2] Abramovich and Perelman were among the members of the Democratic Fraction who, together with W., had excited the indignation of the Democratic Fraction Berlin group by taking part in the consultations with Nahman Syrkin mentioned in the head-note to No. 150. [3] Deichler.
[4] The Berlin group's snipings at W., and generally at the Geneva Information Bureau, starting with the incident described in the above-mentioned head-note to No. 150. [5] The Elberfeld factory. [6] See n. 4 to No. 167.

Aronchik[7] sends his best regards. I have not yet seen all the comrades. I am very tired, as I have been travelling the whole day.

There is hardly anything going on in Heidelberg. There are few Zionists here and they are a very placid lot. There is no militant Zionism in this place. We shall see what happens in Berlin. Write at once, my darling. Should you write immediately after getting this letter, then address it to me in Berlin as follows: Herrn Berthold Feiwel, Schönebergerstr. 2, Berlin, S.W., für Weizmann.

Goodbye, my little darling, my child.

Lots and lots of love.

Your
Chaim

My best regards to Esfir. Do write, my dear, how life is treating you and how you are getting on.[8] Greetings to Nyusya.

170. To Vera Khatzman, Geneva. [*Heidelberg, 23 March 1902*]

Russian: Pcd.: H.W.: W.A.

[Date and place of origin from pmk.]

Best regards. *Gut Purim!*[1]

Chaim

[Also signed by Joseph Klausner and his wife, Fanya, Saul Tshernikovsky, Aaron Perelman, Gregory Abramovich, and two other persons.]

171. To Vera Khatzman, Geneva. *Mainz, 23 March 1902*

Russian: Pcd.: H.W.: W.A.

Gruss aus Mainz[1]
23/III 02

My dearest girl,

Best wishes from here. In an hour's time shall be at Deichler's.

---

[7] Aaron Eliasberg.

[8] 'Do write, my dear . . . how you are getting on.' Formal plur. used throughout, so evidently addressed to Esfir Weinberg, notwithstanding the opening words, 'Regards to Esfir'.

170. [1] Yidd., in orig. in cyrillic characters: 'Good Purim', referring to the approaching Jewish Festival of that name, as to which see n. 5 to No. 8.

171. [1] Printed on the postcard—'Greetings from Mainz'.

From there shall write to you tomorrow in greater detail. Hope to find your letter waiting there.

With a big kiss, darling.

Chaimchik

Best regards to Esfir and Nyusya.

172. To Vera Khatzman and Esther Weinberg, Geneva.
Nieder-Ingelheim, 25 March 1902

Russian: H.W.: W.A.

Nieder-Ingelheim-on-Rhine,
25. III. 1902

My lovely, dearest child,

I arrived here yesterday and found your letter,[1] which gave me much joy. Judging by myself, I have a feeling that you miss me, my darling, because I too can hardly imagine how I shall manage without you for two whole weeks. On the other hand, I am pleased that we are not together just now, so that I am not in any way disturbing your preparations for the exam.[2] But take care, darling; don't drop your studies! Carry on till the end. A shame to waste so much work and effort, and you would not be free in the summer. I should like to see you getting rid of this work. We would then do some work together later in the summer.

Remember, my dearest, my own, don't lose courage and work steadily. Once you are free of examinations, you can take better care of your health; it is not too good, and it worries me a lot.

We did not write to the factory until today.[3] Their reply will come by the end of the week, so that I cannot be at the factory until this time next week. On Sunday and Monday it's Easter, and there will be no one there to talk to. I shall make up my mind today whether to go to Berlin now, or only after Elberfeld. Write to me, darling, both to this address and to Berlin. I think I have already given you my Berlin address: Herrn B. Feiwel, Berlin, S.W., Schönebergerstr. 2. Should I decide to go to Berlin now, I shall be there by tomorrow evening. I have received a letter from Ahad

172. [1] Not found.
    [2] See Nos. 166, 167. From the letter to Esfir Weinberg which follows it can be inferred that she was preparing to face an oral examination.
    [3] See No. 165. The submission to the Bayer Works at Elberfeld of the discovery there referred to (see also n. 5 to that letter) had evidently been deferred pending W.'s arrival at Nieder-Ingelheim for personal consultation with Deichler. No correspondence on the subject between W. (or Deichler) and the Bayer Works has been found.

Ha'am in which he informs me that he intends to work energetically in the cultural field.[4] He writes, among other things, that Bernstein-Koh[an][5] called on him three days ago; this means that the latter is all right, and I don't understand why he does not write to us at all.

Verusya, write to me often; every day, if possible.

It's so dull here; the weather is bad, it's windy and cold.

I had a letter from Sheychik,[6] from Berlin. In his opinion, it's necessary to go there and make peace.[7] We shall see. And so, my little girl. I shall await your letters impatiently both here and in Berlin. Tomorrow I shall let you know my itinerary in detail.

I kiss you many times,

Yours, very much loving you,
Chaim

Dear Esfir,

Thanks for your nice words. So you do miss me? Well, well. I can say the same for myself. It's bad if people[8] get so used to each other that they are unable to part even for a short time. Please do cheer up my Verochka so that she keeps her chin up and is not frightened by the wealth of wisdom with which it is necessary to feed the organism in order to appear before the court [of][9] the great scholars of the city of Geneva.[10] For this and also for your other good

---

[4] W. is referring to Ahad Ha'am's letter of 4/17 March 1902 (copy in A.H. Papers, N.L.). His statement that A.H. had told him 'that he intends to work energetically in the cultural field' is a very free rendering of what A.H. actually wrote. All that A.H. says on the subject of cultural work is, in substance, that the Russian section of the Cultural Commission set up by the Fifth Zionist Congress, which had met in Odessa on 28 Feb./13 March, had decided to begin by getting a clear picture of the existing situation and for this purpose to collect detailed information from the Russian Zionist Societies.—Turning to points raised by W. in his letter of 5 Feb. 1902 (No. 156), A.H., saying nothing about the idea of establishing a Jewish University in Palestine, tells W., with reference to his proposal for the setting up, side by side with this, of a University in Europe, that, while in principle in sympathy with the project, he considers that the time is not ripe for its implementation, since, in the present state of the Jewish people, such a University could not be a truly national institution.

[5] He had taken part in the Odessa meeting mentioned in n. 4 above.

[6] Saul Lurie.

[7] i.e., to put an end to the quarrel between the Democratic Fraction Berlin group, and W. and his Geneva Information Bureau colleagues originating with the dispute mentioned in the head-note to No. 150.

[8] In orig. two words used for 'people'; lit. translation would be 'people, human beings'.

[9] See n. 2 above. In orig. there is an illegible word between 'before the Court' and 'the great scholars'.

[10] A reference to the examination or examinations (apparently oral) awaiting V.K. as a second year medical student and mentioned in the letter to her.

qualities I shall bring a lot of souvenirs from Berlin. How is your health ? Don't be bored! We shall meet soon. Regards to Nyuska.[11]

Yours,
Chaim

173. To Vera Khatzman, Geneva. *Nieder-Ingelheim, 26 March 1902*

Russian: Pcd.: H.W.: W.A.

Nieder-Ingelheim-on-Rhine
26/III 1902

My darling, my good girl,

Tomorrow night I am off to Berlin and shall stay there three or four days; I shall return from there via Cologne and Elberfeld, and from Elberfeld again back here for two or three days, and then back to Switzerland. They are awaiting me eagerly in Berlin and I don't want to delay my departure any longer.

How are things with you, my darling? You have probably sent your letters to Berlin already. When you get this postcard, I'll already be on my way, so write to me there at once. I feel very depressed. I am being looked after[1] as if I were their son, but I am already very bored and anxious to get away. But more than anything, I miss you, my darling girl. I want terribly to have at least a look at you.

Many, many kisses. You are greatly loved by your

Chaim

Regards to Esfir and Nyusya.

Verusenka[2]—just received a postcard from Koh[an]-Bern[stein]. He is all right, but he and his entire family have been ill.

174. To Vera Khatzman, Geneva. *Nieder-Ingelheim, 27 March 1902*

Russian: Pcd.: H.W.: W.A.

Nieder-Ingelheim-on-Rhine
27. III. 02

Dear Verunechka,

Am leaving for Berlin tonight and shall be there tomorrow morning. I hope to find a letter from you there. I hope that time

---

[11] A variant of Nyusya.
173. [1] By Deichler's parents.
[2] It is not clear whether W. wrote 'Verusenka' or 'Verulenka'.

will pass more quickly in Berlin; here it has dragged out endlessly. Write to me about everything, my dear girl, and write a lot. I miss you terribly. I never thought that such longing could come over me.

I kiss you my darling, my lovely, dearest girl.

Your
Chaim

Regards to Esfir and Nyusya.

175. **To Vera Khatzman, Geneva.** [*Frankfurt*], *27 March 1902*

Russian: Pcd.: H.W.: W.A.

[Shown by pmk. to have been posted in Frankfurt.]

27/III 02

Verusenka,

On roule![1] Am off now to Berlin; will be there tomorrow morning. Am feeling rather poorly. This is the third day I've been having headaches. Hope it will pass. What is your news? Write to me often, every day.

Your fervently loving

Chaim

Regards to Esfir and Nyusya.

176. **To Leo Motzkin, Berlin.** *Berlin, 28 March 1902*

Russian: Pcd.: H.W.: C.Z.A.—A126/24/7/2/2

Berlin, 28/III 02

Dear Leo,

Have just arrived in Berlin. Am very tired. Shall be at your place between three and four.

Greetings,
Chaim

177. **To Vera Khatzman, Geneva.** [*Berlin*], *28–29 March 1902*

Russian: H.W.: W.A.

[Written on stationery of Hotel Reich, Berlin.]

28/III 1902   12 midnight

My dear, sweet, lovely little girl,

Despite the fact that I am terribly tired and that this letter will

175. [1] 'We're off'.

not go tonight, I can't help writing to you now. There is so much that is distressing that I would give my soul to embrace you even once and to pour my bitterness in tears upon your breast, my precious darling. I notified Shneerson and Feiwel of my arrival; the latter is not in B[erlin], he is coming tomorrow. Motzkin, of course, is offended, and, generally, exasperates me by his false enthusiasm and his utter worthlessness. Some compromise will surely be reached, but the wound will not heal, since we can no longer have the same attitude to each other as we used to have. Verusya, my darling, it is so difficult for me, who have behaved to Motzkin as you know I have, to experience such a disappointment. It is very, very hard. But what can one do? I would sacrifice everything for the cause not to suffer. There are so few of us; we are surrounded by so many enemies who want to warm their hands at the flames of Zion that we must retain our dignity and refrain from washing dirty linen in public.

I don't know what tomorrow has in store, but I am feeling sad and feel the weight of Monomakh's crown on my brow.[1] My nerves are going to pieces. Verochka, the more difficult the situation I am in, the more I feel that you alone, my darling, and the thought of you, can ease my suffering. Write to me at once, I implore you, do write every day. I keep on imagining now that I am hearing your voice, that I am seeing and kissing your dear, wise eyes.

Please write to me now at Ingelheim at Deichler's address; I shall call there on my return journey. One week separates us. It is hard to imagine that it will pass. Tomorrow I'll write more, and more specifically. Keep well. I cover you with kisses, my beloved little darling.

Your exhausted
Chaimchik

My warm, friendly greetings to Esfir.

29/III   9 a.m.

I have had some rest and am feeling better. Feiwel is coming presently; I have just received a telegram. There is a meeting at 11 o'clock and another at 5.[2] I am depressed. Verunchik, I would not have believed that I could long for you so much. To move to

---

177. [1] An allusion to a line in Pushkin's 'Boris Godunov' where 'Monomakh's cap' symbolizes the regal attributes of the Czar. Vladimir Monomakh was a twelfth-century Grand-Duke of Kiev. The expression 'wearing Monomakh's cap' denotes, in idiomatic usage, a difficult situation or a burdensome responsibility.

[2] Presumably in connexion with the attempt to put an end to the dissensions in the Democratic Fraction.

another town seems impossible now.[3] I don't know what I would do to you if I saw you now. I would kiss you to death, Verunenka, and would die myself. My lovely, delightful darling. Do write to

your fervently loving
Chaim

178. To Vera Khatzman, Geneva. *Berlin, 30 March 1902*

Russian: H.W.: W.A.

Berlin, 20/III 1902   2 a.m.

My precious, my darling, my lovely girl. My adorable Verunechka.

No end of kisses for your lines.[1] Another day of worry, excitement, running about and talk has gone by. Nevertheless, the results will be better and more propitious for our cause. It is difficult to convey the whole atmosphere to you. I am too tired to describe it all. In brief, Motzkin & Co. are an inert power, destructive and pathologically vain, but there are some lively elements here too. They will combine in a Fraction group and will stop the rot that is setting in from the others. I shall put these tactics into operation tomorrow. All the preparations for this are complete. My personal relations with M[otzkin] have, of course, assumed a different character, though he is now doing everything to re-establish friendly feelings. I regard this as labour in vain, [but in any case] the Fraction will be saved from a split. *Tant mieux!* Verunechka, it's impossible to tell you how much bitterness there is. Don't insist on detailed news as a rule. I am writing to you now after a terrible day, and half the night has already gone. Verula, when I come, which I hope will be on Saturday, I'll spend the whole night with you and tell you everything. I shall try to arrive at 7 p.m. How I wish that moment were already here. How I am going to cuddle up to you, you will caress me, warm me, and I shall relax at your home. Verula, I have gone to pieces now. I have to finish. Lots and lots of love, my sweet. Completely, completely, completely

Yours
Chaimchik

Darling child, do study hard, only save Saturday for us. O how I want to see you. I tremble all over at the thought that I'll soon be with you.

---

[3] Orig. does not admit of any other translation, but the allusion is not clear. W. must evidently have considered leaving Geneva for another town, but in no earlier letter which has been preserved does he mention the possibility of such a move.

178. [1] V.K. to W., 27 March 1902, W.A.

179. To Vera Khatzman, Geneva. [*Berlin, 31 March 1902*]

Russian: Pcd.: H.W.: W.A.
[Date and place of origin from pmk.]

No view.[1]
Sincere greetings. Am very tired but perhaps something will be achieved by the journey.

Chaim

[Postscript by Lazare Kunin.]

180. To Vera Khatzman, Geneva. [*Berlin*],[1] *1 April 1902*

Russian: H.W.: W.A.

1/April 1902

My darling girl,

There has been no letter from you today and I am depressed. Here everything is already finished. As far as public affairs are concerned, it is all settled,[2] and it is to be hoped that everything will go on much better from now on. Our personal relations (as I have already told you)[3] can't be restored, although M[otzkin] is making every effort. You can hardly imagine how tired I am, but today is going to be a quiet day and I shall have some rest.

Feiwel is a joy. In his company one can relax. I am still unable to say when I am going to leave, as I am awaiting Deichler's telegram.[4]

Darling, Verunchik, my sweet. Your letters worry me because I am very concerned about your physical condition, but, Verusya— think of the joy when it's all over. You are certain to pass the examinations[5] and, even if you don't, my sweet, you won't be able to reproach yourself. But then we will both have a rest together, my darling. It's quite impossible for me to go directly to Montreux.[6]

179. [1] He seems to be apologizing for its not being a picture postcard.

180. [1] 'Berlin' printed.
[2] See No. 178 as to W.'s efforts to save the Democratic Fraction from disruption. As will be seen from subsequent correspondence, the quarrel was patched up to the extent that there was no secession and Motzkin co-operated in the management of the D.F.'s affairs, though W.'s personal relations with him remained strained.
[3] See No. 178.
[4] He was evidently awaiting a telegram from Deichler about arrangements for a visit to Elberfeld in connexion with the matter mentioned in No. 165.
[5] The examinations on her way to a medical degree mentioned in No. 166.
[6] There is no reference to Montreux in any earlier letter which has been preserved, but from his letter of 3 Apr. (No. 185) it appears that W. was hoping to go there for a few days' rest.

I cannot bear to pass Geneva without calling on you for at least a day. You must give me an evening, and then I want to be <u>only</u> with you, close to you, in you. I want to relax in your arms; Verochka, you will not deny me this. If this is very difficult for you, write to me at Ingelheim. I have bought a lot of pretty post-cards and some good prints, all pictures of Jewish life. If you behave well, you will, of course, get them. There is something for the girls too, for Nyusya and Esfir, but on condition of impeccable behaviour.

With many kisses, my darling girl. Keep well and cheerful.

Chaimchik

Today is a year since the Munich Conference.[7]

[Greetings from Berthold Feiwel and Felix Pinkus.]

181. To Vera Khatzman, Geneva. *Berlin, 1 April 1902*

Russian: Pcd. H.W.: W.A.

Berlin, 1/IV 02

My dear child,

I wrote to you in the morning[1] but now I am by myself. I want to send you greetings again and a fervent kiss.

Nothing new happened during the day. Have not received the telegram yet;[2] as soon as it arrives I leave. And I very much want to leave. Am tired and exhausted, and it's time I got some quiet.

I kiss my Verusya many, many times,

Your fervently loving
Chaim

Feiwel has just brought me your postcard.[3] Many, many thanks, my sweet, my darling. Did I really not write to you for two days? I thought not a day passed without my giving some sign of life. My adorable one, I am already at rest. Shall probably leave tomorrow.

With many kisses,
Chaim

---

[7] The Conference in preparation for the Youth Conference.

181. [1] See No. 180.   [2] See n. 4 to No. 180.   [3] Not found.

182. To Catherine Dorfman and Anne Koenigsberg, Clarens.¹ *Berlin, 2 April 1902*

Russian: Pcd. H.W.: W.A.

Berlin, 2/ɪᴠ 02

[Dea]r good [friends],

I shall probably leave in the evening because there is nothing to do here. Write to me at Ingelheim whether you are going to stay much longer in the lap of nature.

Am feeling better,

Yours
Chaim

183. To Vera Khatzman, Geneva. *Berlin, 2 April 1902*

Russian: Pcd.: H.W.: W.A.

Berlin, 2/ɪᴠ 02

Dear Verulechka, my darling,

I have just sent a telegram to Deichler and shall know in the afternoon exactly when I am leaving.¹ I slept very well and today am feeling better phys[ically], but longing overwhelms me and grows with every minute. I am so glad, Verochka, that it is so and not otherwise; I am so glad that the 'gypsy' in me is dying, and that your lovely, dear, pure image has displaced him, filling the whole of my aching soul. Do you know, I feel much freer now.

I am spending the whole time at Feiwel's. I stayed the night there. He is a wonderful man and is most gifted. It's quite possible that he will come to me for a rest, because he is physically worn out. I have made the acquaintance of a young Zion[ist] Pinkus, a very intell[igent] fellow from Breslau; he has joined the Fraction, is going to Berne and will be in Geneva. Stand firm and take heart, my beloved; finish that undertaking which you began bravely.² I should like to see you free and gay. How I shall cover you with kisses!

Yours, deeply in love with you,
Chaim

182. ¹ Addressed to Clarens but delivered after D. and K. had left and re-addressed to Geneva.

183. ¹ See n. 4 to No. 180.
  ² W. is referring to the impending examinations mentioned in No. 166.

Best regards to Fira[3] and Nyusya. Thanks for their affectionate attitude, which has such a good effect on me in my present state of mind.

Love,
Chaim

[Postscript by Felix Pinkus.]

184. To Catherine Dorfman and Anne Koenigsberg, Clarens.[1] [*Berlin, 3 April 1902*]

Russian: Pcd.: H.W.: W.A.

[Place of origin from pmk. Pmk. date not clearly legible but appears to be 3 Apr.]

Dear [friends],

Am not leaving here until today. Shall be in Geneva on Sunday.

Chaim

185. To Vera Khatzman, Geneva. [*Berlin, 3 April 1902*]

Russian: H.W.: W.A.

[Though the date 5 Apr. 1902 appears on this letter, it is not in W.'s hand and would seem to have been inserted later. That the letter was, in fact, written on 3 Apr. can be inferred from the words 'shall be in Ingelheim tomorrow', read together with No. 189, written from Ingelheim on 4 Apr.]

My darling, my sweet little girl,

I have just learned that the head of our division at the factory is not at Elberfeld at the moment.[1] I am now going to Deichler and will see there where to go next. Possibly I shall not go to the factory myself, and only Deichler will go.

So I am leaving tonight and shall be at Ingelheim tomorrow; I shall probably continue on my way the day after. I am terribly tired. Will it be possible to have at least a few days of rest at Montreux? That is a big question, but I shall try my utmost. This is really essential. Verochka, a terrible longing has overcome me. I simply cannot imagine how I shall survive the days which still lie ahead till I see you. And once I arrive we shall not be able to spend the time as we should both like either.

---

[3] Esther (Esfir) Weinberg.

184. [1] See n. 1 to No. 182.

185. [1] See n. 4 to No. 180.

You are very tired, my little girl. But I do hope that you will relax a few hours for me and so give me a chance to be near you. My heart aches at the thought that we shall not see each other for three more full days or perhaps more.

It's bad to yearn like this. I could never have imagined it, Verochka. I always thought it possible to limit oneself to meetings a few times a year, but nothing of the sort. I had never loved, and now I am in love.

It's dreary here. I very much want to be on the move already, and I am sorry that I shall not be able to be at the factory and see everything for myself. If I have to wait long, however, I shall not do it. Whatever happens, I shall write to you fully tomorrow.

Lots of love, Verochka,

All yours,
Chaimchik

I hope to find letters from you at Ingelheim. My best regards to Esfir and Nyusya. Will be seeing you soon, ladies.

I want terribly to be in Geneva now.

186. To Esther Weinberg and Anna Ratnovskaya, Geneva. [*Cologne*], *4 April 1902*

Russian: Pcd.: H.W.: W.A.

[Shown by pmk. to have been sent from Cologne.]

4/iv 02

Dear girls,

As you see, I am already approaching Switzerland. Tomorrow I shall probably be travelling to Basle. I shall be spending today in these parts. A very interesting fellow is travelling with me;[1] he will stay some days in G[eneva]. How are you feeling? Hope to find you cheerful and gay.

Chaim

[Also signed by Pinkus.]

187. To Vera Khatzman, Geneva. *Cologne, 4 April 1902*

Russian: Pcd.: H.W.: W.A.

Cologne, 4/iv 02

My dear sweet little girl,

I am going to Ingelheim. I'll find out there today how things stand with the factory.[1] Will write from there at once. I am already

186. [1] Felix Pinkus.
187. [1] See No. 185.

consumed with impatience to read your letters. Verula, Pinkus, about whom I've written to you,[2] is travelling to Geneva with me. I am very glad. Feiwel sends you best regards and so does Shneerson. F[eiwel] knows about our relations. He likes me very much, and theref[ore] you too, my little one. He will come to [? visit] us, i.e. you and me.

I kiss you, my joy.
Chaim

[Also signed by Felix Pinkus.]

188. To Vera Khatzman, Geneva. [*Lorelei*],[1] *4 April 1902*

Russian: Pcd.: H.W.: W.A.

4/IV 02

My sweet, my darling,

In ten minutes I shall be at Ingelheim. The journey along the Rhine is magnificent in this weather, and I have been seized by an even stronger longing. Am sending this from the place made so famous by Heine.[2]

Best wishes to my dearly beloved girl.

Your
Chaimchik

189. To Vera Khatzman, Geneva. *Nieder-Ingelheim, 4 April 1902*

Russian: Pcd.: H.W.: W.A.

Nieder-Ingelheim-on-Rhine
4/IV 02

My sweet joy, my dearly beloved one,

And so on Sunday night I shall be with you, with you, with you, my darling. It will not be possible to go to the factory for two or three weeks. We have had a letter from them in which they speak with great interest of our results, but they themselves have to check our tests, and this is going to take them about ten days.[1]

---

[2] See No. 183.

188. [1] 'Lorelei' printed.
[2] In his poem *Die Heimkehr* ('The Homecoming'), from which are taken the words of the Lorelei Song ('Ich weiss nicht was soll es bedeuten').

189. [1] See No. 185 and n. 4 to No. 180.

I'll be arriving on Sunday, i.e. only the day after tomorrow (what bliss!) at 7 p.m. In any case, I'll send a telegram. I don't understand why you did not receive my postcards and letters. Yet I have been writing to you every day, sometimes twice a day. This is the third time today. Do you know, tomorrow morning I am going to Cologne on some private business of Deichler's;[2] I shall be back here again, and then—straight to Basle, where I'll arrive on Sunday morning.

With lots and lots of love.

Chaimchik

Friendly greetings to Firochka[3] and Nyusya.

190. To Catherine Dorfman, Geneva. *Mainz, 5 April* [*1902*]

Russian: Pcd.: H.W.: W.A.

Mainz, 5/IV

My dear Katyushka,

Although nothing definite is yet known at Elberf[eld], what is known so far is excellent. They are pleased with the resul[ts], while the technic[al] outcome will only be known in a few weeks' time.[1] I arrived from Cologne yesterday and am returning there today on Zion[ist] business.[2] From there I shall travel by night via Basle–Heidelberg and shall be in G[eneva] tomorrow. Please call at my place at about half-past eight; I should be there by then. I am tired, tired, tired. As if *Schnellzüge*[3] were running in my head. Regards to Anna.[4] Friend[ly] greet[ings] to Weinstein.[5] Why is the tone of your last postcard[6] so strange?

Yours,
Chaim

[2] The nature of the 'private business' can be inferred from W.'s reference in No. 222 to Deichler's difficulties with his 'quasi-fiancée' in Cologne.

[3] Esther (Esfir) Weinberg.

190. [1] See No. 189.

[2] In No. 189 W. tells V.K. that he is going to Cologne 'on some private business of Deichler's': see n. 2 to that letter. It can safely be assumed that this was W.'s real reason for returning to Cologne.

[3] 'express trains'.

[4] Anne Koenigsberg.

[5] Sonia Weinstein, a Geneva medical student from Kherson and a member of the Geneva Zionist Students Society, *Hashahar*.

[6] Not found.

191. To Vera Khatzman, Geneva. [*Mainz*], *5 April 1902*

Russian: Pcd.: H.W.: W.A.
[Shown by pmk. to have been sent from Mainz.]

5/IV 02

Verunchik,

I have to make another trip to Cologne.[1] Tonight I shall be at Heid[elberg] and tomorrow in Geneva. This second journey was unexpected. I am tired, tired. But tomorrow I'll be with you. Verochka, how wonderful. I am going to Cologne on some [personal] business of Deichler's.[2]

I kiss you.
Chaim

Regards to Fira and Nyusya.

192. To Leo Motzkin, Berlin. *Geneva,* [*8 April*] *1902*

Russian: Pcd.: H.W.: C.Z.A.—A126/24/7/2/2
[Geneva pmk. 8 Apr. 1902. W.'s '8/v' is evidently a slip for 8/IV.]

Geneva, 8/v 1902

Dear Leo,

As we are publishing the news-letter[1] this week, please send us your group's suggestions immediately.

Chaim

193. To Leo Motzkin, Berlin. *Geneva, 13 April 1902*

Russian: H.W.: C.Z.A.—A126/24/7/2/2

Geneva, 13/IV 02

Mr. Leo Motzkin,
Berlin.

Dear Leo,

I have not replied to your *Eilbrief*[1] as I am daily expecting the

191. [1] He had already been there on 4 Apr.—see Nos. 186, 187.
  [2] He had evidently forgotten that he had already told her (see No. 189) that on 5 Apr. he would have to go to Cologne on some private business of Deichler's.

192. [1] The Democratic Fraction Geneva Information Bureau's news-letter No. 4 (copy in W.A.). It was not, in fact, published until 20 Apr.

193. [1] 'express letter'. The letter has not been found, but from a letter dated 14 Apr. 1902 (W.A.), in which Motzkin presses W. for a reply to his enquiry about 'the boy',

arrival of Wertheimer,[2] who is now in Paris. I hope he will get here tomorrow and I shall try to arrange things at once, if this is at all possible.

The news-letter is not quite ready yet.[3] There is such a lot to be printed.

We had a meeting of Fraction members here last night (Pevsner[4] took part too), and we decided that it was essential to have an article about the Fraction—a reply to all the attacks. Will you write [it]? I could also write now. If you have no objection, we could share the job: you would write for one newspaper, I for another.[5] Do let me know at once. We have taken certain decisions with ref[erence] to the organization,[6] which I shall send on to you in a separate report.[7]

On behalf of a section of the Cultural Commission, I propose to circulate the enclosed letter[8] composed by myself, which I am sending you in draft form and on which I would ask you for an expression of your views or, alternatively, for your *Randbemerkungen*.[9] It seems to me that it would be better if we were to write on behalf of a select group (connected with[10] the Fraction). This select group would also comprise members of the *Kultur-A[usschuss]*,[11] viz. Koh[an]-B[ernstein], Buber, Ah[ad]H[a'am] and myself. Then you and Feiwel could sign such a letter,[12] and

it can be seen that his express letter was dated 7 Apr. and asked W. to find out whether arrangements could be made at Geneva for a boy whom it was proposed to send there.

[2] Joseph Wertheimer, Chief Rabbi of Geneva. W. was evidently waiting to consult the Chief Rabbi about the arrangements to be made for the boy.

[3] See No. 192.

[4] Samuel Pevsner was the secretary of the Democratic Fraction Berlin Group.

[5] Nothing came of this project at the time, but, as stated in n. 5 to No. 151, an article on the D.F. by Motzkin appeared in the 5663 (1902–3) edition of the *Luah Ahiasaf* ('Ahiasaf Yearbook') produced by the Warsaw Hebrew publishing house *Ahiasaf*.   [6] i.e. of the D.F.   [7] No such report has been found.

[8] The document referred to's is an undated draft in W.'s handwriting (preserved in W.A., No. 29/0, 6) of a letter for circulation to members of the Cultural Commission set up by the Fifth Zionist Congress, drawing attention to the grave situation created by the mounting obstacles to the admission of Jews to Russian secondary schools and by the tightening up of the conditions for the acceptance of foreign students at Polytechnics and Universities in Germany and Switzerland, pointing out the disastrous consequences of these restrictions for a Movement whose intellectual élite must, in the nature of things, be drawn mainly from Eastern Europe and suggesting that the problem could be solved only by the establishment of a Jewish University.—So far as can be ascertained, no such letter was, in fact, circulated to members of the Cultural Commission.

[9] 'marginal comments'. A wide margin was, in fact, provided for such comments.
[10] Lit., 'alongside the Fraction'.   [11] 'Cultural Commission'.
[12] Motzkin and Feiwel were not members of the Cultural Commission. From a copy of the draft circular, with a marginal note in Feiwel's hand (W.A., Apr. 1902 Box), it can be seen that the draft was sent for comment to Feiwel as well as to Motzkin.

the Fraction would be well represented. Please reply without delay.[13]

Yours,
Chaim

194. To Ahad Ha'am (Asher Ginzberg), Odessa. *Geneva, 20 April 1902*

Russian: H.W.: Ahad Ha'am Papers, N.L.

Geneva, 20/IV 1902
Rue Lombard 4

Mr. A. Ginzberg,
Odessa.

Dear comrade,

I still can't get round to replying to your much-prized letter.[1] There is so much work of various kinds that I am obliged to hold it over, especially as I do not feel like an *über das Knie brechen*[2] treatment of these questions.

I want to inform you of one thing: I hope that it will interest you and that you will co-operate in this venture. We now have an opportunity of starting a weekly publication in Berlin[3] which would serve as an exponent of the aims and aspirations of the Fraction and also (and mainly!) of the reasoning on which Zionism is based.[4] The editorial board is to consist of Buber, Feiwel and one of the comr[ades] from Russia. For this purpose we need means and the sympathy of the best Russian comrades. Can anything be done in this direction in Odessa? Could you advise us whom to turn to? We now want to create a small fund and are, of course, ready to accept any contributions for this purpose.

What is your opinion of this venture?[5] Please write at once. Best wishes for the Festival.[6]

All the very best.

Yours,
Chaim Weizmann

We could also have a Russian section.

[13] No reply from Motzkin has been found.

194. [1] Ahad Ha'am to W., 4/17 Mar. 1902 (A.H. Papers, N.L.); as to which see n. 4 to No. 172.   [2] Lit., 'breaking over the knee'—i.e. rushing it.
[3] See No. 199.   [4] Lit., 'of the scientific bases of Zionism'.
[5] A.H. replied on 19 Apr./2 May 1902 warning W. against launching such a publication unless he had ample resources at his disposal: A.H. Papers, N.L.

[6] The approaching Passover, which came in that year, according to the civil calendar, on the evening of 21 April.

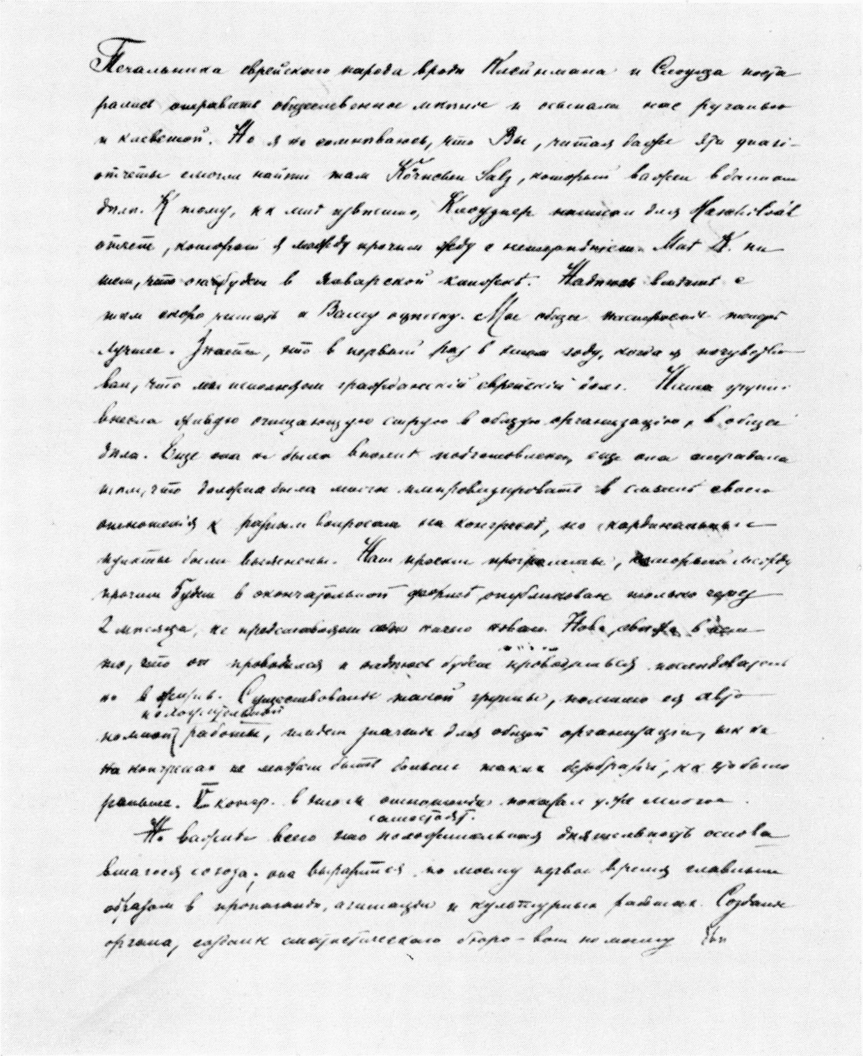

5. Letter to Ahad Ha'am (1902) [Letter 156]

Genève, Rue Lombard 4
4. II. 02.

Herrn Dr. Th. Herzl   Wien

Hochgeehrter Herr Doktor!

Im Anschluß an mein letztes Schreiben erlaube ich mir jetzt Ihnen noch einige Vorschläge über die Hochschulangelegenheit org. zu unterbreiten.

Drei Hauptaufgaben sind es, die nach meiner Meinung schon jetzt in Angriff genommen werden müssen:

1) Die vollständige Ausarbeitung des Projektes.

2) Die Agitation für die Hochschule. Die Agitation wäre am zweckmäßigsten derart einzuleiten daß man zunächst in allen Großstädten (vorzügl. Universitätsstädten) in den Kreisen der Intellektuellen und der höheren Finanz dafür Stimmung macht. Erst, wenn in diesen Kreisen die notwendige Stimmung und Betheiligung vorhanden ist, könnte man die Agitation in die große Masse und die Presse tragen.

3) Erlangung der Bewilligung von den entsprechenden Regierungen für den Bau der Hochschule.

Jedenfalls müßte man auch über die Hauptaufgaben, wie Ort, Dimensionen der Schule, deren innere Organisation vor Einleitung der genannten Schritte im Klaren sein.

Ich glaube, daß man schon in diesem Sommer die akademischen Ferien dazu benutzen könnte um eine Action einzuleiten.

Ihrer geschätzten Antwort entgegensehend zeichne ich mit vorzüglicher Hochachtung und Ergebenheit

Adolf Ehrmann

6. Letter to Herzl (1902) [Letter 207]

195. To Catherine Dorfman, Geneva. [*Geneva, about 20 April 1902*]

Russian: Vcd.: H.W.: W.A.

[Probably attributable to 1902. If so, and if W.'s *Gutjomtev* refers, as is most likely, to Passover, the date would be just before the commencement of the Festival, which came in on the evening of 21 Apr.]

Dear Katyusha,

When you left my place like that today, we did not even wish each other a happy Festival.[1] I now wish you this wholeheartedly. Days of brightness and freedom. Cast off all your neurotic thoughts (they make me think of a decadent song, and a neurotic one!).[2] And may our relations with each other be the same as ever. Once more, away with all this *hametz*.[3]

I warmly press your hand,

Yours
Chaim

Gutjomtev[4]

196. To Vera Khatzman, Geneva. [*Lausanne, 22 April 1902*]

Russian: Pcd.: H.W.: W.A.

[Date and place of origin from pmk.]

My sincere greetings, Verochka, and best wishes for the Festival.[1] Greetings to Esfir and Nyusya.

Chaim

[Greetings added by Felix Pinkus.]

197. To Aaron Eliasberg, Heidelberg. [*Geneva, 24 April 1902*]

Russian: Pcd.: H.W.: W.A.

[Date and place of origin from pmk.]

Best regards and *Gutjomtev*[1]

Chaim

[Also signed by Zvi Aberson, Vera Khatzman, Esther Weinberg.]

195. [1] What had caused the coolness between them is unknown. This was not the first time she had been annoyed with him—see No. 158. As to 'a happy Festival' see head-note.

[2] An allusion to the decadent symbolist literature of the period.

[3] Hebr., in orig. in cyrillic characters, 'leaven', required to be removed from the home as part of the preparations for Passover.

[4] Yidd., in orig. in latin characters, 'compliments of the season'—lit., 'good Festival'.

196. [1] Passover—see head-note to No. 195.

197. [1] See n. 4 to No. 195 and head-note to that letter.

197 A. To Vera Khatzman, Geneva. [? *Geneva*], *24 April 1902*

Russian: Pcd.: H.W.: W.A.

[Picture postcard showing scene on Lake Geneva; unstamped, addressed to 'Mlle C. Chatzmann [*sic*], E.V. [En Ville], 7 Rue Ecole de Médecine'. Evidently written by W. during a one-day local trip and sent to V.K. by hand on his return to Geneva.]

24/IV 02

I send you, darling, my best greetings from the trip.

Your loving
Chaim
V. Khatzman[1]

198. To Leo Motzkin, Berlin. *Geneva, 25 April 1902*

Russian: Vcd.: H.W.: C.Z.A.—A126/24/7/2/2

Geneva, 25/IV 02

Dear Leo,

I am very surprised that up to now I have had no reply to my last letter.[1] Please let me know at once whether you are writing the article, whether you still require the material which I left with you,[2] and in fact please reply to everything in my last letter; I must have a reply. What's happening in the programme committee?[3] Have you had a reply from the other members of the committee? Do I have to write to them? Please return the letter I sent you concerning the *Hochschule*[4] if you have made any comments on it.[5]

I beg you to answer at once.

The boy has arrived. I have taken a room for him for the time

---

197A. [1] No satisfactory explanation can be offered of the appearance, below W.'s signature, of V.K.'s signature, in her own handwriting, in Russian characters.

198. [1] See No. 193.

[2] What 'material' W. is referring to is uncertain, but the context seems to suggest that it has something to do with the article mentioned immediately before, i.e., the article which Motzkin had been invited to write in W.'s letter of 13 Apr. (No. 193). It is possible—though this is only a conjecture—that, while in Berlin early in April, W. had left with Motzkin some material meant to help him with the article on which he appears then to have been working (see n. 5 to No. 151), and that W. is now asking whether M. still needs the material for the purposes of the article mentioned in No. 193.

[3] The Committee appointed by the Youth Conference to draft a programme for the Democratic Fraction.

[4] 'University' (see head-note to No. 113).

[5] No comments by Motzkin have been found.

being and found teachers. There may be some difficulties, but I think it will be possible to arrange things for him.[6]

I am awaiting your immediate reply.

Keep well.

Yours
Chaim

Regards to the comrades.

199. To Aaron Eliasberg, Heidelberg. *Geneva, 26 April 1902*

Russian: H.W.: W.A.

[Begun on visiting-card and continued on a sheet of paper.]

Geneva, 26/IV 02

Dear Aaron,

I don't know where you got the idea that I was talking about the *Isr[aelitische] Rundschau*. I don't know a thing about it.[1] Feiwel definitely informed me of the possibility of having a journal provided we have 800 subscribers and 6000 m[arks]. There is some money already. I passed this on to you without any particular zeal, and I repeat my request that you should do something in this direction. For some reason you are always sceptical. This is terrible!

I also have yet another request. Please find out the *Jahres-etat*[2]

---

[6] See nn. 1 and 2 to No. 193.

199. [1] The letter to which W. is replying has not been found, but what had evidently happened was that Eliasberg had been told by W., in a letter which has not been preserved, about the idea mentioned in his letter to Ahad Ha'am (No. 194) of providing the Democratic Fraction with a weekly organ to be published in Berlin, and that E. had assumed that what W. had in mind was the acquisition of the *Israelitische Rundschau*, the organ of the German Zionists. Early in April there had been discussions (nothing came of them) about a possible transfer of the *I.R.* from its then proprietors, the German Zionist Organization, to the *Jüdischer Verlag*, a Jewish publishing house recently established in Berlin by a group including Feiwel and Buber, both of them prominent members of the D.F. It looks as though some rumour of these negotiations must have reached E. and have led him to suppose that the projected organ of the D.F. was to be the *I.R.* W. now tells him that he was wrong, but it seems at least not unlikely that, though W. was unaware of it, the information mentioned in the letter under notice as having come from Feiwel did, in fact, relate to the proposed purchase of the *I.R.* W.'s 'I don't know a thing about it' would be comprehensible if, as may have happened, Feiwel had merely informed him in general terms of 'the possibility of having a journal', provided that certain conditions could be satisfied. A possible alternative explanation would be that W. did know that the *I.R.* was meant but wanted to conceal this from Eliasberg. Replying on 6 May (W.A.) to the letter under notice, Eliasberg told W. that, in his view, the launching of a D.F. organ must wait until the Fraction was more firmly established. In the event, the project was dropped. [2] Annual budget.

of Heidelberg University, and if you can—that of Karlsruhe as well. Then I must also know: (1) the number of students; (2) the number of Jew[ish] students; (3) the *Lehrpersonal*;[3] (4) and if possible, please find out the running costs of Heidelb[erg] Univer[sity]. All I need is figures, but I need them badly. Please do something in this connection. I ask you to take a serious interest in the matter. This is an important affair. I need as much data as possible. I must forward them to Vienna.[4]

I beg you to reply *postwendend*.[5]

Yours
Chaim

200. To Leo Motzkin, Berlin. *Geneva, 3 May 1902*

Russian: Pcd.: H.W.: C.Z.A.—A126/24/7/2/2

Geneva, 3/v 02

Dear Leo,

I remain without an answer to my letters;[1] in general, Berlin gives no sign of life. I beg you to write to me immediately about everything.

Regards to the comrades,

Yours,
Chaim

It will be possible to arrange things for the boy very well.[2]

201. To Aaron Eliasberg, Heidelberg. *Geneva, 7 May 1902*

Russian: H.W.: W.A.

Geneva 7/v 02
Rue Lombard 4.

My dear Aaron,

Very many thanks for the interesting data promptly

---

[3] Teaching staff.

[4] i.e., to the Central Office of the Zionist Organization, at this time in Vienna. Herzl, who was showing an active interest in the University project, had on 22 Apr. 1902 written to Feiwel (C.Z.A.—H.B. 266) to the effect that it was now essential for him to be provided with an estimated budget for the University. From No. 202 it seems clear (though the letter has not been found) that H. had, on the same date, written in similar terms to W. Writing to W. on 1 May 1902 (W.A.) Feiwel told him that H. had said in conversation that he was prepared to take up the proposal officially with the Swiss Government or with the Sultan. On 3 May, and again on 18 May, H. wrote to the Sultan's secretary, Izzet Pasha, broaching the idea of the establishment of a Jewish University in Jerusalem: *Herzl Diaries*, IV. 1276, 1279. This helps to explain why H. was now pressing for an estimated budget.

[5] 'by return of post'.

200. [1] Nos. 193, 198.   See nn. 1 and 2 to No. 193.

supplied.[1] Little by little I have been accumulating a considerable amount of material. Vienna has asked for an *Aufstellung*[2] on the University,[3] but for the same reasons as those you refer to I am in no hurry; I am not at all willing to let the matter pass out of my hands and hand it over to Vienna, where it will be turned into light literature.

I have every intention of going deeply and seriously into this problem.

I don't know what appeals you refer to.[4] My intention is to arouse the interest only of certain Jews in this matter. I have composed a letter meant for them alone;[5] it is not of the nature of an appeal.

Nothing should be made public before all the necessary authentic material is in our hands.

Please inform Klausner of the Motzkin–Feiwel proposal to get together in Berlin about the 15th–20th.[6]

Keep well. We'll probably meet at Mannheim.[7]

Yours
Chaim

V[era] I[ssayevna] sends her best wishes.

202. To Theodor Herzl, Vienna. *Geneva, 7 May 1902*

German: H.W.: C.Z.A.—Z1/334

Geneva
Rue Lombard 4
7. v. 02

Dr. Th. Herzl
Vienna.

Dear Dr. [Herzl],

I beg to reply as follows to your esteemed letter of the 22nd ult.[1]

At the moment I am not yet in a position to give details of the cost of a University. It is true that I have some very interesting data in my possession, but these I still consider insufficient. There

201. [1] Eliasberg to W., 6 May 1902, W.A. In sending W., in response to his letter of 26 Apr. (No. 199) asking for material for transmission to Vienna, data about Heidelberg University and its students, Eliasberg expresses anxiety about the chaos which might result if the Smaller Actions Committee began dealing with the University project, and deprecates any rushing into a public announcement or appeal at this stage. [2] Exposé. [3] See n. 4 to No. 199.

[4] As to Eliasberg's anxiety about a premature public appeal see n. 1, above.

[5] See n. 8 to No. 193.

[6] As is clear from correspondence in the Motzkin papers in C.Z.A., this refers to the convening of a meeting of the Programme Committee mentioned in No. 198.

[7] i.e., at the German Zionist Conference due to meet in Mannheim on 19–20 May. In the event, W. did not attend the Conference.

202. [1] See n. 4 to No. 199.

are enormous difficulties involved in collecting the necessary material, and we have only now succeeded in overcoming them.

I am in possession of the estimates and other data relating to the Universities[2] of Baden, as well as to Darmstadt and Munich. I should like to wait until I have also collected the corresponding material relating to the Swiss Universities before sending you the detailed statement you require, and this, I think, cannot be done in less than a fortnight.

I should also like to ask if you would be so kind as to let me know what steps you contemplate taking with regard to the matter of the University.[3]

With great respect and with Zion's greetings,

Yours faithfully,

Dr. Ch. Weizmann

cop.[4]

203. To Leo Motzkin, Berlin. *Geneva, 16 May 1902*

Russian: H.W.: C.Z.A.—A126/24/7/2/2

Geneva 16/v 02.

Rue Lombard 4

My dear Leo,

Aberson is preparing for the journey.[1] The delay is due to lack of funds. The point is that my cash-box is at a low ebb, but all the same I shall do my utmost to enable him to leave next week.

There is nothing new here, and I get news from nowhere. Our Fraction members have gone to sleep.

Did K[ohan]-B[ernstein] and Sheinkin reply to you?[2] I have no news from them.

I didn't write to you this week as I had urgent chemical work which I brought to a conclusion. But I am a complete wreck because I had to work with bromine and chlorine, and I am completely hoarse. If I could, I would go to Berlin now too, but never mind. We shall probably meet in about a month and a half. It's

[2] The Baden Universities were Heidelberg and Freiburg. There was also in Baden a Polytechnic at Karlsruhe.

[3] Herzl's reply, dated 17 May, has not been found but is referred to by W. in his letter of 21 May (No. 204), from which its contents can be inferred.

[4] See n. 1 to No. 150.

203. [1] To Berlin, for a meeting of the Programme Committee: see No. 201 as to the Motzkin–Feiwel proposal for a meeting in Berlin in the middle of May. In the event, the meeting was postponed and was held in Heidelberg in the middle of June.

[2] Both were members of the Programme Committee.

a good thing that [they] wrote to Mannheim to take the question of the Fraction off the agenda.[3] Best regards to you and the comrades. I'll send a telegram about Abers[on's] departure.

Yours
Chaim.

204. To Theodor Herzl, Vienna. *Geneva, 21 May 1902*

German: H.W.: C.Z.A—H.vɪɪɪ/915

Geneva 21. v. 02
Rue Lombard 4.

Dr. Theodor Herzl
Vienna.

Dear Dr. [Herzl],

In compliance with the wish expressed in your letter of the 17th inst.[1] I enclose the plan asked for, which I have based on the material I have collected.[2] Every figure has been carefully checked and compared with the official data relating to the various institutes of higher education (Universities and Technical Colleges), so that I am justified in assuming that the estimate of costs is reasonably precise and realistic; it is likely, in reality, to work out somewhat cheaper rather than dearer, although as a rule such estimates are made in order to be exceeded later.

The organization of the University is also described in broad

---

[3] The letter referred to has not been found. The agenda of the impending Mannheim Conference of German Zionists included the question of the setting up of 'Fractions' within the Zionist Movement. The attempt evidently made in the interests of the Democratic Fraction to get this item removed from the agenda did not succeed; the Conference adopted a resolution deprecating the formation of 'Fractions' —*Die Welt*, 23 May 1902.

204. [1] Not found, but contents can be inferred from W.'s reply, and also from a letter of 22 May 1902 from Feiwel to Herzl (C.Z.A.—Z1/335), in which Feiwel, to whom Herzl had sent a copy of his letter of 17 May to W., wrote: 'You are doing a great injustice to Weizmann, and to me also, in accusing us of a lack of seriousness in our handling of the University project, in contrast to the serious attention you are constantly giving it.'

[2] 'Plan for a Jewish University', C.Z.A.—H. vɪɪɪ/915. W. sent Herzl, by mistake, an unsigned and undated copy of this German memorandum, and retained the signed original, dated 21 May 1902 (W.A.), in which he inserted the word 'preliminary' before 'Plan'. The main points can be summarized as follows: (*a*) What is required is a combination of a University providing higher education on the academic plane in a wide range of subjects, with special emphasis on Jewish studies, and a Polytechnic. (*b*) The institution ought, if possible, to be in Palestine. Should this be impracticable, the only alternative calling for serious consideration would be Switzerland. (*c*) Estimated capital cost, 5,473,000 marks; annual budget, 735,000 marks (roughly equivalent, at then rate of exchange, to £274,000 and £37,000).

outline.³ It would be premature to go into details at present,⁴ since for this very serious preliminary study is unquestionably required.

I must emphatically reject the charge of dilatoriness. As I mentioned in my last letter,⁵ the collection of the material presents great difficulties, and not all Universities or authorities were so obliging as to place the relevant publications at my disposal; there were various things which I had to obtain in very roundabout ways.

I take the matter too seriously to be able to act hurriedly, but not a day passes without something being done in connection with the project.

My friends and I are of the opinion that it is only when a scheme has been thoroughly thought out that one can lay it before the public, so that the idea may not become part of that jumbled mass of plans which do not mature.

To get an exact picture of what young Jewish students are like, I have sent a questionnaire to all our trusted friends in all the University towns, and this I enclose for your kind perusal.⁶ A similar enquiry has also been started by the Berlin Stat[istical] Bureau.⁷

Further, we have made all arrangements for collecting and digesting both the technical⁸ material and the vast mass of literature on the University question. Only when this has been done

---

³ The Plan includes a list of the proposed Departments and ancillary institutions, such as Schools of Applied Chemistry and Agriculture and a Teachers' Training College.

⁴ It appears from Feiwel's letter of 22 May to Herzl (see n. 1, above) that Herzl had asked for a syllabus of lectures.   ⁵ No. 202.

⁶ An undated questionnaire in German, in W.'s handwriting, preserved along with the letter under notice in C.Z.A.—H. viii/915, asks the addressee for information about (*a*) the number of Jewish students at his University; (*b*) the subjects they are studying; (*c*) their financial circumstances; (*d*) their ideological outlook; (*e*) their institutions; (*f*) anti-semitism among students and teachers; (*g*) difficulties in gaining admission to Russian Universities.—Though W. here tells Herzl that he has distributed the questionnaire, it seems clear that he had not, in fact, sent it out and was speaking of something he proposed to do as if it had already been done. That he decided, on second thoughts, to wait is evident from the reference to the suspension of 'the *Enquête*' in No. 206 and from his letter to Motzkin of 11 Aug. 1902 (No. 278) explaining his reasons for <u>not</u> having distributed the questionnaire. It was eventually superseded by another distributed some months later: see W. to Michael Aleinikov, 6 Nov. 1902 (text in vol. II of this series).

⁷ The Jewish Statistical Bureau (*Bureau für Statistik des jüdischen Volkes*), set up in Berlin in March 1902 by a committee drawn mainly from members of the Democratic Fraction, including W., had appointed a sub-committee to collect statistical data about Jewish students—Feiwel to Herzl, 22 May 1902: C.Z.A.—Z1/335. The Bureau was later in the year replaced by a new body under the name of The Jewish Statistical Association (*Verein für jüdische Statistik*).

⁸ In orig. *wissenschaftliche*—'technical' seems to be closer than 'scientific' to what W. means.

shall we be able to go ahead and work out in detail a complete project, programme and lecture syllabus.

We are certainly not lacking in initiative or seriousness or good-will, and with the forces at our disposal, which still remain to be organized, we have, after all, already accomplished something in this field.

Your keen interest in the project—one which is, unfortunately, regarded by very many fellow-Zionists as so much fantasy—will encourage us still further in our work.

We are, however, most anxious that you should keep us informed about your activities.

We shall devote all our efforts to the enterprise and we have every reason to assume that we can count on a sympathetic and widespread response in Jewish intellectual circles.

I greatly look forward to hearing from you.

With great respect and with Zion's greetings,

Yours truly,
Dr. Ch. Weizmann.

205. To Theodor Herzl, Vienna. [*Geneva, 21 May 1902*]

German: T.: C.Z.A.—Z1/334

[Date and place of origin as shown on telegram.]

Herzlingen Vienna
Türkenstr. 9.

Report dispatched[1] Zion's greetings,

Weizmann

206. To Leo Motzkin, Berlin. *Geneva, 2 June 1902*

Russian: Vcd.: H.W.: C.Z.A.—A126/24/7/2/2

Geneva 2/vi 02
Rue Lombard 4

My dear Leo,

The state of my health has deteriorated lately to such an extent that *beim besten Willen*[1] I could not attend to affairs as I should have liked. I do not know yet what is in store for me: I am going to the doctor today. My general state of mind is foul too.

I can imagine how unpleasant you find all this delay.[2] If only it

205. [1] See No. 204.

206. [1] 'With the best of good-will.'

　[2] i.e., delay in convening the Programme Committee, as to which see n. 1 to No. 203. Instead of meeting, as at first proposed, in Berlin in the middle of May, the

were possible to get together[3] on Friday. Are you thinking of visiting Switzerland after the committee [meeting] or will you go straight to Berlin ? If you agree to visit S[witzerland], I sincerely invite you to stay with me. Please write to me at once. I'll try to meet you.

Who is the sixth person coming?[4] Write at once and pay no attention to my lack of punctuality due to circumstances beyond my control.

I hope to receive a reply from you. I have suspended the *Enquête*.[5] I sent Herzl the required data in good time, after classifying and working up all the material in the form of an exposé.[6] He rushed me terribly, and I thought he would write to me at once, but to my regret I haven't heard anything from him yet. I am writing to him again today.[7] But he hurried me so much that I sat up for two nights preparing the report for him. What kind of a game is that? To all appearances he seems not to have wanted me to finish the work on time, otherwise he would not have demanded it urgently, giving me only a day and a half.[8]

Keep well. Best regards to the comrades.

Chaim.

207. To Theodor Herzl, Vienna. *Geneva, 4 June 1902*

German: H.W.: C.Z.A.—Z1/335

Geneva, Rue Lombard 4
4. vi. 02

Dr. Th. Herzl
Vienna.

Dear Dr. [Herzl],

Further to my last letter,[1] I now beg respectfully to

Committee held its first meeting in Heidelberg on 16–22 June. From the fact that W. here asks Motzkin if, after the meeting, he will go straight to Berlin, it can be inferred that by this time it had already been decided to change the venue from Berlin to Heidelberg.   [3] i.e., for the Programme Committee to meet.

[4] There were seven members of the Committee, plus one alternate—see n. 6 to No. 161. W. evidently knew of five members who had promised to attend but had heard that there would be six. Who the 'sixth person' was is unknown. In the event, there were only five at the Heidelberg meeting—Aberson, Feiwel, Klausner, Motzkin, and the alternate member, Leib Jaffe.

[5] By 'the *Enquête*' W. means the enquiry into the position of Jewish students at various Universities represented by the questionnaire mentioned in No. 204. As to the words 'I have suspended the *Enquête*' see n. 6 to that letter.

[6] See n. 2 to No. 204.

[7] He did not, in fact, write until 4 June—see No. 207.

[8] W. was evidently unaware that Herzl had already approached the Sultan on the subject of the establishment of a Jewish University in Jerusalem—see n. 4 to No. 199.

207. [1] No. 202.

submit to you some additional proposals concerning the University.

There are three main tasks which, in my opinion, must be taken in hand forthwith:

(1) The complete working out of the project.

(2) Propaganda for the University. The propaganda can most effectively be got under way by arousing interest in the big towns (especially University towns) among the intellectuals and in the world of high finance. Only if and when the necessary interest and support are forthcoming in these circles would it be possible to extend the propaganda to the masses and to the press.

(3) Obtaining permission from the Governments concerned for the building of the University.

In any event, before taking the above-mentioned steps, it would be necessary to be clear about the main points, such as the location and dimensions of the institution[2] and also its internal organization.

I believe that the academic vacation this coming summer could be used to launch a campaign.

Looking forward to your reply, I remain,

With great respect and with Zion's greetings,

Dr. Ch. Weizmann

208. To Theodor Herzl, Vienna. *Geneva, 12 June 1902*

German: H.W.: C.Z.A.—Z1/335

Geneva 12/VI. 02

Rue Lombard 4

Dear Dr. Herzl,

I have, unfortunately, had no answer thus far to my letter of the 21st of last month[1] or to my second [letter] of the 4th inst.[2]

Meanwhile something could be done in the matter, and it would be a pity if the time before the end of the academic year went by without our being clear as to what should be put in hand during the vacation.

Accordingly, should you be disposed to continue corresponding with me on this subject, I would ask you to be so kind as to favour me with your reply.

With great respect and with Zion's greetings,

Dr. Ch. Weizmann

[2] Lit., 'school'.

208. [1] No. 204.   [2] No. 207.

209. To Theodor Herzl, Vienna. *Geneva, 25 June 1902*

German: H.W.A.: C.Z.A.—Z1/335

[Except for W.'s signature, the letter is in the handwriting of Felix Pinkus.]

Geneva 25. VI. 02

Dr. Theodor Herzl
Vienna IX

Dear Dr. [Herzl],

I take the liberty of saying a few words with further reference to your esteemed letter of the 17th.[1] It so happens that I have been able to discuss the matter here with my friend Feiwel. Neither of us could really understand the contents of your letter. The way we look at the work, and are bound to look at it, is that it will for some time to come be of a preparatory nature, and only after months of study shall we arrive at a comprehensive survey of the possibilities of implementation, so that it is absolutely impossible for us to apply our minds to the 'immediate realisation of the plan' of which you, Sir, speak. We propose to engage only in preparatory work, and this we shall do with the greatest interest.

The questions to be considered can be seen to fall under the following heads:

1. The position of Jewish University students in relation to the Russian, German (and, in due course, the other) Universities.
2. A study of the living conditions of Jewish students and of the special problems involved in the organization of a Jewish University having regard to the pre-University schooling and the material circumstances of the students.
3. A study of the University project in relation to Zionism.
4. Organization of the University, having regard to [? the aims of] Zionism.[2]
5. Plan for the University budget.
6. A study of the best possible propaganda for getting the enterprise on its feet.

We believe that only when the preliminary questions have been studied with sufficient care—and this is no easy task—will the project be ripe enough to be put before an official Zionist forum,

---

209. [1] No Herzl letter of 17 June has come to light. W. seems clearly to be referring to Herzl's letter of 17 May—see n. 1 to No. 204. The letter under notice supplements W.'s replies in Nos. 204, 207.

[2] Lit., 'having regard to Zionism'.

i.e. a small or full-scale Congress.[3] In the light of previous experience we consider that harm would be done even by a premature announcement of the project or by its being meantime made a topic for public discussion, whether in a large or a small circle.

You, Sir, are in a position to judge the approximate scope of the work I have organised up to the present. We should like to continue along the same lines as hitherto, and only regret most sincerely that, although you acknowledge the importance of the plan, and although by bringing in our colleagues we are able to achieve great things with small sums, the Actions Committee has placed no funds at all at our disposal.[4] This will needlessly delay the work for many weeks. Once again I beg you to inform me of the steps you are taking or have taken. I am equally anxious to have your comments on the preliminary plan.[5] In any case, since we are, in fact, the initiators of the project and are working at it continuously, we cannot forgo being notified or referred to and consulted about the action you have taken or propose to take. As for the legitimacy of our activities, it is enough that several of those who are collaborating in this matter, such as Dr. Kohan-Bernstein and Buber, are, like myself, members of the Cultural Commission. Finally, might I also take leave to enquire whether you are disposed to let the Congress Bureau[6] be made available for the production, dispatch, etc. of printed material?

With great respect and with Zion's greetings,

Yours truly,
Dr. Ch. Weizmann.

210. To Vera Khatzman, Rostov.[1] *Geneva, 26 June 1902*

Russian: H.W.: W.A.

Geneva 26/VI 02
Rue Lombard 4

My sweet, dear Verochka,

You can well imagine that today has brought nothing happy or

---

[3] The distinction is between a full-scale Congress and the Annual Conference ('Small Congress') convened in the years between Congresses from 1901, when it was decided that Congresses should be held at two-year intervals, instead of, as before, annually: see General Introduction, Appendix II, paras. 3, 4. (p. xxxii).

[4] The Smaller Actions Committee had, on 9 May, rejected an application by Feiwel for a grant in aid of the preparatory work in connexion with the Jewish University project: C.Z.A.—Z1/175.

[5] See n. 2 to No. 204.

[6] i.e., the Vienna Central Office of the Zionist Organization, the official name of which was *Erez Israel, Bureau des Zionisten-Congresses.*

210. [1] She had gone home to Rostov for the summer vacation.

cheerful. I got back from the station last night and fell into bed;
I got up terribly tired today and could not believe that I had seen
you off, that geographically you were now far away from me and
with every minute were moving further and further away. I am
spending the whole day at home, have no wish to do anything or to
think, and somehow it is so depressing, Verulechka. For some
reason or other, Toldy[2] is feeling particularly tired today. He has
spent the whole day sitting, or rather lying, in the room.

Hope to receive a few words from you in the evening. The post
brought nothing today. *Tant mieux.* Tomorrow we are leaving,
we haven't quite decided where for, as the Baron has not yet given
a reply.[3] He is busy and cannot visit Pasmanik as he was asked
to do.

Verunya, I am not showering you with questions about everything you found at home. The reason for this is that I know you'll
write of your own accord. My best regards to Sofochka and Raya,
my dear—my very best, you understand, Verusya?

Keep well, my lovely one. Many kisses from your

Chaim.

There will be long letters from me, too! At the moment, there's
nothing to write.

[Postscript by Berthold Feiwel and Felix Pinkus.]

211. **To Vera Khatzman, Rostov.** *Geneva,* [? *27*] *June 1902*

Russian: H.W.: W.A.

[W.'s dating of this and the next letter (No. 212)—28 and 29 June 1902—will
be found, when these letters are read together with Nos. 210 (26 June) and
214 (30 June), to involve a number of apparent inconsistencies of which the
following are examples: (1) In No. 212, dated by W. 29 June, he writes that
he will be going to Leysin 'tomorrow' [= 30 June], but in No. 214, dated
30 June, he says that he arrived at Leysin 'last night' [= 29 June]; (2) In
No. 214, dated 30 June, W. apologizes to V.K. for not having written to her
'yesterday' [= 29 June], but according to his dating of No. 212—29 June—
he did write to her 'yesterday'. These and some other puzzling discrepancies
disappear if it can be assumed that Nos. 211 and 212 were in fact, written
on 27 and 28 June respectively.]

[2] Berthold Feiwel. So far as can be ascertained, he suffered from heart trouble
originating from overstrain while doing his military service in the Austro-Hungarian
Army towards the end of the 1890s.

[3] In orig., after 'given', 'gone and brought' crossed out. 'The Baron' (presumably
a nickname) cannot be identified, nor is anything known of the matter referred to
in the next sentence.

Geneva 28/vi 02
Rue Lombard 4.

Dear Verochka,

How shall I start this letter? I feel so very depressed. Such emptiness and such weariness, as if lead were flowing through my whole body. And a rather peculiar sensation, too. Dorf[man] and Koen[igsberg] left yesterday. Toldy and Pinkus are leaving together for Leysin[1] now. I shall stay here, as I have not been to the laboratory for a whole week, and I shall not go to see how T[oldy] has settled down till Sunday. My head feels empty, my heart is empty, and I am in a terribly dull mood, but I hope that all this will pass when I can go somewhere in the country and have a change of surroundings.

As for you, my darling, my sweet lovely girl, you are home already having a rest, and I am very happy for you. You will write to me, of course, at once, about everything—how you found things there, because I very much want to know all this.

A postcard has arrived from Motzkin[2] in which he announces that he will write in detail.[3] At the same time, he asks that nothing shall be done about the University without him. The same old story: let's see what he writes.

I have not written home for a long time. I am awaiting news from Deichler about the state of affairs at the factory,[4] and then a great deal will be much clearer. I think everything there ought to be in order now.

I shall stop working by the end of next week without fail, as I am already fed up with everything. Only, Verulenka, don't be stingy with your letters. You have now many more impressions than I, whose life will be quite monotonous. Only I wish I felt less miserable.

Many kisses, dear little girl, lots and lots of them

Your fervently loving
Chaim

My best regards to Sofochka and Raya.

[Postscript by Feiwel.]

---

211. [1] A small health-resort near Montreux.

[2] Not found.

[3] Apparently he did write (see Nos. 223, 225), but the letter has not been found.

[4] i.e., about the Bayer Works' evaluation of the Weizmann–Deichler discovery mentioned in No. 165—see No. 190.

212. To Vera Khatzman, Rostov. *Geneva,* [? *28*] *June 1902*

Russian: H.W.: W.A.

[See head-note to No. 211.]

Geneva 29/vi 02
Rue Lombard 4.

My darling, my good little girl,

Your dear letter from Munich[1] has just arrived. I have been awaiting it impatiently; there were no letters from you yesterday. Nothing new has happened, my sweet one: today I had some news from Buber in Vienna. That is, he has just arrived there for a few days. A pity I didn't know about it earlier; he could have met you. But now it doesn't matter any more; you are already home, my beloved, and have already forgotten all about the journey.

Yes, my darling, I too shall not forget that last evening. It was so good, so cosy, there was so much warmth, love and good fresh sweet bliss. I am so glad you've got to know T[oldy] and that you liked him. For he is the first of my comrades whom you've got to know like this. The others, like Kohan-B[ernstein], adopted a different attitude.[2]

Boredom, dejection all round. There is something heavy in the air. My life is dreadfully empty now. I have no energy. All I want is to get a letter from Deichl[er].[3] I shall shut the laboratory then. As it is, you see, this uncertainty is most unpleasant; and it is no less unpleasant for me that it isn't worthwhile starting a piece of work now. It is really impossible for me to imagine this vacation without you, utterly impossible. I keep imagining that the door is about to open and you will appear and I shall embrace you and cover you with kisses for all I'm worth. *Ne vous faites pas des illusions Mr. le Docteur.*[4]

There is nothing new concerning our cause. True to himself, Motzkin has written nothing yet; consequently it is still impossible to publish a programme.[5] Aberson left today for the Sw[iss] Zionist Conference in Berne. I didn't want to go there at any price.

Verusya, my darling, give my best regards to Sofochka. Tell her

---

212. [1] 27 June 1902, W.A. She had passed through Munich on her way from Geneva to Rostov.

[2] i.e., were less friendly, perhaps because they saw in V.K. the cause of the breaking-off of W.'s engagement to Sophia Getzova.

[3] See n. 4 to No. 211.   [4] Thus in orig.

[5] A programme for the Democratic Fraction had been drafted by the Programme Committee when it met at Heidelberg on 16–22 June, but before being published, it had still to be revised by Motzkin, as to whose procrastination see n. 1 to No. 223.

7. Weizmann (standing) and Feiwel (1902)

8. Chaim Weizmann with his brothers Moshe and Samuel (1902)

everything about me, about my plans, hopes, dreams and longings. I'd write to her now, but I do not want to write in a semi-official tone. You will both write to me, and then I shall write to her, isn't that so, my dearest? Toldy wrote to you yesterday and the day before yesterday; he was very pleased with your postcard.

There will probably be news from them[6] from Leysin today, and I shall join them tomorrow.

No interesting post has come. Keep well, my sweet little girl. Lots and lots of love and many kisses.

Your
Chaim.

My best wishes to Raya.

Best regards to Nyusechka and thank her for thinking of me.

Ch.

213. To Catherine Dorfman, Kherson. [*Leysin*],[1] *30 June 1902*

Russian: Pcd.: H.W.: W.A.

30/vi 02.

My dear,

I have come here with F[eiwel].[2] We have found a marvellous place in a pine forest. I am off to Geneva today and will be back in a week's time. There is no news for the time being. Nothing from Motzkin so far.[3] How was the journey?[4] How do you find things? Best regards to your people.

Dreadful boredom, unbearable. Katyushka, do write. I shall write in greater detail from G[eneva].

Your very depressed
Chaim.

[Postscript by Feiwel.]

[6] 'from them'—presumably Feiwel and Pinkus (see No. 211). It would appear, however, from Nos. 213 and 214 that what actually happened was that Feiwel travelled to Leysin on the evening of 29 June, escorted by W.

213. [1] 'Leysin' printed.
[2] See n. 6 to No. 212.
[3] See n. 5 to No. 212.
[4] Her journey to Kherson.

214. To Vera Khatzman, Rostov. *Leysin, 30 June 1902*

Russian: Vcd.: H.W.: W.A.

Leysin 30/vi 02

My darling, my sweet girl, my joy.

I arrived here last night together with Toldy, who has been staying at Clarens until now.[1] It's marvellous here and T[oldy] is feeling fine. I do not doubt that he will make an excellent recovery here. Forgive me, darling, for not writing yesterday; I planned to write from here last night but on arrival I had a frightful headache, I was sick, etc. Probably because of the great heat during the journey. Now I am perfectly all right. There were no letters yesterday morning; as to today, I don't know, as I shan't be in Geneva until midnight.

Today you are probably already at home. Verunchik, how dreadfully depressed I am. Yesterday, during the journey, we were talking a lot about how lovely it would be if you were to come here in August. We would rent a chalet and would all live together. It is much better than in Montreux. Well, my darling, is it feasible? Perhaps it is. We could be together for a month. Do write to me, please. I hope to have letters from you and Sofochka this week.

From Motzkin not a thing, of course.[2] Toldy wrote him a most abusive letter yesterday.[3] Will it have any effect? I hope so. There is probably post waiting for me at home.

I am looking forward very impatiently to your letters from home. Please write to me about everything, I am terribly impatient. My best regards to Sofochka and Raya. Raya will write too, won't she? Many, many kisses, my darling, my sweet beloved girl.

Your
Chaim.

My love, we have already found a marvellous place, a pension near the sanatorium with a splendid pine-grove (1450 metres), two rooms. I shall move there by the end of the week. I like the place very much.

[Postscript by Feiwel.]

214. [1] See n. 6 to No. 212.

[2] See n. 5 to No. 212.

[3] In a letter to Motzkin dated 27 June 1902 (not 'yesterday'—29 June) Feiwel speaks his mind about the muddle and inertia which, he says, are prejudicing the healthy development of the Democratic Fraction: C.Z.A.—A126/24.

215. To Leo Motzkin, Heidelberg. *Geneva,* [? *end June 1902*]

Russian: Vcd.: H.W.: C.Z.A.—A126/16/2

[Undated, but probably written at the end of June 1902, when Motzkin is known to have been in Heidelberg, having stayed on there after attending the Programme Committee meeting on 16–22 June. This dating fits in with the words 'The laboratory will close soon'—see No. 222 (4 July 1902): 'I closed the laboratory today'.]

Dear Leo,

I am still not quite clear about the immed[iate] steps that have to be taken, by whom and when.

Let me know how you feel, what's your news. What are you doing in Heidelberg? Are you going to stay there a long time?

No special news at my end. The laboratory will close soon, and then *stehe ich zur Verfügung.*[1]

Best regards,
Chaim.

216. To Vera Khatzman, Rostov. *Geneva, 1 July 1902*

Russian: H.W.: W.A.

Geneva 1/vii 02
Rue Lombard 4

My darling Verochka,

I, too, am already writing you my fourth or fifth letter; indeed, I don't remember exactly. Yesterday we[1] wrote to you from Leysin,[2] where Toldy has finally settled down for the whole summer. My only dream now is to join him as quickly as possible, but for the time being my dreams and plans are being wrecked by very formidable financial obstacles. I need 75 roub[les], i.e. 200 francs, to get under way, but I simply have not got them and cannot get them. I can't wait until next month, and moreover my expenses are too heavy. I really don't know where to turn and what to do. This worries me a great deal.

You, my darling, have had quite a long spell in Munich,[3] and I feel as if we hadn't seen each other for a whole eternity, so much that I even feel like writing 'Do come here quickly'. For hours on end I feel a gnawing pain that completely enslaves me, and all my

215. [1] 'I am at your disposal.'

216. [1] W. and Feiwel.   [2] No. 214.
   [3] A reference to V.K.'s letter of 27 June (W.A.), describing her stay in Munich *en route* for Rostov.

efforts to drive my thoughts away and to forget remain futile. If only I could get out of here more quickly.

I am ready to leave even the day after tomorrow, as in any case I can't do a thing at the laboratory. There is no news from anywhere, neither from Herzl nor from Motzkin, nor from any of the comrades. All this adds to and increases my misery. I had a brief note from Father in which he says that he will probably be coming.[4] My sister[5] is at Druskienniki[6] for the time being and will be going abroad afterwards. I'll wait. On the whole, I have some doubts whether I shall be going to Russia. If not, you must come here soon without fail. Verochka, I cannot describe how I long for you. After all, you are at home among your family, your dear ones, while I am completely on my own now and have endless worries!

I have just received a short letter from Saul:[7] he may be coming here soon. My darling, my good little girl. Please write to me at once, a lot, a lot: write every day, as I am doing, because it's difficult even to keep alive. Best regards to Sofochka. Do both write to me. I am waiting so impatiently.

I didn't feel like sending this letter off earlier, hoping that perhaps the post would bring something interesting, but alas, not a thing.

I am finishing this letter now, and I feel like shouting out loud, so loud that you can hear me, Verochka darling: I love you so very very much.

With many kisses,
Always your
Chaimchik.

Best regards to Raya and Nyusya.

217. To Leo Motzkin, Heidelberg. *Geneva, 1 July 1902*

Russian: Pcd.: H.W.: C.Z.A.—A126/24/7/2/2

Geneva
Rue Lombard 4
1/VII 02

Dear Leo,

The letter you mention in your last postcard of the 26th of last

---

[4] Meaning, apparently, coming to Switzerland—see No. 249.
[5] Probably his eldest sister, Miriam (Mariya) Lubzhinsky.
[6] A holiday resort on the border between White Russia and Lithuania.
[7] Saul Lurie.

month[1] has not yet arrived, and meanwhile time marches on. We must get down to work. A programme must be published.[2]

I am staying here just for one week. I shall then go away and it's very doubtful whether I shall be able to work, since I feel very poorly and want to rest for at least a month.

Please do write at once, as I really don't know what to do.

Keep well,
Yours
Chaim.

218. To Catherine Dorfman, Kherson. *[Geneva]*,[1] *2 July 1902*

Russian: Pcd. H.W.: W.A.

Geneva 2/VII 02

Dear Katyusha,

For the moment—just warm greetings, but I should like to write you a very long letter. I feel most miserable, terribly miserable. Oh, to get out of here as soon as possible. There is no news. Motzkin has not written so far. Toldy has already settled down.[2] I simply must go to him at once. I hope you found everything all right at home. Please write me a lot and in detail; do write about everything. It's hard to describe how impatiently I am awaiting news from you and anyhow a letter from you. Once again, my warmest and friendliest greetings to your parents, and also to your sisters and your brother-in-law.[3] So I am waiting for your letter, and I shall write to you within the next few days. Perhaps there will be something more interesting than my own feelings, with which you are already sufficiently familiar. Well, my dear, keep well, cheerful and merry.

Your very down-hearted
Chaim.

219. To Vera Khatzman, Rostov. *Geneva, 2 July 1902*

Russian: H.W.: W.A.

Geneva, Rue Lombard 4   2/VII 02

My joy,

I am writing to you again, my dear darling. I feel slightly better

217. [1] See No. 211.   [2] See n. 5 to No. 212.
218. [1] 'Geneva' printed.   [2] At Leysin—see No. 216.   [3] Fyodor Bromberg.

when I talk to you even by letter. I say 'slightly' because our separation becomes in every way more and more difficult with every hour. I don't know, my young lady, what will happen: I find it difficult to forget, even for a minute, no matter how I should like not to feel such longing—*c'est plus fort que moi*. On the other hand, I am very glad about it: this longing shows how deep is my attachment to you, and I am glad for my own sake that there is at least one person without whom I can't live. Verunya, do write to me every day in detail about everything. Today, at last, a postcard came from Motz[kin][1] saying that until now he has not been feeling well and is going to write soon.[2] Hasn't this man any sense of shame? Toldy is sending very happy postcards. He is feeling well.

In Berne there has been a big row between the Jew[ish] [Students'] Corporation[3] and the Zion[ist] Academ[ic] Society in connection with the Zionist Conference held there.[4] It is not interesting enough to be described in detail. The Acad[emic] *Ver[ein]*[5] was in the right, of course. Pinkus was the chief *makher*[6] in this. This is all the Zion[ist] news I have so far. As you can see, my darling, there is not much. I am driven to despair by the outrageous inactivity of all our 'workers'.

I am waiting most impatiently for a very detailed letter from you, from Sofochka and perhaps (? ?! ?!) from Raya as well. For Ch. W. sends her such warm regards, and V. Kh. has presumably passed on all the greetings. This is all for today; I wrote home, to Deichler, and to many others. It's hard to wait. Write soon, Verusya, to one who sends you fervent kisses and longs for you no less fervently.

Chaimchik.

My very best regards to Nyusechka.

219. [1] Not found.

[2] See n. 3 to No. 211.

[3] i.e., the Zionist student society *Kadimah*.

[4] Student duelling, countenanced by *Kadimah*, was objected to by the Berne Academic Zionist Society, which, furthermore, favoured the Democratic Fraction, whereas *Kadimah* was opposed to it. According to a report in *Hamelitz*, 2 (16) July 1902, disputes between the two groups flared up at a reception given by *Kadimah* on 29 June, and Felix Pinkus, together with other Zionist Academic Society members, demonstratively walked out.

[5] 'Society'.

[6] Yidd., in cyrillic characters, 'moving spirit' (lit., 'maker').

220. **To Vera Khatzman, Rostov.** *Geneva, 3 July 1902*

Russian: Pcd.: H.W.: W.A.

Geneva 3/VII 02
Café du Nord.

No view[1]

I met Herzfeld[2] here. We are sitting and talking about various things. Warm greetings.

Ch.

[Postscript by Herzfeld.]

221. **To Vera Khatzman, Rostov.** *Geneva, 3 July 1902*

Russian: H.W.: W.A.

Geneva 3/VII 02
Rue Lombard 4

My darling, my dear little girl,

I am writing again, my little one. This is my only joy and my only consolation. You cannot imagine how hard things are for me. I find no peace either by day or by night and am simply terrified of this. Last night I went to the Café du Nord, listened to the music for a while, and then walked all alone until I was tired. I thought I should fall asleep after this, but nothing of the sort. I didn't find peace at night either. I am annoyed with myself and scold myself, but nothing helps. I must leave here before long, and O God, if I could only do it; at the moment this is my most cherished dream. I am simply ashamed of myself for letting my longing for you get such a hold on me, absorb me so. The greatest happiness for me would be to know that you were soon coming back and that you would not leave me for a long, long time, and even to think of the day of your arrival—that is too much. I dreamed that you and Sofochka came here, i.e. to us,[1] to Leysin. If only this would come true!

But, my joy, all this is remote, infinitely remote. I am unable to walk across the Plaine.[2] Everything in my room that reminds me of you, of those evenings we spent together, during which we became so attached to each other—all this arouses in me an acute burning pain. My heart aches all the time, gripped as if in a vice,

220. [1] As in the case of No. 179, he seems to be apologizing for this not being a picture postcard. [2] Benjamin Herzfeld, a German Zionist.

221. [1] 'to us'—W. and Feiwel.
[2] The Geneva park known as the Plaine de Plainpalais.

and there is no-one except Toldy—whom I don't see either—to whom I could confide my pain. I never thought myself so soft or capable of such an attachment. I am happy and unhappy, all at the same time. But then my happiness is eternal, while my unhappiness is temporary and passing, because I shall be seeing you, and even soon, perhaps. You will spend a little time at home and then you will come to me. I shall cover you with kisses, embrace you, clasp you in my arms, and I shall be so happy with you, in your arms. But all this is much too good, and I am not going to think about it.

I have been so carried away by my own state of mind that I haven't asked you any questions about how you feel, what you are doing, whether you are having a rest, how you are working, *enfin* everything, everything. Have you started to study Hebrew, and is it going well? You must read the Bible with the teacher without fail. I should very much like you to become acquainted at least to some extent with the spirit of the Book of Books. Tell me of all your plans for the summer. Do you intend to go anywhere, or will you stay in Rostov all the time? It's already four days since I have had anything from you. Verula, write more often. I can't wait long! I wrote postcards to Raya and Sofochka yesterday. Best regards to them and I am awaiting letters from them. Tell me of your whole talk with Sofochka. Verusya, write, write, my little one, my darling, my sweet.

Oh, how I love you! I love you, I love you, I love you.

Chaimchik.

Darling, send me your photo at once without fail, but at once. I should also like to have photos of R[aya] and S[ofochka] but to ask them is rather awkward for me; we are not so well (?)[3] acquainted.

Darling, send it at once. Lots and lots of love. Dengin[4] and Voegtlin are leaving today, and the pension is becoming rather empty.

222. To Vera Khatzman, Rostov. *Geneva, 4 July 1902*

Russian: H.W.: W.A.

Geneva 4/VII 02

Verulya, my adorable darling,

Good day, my darling. I am sure you have already managed to

---

[3] '. . . not so well (?) acquainted'—Thus in orig.: i.e. even 'acquainted' is, in a sense, an exaggeration, W. not having actually met V.K.'s sisters but having only exchanged greetings with them.   [4] A Russian-born chemist.

have a good rest at home and have very likely written me several letters. This interval is unbearable, and sometimes the lack of news from you even worries me. Surely it was possible to drop me a line during the journey, and it is a pity that you have not done so, Verochka. But to make up for it, you will write to me daily from now on, won't you?

I closed the laboratory today, took leave of the prof[essor],[1] who was very nice and promised trainees for the winter, etc. I am going to have the same labor[atory]. I didn't expect all this kindness, and my barometer actually went up a few degrees. I decided to go away tomorrow and started packing today, but my only hope is that 'something will drop out of the skies'. The skies seem to be very capricious, but I am even more so. Never before was my departure so difficult as it is now.

I feel as if the whole year with all its worries and alarms, was dragging at my feet, shackling me with iron chains. But, Verochka, I have firmly decided to lead a more concentrated life from now on, to think more of myself—I mean of us—I want to start building the future we are to have in common. It is difficult for me, Verochka, to live like this, and I am exhausted, exhausted, exhausted. An old man!

Tomorrow I am off, because Toldy is really terribly miserable there[2] and I am already dying, dying to go. There isn't a thing happening in public affairs. There is still no programme.[3] Motzkin is outrageously lazy. I am not writing to him any more and, generally, shall cease to take any further interest in the fate of the Fraction. I am fed up with playing the rôle of an *enfant terrible* who, by the way, is paying out more than anyone else. There has been no reply from H[erzl] to our last letter[4] either, and everything has gone to sleep.

Today a letter came from Cologne, from Deichler's quasi-fiancée.[5] Poor woman, they are having differences again, and D[eichler] is behaving like a coward. I received a letter full of despair, but what can I do? D[eichler] concealed it all from me.

Verusya, please describe in the greatest detail how you are spending your time, whether you are longing for me too much, in short, everything, everything, everything.

I met Herzfeld and we talked for a long time about various matters. We talked quite openly of his relations with E[sfir],[6] and a great deal of it seemed terrible to me. *Enfin!*

222. [1] Professor Graebe.   [2] At Leysin.
[3] See n. 5 to No. 212.   [4] No. 209.
[5] Cf. the reference in No. 189 to 'some private business of Deichler's'.
[6] Herzfeld is the German Zionist mentioned in No. 220; Esther (Esfir) Weinberg later became his wife.

Verusya, my sweet. If you don't write about everything in the greatest possible detail, I shall kiss you so much when you come that you will start screaming.

Best regards to Sofochka and Raya. All the best to Nyusya.

Lots of love to my little darling.

Chaimchik

223. To Catherine Dorfman, Kherson. *Geneva,* [? *5 July* Anne Koenigsberg, Nikolayev. *1902*]

Russian: H.W.: W.A.

[Addressees not named, but one of them was Catherine Dorfman, among whose papers the letter was found. The other can safely be assumed to have been Anne Koenigsberg, likewise closely associated with W.'s work at the Democratic Fraction's Geneva Information Bureau. 'Copy', at the head of the letter, probably meaning 'duplicate', is in W.'s hand.—Dorfman's copy appears to have been sent to her as an enclosure to W.'s letter to her of 5 July (No. 224) —see the opening sentence of that letter, and the same date has been conjecturally assigned to the joint letter.]

Copy

Dear Friends,

First, a joint letter to both of you about business. Don't expect too much news, except that I have been able in my solitude to do a little thinking and to make a few decisions. I don't want to tell you what dreadful days I have gone through. Why depress you?

Motzkin has already finished editing the programme. Tomorrow or the day after I shall be at Feiwel's and shall send the German text from there.[1]

Mr. Motz[kin] 'wants to take the lead in the convening of the Conference, if Geneva agrees to carry out a considerable portion of the work'.[2] How do you like that? Furthermore, he wants to participate in the Enquiry.[3] In what way his participation is to

---

223. [1] See n. 5 to No. 212. W. appears to have been over-optimistic about the early receipt of Motzkin's revised text of the programme of the Democratic Fraction. On 17 July he writes to M. (No. 244): 'The programme has still not arrived'. On 31 July (No. 263) he appeals to M. again: 'I sent you a telegram yesterday asking [you] to let me have the text of the programme.' From the rather confusing correspondence on the subject (see, for example, Nos. 225, 238, 239, 244, 246, 248, 255, 261) it is difficult to extract a coherent picture of what happened in the matter of M.'s revision of the programme, but what is clear is that the printing of the programme in its final form was not put in hand until about the beginning of August—see No. 278. It was eventually published, together with the Constitution of the Fraction, in a pamphlet printed in Berlin (copy in W.A.), undated but shown by W.'s letter to Glikin of 26 Aug. 1902 (No. 299) to have been ready, or almost ready, by that date.

[2] The Motzkin letter from which this seems to be a quotation has not been found.

[3] The projected enquiry into the position of Jewish students at various Universities—see Nos. 204, 206.

express itself I don't know. He will only go to Russia for a month to do propaganda. The others likewise. In other words, I shall have to do all the correspondence and organize the whole thing.

There is nothing from Herzl. I am sending you our letter to him[4] under separate cover.

I shall take the convening of the Conference[5] on myself on condition that I get no directives from anywhere. The reasons for this decision—in a private letter.[6]

I shall write once more from Leysin and send the programme. As you can see, there is little news, but I am sharing with you such as I have myself.

Member of the I[nformation] B[ureau], etc.,
etc., etc., and various other titles,

Ch. W.

224. To Catherine Dorfman, Kherson. *Geneva, 5 July 1902*

Russian: H.W.: W.A.

Geneva 5/VII 02
Rue Lombard 4

My sweet, dear Katyusha,

Rather thin and boring news, isn't it ?[1] Do you remember Feiwel's little song: '*wenn ich einen Galgen hätte und ein Strickelchen hätte . . .*' ?[2] But I would not hang myself, though I know whom I would hang. But, on the whole, one *Galgen* wouldn't be enough. What a nice opening for the first letter you have been waiting for rather impatiently! But, my dear friend, this will tell you what sort of mood I am in, which, by the way, is *relativ*[3] good today. I had a whole week of vacillation, expectations,[4] sad thoughts, and have decided now *einen anderen Kerl vorzustellen,*[5] to undergo a

---

[4] No. 209.

[5] The first Conference of the D.F., whose provisional statutes provided for the holding of such Conferences annually immediately before the Zionist Congress or, in non-Congress years, the Annual Conference.

[6] See No. 224. It looks as though W. must have sent a similar letter to Anne Koenigsberg, but, if so, it has been lost.

224. [1] W. seems clearly to be referring to No. 223 (see head-note to that letter), Catherine Dorfman's copy of which was, in all probability, enclosed with the letter under notice.   [2] 'Had I a gallows, had I a piece of rope. . . .'   [3] 'comparatively'.

[4] Though the meaning is not clear, orig. does not admit of any other translation than 'expectations' or 'anticipations'.

[5] Lit., 'to make a different fellow of myself'—i.e. to turn over a new leaf.

transformation. To begin with, I am not going on holiday. I can't, for some fourteen reasons. The first thirteen[6] you will understand yourself; people like myself don't talk about these. The last one is that I shall be able to do some good work here in chemistry, to work in the library for the *Hochschule*, and that's that. I am talking, of course, of theor[etical] work, for I closed down the lab[oratory] today and took leave of the Professor (he was very, very nice, even more so than I expected). Further, reforms will extend to the character of my work in all its aspects. I shall try to work more sensibly, without attempting to do everything at once. Both the cause and I will gain from this, and my nerves will also improve. *Eh bien!* How do you like all these good intentions? Oh, I'll carry them out. I have come to the conclusion that we— and by that I mean our triumvirate[7]—cannot rely a great deal on the other 'comrades' of the Fraction. They are lazy despite their talk and their good heads, Feiwel will recover and will work, and we shall also get at K[ohan]-B[ernstein], and then Pinkus and Shneerson—that will be the working group.

You know, I have a feeling that I am looking into a new future, and it seems better and fuller to me, and as though all that has happened until now—worry, anxiety—is only a prelude, a prelude which has *ausgeklungen, verklungen.*[8] I am worn out, but I shall rest, find myself; I shall find you (oh, I have already found [you]), and everything will be better.

Don't scold me for not going away. I can't. There is no money and none to be got from anywhere. The people who were supposed to send it[9] are silent in response to the reminders in my telegrams. I am going to carry out some reforms about this, too; *tant mieux.*

---

[6] The words 'The first thirteen [reasons] you will understand' are clearly an echo of the expression *achtzen und dreizen* ('eighteen and thirteen'), sometimes used in Yiddish slang to signify 'cash', and are W.'s whimsical way of saying that he has no money for a holiday.

[7] Catherine Dorfman, Anne Koenigsberg, and himself—the personnel of the Democratic Fraction's Geneva Information Bureau.

[8] 'died out, died away'.

[9] What W. was expecting seems to have been a remittance from Deichler—see his letter to V.K. of 26 July (No. 256): 'My financial problems have sorted themselves out. The deadlock occurred because Deichler sent only 50 instead of 200 (now everything is clear).' It appears from Nos. 87 and 130 that W. had been receiving a salary from the Bayer Works and it may be that the expected remittance represented an instalment of that salary, though why it should have been payable through D. is not clear—possibly (but there is no evidence of this) a salary was payable to W. and D. jointly, it being for D. to send W. his share. That it was not solely a matter between W. and D., the real source of the payment being the Bayer Works, may be inferred from the fact that W. speaks in the plural of 'the people who were supposed to send [money]': so also in No. 225—'The people who should have sent me [money] are not sending it.'

So that F[eiwel] shan't be on his own, I shall be going to him tomorrow, shall spend a few days at his place, shall then return, and back to work. That's why I want to take the convening of the Conference[10] on myself.

I have written you such a lot about myself. I don't want to ask you any questions, and at the same time I am awaiting a most detailed account of all your latest news.

Best regards to all your family, and be sure to give them my best wishes, don't forget. Good-bye, dear Katya. I warmly press your dear, good hand.

Yours
Chaim.

225. To Vera Khatzman, Rostov. *Geneva, 5 July 1902*

Russian: H.W.: W.A.

Geneva 5/VII 02
Rue Lombard 4

My joy,

By tomorrow I expect to have a letter from you from home, but I can't refrain from writing today, especially as there is some news I want to tell you. You see, my dear Verochka, my state of mind was to a large extent reflected in my letters. They, the letters, did not, however, convey even a hundredth part of the depths I have plumbed during this time. Throughout these ten days I have not smiled once, and a terrible sadness took hold of me, an infinite melancholy. Countless thoughts, gloomy thoughts; all these ran in my head and I couldn't connect them all, I could not find my bearings within myself. All I wanted was to talk to you, to talk without end to you, my Verunya. I have been summing up this difficult year, full of all kinds of worries and troubles, and—well, my Verusya, my sweet, the credit side is minute. There is nothing to point to, no halting-place reached, but I haven't lost heart because of this. On the contrary, I have decided that I must now conduct both myself and my activities differently. Everything must be submitted to reappraisal, purification, crystallisation. I don't want any vagueness, any duality that destroys my energy and tears me to pieces. I must regulate my activities in such a way that one thing (Zionism) does not interfere with the other (chemistry); I shall then be healthier and more creative. I shall work and there will be no more financial difficulties. *Je veux en finir.* On this, my Verochka, I stand firm! All this has worn me out too much to

[10] See n. 5 to No. 223.

enable me to forget it for a minute. I shall also get rid of the loafer who is sitting on my back.[1] I have already told my landlady that I shall not pay for the r[oom] any longer.

Things have changed also as regards my trip to the mountains.[2] The people who should have sent me [money] are not sending it,[3] and I am unable to go. I shall leave tomorrow to go to F[eiwel] and shall then return and live here, go for a lot of walks, do some theoretical work, and all will be well and I shall recuperate. Don't be cross with me, Verunya, I have not got the money now. I have it, that is, I will have it in three months' time, but at the moment I have not got the money (some 200–250 francs) which I need to go away and live there in peace. I don't want to stay there and be restless. Verusya, don't be anxious and don't worry. If I do still get the money—which I doubt very much, as I have had no reply not only to letters but to reminders by telegram too—I'll go, but if not, that, too, won't be the end of the world. I assure you that everything will be all right.

Motzkin has at last sent a programme,[4] so that soon it will be possible to send you a copy. As to convening a Fraction Conference, he says (very characteristically) that he is ready to take the leadership on himself if Geneva agrees to carry out a considerable portion of the work,[5] but Geneva doesn't want Mr. M[otzkin]'s leadership. This would mean doing all the work so that M[otzkin] could then write protests.[6] *Tant mieux.* The matter of the University remains in my and Toldy's hands; *c'est convenu.* There aren't any letters from Herzl. Apparently he was angered by our last joint letter.[7] It's possible that we shall write again from Leysin.[8] Toldy is feeling well. My darling, the child[9] sends you his best regards: he doesn't know whether you have left already. His address: Heidelberg, Plöckstr. 64a, should you want to write to him.

---

225. [1] V.K.'s reply to this letter, dated 29 June (12 July) 1902, W.A., shows that the 'loafer' is Zvi Aberson. Aberson was supposed to be writing a book based on a lecture he had given at the Youth Conference in Dec. 1901. As appears from *T. and E.* (p. 89), W. had tried to help him by renting a room for him in Geneva, 'but he never wrote his book'.

[2] See Nos. 216, 224.

[3] See No. 224 and n. 9 to that letter.

[4] See, however, n. 1 to No. 223 as to reasons for doubting whether Motzkin had, in fact, finished his work on the programme.

[5] See No. 223 and n. 2 to that letter.

[6] An obvious allusion to Motzkin's leading part in the Democratic Fraction Berlin group's protest of Jan. 1902—see head-note to No. 150.

[7] No. 209—not, strictly, a joint letter but stated to have been written after consultation with Feiwel.

[8] See No. 241.

[9] Nickname for Aaron Eliasberg.

Verulya, don't scold me and don't worry. If, after this letter, you still insist that I go away, I shall do so.

I give you endless kisses. Try to come as soon as possible. Write every day to your pining

Chaimchik.

226. To Vera Khatzman, Rostov. *Geneva,* [6] *July 1902*

Russian: Pcd.: H.W.: W.A.

[dated by W. 7 July, but pmk. 6 July.]

My address: Rue Lombard 4,
Geneva

Geneva 7/VII 02

I am going away now for a week to Leysin, to Toldy. If I can possibly manage it, I'll stay longer, though I doubt it. I am awfully glad that I am going. Am awaiting letters from Verochka, Sofochka and Raya with great impatience.

Ch.

227. To Catherine Dorfman, Kherson. *Lausanne,* 7 *July* *1902*

Russian: Pcd.: H.W.: W.A.

7/VII 02
Lausanne

Katyusha, my dear,

At last I too am going to Leysin, for the time being for a week, and if something turns up,[1] I shall stay longer. Buber[2] and Esther[3] will also be going there. A disgrac[eful] cowardly letter came from the A[ctions] C[ommittee] in reply to ours.[4] I shall let you know the details from Leysin. I am impatiently awaiting a letter from you. Boredom all round! My regards to all.

Chaim.

227. [1] The money he was waiting for—see No. 225.
[2] Buber did not, in fact, go to Leysin.
[3] Esther Shneerson.
[4] In a letter dated 3 July 1902 (W.A.) Ozer Kokesch and Oskar Marmorek, writing on behalf of the Smaller Actions Committee, told W. that Herzl had asked them to deal with his letter of 25 June (No. 209), and that, feeling that it was not within their competence to take any decision about the Jewish University project, they proposed to bring it up for discussion at the Annual Conference, pending which no official action could be taken in the matter nor any funds allocated for preparatory work.

228. To Vera Khatzman, Rostov. *Lausanne, 7 July 1902*

Russian: Pcd.: H.W.: W.A.

Lausanne 7/VII 02

Verochka,

On roule.[1] At the moment I am going for a week, and then, if the 13 reasons[2] are eliminated, I shall stay longer. I am very worried at having no letter. Please write daily. Regards to S[ofochka] and R[aya].

Ch.

229. To Vera Khatzman, Rostov. *Leysin, [? 8] July 1902*

Russian: H.W.: W.A.

[Dated by W. 9 July, but he speaks twice of not having heard from V.K., whereas, writing to her on 9 July (No. 231) he says 'a postcard came at last last night', from which it may be inferred that the letter under notice must have been written on 8 July.]

Feydey s/Leysin
Pension La Forêt
9/VII 02

My dear Verochka,

Today I am already properly worried because there is no letter from you. Look, darling, I write every day. Not a single day has passed without my having the most urgent need to share the day's events with you. My darling, you could at least have scribbled a few lines during the journey. After all, trains stop long enough at stations in Russia to let you give some sign of life. I am terribly worried in case something happened to you[1] on the journey— terribly worried. This is heightened by the burning feeling of loneliness and an infinite longing which does not leave me for a single moment. You ought to have sensed all this. Finally, there could already be a letter from you from home, if you had written at once; but alas!—apparently you did not write at once. Well it can't be helped, one has to brace one's self with patience and wait, and wait!

---

228. [1] 'we're off'.   [2] i.e., lack of funds—see n. 6 to No. 224.

229. [1] 'You', plur., referring to V.K. and Anna Ratnovskaya, who is known from a photograph (W.A.) taken during their journey together to Rostov to have been her travelling-companion.

I arrived here yesterday and found Toldy somewhat better, although not yet very much. I hope, however, that from now on everything will go well. It's lovely here, very beautiful, the view is marvellous, and there is a fine pine forest. Our house is right in the wood, only, only you are missing. All the time I sit and dream how good everything would be if you were with us. Yesterday Toldy and I talked of nothing but you, and I think that you must be feeling all this and will come to us at once. Verochka, stay home for another two weeks or so, and then come. You will be able to study and rest here very well. Should you come, I shall, of course, stay on here, and later shall go home[2] for three weeks for the Holy Days only.[3] Shneerson is coming here on the 15th, and Buber will be coming too on the 1st.[4] We shall be living here in a little commune.

Won't you really do it? Surely your relatives will have nothing against it. Arrange this, therefore, without fail and write to me immediately on receiving this letter.

I am starting on my chemical studies today. How the money side will work out I do not yet know.[5] If I could get [money] somewhere, I should be most happy.

I don't know now what to write to you about. If I had had your letter, things would have been different; as it is, I have a million questions to ask but shall not ask them until I have a line from you. One thing though—the dominant feature of my life is my boundless longing for you, my beloved. Nothing tastes sweet to me without you, nothing is dear. Oh, if only you were here! How I would recover! I'd listen to you in everything, and so would Toldy. Verochka, come to your Chaimchik.

Verochka, the Geneva post has just arrived and again there was no letter from you. I don't understand, I don't understand, and am very worried. If I were not afraid to start an alarm at your home, I would send a telegram, because my anxiety now knows no limit.

[No signature]

[Postscript by Feiwel.]

---

[2] To Pinsk.

[3] The series of Jewish Holy Days commencing with the New Year, which came in that year, according to the civil calendar, on the evening of 18 Sept./1 Oct.

[4] He did not come.

[5] See Nos. 225, 228.

230. To Aaron Eliasberg, Heidelberg. *Leysin, 9 July 1902*

Russian: H.W.: W.A.

> Feydey sur Leysin
> (Suiss[e], Canton de Vaud)
> Pension La Forêt
> 9. VII. 02

Dear Aaron,

For a great variety of reasons I have been unable to write to you all this time. My health is so poor that I shall only be able to resume work after leading an entirely vegetable existence for a month. Not for a month shall I be able to start thinking of a trip to Russia in general, and to Pinsk in particular.

Where are you planning to spend the summer and how is your health? How is your work getting on? Please write.

And now, business: while still in Heidelberg,[1] we talked about working together on drawing up a University project. Perhaps you know that Herzl insisted on having all the data.[2] Preparing a project appears to him rather an easy matter; he even wanted me to supply him with a *Lektionskatalog*.[3] I am fully convinced that the A[ctions] C[ommittee] is turning the whole issue into an *officielles*[4] *Fressen*[5] and light literature. What I sent H[erzl] is only a *vorläufiger Entwurf*[6] from which an approximate idea can be obtained of the financial side of the project. I made use of details supplied by colleagues and collated by myself, relating to some 12 teaching estab[lishments] of different types (in Switzerland and Germany). But of course this work, though not easy, is nevertheless the simplest. Now I have to see what has been written about *Hochschulwesen*.[7] In the Geneva Lib[rary] there are some valuable works in French and English, which I am studying, but the rich German literature on the subject is unfortunately not available to me. I think you could undertake the preparation of a list of the best works on the history, organisation and planning of Universities. Please do this without fail.

The point is that H[erzl] and the A[ctions] C[ommittee] (as they inform me in their last letter) have decided to refer the whole University issue to the Small Congress.[8] I am opposing this line of

---

230. [1] W. was in Heidelberg in March 1902 (see No. 169).
[2] See n. 4 to No. 199, n. 2 to No. 204.   [3] See n. 4 to No. 204.
[4] Thus—not 'offizielles'—in orig.   [5] 'a fat tit-bit for officialdom'.
[6] 'preliminary draft'—see n. 2 to No. 204.   [7] 'University organization'.
[8] As to the decision to refer the question to the 'Small Congress' (i.e. the Annual Conference) see n. 4 to No. 227.

action with all the means at my disposal. If I cannot forestall this, however, we ought to have some authoritative[9] material to hand. The Small Congress will probably meet in the autumn. Perhaps you have Paulsen's book on *Hochschulstudium*.[10] It would be excellent if I could study it here. I am staying here with Feiwel.

With the help of professors you should be able to find out about the best books in this field and send them. As to the *Enquête*,[11] I shall be getting into touch with Motzkin, to whom, if you wish, you may also show this letter.[12]

Dear Aaron, please write at once.

Keep well. With sincere greetings,

Yours
Chaim.

[Postscript in German by Feiwel.]

231. To Vera Khatzman, Rostov. *Leysin, 9 July 1902*

Russian: H.W.: W.A.

Feydey sur Leysin
Pension La Forêt
9/VII 02

Verusya darling,

Your dear note (a postcard)[1] came at last last night and today I am looking forward to a more detailed letter from you. To my great regret, I shall not be able to read it today, as I am now going off post-haste to Geneva for two days. A letter came from the factory;[2] it looks as if they are leading us by the nose; I am forced to repeat the test once more and to finish off once and for all. This will take a day or two, and that's the end; one way or another I shall know.

Vera, it is terribly difficult for me to leave Toldy. Moreover, I

---

[9] Lit., 'scientific', but W. habitually uses the word in the sense of 'scholarly', 'properly authenticated'.

[10] F. Paulsen: *Die deutschen Universitäten und das Universitätsstudium* ('The German Universities and University Studies'), Berlin, 1902.

[11] See n. 5 to No. 206.

[12] Motzkin was still at Heidelberg—see head-note to No. 215 and No. 258.

231. [1] Not found.

[2] The letter from the Bayer Works has not been found, but it can be inferred from W.'s comments that it amounted to an unfavourable verdict on the Weizmann–Deichler discovery mentioned in No. 165: see also No. 234, from which it appears that the letter was addressed to Deichler, who communicated its contents to W. in a letter which has likewise not been found.

too need a rest so badly, but poverty fetters one so and brings all one's plans to nought: Lord, if only you were here, if I could take one look at you, I should forget everything and live again. Verochka, you must come to me quickly. It's essential! Tomorrow I shall write more; now I am in a hurry. I kiss you, my darling, my sweet, my joy. You and only you are everything in my life.

Yours
Chaimchik.

To Sofochka, and not to Sofia Issayevna,[3] regards from Chaim. Toldy sends his best regards. He is having a rest.

232. To Vera Khatzman, Rostov. *In the train en route for Geneva,* [*9 July 1902*]

Russian: Vcd.: H.W.: W.A.

[Undated but, as can be seen from Nos. 231 and 233, obviously written on 9 July.]

Aigle-Geneva, on the train.

My joy,

Don't be surprised at my writing to you again. Toldy has been insisting that I should keep the whole story from you—that I am going back to Geneva because of the factory,[1] but I can't. To whom but you can I still write like this, and in this difficult moment my anguish grows even more and one wants to confide everything, everything to a beloved being, to say that one's love, one's respect, is stronger than ever. This is now all I have: you and Toldy, the good, fine, really infinitely good Toldy.

The better I know him the more I realise what a wonderful person he is, with a soul pure as crystal.

Verochka, I'll write to you from G[eneva] and tell you what the tests have shown, and now I am repeating my plea: come quickly, this is essential. I can't stand it without you. Your people will understand. For you belong to me too, Vera darling.

Come to your
Chaimchik.

---

[3] W. sends his greetings to V.K.'s sister Sophia under her pet-name, Sofochka, instead of using the formal 'Sofia Issayevna'.

232. [1] See No. 231.

233. To Vera Khatzman, Rostov. *Geneva, 10 July 1902*

Russian: Pcd.: H.W.: W.A.

Geneva 10/VII 02

Verochka, my sweet,

You already know, darling, the reason why I have come here. And so I have checked the experiment and got the same result, and that means that the factory are lying.[1] Either they work carelessly or they are cheating me. *Enfin* we shall see. I am sitting here in a café with Herz[feld] and Monash,[2] and we are thinking of you, dear friends.[3]

But Verochka did not keep her word and did not write a detailed letter. Why? Why? Why? I could even be cross if I were still able to be cross. I worked for 15 hours today and you can imagine how I feel, and all the excitement. O Lord, this pursuit, this badgering. But I shall leave my philosophy for another time, and now I finish.

I am writing just a few lines because I do not want a day to pass without my writing to you. Best regards to S[ofochka] and R[aya].

Chaim.

Cordial greetings to Nyusya.

[Postscript by Herzfeld and Monash.]

234. To Vera Khatzman, Rostov. *Geneva, 11 July 1902*

Russian: H.W.: W.A.

Geneva 11/VII 02
Ecole de Chimie (laboratory)

Verochka, my joy,

Today at last came your detailed letter[1] which I have been awaiting with such impatience. I thank you from my heart, my darling, but at the same time I add a no less heartfelt request that you write to me every day, and moreover—letters. I hate postcards from you. I am delighted that you have found everything in order at home and that you feel calm, quiet and comfortable. You have brought gaiety and joy into your home, and that, Verusya, is very good. But Sofochka is a cross-patch. Why hasn't she written for such a long time? Do scold her, but mildly, nicely, as you can do it.

Your letter, Verochka, found me in exceptionally good spirits. You do know that having received Deichler's long-awaited letter—

233. [1] See No. 232.
 [2] Berthold Monash, an engineer; later practised as a patent lawyer at Leipzig.
 [3] Probably meaning V.K. and Anna Ratnovskaya (Nyusya).

234. [1] V.K. to W., 22 June (5 July) 1902, W.A.

in which he informed me of the results of the tests carried out at the factory[2]—I rushed from Leysin, and we have again checked the basic experiments here and found that my results are correct. The factory is either mistaken or cheating—this will have to be carefully and tactfully ascertained.[3] In any case, I am delighted that I am right. However, I am unable to describe my excitement, Verochka. Yesterday I worked for 15 hours by the clock. At midnight I was still at the laboratory. Today I have been here since 7 a.m., but I am finishing today too and am leaving tomorrow morning. I shall, of course, write to the factory and I hope they will understand now that they must behave differently. Toldy also was very excited all the time because of all this business, and I have just sent him a telegram saying that all is well.

In this difficult time Levinson[4] did me a very great favour by working with me through all these hours. I was terribly upset. I shan't start writing to you now about the Conference[5] and the University, my darling. I shall leave it till the day after tomorrow, when I shall have calmed down and be rested. Last night I hardly closed my eyes. Now I am going home and will tumble into bed until tomorrow. If it's possible, I'll send Sofochka a copy of the project I had prepared for Herzl.[6]

Tomorrow I shall take your dear letter to Toldy. He will be very pleased. We recall you, Verusya, almost hourly, but he is going to get a good laugh at your German dialect.[7] Verusya, my poor little German girl. Oh, would I kiss you: three or four kisses for each little mistake. Oh, what a long time I would have to kiss you, Verusik, till you were black and blue all over, Veronka.

My darling, I don't agree, don't agree, don't agree—I am talking of your plans for coming here. You must understand, sweetheart, that it is terrible for me to think of it. You must understand that I am persistently haunted by a terrible, aching, wringing pain. I can't take a single step without feeling your absence all the time, and the fact that you will be coming three weeks earlier is no consolation to me.[8] Verulya, if you only knew—but this is impossible to describe.

---

[2] See n. 2 to No. 231.

[3] How the discussions with the Bayer Works ended is unknown. Later references to the subject, ending with No. 274, leave the matter in the air.

[4] Samuel Levinson.

[5] The projected Democratic Fraction Conference.   [6] See n. 2 to No. 204.

[7] V.K. had added to her letter a few lines in German for Feiwel.

[8] V.K. wrote in her letter: '. . . Despite my ardent wish, I cannot come to you in August. . . . I shall come to you three weeks before the term starts, that is on October 1st.' (In his letter to V.K. of 30 June (No. 214) W. had suggested her coming in August.)

I write to you every day, and sometimes in the evening a post-card in addition to the letter, so that you know everything that happens to me. And I beg you to do exactly the same. For me this is as indispensable as air.

I have already written to you about Herzl's letter.[9] I have not yet replied because he is in London.[10]

Verochka, write to me about the Rostov 'comrades'.[11]

So Lyolya is a Zionist.[12] That means there are two black sheep in the family, that's good! Darling make him into a member of the Fraction. The programme is already in existence. I'll send it to you when it is printed in full.[13]

Well, I am closing. I have to go and filter.

Good-bye, my darling, my good one, be happy, gay, and know that far away from you there lives and loves you very much

Yours
Chaimchik.

Regards to Raya and Sofochka.

A letter from Saul has just arrived: he makes many enquiries about you. His address: Darmstadt, Dieburgerstr. 55.

235. To Vera Khatzman, Rostov. *Geneva/Leysin, 11/23 July 1902*

Russian: Pcd.: H.W.: W.A.

[The contents explain how this postcard, dated Geneva, 11 July 1902, came to be posted by W., as shown by pmk., on 23 July from Leysin, the words down to 'how dreadful, Verochka' having been written in Geneva and the rest added in Leysin.]

Geneva 11/VII 02
Rue Lombard 4

Dear Verochka,

I have just received your letter,[1] my darling. How dreadful,

---

[9] W. probably means the Smaller Actions Committee letter of 3 July 1902 mentioned in n. 4 to No. 227.

[10] He had gone to London to give evidence before the Royal Commission on Alien Immigration.

[11] A mildly ironical reference to the Rostov Zionists.

[12] V.K. had told W., in her letter, that according to her sister Sophia, her brother Lyolya was a Zionist.

[13] As to the final revision and printing of the programme of the Democratic Fraction see n. 1 to No. 223.

235. [1] The letter of 22 June (5 July) mentioned by W. in his letter of 11 July (No. 234).

Verochka.[2] I have just now (23/VII) found this beautiful postcard which I started to write in Geneva a fortnight ago, but which remained in my pocket. I have just found it and I am posting it on to you.

I have just sent you a letter,[3] and therefore am writing only a brief note of greetings.

Lots and lots of love.
Chaim.

236. To Vera Khatzman, Rostov. *Lausanne, 12 July 1902*

Russian: Pcd.: H.W.: W.A.

Lausanne 12/VII 02
(railway-station)
Address at Leysin (Vaud)
Pension La Forêt

Verochka,

At Geneva I wrote just a couple of words;[1] am continuing from Lausanne. I am on my way and will be in Leysin at 9 o'clock, where I should like to remain as long as possible. It's difficult, my darling, to describe how tired I am. I worked so hard, but I am glad that the results are good. I don't know how things will turn out with the factory,[2] but for the time being I am not worried. I shall probably stay a whole week in bed. I haven't slept for 2 nights. Best regards, Verunya, many greetings to Sofochka.

Chaim.

I have received a very nice letter from my sister. She is at Druskienniki for the time being.[3]

237. To Vera Khatzman, Rostov. *Leysin, 13 July 1902*

Russian: H.W.: W.A.

Feydey s/Leysin
13/VII 02
Pension de La Forêt

Toldy has replied to you in not entirely class[ical] German, but all the same, Verochka, keep on writing in German always. Toldy will

---

[2] In her above-mentioned letter V.K. had told W. that she had seen an elderly Jewish traveller molested in the train in which she (V.K.) was going through Austria *en route* from Geneva to Rostov.   [3] No. 249.

236. [1] See No. 235.   [2] See n. 3 to No. 234.

[3] See nn. 5 and 6 to No. 216.

correct your mistakes. This is very useful, my wicked girl, my good girl! Regards to Sofochka and Raya.[1]

Chaimchik

Dear Verochka,

I shan't trouble you, Verochka, with requests to write to me more often. Apparently, for some reason totally incomprehensible to me, you are writing rarely. In all, I have had two letters from you[2] (I don't count postcards), while by now you must have had about 15 from me. If you would only think a little about my state of mind, you would always find an opportunity to write to me. But I am not going to say another word about this.

I arrived here last night. I feel terrible after all I had to go through during that damned week;[3] nevertheless, I am calm now. My only wish at the moment is to have the means to stay here longer, but I have grave doubts on this score.

Verochka, if you are not thinking of coming until 1st Oct[ober], then this is complete nonsense, since by then we shall all be on the move and this would mean extending our separation even further.[4] I still have a spark of hope that you will think it over and come here sooner.

I can't write a great deal at the moment, my darling, my lovely one, because the pen is falling out of my hand. When I get a letter from you, my spirits will improve.

Good-bye my darling. With many kisses.

Chaim.

[Postscript by Feiwel.]

238. To Catherine Dorfman, Kherson. *Leysin, 14 July 1902*

Russian: H.W.: W.A.

Leysin-Feydey,
Pension Forêt,
14/VII 02

Dear good Katya, my friend and comrade,

Thanks for your news. In the meantime you must have received

237. [1] Added at head of letter.
  [2] From Munich, 27 June, and from Rostov, 22 June (5 July), both in W.A.
  [3] See No. 234.
  [4] See n. 8 to No. 234. What W. is saying is that, if V.K. carried out her intention of arriving in Geneva on 1 October, this would be pointless, since by that time he would have gone to Russia. As to W.'s plans for a propagandist campaign in Russia see n. 24 to No. 238. He did, in fact, go to Russia at the end of August and was not back in Geneva until the beginning of November.

my letter.[1] Not a great deal has happened since, apart from un-pleasant things. I rushed to G[eneva] again from here, because I received an unpleasant letter from the factory which stunned me:[2] but all the same, I was right, my data were correct, and they are thieves and want to drain the last drop of blood out of me. I shall try to resist.[3] Now I hope I am here *definitiv*.[4] I have been having a rest for a day and a half: I can't describe to you how hard I worked, I even had my meals in the labor[atory] and slept only 4 hours a day, and this went on for 4 days.[5] But let's leave it, I want to forget it and not think about it any more.

What's wrong with your Mother?[6] Why don't you write to me in greater detail? Katyusha, my dear write immediately everything about your family, about those people who are so dear to me.[7] I am not asking any questions for I am quite sure that you yourself will write, and you will, won't you?

My dear, through Sonia W[einstein] you will receive 'part' of the programme (shame!). Mr. Motz[kin] is still not ready.[8] Well, I won't start venting my indignation and my irritation. I have received Nietzsche,[9] but do you know, it wasn't what I wanted, and I had to send it back. If I get it before W[einstein]'s departure, I shall be very pleased, as I very much want you to have it as soon as possible. An entire colony is gathering here, but a different one, our own.[10] Buber is coming on the 1st, Shneerson on Wednesday, Pinkus on the 20th, Sheychik too.[11] Not bad, is it? Kasteliansky and Aaron[12] are collecting material on the Universit[y]. We shall get the books here and shall all work. Toldy is getting better, though his progress is not too quick. Esther[13] will come and take him in hand, I am no good for it. Soon (in 3 weeks' time) the miscellany[14]

---

238. [1] No. 224.   [2] See n. 2 to No. 231.

[3] See No. 249.   [4] 'for good'.   [5] See No. 234.

[6] Her mother was seriously ill and died later in the month—see No. 255.

[7] He had met them when in Kherson in Aug. 1901.

[8] See n. 1 to No. 223.

[9] See No. 255, from which it appears that the book which W. meant to send to Catherine Dorfman did not, in fact, arrive in time to be taken to her by Sonia Wein-stein. There is nothing in W.'s correspondence with her to show which of Nietzsche's works he wanted her to have.

[10] 'our own'—i.e., not like the Jewish student colony in Geneva, in which the Zionists were a minority.

[11] Buber did not, in fact, join them at Leysin, nor did Saul Lurie ('Sheychik')—see No. 265.

[12] Aaron Eliasberg—see No. 230.   [13] Esther Shneerson.

[14] By 'the miscellany' W. means the *Jüdischer Almanach*, the first publication (Berlin, Sept. 1902) of the Berlin Jewish publishing house, *Der Jüdischer Verlag*, founded in 1902 by Buber, Feiwel, Ephraim Lilien, and David Trietsch. It was taken over in 1907 by the Zionist Organization.

will appear, it will be a splendid edition, also Morris Rosenf[eld].[15] Everything is already with the printers. I have subscribed for all of us (i.e. the three of us[16] one copy each, of course on the best paper. Buber and Lil[17] are working hard. I am sending you the *J[üdischer] V[erlag]* prospectus.[18] Perhaps you can do something about it at Khers[on]. You'll find all the information there. It's hardly necessary to tell you that T[oldy] sends his best regards. He also is very sorry that [we] were unable to spend more time together.[19] But he will probably stay here for the winter too, as he intends to take his docto[rate] in Berne. We haven't written to the A[ctions] C[ommittee] so far, as H[erzl] is in London, taking part in the *Alien-enquête*[20] I imagine the היגטערן אויוון פאליטיקער[21] of the synagogues have decided that he has been invited to rule England in place of the ailing Edward.[22] פאר אס ניט?[23] I am still not clear as to what is happening to the Fraction. Such indolence and utter indifference. I don't know yet who is going to R[ussia] and when. I am waiting for news from Jacobson.[24] I shall also send you the Univ[ersity] project.[25] What do your—our—Kherson comrades think about the question? I am especially inter[ested] in the views of your sister[26] and Bromberg; please convey to them my heartfelt greetings.

I shall write to Anna[27] today. Perhaps מויד[28] will come over to us

---

[15] *Lieder des Ghetto*, another *Jüdischer Verlag* publication, being Feiwel's German translation from the original Yiddish of 'Songs of the Ghetto' by the Jewish poet Morris Rosenfeld (1862–1923). It did not, in fact, appear until 1903.

[16] W., Catherine Dorfman, and Anne Koenigsberg.

[17] Affectionate abbreviation of Lilien.

[18] See n. 14 above. The prospectus (copy in C.Z.A.—A102/10/1/4) invited financial support by way of (*a*) subscriptions for projected publications, or (*b*) contributions to a guarantee fund.

[19] Feiwel had been in Geneva in the latter part of June before going to Leysin at the end of that month—see Nos. 210, 213.   [20] See n. 10 to No. 234.

[21] Yidd., 'Armchair politicians'—lit., 'politicians behind the oven'. At or after synagogue services in Russia the congregants had a way of gathering round the stove for a chat about the events of the day—hence this Yiddishism.

[22] The press had reported the postponement of the Coronation of King Edward VII because of his having to undergo an operation for appendicitis.

[23] Yidd., 'And why not?'

[24] From a letter of 25 July (7 Aug.) 1902 from Victor Jacobson to Ussishkin (C.Z.A.—A24, vol. 17) it appears that W. had written to Jacobson, at this time director of the Russian Zionist Information Centre and Zionist regional leader in the Simferopol area, announcing that he (W.) and other members of the Democratic Fraction intended touring Russia that summer in the interests of Zionist propaganda, and asking that the proposed itinerary should be communicated to the regional leaders.

[25] The preliminary plan mentioned in n. 2 to No. 204.

[26] Catherine Dorfman's sister, Anastasya (Esther) Bromberg.

[27] Anne Koenigsberg.

[28] Yidd., *Yud*, meaning *Der Yud* ('The Jew'), a Warsaw Yiddish weekly edited by Joseph Lurie.

after all. We have had some interesting news from Eliashev[29] in this connection. We need some 5,000 r[oubles] and we shall scrape them together.

Latest news: 'Russian' girls are no longer admitted to Berlin Univ[ersity].[30]

Keep well, my dear, write often. Regards to all [your] dear ones! Your loving and respectful, and very weary

Chaim.

The prospectus[31] is under separate cover.

[Postscript by Feiwel.]

239. To Vera Khatzman, Rostov. *Leysin*, [? *14 July 1902*]

Russian: H.W.: W.A.

[Date 19 July 1902 inserted in an unidentified hand, but contents point to 14 July as a more probable date.]

Leysin-Feydey (Vaud)
Pension Forêt

Dear Verochka, my girlie,

I have just received your postcard[1] which made me very happy. Verusya, don't write postcards; they irritate me. There is nothing new to report since yesterday, of course; the post didn't bring anything special. I keep waiting for Sofochka's letter, but she is taking a long time over it, and Raya keeps on laughing [? at us]. Look, Verochka, tell her that something like this could happen to her too, and then we old people, you and I, will laugh at the young. I don't want to start that old song again—that I long for you infinitely, that everything would be much better if you were here; your caresses, your words, your eyes—all of you, Verochka, has so become part of me that I feel incomplete, cut off, uprooted, artificially shackled, morally amputated. At such a distance my

---

[29] Eliashev had interested himself in a project (nothing came out of it in the end) for making *Der Yud* the organ of the D.F.: see Lurie to Motzkin, 6 June 1902 (C.Z.A. —A126/24/7/2/1) and subsequent correspondence between Motzkin, Lurie, and Feiwel, ibid.

[30] 'Russian' in quotation-marks in orig.—i.e. 'Russian' means Russian-Jewish. Severe restrictions were reported in the Jewish press of the period to have been imposed by Berlin University on the admission of women students from Russia, but there appears to be no evidence that they did, in fact, amount to an absolute ban on the admission of such applicants generally or of Jewish applicants of this category.

[31] See n. 18 above.

239. [1] Not found.

pen is unable to transmit the nervous tension I am under in my effort to forget a little, and the days seem to crawl, to drag endlessly. Toldy feels a little better and he very much wants to see you, as you can judge for yourself from his letter. These last days he has had to work for the *Verlag*. Sumptuous editions will soon come out: the Jewish miscellany and Morris Rosenfeld's poems in Toldy's translation.[2] I shall have a splendid copy of each, and you will get one too from Toldy. We shall read it together in the winter. Did I say 'winter'? No, no, no: in summer, summer, summer! I have ordered some typed copies of the unfortunately unfinished programme[3] and of the University draft project.[4] I should have them the day after tomorrow, and shall send you [? a copy] at once. I am sending you under separate cover the prospectus of the *Jüdischer Verlag*.[5] Perhaps we could get a few subscribers. The subscription is 20 marks. But all this can be found in the pro[s-p]ectus. The money is to be sent to Berlin. The address is at the bottom of the prospectus. Sheychik will come here in ten days' time. He complains about your silence. Buber will be here on the 1st.[6] Esther Shneerson and Pinkus probably on the 20th. Well, Verusya, doesn't all this attract you? Kasteliansky (I think I told you about him, he is a very good man) and Aaronchik[7] are preparing a bibliography on the University question. All this will be sent to Leysin and will be put together here. We have not yet replied to the A[ctions] C[ommittee],[8] as Herzl is in London: he is taking part in the Parliamentary *Enquête* into the Jewish question.[9] You know, of course, my dear, that a Bill has been introduced to stop the entry of Jews into England.[10] Their Parliament decided to hold an *Enquête* into the influence of foreign Jews (Russians and Roumanians) on the life of the local population, and Herzl has been invited in the capacity of an expert on the Jew[ish] question.[11] Very interesting, isn't it? I can imagine all the comments of the half-baked Synagogue politicians. They have probably decided that because of Edward VII's illness, Herzl has been invited to rule England for the time being; and why not?[12]

How do you spend your days? Do you study with Nyusya, to

[2] See nn. 14 and 15 to No. 238.   [3] See No. 238, 3rd para.
[4] See n. 2 to No. 204.   [5] See n. 18 to No. 238.
[6] See n. 11 to No. 238.   [7] Aaron Eliasberg.
[8] i.e. to the S.A.C.'s letter of 3 July 1902—see n. 4 to No. 227.
[9] See n. 10 to No. 234. This expression 'Parliamentary *Enqutêe*' is inaccurate; the body in question was a Royal Commission.
[10] No such Bill was, in fact, before Parliament at this stage.
[11] See No. 247.
[12] Cf. the almost precisely similar paragraph in W.'s letter of 14 July to Catherine Dorfman (No. 238); and see nn. 21 and 23 to that letter.

whom I send my warmest regards? Will Nyusechka stay long in Rostov? Or will she go soon to Peter?[13] Another news item. Berlin Univ[ersity] will no longer accept 'Russian' girls.[14] Things become worse almost hourly. I'll finish now, as I still have many letters to write. Keep well, my beloved Verusya. I give my little girl, my little darling, many, many kisses. Toldy sends his best regards and asks you to come as soon as possible. I agree with the last speaker. Write to me about the R[ostov] Zionists.

> Your, your
> Chaimchik.

If any money is avail[able]—send it.

[Postscript by Feiwel.]

240. To Vera Khatzman, Rostov. *Leysin, 15–16 July 1902*

Russian: H.W.: W.A.

> Leysin, 15/July 1902[1]

Verunchik, my darling girl,

Today is the first time that I haven't managed to write in time to catch the post, and so a day will pass without your receiving a letter from me. I hope you won't be worried. I have done a whole day's work on chemistry (theoretical) and there were many letters to deal with too. I want to finish the day with a letter to you, Verochka. Today I received a picture postcard from you[2] (the view is not particularly beautiful). Thanks to all those who signed. But really, Verochka, can't you write a letter every day?

There is little news here. We live, work and rest. The day passes very quickly, and at times, especially when Toldy begins to feel unwell, I feel rotten, miserable, depressed. Moreover, there are also extraneous circumstances which prevent me from enjoying the peace and quiet, but what can one do? I am beginning to content myself with what there is, and for the time being do not think about how much better it might be.

We have prepared a pamphlet on the University question. We shall have it printed and will send it on to a number of people. It will be in the form of a report and will also include my outline

[13] St. Petersburg was often referred to in Russian as 'Peter'.
[14] See n. 30 to No. 238.

240. [1] '1902' printed.   [2] Not found.

plan.³ We need money for printing and we go about begging everywhere. If you can get anything at R[ostov], send it to us. Should you get an amount worth considering, say 25–50 roubles, send a telegram to Feiwel at Leysin with the one word *Ja.*

Well, Verochka, you are not pampering me with letters. You are probably missing me less than I miss you. *Tant pis* for me.

Shneerson is coming the day after tomorrow. She will bring plenty of interesting books. Buber will certainly be here by the 1st.⁴

As for other news, I can report that there is a flood in the Rhône Valley; this can be clearly seen from our mountain (1450 metres). In Berne, the railway-station burnt down. Salisbury has resigned.⁵ There is a violent storm here, which is amazingly beautiful. Tomorrow there will be a *mer de brouillard*. Our landlady is very good and looks after us well.

Toldy is feeling better now; his appetite is good but the poor chap will have to live on milk for another month.

I am ending for the time being; will write more tomorrow. With many, many kisses, Verochka, my wicked one, my darling girl,

Chaimchik

[Postscript by Feiwel.]

16/VII

My sweet darling,

Your dear letter,⁶ your photograph and Sofochka's letter arrived today. This made me terribly happy, and I thank you with all my

---

³ Published in Berlin later in 1902 under the title *Eine Jüdische Hochschule*. Buber, Feiwel and W. are named as the authors, but Buber's participation appears to have been purely nominal; in No. 257 W. describes the pamphlet as consisting of 'my plan with Toldy's commentary'. The work was done by W. and Feiwel—see No. 257. Pt. I, probably attributable mainly to Feiwel, after describing the ever-increasing difficulties encountered by Jewish students in Eastern Europe in obtaining access to higher education, argues the case for the establishment, as a matter of urgency, of a Jewish University (*Hochschule*)—if possible in Palestine, but if this should be, for the time being, impracticable, then—since the need is pressing—in some other country, which might be England or Switzerland, but only as a temporary measure and on the understanding that it was intended eventually to move the institution to Palestine.—Pt. II consists of a slightly amended version of the 'preliminary plan' submitted by W. to Herzl in May 1902 (see n. 2 to No. 204), the main difference being that England is added to Switzerland—apparently with a bias in favour of England—as a possible second-best, should it be unavoidably necessary to consider a temporary alternative to Palestine.   ⁴ But see n. 11 to No. 238.

⁵ The British Prime Minister, Lord Salisbury, resigned on 11 July 1902.

⁶ Shown by V.K.'s letter of 29 June (12 July) 1902, W.A., to refer to a letter (not found) of 27 June (10 July).

heart. Yes, Verochka, you are right: we are not going to have such separations ever again; every hour it becomes more and more difficult, and it feels as if a whole eternity lies ahead of us before our reunion. . . . I shall be alone this evening, as Toldy is leaving to meet Shneerson; she will be here tomorrow morning. I am not writing a lot to you now, either. I shall answer Sofochka today but shall not post the letter until tomorrow; it is a long one. My chemistry studies are going well. Verochka, tell Raya that by V. Kh. I mean her sister Verochka. What a girl! She was trying to be clever at my expense.

I kiss you, my sweet, my lovely one, my dear beloved darling, and I love you, love you, love you. I haven't been able to tear myself away from your dear picture all day long. We shall have our photographs taken one of these days. We have got a photographer at the pension. My sweet, keep well, and love your loving Chaimchik who longs for you terribly.

These hieroglyphics represent regards from Toldy.

[Postscript written in margin by Feiwel.]

241. To Theodor Herzl, Vienna. *Leysin, 16 July 1902*

German: H.W.: C.Z.A.—Z1/337

> Leysin, Pension de la Forêt
> (Switzerland)
> 16/VII 02

Dr. Theodor Herzl
Vienna

Dear Dr. Herzl,

We are extremely sorry to have received from the Actions Committee a communication on the subject of the Jewish University which makes it clear that you wish to hold over the whole matter for the time being until the Small Congress.[1]

We are not blind to the fact that through the medium of the Small Congress—to which, incidentally, it could not be submitted by way of a resolution[2]—the matter could, in other circumstances, be given a certain impetus. Nevertheless, we who today still have the fullest grasp of the subject must say clearly that it would be entirely inappropriate, indeed positively harmful, to bring the

241. [1] See n. 4 to No. 227. As to the 'Small Congress' see n. 3 to No. 209.
[2] Decisions on questions of principle were reserved for the Congress and were not within the competence of the 'Small Congress'.

matter up at a time when it is so unripe for discussion. Even the preliminary plan previously submitted[3] cannot, in our opinion, be treated as something to build on, or an adequate point of departure in this extremely complicated question.

We beg again to refer most emphatically to our last letter, sent to you on June 25th[4] and would ask you to re-examine the arguments put forward in that letter.

We also take the liberty of informing you that we are still working on the project as energetically as before and have enlisted the collaboration of a group of people with whose help we are carrying out the preparatory work along the lines indicated in our letter of the 26th.[5]

In view of the fact that we were not granted any funds for our initial activities,[6] and because the position of Jewish students at the Universities is becoming more and more complicated from month to month,[7] it is impossible to determine in advance when this work will have made sufficient progress for us to submit it to public scrutiny.

We shall take it upon ourselves, should you so wish, to keep you informed about the progress of our work.

With Zion's greetings,
In the name of Mr. B. Feiwel and myself,
Yours faithfully,
Dr. Ch. Weizmann

242. To Catherine Dorfman, Kherson. *Leysin, 17 July 1902*

Russian: Pcd.: H.W.: W.A.

Leysin, Pension Forêt
17/VII 02

Dear Katyusha,

I am sending you part of the programme through Weinstein. Mr. M[otzkin] has not sent us the rest yet.[1] Please forgive me for writing a postcard, but I am in a hurry. We have decided to publish a pamphlet about a Jew[ish] Univ[ersity], not of a propagandist

---

[3] See n. 2 to No. 204. [4] See No. 209.
[5] '26th' is obviously a slip for '25th'.
[6] See n. 4 to No. 209 and n. 4 to No. 227. [7] See n. 30 to No. 238.

242. [1] A repetition of what he had already told her, in his letter of 14 July (No. 238), about his sending her, through Sonia Weinstein, so much as was to hand of Motzkin's revised version of the programme of the Democratic Fraction.

character, but intended only for distribution among individuals. This will contain an account of the position of Jewish students, the aim of the Univ[ersity],[2] etc. Money is needed to issue this thing. Perhaps you can get something (25–30 roub[les]). If so, please send a cable to Feiwel, Leysin: *Ja.*

There is nothing new here. Am conscientiously working on chemistry. Shneerson arrived today. I haven't had a chance to speak to her yet.

Please write fully about everything that is happening at home. How is [your] Mother?[3] Is she staying on at Kherson? Don't stint your words and write.

F[eiwel]'s health is better and mine is rather middling. I very much hope to recuperate, although I have rather a lot of work to do.

Best regards to you and all yours; do write, Katyusha.

Yours
Chaim.[4]

Please forgive my absent-mindedness. Did you read Herzl's reply in No. 28, *Die Welt*?[5] We have replied to the A[ctions] C[ommittee].[6] I shall send you a copy of the letter tomorrow.

243. To Vera Khatzman, Rostov. *Leysin, 17 July 1902*

Russian: H.W.: W.A.

Leysin, Pension de la Forêt
17/vii 02

Sweet, dear, good Verochka, my precious darling,

There has been no letter from you today, and I am feeling very melancholy. The weather is melancholy too; we are swimming in a *mer de brouillard,* and although this is very beautiful, the sun should have appeared by this time. Yes, Verochka, of course next year we shall be together every day, we shall work together, but how can we quickly reach the time when we shall be beside each other, with one another, in one another? O Lord, there is still a whole, whole eternity, and I can't think of it without horror.

Why this torment, why such imperfection?[1] It is difficult for me

---

[2] See n. 3 to No. 240.   [3] See n. 6 to No. 238.
[4] Signature 'Ch. Weizmann' deleted by W. and 'Chaim' substituted.
[5] No. 28 of *Die Welt*, 11 July 1902, contained a summary of Herzl's evidence before the Royal Commission on Alien Immigration, as to which see n. 6 to No. 247.
[6] See No. 241.

243. [1] 'imperfection' reads awkwardly, but orig. does not admit of any other translation.

even to write about it, the pain flares up in me so, but I can't keep silent about it either.

Yes, Verusya, those are the thorns of our love, of our fine love, which, my Verunchik, my darling, my sweet, I have never doubted.

I am getting on quite well with my chemistry. I am always in the open and smoke very little. Of course I am feeling much better, but it is rather difficult to cast all cares aside. Toldy's health is better; he sends his best regards. He is sleeping now.

Shneerson came today. She looks very poorly, but she will soon recover here.

My work is going on excellently and I am burrowing in chemical literature with great pleasure, filling up the gaps. You know, of course, that this has been worrying me a great deal, and so I now feel great satisfaction.

Please write, my joy, of your studies and especially of your Hebrew. Are you studying the Bible?

Yesterday I answered Sofochka with a long, long—but, I fear, rather disjointed—letter. My thoughts ran ahead of my pen and I did not finish anything off.

Verulya, give my regards to all our, your, family. Tell Rayka[2] that she could write all the same.[3] And you, my darling, my child, write every day, and not postcards. Regards to Zina[4] and Nyusya.

Good-bye, my sweet, my darling, my lovely one.

Many kisses.
Your
Chaimchik

244. To Leo Motzkin, Heidelberg. *Leysin, 17 July 1902*

Russian: H.W.: C.Z.A.—A126/24/7/2/2

At[1] Leysin, Pension de
/la Forêt
17/VII 02

Mr. L. Motzkin
Heidelberg.

Dear Leo,

The programme has still not arrived[2] and I really do not know

[2] V.K.'s sister Raya.
[3] 'all the same'—What W. is alluding to is unknown.
[4] Agnes (Zina) Brailovsky.

244. [1] In orig., *z. Zt.* ('temporarily'). [2] See n. 1 to No. 223.

what to do now, when we are being showered with letters from everywhere, asking about the programme. Not a single decision has been implemented as yet.[3] Who is going to Russia?[4] When? I have to know this to get into touch by letter with those people and also with our representatives.

As to the Conference,[5] I don't think it can be convened by October and in Russia. Don't forget that studies start everywhere in Oct[ober] and moreover, in Russia, under present conditions, it is rather doubtful whether it would be possible to confer in peace.[6]

I earnestly ask you to send the programme at once, to write when and how the first official announcement is to appear, your views about the Conference. It is essential to issue the programme and Conference announcements at once, stating the time and place.

I am awaiting your reply by return of post. F[eiwel] sends his best regards. He is not well but on the whole he is better.

With best wishes,

Chaim.

245. To Vera Khatzman, Rostov. *Leysin, 18 July 1902*

Russian: H.W.: W.A.

Leysin, 18/VII 02.

My sweet darling,

Today is a sad day with us. Toldy has been in bed the whole day and he has not said a word; he is feeling ill, and this affects my state of mind too. I hope he will be better by the evening. He meant to write to you but has put it off till tomorrow.

---

[3] The decisions referred to are those taken by the Democratic Fraction Programme Committee at its Heidelberg meeting on 16–22 June. From a printed sheet, *Aus dem Protokoll der Demokratisch-Zionistischen Fraktion*, (W.A.), it can be seen that the main points dealt with were the publication of news-bulletins, the drafting of a programme of work, the enrolment of new members, and arrangements for the Fraction's first Conference, pending which the Programme Committee was to function as the Executive Committee.

[4] As to the proposed propagandist campaign in Russia see n. 24 to No. 238.

[5] See n. 3, above.

[6] W. does not appear to have in mind any special circumstances which would make it more difficult at that time than at other times to hold the Conference in Russia. He seems to be referring simply to the obstacles presented by the repressive legislation then in force—the unlikelihood of official permission being obtainable for the Conference and the danger of police intervention if it were held without such permission. (Nevertheless, the Russian Zionist Conference held at Minsk a few weeks later was officially sanctioned and not interfered with.)

Otherwise nothing special. I am studying, do a bit of walking, the day passes rather quickly, but most of all I am longing for you, my darling. There have also been some unpleasant things during this time. I don't know what was the reason, but I had very nasty letters from Berne,[1] of such a nature that I did not even answer them. This has been poisoning my life, and I want all the more to have you here. In fact, Verochka, my darling, everything seems to stand out in stronger relief in your absence.

I am still hoping very much that there will be a letter from you today; there ought to be one. Please write, my little one; perhaps you have all decided differently about your coming here.

I don't know how much longer I shall stay here. I think another three weeks or so. I'll be very sorry to leave this place if only because one can study here marvellously. I am making very good progress. I have already prepared about six lectures, and this, moreover, is also of enormous benefit to myself.

I have still had no letter from Deichler nor from the factory and am awaiting it with great impatience.[2] One hopes that things will be all right now. About time, too.

Darling Verunchik, write, write, write to your ever deeply loving

Chaimchik.

246. To Vera Khatzman, Rostov. *Leysin, 20 July 1902*

Russian: H.W.: W.A.

Leysin, Pension de la Forêt
20/VII 02

My sweet Verochka,

In yesterday's letter[1] to you I unwittingly, and despite myself, let my low spirits break through, probably conveying this mood to you, my darling, from afar. Now it's over, my dearest, and I feel better today, more cheerful and gay, and should like to drive away the sad little thoughts which this has cast over you, my beloved.

245. [1] Almost certainly from W.'s former fiancée, Sophia Getzova, at this time residing in Berne. This supposition is confirmed by V.K.'s letter to W. of 10 (23) July 1902, W.A.: '. . . I simply cannot understand what sort of nasty letters you could receive from Berne or what reason there is for them. After all, everything has been clarified, and you have remained friends, I think.' As to the last point, see n. 22 to No. 140.
[2] See n. 3 to No. 234. Nothing is known of any further communication from Deichler or from the Bayer Works with reference to the matter.

246. [1] No letter dated 'yesterday' (19 July) has been found. He may possibly be referring to his letter of 18 July (No. 245).

And why such moments come over me is really difficult for me to define. All that I have gone through, all that I have suffered and endured, finds its outlet in boundless sadness and even in tears, and I must relieve my heart sobbing out the grief which I cannot put into words. That's how it has been with me, Verusya, these last days, and I haven't been able to find peace, while you, your image, has been following me everywhere—if I may put it paradoxically—with its absence.

What wouldn't I give to see you, Verusya: all the beauty of Switzerland for one instant with you. Toldy has been feeling better recently, and we discussed the University project thoroughly and at length. To begin with, we need money, which would give us a certain freedom of movement. In the autumn both he (when he recovers, of course) and I will be in Russia,[2] and then we shall obtain the necessary means to carry out the project on a large scale and independently of the will of the A[ctions] C[ommittee] or any other potentates of the Zionist world. I have been unable to let you have the programme so far, as I haven't got it yet, but Pinkus will send it tomorrow,[3] and I shall then post it on to you at once. P[inkus] is still in Berne, but he is coming over this week.

What is your news? When will you write to me in such a way that I won't have to ask questions, though I know, Verulya, that I shall always ask questions, just as I shall always devour all your letters. How are your studies? All the same, Verochka, do write precisely and definitely when you expect to leave.[4] My work is going very well indeed. Last week I managed to do a great deal, and if it goes on like this, I shall succeed in filling all the gaps, which would make me infinitely happy.

Verunya, I am closing now. Lots and lots of love. Keep well and write often to your

Chaim.

[Postscripts by Esther Shneerson and Feiwel.]

---

[2] As to the projected propagandist campaign to be undertaken in Russia by members of the Democratic Fraction see n. 24 to No. 238. Feiwel had not been mentioned by W. to Jacobson as one of those proposing to take part in the campaign. In the event, W. went to Russia that summer, but not Feiwel.

[3] As to the repeated disappointment of hopes of the imminent receipt of Motzkin's revised text of the Democratic Fraction programme see n. 1 to No. 223. In saying that 'Pinkus will send it tomorrow', W. is evidently referring to a part of the revised text ('the unfortunately unfinished programme' mentioned in No. 239) which had reached him from Motzkin, and which he had sent to Pinkus, then in Berne, to have copies made there—see No. 248 and n. 6 to that letter.

[4] See No. 234 and n. 8 to that letter.

247. To Vera Khatzman, Rostov. *Leysin, 21 July 1902*

Russian: H.W.: W.A.

Leysin, Pension Forêt 21/vii 02

My sweet darling, my lovely little girl,

Your dear letter[1] arrived today. I cannot tell you, my joy, how I hate myself for causing you distress and poisoning your stay at home.[2] It is true that this is wrong, but I am at times so hopelessly despondent that I simply cannot keep silent and have to write to you. Forgive me, my darling, I realise only too clearly that it is difficult for you to come,[2] and I shall adapt myself to these circumstances and impatiently await that happy day when we find ourselves together again in the good old way. All I am asking you, my dearest, is not to worry and to write to me as often as possible. I also thank you sincerely for the money.[2] The fact is that Toldy's affairs are in none too good a state either, and you have rescued both of us; now everything will be all right.

My darling, you will find answers to all the questions you ask[3] in the letters I have written during the last weeks and which must have reached you by now. There is nothing that I haven't written to you about. I do not worry at all about the factory now; I am fully convinced that I am right, and consequently all will be well.[4]

But you, Verusya, are not writing much to me about how you are spending your days, how your studies are progressing, in short your whole life in Rostov—whom you meet, who comes to see you, etc., etc.

It's difficult to say how long I shall be staying here. I shall let you know in good time, of course. If I am in Russia,[5] you would go by way of Warsaw, and we could meet either at Pinsk or in Warsaw.

---

247. [1] V.K.'s of 1 (14) July 1902, W.A., in which (perhaps referring to such letters as Nos. 221, 225) she tells him that his letters have grieved her. She explains that one reason why she is unable to hasten her return to Switzerland is that her family do not know of her ties with W. She reminds W. that before her departure for Rostov she had offered to remain with him in Switzerland but had told him that in that case she would have to tell her family about their relationship, and W. had not then agreed to her doing so. She asks whether W. is going home to Pinsk for the Holy Days and says that she proposes to return to Switzerland a month before the start of the University term if he should not be going to Russia. She also says that she is sending him some money she has borrowed on his behalf.

[2] See n. 1, above.

[3] In her above-mentioned letter V.K. enquires about Feiwel's health and the length of his stay in Switzerland, and asks why W. has not said anything in his letters about Pinkus; how his chemical experiments are progressing; and whether the Bayer Works are going to extend his contract—see n. 15 to No. 55.

[4] See, however, n. 3 to No. 234.   [5] See n. 24 to No. 238.

In spite of everything, I already comfort myself with the thought that we shall see each other soon and that in any case a good stretch of time is behind us. I, too, count the days and am glad when they pass.

Verulya, I advise you most strongly to study issues Nos. 28 and 29 of *Die Welt* with somebody who knows German; there you will find Herzl's reply to the members of the Parliamentary Commission. This is all extremely interesting—how the English statesmen see the position of the Jews, and how shockingly Herzl defined Zionism and the Jewish nation. Some of his answers are very intelligent, some are purely journalistic and show the dilettantism of a journalist who, having such an important mission, has not prepared himself for it. He did not produce a single fact to describe the legislation affecting Russian Jews.[6] Furthermore, he had the opportunity to finish off the J.C.A.[7] right in front of the Brit[ish] Parliament, where some of the J.C.A. gentlemen (like Lord Rothschild)[8] have seats, but he did feebly. Moreover, it is clear from the questions asked by the English that they haven't even an approximate idea of the terrible plight of the Jews in Russia. Herzl did nothing whatever to explain matters in this connection. Note also

---

[6] The evidence given by Herzl on 7 July 1902 before the Royal (not 'Parliamentary') Commission on Alien Immigration was summarized in *Die Welt*, vol. vi, No. 28 and set out almost verbatim in a German translation (it was given in English) in No. 29 (11 and 18 July 1902). It is printed in the Minutes of Evidence (Command Paper 1742 (1903)) at pp. 211–21. As to the objects of the Zionist Movement Herzl said: 'We have a programme formulated at the Basle Congress, and that states that the aims of Zionism are to create a legally assured home for the Jewish people in Palestine. . . . But there may be moments when immediate help or a step forward is indispensable, and so Zionists believe that, maintaining always their principle and programme, they should in the meantime try to alleviate the hard conditions of depressed Jews by adequate means. Asked about his conception of Jewish nationalism, he said that he would define a nation as 'an historical group of men of a recognisable cohesion which is held together by a common enemy', the common enemy being in this case the anti-semite. He outlined in general terms the effect of the repressive legislation directed against the Jews in Russia but did not go closely into details. Herzl himself recognized that he had not been at his best in his evidence and had made errors of judgement (*manchen Fehler der Vorsicht*): *Herzl Diaries*, iv. 1295.—W.'s remarks about the 'dilettantism of a journalist' are a barbed allusion to the fact that Herzl had made a name as a journalist before immersing himself in Zionism.

[7] As to the reasons why the Zionists were antagonistic to the Jewish Colonization Association see n. 7 to No. 81 and n. 8 to No. 113. For Herzl's replies to questions about the activities of the I.C.A. and his estimate of their value to the Jewish people see Minutes of Evidence, p. 217.

[8] The first Lord Rothschild (the father of the Lord Rothschild to whom the Balfour Declaration was communicated) was a member of the Royal Commission. He had been allotted a token share in the I.C.A. on its incorporation as an English company in 1891, but he was not in 1902, nor had he ever been, a member of the governing body. He asked Herzl some searching questions, as (for example) whether a Jew could be a Zionist and at the same time a good citizen of his native country.

the timidity of Lord Rothschild, a wonderful product of assimilation.[9] Altogether I find all this extremely interesting and particularly draw your attention to it, my beloved; it is most instructive.
There are rumours that the next Congress will take place in
America.[10] I am convinced that this is being done mainly with the
aim of shaking off certain undesirable elements.[11] But it won't
work; we shall set sail and hold meetings during the voyage.

I feel fine, Verunechka, my studies are progressing very well and
I am very glad about it. You do know, don't you, my little darling,
how it always tormented me to be unable to devote as much time
as I wished to chemistry. I am going to fill in those gaps now. It has
been cold and cloudy here for the third day running, but as soon
as it clears up we shall have our photographs taken and I'll send
you one. Keep well, my joy and don't worry.

I give you endless kisses and warmly press your dear, lovely
hand. Loving you with all my heart, believing in you, most deeply
respecting you,

Your
Chaimchik

Warm regards to Sofochka and Rayechka.

248. To Vera Khatzman, Rostov. *Leysin,* [? *22*] *July 1902*

Russian: H.W.: W.A.

[Dated by W. 21 July, but '21' is probably a slip for '22'; 'yesterday' ('Yesterday . . . I had two letters from you') can hardly be *20* July, since in his letter
of that date (No. 246) W. makes no reference to the arrival of any letter from
V.K., and on 21 July (No. 247) he acknowledges the receipt of one letter only.
It seems clear, therefore, that he cannot have received two letters on 20 July
and that the two letters reached him on the 21st, his letter of that date,
acknowledging the receipt of one letter, having been written before the
delivery, on the same day, of a further letter from V.K.]

Leysin, 21/VII 02
Pension de la Forêt.

Verochka, my dear, sweet, lovely darling,

I feel like writing to you, but there is so little news here. Day in

---

[9] When W. made these remarks about Lord Rothschild he was not aware that
Rothschild had on 5 July had an exchange of views with Herzl at an interview which,
after an inauspicious start, had ended on a by no means unfriendly note: *Herzl
Diaries*, iv. 1290–4.

[10] It was, in fact, held at Basle in Aug. 1903.

[11] i.e., the 'Young Zionists'.

day out nothing ever changes, it is peaceful and quiet and this has a wonderful effect, one can relax and work, and doing some good chemical work my brain gets a complete rest. Thus for inst[ance], today I have already worked for eight hours, and I am not tired at all. On the contrary, the feeling that I am noticeably filling up the gaps every day cheers me up very much.

Yesterday was a good day, Veronka: I had two letters from you,[1] but I fear that because of this you may not write to me for two days. I, too, my darling, wait impatiently for the post. Once more, thanks for the money,[2] which came at the right moment (surprising!). It looks now as if things are going to improve generally.

Do you know, darling, I have already prepared the lectures for almost half the term. I shall hardly have to prepare any lectures during the year, as I am now putting everything in writing, partly in French, partly in German; I shall translate later.

You ask about Pinkus.[3] He isn't here yet, but he will probably arrive one of these days. I think that Sh[neerson]'s presence here may be keeping him away. Do you know, I don't like the way she pokes fun at him. It's awfully unjust and cruel. Toldy is also unfair, I think, and I am going to tell him this, because all this upsets me a great deal. I don't know, but though I usually like to make fun of others, I would never allow myself to do so in such matters. I am only sparing T[oldy], who undoubtedly does it just to conform (because Sh[neerson] does it); otherwise I would have mentioned this long ago. Altogether, I like Sh[neerson] less now than before. Berlin has had a bad influence on her[4] and she seems to look down on everything a bit too much. But enough gossip. Tomorrow I shall probably go by mail-coach to a place a few miles from here to see my brother-in-law's partner.[5] Do you know, my brother-in-law was in Paris again a few days ago, and I didn't know it. What a dirty trick!

I have not yet received the programme. I sent it off to be typed

248. [1] See head-note. One of the two letters from V.K. is probably that dated 1 (14) July 1902, as to which see n. 1 to No. 247, and the other, as can be inferred from the words 'You ask about Pinkus', a letter dated 2 (15) July (W.A.), in which V.K. writes, with reference to Pinkus: 'How are his affairs of the heart ? Where is he ?'

[2] See n. 1 to No. 247.

[3] See n. 1, above.

[4] See n. 18 to No. 140 as to Esther Shneerson's contacts in Berlin with Syrkin's Zionist-Socialist '*Hessiana*'.

[5] The brother-in-law is Chaim Lubzhinsky, the husband of W.'s eldest sister, Miriam (Mariya), at this time resident in Warsaw. He was engaged in the timber-trade, carrying on a successful business in which W.'s father, Ozer Weizmann had an interest (see *T. and E.*, p. 24). The partner referred to cannot be identified with certainty but is believed to have been a certain Oxner, the father-in-law of Nahum Sokolow's son, Florian.

in Berne,[6] but a press congress is taking place there now,[7] and you can imagine how busy all the typing people are.[8] And I wanted so much to send it to you. I wrote postcards to Sofochka and Raya yesterday.

Verunechka, lots and lots of love. Oh, how I shall cover you with kisses when I see you, Verochka. I dare not even picture this.

Your
Chaimchik.

[Postscript by Feiwel.]

249. To Vera Khatzman, Rostov. *Leysin, 23 July 1902*

Russian: H.W.: W.A.

Leysin, 21/vii 02
Pension de la Forêt

My sweet Verochka,

You cannot imagine, my joy, how vexed I am by what you tell me, that you had no letters from me for two days.[1] I write to you every day and I do not recall a single day without having written to you. This disgraceful post infuriates me. I well understand your disappointment, as I, too, am very worried if a day passes without a letter from you. I hope that you will now receive [letters] more regularly, but if this goes on, I shall start writing by registered post.

Today we received 50 roub[les] from Tyomkin towards the

---

[6] It seems clear that 'the programme' [of the Democratic Fraction] means the incomplete text mentioned in No. 239 (14 July 1902)—'I have ordered typed copies of the unfortunately unfinished programme'; on 31 July the full text of the programme, as revised by Motzkin, had still not reached W.—see No. 263. In No. 239 (as also in No. 263) W. uses an expression of which the only possible translation is (lit.) 'by typewriter'. Here he uses a different expression capable of denoting either typing or printing. In the light of No. 239 (see above), and because it is highly improbable that W. would have incurred the expense of printing an incomplete text, it is almost certain that he means 'typed'. The expression rendered 'typing people' would not normally be used either for typists or for printers but must here, it would seem, be taken to denote typists. From the letter under notice, read together with Nos. 239 and 246, it can be inferred that what happened was that W. sent the 'unfinished programme' to Pinkus, then in Berne, to have it copied there. W. was at this time at Leysin, and this may explain why he did not have the copying done in Geneva instead of relying on Pinkus to get it done in Berne. No copy, typed or printed, of the 'unfinished programme' has been found.

[7] The International Congress of Journalists, Berne, 20–25 July 1902.

[8] See n. 6, above.

249. [1] V.K. makes this complaint in a letter of 29 June (12 July) 1902, W.A. Because of erratic posts, this may well have reached W. after he had already received the letters bearing later dates acknowledged by him in No. 248—see n. 1 to that letter.

publication of the University pamphlet,[2] and we shall shortly pass it on to the printers. Lilien will be working on it, and it should, therefore, be beautifully produced. My project[3] will be included in full.

We are taking photographs today; so far the weather has been very cold and dull all the time. Yesterday and the day before we had to have a fire. There is a lot of snow on the mountains.

I am awaiting your picture impatiently, Verulya. My darling, Father will soon be abroad and may pay a visit here. I shall be happy to have him here with me. I didn't send my reply to the factory until today, as there was something I was waiting for.[4] I hope everything will be all right now.

Forgive me, my love, for this scrappy letter. I still have a lot of writing to do, and am therefore in a hurry.

Regards to Nyusya and thanks for [her] greetings. I shall write soon. Regards to Zina. Never-ending kisses to my dear, sweet, lovely darling, never-ending kisses and a tight, tight embrace.

Write often.
Chaimchik.

My warm regards to Sonia(fochka).[5]

250. To Aaron Eliasberg, Heidelberg. *Leysin, 24 July 1902*

Russian: H.W.: W.A.

Leysin, 24/VII 02
Pension de la Forêt

Dear Aaron,

Your letter[1] would be funny if it weren't so sad. You preach truths to us that we repeat to ourselves every day with our every action, and we do not stop at preaching them, but attempt to act upon them. I am not going to adduce all the proofs I have; I could send you copies of all our letters to Herzl and the A[ctions] C[ommittee], in which we protest in most energetic terms against the project being launched now, in which we most energetically demand that the prelim[inary] memorandum sent to Herzl be not made the

---

[2] See n. 3 to No. 240. [3] See n. 2 to No. 204.
[4] See n. 3 to No. 234. It is not known what he was waiting for, nor has his letter to the Bayer Works been found. [5] Thus in orig.

250. [1] W. is replying to a letter of 22 July 1902 (W.A.) in which Eliasberg severely criticizes his handling of the University project. The nature of the criticism can be inferred from W.'s reply.

basis of discussion, in which we insist on the incompetence of all the gentlemen from Vienna to decide such matters, in which we also set forth in much greater detail than you a whole series of questions that must be decided before the undertaking can be launched, and in which we assess the statistics exactly as you have done.[2]

The memor[andum] sent to Herzl was marked *Vorläufig*.[3] In the covering letter[4] I strongly emphasised that the report covered only the financial aspect of the matter, and I laughed no less than you at the syllabus of lectures.[5] Let me add that H[erzl] insistently demanded these data;[6] and through the fault of others pressure was brought to bear upon me, in spite of my opposition. What I submitted, *das kann ich verantworten*;[7] it was compiled thoroughly and correctly. I don't know whether you have seen it or not, but it doesn't matter. You could have criticised it without even seeing it, for it is much easier and cheaper to criticise than to do anything. In my view, the project requires not six months but more. I have also my own obligations which force me to divide my interests. I have less chance than you of living peacefully in the future, of being able to work in peace.[8] I have to combine this with being a chemist who sells the best of his time for a piece of bread, and I devote to the cause only my leisure time, all of it, without giving a thought to the consequences except when they suddenly confront me; and only in this way can we work.

If you cannot work now, that is your business.[9] When you decide for yourself that you can work, then I hope you will let us know. I never considered the compilation of a bibliographical list as 'work'.[10] However, you did not do even this, this 'non-work'.

[2] See Nos. 204, 207, 209, 241—all to Herzl, but though not directly addressed to the Actions Committee, No. 241 (16 July) is, in effect, a reply to the A.C.'s letter of 3 July mentioned in n. 4 to No. 227.

[3] 'preliminary'. In fact, the word 'preliminary' did not appear in the heading to the document sent to Herzl. What happened was that W. sent him, by mistake, an unsigned copy and retained the document intended for Herzl, in which he inserted 'preliminary' before 'plan'—see n. 2 to No. 204.

[4] See No. 204.

[5] See No. 230 and n. 4 to No. 204.

[6] See n. 4 to No. 199 and Nos. 201, 202.

[7] 'for that I can take responsibility'.

[8] Eliasberg came of a well-to-do family.

[9] Eliasberg had said in his letter that he could not at present find time for serious research work, which would need five or six months, but would be prepared to undertake it when he was free.

[10] In his letter to Eliasberg of 9 July (No. 230) W. had asked him to compile a list of the best German works on Universities, to which Eliasberg's reply was that this could not seriously be called 'work'.

I appealed to you, believing that extensive literature on the subject could be found in Heid[elberg]. I did not wish to confine myself to the titles of books; what interested me was their content. But everything I write is superfluous. . . .

Yours
Chaim.

251. To Vera Khatzman, Rostov. *Leysin, 24 July 1902*

Russian: H.W.: W.A.

Leysin 24/VII 02

My sweet Verochka, my joy,

I received your dear letter[1] last night and kept on reading and re-reading it. Verochka darling, I have not taken any decision yet about my journey home. I shall be faced with the same struggle you are experiencing now.[2] You know how they love me at home and how impatiently Mother and all the children, including Yehiel,[3] are waiting for me. Not to go would mean disappointing them all greatly. On the other hand, everything you write is so tempting, and my heart leaps with joy at the thought of the three of us—I mean Toldy—spending a month together somewhere in a quiet spot, with you, with you, with you, my beloved.[4]

251. [1] In addition to the letter from V.K. dated 2 (15) July 1902 mentioned in n. 1 to No. 248, there is also in W.A. another V.K. letter of the same date, and this is probably the 'dear letter' here referred to. It is easy to understand why W. should have 'kept on reading and re-reading' this moving love-letter, in which, after telling him how he has transformed her outlook ('You have made me a Jewess'), V.K. goes on to assure him of her longing for him and of her hope that they may not again have to endure so long a parting. She cannot, she says, feel entirely happy at home because of the conflict between her attachment to her family and her still stronger feeling for W. She has not, she goes on, confided even in her sister Sophia about the ties between them—'Somehow I do not know how to tell her—but anyhow she knows.' It is to this that W. would seem to be alluding in the last part of the letter under notice—'Why don't you tell your sisters? I should very much like them to know, only them'—The two V.K. letters of 2 (15) July, though bearing the same date, were not necessarily posted on the same day, and a later posting of the letter here summarized could account for its not having reached W. until 23 July ('last night'), whereas the other appears from No. 248 to have reached him on 21 July.

[2] See n. 4 below.

[3] W.'s youngest brother, then aged ten.

[4] In his letter of 30 June (No. 214) W. had asked V.K. whether there was any possibility of her joining him and Feiwel at Leysin in August—'we could be together for a month'. On 5 July (see n. 8 to No. 234) V.K. had replied that it would be impossible for her to come in August, but she would come 'three weeks before the term starts, that is on October 1st'. W. appears to be referring here to her letter of 1 (14) July, summarized in n. 1 to No. 247, in which she says that, if W. does not propose to go home to Pinsk for the Holy Days she would come to Switzerland a month before the

You have no idea, Verochka, how deeply you have affected me; how you have become one with me, inseparably so; how my thoughts hover round one wish, to give you as much happiness as possible, good pure happiness; how I should like to work twice as hard for you; how deep in my heart I dedicate every single action to you.

I am so infinitely happy that I am capable of loving a human being like this. I should like you not only to believe me, but also to have confidence in me, and then I myself shall be stronger.

We had our photographs taken yesterday; as soon as they are ready I shall send them to you.

I have just sent part of the University pamphlet[5] to the printers. This is the first more or less public step.

Cambridge and London Universities are of an interesting type, and I wrote yesterday asking for some material.

Oh yes, there was a letter yesterday from Herzl,[6] in which he announced that he is doing everything in his power to achieve some practical results in the University matter. At the same time, he asks us to continue our work energetically, and expects results from a personal meeting with us. All very diplomatic!

All three of us[7] are sending you today a box of fresh flowers which we picked on our mountain. I don't know in what condition they will reach you, but I ask you to appreciate our good intentions.

That, my joy, is all the news for last night and this morning. I am now going to Levin[8] for a few hours. Her parents are there, and the whole family.

Why don't you tell your sisters? I should very much like them to know, only them. The others don't matter to us, but you ought to tell your sisters everything, about my past, my character, everything.[9] I don't want anything to be concealed from them.

beginning of the University term. This, however, would involve a postponement of W.'s visit to his family, who, he says, are eagerly awaiting him; hence, it would seem, his allusion to 'the struggle you are experiencing now'—i.e. the emotional conflict of which V.K. speaks in her letter of 2 (15) July summarized in n. 1 above.

[5] *Eine Jüdische Hochschule.*

[6] Herzl to W., 20 July 1902, W.A. Referring to W.'s letter of 25 June (No. 209), Herzl wrote: '. . . My attitude to this question differs from yours—I want to achieve something concrete as soon as possible . . . I am awaiting our next meeting so that I can explain to you orally how I envisage the matter. If you are impatient, then you can do whatever you think proper at your discretion.'

[7] W., Feiwel, and Esther Shneerson.

[8] Possibly the Geneva student who appears under the name of Lewin in a list of members of the Zionist student society *Hashahar* in C.Z.A.—A139/6.

[9] In her letters of 1 (14) and 2 (15) July (see n. 1 to No. 247 and n. 1 to No. 248) V.K. had told W. that she was embarrassed by her family's unawareness of the relations between them, about which she had not spoken frankly even to her sister, Sophia.

Sofochka will know from my last letter. Show her this letter, give her my best regards and to Raya too.

I love you dearly.
Your
Chaimchik.

I am writing this letter at the post-office. Toldy and Shneerson send you their best regards and ask you to come (I am passing on their message without any comment from me).

252. To Catherine Dorfman, Kherson. *Leysin, 24 July 1902*

Russian: Pcd.: H.W.: W.A.

Leysin 24/vii 02

Dear Katyusha,

Just a line to let you know that I shall write you a more interesting letter tomorrow.[1] I am writing sitting in a coach, as I am going to pay a visit in the neighbourhood.[2] We have already sent off the prospectus[3] to the [pr]inters.

Lots of love,
Chaim.

253. To Vera Khatzman, Rostov. *Sepey, 24 July 1902*

Russian: Pcd.: H.W.: W.A.

Sepey near Leysin
24/vii 02

My sweet Verochka,

I am on my way to Diablerets (don't get scared of the name!)[1]

252. [1] No such letter has been found.   [2] See No. 253.
[3] The only 'prospectus' hitherto mentioned in W.'s correspondence with Catherine Dorfman is the *Jüdischer Verlag* prospectus referred to in his letter to her of 14 July 1902 (No. 238). There, however, he appears from the context to be speaking of a prospectus in printed form, whereas here he writes: 'We have already sent off the prospectus to the printers.' On the other hand, nothing is known of any other prospectus to which W. can be supposed to be referring when he tells C.D., obviously assuming that she will know what he means, that 'the prospectus' has gone to the printers. It looks as though 'the prospectus' may be simply a slip of the pen for 'the project', i.e. the 'University project' mentioned, together with the *J.V.* prospectus, in W.'s above mentioned letter to C.D. of 14 July, meaning either the pamphlet *Eine Jüdische Hochschule* or W.'s 'Plan for a Jewish University' (see n. 2 to No. 204), which was to form part of the pamphlet. The words in the letter under notice, 'We have already sent it . . . to the printers' would then fit in with W.'s letter of the same date, 24 July, to V.K., in which he writes: 'I have just sent part of the University pamphlet to the printers.'

253. [1] 'Diable' resembles the Russian word for 'devil'.

to see Mme Berlin.[2] The road is beautiful, and the journey in the mail-coach most interesting. I wrote you a letter from Leysin. Toldy and Esther will also write to you today.

With best wishes and a kiss,

Chaim

254. To Vera Khatzman, Rostov. *Diablerets, 25 July 1902*

Russian: H.W.: W.A.

Diablerets, 25/VII 02

My dear darling,

I wrote yesterday on the journey to say that I was coming here.[1] There is probably a letter from you waiting at home, but I cannot wait till Leysin to write to you I shall not be there until the afternoon at 4, and so I write now, especially as it's terribly boring here with these people, and the best thing I can do, Verochka, is to write a few lines.

You can see already from this preface, my sweet, my darling, that there is nothing interesting here. There is only one good thing: I got hold of a Jew here who was at the Youth Conference.[2] He has a tender spot for us, to the extent of expressing it tangibly by forking out a hundred roubles towards the printing of the University pamphlet.[3] At the same time he also promised to give more when it is needed, even a few thousands. This is a real success! His name is Mr. Shriro, a wealthy and very agreeable man from Baku. And so, beyond expectations, my trip to Diablerets has proved very useful. But what I am not very pleased about is that on Sunday I shall have to come here again, as the same gentleman insisted that I should have dinner with him, and of course, out of mere courtesy, I could not refuse. This is the sum-total of what has actually happened at Diablerets.

I am going back presently, as this is a very inane *milieu*, and the people are dull, and there is such a difference, as you can well imagine, between the spiritual atmosphere in which we live with Toldy and the vegetable-animal kingdom here, where everything spiritual is expressed in empty talk about one thing or another.

I shall write more from home,[4] my joy, and for the time being

[2] Not identified.

254. [1] No. 253.
[2] The Basle Zionist Youth Conference, Dec. 1901.
[3] *Eine Jüdische Hochschule*—see n. 3 to No. 240.
[4] Meaning apparently, Leysin, from which he wrote to her the next day—No. 256.

I only send you very warm greetings. Lots and lots of love, my dear sweet darling. Regards to Sofochka and Raya. A kiss for my Verochka.

Chaimchik.

O yes, listen my darling. I thought a lot last night about how to arrange things, and most likely I shall not go home at all, especially if Father manages to come to me. And then, my joy, you can come by the end of August.[5] This you must do for me, and we shall stay about three weeks in the mountains, and then on to Geneva, where I want to attend the scientists' meeting in September[6] and work in the library.

If you can come by the end of August, new style, then it will be perfect. You see, Verochka, for this I shall even give up taking part in the All-Russian Zionist Conference.[7] This will be the first time I shall have forsaken a publ[ic] duty because of my private life.

Reply at once
to your Chaimchik

255. To Catherine Dorfman, Kherson. *Leysin, 26 July 1902*

Russian: H.W.: W.A.

Leysin, Pension Forêt
26/vii 02

My dear good Katyusha,

Your postcard[1] has just arrived. What can I say to you? All the trite words of comfort are so insignificant that I shall refrain from them and so convey my deep deep sympathy with the grief that has befallen you. I remember so well the lovely pure image of your dear Mother that I feel deeply at one with you. Katyusha dear, how my heart aches for you, for all your family. Everything happens so wickedly, so senselessly.

I don't want now to write anything about myself. Things are not too bad. There is nothing new. Stagnation, peace and quiet. The programme is not yet ready.[2] Motzkin has been ill. I shall wait a few days and then write again. I don't want to worry you with essentially trifling things; nothing of importance has happened.

---

[5] See No. 251 and n. 4 to that letter. As to the prospect of his father's coming to Switzerland see No. 249.

[6] The annual meeting of the Société Helvétique des Sciences Naturelles, 7–8 Sept. 1902.   [7] Minsk, 4–10 Sept. (N.S.) 1902.

255. [1] Not found.   [2] See n. 1 to No. 223.

Take courage, my dear; but I needn't say this to you. I understood everything from your postcard, and your brave behaviour does honour to you and to the dear departed. I send the profound condolences of a friend to all the dear good members of your family.

I press your hand and kiss you, Katyusha.

Yours
Chaim.

[Postscript by Feiwel and Esther Shneerson.]

My nice Katenka,

The Nietzsche[3] has been lying here for several days, and I am unable to forward it to you. Shall I wait till you come?

256. To Vera Khatzman, Rostov. *Leysin, 26 July 1902*

Russian: H.W.: W.A.

Leysin, 26/VII 02
Pension Forêt

My dear sweet girl, my wonderful Verochka,

I have just received your letter.[1] Such an enormous distance separates us that an exchange of letters proves almost impossible, especially with a person like me, whose mood is more changeable than the weather. You will have found answers to all your questions in all my letters which, my darling, you will have received after that unfortunate one.[2] I'll be glad to learn that you have calmed down even before this letter reaches you. You do realise, my beloved, my one and only Verochka, that I didn't mean to grieve you, but I was so wretched at that moment, I felt so lonely, such a stranger in the big wide world, so cut off from everything, that it seemed cruel that I hadn't had several letters a day from you. It seems to me that in spite of the distance you should have sensed what I was going through. Forgive me, my little one, if I said anything I shouldn't have said which pained you; forgive me, my sweet good darling Verochka. Things would be much easier, of course, if we didn't love each other so much; time would pass quickly and everything would be all right. But I'd rather go through all these tortures than have this 'all right'. It is understandable, of course, that life even in such beautiful surroundings as I am

---

[3] See No. 238.

256. [1] Not found. After the letter of 2 (15) July mentioned in n. 1 to No. 248, no V.K. letter has been preserved earlier than that of 8 (21) July referred to by W. in No. 257.

[2] Probably his rather testy and dismal letter of 13 July (No. 237).

living in now offers no compensation, does not offset the pain. This seems to me impossible. I am perfectly able to enjoy life in Toldy's company, without any social contacts,[3] in a whole range of spiritual interests, but Verochka (and this must be quite clear to you), the better I feel in one respect, the heavier my heart, the deeper my awareness of your absence. I never felt last year such a burning, strong, passionate need to share everything with you as I do now. I analyse all these developments with delight and believe ever more in a harmony which grows slowly, little by little, but takes deep root, rather than in the passionate impulsive love which rushes like a tornado over the infatuated lovers' heads but leaves nothing behind it but memories,—pleasant ones perhaps, but nevertheless only memories. With us, I dare hope, it will be different. Not only will it be, but it is. Moreover, Verochka, since you became one with me in the cause too, since you told me that you are a Zionist, since then, Verochka, our spiritual union has grown stronger, and what in other cases springs from passion, in our case, to my mind, has grown from a spiritual affinity. The difference between the two is, of course, enormous. The one is transitory, the other keeps on growing. The one always leaves a *Beigeschmack*,[4] the other brings spiritual poise, integrity, strength. Is my assessment correct, Verochka? I beg you most earnestly to write to me about this.

One more thing, my beloved. I always wanted to love the disciple in you too, so dear and so pure, with a pure, simple soul unstained by anything; to cleanse you, my joy, of all assimilation, to lead you into the Movement. I never spoke to you about it directly, yet I followed with a watchful eye every stirring of your soul, without ever, ever—do you remember, Verochka?—wishing to penetrate it, without ever wishing to bring any pressure to bear.

I believe in the victorious force of the Idea, in the cogency of my arguments and of my Zionist life which you have had an opportunity to observe. I am writing to you at length about this, my joy, because I ponder almost daily on the meaning of our relationship, and I want to let you know my conclusions. These are by no means all the conclusions I have drawn, but I don't want to write about everything at once.

As to smoking, my darling: the rumours that have reached you from Switzerland seem to be correct. I promise you not to smoke more than two.[5] (But I can see that you don't believe me!).

---

[3] Lit., 'outside society'.   [4] In orig. in cyrillic characters—'after-taste'.

[5] In her letter of 2 (15) July (see n. 1 to No. 248) V.K. had asked W. to give up smoking. She had evidently returned to the subject in the lost letter to which W. is now replying.

My financial problems have sorted themselves out. The deadlock occurred because Deichler only sent 50 instead of 200[6] (now everything is clear!) And Deichler himself has really run aground.[7]

I wrote to you yesterday from Diablerets that I have hooked a 'bream' (as they say in Pinsk) who gives money away. I also wrote about your coming here.[8] If you tell your sisters everything,[9] can there really be further obstacles to your being here by the beginning of September N.S.?

Verochka, I am not being morose, definitely, most definitely not. I only feel despondent, for this feeling isn't just melancholy. I only feel a terribly strong pain which at times becomes dreadfully acute, and no power in the world can alleviate it. I am writing this quite candidly, Verusya, without the slightest intention of bringing pressure to bear on your family. I know the weight of your arguments and fully respect them, my dear girl.[10] But, but, but things are not easy for me, and that's why I write to you so often about your coming over. Try to understand this, my beloved, and don't be cross with me.

One more thing: the comparison between last year and this year is inappropriate. Last year I could leave Kharkov, a thing which could not happen now. This is natural and obvious after everything I have written to you in this letter.[11]

I wrote to Sofochka immediately I received her letter, replying in full. My best regards to Nyusechka, and I am grateful for her warm greetings. You can tell her everything about me, my joy. Well, I kiss you an infinite number of times. Write everyday to your

Chaimchik.

Toldy and Esther[12] send their best regards.

---

[6] Currency not specified—probably either marks or Swiss francs. What the remittance represents can only be a matter of conjecture, but see n. 9 to No. 224.

[7] i.e., he has his own financial troubles.

[8] See No. 254.

[9] See No. 251: see also n. 1 to No. 247.

[10] See n. 1 to No. 247.

[11] During his visit to Russia in the summer of 1901 W. had more than half-promised V.K. to visit her at her home in Rostov: see No. 115. Just before going to Kharkov he told her that he would there decide whether to go on to Rostov or to Pinsk, and in the end he decided in favour of Pinsk and never went to Rostov—see Nos. 125, 128. Evidently referring to something in V.K.'s lost letter under reply, W. now tells her that there is no question of anything like this happening again, as is obvious, he says, 'after everything I have written in this letter', clearly alluding to the opening passage ending: 'I never felt last year such a burning, strong, passionate need to share everything with you as I do now.'

[12] Esther Shneerson.

257. **To Vera Khatzman, Rostov.** *Leysin, 28 July 1902*

Russian: H.W.: W.A.

Leysin, Pension Forêt, 28/VII 02

My dear little girl Verochka,

We were terribly pleased to receive your beautiful postcard[1] today, but I thank you even more for your nice letter[2] which I didn't manage to answer yesterday. Forgive me, my Verochka, for my letter being a day late. The last post leaves here at six in the evening, and often, when I have very many urgent letters, I can't manage to send yours in time. To think that I was trying to punish you was unjust, Verochka.[3] Never, Verulya. [It is] just that, as I have already written to you once before, I feel downhearted when there is no letter from you, though I know very well that you always write to me, or at least always mean to do so. But enough of this. My dear child, you ask me a lot of questions, but I think you must have had all the answers in my letters. I positively write everything in them, Verulya, I tell you everything about us, and about myself in particular. Do you know, my darling, it's quite likely that I shall be going to you in Rostov, and to Baku.[4] I have met some people who guarantee, if I go there, a collection amounting to 2 or 3 thousand r[oubles] towards the University. That's why I want to settle by letter with the various individuals concerned, and then I shall leave. I shall leave here by the end of August (n[ew] st[yle]), and shall go to Pinsk, then to Rostov, Baku, Yekaterinoslav, Kharkov and Poltava, so that I could be in Rostov by the end of September n[ew] style. For the time being, all this is strictly secret as far as the local Zionists are concerned, for it is essential that they should not know who, what, what for and why.[5] It's quite possible that I shall

257. [1] Not found.

[2] 8 (21) July 1902, W.A., promising to try and enrol subscribers for the *Jüdischer Verlag* (see n. 18 to No. 238), assuring W. that she meant to study German seriously with his help and much more regularly than she had studied Hebrew last year, and drawing attention to the weakness of Zionist propaganda in Rostov. She also said that she was happy to receive two letters from him (probably those of 14 and 15–16 July, Nos. 239, 240); from the tone of the letter she had had from him the day before (presumably that of 13 July, No. 237) she had inferred that he was displeased with her and meant to punish her.

[3] See n. 2, above.

[4] See No. 254 as to his encouraging encounter at Diablerets with the wealthy Samuel Shriro from Baku.

[5] Presumably so that those unfriendly to the Democratic Fraction should not be forewarned and organize opposition, or possibly simply because he did not want to be bothered by the local Zionists, at all events not immediately on his arrival.

go first to B[aku], and then I would stop at R[ostov] only with you
and for you. I shall send you a telegram when I know everything
for certain, which will be in about a fortnight.

We are not printing all the material in the pamphlet,[6] only my
plan, with Toldy's commentary, in which we substantiate everything. We already have 150 r[oubles] towards the printing costs;
that's enough for the German ed[ition]. But we need more for the
Hebr[ew] and Russian ed[itions],[7] for which I have received (begged)
another 100 r[oubles]. As you see, I know how to wheedle money
out of people, but all the same, if you get some send it, because it is
needed and we need more and more. The programme[8] is not ready
yet. But it soon will be. It must be ready before my arrival in
Russia, otherwise I won't go. This is a *conditio sine qua non.* I'd be
ashamed to show myself without a programme, as, more than anyone else, I shall prove to be the scapegoat and the target for all
attacks. I was in Russia before the Conference,[9] and unfortunately
the state of affairs is worse after the Conference than before it, and
our opponents will point at me. The area I have to tour is Ussishkin's[10]—you realise what that means.

My dear child, from Raya's postscript I gather that you have
told them,[11] and I am very glad of it, Verulya. But only them, my
girlie. I shall not tell my parents yet, and that's why I don't want
any wide publicity. We are not concerned with the others, with the
general public. But she knew before we did ourselves, didn't she?

Sheychik hasn't arrived yet; he will not be here until the 5th.[12]
We shall probably stay here till the 15th and then move to Zermatt.
Verochka, this also depends on Toldy's state of health; to my great
regret, he has been feeling worse lately.

My studies are going very well, and I shall be more than ready
with my whole course in a fortnight. I shall only have to supplement the current literature in G[eneva]. I am very pleased about
this.[13] If we succeed in collecting a few thousand in Russia, we

[6] *Eine Jüdische Hochschule*—see n. 3 to No. 240.

[7] In the event neither a Russian nor a Hebrew edition was published—see n. 4
to No. 269.

[8] As to the delay in the completion and printing of Motzkin's revised version of
the Democratic Fraction programme see n. 1 to No. 223.

[9] The Zionist Youth Conference, Dec. 1901.

[10] Ussishkin, at this time the Zionist regional leader for the Yekaterinoslav area,
was opposed to the D.F., objecting in principle to the formation of parties within the
Zionist Organization.

[11] i.e., that she had told her sisters about the ties between herself and W.—see No.
251 and n. 9 to that letter.

[12] He did not come—see No. 265.

[13] W. passes abruptly from the preparation of his lectures to an entirely different
topic—the Jewish University project.

shall set up an office and be able to afford a secretary.[14] I should then get rid of a great deal of work, though there would probably still be a lot of it, my darling. The deeper you go into the forest, the more trees you see. But you will help me, my sweet. For this, as for everything else, my darling, you have to know German. However, judging from your letters to Toldy, you are making very good progress, which pleases me infinitely. When you can read German, I'll get a wonderful edition of Nietzsche's 'Zarathrustra'[15] for you, but a really wonderful one. So go on, my sweet, and we shall read it regularly and without fail. The fact that we didn't do it regularly last year was due to reasons beyond my control. Now it will be quite different, you'll see, my love.

And so keep on writing and writing. If you wish, my darling, you can show the letters to Rayechka. Give her a big kiss on my behalf and tell her that I am very fond of her and let her write to me. Heartfelt greetings to Sofochka. I shall write to her later in the week.

Keep well, my darling. Lots and lots of love.

Yours
Chaim.

Best regards to Nyusechka. I don't write to her because I am sure that you tell her everything and that I always send her my most sincere good wishes. *Ça va sans dire.* Toldy is writing to you separately. You are exchanging letters with strange men!

[Postscript by Esther Shneerson.]

258. To Leo Motzkin, Heidelberg. *Leysin, 28 July 1902*

Russian: H.W.: C.Z.A.—A126/24/7/2/2

Leysin, Pension de la Forêt
28/vii 02

Dear Leo,

I have been unable to write for a number of different reasons beyond my control. From your last communications I learnt that you had been ill. I hope that you are better now and that you will recover your strength quickly and completely. What was wrong with you? How is your health now? Are you going to stay in Heidelberg much longer?

---

[14] A Jewish University Office (*Bureau Jüdische Hochschule*) was set up in Geneva in Nov. 1902.   [15] See n. 1 to No. 52.

Nothing new at this end. F[eiwel] is taking a very long time to get better and we are simply in despair. He is very weak.

I am staying here another three weeks at the m[ost], and then am going to Russia. I haven't had replies from the regional leaders yet but hope that they will come soon.[1] My propaganda area will probably cover the South. When are the others leaving? Where is Jaffe? I must know everything about their trips at once, for I must get in touch with them by letter, and there is little time left. It is essential to have the programme printed before my departure for R[ussia],[2] otherwise it will be useless to show one's face. Can't you possibly get something towards it? I shall also get some money, and in the meantime we will send it to the printers. I therefore ask you to send the text at once, in its final form, ready for the press. Everything has to be done during the next three weeks.

Write what you think about the Conference.[3] Write at once. F[eiwel] sends you his best regards.

> Yours
> Chaim.

259. **To Vera Khatzman, Rostov.** *Leysin, 29 July 1902*

Russian: H.W.: W.A.

> Leysin, Pension Forêt   29/VII 02

My dear lovely darling,

Your letter[1] with Sofochka's postscript arrived today, my darling. Your letter is very short, and reading it even 2 or 3 times I got through it very quickly. As you have seen for yourself, my joy, you are receiving my letters irregularly only through the fault of the post. I write regularly every day; I feel such a need to write to you that it can't be otherwise, and I impatiently await the post to bring me news from you. You ask about my health: it is good, but I worry more about yours, my darling. It is so hot in your part of the world that you will hardly recuperate, and I fear that you will return here again looking pale, and most important, my dear child,

---

258. [1] As to his projected propagandist visit to Russia see n. 24 to No. 238.

[2] As to the printing of the Democratic Fraction programme as revised by Motzkin see n. 1 to No. 223; see also n. 6 to No. 248.

[3] The first D.F. Conference, which still hung fire—see n. 5 to No. 223.

259. [1] 10 (23) July 1902, W.A.

your nerves. Do you remember how you fell down when I just pushed you with one finger? Do you remember, my dearest? This must not happen again, and I want you to be healthy, strong and not jumpy. What a pity, Verochka, that you haven't had your photograph taken yet. I am looking forward to your picture so impatiently, and I have also asked for Raya's phot[ograph]. I am afraid to ask Sofochka. I have put your old photograph into a very elegant frame and it stands on my table constantly before me. I cannot tear myself away from it and always take a long, long look at it. Please, my darling, have a photograph taken as soon as possible and send it to me. Our photographs will be ready on Friday and I shall send them to you at once. You will find in this envelope a picture of Leysin, which is very true to life. The little house at the highest point is the one we are living in. It's beautiful here, it's wonderfully sunny during the day and rather cool at night. The weather is excellent now. Half-a-minute away from us there is a lovely pine-forest and the mountains. The mountains are infinitely beautiful. There is a small village here (about 500 metres above us), and we live at a height of 1500 m. From it we can see the whole of Lake Geneva, the river Rhône as it falls into it, Montreux, and in very clear weather even as far as Lausanne. I haven't been in the neighbourhood; you know that I am slow to move, but I shall go all the same when Sheichik arrives; I don't feel like going anywhere on my own, and Toldy can't. His health is improving noticeably. He will soon stop this accursed *Milchkur*.[2] Whether it will be possible to get him over to G[eneva]—that is the question.[3] I wish it with all my heart, of course. I'll try very hard. Your postcards have come. T[oldy] was delighted and the picture stands in front of him all the time and inspires him. If you could see it now, my little one. Esther picked some flowers for us, and we decorated the photographs standing on our desks. By the way, Esther slandered me yesterday; don't you believe her at all.[4] I do work, but not all day long, far from it, just as much as I feel like, without forcing myself in the least, that's the best way. I received the information yesterday from Cambridge[5] (not yet exhaustive), and do you know, Verulya, I am managing the English lingo very well. Toldy will write to you today. He bought a whole series of postcards for you, is adding some doggerel and is going to send them to you. No news

[2] 'milk diet'.
[3] V.K. had suggested in her letter that Feiwel should move to Geneva.
[4] In a postscript to W.'s letter to V.K. of 28 July (No. 257) Esther Shneerson wrote: 'Our party is not a very jolly one. Chaim, for instance, has the nerve to work all day long, and the others—including your obedient servant—are just bored.'
[5] In reply to the request for material mentioned in No. 251.

whatsoever. No letter so far from Elber[feld],[6] and in fact I am not waiting for it so impatiently any more. I have got a whole lot of new chemical ideas. Will anything come out of them? If so, it will be very good. Why does Sofochka feel shy about writing to me? I can't understand it. But Raya is a bold one! Let her write. Verulya, send us the photogr[aphs] immediately. I have already picked a wonderful frame. Have the picture made larger than the one I have now. Keep well, my joy. Many, many kisses for you, regards to Raya and Sofochka.

Your
Chaimchik.

260. To Vera Khatzman, Rostov. *Leysin, 30 July 1902*

Russian: H.W.: W.A.

Leysin, Pension Forêt
30/vii 02

Dear Verochka, my lovely one,

No letter from you today. I hope it will still come in the course of the day, but I want to write to you without waiting for it. I always feel better when I write to you, my beloved darling. All the more since I want to share with you my impressions of a very serious conversation with Toldy. I not only want to share them with you, but I consider it <u>very important</u> to know your views on the matter immediately.

You see, my lovely one, as I told you at the time, we are printing a pamphlet on the University project;[1] in so doing, we are addressing ourselves to the public, though not a very extensive one. We shall collect some five or six thousand roubles to enable us to open an office which will deal with the matter,[2] i.e. with propaganda, the working out of the project, the establishing of contacts with various individuals in various countries. The undertaking is on a grand scale, and the activity must be conducted accordingly. Who will direct all these affairs?—I. Such is my reply, such will be, I think, your reply, Verulya my darling, such was also Toldy's answer. He, Buber and the others will, of course, help, but, my

---

[6] See n. 3 to No. 234.

260. [1] *Eine Jüdische Hochschule*—see n. 3 to No. 240.
[2] See n. 14 to No. 257.

lovely one, there must be one hand holding all the threads of the venture. It will be necessary, as is already becoming clear, to go to England and to America and to set things in motion there. It will be necessary to fight a whole pack of dogs from various camps and of various kinds. In short, one lifetime isn't enough for such work. I know, Verochka, that you will help me with all your strength; I know what you mean to me, I know it better now than ever. Toldy and I took this into consideration; we also took into consideration that, in the first place, you haven't had much experience yet, and in the second—that you must never engage in Zionist work to the detriment of your University studies, as your work for the Jewish people[3] is still to come, and you are now preparing for it. But I have to choose: either—or. If the Univer[sity] venture goes well, then it is unthinkable for me to work on my chemistry at the same time. I don't have to tell you this in so many words: you yourself know very well what chemistry means to me, the laboratory with all its joys and sorrows; but at the same time you know, my lovely one, that the idea of the University is no less dear to me, if not more. Chemistry is my private affair, an activity in which I rest from my public duties. Let me put all material considerations aside and ask you the question from a purely moral point of view. The choice is difficult, deadly difficult, and I don't want to conceal the problem from you and am putting it to you in its plain unadorned form, as it stands before my own eyes.

Having linked your life with mine, you must have your say, my darling, you must declare your attitude, and I am waiting for it.

I don't have to add how impatiently I shall wait for your answer to this letter.[4] It's also superfluous to state that at this moment I'd be prepared to do anything just to see you for an hour, even for half-an-hour!

Nothing new has happened since yesterday. Our life here, though very full, is monotonous but far from being boring. It's amazingly beautiful here, real heaven; I have never in my life seen such lovely days, and I am really tormented by the fact that you are not here. Everything has turned out so revoltingly stupid, and I blame myself right through and am paying dearly for it.[5]

And so it is practically certain that I am leaving for Russia by the end of August, n[ew] st[yle], but I don't yet know my exact

---

[3] Lit., 'your national activity'.

[4] For her answer see n. 1 to No. 280.

[5] What W. seems to be saying is that they might have been together in Switzerland but for his own wish that, except for her sisters, her family should not know of the relations between them, and his vacillation about going home to Pinsk: see n. 1 to No. 247, n. 4 to No. 251, No. 254, No. 257.

itinerary. If Herzl is in Vienna (he is in Constantinople now),[6] then I shall go via Vienna.[7] If not, then Berlin–Aleksandrovo–Warsaw, and afterwards Pinsk–Minsk–Kharkov–Rostov–Baku–Tiflis–Yekaterinoslav–Kiev–St.Petersburg–Moscow, if I can manage to do it all.

Such are my plans, my joy. I feel vigorous enough to start my wanderings, and I go into raptures at the thought that I shall see you and all your family. You will come to meet me, Verusya, won't you?

But I don't want to anticipate. First of all, I must hear from you. I therefore earnestly beg you to write to me at once.

Why doesn't Sofochka answer me? Let me know, Verochka, about the state of your health, how you feel, what you are doing. Write at once about everything to your fervently loving

Chaim.

[Postscript by Feiwel.]

261. To Catherine Dorfman, Kherson. *Leysin, 31 July 1902*

Russian: H.W.: W.A.

Leysin, Pension Forêt
31/vii 02

Katyusha, my dear,

I haven't the courage to write to you about current business, but knowing your attitude to it, I hope that it won't add to your grief.[1] I do not ask any questions about you; you will understand yourself, my darling, why. I do not want to put into words what you will understand better through my silence.

As to business, the University pamphlet, the *exposé* is already being printed.[2] We scraped the money together, somehow, and it will come out very well. The programme is ready: I have ordered 25 typewritten cop[ies], and I shall forward it to you as soon as

---

[6] Herzl, accompanied by David Wolffsohn, went to Constantinople at the end of July 1902 for discussions with the Turkish Government. As to his proposals and their failure see n. 12 to No. 302.

[7] In the end he decided to make the outward journey via Berlin—see No. 291. He took in Vienna on his way back—see No. 320.

261. [1] She had just lost her mother—see No. 255.

[2] *Eine Jüdische Hochschule*—see n. 3 to No. 240.

available.[3] You see, once it is in my hands, I shall not be so worried.[4] I have made every possible effort to get the pamphlet, as well as the programme and a *Lebenszeichen*[5] from the Statist[ical] Bureau,[6] in advance of my departure for R[ussia]. Now everything is in motion and I'll appear there at least with something.

As regards the Conference,[7] you are absolutely right. It is utterly impossible to convene it now. Mr. Motz[kin] hasn't yet given me a clear answer, but to blazes with him.

There is no point in discussing the University with H[erzl] for the time being. He gives an assurance in his letter that he is very interested in the undertaking and intends *etwas Praktisches erlangen*,[8] but at the same time he asks for the work on it to be continued.[9] I hope that the small Congr[ess] won't spoil things, especially as our pamphlet will be published before it meets. I hope that the public will react favourably, as the tone of the pamphlet is restrained and dignified; the edition is very beautifully produced. We have enough money for the Russian and Hebrew editions.[10] I got hold of a 'Maecenas' here in the mountains[11] and stripped him of everything I could.

I am being summoned to the South and guaranteed a few thousands towards the Univers[ity] project.[12] You understand, of course, that I shall not be backward about travelling, and I'll set out by the end of Aug[ust], n[ew] st[yle].

Now about myself. It looks as if my intentions are going to be fulfilled. I have been very successful in my chemical work. I have prepared almost all the lectures, some 150 typewritten p[ages], from various sources. I am going to go to G[eneva] one of these days to look up periodicals. All this gives me great satisfaction and relief. I have also made a step forward as far as the University project is concerned: I have exchanged letters with everybody, in

[3] See W.'s letter of the same date, 31 July, to Motzkin (No. 263), asking for the text of the Democratic Fraction programme and explaining that, if it cannot be printed immediately, he wants to have typewritten copies made for use in connexion with his impending visit to Russia.

[4] Lit., 'I am not so worried', but, since the programme was not already in his hands, fut. tense seems to be required.   [5] 'a sign of life'.

[6] As to the Jewish Statistical Bureau see n. 7 to No. 204. W. had now seen the first-fruits of its activities—see n. 3 to No. 262.

[7] The first D.F. Conference, the arrangements for which were still undecided: see n. 5 to No. 223, No. 224. It was, in fact, never held.

[8] 'to achieve something practical'.

[9] As to Herzl's letter of 20 July 1902 see n. 6 to No. 251. As to W.'s misgivings about the Smaller Actions Committee's proposal to submit the University project to the 'Small Congress' (Annual Conference) see No. 241.

[10] See, however, n. 7 to No. 257.

[11] Mr. Shriro of Baku—see No. 254.   [12] See No. 257.

short—I have stopped moping and have worked consistently and regularly.

Katenka, smile with me for a moment.

Toldy feels much better, and is working well, despite my protests. Rosenfeld[13] will soon be ready; we have received all the proofs already. The miscellany[14] is in the press. It's very good that all this is going to appear now—it is something after all.

As soon as I receive replies from the regional lead[ers], I shall be able to decide on my itinerary.[15] In any case, I shall try to see [you]. We shall send you our photograph soon (a group).

Write to me, Katyusha, immediately after receiving this letter, tell me everything. I expect you to write without trying to spare me. I'd like to know everything that is going on in your heart.

Warm regards to all your family.

Keep well and be cheerful and strong.

Lots of love.
Yours
Chaim.

Toldy and Shneerson
send you their best wishes.

262. To Vera Khatzman, Rostov. *Leysin, 31 July 1902*

Russian: H.W.: W.A.

Leysin, Pension Forêt
31/VII 02

Dear Verochka, my darling, what has happened? This is already the third day that I haven't had a letter from you, and I am very worried. Is everything all right? You should never do this, my darling, knowing how much your silence torments me. My whole day is poisoned because of it, and surely it isn't difficult for you to write a couple of words. The thought that the letter might have got lost is my only comfort.

Verulya, Verunchik, I implore you to write to me daily. This sweetens the whole bitterness of separation at least to some extent, a bitterness which I cannot describe to you. I quiver with emotion when I think that two more full, long, interminable months separate us from each other, and such a deadly great distance. O Lord,

[13] The German translation of Morris Rosenfeld's Yiddish poems, 'Songs of the Ghetto'—see n. 15 to No. 238.

[14] The *Jüdischer Almanach*—see n. 14 to No. 238.

[15] He was awaiting the views of the Russian Zionist regional leaders, to whom the proposed itinerary of his propagandist tour had been submitted—see n. 24 to No. 238.

why these tortures, when it could have been otherwise, and so infinitely good!

As for me, I don't miss a single day, and even if I am swamped with work, I always find an hour or so to be with you, my darling.

Sofochka doesn't write either. You can't imagine how all this worries me.

Here there is nothing new. Today the proofs of the first part of the pamph[let][1] came. It will be very good when it is all printed. I have also received a whole list of books on the University question,[2] all very good books and the price of many of them makes them quite accessible. I have also received the first publications of the Jew[ish] Statistical Bureau in Berlin.[3] I would send you all this, but in the first place we have only one copy each, and in the second place, I am somewhat angry now, Verochka, I admit. When we finish reading everything, I shall send it on to you; by then my 'anger' will have subsided, especially as I still cherish a tiny hope of getting a letter from you today.

Verochka, I don't reproach you, but you don't even realise what terrible torments your silence makes me go through. Try to understand, my child, that I cannot find peace for a single moment; both night and day I see you, feel you, think about you to distraction, till I get angry with myself and reproach myself for being as I am and not stronger. If you knew all, you could not let a day pass without writing to me. O Lord, but distance paralyses everything.

You must understand, too, that I am not surrounded by the warm atmosphere which you have.

But I have said this a hundred times already in my letters and you probably do not 'believe' me. God be your judge, Verochka! I cannot imagine a situation in which I wouldn't write to you. I write at home, in the train, at the railway-station, in coaches, wherever I can get hold of a bit of paper and a drop of ink. I do not fail to share the slightest stirring of my soul with you, and yet— I repeat—you do not respond to it. Why, I really don't know, and it torments me.

If you only knew how I need your caresses, your warmth, how cold and frightened I feel at times—but I shall not torture both you and myself any longer. Let the time pass quicker, and once I hold

262. [1] *Eine Jüdische Hochschule*—see n. 3 to No. 240.

[2] Perhaps from Eliasberg, whom he had asked to compile such a list—see No. 230.

[3] So far as is known, what had up to this time been produced by this body consisted only of rules for investigators and instructions for bibliographical research— see Abraham Kasteliansky to Schachtel, 28 July 1902: C.Z.A.—A102/10. In No. 278 (11 Aug. 1902) W. complains to Motzkin that the Statistical Bureau has, up to that date, achieved nothing.

you in my arms, I'll not let you go any more. I can't picture our meeting at all; *c'est plus fort que moi.*[4]

If our photographs are ready today, they will be sent off today.

Keep well, Verochka, don't forget for a single moment the state of your lovesick

Chaimchik.

Regards to everybody.

263. To Leo Motzkin, Berlin. *Leysin, 31 July 1902*

Russian: Pcd.: H.W.: C.Z.A.—A126/24/7/2/2

Leysin, Pension Forêt
31/VII 02

Dear Leo,

I sent you a telegram yesterday asking you to let me have the text of the progr[amme].[1] If we fail to find the means to have it printed without delay, then I want to have about 20 typed copies made and forwarded to Russia, where I am going in 2 or 3 weeks' time.[2] We have not yet agreed on a single question, and this ought to be done before my journey to R[ussia]. That's why I am waiting for an answer to my letters. Who else is going? What about the Conference?[3]

I shall probably go by way of Vienna,[4] so we shall have to settle everything by letter. There is very little time left.

Yours
Chaim.

264. To Vera Khatzman, Rostov. *Leysin, 1 August 1902*

Russian: H.W.: W.A.

Leysin, Pension Forêt
1/VIII 02

Dear Verochka, my darling,

Another day has gone by, and there is no letter from you. I don't want to describe to you how terribly all this tortures me. I can't

---

[4] Thus in orig., but exactly what is meant is not clear.

263. [1] The Democratic Fraction programme. [2] See n. 24 to No. 238.
[3] The projected D.F. Conference (in the event, never held)—see Nos. 244, 258.
[4] What actually happened was that he made the outward journey via Berlin (see No. 292), returning via Vienna.

even imagine what may have happened. O Lord, let it be just negligence, as long as all is well with you. I don't want even to entertain the thought that there is something amiss, though I can't find a moment's peace and had a terrible night.

I am not writing all this to you in order to make you write every day, as I have already implored you many times. This won't help, and I don't want to plead and beg for letters, my friend. You, who are so concerned about my peace of mind, are doing your utmost to prevent me from calming down; but I don't want, don't want, don't want to reproach anyone. It's just that my nerves have been torn to shreds. I repeat once more: I understand that you may not be in the mood for writing, that you may have no wish to do so. I do understand, and I ask you, Verochka, not to force yourself in any way and to write only when you feel like it. I have received a lesson in patience from you, and shall be a very obedient pupil. I'll wait without grumbling. *Nicht klagen — tragen!*[1] But I have to know, and then I shall be more at peace. At the same time, please do not worry if I write to you once a week. I realise that if you cannot write, it must be unpleasant for you to receive such letters from me so often. Whatever effort this may mean for me, I shall train myself to do it. The separation will, perhaps, be easier if salt is not being constantly rubbed into the wound. *Tant pis!* I am sending the photographs separately.[2] And so don't worry. One thing more: if you are hiding something from me and that is why you don't write, then you don't realise yourself what you are doing. Any truth is better than this terrible [? uncertainty].[3] Once and for all, Verochka. Regards to all.

With many kisses,
Chaim.

265. To Vera Khatzman, Rostov. *Leysin, 2 August 1902*

Russian: H.W.: W.A.

Leysin, 2/VIII 02

My darling, my good sweet Verunchik, my joy,

I doubt, Verochka, whether my vocabulary has enough tender words to express all that I would like to say. Yesterday came the

264. [1] 'Don't complain—bear it.'

   [2] See No. 262, near end. There are in W.A. two photographs taken during W.'s stay at Leysin, showing respectively W. and Feiwel, and W., Feiwel, and Esther Shneerson.

   [3] The Russian word for 'incredibility', which appears in the orig., would seem to be a slip of the pen for the rather similar word meaning 'uncertainty'.

joint letter[1] in which, my dear ones, you all ask me to come to Rostov. Is it really necessary to plead with me like that? Were my wings stronger now, I would have flown to you long ago, my darling Verochka, whom I miss so terribly. My letters of the past week— sent before I received your letter yesterday—should have convinced you, my darling, how I crave to see you and what plans I am forging to overcome all that lies between us. And so it is decided: I shall leave here not later than the 20th or 22nd n[ew] st[yle], and shall travel not by the way of Vienna but via Berlin.[2] Father will be waiting for me there and we shall go together to Pinsk via Warsaw. I shall reach Pinsk, therefore, not later than the last days of August, n[ew] st[yle]. I'll stay in Pinsk until September 1st o[ld] st[yle] and shall set out on the 1st. I don't know how things will turn out at the Minsk Conference,[3] but this should not take more than four days of my time. I'll stay three or four days in Kharkov and shall probably be in Rostov between the 10th and 15th of September, and from there on to Baku. It's difficult to determine whether I'll stay long in Rostov. Verochka, you will have to travel to meet me, without fail. Such is the plan. This is, of course, a *tour des forces*,[4] but it is unavoidable and I can't arrange it differently. I expect great things from my trip. I would leave here sooner, but I cannot do so before everything is printed, i.e. the programme[5] and the pamphlet,[6] and this will certainly take another two weeks. Besides, a great deal of money is still needed, but we shall have it. It will drop from the skies again.[7] True, my nerves are not composed yet, and now once more I cannot live quietly because I am preparing for the journey. I am on the point of going to G[eneva] for two days, shall do some work in the library and will see Esfir[8] off.

Father is now in Thorn-Bromberg-Danzig[9] and will travel to Berlin to meet me.

Darling, my good girl, I sent you a nasty letter[10] yesterday. I felt

265. [1] V.K. to W. 13 (16) July 1902, W.A., with friendly messages added by her aunt, Maria Mamurovskaya, and by her friends, Agnes (Zina) Brailovskaya and Anna (Nyusya) Ratnovskaya. V.K. wrote that her sisters, Sofia and Raya, and her brother Michael (Misha) were looking forward to seeing W. in Rostov.

[2] He had told V.K. (No. 260—30 July) that he might travel via Vienna.

[3] The Russian Zionist Conference due to be held in Minsk at the beginning of September.   [4] Thus in orig.

[5] As to the printing of the Democratic Fraction programme see No. 263.

[6] *Eine Jüdische Hochschule*—see n. 3 to No. 240.

[7] As to gifts by, and further expectations from Mr. Shriro of Baku and other Baku sympathizers, see Nos. 254, 257—see also No. 276.

[8] Esther (Esfir) Weinberg was about to leave for Rostov.

[9] W.'s father, Ozer Weizmann, regularly paid business visits to those towns in connexion with his activities in the timber-trade—see *T. and E.*, pp. 18–19.

[0] See No. 264.

terribly bitter and down-hearted not having had a letter from you for three whole days. Did you get the flowers,[11] Toldy's letter, the postcards, the picture of Leysin? Go on writing to this address for the time being. I shall let you have addresses in good time, so that letters will not be delayed.

Nothing new has happened to us. We are living as usual and working quite well. Sheychik, the beast, has pulled a fast one and left for Kissingen.[12] His stomach is playing him up and he intends to put it right. I really quarrelled by letter with the 'baby',[13] but not to the bitter end. I shall box his ears when I pass through Heidelberg. Sheychik will meet me in Frankfurt, and Deichler too. Well, that's all for the time being. I'll write from G[eneva]. Through Esfir you will receive regards and Nietzsche.[14] If I have any money I'll send something nice for Raya and Sofochka.

Do write, write to your loving-to-distraction

Chaimchik.

Best regards to Nyusechka and Zina. Till we meet again!

Greetings to Sofochka, Misha and Raya, to whom I wrote three postcards yesterday.

266. To Vera Khatzman, Rostov. *Geneva, 3 [August] 1902*

Russian: H.W.: W.A.

[It is obvious from the contents, including the reference to 'yesterday's letter', clearly meaning No. 265, that W.'s dating '3/vii' is a slip for '3/viii'.]

Geneva, 3/vii 02
Rue Lombard 4

My dear Verochka,

As you already know from yesterday's letter,[1] I came here for a couple of days to the library and am leaving tomorrow. I met Esfir[2] yesterday. I was feeling so miserable, my darling, so very miserable, that I was afraid of some sort of attack of nerves. I didn't know where to begin and without stopping kept telling Esfir about you, about our relationship, about this and that; we dreamed and planned how things would be at Rostov, how we should meet,

---

11 See No. 251.

12 Saul Lurie ('Sheychik') had been expected at Leysin—see No. 257.

13 Nickname for Aaron Eliasberg; as to the 'quarrel' see No. 250.

14 See n. 8 above. She was to bring V.K. a copy of Nietzsche's *Also sprach Zarathustra*—see No. 257.

266. 1 See No. 265.   2 Esther (Esfir) Weinberg—see n. 8 to No. 265.

how we should see each other. Verochka, Verochka, my joy, my beloved, beware of me: I shan't leave you alive after I get at you. My head is swimming at the mere thought of it.

Verula, my joy, I am sending you Nietzsche:[3] learn to read and understand him. This is the best and the finest thing I can send you. To dear Rayechka and Sofochka I am sending my prints: *Judengässchen*[4] for Raya and 'Moses' for Sofochka. I hope that this will give them at least a little pleasure.

I shall probably take the books out of the library and leave by tomorrow morning. You can't imagine, Verochka, how difficult it is for me here in this room, where everything reminds me of our evenings, of you, of your caresses. I keep on hearing your voice, seeing your dear face, embracing you, feeling you, and all this lashes my nerves without mercy. I can no more live without you than without air, and sometimes, when I am on my own, I am frightened of seeing things.

Verochka, my sweet, my only love: love me, for you hold my life in your delicate, but strong and pure hands. Verochka, I have become a much better person; your love, our love, has freed me— I know it has—from a kind of staleness. I have a corner of my own, I am not a gypsy, I have found a haven, I have found my infinitely beloved, my pure darling, my, my, my Verochka.

Chaimchik.

Esfir will tell you everything. I can't write any more now. I am too excited.

267. To Vera Khatzman, Rostov. *Geneva, 4 August 1902*

Russian: H.W.: W.A.

Geneva 4/VIII 02
Rue Lombard 4

Dear Verochka,

The post forwarded from Leysin has just arrived. Among the letters there was none from you. That means two days again—the third day that I have had no news from you, and I cannot but ask myself why you don't feel the same need to write as I do. But I have already put this question to myself many times, and it remains a disagreeable and agonising problem for me.

---

[3] See n. 14 to No. 265. As to W.'s enthusiasm, at this time, for Nietzsche see n. 1 to No. 52.   [4] 'Jews Alley'.

Indeed, I should be much stronger if my spirits were not so closely dependent on the arrival or non-arrival of a letter from you. I have done some work in the library here, but my most successful step was to take out from the Chemistry [? Department] a number of indispensable books to take to Leysin, where I'll do all I need much more peacefully.

I have been even more melancholy here than in Leysin. I have been spending most of my free time in the company of Esfir and Herzfeld. Esfir is leaving today and will not be in Rostov until Sunday. She promised me she would come to see you at once, without fail. I have not been able to discover anything for the moment at the University, since everything is closed; there isn't a soul in the whole building. I'll go in again today. If I find out anything, I'll pass it on through E[sfir]. I have no doubt, however, that Sofochka will be admitted without any difficulty.[1] I can't write anything about myself at the moment as there is absolutely nothing new to say, nor does your silence give me much food for writing. However unwillingly, I must finish this letter. Maybe it is a silly letter, but it turned out like this because of my silly mood. Keep well, Verochka, I am again standing fast and do not ask you to write, consoling myself with the thought that soon, perhaps, it may no longer be necessary to beg you for a letter—that we shall see each other, and then there will be work and I may be cured to some extent at least from my boundless melancholy. In fact, half the time has already gone, and if during the first half you were unable to comply with this essentially paltry request, then all hope is lost, and I am merely ridiculous with my frequent pleas for a letter, as though it were a favour. I am going back today and shall spend exactly two weeks there,[2] and then I am off. If only it were sooner! Another such morning as today's and my entire 'recovery' is as good as if it had never been. And such mornings recur often. It's neither rest nor work, but I have known for a long time that it is the others who can and must rest. As for me, I shall rest too, but somewhere else, where there will never be any anxieties or other worries. But why am I writing all this to you? It doesn't make things easier for anyone, neither for you nor for me. All last week I wrote to you practically twice a day. Letters to R[ussia] may get lost, but letters from R[ussia] never go astray, so that if you wrote every day I should have received a letter a day. But during the whole week I only received three letters and, today being Monday, I only

267. [1] Writing to W. on 12 (25) July 1902, W.A., V.K. had asked him to inquire about the chances of her sister Sophia being admitted to Geneva University.
  [2] At Leysin.

received 3 letters in 8 days. But I am a fool, a fool, for writing such childish things, such trifles. You are not obliged to pander to my whims. A big kiss, Verochka.

Your
Chaimchik.

Regards to Sofochka and Raya. I am not asking them to write any more either, as if I do I am afraid I shall simply be a nuisance.

268. To Vera Khatzman, Rostov. *Lausanne, 4 August 1902*

Russian: Pcd.: H.W.: W.A.

Lausanne 4/VIII 02
At the railway-station
on the way to Leysin

I have 15 minutes and the best I can do is to scribble a few words. One doesn't feel so sad when writing. You will receive all the news through Esfir, to whom I have just said goodbye and who is leaving tonight. She will tell you how I feel, what I think, etc., etc. If I could only find a letter from you at Leysin; otherwise it's simply awful.

I shall work for another two weeks and then off on my way.[1] Do try, Verochka, to write regularly, at least these last days. Your silence really poisons my existence. Regards to everybody. With very many affectionate kisses.

Yours Chaimchik.

If I don't get a letter today, I shan't write for a whole week. *Tant pis!*

269. To Vera Khatzman, Rostov. *Leysin, 5 August 1902*

Russian: H.W.: W.A.

Leysin, Pension Forêt
5/VIII 02

Dear Verochka,

I arrived here last night, and found your letter and postcard,[1]

268. [1] To Russia.

269. [1] Probably V.K.'s letter dated 16 (29) July and postcard 14 (27) July 1902, both in W.A.

and today, my darling, came your registered [letter] with the cheque.[2] Everything disappeared, of course, in a flash as if removed by a magic wand, and I feel myself again. My dear lovely darling, you do not realise that for me your letters are like air without which it's impossible to live. I don't know what to write to you today. So little has changed, there is so little new, and all my thoughts revolve around a single point, that I am on the verge of setting out on my journey, that the distance which separates us will diminish and that later we shall be together: and this for me is the utmost. My thoughts go no further, and indeed I cannot imagine what will happen to me when I see you, am able to embrace you and press you to my heart.

Esfir will tell you all about my state of mind, and you will be able to have some idea of it; letters can't convey it all.

My darling, I believe I have already written to you that the pamphlet[3] will be translated into three more languages: Hebrew, Russian and English.[4] In general, you will find all the news concerning the University in my letters of last week. If only letters would arrive more quickly! It's dreadful; an exchange of letters takes no less than two weeks. It's agonising. How many times have I been on the point of sending you a telegram but held back for fear of frightening you.

I am very glad that the flowers arrived after all.[5] By now you will also have received the photos, which went off on Friday, I think.

I shall not be staying here much longer. I'll let you know by telegram of my departure from Switzerland, so that you'll always know where I am.

I have not yet received precise information from Father as to the date of our meeting.[6] Samuil is now in Kiev; the poor chap is pre-

---

[2] The registered letter has not been found, but from V.K.'s above-mentioned letter of 16 (29) July it can be inferred that the cheque was for 30 roubles collected by her in Rostov towards the cost of printing *Eine Jüdische Hochschule* (as to which see n. 3 to No. 240).

[3] *Eine Jüdische Hochschule*—see n. 3 to No. 240.

[4] No such translations were, in fact, ever published. It would seem, from W.'s correspondence with Joseph Lurie, that during W.'s visit to Warsaw in Aug. 1902 Lurie promised him to have the pamphlet translated into Hebrew. From W.'s letter to V.K. of 25 Aug. 1902 (No. 297) it can be seen that he hoped that this translation would be ready in time for the then impending Russian Zionist Conference in Minsk, but this did not happen, nor did the projected Hebrew version ever see the light. Later in the year the pamphlet was translated into Russian (see W. to Idelson and Kroll, 8 Nov. 1902—text in vol. ii of this series), but the Russian version was never published. There was never any English translation.

[5] See No. 251.

[6] See No. 265.

paring for the exams, for the third time now.[7] Moisey is at home. Some of the children are at Motol,[8] the others in Pinsk.

Well, that's all for today. I shall write more tomorrow. Regards to all.

I kiss you endlessly and clasp you very tightly, my Verulya, my beloved girl. Toldy and Shneerson send you their best regards.

Your
Chaimchik.

270. To Leo Motzkin, Berlin. *Leysin, 5 August 1902*

Russian: H.W.: C.Z.A.—A126/24/7/2/2

Leysin, Pension Forêt
5/VIII 02

Dear Leo,

I remain without a reply to all my letters, questions and enquiries.[1] I really don't know why. This is a busy time and it is necessary to know everything and to do a lot of work. I am travelling to the Minsk Conference[2] via Berlin. I could take the programme with me. Is it being printed? If not, it's essential to make at least ten typed copies, but for goodness sake let me know whether these will be ready for the Conference.[3] Who else is going to Minsk? I have been told that on the *Tagesordnung*[4] there is an item: 'Attitude to the Fraction and to *Mizrahi*.'[5, 6] I want to read a pap[er] on the Fraction at the Conference.[7]

Please write immediately about everything

to yours
Chaim.

[7] 'for the third time'—An earlier unsuccessful attempt by Samuel Weizmann to pass the entrance examination for the Kiev Polytechnic is mentioned in No. 130 (see n. 7 to that letter), but nothing is known of a second failure. He was eventually admitted—see n. 17 to No. 100.

[8] Presumably staying with relatives or friends in Motol, the Weizmann family's former home, during the summer holidays.

270. [1] See Nos. 258, 263.

[2] The All-Russian Zionist Conference due to be held in Minsk at the beginning of September.

[3] As to W.'s urgent need for copies of the Democratic Fraction programme see No. 263.

[4] 'agenda'.

[5] This is one of the items in a Minsk Conference agenda dated 30 June (13 July) 1902. Another agenda, undated but probably later, contains a similar item, mentioning Ussishkin as the opening speaker. Both documents are in C.Z.A.—A1/380.

[6] Meeting at Vilna in March 1902, under the leadership of Rabbi Isaac Jacob

271. To Vera Khatzman, Rostov. *Leysin, 6 August 1902*

Russian: H.W.: W.A.

Leysin, Pension Forêt
6/VIII 02

Verochka, my love, my joy,

Your letter arrived today[1] and the telegram[2] this morning. I understand your having been taken aback by the way I reproached you in my letter.[3] But darling, if you only had some idea of my state of mind on the days when I do not get your dear, sweet, wonderful letters. All this defies description. My heart aches the whole day and I wander aimlessly from pillar to post. In your hands alone lie my pleasure in life and the state of my nerves. You must understand, my little one, my beloved, that there is no force which could, even for a moment, even in part, displace you who fill my whole, whole being. You pervade everything I do, write, feel, think—all is refracted through the prism of your crystal-clear soul. And Verochka, the day when I press you to my heart, when I rest[4] on your breast, will be the brightest in my life. O God, how many caressing, infinitely tender words I should like to say to you, my Verochka, my love, my friend, both my beloved darling and at the same time my sister. The whole past seems to me so insignificant in comparison with those sacred feelings which now fill

Reines, a group of Russian Zionists firmly attached to traditional Judaism and, while in full accord with the aims of the Zionist Movement, resolved to ensure that it should conduct its activities with due regard to the convictions of Orthodox Jews and should not deviate from its declared neutrality on religious questions, decided to form themselves into an organized Party within the Zionist Organization under the name of *Mizrahi*, representing the Hebrew words *Merkaz Ruhani* ('Spiritual Centre'). From Russia the *Mizrahi* Movement spread rapidly to other countries. One of its main purposes was to serve as a counterpoise to the Democratic Fraction, and, in particular, to block the development of 'cultural work' as part of the Zionist programme—see n. 10 to No. 86. There were many Zionists who were opposed on principle to the formation of Parties, whether of the *Mizrahi* or of the Democratic Fraction type, within the Zionist Organization.

[7] From a letter of 31 July (13 August) from the organizers of the Minsk Conference, Isaac Berger and Simon Rosenbaum, to Ussishkin it appears that W. had suggested to them that he should speak on 'The Fraction and its tasks', but he did not, in fact, address the Conference on this subject—presumably because the proposed discussion of its attitude to the D.F. and the *Mizrahi* was dropped, nor does he seem, in the event, to have read a paper on the subject mentioned in his letter of 6 Aug. (No. 271), 'The tasks of the young generation.'

271. [1] Probably her letter of 18 (31) July, W.A.

[2] From V.K.'s letter of 25 July (7 Aug.), W.A., it appears that, having received W.'s letter of 1 Aug. (No. 264), in which he complained of not having heard from her, she sent him a telegram (not found) to reassure him.

[3] See No. 264.   [4] 'rest' underlined in orig.

my soul. I feel now that love is something absolute and powerful, filling one's whole person, with no end and no beginning, something complete in itself, harmonious, something that cannot and must not be profaned by words.

Of course I'll be with you, with you, with you, my joy, and oh, how much we shall then say to one another, my darling. May this day come soon, soon.

Here there is one big rush. I am preparing all the material for the Minsk Conference on 22nd August, o[ld] st[yle], where I shall read a paper on 'The tasks of the young generation'.[5] The pamphlet[6] will be signed by Buber, Feiw[el] and myself. Work again. Of course, my darling, you will start working next year from the very first day. If I open a *Jüdische Hochschule* Bureau,[7] I shall take a special room for it near your place, and you and I will work there part of the time.

Won't it be lovely, my darling? Do try to imagine in some measure at least how full and warm our life will be. My head is spinning with joy and my agonies increase because it isn't so now. But I shall work, work for all this to come about even better and more fully, and my darling, my beloved, how good everything is!

Well, my darling, I close with endless kisses and declare once more my boundless, boundless love for you. I kiss you, my little one. Toldy sends you his best regards.

Your
Chaimchik.

Best regards to Sofochka and Raya.

272. To Vera Khatzman, Rostov. *Leysin,* [7] *August 1902*

Russian: H.W.: W.A.

[From the opening sentences of Nos. 274, 275, both dated 8 Aug. 1902, it would seem that this letter, though likewise dated by W. 8 Aug., must have been written on 7 Aug.]

Leysin, Pension Forêt
8/VIII 02

My Verochka, my darling, my true love,

I received your postcard[1] today. Thank you, Verulya, for writing

---

[5] See n. 7 to No. 270.   [6] *Eine Jüdische Hochschule*—see n. 3 to No. 240.
[7] See n. 14 to No. 257.

272. [1] Not found.

every day now. My darling, the hour of our reunion is gradually approaching, and the day I weigh anchor here will be like a holiday for me, for this will be the beginning of my coming nearer to you. In all probability, this is what will happen: on the 15th we shall all make a move from here. I'll go to Geneva for a day to pack my things. On the 16th I shall be at Nieder-Ingelheim,[2] on the 18th in Berlin, and on the 21st at home.[3] My dear, do work out the posting of your letters so that I find 2 or 3 letters from you in Berlin. My address will be as follows: Herrn Dr. Ch. Weizmann, Berlin, N.W., *Postlagernd, Postamt*[4] 7, Dorotheenstr. Up to the 15th you can go on writing here. All the dates are, of course, new style. Keep that in mind, my little one. I shall spend about 10 or 12 days at home, and then on to Minsk, Kharkov and Rostov. This is what I propose, let's hope God won't dispose otherwise. In any case, I shall be with my Verochka, my adorable girl, and the only thing that keeps me alive is that you will reward me, that we shall reward ourselves, for the time irretrievably lost. Verulya, you will caress me fondly, fondly, as never before and oh, Verochka, if you only knew how your caresses, your tender embraces affect me, how Verulya, they fortify and encourage me. And now I am no longer afraid of these passionate outbursts; do you remember, Verochka, we talked about it, my child. I have not squandered my caresses, have preserved them, and that's why they overflow now so luxuriantly. You must understand this, my girl whom I love so ardently, understand and love me as I am and not as I might have been. Verulya, my pure one, my beloved, how much we shall have to say and tell each other when we meet. There is so much that at first we are sure to be silent for hours on end without finding [words]. That's how it sometimes happens, my darling.

Verochka, I have already written to you that Father will be waiting for me in Berlin[5] and that we shall travel home together from there. Father has concluded a good business deal and is pleased. My sister is at Druskienniki[6] and is going to Wiesbaden in the autumn. I wrote you that Sheychik is in Kissingen; he never came here, the brute.[7]

The pamphlet should be ready by the beginning of next week.[8] I am very impatient already. Write and tell me, Verchik, how you liked Nietzsche.[9] Are Rayechka and Sofochka pleased with the

---

[2] Deichler's home.
[4] 'Poste restante'—'Post Office'.
[6] See nn. 5 and 6 to No. 216.
[8] As to the printing of *Eine Jüdische Hochschule* see No. 265.
[9] See n. 14 to No. 265.

[3] i.e. at Pinsk.
[5] See No. 265.
[7] See No. 265.

prints ?[10] I shall bring the postcards with me. If everything turns out the way I want, I'll also bring my Verochka something very pretty. Verulya, Verulya, Verulya, that photograph—you know, my darling, I don't like the photograph where you are all together with H. Pick, etc.[11] I don't like it for some reason. I want only Verochka, and there you aren't mine.

Kisses, endless kisses.

Your

Chaimchik.

My best regards to Sofochka.

273. **To Vera Khatzman, Rostov.** *Leysin, 8 August 1902*

Russian: H.W.: W.A.

Leysin, 8/VIII 02

My little darling,

Today no[1] letters from you, and we were all awaiting them. Incidentally, you said in your postcard[2] that you would write a letter 'tomorrow'. Those 'tomorrows'! I too, when I don't feel like writing, get out of it with a postcard on which I write 'tomorrow'. Toldy was also waiting for an answer to his postcards over which he took so much trouble, looking for rhymes for each picture.

I don't know, my darling, what to write to you today. These last few days the post has not brought us anything interesting, and as a matter of fact we are pleased, for we have enough to do as it is, and everything has to be settled before my departure, which is coming perceptibly nearer.

I should like to be travelling already, since in any case I am unable to do a thing, and when one is in such a fever, resting doesn't do any good either. There is no reply nor sign of life from Motzkin, and I don't know what is going to happen if the programme is not ready by the time I leave.[3] It's so disgusting that it is difficult to describe. We shan't be able to show our faces anywhere.

I am sending a telegram to Berlin today, for the third time.

---

[10] See No. 266.

[11] A photograph (in W.A.) taken in Geneva of a group including V.K. and Hermann Pick.

273. [1] Lit., 'zero'.

[2] Presumably the postcard (not found) mentioned in No. 272.

[3] See W.'s letter of 31 July to Motzkin (No. 263) urgently requesting that, if there is to be any delay in the printing of the Democratic Fraction programme, he may be furnished with typed copies for use in connexion with his impending visit to Russia.

Perhaps it will help. I am also sending a telegram to Dr. Jacobson to find out about the itinerary.[4]

The programme of the Minsk Conference is out already. Apart from purely business matters, both the Rabbinical Fraction and ours will come up for discussion. I have written to Minsk, but haven't had a reply yet.[5]

Herzl and Wolffsohn have been in Constantinople for two weeks. I don't know what they will achieve there.[6] The Small Congress will probably be held in the autumn.[7] Apparently it will be necessary to tear oneself into several pieces in order to be everywhere. Well, my darling, I am not writing any more. Should there come a letter from you today, I'll write again. I love you madly, my beloved, kiss you endlessly, and smother with all my strength my pretty little, lovely Verulechka. Best regards to all.

Chaimchik.

274. To Vera Khatzman, Rostov. *Leysin, 8/9 August 1902*

Russian: H.W.: W.A.

Leysin 8 VIII 02
Pension Forêt

My dear Verochka, my darling,

Your letter[1] which I was awaiting so impatiently arrived this evening, and, true to the promise I gave you in this morning's letter,[2] I want to write again. You do know, darling, that I am capable of writing to you several times a day. The only trouble is that life is not rich enough in events to fill several letters. But I always take advantage of an opportunity to write at least a postcard in addition to the letter. I always feel that with the sealing of the envelope something is being torn away from me, is being carried far away to you, my little one. O Lord, I can't imagine that fate would be so cruel as to separate us ever again. It's difficult to convey to you, my dearest, what agonising minutes, hours and days I

---

[4] See n. 24 to No. 238. [5] See nn. 5 and 7 to No. 270.

[6] See n. 6 to No. 260. Nothing was achieved by the visit to Constantinople.

[7] The Zionist Annual Conference ('Small Congress') met in Vienna at the end of October 1902.

274. [1] V.K. to W., 20 July (2 Aug.) 1902, W.A. asking (*inter alia*) why there was such delay in printing the Democratic Fraction programme, whether Aberson's lecture (see n. 1 to No. 225) had been printed, and whether it was proposed to print the minutes of the Dec. 1901 Zionist Youth Conference.

[2] No. 273.

have experienced, how infinitely difficult they are for me even now, especially the evenings. During the daytime one still works, there is the post, there are things to do, but when the day ends and twilight falls, there are times when my heart is so heavy that nobody and nothing can help. You ask, my sweet darling, whether I am better. Well, how can I put it to you? I do not feel fatigued, but on the whole I am not too well; in particular, the smallest thing makes me terribly irritable and upsets my equilibrium, and I see everything larger than life. The colour of my face—well, I suppose it is not green but rather brown, or so I am told, for I myself have never paid any attention to it, but by the time I arrive at your home it will turn pale green. But, my darling girl, all this is unimportant; if one only had one's peace of mind. True, I am calm now on the whole and see many things more clearly. I think I shall work better and more fruitfully in the coming year. As for Toldy, on the whole he is much better, gayer, livelier and stronger, but he gets bad attacks of nerves; do you know, Verochka, they are very much like those you used to have in the winter—do you remember, my sweet, my darling? He is definitely staying on in Sw[itzerland] and will not go to Berlin for the winter.³ That would be fatal for him.

Please write to him about this. He likes you very much and will listen to you, although he pays pretty good attention to us too. I have already written to you, my dearest friend, that the pamphlet is at the printers and will appear in a matter of days, and that it will be translated into Russian.⁴ The affairs of the Fraction, the papers, the minutes etc.—everything is in just the same state,⁵ and no force can make this bunch of good-for-nothings move. We shall have to drop them and start a new life.

Yes, Verochka, hard as it is for me, that's how it is. How much strength has been wasted, how much fresh energy spent, how many hopes frustrated. Apparently this generation is not yet fit; evidently it was not born to 'act',⁶ to build, to create. Men of the Diaspora, assimilationists—a prey to phrases, to forms of words, to stereotypes. Small people, with small brains and small ambitions. There is no boldness, no daring urge to assume responsibility for the honour of the cause. *Flickschneider*,⁷ meaning those who can only

³ After leaving Leysin and spending a short time at several other resorts, Feiwel moved in the autumn of 1902 to Zurich.

⁴ See n. 4 to No. 269.

⁵ See n. 1, above. By 'the papers' W. probably means the papers read at the Youth Conference.

⁶ In orig. 'act' in quotation-marks—probably an echo of the preoccupation of contemporary Russian writers with the idea of 'action' as against mere talk.

⁷ 'botchers'.

put on patches, tailor suits for Trishka[8] with all the seams beginning to split as soon as one turns round. I sent a telegram to Berlin this morning about the programme; a reply could be here already, but there is still nothing, not a thing.[9] What can you do with such little men? And as for Aberson, he isn't even worth mentioning.[10]

No, no, Verochka! All this must be a lesson to us. We have to work more, to work for the good-for-nothings as well. There is an old Jewish tradition, כל ישראל ערבים זה בזה[11]—all Jews are responsible for one another, and you and I, my darling, my dearly beloved, have to pay with our nerves for the sins of others. You write that your Zionism is platonic.[12] Yes, that's what it used to be while you were a novice. I did not want to drag you into the whirlpool of the cause, and do you remember, my joy, how I gradually made you interested in current affairs and how before your departure there wasn't a single letter, however brief, that you didn't know about? Now it will be different. We are going to work, and my Verochka is going to suffer and rejoice together with me. Verochka, my sweet, if you only knew how dear your convictions are to me, if you only knew how I fostered this. I see this as a flower which yields good fruit. Verusya, this fruit is the generation which will work, which will represent something genuine, good, strong and thoroughly Jewish. You have understood me—and this is the most intimate thing I can tell you, my beloved, the most sacred thought which I allow myself only in such hours of spiritual communion with you.

We shall soon see each other. The days are passing. Let them. If only the hour would come more quickly when I shall see you, embrace you. Am I going to cover you with kisses? Well, I am afraid nothing will be left of you, absolutely nothing, my child. I'll smother you, pinch you, bite you. But God, beware, my darling, for I am a savage!

Although our temperaments do not match now, Verochka, they shall. You, Verulya, love me as you used to do, but now, you know it seems to me that I really love you more than you love me. You keep asking about Azayts.[13] He hasn't much more work now. I

---

[8] An allusion to Krilov's fable *Trishka's Suit*.

[9] As to the attempts already made by W. to obtain from Motzkin copies of the final text of the D.F. programme see Nos. 270, 273.   [10] See n. 1 above.

[11] A Talmudical maxim (Shevuot 39a), translated by W. himself in the next sentence.

[12] In her letter to W. of 18 (31) July 1902, W.A., V.K. wrote: 'After all, my Zionism is very platonic', and went on to ask to be given some Zionist work to do in the winter.

[13] Not identified, except that in a much later letter from W. to V.K. (27 June 1905, W.A.) a person of this name is mentioned as a friend of theirs.

helped him a little and now he is all right again. On the whole, he
is quite happy. I like him immensely.

Esfir[14] has probably managed to tell you everything, to pass on
all [? the messages], and you have already had an answer to all
your questions.

I am breaking off our talk for today. In any case, the letter will
not go today. I just felt like having a little chat with Verulya.

Tomorrow (?)[15] your letter will come, and I shall continue then,
and for the time being, my little one, good-night, I am tired and am
going to bed. There is a violent thunderstorm here; it has turned so
cold that it's probably going to snow. Did you, Sofochka and Raya
receive my registered letter and the innumerable postcards?[16]

9/VIII. Darling, your letter[17] and Sofochka's postcard arrived
today.[18] I gather from its contents that you have not received two
of my letters,[19] otherwise you would know already that I am coming.
Perhaps they will still reach you. I didn't miss a single day, and
consequent[ly] there must be letters; and where the postcards are
I have no idea. Apparently they are all being stolen. This is outrageous. Thank you, my little darling, for intending to send me
the photograph, but see that you do it as soon as possible. As for
the experiments, don't be afraid, my darling, I shall manage.[20]
But look, darling, two weeks—that's absolutely impossible.[21] My
time is strictly limited and you'll see from my letters which, I hope,
you'll have already received by now, what I have to do. But
we shall meet, spend a few days together, and part only for a
short time.

My darling, there is nothing to add to yesterday's letter,[22]
nothing has happened during the night. Keep well, bear in mind
that we shall be meeting soon and think of all the delights of that
meeting. Many, many kisses. Best regards to Sofochka. Thanks to
her for remembering.[23]

> Your
> Chaimchik.

[14] Esther (Esfir) Weinberg—see No. 265, last paragraph.
[15] 'Tomorrow (?)'—thus in orig.
[16] Probably his letter of 2 Aug. (No. 265) and the postcards mentioned in the postscript thereto.
[17] Not found.
[18] 22 July (4 Aug.) 1902, W.A.
[19] Probably, from the context, Nos. 257, 260.
[20] The reference is probably to experiments necessitated by the Bayer Works'
doubts about the discovery submitted to them by W. and Deichler. As to W.'s
'I shall manage', see n. 3 to No. 234.
[21] V.K. had evidently suggested his spending two weeks at Rostov.
[22] i.e., the first part of the letter under notice.
[23] Meaning, presumably, 'Thanks for remembering [me]'.

275. To Vera Khatzman, Rostov. *Leysin, 9 August 1902*

Russian: Pcd.: H.W.: W.A.

Leysin, Pension Forêt
9/VIII 02

My little darling,

How sorry I am that you did not receive my two letters![1] Maybe you'll still get them. I think I wrote everything about my journey in them. And now, my darling, you have calmed down, haven't you? I, too, feel a little better now at the thought that I too am about to set out and that I shall see you. Will all your family be in Rostov by then? I want to make the acquaintance of them all.

I have been feeling rather poorly these last few days, but I am all right now. I don't know what it was. Yesterday I had a rather sharp exchange on politics with Sh[neerson]. This is causing me a great deal of unpleasantness.

I have already written and told you several times, my darling, that Pinkus isn't here and hasn't been here.[2] Sh[neerson]'s attitude to him = 0.

I shall bring the postcards myself, my sweetest, although I don't know whether I can take many of them.[3] Let me know whether you received everything sent with Esfir.[4] Keep well, my child.

With lots and lots of love,

Your
Chaimchik.

Darling, don't dare to nag me! After all, it isn't my fault if I haven't recovered completely.

276. To Vera Khatzman, Rostov. *Leysin, 10 August 1902*

Russian: H.W.: W.A.

Leysin, 10/VIII 02
Pension Forêt

My dear Verochka, my joy,

If only I could, I would fly to you at once, embrace you, cover you with kisses and say: 'Verochka, you still don't understand your

---

275. [1] See No. 274 and n. 19 to that letter.

[2] As to V.K.'s enquiries about Pinkus see n. 3 to No. 247.

[3] In the letter of 18 (31) July mentioned in n. 1 to No. 271, V.K. has asked for picture postcards. W. is apparently not sure of getting them through the Russian censorship at the frontier.   [4] See No. 265, last paragraph.

Chaimchik.' How could you, my sweetheart, have read anything offensive into the phrase 'to your sisters only'?[1] That was the last thing I had in mind. You have seen, my dear friend, that of late I have concealed nothing from people who are really close to us, people of whom I did not fear that they would vulgarize our relationship. If I wrote this to you, it was only because of not wanting nasty tongues to talk about us, and that's all there is to it. I cannot tell my family yet—and you must understand this—in view of all that happened in the past,[2] and this is the only, the one and only reason. But I am impatiently awaiting that wonderful day when you will come to us and be a sister to my sisters and brothers, a daughter, and I am sure a beloved daughter, to my, our Verochka, dear parents. Don't you know, Verusya, my lovely one, how I dream of this, and how could you suspect me of meaning to say something offensive to you? O Lord, if only I could be with you now, you would give me one look and would understand. All my thoughts are concentrated now on how to make my beloved girl happy with a happiness worthy of us both. I know full well that the path, the path of Jews—Zionist Jews[3]—is not strewn with roses, but I leave roses to rosy simpletons—roses exist only in novels. The good things in our life will be better than in the case of other people, and the bad things will at least be hidden[4] and won't debase you and me, my sweetheart. Verochka, you must understand that for me you are at one and the same time both a comrade whom I deeply respect, and a sweetheart; both ethically and aesthetically you are a creature[5] of whose love I am proud. My God, you yourself are not the reason for my request, but circumstances beyond our control. Besides, perhaps I see this differently, but, my child, the whole *cas* is essentially trivial and not worth mentioning again. Please, my friend, keep in mind these words of mine: 'The whole aim of my life will be to serve our common cause together with you.' We shall make this the basic theme of our life, and, Verochka, how much roughness is already behind us; further and smaller [? difficulties] will disappear, and our love will crystallize in ever purer forms. Do understand, do respond to these words, into which I put all my soul and my whole mind; I can do no more. Love me with

276. [1] In a letter of 22 July (4 Aug.) 1902, W.A., V.K. told W. that she was distressed by his request, in his letter of 28 July (No. 257), that she should tell only her sisters about the ties between them.

[2] His engagement, broken off in 1901, to Sophia Getzova.

[3] Lit., 'Jews-Zionists'.

[4] The meaning is obscure, but the Russian word here represented by 'hidden' admits of no alternative translation other than the still more unsatisfactory word 'deep'.   [5] Lit., 'you are an ethical-aesthetic creature'.

my shortcomings and believe that I am trying hard to improve myself.

Darling, a further point: don't worry about my health and about my working beyond my strength. There is a wonderful saying of a Jew[ish] sage, Rabbi Hillel, who was known for his meekness and modesty (Renan, for some reason, considers him the first Christian),[6] and this modest man made the following immodest remark:[7] אם כאן כולם כאן אני כאן, אם אני כאן מי כאן אין which means: 'If I am not here, who then is here? If I am here, everyone is here.' This saying by such a meek and diffident, yet profoundly wise, person as Rabbi Hillel is of deep significance for our times too, my darling, when our numbers are limited. You know that it isn't work that wears one out, it is other things that wear one out. You know me well enough to say: 'If my Chaimchik is going to work fruitfully together with me, he will be in good health.' However, apart from Kharkov, where my presence is imperative,[8] I shall probably not go anywhere else (except Rostov and Baku, of course). And you and I together will be inseparably joined in creative work, and I can feel that it will turn out well. But, Verochka, should we (and I am not referring to myself only, being indeed convinced that you are going to work better than I)—should we be unable to go on after some years, then we shall both withdraw, but we shall say: 'We had a good life, even though a difficult one.'

I will write to you no more about this, and I believe you have understood the sacred feelings which fill my whole being in regard to you.

In conclusion, forgive me, Verochka, if I ever caused you sorrow. Take me *tel qu'elle*.[9]

And now, my child, the following: send your repiy to this letter to Berlin at this address: Dr. Ch. Weizmann, Berlin, N.W., Postlagernd, Postamt[10] 7, (Dorotheenstr.)

We are leaving on the 14th and I shall be in B[erlin] from the 20th to the 22nd. There I shall find three letters from you, shan't I?

Just imagine, Verulya, this g[entleman] from Baku who gave the 100 roub[les] has sent another 200 and opened an 800 roub[le]

---

[6] *Vie de Jésus*, Paris, 1863, p. 35.

[7] Hebr., paraphrased by W. himself in the next sentence: the Talmudical source is Succah, 53a. A more exact translation would be: 'If I am here, everyone is here, but if I am not here, who is here?'

[8] W. had reason to attach special importance to Kharkov as a potential source of support for the University project—see Nos. 128 and 319.

[9] Thus in orig.   [10] 'Poste Restante'—'Post Office'.

credit account, and all this in such a marvellous way.[11] Well it fell from heaven. ‏גאָט וועט העלפן, וואָס‏[12]

You will understand our joy; we can now work independently of all offic[ial] Zionist big-wigs. The pamphlet[13] is ready. It has been published at the *Jüd[ischer] Verlag*, very nicely too. The programme too. I'll bring everything with me, and many other things as well. Toldy is staying on in Switzerland for another three m[onths], so I am sure we shall keep him here for the whole winter. Both he and I will help you with the German. You can't imagine what infinite pleasure you have given us all by your tenderness to Toldy. Esther (with whom I have already made peace)[14] and Toldy are writing to you, and I'll finish now. Keep well, goodbye.

I send Sofochka my best regards and heartfelt thanks for the invitation and welcome. Of course, of course I shall come. Warm greetings to Nyusya and Esfir.

With lots of love,
Your
Chaimchik.

277. To Vera Khatzman, Rostov. *Leysin, 11 August 1902*

Russian: H.W.: W.A.

Leysin, Pension Forêt
11/VIII 02

My dear Verochka,

Today I received your letter,[1] the contents of which did not come to me as a surprise. This letter couldn't have fitted in better with the whole of today's post, consisting of 10 letters, one more unpleasant than the other. These were all Zionist letters and I cannot write all about them—I'll tell you in person. All I can say is that I have always been considered a big fool who believes in people, while most of them are good for nothing. The writers are Mr. Motzkin, Pevsner, Aberson, the Actions Committee,[2] etc., etc.,

---

[11] W. is reporting the contents of a letter received by him from Mr. Shriro mentioned in No. 254. Shriro's letter, dated 8 Aug. 1902, is in W.A. W.'s '200 roubles' represented a promised remittance of 532 francs.

[12] Yidd., 'God will help—what?'

[13] *Eine Jüdische Hochschule*—see n. 3 to No. 240.

[14] As to his 'sharp exchange on politics' with Esther Shneerson see No. 275.

277. [1] Not found.

[2] The Smaller Actions Committee had circulated to the members of the Cultural Commission set up by the Fifth Zionist Congress a note dated 7 Aug. 1902 (C.Z.A.—Z1/211), (i) enquiring whether the Commission had duly organized itself and had elected a Chairman; (ii) asking that, if this has not been done, the organization of the

and the whole lot are disgraceful[3]. I have to reply today to twenty letters, and my hands are shaking from excitement; that's how all this has got me down.

And you, Verochka darling, should have known by now that I have been writing to you every day, and that I am incapable of not writing to you daily, all the more so since you are absolutely right and I am wholly to blame for giving way to my nerves and not pulling myself together. Perhaps Esfir will justify me somewhat in your eyes; she saw the state I was in on those days when there were no letters from you.[4] Distance is particularly apt to aggravate and complicate insignificant trifles. I don't want to write about the way I was worrying myself. Both Esther and Toldy rebuked me for the reproaches levelled at you. But now, of course, as you have seen, I have been and am writing oftener than every day. Darling, do reply to this letter too, addressing the reply to Berlin and the next letters to Pinsk, *poste-restante*. Everything is ready for my departure and there are no obstacles to my tour of Russia. I'll be at your home no later than mid-September, n[ew] st[yle]. You know already that I have received 1000 r[oubles] for propaganda.[5]

Lots and lots of love to my darling, my own.

Your

Chaimchik.

Regards to Sofochka. Shall probably write once more.

278. To Leo Motzkin, Berlin. *Leysin, 11 August 1902*

Russian: H.W.: C.Z.A.—A126/24/7/2/2

Leysin, Pension Forêt

11/VIII 02

Dear Leo,

I received today your letter of the 8th[1] to which I should like to reply in detail, for I see that a great deal is not clear.

Commission should be completed, and the S.A.C. informed of the action taken, within two weeks; (iii) intimating that the Chairman would be expected to present a progress report at the forthcoming Annual Conference ('Small Congress').—At the Annual Conference (Oct. 1902) statements (though they could hardly be called progress reports since there was no serious activity to be reported) were made by representatives of the four regional sections of the Commission—Sokolow (Russian Poland), Buber (Austria), W. (Switzerland), Theodore Zlocisti (Germany).

[3] Except for the S.A.C. circular, none of the letters referred to by W. have been found, nor is anything known of their contents except to the limited extent to which these can be inferred from Nos. 278, 279.

[4] See No. 266.   [5] See No. 276 and n. 11 to that letter.

278. [1] Not found.

You write about a detailed letter from Heidelberg.[2] The letter is in my possession and I admit that I did not obtain even an approximate idea of what work is supposed to be done and how. I only formed the impression that such utter disorganization set in after the Heid[elberg] meeting[3] that the only way out as a means of saving the Fraction and its honour was the immediate convening of the Conference. There is no point in talking about it now as there is no time and we are once again faced with new problems.

None of the Fraction members write anything to me at all for the simple and very obvious reason that they said 'Amen' to the Fraction as a whole long ago. After all, it's already three months since a news-letter came out,[4] and this is entirely the fault of the committee, or the fault of those members of the committee who made themselves responsible for disseminating information.[5] Where is the report on the activities of the committee, its decisions, etc.? (In what way can I keep in touch with Fraction members when I myself have no idea what has been done and who is going to carry on the work in the future?) A report should have appeared immediately after their return from Heidelberg. Absolutely everything depended on that. Those who made themselves responsible for propaganda should have notified the Bureau of their intentions, as I repeatedly asked them to do. Nobody responded, and Mr. Jaffe, who had himself been at Heid[elberg], did not bother to inform us about it. What am I to do? All this time I have not received תמונת אות[6] from either Sheinkin,[7] Glickman,[8] or others, and I consider it ridiculous to write page after page in vain when nobody has the least interest in the cause and everything suffers terribly from endless delays. I wrote, begged, sent telegrams, and from nowhere did I get either an answer or a greeting, and then— reproaches are showered upon me as easily as anything. I consider, therefore, that the game is not worth the candle. Everything is so rotten that there is no hope of accomplishing anything. *Sauve qui*

---

[2] Presumably the letter from Motzkin (not found) referred to by W. in Nos. 223, 225.

[3] The Heidelberg meeting of the Democratic Fraction Programme Committee, 16–22 June.

[4] The D.F.'s Geneva Information Bureau produced its fourth (and last) news-letter on 20 Apr. 1902.

[5] A printed document setting out certain decisions taken at the Heidelberg meeting (W.A.) shows that Motzkin and Feiwel were charged with arrangements for the production by the Committee of reports on the activities of the D.F.

[6] Hebr., 'a sign of life' (lit. 'the form of a letter'—'letter' in the sense of a letter of the alphabet).

[7] Menahem Sheinkin was a member of the D.F. Programme Committee but did not take part in the Heidelberg meeting.

[8] Probably David Glickman, a member of the D.F. Berlin Group.

peut! If anyone wants to work, let him do so in the same way as he has been doing. If anybody takes upon himself the convening of a Fraction Conference even by December, then perhaps something will still be saved. Until that time there is no Fraction. Where am I to get money for the programme?[9] If Fraction members would pay up their dues—of which I am ashamed even to remind them— this would be enough. I decline all responsibility and have no intention of wasting either more words or time or money on a game of blind-man's-buff when I see that there are no people able and willing to work. During all this time Berlin has sent 35 fr[ancs];[10] the others did not send even that. How the correspondence was conducted all the time Heaven only knows.

Is it possible to think of any work whatsoever when the programme is only now being printed; when up to the present there has not been one word about the Fraction in the press, and, except for *Schimpfliter[atur]*,[11] people know nothing whatever about us? I have been told that you are writing an article—it has not yet arrived, and for that reason I could not write,[12] and how could I write when a statement was about to be made at any time? And this period of waiting, delays, and complete inactivity has lasted 3 months already. No words are needed to demonstrate the obvious—the reproaches I shall receive from all sides and the kind of journey to Russia I shall have.

Enquête: At the insistence of these very Berlin comrades, though I had the leaflets printed as early as the beginning of June, I held up distribution because of the same committee.[13] It was pointless to start an *enquête* in July, especially at the end of the month, when everything was already coming to an end in the circles in which the questionnaires were relevant. For in Russia the Universities are empty in July. You wanted to take part in the *enquête* and had an opportunity of doing something at the Statist[ical] Bureau in

---

[9] It appears from No. 279 that Motzkin had complained of W.'s failure to raise money to pay for the printing of the D.F. programme.

[10] In his letter of 10 March 1902 to the Berlin Group (No. 162) W. acknowledges 'the receipt of 37 francs from comrade Pevsner'.

[11] 'lampoons'.

[12] As to the proposal that Motzkin and W. should each write a newspaper article about the D.F. see No. 193 and n. 5 to that letter.

[13] By the *Enquête* W. means the collection of information about Jewish University students referred to in No. 204, see n. 6 to that letter as to the probable explanation of the discrepancy between W.'s statement that he had already sent out his questionnaire (here referred to as 'the leaflets') and what he now writes about having held up its distribution. Though nothing is known of the matter, it can be inferred from the letter under notice that the Berlin members of the D.F. had urged the holding over of the *Enquête* until after the meeting of the Programme Committee at the end of June.

Berlin. What has been done there? Not a thing. God, I am tired of this way of doing things. Work should be done briskly, but with us there is nothing but words, or at best—letters and endless delays.

Hochschule: Feiwel and I have managed to do something for it. First, we prepared an *exposé*[14] on this subject. Secondly, it is now necessary to obtain 10,000 roubles in order to go ahead with research and the preparation of the project. I have a source of money and we shall have part of it in October. 1000 r[oubles] are already at my disposal for this purpose,[15] and I shall bring more from Russia.[16] The *exposé* is being printed and will probably be ready tomorrow. F[eiwel] and I are now working without any support from any quarter, nor has one of the gentlemen of the Fraction responded to the call.

Minsk: What is going on there is dreadful. We shall be forced to defend what, in essence, it is impossible to defend. Everything that will be said there will be true.[17] That's how things are. I have still had no clear reply from Jacobson,[18] but it will probably come within a matter of days. I wrote to him 4 times and telegraphed once.

Shall be in Berlin on the 20th.

The entire contents of this letter are known to Feiwel and he is in complete agreement.

> Keep well.
> Yours
> Chaim.

279. To Vera Khatzman, Rostov. *Leysin, 11 August 1902*

Russian: Pcd.: H.W.: W.A.

Leysin, 11/viii 02

Dear Verochka,

I have just completed my correspondence, and I still want to drop a line to my Verochka who is so cross with me.[1] My darling,

[14] *Eine Jüdische Hochschule*—see n. 3 to No. 240.
[15] See n. 11 to No. 276. [16] See No. 257.
[17] See nn. 5 and 7 to No. 270 as to the attack on the D.F. foreshadowed by the agenda of the forthcoming Russian Zionist Conference at Minsk, and the eventual dropping of this item from the agenda.
[18] As to W.'s request to Victor Jacobson for information about an acceptable itinerary for his propagandist visit to Russia see n. 24 to No. 238.

279. [1] Probably an allusion to the letter from V.K. (not found) referred to by W. in No. 277 as fitting in with various unpleasant letters from other sources.

I have already replied to the A[ctions] C[ommittee][2] and to Motzkin.[3] This time I gave both of them the truth without any sugar coating, and so much of it that both they and Motzkin will sever all relations with me. M[otzkin] reproaches me for not writing anything to him about the *Hochschule*, for not getting the money for printing the programme, and so on and so forth. What impudence! I have been writing my fingers off, and he doesn't do a single thing. Nor is he going to Russia: he is tired. How do you like that? The A.C. asked me what the Cultural Comm[ission] had done.[4] My answer was (literally) that it was about time to drop the comedy. When the Cultural Comm[ission], in the persons of Ahad Ha'am, Koh[an]-Bernst[ein], Buber, Toldy and myself, wanted to do something, the A.C. immediately strangled everything;[5] so why aren't you ashamed to ask now? Everything that has been accomplished has been done <u>by us</u> as private individuals and despite your interference. . . . These are, literally, the main points of my reply.

I have told Motzkin that I am not taking any responsibility for the inactivity of the others and am doing everything myself. The Fraction is, for the time being, only a ghost. If he wants to convene a conference of Fraction members, well and good, but on his own. If, however, he wants to take over the 'leadership' while I take over the work, then nothing doing. I do not need any 'directives'. I can do everything <u>myself,</u> independently. In other words, *adieu*!

That's all, my sweet. The other letters are not even worth mentioning. All this is painful and unpleasant. Aberson has reproached me for not treating him with enough consideration.[6] What's the use of talking? What people!

My Verulya, many kisses. Toldy particularly asks to be remem-

---

[2] W.'s reply to the Smaller Actions Committee's circular mentioned in No. 277 has not been found.

[3] See No. 278.

[4] See n. 2 to No. 277.

[5] As to the S.A.C.'s rejection, in May 1902, of an application by Feiwel for a grant towards the preparatory work in connexion with the Jewish University project see n. 4 to No. 209. The S.A.C. had also refused to accede to a demand by the Russian section of the Cultural Commission for an assurance that Zionist regional leaders in Russia would publish in their bulletins the full text of any decisions taken by the Commission and of any enquiries it might desire to address to Zionist societies—see minutes of meeting of the C.C., 28 Feb. (13 March) 1902: C.Z.A.—Z1/233; S.A.C. circular, 1 Apr. 1902: C.Z.A.—Z1/211. So far, however, as this second rebuff is concerned, W., Feiwel, and Buber had nothing to do with the rejected proposal; Feiwel was not a member of the Cultural Commission, and W. and Buber, though members of the Commission, were not members of its Russian Section.

[6] As to the withdrawal of W.'s assistance to Aberson see n. 1 to No. 225.

bered. He can't write now; he is busy. E[sther] Sh[neerson] also sends regards, and I too send you endless kisses.

Your
Ch.

Best regards to Sofochka.

280. To Vera Khatzman, Rostov. *Leysin, 12 August 1902*

Russian: H.W.: W.A.

Leysin, Pension Forêt
12/VIII 02

My sweet darling, my dear Verochka,

The long-awaited reply[1] came today. It's strange that letters arrive so unpunctually. All these, my dear friend, are questions which it is difficult to explain in writing, and, as you can imagine, I should like with all my might to drag closer[2] the hour when, sitting side by side, we shall be able to talk and tell each other everything.

Verochka, there is no need for you to worry about my coming. You can rest assured that I am doing everything in my power to be near you as soon as possible, but at the same time you must understand that I cannot shirk my responsibilities. People are waiting for me everywhere; you know well enough how many people I shall see on the way, and with all of them there is business to discuss. I'll arrange to be in Rostov as long as possible. You have thought of leaving on the 10th, i.e. 23rd September;[3] well, my darling, you are not going to, and you will leave later. As to travelling together to G[eneva], I can't say anything. Verochka, my dear friend, never, until the last moment, can I be sure of my route: Vienna or Berlin or God knows [where]. Everything is blowing about, and my head being all in a whirl,[4] I can't say anything.

---

280. [1] Replying on 24 July (6 Aug.) 1902, W.A., to W.'s letter of 30 July (No. 260), V.K. said that she had no wish to stand between him and the University project but feared that all the work would devolve on him and that this might be too severe a strain on his health. This, she explained, was what made it impossible for her to reply 'yes' to the question whether she would approve of his devoting his energies to the projected Jewish University Bureau, even at the expense of his chemical work. Telling W. that she felt that she had a right to withhold her consent, she urged him not to neglect his chemistry, thus being obliged to accept money from Jewish sources and to run the risk of finding himself in the same position as Bernstein-Kohan, who 'had his fill of sorrow when he served the Jews [i.e. when he directed the Zionist Correspondence Bureau at Kishinev]. People said he was getting something for each good deed.'   [2] Lit., 'I should like to drag closer with my teeth'.
[3] 10/23 Sept.   [4] Lit., 'when there are so many winds in one's head'.

Don't be afraid, my darling, that I shall give up to no purpose the chemistry which is so dear to me. All your arguments are quite correct, and I am bearing all this in mind, and anyhow there can be no question of it this year. Vera, Vera, the whole aim of my letter was to tell you everything. I did not want to make any decisions without the boss. How, then can you speak of a 'right'?[5] Is our relationship based on 'rights'? You and I are both bound to tell each other everything, to communicate [? everything]; this is simply a categorical imperative. I have already written to you that Toldy will probably stay in G[eneva], and so I shall not start writing about plans.[6] There will, of course, be plenty of work, but, darling, I am well able to work and am by no means as weak as you think. I am grieved that your happy moments are poisoned by thoughts about the state of my health. This must not be. I shall take care of myself, my darling, and if I have a definite piece of work, I shall not squander my energies in all directions, and all will be well. As for the financ[ial] side, I shall never get into Koh[an]-Bernstein's position:[7] Zionism is developing differently, and I shall not be dependent on Jews.

My little one, send the reply to this letter to Pinsk (*poste restante*). I am sending Sofochka a postcard today. Those were idle thoughts of yours about being punished (?!!??!).[8] You will see for yourself that I have been writing to you even more frequently than every day. I warn you, my darling, that from now on you will be getting more postcards, as I am off at a gallop: Geneva, Mainz, Frankfurt a/M, Berlin, Warsaw, Pinsk—and it is difficult to write letters while travelling. I am madly in love with you and I kiss you endlessly, my Verulya, my dear little girl. Best regards to Sofochka; thanks for the many postscripts. Keep well, my darling.

Don't be nervous (oho!) Think that we shall soon see each other and it will be so wonderful, so utterly wonderful, my beloved. Make a good recovery, Verusya, have a good rest, because, when I arrive, I shall wear you out completely. I am not going to find you

---

[5] See n. 1, above.

[6] See Nos. 259, 274. In the event, F. moved, in the autumn of 1902, to Zurich.

[7] From the biographical material in *Sefer Bernstein-Kohan* ('The Bernstein-Kohan Book'), Tel Aviv 5706 (1945/46) it appears that, having used up all his own savings in paying the expenses of the Kishinev Correspondence Centre, K.-B. was given an annual expense allowance of 2,000 roubles (rising later to 6,000) by the Zionist Organization. It also appears that his preoccupation with his Zionist work caused him to neglect his medical practice, with the result that he got into serious financial difficulties.

[8] In the letter of 24 July (6 Aug.) to which W. is replying V.K. says nothing about being 'punished', but W. may be referring to an earlier letter—that of 8 (21) July (see n. 2 to No. 257)—in which she writes that she fears that he is annoyed with her and means to punish her—i.e. by not writing.

looking pale, nor will you collapse from the pressure of my finger,[9] nor will you be jumpy, my darling, my sweet Verochka. Toldy will write to you at length in a few days' time. He is very busy, but you ought to know that he does not forget you for a moment. This is not surprising. Your name crops up so many times during the day, and he so often teases me for longing for you so much. I am so glad, my beloved, that he likes and knows you so well.

Darling, give my best regards to Nyusechka, Zina and Esfir. I hope she[10] has arrived safely by now. Have you received the Nietzsche[11] and do you like it? I should very much like to know whether Sofochka and Raya were pleased with the print[s].[12] I have no idea at all of their taste and relied on my lucky star. Well, enough for now. Keep well. Lots and lots of love.

Chaimchik.

Father is in Berlin today. I shall meet him either at Thorn or in Danzig.[13]

[Postscript by Feiwel.]

281. To Vera Khatzman, Rostov. *Leysin, 13 August 1902*

Russian: Pcd.: H.W.: W.A.

Leysin, 13/VIII 02

My sweet darling,

At last a happier letter[1] has come from you today. Forgive me for writing a postcard. We are packing already; there is terrible disorder in the room. You can well imagine how many papers, letters, manuscripts, etc., etc. have to be packed. We leave to-morrow morning and, as I have already told you, Toldy, with Esfir[2] and Pinkus, will be at Bioux,[3] near Lausanne, in a very pretty spot. Toldy has already finished his *Milchkur*[4] and on the whole has made a good recovery. We shall find him in Geneva yet.[5] My little one, I have already written to you about plans, but it will be best to wait till we meet: things will be clearer, and we shall try to

---

[9] See No. 259: 'Do you remember how you fell down when I just pushed you with one finger?' [10] Esther (Esfir) Weinberg.
[11] See No. 265. [12] See No. 266.
[13] It had previously been intended that they should meet in Berlin—see No. 272.

281. [1] V.K.'s letter of 25 July (7 Aug.) 1902, W.A.
[2] Esther Shneerson.
[3] Bioux is not, in fact, mentioned in any earlier letter which has been preserved.
[4] 'Milk diet'. [5] See n. 6 to No. 280.

arrange everything in the best way—you'll see, Verochka. 500 fr[ancs] are due to arrive in time for my journey,[6] and this should do for the entire *tour*. Although I need a great deal, I have enough and Toldy does not expect any financial worries either, so everything is all right. I have not forgotten Nyunechka,[7] my de[ar]............................

Hurrah! Hurrah! Hurrah![8]

While writing this postcard I have this very minute received the money-order telegram.[9] I am on my way, on my way, no obstacles! Well, things do drop from Heaven. I tell you, Verusya, *fein!* Heartfelt greetings to Nyusechka. By the way, I do not know who is offended with me: 'Nyusechka' or 'Nyunechka'.[10] Verulya, let them not so much as think of being offended. I send my warmest greetings to everybody, everybody, and I think about everybody too much to be suspected of lack of attention. Verulya, don't you dare lose your appetite. Keep happy and well. With lots of love

Your
Chaimchik.

Best regards to Sofochka. I have not fallen for Rayechka yet,[11] but—

282. To Vera Khatzman, Rostov. *Leysin, 13 August 1902*

Russian: Pcd.: H.W.: W.A.

Leysin, 13/VIII 02 (after dinner)

Dear Verochka,

This morning I wrote to you about leaving.[1] Everything is packed, letters and telegrams have gone off in all directions, to all points of the compass. How good it is to have weighed anchor! I'll be in Geneva tomorrow morning, shall probably stay there no longer than a day, and then will be on my way.

[6] W. is referring to the remittance of 532 francs then on its way to him from his Baku benefactor, Shriro—see n. 11 to No. 276.

[7] In her above-mentioned letter (n. 1) V.K. had written that 'Nyunechka' (her sister Anna) was hurt because W. had not enquired after her—see n. 10 below.

[8] Words about Shriro's gift here interposed in the writing partly of Feiwel and partly of Esther Shneerson.

[9] See n. 6, above.

[10] W. pretends jokingly not to be sure whether V.K. meant Nyusechka (V.K.'s friend, Anna Ratnovskaya) or Nyunechka (Anna Khatzman).

[11] In her above-mentioned letter V.K. had said: 'You sent three postcards to Raya and only one to each of us. You have already been unfaithful to me.'

282. [1] No. 281.

What can I tell you, dear heart? I am all afire, and you will probably see me burnt out. My nerves are terribly tense and I hope that the beat of the wheels will soothe them. So much has been gone through, so much work done, and ahead—there is an interesting time too. Verusya darling, we were very lucky, and we have made a good start with the University venture.[2]

There is nothing else to write now. As I already warned you yesterday,[3] it will be difficult for me to write letters while travelling, but you will be kept informed about everything by letter, postcard or telegram. In any case, I shall not give up writing to you every day.

I kiss you many times, my dear child, I kiss you endlessly. The hour of our meeting is approaching, and from tomorrow onwards, the distance between us will begin to diminish.

Keep well. All good wishes.

Your
Chaimchik.

Regards to all.

283. To Catherine Dorfman, Kherson. *Aigle, 13 August 1902*

Russian: Pcd.: H.W.: W.A.

[Date and place of origin from pmk.]

Katyusha,

There has recently been so much work that it was difficult to write, and moreover everything is *im Werden*.[1] Briefly, I leave for home tomorrow by way of Berlin. Write to me there. I shall try to write to you while travelling. I have got 1000 r[oubles] for this journey from a Maecenas; they fell from Heaven.[2] The pamphlet[3] will be ready by the time I reach B[erlin]. I sent you my photograph yesterday.[4] Toldy and Shneerson send you their greetings and are moving to Bioux, Vallée de Joux (Jura), where Toldy is going to stay until October, so that I shall still find him.[5] As to the *Hochschule*, I shall get into touch by letter with your brother-in-law[6] and will, most likely, be seeing him.[7] I kiss you warmly, my dear.

---

[2] See, as to Shriro's gifts, n. 11 to No. 276 and No. 281.　　　　[3] No. 280.

283. [1] 'in the making'.　　　　[2] The reference is to Shriro's gifts—see No. 276.

[3] *Eine Jüdische Hochschule*—see n. 3 to No. 240.

[4] Possibly one of the two photographs mentioned in n. 2 to No. 264.

[5] i.e., he will still be there when W. gets back to Geneva.

[6] Fyodor Bromberg.

[7] They did, in fact, meet at Minsk at the Russian Zionist Conference at the beginning of September—see No. 309.

Best regards to your family. Thank you for the invitation from the bottom of my heart. I shall do all I can to visit you.[8]

Love,
Chaim.

284. To Vera Khatzman, Rostov. *Lausanne, 14 August 1902*

Russian: Pcd.: H.W.: W.A.

Lausanne, 14/VIII 02

Dear Verochka,

We are now all on the way from Leysin. I am going to Geneva, and I shall leave there for Berlin tomorrow. Toldy, Esther, and Pinkus, who met us[1] here today, are off to Bioux. My darling, even before receiving your letter I asked you and Sofochka to forgive me and I now do so again. As to whether I believe you, there can't be any doubt, and you don't need my answer.[2] My dear, I'll probably write more to you tomorrow. Don't be cross because this letter is so short. Many, many kisses.

Your
Chaim.

[Postscript by Pinkus, Feiwel, and Shneerson.]

285. To Vera Khatzman, Rostov. *Geneva, 14 August 1902*

Russian: H.W.: W.A.

Geneva
14/VIII 02
Café du Nord.

Dear Verochka,

Your letter came today,[1] and while reading it I felt like boxing

---

[8] As it turned out, W. did not go to Kherson.

284. [1] 'Met', in orig. in masc. sing. form, referring to Pinkus. What W. is saying is that P. met him (W.), Feiwel and Esther Shneerson at Lausanne, and from there F. and E.S., together with P., went off to Bioux.

[2] In his letter of the same date, 14 Aug. from Geneva (No. 285) W. again speaks of having been asked by V.K. whether he believes her, evidently meaning—as appears from the context—whether he believes her explanation of her failure to write more frequently. It looks as though he must be referring, in both cases, to the same letter, being one which has been lost, for no such question is asked by V.K. in any of her letters which have been preserved.—As to the words 'I asked you and Sofochka to forgive me' (i.e. to forgive such reproaches to both of them as are contained in his letter of 4 Aug.—No. 267), no apology to Sofochka can be traced, but W. does, in effect, excuse himself in his letters of 6 and 10 Aug. (Nos. 271, 277).

285. [1] See n. 2 to No. 284.

my own ears. From my subsequent letters you must already have been able to judge how I reproach myself.[2] Once again, my darling, I want to justify myself by pleading that I don't know myself on the days when I receive no letter from you. What a blessing that letters now arrive every day; you can't even imagine what a blessing this is. Of course, Verochka, letters don't satisfy me either—far from it. No amount of letters can be a substitute for even one moment of the meeting face to face which seems to me so infinitely desirable, so infinitely blissful[3] that I don't even want to write about it. It goes without saying that I shall make every effort to prolong it as much as possible. You ask me to tell you 'whether I believe you'. My sweet child, you know how I trust you, and don't you dare to ask such things.

I'll be leaving tomorrow at 5 p.m. At 9 o'clock I shall be in Berne, where I'll probably stay until 2 on Saturday (it's Thursday evening now). Then I'll go on to Deichler's,[4] where I will be on Sunday. On Monday I shall be in Berlin and shall stay there till Wednesday. On Thursday I'll be in Warsaw and on Friday—home.

I will send you a telegram either from Berlin or from Frankfurt.

The programme[5] and the pamphlet[6] have been printed.

My little one, from today I'll not see your letters until Berlin. Anything arriving at Leysin will also be sent on to Berlin, and so till Monday or Tuesday—a fast. This is *hart*.[7] Toldy will write to you all the time. His address: Bioux, (Vallée de Joux), Suisse.

My joy, you cannot imagine how hard it was for me to part from him at Lausanne today. We have become so intimate, we have worked so well, we have come to know and like each other so much. All of us, Esther, Toldy, Pink[us] and I, were swallowing tears and trying to conceal [our] emotions from each other.

My best regards to Sofochka and heartfelt thanks for giving evidence. Though totally unnecessary, it is strictly correct.[8] And so, Revekka, Rivochka,[9]—do you remember, Verunya, how annoyed you were when I called you that? It was in those days—in that awkward period—when you seemed a stranger to me. How strange it seems now! How could it have been so? My darling, Sheychik wasn't with us; I wrote and told you that.[10] Maybe he

---

[2] Ibid.   [3] Lit., 'infinitely good'.

[4] i.e., Deichler's home at Nieder-Ingelheim.

[5] As to the concluding stages of the long drawn-out struggle for the printing of the Democratic Fraction programme see Nos. 270, 278.

[6] *Eine Jüdische Hochschule*—see n. 3 to No. 240.   [7] 'hard'.

[8] V.K.'s letter having been lost, it is not possible to explain the allusion.

[9] V.K.'s Hebrew name, Rebecca—spelt and pronounced in Russian Revekka—diminutive, Rivochka.   [10] See Nos. 265, 272.

will come to meet me from Kissingen, and we will meet in Frankfurt a/M. I have had a letter from Dr. Jacob[son], in which he very persuas[ively] asks me to come to the Crimea,[11] but I won't do it.

Tyomkin invites me to his district.[12]

I kiss my dear, sweet, angry Rivochka, my darling girl.

Your
Chaim.

Regards to all.

286. To Vera Khatzman, Rostov. *Geneva, 15 August 1902*

Russian: Pcd.: H.W.: W.A.

[Pmk. 'Ambulant'. Shown by contents to have been written in Geneva.]

15/VIII

My sweet darling,

I wrote you a letter yesterday.[1] My things are packed and I am leaving at 5. I am tired because there was a lot of running round. Father is waiting for me in Berlin.[2] He has done some good business there, and I am very pleased. Here there is noise, uproar, a crush, a circus, music, crowds—disgusting.[3] I am running away.

Endless kisses for Verusya.

Chaim.

287. To Vera Khatzman, Rostov. *Berne, [16] August 1902*

Russian: Vcd.: H.W.: W.A.

[Date should strictly be 16 Aug., since written after midnight 15/16.]

Berne, 15/VIII 02
12.30 a.m.

My dear darling,

I feel like sending you another few lines. My darling, I arrived

---

[11] W. had telegraphed to Jacobson about his itinerary in Russia—see No. 273. Jacobson, who was the Simferopol (Crimea) regional leader, was well-disposed towards the Democratic Fraction.

[12] Tyomkin was the Yelizavetgrad regional leader.

286. [1] No. 285.

[2] In No. 280 W. speaks of meeting his father in Thorn or Danzig, but they had evidently now decided to meet, as earlier intended (see No. 265), in Berlin—see, however, No. 288.

[3] The postcard bears the printed words: *Concours National et International de Musique, Genève, 16, 17, et 18 Août 1902.* W. was evidently writing from a public place on the eve of the Festival.

here at 9 in the evening, and until now we have been sitting and talking about much that was painful.[1] However, I feel much better now than I had, in fact, expected. I am leaving tomorrow and am still faced with a visit to Deichler, which is not particularly pleasant either,[2] and I'll try to stay there as short a time as possible, for I want to get to Berlin as soon as possible and Father.[3] On the whole, I should now prefer not to make any stops and I should have liked best to jump into a railway-carriage and go right through to Pinsk, or even further. Forgive me, my joy, for writing to you little and briefly. You can imagine that I have nothing to write to you from here, and altogether these are such painful impressions that it's better not to write about them.

Darling, Toldy did not like it at Bioux,[4] and he is now going to live at Colline, where we stayed last year.[5] It's already very nice now over there. My little one, please write every day, so that when I arrive I'll find letters from you. I feel terribly depressed, having had no letter from you today—that is, I could not have had one; I have redirected my Leysin mail to Berlin too.

Keep well, my sweet Verochka. I give you endless kisses. O God, when I am going to see you at last? My longing grows and is going to become a disease.

Regards to Sofochka and to everybody.

Your
Chaimchik.

288. To Vera Khatzman, Rostov. *Mainz, 17 August 1902*

Russian: H.W.: W.A.

Mainz, Railway-station,
17/VIII 02
8 a.m.

Verochka, my little darling,

As you can see, I am already on the move. I have left wonderful Switzerland, and am in the *Vaterland*[1] now. In an hour's time I

287. [1] W. does not name the person he has been with but appears to take it for granted that V.K. will know who is meant—viz., as can safely be assumed, his former fiancée, Sophia Getzova.　　[2] See Nos. 222, 256; see also No. 288.

[3] See n. 2 to No. 286.　　[4] See No. 285.

[5] 'Colline' is the name of the pension at which V.K. is known to have stayed while at Clarens-Baugy in March–Apr. 1901. During his short visit to Clarens-Baugy towards the end of March (see head-note to No. 66) W. evidently stayed at the same pension—hence 'where we stayed last year'.

288. [1] In orig. in cyrillic characters.

shall be at Deichler's,[2] where I shall stay until the evening. I'll be going to Berlin by the night *Schnellzug*[3] and will get there tomorrow (i.e. Monday) morning.

In B[erlin] there will be a lot of worries and scurrying around. I intend calling on a lot of people and shall, therefore, spend 3 or 4 days there. I'll catch up on my sleep a bit, as up to now I have had to travel by night; it seems a pity to waste daytime on travelling. In Berlin I'll visit some Jewish professors and shall try to acquaint them with the Jew[ish] University idea and awaken their interest in it. Raoul Pictet is there now, and this suits me very well. I shall see Father either in B[erlin], or in Bromberg, or Danzig; that will become clear in Berlin.[4]

About myself, my darling, there is nothing to say, except that I am very much in a travelling mood, and this, as far as I am concerned, amounts to a very good mood. Everything is so familiar, as I am going through the same places for the hundredth time, and I know all the *Kellners*[5] at the railway-stations. Consequently, travelling impressions zero.

There is one thing, my darling: I am burning with impatience to have a letter from you. Do you know, this is already the fourth day without my having had [? a letter] or seen your handwriting,[6] and I shall attack tomorrow's post in Berlin in a frenzy.

I shall write from B[erlin], i.e. I shall write every day. Darling, even when on the move I have contrived to write to you often, thanks to the fact that I have my fountain-pen with me, and so it is possible to have a chat with Verochka in a railway-carriage.

As you see, I shall arrive both in B[erlin] and at home two days sooner than I expected,[7] and I am very pleased about it. I'll be able to stay a bit longer at home. Mother always complains about her gypsy who is too restless to stay at home. At the Deichlers' I have lengthy discussions in store and delicate conciliatory missions between father and son, etc.

Well, Verusya, this has turned out to be rather a silly and sleepy letter; I haven't slept for two nights—but don't let this worry you, my baby.

Darling, I dream of you every time I doze off, and I recreate your

---

[2] i.e., at Deichler's home at Nieder-Ingelheim.

[3] 'express'—in orig. 'Schnellzug' in latin characters with Russian suffix ('om') denoting 'instrumental' case of the noun.

[4] See n. 2 to No. 286.

[5] 'waiters'—in orig. *Kellner* with Russian plural suffix.

[6] The awkwardness of the orig. is probably to be accounted for by W.'s having accidentally omitted to write 'a letter' after 'having had'.

[7] He would now be arriving in Berlin on 18 Aug. instead of—as he had expected (see No. 267)—the 20th.

image in all the various forms in which I have been able to see you.

Verochka, I am sure you cannot even imagine how I am going to kiss you when I arrive. You will be screaming; wait and see, my child.

I kiss you endlessly. Do write every day to Pinsk about everything.

My sincere greetings to Sofochka and Raya. Regards to Nyusya and Esfir.

Your
Chaimchik.

289. To Vera Khatzman, Rostov. [*Mainz*], *17 August 1902*

Russian: Pcd.: H.W.: W.A.

[Shown by pmk. to have been posted at Mainz.]

17/viii

Verusya,

I send you my best regards. I wrote you a letter from Mainz.[1] On my return from Ingelheim I'll send you a telegram from Frankfurt.

Love,
Chaim.

Regards to Rayechka.

290. To Vera Khatzman, Rostov. *Between Frankfurt and Berlin, 17 August 1902*

Russian: Pcd.: H.W.: W.A.

[Picture postcard with view of Frankfurt. Railway pmk. dated 18 Aug. 1902. Apparently written in the train *en route* for Berlin on the night of 17/18 Aug. 1902.]

17/viii

In the morning at Mainz, in the evening in Frankfurt, and tomorrow morning in Berlin. I kiss Verulya. Am off in 5 minutes.

Chaimchik.

289. [1] No. 288.

291. To Vera Khatzman, Rostov. *Berlin, 18 August 1902*

Russian: Vcd.: H.W.: W.A.

Berlin N.W. 18/VIII 02

My dear darling,

I have just arrived in Berlin, have already seen Trietsch and Lilien, and have managed to get some idea of the state of affairs. I found two letters at the post-office as well as a postcard from you, and also Sofochka's card,[1] which gave exceptional pleasure. Now it's my turn: my darling Verulya, I never dreamed of punishing you[2] and wrote more than once a day all the time, even when travelling. I have no doubt that you will find out that it's so, as in the end you will receive all the letters. It's simply due to forgetfulness that I did not write in reply to your question about the University.[3] This is superfluous now, as I shall send you the pamphlet,[4] from which all will be clear to you.

It's ridiculous, Verusik, to think about punishments. How could I do this? Even if occasionally I am angry, this is only momentary and it disappears: the whole essence of my life is my infinite love for you. Where could Esfir have disappeared to for such a long time?[5] This is beyond me. Can she have been in Vienna all this time? And I thought that you had already seen her long ago. Toldy has probably written to you. His address is definitely: Glion-sur-Territet (Suisse), Hôtel du Parc.

In Pinsk I shall, of course, again find letters from my darling Verusya. Sofochka asks where we find so much to write to each other about. Tell her, my little one, the name of that wonderful, fresh, pure source.

Tomorrow I shall write more, but today I am terribly tired from the journey and I still have a lot of work.

I kiss my infinitely beloved darling. Regards to Sofochka.

Chaimchik.

291. [1] None of these has been found.

[2] See n. 8 to No. 280. It seems doubtful, however, whether, writing on 18 Aug., W. would have reverted, after so long an interval, to V.K.'s letter of 8 (21) July, and it looks as though, in one of the (lost) letters awaiting him in Berlin, she must again have said something about his 'punishing' her by not writing—possibly in response to the postscript to his postcard of 4 Aug. (No. 268): 'If I don't get a letter today I shan't write for a whole week.'

[3] It is not possible to infer from the context what the question was. In the letter of 16 (29) July, mentioned in n. 1 to No. 269, V.K. had asked various questions about the University project. It may be that V.K. had reminded W. of some particular point not fully covered by No. 269.   [4] *Eine Jüdische Hochschule*—see n. 3 to No. 240.

[5] Esther Weinberg had left Geneva for Rostov at the beginning of August (see No. 267) but had evidently not arrived there. W. had relied on her to take messages and a gift to V.K. (see Nos. 265, 275).

292. To Vera Khatzman, Rostov. *Berlin, 20 August 1902*

Russian: H.W.: W.A.

20/VIII 02   Berlin.

My dear darling,

Do you know that I have had so much scurrying, such a rush, and so much to do that I have entirely forgotten whether I have written to you or not? But I am sure you are not worried and understand that I am busy. It's difficult to tell you about all this rush. I'll be happy when I leave B[erlin]. The change after Leysin is extremely harsh and I can hardly stand it. I have received all your letters, my darling. All this is far above all thanks and I do not thank you. I am not writing anything now, as I don't know where to start. I'll try to come to you sooner and am quivering all over at the feeling that I'll be at your home, that you will embrace me and nestle in my arms like a little bird. My nerves have gone utterly to pieces, thanks to Berlin. I am very glad that Esfir has arrived at last.[1] Give my regards to Sofochka. I kiss you endlessly, with deep, deep affection. Regards to Esfir and Nyusya. I shall, of course, stay with you. Verulya, forgive me for being so brief.

Your
Chaimchik.

293. To Vera Khatzman, Rostov. [*Berlin*], *20 August 1902*

Russian: H.W.: W.A.

[Place of origin from pmk.]

My dear darling,

I scribbled a few disjointed words—lines[1] to you today in a great hurry,[2] just to give you a sign of life and to tell you that as I get nearer to you my passionate desire to see you, to take a long look at you, to talk to you, to kiss you, grows stronger. I am incapable of describing this to you, and because of it my whole being is so highly charged that at times I feel simply unbearable pain and have to restrain myself from jumping about.

I hope I shall succeed in doing something for the *Hochschule* today. The pamphlet[3] has gone off in the post. I'll bring you another

292. [1] See No. 291.

293. [1] Thus in orig.   [2] No. 292.
[3] *Eine Jüdische Hochschule*—see n. 3 to No. 240.

copy. Motzkin is ready at last,[4] and everything will be delivered to you. I have made contact here with leading Jewish professors at this University—with Senator,[5] Levin,[6] Landau[7] and others. I don't yet know what will come out of all this, but my luck holds and I trust my star. Mme and M. Pictet are here, and I shall be seeing them tomorrow. Today I am meeting their assistant, Dr. Altschul, who is an old friend of mine.

I am being torn to pieces here, and I should surely have lost my nose were it not for catarrh, thanks to which I always feel that it is still there. You are probably getting news from Toldy; his address: Glion s/Territet, Hôtel du Parc. Pinkus is just a big boy.[8] I am waiting now for a certain Jew[ish] banker of my acquaintance—he has [? just] arrived—perhaps he will bite.[9]

Darling, my angel, my sweet, don't be cross with your very weary Chaimchik. He is exhausted, he has seen so much that his head is spinning, but he loves you without limit and without end and feels happy that we love each other so.

Chaim

20/VIII

294. To Regina Schimmer, Berlin. *Berlin, 20 August 1902*

German: Pcd.: H.W.: C.Z.A.—A110/29

Berlin 20/VIII 02   The Café Monopol would suit me very well.[1]

Dear Miss Schimmer,

    I have greetings to convey to you from Esther[2] and Feiwel. Un-

---

[4] i.e., Motzkin's revised version of the Democratic Fraction's programme, as to the printing of which see Nos. 270, 278.

[5] Hermann Senator (1834–1911), a distinguished German Jewish physician; appointed Honorary Professor, Berlin University, 1899.

[6] Louis Levin (1850–1929), pharmacologist and toxicologist; appointed Extraordinary Professor, Berlin University, 1894.

[7] Leopold Landau.

[8] Writing to Feiwel on 9 Nov. 1902 (text in vol. ii of this series), W. says about Pinkus: 'Ever since the Bioux affair I have known what to think of this dear frivolous fellow.' In the summer of 1902 Pinkus spent a short time at Bioux (Switzerland) with Feiwel and Esther Shneerson but the nature of the 'Bioux affair' is unknown. As to W.'s favourable first impression of Pinkus see Nos. 183, 186, 187.

[9] The person mentioned as a potential supporter of the Jewish University project is, perhaps, Heinrich Meyer-Cohen (1855–1905), a Berlin Jewish banker and philanthropist actively interested in Jewish education and, in the 1890s, a supporter of the *Hibbath Zion* movement and of Berlin Jewish student societies in sympathy with Jewish nationalism.

294. [1] Written, as shown in text, at the top of the card. The Café Monopol was a favourite meeting-place for Berlin Zionists.   [2] Esther Shneerson.

fortunately, it is impossible for me to come out to see you. Would you be so kind as to fix an appointment for tomorrow midday ?

Yours truly
Dr. Ch. Weizmann.

Hotel Reich,
Dorotheenstr.

295. To Vera Khatzman, Rostov. *Berlin, 21 August 1902*

Russian: H.W.: W.A.

Berlin N.W.
21/VIII 02

My joy,

I now have a few free moments at my disposal and I am taking advantage of them to scribble a few words to my beloved girl. I am leaving here today at last and by tomorrow shall be in Warsaw. I have had some success here; I have succeeded in making contact with some leading professors.[1] It is understandable that I am hopelessly tired; have run about a great deal and have gone stupid from endless discussions and negotiations. I'll jump into a railway compartment with delight in the knowledge that I shall be able to sit there a few hours in peace.

I am now going to send a wire to Father in Thorn and will decide with him what train to take.[2]

It will be possible to do something here for the *Hochschule* by October, and clearly I shall again be going by Berlin on my way back.[3] It would be splendid, of course, if we could travel together, but would you want to get entangled with someone who never knows his exact route ? There is, of course, much that is interesting here, but I have been living in such a daze, and my days from 9 in the morning to 3 o'clock at night have been so full, that I have not once been either to the theatre or to a concert. Altogether, I like Berlin less now, and the Germans as well. They are coarser, even though more cultured, than the Swiss. I have news from Toldy every day;[4] he is very dejected, but we shall still find him [? in Switzerland] when we get there. Well, Verulya, my little friend, it will be good to be together, and perhaps Sofochka will come too.[5]

295. [1] See No. 293.   [2] See No. 280.
   [3] He did not, in fact, travel via Berlin on his way back from Russia to Switzerland.
   [4] All the letters here referred to have been lost.
   [5] W. may have been thinking of Sofochka's proposed application for admission to the University of Geneva—see n. 1 to No. 267.

Please let me know, my darling, why and how I have almost managed to get into Mother's bad books?[6] I can't imagine such a *cas*. Best wishes to Sofochka. I am not writing to her separately now but shall write to her from home. I shall stop in Warsaw for a day and a half,[7] and on Sunday morning shall be at home. Mother is already awaiting me with terrible impatience.

Lil[8] is taking my photograph today and we shall send it to you. He wants to see you terribly, so does his fiancée,[9] and I told him that we shall be here on the way back and he will prepare a sumptuous feast in his *atelier*.

I give you endless kisses, my beloved darling, my lovely little girl. I am so glad that you are buying a simple little round hat. The ideal is coming true. But see that it is elegant and smart. I am sure that in spite of your assertions about a 'broad' face and the need for a hat with a diameter of several kilometres, a tiny smart simple hat will do nicely, as 'they say'.[10]

What a lot of nonsense! I kiss you, my angel, affectionately, tenderly.

Chaimchik.

Father is calling me on the 'phone, here I go. . . .

296. To Vera Khatzman, Rostov. [*Warsaw, 23 August 1902*]

Russian: Pcd.: H.W.: W.A.

[Date and place of origin from pmk.]

Dear Verochka,

I arrived here today and am leaving tomorrow. Have seen a lot of people[1] and am now sitting among friends and thinking a lot of you. Regards to Sofochka.

Chaim.

[Postscript by Lazare Kunin.]

[6] Evidently an allusion to something in a V.K. letter which has been lost.

[7] W.'s eldest sister, Mariya, was now living with her husband, Chaim Lubzhinsky, in Warsaw.

[8] Ephraim Lilien.

[9] The Mme Braff favourably spoken of by W. in No. 302.

[10] In orig., quotation-marks as shown in text.

296. [1] In his letter of 27 Aug. to Catherine Dorfman (No. 300), W. tells her that in Warsaw as well as in Berlin he has tried to arouse interest in the University project.

297. To Vera Khatzman, Rostov. *Pinsk, 25 August 1902*

Russian: H.W.: W.A.

Pinsk, 12/25 Aug. 1902

My dear beloved little girl, my darling Verusik,

I only arrived home yesterday. You will already have learnt this from the telegram sent to you from Warsaw. I was so tired from the journey and felt so ill that I was incapable of writing to you. Moreover, talks, questioning, relatives, acquaintances, etc. Besides, it was Sunday, and I experienced the torments of Tantalus, knowing that your letters were waiting at the post-office and I could not get them. At home I found everyone and everything in good shape. Samuil is in Kiev and is going to try his luck: the examinations start in a few days' time.[1] Kilichek[2] is a fine boy; he is already studying the Talmud, has an excellent knowledge of Hebrew and writes delightful rhymes. He was ill with pleurisy for six weeks and raved in Hebrew verse. He still knows no Russian—that is of no interest to me. Astonishing studiousness, though a terrible rogue. The girls[3] have grown and developed; they are pursuing their studies and grasping them very well. Father and Mother are feeling well, and a happy harmony reigns in the house. I have somewhat outgrown all the trifles of life, but this makes no odds. I haven't seen anything of Pinsk and it doesn't interest me. Such acquaintances as interest me (there are two of them!)[4] have called to see me. I was in bed and we talked until 1 o'clock in the morning about the approaching Conference[5] and about Zionist affairs generally. The Conference promises to be a terrible *golus*[6] product. The Rabbinical party is organising itself in Jesuit fashion,[7] and I think of their machinations with disgust. Everything is vulgar and foul. I am amazed that the cause could have degenerated into such a tragicomedy. However, this is only a cursory impression based on rumour and conversations. I know that stupidity reigns supreme, and ignorance, and the darkness of Egypt, and our half-baked

297. [1] See n. 7 to No. 269.

[2] W.'s youngest brother, and the youngest member of the family, Yehiel Mikhal, at this time aged 10.

[3] Presumably W.'s youngest sisters, Anna, Masha, and Minna, at this time aged 16, 14, and 12 respectively.   [4] Not identified.

[5] The Russian Zionist Conference due to open in Minsk at the beginning of September.

[6] 'golus' (in orig. in latin characters) represents the Ashkenazic pronunciation of Hebr. 'galuth' ('diaspora'—lit., 'exile').

[7] How energetically the 'Rabbinical party' (i.e. the *Mizrahi*) was electioneering in preparation for the Minsk Conference can be seen from the collection of *Mizrahi* pamphlets in the Jewish National and University Library, Jerusalem.

intelligentsia, such as the medical men and others, make up to all this wretchedness. This hurts me and I am terribly ashamed, but I have promised myself not to get uselessly excited at the Minsk Conference and to pursue my own line independently and calmly. On the Fraction's behalf there will probably be Motzkin and all the Russian [? colleagues]. I know that in many quarters there are people greatly in sympathy with us, but this is all *im Werden*[8] and perhaps at Minsk it will be possible to create a nucleus.[9]

Verulik, my darling, you don't know how it hurts me to hear that you are so irritable and nervous.[10] Verochka, my dear, I implore you to be calm and not to behave like that. I understand you perfectly well and I feel all this myself, but, my dear heart, the hour when we shall be in each other's arms is very near, and just think how good, what a delight, that will be. Of course, I'll be in Rostov *incognito* on the first day: you alone will meet me. I shall only be busy in the evenings; the days and the nights will be ours. My sweet, I have not yet been able to fix the day, but I shall know in Minsk and will send you a telegram immediately. Forgive me, my joy, for writing to you little and briefly these last few days. You know, Verochka, how busy I was. In Warsaw I had no chance either, as it was necessary to make a lot of arrangements. The pamphlet is being translated[11] and will, perhaps, be ready in time for the Minsk Conference. I am sending the pamphlet in a small package for you, Sofochka, and Nyunya, and also—for you— Lilien's photogr[aph],[12] which he sends you with many friendly regards and requests to be included in the company of our friends. Please forgive me, and Sof[ochka] and Nyunya[13] too, for sending only one copy. I only brought 4 copies across the border, the rest are at the Censorship,[14] and some of them I'll receive in a matter of days. Of course, I shall then send you copies for everybody. Within the next few days you will certainly get the programme from Berlin.[15] I have only the first proof here.

[8] 'in an inchoate state'.

[9] At the Minsk Conference the Democratic Fraction leaders did, in fact, decide to open a D.F. centre in Moscow.

[10] It is not clear whether W. had heard this from V.K. herself (if so, the letter has been lost) or from some other source.

[11] No Russian translation of *Eine Jüdische Hochschule* was at this time in sight, and what W. must be thinking of here is Joseph Lurie's promise to arrange for a Hebrew translation, as to which see n. 4 to No. 269.

[12] i.e. a photograph of Lilien himself. As to L.'s failure to keep his promise to photograph W. see No. 302.   [13] V.K.'s sister Anna.

[14] Imported printed material had to be passed at the frontier by the Russian Censor.

[15] The Democratic Fraction programme had at last reached the point of being ready for the press and was now being printed in Berlin.

Please give my regards to Esfir, Zina and your sisters. I'll write to them tomorrow; today I still have heaps of work, a mass of neglected correspondence.

Keep well, my child, and see that you are not despondent; don't dare to be in a state of nerves. I want to find you bright, cheerful and strong. I shall wear you out all right.

Lots of love, endless kisses.

Your

Chaimchik.

298. To Moshe Glikin, Berlin. *Pinsk, 26 [August] 1902*

Russian: Pcd.: H.W.: C.Z.A.—A179/3

[W.'s dating omits the month which can be seen from pmk. to be August.]

Pinsk, 13/26 1902

Dear Glikin,

For goodness' sake send the programme at once.[1] Absolutely essential. Please send one copy to Berger[2] too. Is Motzkin going?[3] Let me know immediately. I implore you, Glikin, immediately, at least the proofs.

Yours

Chaim

[The Programme of the Democratic Fraction, now at last ready, or almost ready, for distribution, was printed in Berlin and published in German, together with the Constitution ('Organization Statute') of the Fraction, in the form of a 24-page pamphlet—copy in W.A. Starting with an exposition of what the Fraction conceives to be the basic principles and objects of Zionism, which must—it is declared—keep inviolate its character as a national movement not concerned with religion, the programme goes on to explain why, far from being inconsistent with loyalty to the common purpose, it is, on the contrary, natural and desirable that various bodies of opinion should be represented by organized Fractions within the Zionist Movement. After sketching the historical background to the establishment of the Fraction and affirming its adherence to the Basle Programme, the programme proceeds to set out the main objectives of the Fraction, among the salient points being the following:

(i) The Movement must rid itself of the cult of personality (*Personenkultus*) and democratize itself.

298. [1] Moshe Glikin was the director of a temporary Information Office opened in Berlin by the Democratic Fraction in Aug. 1902, mainly for the purpose of distributing the D.F. programme.

[2] Isaac Berger was the secretary of the committee in charge of the preparations for the Russian Zionist Conference about to open in Minsk. In orig. 'Motzkin' crossed out and 'Berger' substituted.

[3] i.e. to the Minsk Conference. (Motzkin did go—see No. 308.)

(ii) To this end, there must be drastic reforms in (*a*) Congress procedure, (*b*) the manner in which the governing bodies of the Zionist Organization are elected, (*c*) the control of the Jewish Colonial Trust.

(iii) In the future Jewish homeland the land must be nationally owned, and colonization must be on collectivist lines (. . . *soll vor allem das assoziative Prinzip zur Geltung kommen*). It is urgently necessary that the Z.O. should apply itself forthwith to the acquisition of as much land as possible.

(iv) Cultural work, including in particular, the encouragement of the use of Hebrew and the study of Hebrew literature, must be vigorously taken in hand in the Diaspora and also in Palestine. There must be a campaign for the establishment of a Jewish University (*Hochschule*) for general and Jewish studies.

(v) Zionists must bring the strongest pressure to bear on the Jewish Colonization Association to compel it to co-operate, and they must also fight the assimilationist activities of the Alliance Israélite.]

299. To Vera Khatzman, Rostov. *Pinsk, 26 August 1902**

Russian: H.W.: W.A.

Pinsk, 13 Aug. 1902

Verulya, my joy,

I received your letter today[1] and am so glad that you are feeling better. My dear, my heart is much lighter now, for I know how short a time remains before we see each other—are close to each other. Even when I was in Berlin it seemed to me that we were terribly far apart, but now I am only trying not to fan my impatience and keep calm. Altogether, I have to make an effort to keep my nerves under control. Minsk, Minsk[2] . . . but I shall be completely calm. Intelligent Zionists will be in a frightful minority there. Verulya, just see that you get well, for it will hurt me greatly to see you pale and nervous and, God forbid, suffering palpitations. My darling, my darling! Please write to me here direct and not *poste-restante*.[3] I shall leave Pinsk on the 19th or 20th and shall, therefore, be in Minsk on the 20th or 21st. My address there: Isaak Berger, for Dr. Weiz[mann], Torgovaya street, pr[ivate] h[ouse], Minsk. I sent you the pamphlet[4] and Lil's photograph[5] by registered post yesterday. You may still receive the pamphlet from Berlin,[6] if the censorship will let it through.

I do not yet know my exact itinerary and therefore, my darling,

---

299. [1] From V.K.'s letter of 10 (23) Aug., W.A., it would appear that W. is referring to a letter (not found) of 9 (22) Aug.

[2] The Russian Zionist Conference about to open in Minsk.

[3] i.e. to his parents' home in Pinsk. In his letter of 11 Aug. (No. 277) he had asked her to send letters to Pinsk *poste-restante*.

[4] *Eine Jüdische Hochschule*—see n. 3 to No. 240.

[5] A photograph of Lilien, not of W.—see n. 12 to No. 297.

[6] Presumably from the publishers, the *Jüdischer Verlag*.

cannot fix the date of my arrival at your home, but I'll let you know from Minsk. I spent all day yesterday reading the circulars issued by the regional leaders.[7] God, what trash, what poverty of thought, what stupidity, pettiness and lack of everything! If the leaders write like that, what can the groups[8] be like? We shall see it all in Minsk, where 500 people will be meeting. Koh[an]-Bern[stein] is coming here for a day and we shall travel together from here.[9] I had a letter from Toldy today. He sends you his best regards and is going to write to you 'tomorrow'.

My sweet, I implore you not to get nervous, be bright and gay. I suffer when I think of your sufferings over there. Samuil and Moisey will also be in Minsk, as well as the whole of the Kiev *Kadimah*.[10] Sam[uil] will already have finished his exams. Whether he will get in still remains a big question.[11] If he is turned down, he will do his military service[12] and will then go either to the (new) Danzig Technical College[13] or to Geneva. It's terribly, deadly boring in Pinsk. I don't want to see any of the Zionists; they disgust me to the bottom of my heart. They are destroying the cause. A letter came from Buber; he is delighted with the pamphlet.

The 1,000 roub[le] Jew[14] is evidently a very sincere person. Wasn't it a piece of luck?

Sheychik has really behaved like a swine. When he was here he didn't even bother to call on us to pass on the kind remembrances. How do you like that? Well, my little darling, goodbye. Until tomorrow. Everything is so monotonous here that I can't write the way I did from abroad. O God, how I have lost the habit of it all! I kiss, kiss, kiss you endlessly.

Your
Chaim.

My best regards to Nyusechka and Fira. I'll tell you about Herz-f[eld].[15] He did not feel too badly.

Send me the water-melons and all sorts of herrings. I shall take home the barrel of water-melons.

[7] i.e., circulars distributed by the Zionist regional leaders in Russia to Zionist societies within their respective areas.   [8] Local Zionist societies and the like.

[9] In the event, he was prevented by illness from going to Minsk.

[10] The Kiev Zionist student society of that name.

[11] As to Samuel's efforts to qualify for admission to the Kiev Polytechnic see n. 7 to No. 269. As to the outcome of this attempt see No. 317. In spite of the misunderstanding there mentioned Samuel was eventually admitted—see n. 17 to No. 100.

[12] As to the expression here rendered 'do his military service' see n. 8 to No. 115.

[13] Then being planned: opened 1904.

[14] Samuel Shriro—see No. 276 and n. 11 to that letter.

[15] The Benjamin Herzfeld mentioned in No. 220 and, in a comment on his relations with Esfir Weinberg, in No. 222.

300. To Catherine Dorfman, Kherson. *Pinsk, 27 August 1902**

Russian: H.W.: W.A.

Pinsk, 14/VIII 02

Dear Katyusha,

After long wandering across Europe I reached home only yester-day;[1] I shall stay here exactly a week and then go to Minsk. I have a mandate.[2]

I can write little of my travelling impressions. In Berlin and in Warsaw I tried to get the public interested in the *Hochschule* and scored some success. My greatest expectations are from my journey through Russia. The itinerary has not yet been fixed. It's difficult to say what the Conference will be like. I don't expect anything from it for a number of reasons. So many *Mizrahi* people will be assembling, there will be so much ignorance, that in such a con-centration the putrefying bacilli of reason and culture will not be able to survive.[3] I shall, of course, write to you from Minsk and tell you my impressions. There has been nothing new since Leysin. If you only knew, Katyusha, how sharp the transition is from Leysin, from the life and environment there, to Pinsk, to the Pale.[4] But this is our real life. Within the next few days I shall send you the pamphlet[5] and the full programme.[6] Write to me here the whole time. As soon as I know my route I'll send you a telegram.

Katyusha, I shall not reply now to your dear letter which I received at Leysin just before my train left. It is too nice to be answered cursorily, and I am not now in a fit condition to write at length. I am worn out and in a state of *allgemeine Depression*.[7] I should like to convey to you Berthold's and Esther's[8] very sincere regards—to you and to Koenigsberg. Who is coming[9] from Kherson?

---

300. [1] W. in fact arrived at Pinsk on 24 (not 26) Aug.—see No. 297.

[2] From a letter of 10 (23) Aug. 1902 to Moshe Glikin from an unidentified person named Levin, C.Z.A.—A179/4, it appears that Isaac Berger had arranged for W. to receive a mandate (credentials as a delegate)—on whose behalf is not known—for the Minsk Russian Zionist Conference. In No. 304 W. tells V.K. that he has received five mandates.

[3] As to the rallying of the *Mizrahi* forces see No. 297 and n. 7 to that letter. The reference to 'putrefying bacilli' is, of course, ironical—'putrefying' in Mizrahi eyes.

[4] The Jewish Pale of Settlement: see n. 3 to No. 63.

[5] *Eine Jüdische Hochschule*—see n. 3 to No. 240.

[6] The full text of the Democratic Fraction programme in its final form (see bridge-note following No. 298), as contrasted with the 'part of the programme' sent to her in the middle of July—see No. 242.

[7] 'general depression'.

[8] Esther Shneerson.   [9] i.e. to the Minsk Conference.

If only Bromberg would come![10] Lots and lots of love. Regards to your family. A brotherly greeting from

Chaim.

Did you get our phizzes![11]
Best regards to Weinstein.

301. To Vera Khatzman, Rostov. *Pinsk, 27 August 1902**

Russian: H.W.: W.A.

Pinsk, 14 Aug. 1902

My sweet darling, Verunya, my joy,

There was no letter from you today, and for me this is a great deprivation. I hope that tomorrow there will be one, and I shall patiently await tomorrow. You ask me, little darling, to fondle you, if only by letter. Verochka, my dear, this is what I do in every word of mine, with every sound. But no such caresses can satisfy me. I hope, however, that when we meet we shall make up for it, and during those days we will not leave one another's side, we will be always together, and our happiness will know no bounds. Verulya, you really cannot complain about me now: I have been writing to you so often, more often would really have been impossible, and there was nothing in my life that I did not share with my beloved darling: you have always known of the good and of the bad. This is already my fourth day at home, and everything is very quiet. I am not used to such calm days, during which I get very few letters, hardly any telegrams, sleep a lot and soundly and relax, awaiting great days in Israel in the t[own] of Minsk.[1] But everything here is alien to me, terribly alien, and during this one year I have moved further away from this life than in five years. Another two or three years abroad, and I'll be *sans patrie* in the full meaning of the word. My dearest, you have got the pamphlet[2] already and I beg you, my dear, to write me your impressions immediately, at once, do you hear? Author's vanity! The article on Zionism you write about is in *Russkoye Bogatstvo* and not in

---

[10] Fyodor Bromberg did go to Minsk.

[11] In No. 283 he tells her that he has sent her his photograph. If, as seems probable, what he had sent her was one of the two photographs mentioned in n. 2 to No. 264, showing respectively (*a*) W. and Feiwel, and (*b*) W., Feiwel and Esther Shneerson, this would explain the reference to 'our phizzes' (plur.).

301. [1] The Russian Zionist Conference was due to open at Minsk on 4 Sept.
[2] *Eine Jüdische Hochschule*—see n. 3 to No. 240.

Mir B[ozhiy].[3] I have read about it, as well as extracts from it, and it's complete rubbish: the pettiness of an assimilationist, the sweet-and-sour jabbering of a Jew who is a candidate for conversion or already converted. In vain, my darling, can you seek anything new there, and what is old in it is nasty. I have written to the Minsk Conference Bureau telling them that they would be acting tactlessly if they discussed the Fraction without having a report from any Fraction member.[4] How this *Pack*[5] can talk about us without knowing either our programme or our aims or intentions—it's enough to make a chicken laugh. Yet again there will be invective and nothing more. Then we shall all decline to take part in the debate and shall let them do as they like. Tell me, my little girl, you are no longer pining for me as terribly as you did, are you? You do know, don't you, that I think of you every second, that it is you I live, think and breathe. You are not going to be upset and cross but will write me nice, tender letters and will love me dearly, kiss and caress me when I am with you, won't you, Verochka? Keep well, my joy, and write to me every day regularly, or I shall get very miserable.

Regards to all and love to my dearly beloved Verusenka.

Your
Chaimchik.

302. To Vera Khatzman, Rostov. *Pinsk, 29 August 1902**

Russian: H.W.: W.A.

Pinsk, 16th/Aug. 1902

Verunchik, my little darling,

For two days there were no letters from you, but, as if to make up for it, today I got two letters and a postcard.[1] You are unfair, my love, if you are cross with your Chaimchik for not writing to you as fully as you would have liked. Verochka, you must admit that no matter how full my letters were, you would still find them unsatisfactory. I am well aware of it from experience, but you

---

[3] From references to the same subject in later letters from V.K. preserved in W.A. it would appear that W. is here replying to a letter (not found) dated 9 (22) Aug. 1902 mentioning a critical analysis of Zionism, on assimilationist lines, in an article by J. Bickerman published in the July 1902 issue of the Russian monthly *Russkoye Bogatsvo* ('Russian Wealth').

[4] As to the proposal (eventually dropped) that the Minsk Conference should define its attitude towards the Democratic Fraction see No. 270 and nn. 5 and 7 to that letter.   [5] 'rabble'.

302. [1] Dated respectively 10 (23), 11 (24), 12 (25) Aug. 1902—all in W.A.

should have borne in mind my extreme fatigue. My dear good
friend, I knew that the letters were unsatisfactory but preferred
to scribble a few lines rather than not write at all. Besides, I got
nothing concrete out of my wanderings through Berlin: I have been
simply probing and probing. To write all this was difficult for me.
It will be different when we are sitting side by side. Then I will
embrace you, cover you with kisses; you will look at me, and I'll
talk to you for ever, Verulya, about everything,—everything. Just
think how good it will be. God, if only it were sooner! I am terrified
at the thought that there is still so much to go through before we
meet. But how sweet it will be. Verochka, you will lavish caresses
on me, won't you my darling? I don't correspond with anyone at
Rostov. How is it that the local Zionists know of my arrival? The
local representative must have written to them.[2] In any case,
Verochka alone will meet me. Don't you understand yourself,
darling, how much I want to see you? You reprove me unjustly
for something that is really my ardent desire.

As for Bickerman's article, I haven't read it yet but shall read it
tomorrow.[3] However, I am aware of the author's basic premise and
conclusion. All this makes me so disgusted that it's unpleasant
even to write about it. The man denies the existence of the *Juden-
not*[4] and does not, therefore, find any justification for the existence
of Zionism. He solves the Jew[ish] prob[lem] by what is almost
tantamount to conversion. The article may arouse some interest
among such *goyim*[5] as the Jews of Rostov. I regard this as the
chatter of a servile Yid[6] and I am disgusted. Incidentally, you do
know, my darling, that I don't intend, on principle, to enter into
an argument with assimilationists in the non-Jewish press. I can
only write in Jewish or Jewish-German journals.[7] If I have time,
I shall write a reply in *Ost und West*,[8] but I hope that one of the

[2] See n. 3, below. By 'the local representative' W. means, presumably, the regional
leader, who, in the case of the Yekaterinoslav region, to which Rostov belonged,
was Ussishkin.

[3] What W. wrote about Bickerman in his letter of 27 Aug. (No. 304) was, as he
there explains, based on what he had read about the article and on extracts from it.
In the letters mentioned in n. 1, above, V.K. tells W. that everyone in Rostov is
talking about Bickerman's attack on Zionism, and that a local Zionist, Isaac Rothstein, has promised to call a meeting during W.'s stay in the city. 'You will have', she
writes in her letter of 12 (25) Aug., 'to reply to the article here—everyone will pester
you to do so.' [4] 'the Jewish predicament'.

[5] In orig., the Russian transliteration of *goyim* (Yidd., 'gentiles') in cyrillic
characters. [6] 'Yid'—in orig. 'Zhid', opprobrious Russian word for 'Jew'.

[7] The distinction seems to be between Jewish papers published in Russia in Hebrew,
Yiddish, or Russian, and Jewish papers in the German language.

[8] *Ost und West* ('East and West') was a Jewish illustrated monthly founded in 1901
in Berlin. It did not, in fact, publish any reply to Bickerman by W., and there is no
evidence of his having submitted one.

comr[ades], Jaffe or Idelson, will reply: they are 'Russian' journalists.[9] On the whole, I detest the métier of a journalist[10] and
consider it beneath my dignity *zu polemisieren mit Hunden in
kleinen Journalen* (Heine said it).[11] If I am challenged at Rostov,
then I shall certainly be ready to lash out.

You have been asking me about Herzl's negotiations. I know
little about them. It's true they were not about Palestine; whether
they concerned Mesopotamia I do not know. It is not true as far as
I know, that Herzl [? would] not conclude a treaty if it were not
Palestine but a neighbouring country.[12] At any rate, I do know that
there have been very serious *Unterhandlungen*,[13] and these are still
in progress. On Monday I am going to Minsk. I shall live for a week
in a daze and shall write to you about everything from there.

I am anxious—very anxious—to know what you think of the
pamphlet.[14] Altogether, we have so many things to talk about that
we won't have enough days or nights. Lil, the brute, didn't manage
to take my photograph.[15] His fiancée, a Mme Braff, makes a very
pleasant impression. She is a very good-looking woman and already
has two children. She is divorced from her husband and lives in
Berlin. I'll make every effort to see that we travel together.[16] My
dearest, I want it so much myself that it's quite unnecessary for
you to make such repeated requests for it. I'll try to get acquainted
with Rothstein at the Conference.[17]

Regards to Sofochka, Raya, Misha and the recent arrivals.[18]
Misha shouldn't laugh; pamphlets like these are not the only ones
we have coped with.[19] There have been even more interesting

[9] 'will reply'—i.e. in the non-Jewish press. 'Russian' in quotation-marks because
they are not really Russians but Russian Jews.

[10] Cf. his unflattering references, in No. 247, to 'the dilettantism of a journalist'
reflected, as he sees it, in Herzl's evidence before the Royal Commission on Alien
Immigration.

[11] 'to enter into polemics with dogs in minor periodicals'. The reference to Heine
has not been traced.

[12] This refers to Herzl's visit to Constantinople at the end of July 1902, as to which
see Bein, 'Theodor Herzl', p. 392: 'Herzl was asked to submit his plan for the unifica-
tion of the Ottoman Debt. Herzl made his proposal . . . and asked, as recompense, the
granting of a Charter for Mesopotamia and for the territory of Haifa in the region of
Palestine.' Nothing came of these discussions.

[13] 'negotiations'.

[14] *Eine Jüdische Hochschule*—see n. 3 to No. 240.

[15] See No. 295: 'Lil is taking my photograph today and we shall send it to you.'

[16] i.e., for W. and V.K. to travel back together to Switzerland.

[17] See n. 3, above.

[18] V.K.'s sister, Anna, and her sister-in-law, Sophia, the wife of her brother Lev
(Lyolya), had recently arrived at Rostov—V.K. to W., 11 (24) Aug. 1902, W.A.

[19] In her letter of 10 (23) Aug. 1902, W.A., V.K. quotes her brother Misha (Michael)
as having said: 'If Chaim routs Bickerman . . . then I'll become a Zionist.' As to
Bickerman, see n. 3, above. 'Pamphlets like these' seems to be just a loose description

opponents, and they too, vanished. There will be none more serious than Davidson, Ratner of Kiev,[20] or Edward Bernstein. I had a long talk with Bernstein (the famous one) and his daughter in Berlin. I took him to task for taking up the cause of the Armenians and not taking up the Jewish cause.[21] He declared: *Wenn ich jüdisches Gefuehl haette, ich waere Zionist. Vielleicht kommt es.*[22] Together with him, we[23] cursed the assimilationists. In the journal we shall be publishing Bernstein will write against the assimilationists: he is on the road to Zionism,[24] and his daughter has paid her shekel. Kastelian-sky has been working on them adroitly. I can't say a thing about the scientific bases of Zionism.[25] You should have heard how Bernstein laughed at that. After all, the 'scientific character' of Socialism has been wrecked completely,[26] and people are only looking for slogans, *Eh bien!* And Mr. Bickerman *wird abfallen* too.[27] *Passé.*

Verusya, my joy, I send you many, many kisses and hold you in a tight embrace. Kiss me, Verochka.

Your
Chaimchik.

Best regards to Nyusya, Esther, Zina and Co.

303. To Moshe Glikin, Berlin. [*Pinsk*], [? *31 August 1902*]

Yiddish: Pcd.: C.Z.A.—A179/3

[Undated. Pinsk pmk. missing. Berlin (Charlottenburg pmk. 2 Sept. 1902).]

Dear Glikin,

My brother-in-law, Mr. Ch. Lubzhinsky, is in Berlin, Central

of anti-Zionist propaganda. Bickerman's attack was in a magazine article, not a pamphlet.

[20] Eliahu Davidson and Mark Ratner were Jewish socialists opposed, at this time, to Zionism, though not long afterwards Ratner softened in his anti-Zionist views. For earlier references to Davidson, a former Zionist turned anti-Zionist, see Nos. 55, 144.

[21] The German Revisionist Socialist leader, Edward Bernstein, had taken an assimilationist and anti-Zionist line in numerous articles on Jewish questions contributed to *Neue Zeit*, the theoretical organ of the German Social-Democratic movement, and to other papers. He had been prominently associated with protests against the Turkish persecution of the Armenians.—The lady referred to by W. as his daughter was, in fact, his stepdaughter.

[22] 'If I had any Jewish feeling, I should be a Zionist. Perhaps this will come about.'

[23] i.e., W. and Bernstein's stepdaughter.

[24] Bernstein did, in the end, develop some sympathy with Zionism, and especially with the Jewish Labour movement in Palestine, but not until the 1920s.

[25] In her above-mentioned letter of 10 (23) Aug. 1902 V.K. had said that Bickerman was quite right in remarking in his article that Zionism still lacked a 'scientific basis'.

[26] Bernstein had, in 1901, critically examined the basic postulates of Marxism in an address to a Berlin students society entitled 'Is scientific Socialism possible?'

[27] 'will fade out' (lit., 'will fall away').

Hotel. You can give him everything you have for me, both the programme[1] and the University pamphlet.[2]

Best wishes,
Chaim.

304. To Vera Khatzman, Rostov. *Pinsk, 31 August 1902**

Russian: H.W.: W.A.

Pinsk, 18.VIII.02

My sweet Verochka, my beloved little girl,

Let me first of all ask your forgiveness, my dear, for not having written to you regularly; I let two days lapse, and I am perfectly aware of having caused you annoyance, against my and your will, of course. And so I didn't write to you yesterday, my dear child, because it was my first Saturday at home; people kept coming, and, moreover, Moisey and I and another acquaintance were busy the whole day translating the Fraction programme into Russian.[1] Do you know, I spent the whole of six hours dictating to Moisey. You see, my little darling, I want you to understand the validity of this excuse and to forgive your deeply loving Chaimchik, who never forgets you for a single second and who always and every-where thinks of you, lives by you, my beloved dear little darling, Verochka. Tomorrow, Monday, I shall be leaving for Minsk at last.[2] My paper on the Fraction[3] has been fixed for Saturday, outside the session,[4] and I shall probably speak at the Conference as well.[5] When, I do not yet know.

I'll try to write to you from Minsk every day about everything, or several times a day, so that you are *auf dem laufenden.*[6] There will still be alterations in the agenda of the Conference.[7]

I have absolutely nothing to say about my life in Pinsk. You can

303. [1] The programme of the Democratic Fraction.

[2] *Eine Jüdische Hochschule.*

304. [1] The Russian translation of the Democratic Fraction programme was never published, but a Hebrew translation known from a letter of 15 (28) Jan. 1903 from Abraham Idelson to W., W.A., to have been commissioned by the D.F. Centre in Moscow appeared in 1903—copy in W.A.

[2] To attend the impending Russian Zionist Conference.

[3] See n. 7 to No. 270.

[4] 'outside the session'—i.e. not as part of the proceedings of the Conference.— There was a D.F. meeting in Minsk on Saturday, 6 Sept., but there is no record of any paper having been read by W. on that occasion, and it is doubtful whether he ever did read his paper.

[5] W. took part in a debate on cultural work at a meeting of the Conference on 9 Sept., as to which see head-note following No. 308.

[6] 'in the know'—'au courant'.

[7] As to the eventual dropping of the proposed debate on the *Mizrahi* and D.F. see n. 7 to No. 270.

judge yourself by Rostov. Indeed, I am a visitor here, and with the exception of a close family circle and two acquaintances,[8] I have nothing in common with anybody. I feel so contented at home that I don't need anything else here. [? You want me] to tell you about the family, Verusya. I have already written to you about a few things, my darling. Samuil is at present in Kiev. He got top marks in physics; the other exams are still to come.[9] He will still be sitting for them before the Conference and will probably come to Minsk. Thus there will be four of us from home,[10] and Father will probably come to my Saturday lect[ure].[11] My parents feel quite well. Business is so-so. Mother did once start saying that it's time for her son to . . .[12] there is a dowry of 50,000, but I retorted that it seemed to me that I already had a fiancée, and moreover I wanted to establish a Jew[ish] Univ[ersity] first. All the children are at home now, but they will soon be going away. Yehielke[13] does not want to prepare for entering school—עס איז איבעריג,[14] he says. He proposes to come to me and then go to the Jew[ish] Univ[ersity].

Yes, my little one, soon we shall be together too; let's only get rid of the Minsk Conference, and that is very soon indeed. Once I am on my way I'll tear along to you like a shot. Surely you do believe that I shall do all I can to find myself near you as soon as possible.

I have got five mandates for the Conference; evidently the Fraction has many sympathisers. But many people intrigue against us terribly—G. Bruck,[15] etc. etc. Well, my little darling, once more I earnestly beg you not to be fretful, not to be cross, but to love me, love me dearly. Verusya, I love you beyond words and I kiss you again and again. Best regards to all, especially to Sofochka.

I embrace and kiss you passionately, Verusya, even if it hurts.

Chaimchik.

Toldy and Pinkus are staying together now at Chailly, Pension Mury, and they send you their best regards.[16]

[8] Presumably the two persons (not identified) mentioned by W. in No. 297 as the only Pinsk acquaintances who interested him.   [9] See n. 7 to No. 269.
[10] Probably meaning, in addition to W. himself, his brothers Moshe (Moisey) and Samuil and (see No. 305) his brother-in-law, Abraham Lichtenstein.
[11] See n. 4, above.   [12] 'for her son to . . .'—Thus in orig.
[13] W.'s youngest brother, Yehiel Mikhal, at this time aged 10, of whom W. writes in No. 297 that, though good at Hebrew, he knows no Russian. A knowledge of Russian would have been necessary—as it was in W.'s own case—for his admission to the Pinsk Secondary School, and the words 'prepare for entering school' may refer to this.
[14] Yidd., 'unnecessary'.
[15] Gregory Bruck, who was a member of the organizing committee for the Minsk Conference, was opposed to the formation of Fractions within the Zionist Movement, and also to the inclusion of cultural work in the Zionist programme.
[16] W. knew this from a letter from Feiwel dated 27 Aug. 1902, W.A.

305. To Vera Khatzman, Rostov. *Pinsk,* [? *1 September 1902*]

Russian: Pcd.: H.W.: W.A.

[W.'s dating cut out, but from the words 'I wrote to you last night' in No. 306 it can be inferred that this postcard was written on 1 Sept. Pinsk pmk. missing, a corner of the postcard having been cut off. Rostov pmk. 22 Aug. (= 4 Sept.). The ends of the first four lines have been snipped, the resulting mutilations being indicated in the printed text by dots enclosed in square brackets.]

Pinsk, [date cut out]

My dear little darling,

Am scribbling a few [. . . . .]nsk.[1] I was unable to write to you during the day, I was at [. . .] my sweet darling for writing only a post[card . . .] and my brother-in-law (Chaya's husband)[2] are also going to the Conference [. . .]. During the day we shall reach Minsk, and in the evening we'll immediately have a preparatory session and probably elections for the *Permanenz-Ausschuss*.[3] My darling, my own, you too [? are writing] irregularly: the whole week I have been getting letters from you every other day. Tomorrow in Minsk there may be a letter from you. I am waiting most impatiently for your comments on the pamphlet. I read Bickerman's article;[4] it's quite well written, though with the utmost impudence. He will get a fitting answer. I may be able to send you a copy of the programme[5] as soon as I get to Minsk. I'll do my very best. My Verunya, I was thinking of you the whole night. I can't imagine at all what you look like—very well, I imagine. It seems to me that if I were to see you now, if I were to hear your voice, something awful would happen to me out of sheer happiness. That's the extent to which my nerves go to pieces when I think of Verusya. My sweetheart, my little one, what have you done to me? Naturally, I'll try to find out my itinerary at once and fix it.

No news of any kind. Trietsch will probably come from Berlin tomorrow; 1000 delegates are expected.[6] It's dreadful; nothing can be done in a few days with such a mob.

And so, after all, I did manage to move Raya with all my postcards, with all my pleas for a letter. Oh, well, I'll settle my accounts with her in Rostov. Give my best regards to Sofochka, Misha,

---

305. [1] 'nsk' is merely a transliteration of the three letters left from the mutilated word.

[2] Abraham Lichtenstein.

[3] 'Standing Committee'—the most important of the Conference committees.

[4] See n. 3 to No. 301 and No. 302.

[5] The Democratic Fraction programme.

[6] There were, in fact, some 500 delegates at the Minsk Conference.

Nyunechka. To Nyusya and Fira too. When you get this letter, write again to Pinsk: I'll stop for a day at home again on my way back. My dear little girl, you will be pleased with this postcard: you'll have to get hold of a magnifying glass to decipher these hieroglyphics.

You may, perhaps, have seen Gregory Lurie. I only found out today that he was in Rostov. Had I known sooner, I would have asked him to convey my regards to Verusya. Well, I am closing. The coachman is here, it's time to go. I give you endless kisses and hold you in a tight embrace.

Your
Chaimchik.

Samuil sat ιor two exams and got top marks in each.[7]

306. To Vera Khatzman, Rostov. *Near Minsk, 2 September 1902**

Russian: Pcd.: H.W.: W.A.
[Pmk. reads: 'Railway-carriage, 21.VIII.02']

Near Minsk 20/VIII 02

Dear Verochka,

I met Motzkin on the way. He is very angry, of course, at having been by-passed about the pamphlet,[1] but I soon made him see reason. I don't know how to manage things with the Fraction now, but I think that perhaps something can be done.

In any event, I shall be careful.

I wrote to you last night[2] and therefore am not writing now.

Lots and lots of love.

Your
Chaimchik.

Warmest regards to everybody.

[7] In No. 317 W. tells V.K. that in the entrance examinations for the Kiev Polytechnic Samuel got 19½ marks out of 20.

306. [1] Motzkin had had no part in the authorship of *Eine Jüdische Hochschule*, as to which see n. 3 to No. 240.　　　　[2] See No. 305.

307. To Vera Khatzman, Rostov. *Minsk, 3 September 1902**

Russian: Pcd.: H.W.: W.A.

Minsk 21/VIII 02

Dear Verochka,

Best regards from the fair.[1]

Chaim.

[Signed also by Moses Weizmann, Nahum Stiff and Leib Beham.]

308. To Vera Khatzman, Rostov. *Minsk, 3 September 1902**

Russian: H.W.: W.A.

Minsk 21/VIII 02

My dear Verochka,

Today I only wrote you a hurried postcard.[1] I hope you aren't cross with me for not writing much these days. You should know, my dear, that I don't for a moment stop thinking of you. Tomorrow we start. The Fraction hasn't organised itself yet.[2] Motzkin is here, but he is repulsive to me, and I try to have little to do with him. There are some 60 pe[ople] who sympathise with the Fraction, all of them quite good, but can one knock something together from this material?—that is the question. There is no-one fit for leadership.[3] Kohan-Bern[stein] is arriving tomorrow,[4] Ahad Ha'am also. The idea of the *Hochschule* is arousing immense sympathy, and it will probably be possible to pass a favourable resolution,[5] and even maybe something practical.

307. [1] W.'s ironical name for the Minsk Conference.

308. [1] See No. 307.

[2] The Democratic Fraction was not represented at the Minsk Conference by any delegates of its own, but, according to a report in the Hebrew journal *Hatzefirah*, 25 Aug. (7 Sept.) 1902, the chairman of a meeting held under the auspices of the Fraction on 3 Sept., just before the opening of the Conference, invited all those in sympathy with the D.F. programme to signify their general approval of its aims. According to a report from the Moscow Office of the D.F. (W.A., No. 30/0, 41), 54 persons were registered at Minsk as actual members of the Fraction. The figure of 54 comes close to W.'s estimate, in the letter under notice of 'some 60 people who sympathize with the Fraction'. In No. 310 (4 Sept.) W. writes: 'The Fraction has about 50 people', evidently referring to persons registered as members. The total number of delegates was about 500.

[3] i.e., leadership of the D.F. movement in Russia.

[4] Kohan-Bernstein was prevented by illness from going to Minsk.

[5] On the motion of Nahum Sokolow, the Minsk Conference adopted a resolution (one of a group of resolutions on cultural matters) expressing sympathy with the initiators of the Jewish University project—see list of resolutions, C.Z.A.—Z1/380.

I feel quite well. My itinerary[6] is not yet fixed; as soon as it is I'll let you know. Why isn't there a letter from you, my dearest? I think there will certainly be one today. I kiss you again and again. Regards to all. I am not writing separately to Sofochka; there is nothing to say at present. Verusya, for God's sake, write!

Your
Chaimchik.

[The letters which follow, Nos. 309–13, were written during the Russian Zionist Conference at Minsk, 4–10 Sept. 1902. No minutes of the Conference have been preserved, but its proceedings were extensively reported in the Jewish press, the fullest accounts being those provided by *Hatzefirah* and *Hamelitz*. Though not expressly so described in the reports, W. appears to have been a member of the main committee, the '*Permanenz-Ausschuss*'. W. and Motzkin spoke on behalf of the Democratic Fraction in a debate on cultural work on 9 Sept., W. insisting on the high priority which ought to be given to such work and inveighing against those Zionists who thought that fund-raising should come first. He opposed a proposal by Ahad Ha'am for the setting up of a separate body for the advancement of cultural work, to function independently of the Zionist Organization, but he supported Ahad Ha'am's alternative suggestion that the Conference should set up two distinct Cultural Commissions, representing respectively the religious and the secular approach to cultural activities. Repudiating the charge that the D.F. was anti-religious, W. insisted on the importance of amicable relations between the two schools of thought and called for co-operation between them within the framework of the Zionist Movement. The Conference elected two Cultural Commissions as proposed by Ahad Ha'am, and the compromise resulted in a relaxation of tension at the Conference, at the close of which W. was publicly embraced by the *Mizrahi* leader, Rabbi Reines.—So far as can be ascertained, neither of the two Commissions made any significant contribution to the promotion of cultural activities. As late as April 1903 the Hebrew periodical *Hazman* is to be found complaining that, since the Minsk Conference, 'nothing has, up to the present, been heard about the activities of the [Cultural] Commission'. (*Hazman*, 27 March/9 Apr. 1903).]

309. To Catherine Dorfman, Kherson. [*Minsk*], *4 September 1902**

Russian: Pcd.: H.W.: W.A.

22/VIII

Katyusha,

I am still alive. Noise, uproar, confusion. For the time being we all keep mum. I don't know what will happen next. Fedya[1] and I are spending a lot of time together.

Chaim.

---

[6] For his Russian tour.

309. [1] Fyodor Bromberg.

310. To Vera Khatzman, Rostov. [*Minsk*], *4 September 1902**

Russian: Pcd.: H.W.: W.A.

Without a view. Assembly Hall 22/viii

Dear Verochka,

Muddle, noise, disorder. Terrific crowd. I cannot write a long letter. The Fraction has about 50 people,[1] but there will be more. Rothstein[2] is for us. The composition of the Praesidium is stupid.[3] Klausner and I were proposed but we refused. I'll read [a paper] on the University.[4] Verulya I am absolutely calm. My dear little friend, don't ask me for a detailed letter. If I can, I'll write. I shall probably go direct to Rostov and will take in Kharkov on my return journey. Warm regards to all.

Lots of love.
Chaim.

311. To Vera Khatzman, Rostov. *Minsk, 4 September 1902**

Russian: Pcd.: H.W.: W.A.

22/viii Minsk midnight
Assemb[ly] Hall

Dear Verochka,

Strong opposition [to the] A[ctions] C[ommittee][1] I have already joined the battle twice—successfully, I think.[2] I feel quite well.

310. [1] See n. 2 to No. 308.

[2] The Isaac Rothstein of Rostov, mentioned in No. 302.

[3] There were disputes as to the principles on which the 'Praesidium' (the supreme authority of the Conference) should be constituted. In the end, it was composed of the Russian Zionist regional leaders, with the exception of Gregory Bruck, plus Simon Rosenbaum, the regional leaders being brought in so as to avoid the allocation of seats on the Praesidium by reference to the strength of the various organized groups represented at the Conference.

[4] W. did not, in fact, address the Conference on this subject nor does it appear from the press reports mentioned in the bridge-note following No. 308 that he referred to it in his contribution to the debate on cultural work on 9 Sept. It would seem, however, from his letter of 15 Sept. to Herzl (No. 316) that he was active behind the scenes in trying to enlist support for the University project.

311. [1] i.e., to the Greater Actions Committee, as represented by the Russian regional leaders present at the Conference, all of whom were members of that body. Their reports were severely criticized in the debate on their activities.

[2] According to a report in *Voskhod*, 28 Aug. (11 Sept.) 1902, W. commented adversely on the report of the Russian Zionist Information Centre, pointing out that it made no mention either of the Cultural Commission or of the Colonization Commission set up by the last Congress.

The Conference affairs are not progressing too badly. Tomorrow, a report on organization—the most important.[3] The Fraction cuts rather a poor figure. Motzkin walks about wearing a hang-dog look. I don't know the reason. Sympathy for the Univer[sity] venture is great. I have yet to speak on the subject.[4] Composition and level of the delegates—poor.

I like Rothstein. The Praesidium, in the person of one of the chairm[en], Rosenbaum, is behaving disgracefully.[5]

Darling, my dear darling, forgive your weary

Chaimchik.

Regards to all.

312. To Vera Khatzman, Rostov. *Minsk, 5 September 1902**

Russian: Pcd.: H.W.: W.A.

23/viii Minsk

Dear Verochka,

The criticism of the report[1] goes on. I am sitting next to Roth-stein and S. Ginzburg. Comrade Avinovitzky is speaking at the moment—you know what that means.[2] Best regards to everybody.

Chaim.

[Postscript by Simon Ginzburg and Isaac Rothstein.]

313. To Vera Khatzman, Rostov. [*Minsk*, (?) *6 September 1902*]

Russian: Vcd.: H.W.: W.A.

[Undated. Date conjectured from contents.]

Dear Verochka,

My sweet, you are cross with your Chaimchik, and you are

[3] Ussishkin's report on organization was, in fact, presented on 6 Sept. not 'tomorrow', 5 Sept.

[4] See n. 4 to No. 310.

[5] From a report in *Hatzefirah*, 30 Aug. (12 Sept.) 1902, it appears that at the evening session on 4 Sept., Simon Rosenbaum, as chairman, disallowed a point of order which W. tried persistently to raise.

312. [1] Apparently a reference to the discussion of the reports of the regional leaders (see n. 1 to No. 311), which, according to Mordekhay Nurock's account of the proceedings of the Minsk Conference (Riga, 1902), was continued on 5 Sept.

[2] As to Avinovitzky's views on cultural work see n. 3 to No. 134. He was now, as was to be expected, strongly opposed to the Democratic Fraction.

hurting him very deeply.[1] I am so exhausted, my darling, that it is all I can do to give a sign of life. Motzkin's behaviour is foul,[2] and so the Fraction is not very effective. These intrigues are wearing me down. In the evening, organization.[3] The *Permanenz-A[usschuss]* will select the committees today. Culture and *Hochschule* tomorrow evening.[4] Darling, I don't forget you for a moment, and I write as much as I can manage. We shall make it up after I arrive. Regards to all.

Your
Chaim.

314. To Menahem Ussishkin, Yekaterinoslav. *Pinsk,*

*14 September 1902**

Russian: H.W.: C.Z.A.—A24/vol. 17

Pinsk 1 Sept. 02

Dear comrade,

I am sending you the pamphlet *Jüdische Hochschule*; please read it and let me have your comments on it at Rostov-on-D[on], c/o Miss Vera Issayevna Khatzman.

If you write to me at once, your letter will find me there.

If, in your opinion, it is possible to interest anyone in Yekater[inoslav] in this cause, I am ready to come for this alone.[1]

Best regards,
Yours
Ch.W.

---

313. [1] W. may be referring to a letter dated 21 Aug. (3 Sept.) 1902, W.A., in which V.K. finds fault with him for criticizing Bickerman before having read his article (see No. 301).

[2] It is not known exactly what W. is alluding to. For his generally antagonistic attitude to Motzkin see Nos. 308, 311.

[3] i.e. the presentation and discussion of the report on organization mentioned in n. 3 to No. 311.

[4] At the evening session on 7 Sept. Ahad Ha'am gave an address on 'The Nationalization of Jewish Education' (i.e. the remoulding of Jewish education on nationalist lines).

314. [1] No reply from Ussishkin has been found. W. did not go to Yekaterinoslav.

315. To Moshe Glikin, Berlin. *Pinsk, 14 September 1902**

Russian: Pcd.: H.W.: C.Z.A.—A179/3

Pinsk 1/Sept. 02

Dear Glikin,

Please send 2 copies of the programme[1] at once to M. Lieberman,[2] <u>Pinsk, Albrekhtovo</u>, and to Dr. A. Lichtenstein, <u>Pinsk</u>, but for goodness' sake at once, absolutely necessary. One copy also to Vera Issayevna Khatzman, Rostov-on-Don.

Best wishes.
Ch. Weizmann.

I beg you to fulfil my request immediately; it's absolutely essential. I shall soon send you 50 roub[les].[3]

316. To Theodor Herzl, Vienna. *Pinsk, 15 September 1902*

German: H.W.: C.Z.A.—Z1/337

[W.'s '15 September' can safely be taken to be an N.S. and not an O.S. date, even though, to avoid any possible ambiguity, he expressly says '25 Oct., N.S.' in informing Herzl of the date on which he could be in Vienna. He is writing from Pinsk, before his departure for Rostov. It follows that 15 Sept. must be an N.S. date, since 15 Sept., *O.S.*, would be about a week after his arrival in Rostov. From what is known of W.'s movements it is clear that, consistently with the N.S. dating of the letter, the dates mentioned in the postscript are likewise N.S.]

At[1] Pinsk,
15 Sept. 02

Dear Dr. [Herzl],

[My] friend Feiwel has sent you the brochure entitled 'A Jewish University'. I do not know whether he has written to you about our further plans with regard to the University project;[2] in any case, I should like now to do so very briefly. What we want to do is to arouse interest in the question among thinking people here in

---

315. [1] The Democratic Fraction programme.
  [2] Meir Lieberman, the manager of a Pinsk lamp factory and a leading local Zionist.
  [3] Probably towards the expenses of the D.F.'s recently established Berlin Information Office—see n. 1 to No. 298.

316. [1] In orig. z[ur] Z[eit]—'temporarily'.
  [2] No such letter from Feiwel has been found.

Russia and to raise money for the further preliminary work as described in our scheme.

In Minsk I had the opportunity of interesting various people in the matter and met with some success, so it is necessary, as I see the situation, to start a suitable propaganda campaign. Motzkin is, therefore, going to Petersburg and Moscow, and I am setting off today for Kharkov, Rostov-on-Don, Baku (where I'm told that several thousand roubles are in sight),[3] Tiflis, Odessa and Kiev.

In the atmosphere prevailing at the moment (in Minsk there was a reconciliation between the Parties[4]) we shall, I hope, succeed in arousing interest in the question.

From a very responsible quarter has come the suggestion that a society be founded for the establishment of a Jewish University, with a subscription of 1000 roubles; in Baku one might find 20 such people who would take the initiative[5] I intend to study the question on the spot.

I should be very happy, Sir, if you would be so kind as to let me know your opinion of our present activities on behalf of the University.

I could be in Vienna on Oct. 25th N.S., if I am given the chance of reporting to the A.C. about the University project or of taking part in the relevant session of the Small Congress.

I shall impatiently await your reply[6] and would ask you to be so good as to send your letter (by registered post) addressed as shown below.

I would add that your reply will reach me in Rostov-on-Don if you send it by return of post; I am most anxious to have your views before I get to Baku.

With great respect and with Zion's greetings.

Yours truly
Dr. Ch. Weizmann.

My address:

Till 28th Sept., c/o Mr. I. Khatzman, Rostov-on-Don.

Till 4th Oct., c/o Mr. S. Shriro, Baku.

[3] See No. 257.

[4] See bridge-note following No. 308.

[5] It is not known with certainty who made this suggestion, but the mention of Baku suggests that it probably came from Samuel Shriro—see also bridge-note following No. 317.

[6] No reply from Herzl has been found, but W. did speak on the University question at the Annual Conference ('Small Congress') on 30 Oct. 1902—see n. 4 to No. 320.

317. To Vera Khatzman, Rostov. *Pinsk, 16 September 1902**

Russian: H.W.: W.A.

Pinsk 3 Sept. 02

My dear little darling,

Verusya, you have been quite cross with me for not writing regularly these last few days, but all this is due to circumstances beyond my control. The Conference in Minsk ended 2 days later than we expected.[1] I was so exhausted during the Conference and caught such a bad cold that I utterly lost my voice and was in no condition to undertake such a long journey.[2] On my arrival in Pinsk a number of surprises awaited me. First of all, I found Mr. Evans-Gordon here (see *Die Welt*), a member of the British Parliamentary Commission which questioned Herzl. Gordon has been commissioned by Parliament to study the Jew[ish] prob[lem] in Russia. He was directed to Petersburg, and from there to Vilno–Pinsk–Warsaw. In Pinsk he had my address and, in spite of my poor physical state, I toured the Jew[ish] settlements of the Pinsk neighbourhood with him for 30 hours, by steamer and boat, all over the local swamps.[3] You can well imagine that this did not improve my health, and having returned home, I formally took to my bed. Yesterday I felt ready to travel and, notwithstanding my family's expostulations, I packed my trunk and was *reisefertig*.[4] Suddenly, like a bomb, comes the following news: 'Misunderstanding over Samuil's admission.' This is terrible. Samuil has been parading in his uniform for two weeks, and was admitted to the engineering [faculty], as he got $19\frac{1}{2}$ out of 20. I don't understand what the misunderstanding can be about.[5] You can well imagine what is going on at home.

317. [1] It ended on 10 Sept.

[2] i.e., to Rostov.

[3] Major (later, Sir William) Evans-Gordon, M.P. (1857–1913) was a member of the Royal Commission on Alien Immigration, 1902 (erroneously called by W. 'the Parliamentary Commission'). As to Herzl's appearance before the R.C. see No. 247. W.'s 'see *Die Welt*' refers to the report of Herzl's evidence in *Die Welt*, No. 29, (18 July 1902). The Commission stated in its Report: 'One of our body, Major Evans-Gordon, visited many places, principally in Russia and Poland, for the purpose of obtaining information upon the subjects submitted to us for consideration:' Command Paper 1742 (1903), vol. i, p. 1. Evans-Gordon's visit to Pinsk and neighbouring towns is mentioned in his account of his tour: ibid., vol. ii (Minutes of Evidence), pp. 451–7.

[4] 'ready to travel'.

[5] As to Samuel's entrance examinations for the Kiev Polytechnic see postscript to No. 305. Whatever may have been the 'misunderstanding', he did, in the end, gain admission to the Polytechnic: from his lettter to W. from Kiev dated 21 Apr. (4 May) 1903, W.A., it can be inferred that he was a Polytechnic student at that date.

I therefore decided to go to Kharkov via Kiev, and I am setting out today. Consequently, my itinerary is like this: tomorrow, Wednesday, morning, I shall be in Kiev. On Wednesday evening I continue my journey, and on Thursday at noon will be in Kharkov. I shall stay there Friday and Saturday and should be in Rostov by Sun[day] or Mon[day]. I am bringing the programme[6] with me. I shall not start to describe all my impressions now. My head is in a muddle, and I only hope that I shall have a rest at your home, my sweet; we shall sort out all my experiences together, and there are an awful lot of them.

Verochka, my dearest, meet me at Taganrog; from there we shall try to find an empty compartment so that we can talk in peace until Rostov. You will get a telegram from me. Rothstein will be notified too, but he will not come to meet me; we agreed on that.

From Rostov we shall travel together to Baku[7] and will fix our itinerary. I must finish; it's time for me to leave.

I am very surprised that I have not had a word from Raya all this time. Anyway, never mind. My very best regards to Sofochka, Esfir, Nyusya. How I have wanted to meet them all before! But now I know that I am coming. Four days ago I still had serious doubts. I kiss my dearly beloved girl, my Verochka. Best regards to all.

Chaim.

[During the second half of September and the early part of October 1902 W. visited Rostov and Baku. In Baku his appeal for contributions towards the cost of preparatory work for the furtherance of the Jewish University project produced promises of more than 4,000 roubles, including 2,000 pledged by Samuel Shriro, and he also received promises of 400 roubles in Rostov—see Jewish University Bureau bulletin, May 1903, W.A.]

318. To Vera Khatzman, Rostov. *Kharkov, 13 October 1902**

Russian: H.W.: W.A.

Kharkov 30/Sept. 02

My dear, sweet, lovely Verusechka.

I am annoyed with myself for not writing till now, though I have been in Kharkov two days. But, my little one, you must forgive

---

[6] The Democratic Fraction programme.

[7] In a letter dated 25 Aug. (7 Sept.) 1902, W.A., V.K. had suggested to W. that they should travel together to Baku. (Her brother Michael was living there at the time.)

your Chaimchik, for you know how busy I can be when I come to a town, especially a town like Kharkov. Even now I am not writing by any means as I should have wished. I should like to tell you a lot, and most of all to thank you and all our family,[1] in your person, for the warm and cordial welcome extended to me by everyone,[2] but I cannot do this now. I am restless and tired. I was very well received here. Altogether, the people of Kharkov are a fine lot. There was a mammoth discussion-meeting yesterday. Some 300 p[eople] attended. Very many students. Our opponents were not very good, though better than in other towns. But they got it so hot that they later tried to explain their defeat by timidity. The evening made a tremendous impression. It cost me a great deal, as the conditions at the meeting were terrible; a crush, a throng, no air whatsoever, perspiration, and a highly wrought-up atmosphere.

Incidentally, the comr[ades] here forced me to go to a doctor, who, after examining me, did not find anything except general weakness and exhaustion and even allowed me to smoke, though I did not ask his permission. Today the *Hochschule*.[3] I don't know what it will be like. At any rate, it will be possible to do a lot in Kh[arkov], if not now, then some time later. Verulik, my dear, my angel, my sweet. I miss you again outrageously. I cannot live without you, without feeling your constant presence, and I impatiently await our reunion. My joy, give a warm kiss[4] to Nyunechka, Sofochka, Rayechka, to your aunt,[5] to the children,[6] to your parents. Give my regards to your grandmother.[7] I shall write to all at home separately; at the moment it's impossible.

I send kisses, endless kisses to my Verulya.

Chaimchik.

---

318. [1] Lit., 'ours'—i.e. V.K.'s family, with which he now identifies himself.

[2] In the course of his Russian tour W. had, as planned, visited V.K.'s home in Rostov, meeting her family for the first time. He is known to have arrived at Rostov about 20 Sept., N.S. Exactly how long he stayed there is not quite certain, but from the postscript to No. 316 it can be inferred that his programme required him to leave for Baku on the 28 or 29 Sept. He is known to have been in Baku on or about 1 Oct. (this appears from a letter dated 18 Sept. (1 Oct.) 1902 from Michael Rabinovitz, of Rostov, to Ussishkin—C.Z.A.—A/24, vol. 17. A letter from V.K. to W., dated 28 Sept. (11 Oct.) 1902, W.A., shows that, after leaving Baku, he made another short stay at Rostov before leaving for Kharkov on 10 Oct.

[3] See No. 319.

[4] Lit., 'a huge kiss'.

[5] Her mother's sister, Maria Mamurovskaya.

[6] V.K.'s cousins, Lydia and Deborah Chernin, daughters of Maria Mamurovskaya.

[7] V.K.'s maternal grandmother, Apolinaria Fluxman.

319. To Vera Khatzman, Rostov. *On the Kharkov–Kiev train 15 October 1902**

Russian: H.W.: W.A.

[Written on stationery of the *Bureau Jüdische Hochschule.*][1]

Kharkov–Kiev (railway-carriage)
2/Oct. 02

My dear, dearest, sweet darling,

I have finished my business here, and what can I tell you, Verochka? I don't know whether I should be proud of it or not, but everything I have done so far is going well, it seems to me almost uncanny. Both my general Zionist work and my activity on behalf of the *Hochschule* have been extremely successful. Both the Kharkov people and I are exultant. The Univ[ersity] was received with unexpected sympathy here. I managed to read my paper brilliantly and to arouse the interest of people who were completely outside any sort of activity.[2] A group has been organised here which may play a most important rôle in every respect. Notable representatives of the Khar[kov] financial and learned world have started to participate actively in the Committee for promoting and elaborating the Jew[ish] University project,[3] and some non-Jewish professors are joining too.[4] We haven't started to collect money yet, as the venture has to be organised, and it will provide quite a tidy sum, but I have already found some people whose names are famous in Russia and whose collaboration will prove most valuable. This morning I received a telegram from Prof. Mandelstamm[5] reading: 'certain of Brodsky success, imperative you come',[6] and so to-

319. [1] W. was evidently writing on Bureau stationery ordered before the actual opening of the Bureau early in Nov. 1902 (see bridge-note following No. 320).

[2] i.e. people who had taken no part in the affairs of the Jewish community.

[3] The Committee is known to have had over twenty members, but no complete list has been found. The names of those known to have joined it are as follows: Dr. B. Greidenberg (Chairman), Michael Aleinikov (Secretary), Dr. Israel Breslav, Dr. Michael Futran, G. S. Levinsohn, Alexander Nemirovsky, and (in Feb. 1903) Vladimir Idelson.

[4] *Der Yud*, 6 Nov. 1902, mentions two Kharkov University professors (not Jews) as having promised their support.

[5] Max Mandelstamm was not, in fact, a professor, though often referred to as such.

[6] The brothers Lazar and Leo Brodsky, of Kiev (it is not certain which of them is meant) occupied a leading position in the sugar industry. According to the Jewish University Bureau bulletin of May 1903 (W.A.) mentioned in the bridge-note following No. 317: 'In Kiev, with the help of Dr. Mandelstamm, the support has been enlisted of one of the most prominent manufacturers in the city, with the likelihood of his contributing a substantial sum (approximately one million francs).' The prospective donor was not, in fact, called upon for his contribution, since this was not intended to subsidize the preparatory work but to help in financing the actual establishment of the University—a stage not reached until some twenty years later.

morrow I shall be in Kiev. We shall see. Tomorrow evening I continue my journey, and the day after tomorrow shall be in Pinsk. There I will find a letter from my Verochka. My little darling, I miss you infinitely; I cannot picture a single minute free from work without being together with you. Only when I am working do I feel less pain.

Verochka, my joy, I shall never forget how you received me, how you met me, the atmosphere you surrounded me with in Rostov, how every movement of yours, every word, was filled with love and warmth. Your vile Chaimchik knows how you love him, but believe him that he loves you no less, quite apart from his infinite respect for your person. Altogether, I had the feeling that I was among a family of my own. I kept fearing beforehand that I should prove a stranger in your family, but it turned out quite differently. The best proof of it is the longing for all our family[7] which has been gripping me ever more strongly.

My little darling, I shall immediately send you a telegr[am] from Pinsk about my departure; don't get excited and don't worry.

My dear Verochka, give my regards to your parents, and kiss them warmly[8] for me, and also your aunt[9] and Lidochka and Deborochka.[10] And, without fail, greetings to Granny.[11]

Your
Chaim.

Rayechka, my sweet, your little knife is safe, and <u>you</u> will receive it by post. I am very sorry that you forgot it, but it was too late to pass it on to you. Verunchik will tell you how everything was in Kharkov: it was all very important, and we talked about Volod'ka[12] with the Nemirovsky's, with whom I spent most of my free time. Thank you, dear little one, for your parting words. I send you brotherly greetings and love.

Chaim.

---

[7] Lit., 'for all ours'—see n. 1 to No. 318.
[8] Lit., 'give them a huge kiss'.
[9] Maria Mamurovskaya—see n. 5 to No. 318.
[10] Lydia and Deborah Chernin—see n. 6 to No. 318.
[11] See n. 7 to No. 318.
[12] Probably the Vladimir Idelson, a lawyer and an active Kharkov Zionist mentioned in n. 3, above as a member of the Kharkov Committee for the Jewish University.

320. To Vera Khatzman, Geneva. *Vienna, 29 October 1902*

Russian: H.W.: W.A.

Vienna[1] 29/Oct. 02

My dear, good, lovely darling,

I greet you, my angel, in your *Alma Mater*[2] and wish you a good fresh start in your studies. I wish, my dear, dearly beloved little girl success, strength and fortitude.

You are my hope and my pride, and this, I am certain, you will always remain.

The session opened this morning. Herzl read a very sad report.[3] I cannot commit it to paper and will tell you all about it later; for the time being, keep even these words secret. Herzl's attitude to us is very good. Why? My successes have greatly impressed him.

My paper and Buber's—probably tomorrow morning.[4] I want to

---

320. [1] The Annual Conference of the Zionist Organization ('the Small Congress') met in Vienna on 29–30 Oct. 1902. It was attended by W. as the representative for Switzerland of the Cultural Commission set up by the Fifth Congress. In his letter of 15 Sept. (No. 316) W. had told Herzl that if he came to Vienna it would be on the understanding that he would have an opportunity of speaking on the University question at the appropriate session of the Annual Conference.

[2] Geneva.

[3] The Conference minutes (C.Z.A.—Z1/168) show that, reporting on 29 Oct. on his political activities, Herzl told the Conference of the failure of his discussions with the Turkish Government (see n. 12 to No. 302) and said that he could see no prospect of any improvement in the situation in the foreseeable future.

[4] W. addressed the Conference on the University project, and Buber reported on the activities of the *Jüdischer Verlag* and of the Jewish Statistical Bureau. It is clear from the report in *Die Welt*, 31 Oct. and 7 Nov. 1902, that both spoke on the second day of the Conference, 30 Oct. In moving a resolution standing in the joint names of himself and Buber, W. gave an account of the preparatory work already done on the University project, described the encouraging response to his propaganda in Russia, and said that most of the money required for a Jewish University Bureau was already assured. (The Bureau was opened in Geneva almost immediately after the close of the Conference.) The resolution read: 'The Annual Conference notes with satisfaction the information communicated to it by Mr. Buber and Mr. Weizmann on the question of a Jewish University [*Hochschule*], declares itself in sympathy with their aspirations, [and] requests members to support the project to the best of their ability, in collaboration with the Jewish University Bureau in Geneva. The Actions Committee is enjoined, likewise in collaboration with the above-mentioned Bureau, to send circulars on the subject, if and when appropriate, to Societies and responsible representatives [*Vertrauensmänner*]. The Conference enjoins the Actions Committee to leave nothing undone to facilitate the establishment of the Jewish University in Palestine.' Though the resolution spoke of a Jewish University in Palestine, it appears from the Conference minutes (see n. 3 above) that, consistently with the views expressed in *Eine Jüdische Hochschule* (see n. 3 to No. 240), both W. and Buber made it clear that they did not regard it as axiomatic that in no circumstances could any alternative to Palestine be considered. The Conference refused to be satisfied with the Weizmann–Buber resolution and, in its place, adopted a Farbstein–Ussishkin resolution reading as follows: 'The Annual Conference enjoins the Actions Committee to leave nothing

leave tomorrow evening. For the time being, deadly boredom. Let's pray that it will be better later on. We shall see.

I have no more to say for the moment. Koh[an]-Bern[stein] is here and looks very well. From Russia also Belkovsky, Bruck, Ussishkin, Sokolow and some others less interesting. General mood = zero, but a good thing it isn't below zero.

I kiss you Verik, and thanks for the postcard. Best wishes to Nyusechka and Zina. Every single nerve of mine craves for you.

I kiss and embrace Verusik.

Chaimchik

[After his return to Switzerland at the beginning of November 1902, W. opened at Geneva a Jewish University Bureau (*Bureau Jüdische Hochschule*) for the handling of the preparatory work (including the raising of funds) for the launching of the project. In the direction of the Bureau W. was assisted by Samuel Levinson, replaced in the spring of 1903 by Saul Stupnitzky. Feiwel in Zurich, Buber in Vienna, and Trietsch in Berlin were in close contact with the Bureau, and so was Glikin, first in Berlin and from Jan. 1903 in Zurich. Much of the extensive correspondence conducted by the Geneva Bureau has been preserved.]

★ ★ ★ ★ ★ ★ ★ ★

undone to facilitate the establishment of the Jewish University [*Hochschule*], but only in Palestine.' The voting in favour of this resolution which, it will be noticed, made no mention of W., Buber, or the Geneva Bureau, was 7 to 5. The figures are not recorded in the minutes but are given by W. in a letter of 5 Nov. 1902 to Samuel Shriro—text in vol ii of this series. (Both resolutions, as here set out, are translated from the orig. German.)

BIOGRAPHICAL INDEX

ABBREVIATIONS

D.F. = Democratic Fraction
G.A.C. = Greater Actions Committee
H.Z. = Hoverei Zion (Lovers of Zion)
I.C.A. = Jewish Colonization Association
J.C.T. = Jewish Colonial Trust
J.N.F. = Jewish National Fund
K.H. = Keren Hayesod (Palestine Foundation Fund)
Minsk Conference = Conference of Russian Zionists, Minsk, 1902
S.A.C. = Smaller Actions Committee
W. = Chaim Weizmann
Z.C. = Zionist Congress (I Z.C. = First Zionist Congress)
Z.E. = Zionist Executive
Z.O. = Zionist Organization
Z.Y.C. = Zionist Youth Conference, Basle, 1901

ABERSON, ZVI (1875?–1951). B. Dubrovna, Byelorussia. M. 1905 Rosa Grinblatt (q.v.). Having started in Russia as a Bundist, attracted to Zionism while studying in Paris and became an active Zionist after moving in 1901 to Geneva, where he joined the Zionist group *Hashahar*. Became widely known by devastating attack on Bund at Z.Y.C., 1901. Among founders of D.F., member of its Programme Committee, and member of D.F. group of delegates at V and VI Z.C. (1901, 1903). Delegate to VII Z.C. (1905). After establishment of League of Nations, resident representative at Geneva of Committee of Jewish Delegations, and subsequently (1922–5) of Z.O.

ABRAMOVICH, GREGORY (1880?–1933)—also known as Zvi Abrahami, Zvi Farbman, Michael Farbman. Journalist and author. Orig. Odessa. Studied Munich and Zurich. Helped to organize Z.Y.C., 1901. In 1902 or 1903 joined Syrkin's Zionist-Socialist group, *Cheirus*. On the 'Uganda' issue seceded (1905) from Z.O. and joined the Territorialists, identifying himself with the Zionist-Socialist Workers' Party ('Z.S.') and becoming a leading exponent of its ideas. Wrote for the press on economic questions and Jewish emigration. Later went into publishing in Russia, but in 1915 abandoned this and settled in England, where by his writings he established himself as a recognized expert on U.S.S.R. affairs.

AHAD HA'AM—Hebr. pseudonym, meaning 'One of the people', of Asher Zvi Ginzberg (1856–1927). By the Hebrew writings in which he developed his conception of Spiritual Zionism established himself as a leading figure among the Jewish thinkers and men of letters of his day. B. Skvira, Ukraine. Settled 1886 in Odessa and became member of Odessa Committee of *Hovevei Zion*. Founded *Bnei Moshe* 1889. Began literary career with essay in Hebrew journal *Hamelitz*, 1888. Visited Palestine in 1891 and again in 1893. First volume of collected essays published under title *Al Parashath Derachim* ('At the Crossroads'), 1895. Founded 1896, and edited until 1902, Hebrew journal

Hashiloah. Attended I Z.C., 1897, but did not join Z.O., being out of sympathy with Herzl's Political Zionism. Gave principal address at Minsk Conference, 1902, and served on Cultural Commission set up by the Conference. Settled in London, 1908, as representative of Russian-Jewish firm of tea-merchants (Wissotzky's). Fourth (and last) volume of his collected essays published 1913. Appointed member of Curatorium of Haifa Technical Institute and actively involved, on the Zionist side, in the controversies of 1913–14 concerning its educational policy. One of W.'s intimate advisers in the discussions leading to the Balfour Declaration, 1914–17. Settled in Palestine, 1922, and lived in Tel Aviv until his death in 1927. Among his writings available in English translations are *Selected Essays*, Jewish Publication Society of America, 1912; *Ten Essays on Zionism and Judaism*, Routledge, 1922; *Ahad Ha'am: Essays, Letters, Memoirs*, East and West Library, 1946.

BEHAM (also known as BOEHM), ARIEH LEIB (1877–1941). Physician. B. Kovno Province. As Kharkov student, founder of *Bnei Zion* Society and member of Kharkov *Kadimah* Society. Delegate to IV Z.C., 1900, and to Minsk Conference, 1902. Supporter of D.F. After settling in Palestine in 1913, took active part in Jewish affairs in the fields of public health and education.

BELKOVSKY, GREGORY (MOSES ZVI) (1865–1948). Lawyer. B. Odessa. An active Zionist from his student days. Professor of Roman Law at University of Sofia, 1893–7. After returning to Russia, served as Zionist regional leader for St. Petersburg area. Elected to G.A.C. at III, VI, and VIII Z.C., 1899, 1903, 1907. Member of delegation sent to Herzl by Kharkov Conference of Russian Zionists, 1904, to protest against the 'Uganda' project. Chairman, 1918–19, of Central Council of Russian Jewish Communities, and Chairman, 1922–4, of clandestine Russian Zionist Centre. Expelled from Soviet Union, 1924, and settled in Palestine, where actively associated with Union of General Zionists.

BENDERSKY, SOLOMON (1866–1908). Physician. B. Kishinev. Early adherent of *Hovevei Zion*. From 1899 to 1903 member of G.A.C. and Zionist regional leader for Bessarabia-Volhynia area.

BERGER, ISAAC (1875–1945). B. Minsk. Among founders of Minsk *Poale Zion*. Elected head of central organization of *Poale Zion* societies of the Minsk type at their Minsk Conference in 1901. Attended Z.Y.C., 1901, and joined D.F. *Poale Zion* delegate to V and VI Z.C., 1901 and 1903. One of organizers of Minsk Conference, 1902. When, on 'Uganda' issue, the Minsk *Poale Zion* sided with the Territorialists, Berger left them and identified himself with the General Zionists. Active in fund-raising efforts of K.H. in Poland and Bessarabia, 1921–34. Settled in Palestine, 1935.

BERGER, JUDA LEIB (1867–1917). B. Minsk. Elder brother of Isaac Berger (q.v.). Attended Odessa *Hovevei Zion* Conference, 1890. Member of *Bnei Moshe*. Leading Zionist worker in Pinsk in 1890s and among founders of Pinsk 'reformed' (i.e. modernized) *heder*. Delegate to I Z.C., 1897. Itinerant propagandist for J.C.T. and J.N.F. Later, prominent in Zionist activities, Vilna and Moscow. Settled in Palestine, 1912.

BERNARD-LAZARE—*see* LAZARE, BERNARD.

BERNSTEIN, Leon (Leib) (1877–1962). Journalist. B. Vilna. Actively associated, in the 1890s, with Jewish labour movement in Kovno and Vilna. Later, member of Bund Central Committee. Manager, 1900–1, of Russian Social-Democratic Union press in Geneva, where in 1901 he organized a Bundist group.

BERNSTEIN-KOHAN, Jacob (1859–1929). Physician. B. Kishinev. Founded Jewish nationalist students society, Dorpat University, 1884. At I Z.C., 1897, elected to G.A.C., on which he continued to serve until 1905. Director, 1897–1901, of Zionist Correspondence Centre at Kishinev. Prominently associated with Z.Y.C., 1901. Among founders of D.F. and member of its Programme Committee. At Minsk Conference, 1902, elected to serve on Cultural Commission set up by the Conference. On the 'Uganda' issue (1903–5) one of the leading *Zione Zion* (anti-Ugandists). Member of S.A.C., 1905–7, and of G.A.C., 1907–11. Went to Palestine in 1907 but in 1910 returned to Russia, where he resumed his Zionist activities. After a second unsuccessful attempt, in 1925, to settle in Palestine, again returned to Russia, where he devoted himself to medical work in the Jewish colonies in the Crimea.

BICKERMAN, Joseph (1867–1945). Journalist. B. Podolia, Russia. Active anti-Zionist from student days in Odessa in late 1890s. His critical analysis of Zionism in the monthly *Russkoye Bogatstvo* (July 1902) attracted much attention in Russia and abroad. From 1905 lived in St. Petersburg, where he wrote for the Russian liberal press. After 1917 Revolution, associated with Russian monarchist *émigré* circles in France.

BIRNBAUM, Nathan (1864–1937). Writer. B. Vienna. One of the founders of Vienna Jewish Zionist students society, *Kadimah*, 1882. Edited Jewish nationalist journal, *Selbstemancipation*, 1885–6, 1890–3, and the Berlin Jewish German-language monthly *Zion*, 1896–7. Took part in I Z.C., 1897, and served for a time as secretary of Z.C., but later discarded Zionism in favour of the view that what was needed for Jewish national regeneration was cultural autonomy for a Yiddish-speaking Jewry in the diaspora. About 1918 turned from this to religion, becoming an active adherent of the ultra-Orthodox Jewish organization, *Agudath Israel*.

BLANK, Reuben (1866–c. 1954). Writer. B. Kishinev. Studied at Zurich, Paris, and Berlin. Secretary, 1902, of Berlin non-partisan committee for helping Russian Jews studying at German Universities. After settling in St. Petersburg in 1905, published writings on Jewish subjects and was also a frequent contributor to the Russian general press. During part of First World War was Petrograd correspondent of the Anglo-Jewish Association. Spent part of the war years in England. Later moved to Berlin, and finally to New York.

BODENHEIMER, Max Isidore (1865–1940). Lawyer. Among founders of German Zionist Federation and Chairman of its Central Committee, 1897–1910. Member G.A.C., 1897–1921, and President of J.N.F., 1907–14. During First World War, member of *Komitee für den Osten*, designed to serve as intermediary between Jews and German authorities in occupied parts of Eastern Europe. After the War, identified with Zionist-Revisionist movement until its secession from the Z.O. in 1935. Settled in Palestine, 1935.

BORUKHOV, AARON (1869–1946). Teacher and writer. B. Vilna. Entered Berne University, 1899. Took part in Munich preparatory conference (Apr. 1901) for Z.Y.C. Member of D.F. group of delegates at V Z.C., 1901. Delegate to VI Z.C., 1903. Appointed secretary of *Hovevei Zion* Odessa Committee, 1906, and later, of Russian Zionist Centre, Vilna. Settled in Palestine, 1912.

BRANDT, BORIS (BARUKH) (1860–1907) (pseudonyms, Arendt, Arndt, Yevrei). Economist and writer (Russian, Hebrew and Yiddish). B. Ukraine. Early adherent of *Hovevei Zion* and, as graduate student in Berlin in early 1890s, member of Russian Jewish Academic Society. Took part, under assumed name, in I Z.C., 1897. Wrote on Jewish matters for Russian general press. From 1897 an official of the Russian Ministry of Finance.

BROMBERG, FYODOR (FEIVEL) (1862–1941). Teacher and journalist. B. Odessa. M. sister of Catherine Dorfman (q.v.). From 1897 prominent among active Zionists in Kherson. Delegate to Minsk Conference, 1902. Joined Zionist Socialist party ('Z.S.'), 1921.

BRUCK, GREGORY (ZVI) (1869–1922). Physician. B. Chernigov, Ukraine. Early adherent of *Hovevei Zion*. Member of G.A.C., 1899–1905, and during that period Zionist regional leader for Homel area. Appointed Crown Rabbi, Vitebsk, 1901. At Minsk Conference, 1902, delivered opening address, coming out strongly against D.F. Member of first Russian Duma, 1906. Disapproved of Zionists figuring as separate party at Duma elections and on that issue seceded from Z.O., but later rejoined it and was delegate to X and XII Z.C., 1911 and 1921. Went to Palestine in 1920, but returned to Europe in 1921 and died in Berlin.

BUBER, MARTIN (MORDECAI ZEEV) (1878–1965). B. Vienna but spent early years in Lemberg. Studied at Leipzig, Berlin, and Zurich and finally graduated at Vienna (Ph.D., 1904). Joined Z.O. 1898 and took part in III Z.C., 1899. Appointed editor *Die Welt*, 1901. A leading member of the group of D.F. delegates at V and VI Z.C., 1901 and 1903. A founder, and member of the first board of directors of the *Jüdischer Verlag* (estab. 1902). Active supporter of Jewish University project in its early stages (1902–3) and again on its revival in 1913. On 'Uganda' issue (1904–5) anti-Ugandist. Founder and editor of the Berlin monthly *Der Jude*, 1916–24. After collapse of D.F. in 1904 withdrew from Zionist politics, but eventually gravitated towards the socialist *Hapoel Hazair* and at XII Z.C., 1921, moved on their behalf, a conciliatory resolution, which the Congress adopted, on the Zionist attitude towards the Arab people. Later, actively associated with the efforts of *Ihud* and like-minded groups to promote Jewish-Arab understanding. The publication in 1922 of *Ich und Du*, the most widely-known of his prolific output of works on the borderland between theology and philosophy, was followed by his appointment, in 1924, as lecturer in the history of the Jewish religion at the University of Frankfurt, which in 1930 made him an honorary professor. This appointment terminated with Hitler's rise to power in 1933, and, after serving for a time as Principal of the College of Jewish Studies in Frankfurt, he settled in Palestine in 1938. Professor of Sociology and Philosophy at the Hebrew University from 1938 until his retirement, in 1957, with the title of professor emeritus.

411

BUKHMIL, Joshua Heshel (1869–1938). B. Ostrog, Volhynia. Active member of Zionist Students Society at Montpellier University. Sent by Herzl, 1897, on mission to Russia to work for *Hovevei Zion* participation in I Z.C. Addressed Z.Y.C., 1901. Member of D.F. and of its Programme Committee. A leading supporter of Syrkin's *Cheirus* movement so long as main object was to extract funds for Zionist purposes from I.C.A., but took no part in its later Zionist-Socialist activities. On 'Uganda' issue (1903–5) sided with anti-Ugandists. Later, engaged in Zionist propaganda in Russia and in fund-raising for K.H. Settled in Palestine, 1923.

DAVIDSON, Eliahu (1870?–1923). B. Mohilev. As Berlin student in 1890s, a leading member of the Russian-Jewish Academic Society, member of *Bnei Moshe*, and interested in movement, promoted by 'Jargon Committees', for dissemination of Yiddish literature. Delegate to I Z.C., 1897. After II Z.C., 1898, left Zionist Movement, identified himself with the Bund, and engaged in anti-Zionist propaganda among Jewish student colonies in Germany and Switzerland. In 1901 severed connexion with the Bund and thereafter conducted anti-Bundist campaign within the Social-Democratic movement. Returned to Russia after Oct. 1917 Revolution and became a University professor at Kiev.

DEICHLER, Christian (?–?). German chemist. Came into contact with W. in Berlin in later 1890s. His associate in early chemical researches and in all patents taken out in the period 1900–3. Later, practised as patent lawyer in Berlin.

DORFMAN, Catherine (Gittel) (1881–1935). Physician. Orig. Kherson. Entered Geneva University 1900. Joined Geneva Zionist students group, took active part in preparations for Z.Y.C., 1901, which she attended, and assisted W. in D.F.'s Geneva Information Bureau. Member of Geneva Zionist Students Society, *Hashahar*, 1902–3. From 1906 practised medicine in Russia, where she later joined the Zionist-Socialist party ('Z.S.'). Settled in Palestine, 1925 and did medical work in the *Emek* (Valley of Jezreel) settlements and in Jerusalem.

DUBOSARSKY, Joseph (1880–1944). Physician. B. Kerch, Crimea. As Berlin student, joined Zionist students society, *Kadimah*. Member of Berlin group of D.F. After returning to Russia, seceded from Z.C. on 'Uganda' issue and became a Territorialist. Moved, 1924, to Paris, where actively associated with Jewish Refugee Aid Committee. Died at Auschwitz.

ELIASBERG, Aaron (1879–1937). B. Pinsk. Studied Leipzig and Heidelberg. Member of D.F. Delegate to V Z.C., 1901. Helped in preparatory work for Jewish University project (1902). Director *Jüdischer Verlag*, 1911–20. Settled in Palestine, 1933 and joined staff of K.H.

ELIASHEV, Isidore (Israel) (1873–1924). Physician and writer. Pioneer in field of Yiddish literary criticism. B. Kovno. Studied Berlin and Heidelberg. Member of Berlin Russian-Jewish Academic Society. Interested in 'Jargon Committees' movement for dissemination of Yiddish literature. Took part in I Z.C., 1897. Moved to Warsaw, 1901. Addressed Z.Y.C., 1901, and in same year member of D.F. group of delegates at V Z.C. Joined Syrkin's *Cheirus* movement, 1902. In later life resided in Petrograd, Berlin, and Kovno.

412

ESTERMAN, Leo (Yehuda Leib) (1869–1940). B. Telsiai Province, Lithuania. Studied Berlin and Heidelberg, 1890–5. Active member of Russian-Jewish Academic Society (Berlin), of Jewish nationalist society 'Young Israel' (Berlin) and of *Bnei Moshe*, and, later, founder-member of Berlin Zionist students society *Kadimah*, 1898. Manager of pharmaceutical business, Hamburg, 1898–1920. One of the founders of the German Zionist Federation. Settled in Palestine, 1920. Manager, General Mortgage Bank, 1922–35.

FARBSTEIN, David Zvi (1868–1953). Lawyer. B. Warsaw. Early adherent of *Hovevei Zion*. In early 1890s member of Berlin Russian-Jewish Academic Society. From 1894 lived in Switzerland. Joined Social-Democratic party, 1897, and served as a representative of the party on various Swiss public bodies, including the Federal Council. Took part in I Z.C., 1897, and was one of founders of Swiss Zionist Federation. Though a Social-Democrat, opposed to separate organization of Zionist-Socialists. Founder-member of Jewish Statistical Society, 1902. Favoured Jewish University project. At VI Z.C., 1903, sided with the 'Ugandists'. After Herzl's death (1904) withdrew for a time from active part in Zionist affairs, but later became president of the Swiss branch of K.H. Prominently associated with the organization of the Jewish communities in Switzerland.

FEIWEL, Berthold (1875–1937). B. Pohorlits, Moravia. M. 1906 Esther Shneerson (q.v.). Delegate from Brno to I Z.C., 1897. Editor, *Die Welt*, 1900–1. Elected to G.A.C. at IV Z.C., 1900. Among founders of D.F. group of delegates at V and VI Z.C., 1901 and 1903. One of the founders, and from 1902–7, a director of the *Jüdischer Verlag*. Principal author of brochure (*Eine Jüdische Hochschule*) arguing the case for a Jewish University (1902), and W.'s most intimate collaborator in activities connected with the project. Joined Z.O. secretariat at Cologne, 1906. In banking business in Strasbourg, 1909–12. In 1919–20 served on G.A.C. and as member of Z.O. Administrative Committee and, later, of Z.E., at Zionist headquarters in London. Member of Zionist Financial and Economic Council, with voting rights in Z.E., 1921–7. Managing Director of K.H. from its establishment in 1920, and a Director (1929–31, Managing-Director) of J.C.T., 1920–33. From 1929 member of Administrative Committee of Jewish Agency for Palestine. Settled in Palestine, 1933.

GASTER, Moses (1856–1939). B. Bucharest. Graduated Bucharest University, 1874. Rabbinical diploma, Breslau Jewish Theological Seminary, 1881. Lecturer in Rumanian history and literature, Bucharest University, 1881–5. Early adherent of *Hovevei Zion* and helped to establish two of the first Jewish settlements in Palestine—Zikhron Ya'akov and Rosh Pinah. Because of prominent participation in protests against Jewish disabilities, expelled from Rumania, in 1885, and settled in England. Haham (Chief Rabbi) of Sephardic Jewish congregations in England, 1887–1918. One time President, English Folklore Society and Vice-President, Royal Asiatic Society. Presided over first public meeting addressed by Herzl, London, 1898. A Vice-President of I, II, IV, and VII Z.C., 1897, 1898, 1900, 1905. On 'Uganda' issue, 1904–5, an anti-Ugandist. President of English Zionist Federation, 1907–9. Prominent in early stages of discussions leading to Balfour Declaration but subsequently at variance with the Zionist leadership and withdrew from Zionist activity.

GETZOVA, Sophia (or Sonia) (1874–1946). Physician. B. Svisloch, near Minsk. W.'s first fiancée—engagement broken off, 1901. An active Zionist in student days at Berne. Delegate to II Z.C., 1898, and member of D.F. group of delegates at V Z.C., 1901. After completing her studies, engaged in research in Berne, Basle, and Paris. Settled in Palestine, 1925. Appointed, 1927, Professor of Pathological Anatomy at Hebrew University.

GINZBERG, Asher—*see* s.n. AHAD HA'AM.

GINZBURG, Simon (1871–1950). Chemical engineer. B. Shuya, Russia. Connected with Baku oil industry. Delegate to Minsk Conference, 1902. Supported Jewish University project. Member (and, in 1917, Chairman) of Baku Zionist Committee. Left Russia, 1920, and, after living in England, France, Germany and Egypt, settled in 1932 in Palestine, where engaged in bibliographical work at Weizmann Institute, Rehovoth.

GLIKIN, Moshe. B. Moscow, 1874. A *Hovev Zion* from his youth. Agricultural labourer in Palestine, 1892–4. Entered Leipzig University, 1899. Secretary of Leipzig *Ziona* society. Took part in Munich preparatory conference for Z.Y.C. and in Z.Y.C., 1901. Joined D.F. Delegate to V and VI Z.C., 1901 and 1903. Took charge, 1902, of D.F. Berlin Information Office. After working for a time in Berlin for Jewish University project, accepted, early 1903, appointment to J.U. Bureau at Zurich. After return to Russia in 1903, employed in management of St. Petersburg Yiddish daily, *Der Fraind* and, subsequently, of the Russian-language Jewish weekly, *Raszviet*. Settled in Palestine, 1908 and for some twenty-five years managed the Migdal agricultural settlement. A member of the Jewish Elected Assembly (*Asefat Hanivcharim*) set up in 1920. One of the founders of the Hadar Hacarmel quarter of Haifa.

GOURLAND, Aaron (1881–?). Writer. B. Vilna. As Heidelberg student, helped to organize, and took part in, Z.Y.C., 1901. Joined D.F. Visited Palestine, 1902. Engaged in literary work in St. Petersburg, 1909–15. From 1915–17 in England and U.S.A. Joined one of the Jewish Battalions of the British Army and went with it to Palestine in 1918. Left Palestine 1920, after which nothing known of him except that he lived for a time in Vilna and Berlin.

GRINBLATT, (later ABERSON), Rosa (1877 ?–1943). Orig. Vitebsk. M. 1905 Zvi Aberson (q.v.). Delegate to founding conference of Bund, 1897. Later, became a Zionist while a student at Berne and Geneva. General Secretary of Geneva League of Jewish Women, 1921–42.

GUREVICH, Boris (Chaim Dov) (1865–1927). Journalist. B. Gorki, Byelorussia. Studied in Berlin, where interested in 'Jargon Committees' movement for dissemination of Yiddish literature and was member of Zionist students society, *Kadimah*. Actively concerned in preparations for and took part in, Z.Y.C., 1901. Joined D.F. At Minsk Conference, 1902, made his mark by address on place of economic questions in Zionist programme. From 1903 to 1911 a leading contributor to St. Petersburg Yiddish daily, *Der Fraind*. Later, became editor (1919) of a Zionist periodical in Minsk. Under Soviet régime, worked in State economic institutions and wrote for the Russian press.

HERZL, THEODOR (BENJAMIN ZEEV) (1860–1904). Journalist and playwright. Founder of political Zionism. B. Budapest, but lived mainly in Vienna. Publ. 1896, his brochure *Der Judenstaat*. The First Zionist Congress (1897), over which he presided, resulted in the formation, under his leadership, of the Zionist Organization, which he headed until his death in 1904, commanding throughout that period an unchallengeable ascendancy as the dominant figure in the Movement. Full-scale biography by Alex Bein: English translation, Philadelphia, Jewish Publication Society of America, 1945.

HICKEL, MAX (1873–1924). Publisher. B. Moravia, where he was one of the earliest adherents of the Z.O. Founded in Brno, 1900, a German-language Zionist fornightly, *Die Jüdische Volkstimme*.

IDELSON, ABRAHAM (1865–1921). B. Kovno. As Moscow student, joined *Bnei Zion* society. Member of *Bnei Moshe*. After I Z.C., 1897, founded Zionist students society, *Kadimah*, in Moscow. Took part in Z.Y.C., 1901. Member of D.F. and of its Russian Central Committee. Elected to Cultural Commission set up by Minsk Conference, 1902. Editor of Russian-Jewish periodicals *Yevreiskaya Zhizn* and *Raszviet*. Took part in formulation (Dec. 1905) of the 'Helsingfors Programme', committing Zionists to campaign for national autonomy for Russian Jewry. Elected to G.A.C. at XI Z.C., 1913. After Russian Revolution of March 1917, took a leading part in Zionist activities in Russia. After First World War, worked in Paris with the Committee of Jewish Delegations. In 1920 co-opted to Z.E. and came to London to edit its Hebrew weekly organ, *Ha'olam*.

JACOBSON, VICTOR (AVIGDOR) (1869–1934). B. Simferopol, Crimea. As Berlin student, member from 1891, and in 1894 secretary, of Russian-Jewish Academic Society. Returned 1895 to Simferopol, which he represented at II Z.C., 1898. Member of G.A.C., 1899–1900 and 1901–7. Zionist regional leader for Simferopol area, and from end of 1901 director of the Russian Zionist Information Centre at Simferopol. Member of Council (*Aufsichtsrat*) of J.C.T., 1902. Manager from 1906 of Beirut branch of Anglo-Palestine Company. From 1908 to 1915 in Constantinople as Manager of another J.C.T. subsidiary, the Anglo-Levantine Banking Co., and, in effect, as political representative of the Z.O. Member of S.A.C., 1911 to end of First World War. From early 1916 directed Zionist Bureau at Copenhagen. Appointed by Z.O., 1925, as its political representative at League of Nations headquarters in Geneva.

JAFFE, LEIB (1875–1948). B. Grodno. *Hovev Zion* from his youth. Studied Heidelberg, Leipzig, Freiburg. Attended I Z.C., 1897, and Z.Y.C., 1901. Member of D.F. group of delegates at V and VI Z.C., 1901 and 1903, and member of D.F. Programme Committee, 1902. Elected 1906 member of Russian Zionist Centre. Elected to G.A.C. at VIII Z.C., 1907. Settled in Palestine, 1919, and associated with the Zionist Commission. Later, Chairman of Board of Directors of K.H. Killed by Arab bomb in Jerusalem, 1948.

KASTELIANSKY, ABRAHAM (1877–1934). Economist. B. Slonim, Byelorussia. Studied at Heidelberg and, later, in Berlin, where, in 1902, he joined the Zionist students society, *Kadimah*. Secretary of Central Committee of Berlin Jewish Statistical Society, 1902. On 'Uganda' issue seceded, about

1905, from Z.O., and joined the Zionist Socialist Workers Party (Territorialists). Immediately before First World War moved to England, where employed in Government service during the War as an inspector of supplies. In 1926 took part in Conference on economic and financial problems concerning Zionist work in Palestine. Later, settled in Palestine, where engaged in citrus export trade.

KHATZMAN (later WEIZMANN), VERA (1881–1966). B. Rostov-on-Don. M. 1906, Chaim Weizmann. Sixth of the seven children of Isaiah Khatzman and his wife Theodosia (née Fluxman). Medical student, 1900–6, at Geneva, where met W. and under his influence joined Zionist students society, *Hashahar*. After marriage to W. in 1906, lived with him in Manchester, where from 1913 to early in 1916 she served as a Medical Officer under the Manchester Corporation. Actively interested in social welfare work in England and, later, in Palestine. One of the founders of the Women's International Zionist Organization (1918) and of Magen David Adom (1930), and from the early days of the Youth Aliyah Movement (established 1934) prominently associated with its activities. From 1943 a member of the Board of Governors of the Weizmann Institute of Science.

KHISSIN, CHAIM (1865–1932). Physician. B. Mir, Byelorussia. Went to Palestine with group of Russian Jewish students (*Bilu*) in 1882, but returned to Russia in 1888. In late 1890s became medical student at Berne, where served as Chairman of the Zionist Academic Society. Took part in Munich preparatory conference for Z.Y.C. (Apr. 1901) and in Z.Y.C. (Dec. 1901). Member of D.F. group of delegates at V and VI Z.C., 1901 and 1903. Visited Palestine in 1902 and settled there in 1905. Representative in Palestine of Odessa Committee of *Hovevei Zion*. A leading figure in colonization activities of Z.O. and one of the founders of Tel Aviv.

KLAUSNER, JOSEPH GEDALIAHU (1874–1958). B. Olkiniki, Lithuania. While studying at Heidelberg, where he was an active member of Zionist students groups, came to I Z.C., 1897. A disciple of Ahad Ha'am (q.v.), he strongly advocated the recognition of 'cultural work' as an indispensable part of the Zionist programme. Began contributing to the Hebrew press in 1893 and in 1903 succeeded Ahad Ha'am as editor of *Hashiloah*. Took part in Z.Y.C., 1901. Member of D.F. group of delegates at V Z.C., 1901 and served on D.F. Programme Committee. Elected member of Cultural Commission set up by Minsk Conference, 1902. On 'Uganda' issue (1904–5) sided with anti-Ugandists. From 1906 worked actively for Zionism and the Hebrew language movement in Odessa. Settled in Palestine, 1919. Appointed in 1925 Professor of Hebrew Literature at the Hebrew University and in 1944 Professor of the History of the Second Temple period.

KLEINMAN, MOSES (1871–1948). B. Ukraine. Delegate to II Z.C., 1898 and to all succeeding Congresses up to and including the Twelfth (1921). Delegate to Minsk Conference, 1902. Member of Odessa Committee of *Hovevei Zion*, 1906–16. Editor of Jewish periodicals in Lvov and Odessa, 1908–16, and of Moscow Jewish daily *Ha'am*, 1917–18. Moved to London in 1923 and, after living there until 1935, settled in Palestine. Editor for many years of *Ha'olam*, the Hebrew weekly organ of the Z.E.

KOHAN-BERNSTEIN, Jacob—*see* BERNSTEIN-KOHAN.

KRINKIN, Boris (Meir) (1867–1931). Physician. B. Druya, Lithuania. Became a Zionist while a student at Kazan University threw himself into Zionist propaganda in the Volga region, and continued his Zionist activities while engaged in post-graduate studies in Vienna, Zurich, and Berlin. Settled in Palestine, 1911. Vice-President of Palestine Jewish Medical Association and founder of Oculists Association.

KUNIN, Lazare (1875–?). B. Krucha, Byelorussia. Joined Russian-Jewish Academic Society while a student in Berlin. Attended I Z.C., 1897. Member of Berlin group of D.F.

LANDAU, Leopold (1848–1920). Gynaecologist. B. Warsaw. *Privat-Docent*, 1893–1902, and from 1902, Extraordinary Professor at Berlin University. Joined the Berlin *Hovevei Zion* society *Ezra*, 1896. Served on Berlin Committee for Jewish University, 1903, and supported University project on its revival in 1913.

LAZARE, Bernard (sometimes known as Bernard-Lazare) (1865–1903). B. Nîmes (France). Publ. book of poems, 1892, and works on anti-semitism (1894) and on Jewish nationalism (1898). Immediately after first Dreyfus trial (1894) threw himself into campaign for rehabilitation of Dreyfus. On establishment of Z.O. in 1897 immediately joined it and was elected member of G.A.C., but because of differences of opinion on questions of policy withdrew in 1899. Declined invitation to address Z.Y.C., 1901, but helped in activities of *Jüdischer Verlag* after its establishment in 1902. Visited Rumania in 1902 to investigate the position of the Jews.

LEVINSON, Samuel (?–?). Chemist. Orig. Romny, Ukraine. At end of 1890s student in Berlin and leading member of *Bildung* Society for dissemination of Yiddish literature. Lived in Geneva from c. 1900 to 1903. Secretary, Jewish University Bureau, Geneva, 1902–3. Settled in U.S.A., 1903.

LICHTENSTEIN, Abraham (1869–1926). Teacher. B. Courland. M. W.'s sister, Haya Weizmann (q.v.). Secretary and later Chairman of Berne Academic Zionist Society. Teacher and bookseller in Pinsk, and later, teacher in Warsaw. Appointed, 1909, teacher of German and Vice-Principal, Pavel Cohen Secondary School, Vilna. Settled in Palestine, 1921. Employed as bookkeeper in a building firm and later in General Mortgage Bank.

LILIEN, Ephraim Moses (1874–1925). Artist and lithographer. B. Orohbycz, Galicia. Settled in Berlin but lived at intervals in Palestine, 1906–14, and for some time connected with Bezalel School of Art, Jerusalem. Member of D.F. group of delegates at V Z.C., 1901, and delegate to VI Z.C., 1902. One of the founders of the Berlin *Jüdischer Verlag*, 1902.

LOEWE, Heinrich (Elyakim) (1869–1951). Librarian. B. Gross-Wanzleben, near Magdeburg, Germany. One of the earliest Zionists in Germany. The only German Jew belonging to the Berlin Russian-Jewish Academic Society. Founded the Berlin Jewish nationalist society, 'Young Israel', 1892. Editor of Jewish nationalist monthly *Zion*, 1895–6. Visited Palestine three times between 1895 and 1898. Attended I Z.C., 1897. Editor German Zionist

Federation organ, *Jüdische Rundschau*. Elected at XI Z.C., 1913, member of Preparatory Committee for establishment of Hebrew University. Co-operated in the building up of the Jewish National Library in Jerusalem. Settled in Palestine, 1933, becoming Director of the Tel Aviv Municipal Library.

LUBZHINSKY, CHAIM (1864–1919). B. near Lomza, Poland. M. 1888 W.'s sister Miriam (q.v.). From 1886 associated with W.'s father, Ozer Weizmann (q.v.) in his business as a timber-transporter. Moved, *c.* 1896, to Warsaw, where engaged in timber-trade on his own account and built up prosperous business, in which his father-in-law had an interest. Helped members of W. family in their education. Left Warsaw at outbreak of First World War and went to Russia. Died in Petrograd.

LURIE, GREGORY (1861–1917). A member of the well-to-do Pinsk family of that name mentioned in head-note to letter No. 3 (4 Sept., 1890). Studied at Karlsruhe Polytechnic. After living for several years in Paris, returned to Pinsk. A *Hovev Zion* from his youth and later active in Zionist work in Russia. Delegate to first five Zionist Congresses, 1897–1901. Member of first Board of Directors of J.C.T. At V Z.C., 1901, supported demand for greater emphasis on cultural work.

LURIE, JOSEPH (1871–1937). Educationalist and journalist. B. Pompyani, Lithuania. As Berlin student a leading member of Russian-Jewish Academic Society. Member of *Bnei Moshe*. Headmaster from 1896 of 'reformed' (i.e. modernized) *Heder*. Delegate to I, III, IV and VIII Z.C., 1897, 1899, 1900, 1907. Editor Warsaw Yiddish journal *Der Yud*, 1899–1902. Active supporter in Warsaw of D.F. and of Jewish University project, 1901–3. Joined editorial board of St. Petersburg Yiddish journal *Der Fraind*, 1903. Member Vilna Russian-Zionist Centre, 1906–7 and Editor of Yiddish Zionist weekly *Dos Yiddishe Volk*. Settled in Palestine, 1907 and became Chairman of Teachers Organization (*Merkaz Hamorim*). During mandatory period served at various times as Director of Z.E. Education Department, Inspector of Jewish secondary schools, and Director of Education Department of National Council of Jews in Palestine (*Va'ad Leumi*).

LURIE, OVSEY (HOSEA) (1875–1941). B. Pinsk. As to his family, and W.'s association with them, see head-note to letter No. 3 (4 Sept. 1890). Educated at Mitava (Mitau) and Riga. Worked until 1914 in his father's business. In 1920 settled in London, becoming associated in business with his brother Saul (q.v.).

LURIE, SAUL. B. Pinsk 1879. Younger brother of Ovsey L., (q.v.). Coached by W. while pupil, with him, at Pinsk Secondary School from *c.* 1888. Student at Darmstadt Polytechnic, 1897. Attended I Z.C., 1897. In 1901 went to Geneva and worked in W.'s laboratory. Returned to Darmstadt, where among founders of Zionist students' society, *Maccabea*. Engaged in business in London, 1905–39. Later settled in U.S.A.

MAKHLIN, DAVID (?–?). Orig. Ukraine. As Berlin student in mid-1890s actively interested in *Bildung* Society for dissemination of Yiddish literature. In 1900 joined the Bund, for which he worked in Berlin, from 1904 in Berne, and from 1906 in Russia.

MANDELSTAMM, MAX (EMANUEL) (1838–1912). Ophthalmologist. B. Zhagory, Lithuania. An early *Hovev Zion*. Attended I Z.C., 1897, at which elected as one of the four Russian representatives on G.A.C. Director of Russian Zionist Finance Office, regional leader for the Kiev area, and member of Board of Directors of J.C.T. Supported Jewish University project, 1902–3. A fervent 'Ugandist', he seceded from Z.O. after split on that issue in 1905 and became one of the leaders of the Jewish Territorial Organization (I.T.O.).

MOTZKIN, LEO (1867–1933). B. Brovari, near Kiev, Ukraine. Lived in Germany from age of 15. As Berlin student principal founder of Russian-Jewish Academic Society, 1889. Attended I Z.C., 1897. Founder and first Chairman of Berlin Zionist students' society, *Kadimah*, 1898. One of the leaders of the 'Young Zionist' critics of Herzl at III, IV, and V Z.C., 1899, 1900, 1901. One of the founders of D.F. and principal draftsman of its pro-gramme, 1902. Attended Minsk Conference, 1902. Publ. study of Russian pogroms, 1910. Among principal promoters of Hebrew Language and Culture Conferences, Berlin, 1909 and Vienna, 1913. Director of Zionist Organization Copenhagen Bureau, 1915. After end of First World War became Secretary-General of Committee of Jewish Delegations at Peace Conference (1919) and took a leading part in organizing the campaign for minority rights for the Polish and other East European Jews and for national minorities generally. Member Z.E. 1921–3. Chairman G.A.C. 1925–33. Presided at XVII and XVIII Z.C., 1931, 1933.

NEMIROVSKY, ALEXANDER (?–? 1921). Lawyer. Chairman Kharkov Zionist Committee, 1898–1904. Joined Kharkov Committee for Jewish University, 1902. Appeared for the defence at trials of a number of Zionists charged with political offences on eve of and during First World War.

NEMSER, ALEXANDER (?–? 1906). Engineer. Member of earliest Zionist students' group at Kharkov. As student at Munich Polytechnic a leading member of the Zionist students' society, on whose behalf he helped to organize Munich Preparatory Conference leading to Z.Y.C., 1901, which he attended as a delegate. Member of D.F. Returned to Russia and was an active Zionist worker in St. Petersburg until his death about 1906.

NORDAU, MAX (1849–1923). B. Budapest. Lived from 1880 in Paris. As author of (among other works) *Die conventionellen Luegen der Kulturmenschheit* ('The Conventional Lies of Civilized Mankind'), 1883, and *Entartung* ('De-generation'), 1893, already a European celebrity when, on reading *Der Judenstaat*, he at once assured Herzl of his support. In tribute on 70th birth-day (1919), described by W. and Sokolow as 'the co-founder of the Zionist Organization'. Attended I Z.C., 1897, taking a leading part in formulation of Basle Programme, and was one of the principal speakers at this and all succeeding Congresses up to the Tenth (1911). Presided at VII, IX, and X Z.C. (1905, 1909, 1911). Came out in opposition to S.A.C., dominated by 'Practical Zionists', elected at X Z.C., 1911, and absented himself from XI Z.C., 1913. During First World War lived in Spain. Attended London Zionist Conference, 1920, and elected Honorary President. Did not attend XII Z.C., 1921 and, offended by rejection of 'Nordau Plan', calling for immediate mass settlement of Jews in Palestine, withdrew from active participation in Zionist affairs.

NOSSIG, ALFRED (1864–1943). B. Lvov. Pre-Herzlian Zionist. Joined Z.O. but, contrary to the accepted Zionist policy, pressed for immediate colonizing activity. Member of first Board of Directors of *Jüdischer Verlag* (est. 1902) and member of editorial board of *Palästina*, the organ of the Berlin *Komitee zur wirtschaftlichen Erforschung Palästina*. Chairman, 1902, of Central Committee, Jewish Statistical Society and member of Berlin Committee for Jewish University. Member of D.F. Delegate to VI Z.C., 1903. Founded in Berlin, 1908, *Die Allgemeine Jüdische Kolonisations-Organisation* and, in 1911, an English subsidiary, The Orient Colonizing Company. At IX Z.C., 1909, his activities were publicly disowned by the Z.O., after which he ceased to have any part in Zionist affairs. During Second World War resident in Poland, where accused of collaboration with the Nazi authorities and executed by the 'Jewish Combat Organization' in the Warsaw Ghetto.

PASMANIK, DANIEL (1869–1930). Physician. B. Gadyach, Ukraine. Appointed at end of 1890s *privat-docent* in medicine at Geneva, where he took part in Zionist activities. Served for a time on preparatory committee for Z.Y.C. but in mid-1901 came out in active opposition to the holding of the Conference. At V Z.C., 1901 opposed creation of parties in Z.O., with special reference to D.F. Contributed from 1904 to Jewish journals in Russia, *Raszviet* and the Zionist organ *Yevreiskaya Zhizn*, acquiring a reputation as a leading exponent of Zionism in Russia. During post-1917 civil war in Russia supported the 'White' General Denikin. Worked for a time with Committee of Jewish Delegations at Paris Peace Conference, 1919. His association with Russian monarchist *émigré* circles led to his disappearance from Jewish public life.

PERELMAN, AARON (?–?). Orig. Odessa. As Karlsruhe student member of Zionist students' society, *Kadimah*. Took part in organization of Z.Y.C., 1901. Joined D.F. While studying at Zurich, 1902–3, joined Syrkin's *Cheirus* group. After Russian revolution of 1905, moved away from Zionism to join the 'Popular Party' founded by Simon Dubnow, with programme of full civic rights for Jews coupled with the recognition of their separate national identity within the Russian State.

PEVSNER, SAMUEL JOSEPH (1878–1930). B. Propoisk, Byelorussia. M. Leah Ginzberg, daughter of Ahad Ha'am (q.v.). While a student in Berlin, where he was a member of a Zionist students society, attended I Z.C., 1897. Contributor to Ahad Ha'am's Hebrew journal *Hashiloah*. Attended Z.Y.C., 1901. Member of D.F. group of delegates at V Z.C., 1901 and secretary of D.F.'s Berlin group. Attended Minsk Conference, 1902. In 1905 settled in Palestine, where made important contribution to expansion and industrial development of Haifa as a director of the *Atid* oil factory and a promoter of the citrus trade. During First World War resided in U.S.A. After returning to Palestine, active in Jewish affairs during mandatory period as delegate to Jewish Elected Assembly (*Asefat Hanivcharim*) and member of National Council of Jews in Palestine (*Va'ad Leumi*).

PICK, HERMANN (CHAIM) (1879–1952). Orientalist and librarian. B. Schildberg, Germany. Joined Z.O., 1898. Librarian, Prussian State Library, Berlin, 1906–20. Elected to Central Committee, German Zionist Federation, 1911. Member of Central Committee of World *Mizrahi* Organization, 1919–25. Resided in Palestine, 1921–7; member of Palestine Z.E. and head of its

Immigration Department. After returning to Germany resumed position at Prussian State Library, 1927, relinquishing it in 1933, when he settled permanently in Palestine.

PICTET, Raoul (1842–1929). Physicist. B. Geneva. Professor of Industrial Physics at Geneva University from 1879 to 1886, when he moved to Berlin, where he set up a liquid gas factory. In contact, in Berlin, with W. during his student days at Charlottenburg and tried, though without success, to help him to market his first discovery in dyestuffs chemistry.

PINKUS, Felix Lazar (1881–1947). B. Breslau. Entered Berne University, 1899; later studied at Breslau. At both Universities active in Zionist student circles. Joined D.F., 1902 but left it in 1903. Settled in Switzerland; member, 1902, of Central Committee, and later President, of Swiss Zionist Federation. After First World War edited various periodicals in Switzerland, France, and Germany.

PORTUGALOV, Gregory (?–?). In early 1900s student, and active Zionist, in St. Petersburg. Interested in organization of Z.Y.C., 1901, though not known to have attended it. Editor, 1909–11, of the St. Petersburg Jewish periodical (neutral on the Zionist question), *Yevreisky Mir*. Towards end of First World War returned to Zionist activity and by 1917 had become a leading member of the Socialist wing of the *Zeirei Zion* party.

ROSENBAUM, Simon (Shimshon) (1860–1934). Jurist. B. Pinsk. A *Hovev Zion* in student days in Odessa and Vienna. Delegate to I Z.C., 1897, and to all succeeding Congresses up to and including the Eleventh (1913). Elected to G.A.C. at IV Z.C., 1900. Zionist regional leader for Minsk area. One of the organizers, and Vice-President, of Minsk Conference, 1902. Member of deputation sent to Herzl by Kharkov Conference of regional leaders, 1903, to protest against 'Uganda' project. Member of first Duma, 1906. After First World War, member of Lithuanian Government as Deputy Foreign Minister and, later, as Minister for Jewish Affairs. Member of Committee of Jewish Delegations at Paris Peace Conference, 1919. Chairman of Lithuanian Zionist Centre. Settled in Palestine, 1924. Lithuanian Consul in Palestine and Chairman of Jewish Arbitration Tribunal.

ROTHSCHILD, Baron Edmond (Abraham Benjamin) de (1845–1934). Head of French branch of House of Rothschild. The first to give financial and practical support on a large scale to the movement for the re-settlement of the Jews in Palestine. By his munificent benefactions, beginning in 1882, he saved the earliest Jewish agricultural colonies from collapse and subsequently founded or supported a large number of other colonies. He provided the settlers with schools, medical services and facilities for the satisfaction of their religious needs. He encouraged intensive farming and laid the foundations of the Palestine wine industry. He set up his own administration for his colonies but in 1900 transferred their management to the Jewish Colonization Association (I.C.A.). In 1924 he founded the Palestine Jewish Colonization Association (P.I.C.A.) to take over this function from the I.C.A. and to continue and extend his work in Palestine under the direction of his son, James de Rothschild. Active supporter of the University project on its revival in

1913. Acclaimed as 'The Father of the *Yishuv*', he was, on the establishment in 1929 of the Jewish Agency for Palestine, elected Honorary President of the Agency.

ROTHSCHILD, Nathaniel Mayer (The First Lord Rothschild) (1840–1915). From 1879 head of London banking firm of N. M. Rothschild and Son. M.P. for Aylesbury, 1865, until elevation to peerage in 1885, being the first Jew to sit in the House of Lords. For many years the lay leader of the Anglo-Jewish community. Took a leading part in efforts to secure relaxation of Jewish disabilities in Russia and to ease the position of Russian Jews settling in England. Member of Royal Commission on Alien Immigration, 1902, when he first came into personal contact with Herzl, after which, though not in sympathy with Jewish nationalism, he showed a friendly interest in the El Arish and, later, in the 'Uganda' projects. Joined International Council of Jewish Territorial Organization (I.T.O.), founded in 1905, under the leadership of Israel Zangwill, for the purpose of establishing an autonomous Jewish settlement in any part of the world. Near the end of his life, in the changed situation created by the outbreak of war, he became favourably disposed to the idea of a Jewish home in Palestine under British protection.

ROTHSTEIN, Isaac (?–?). Engineer. A leading Rostov Zionist in the early 1900s. Supporter of D.F. and of Jewish University project. Delegate to Minsk Conference. Later, member of Zionist Centre for South Russia.

SALKIND, Jacob Meir (1875–1937). B. Kobryn, Byelorussia. In student days one of founders of Berne Zionist students' society, *Kadimah*. Delegate to Z.Y.C., 1901, but did not join D.F. Later (*c.* 1904) moved to England, where edited London Yiddish journals, *Yiddishe Stimme* and *Arbeiter Fraind*, officiated for a time as Rabbi in Cardiff. British delegate to VIII Z.C., 1907. Went to Palestine, 1913, and took part in foundation of colony of Karkur. Returned to England, where, during First World War, engaged in pacifist propaganda. Settled permanently in Palestine in early 1930s.

SCHIMMER (later BRITSCHGI), Regina (Ina) (1881–1949). B. Vienna. On clerical staff of *Jüdischer Verlag*, Berlin, 1903, and, later, of German Zionist Federation and of Publication Department of Z.O.'s Hebrew weekly organ, *Ha'olam*. After settling in Palestine in the 1930s, actively associated with *Aliya Hadasha* (German Immigrants Association) and *Ihud* (movement for Jewish-Arab understanding).

SHEINKIN, Menahem (1871–1924). B. Vitebsk. Delegate to I Z.C., 1897. Among founders of earliest Odessa society to be affiliated to Z.O. Visited Palestine 1900. Attended Z.Y.C., 1901. Member of D.F. and of its Programme Committee. Crown Rabbi, Balta, 1901–5. Elected to G.A.C. at VI Z.C., 1903. Zionist regional leader for area comprising Podoloa, Volhynia, and Bessarabia. Again visited Palestine in 1905 and settled there in 1906, becoming member of *Hovevei Zion* Information Bureau. One of the founders of Tel Aviv. During First World War went to U.S.A. but in 1919 returned to Palestine, where appointed Director of Z.E. Immigration Department.

SHERMAN, Isaac (1883–1955). B. Odessa. Student at Munich and Heidelberg Universities. Attended Z.Y.C., 1901. Member of D.F. Served as link between W. and Zionist youth groups in South Russia. After outbreak of First World War settled in U.S.A.

SHERMAN, Moses. Physician. Brother of Isaac Sherman (q.v.). B. 1881, Nikolayev. Active Zionist from 1898. Student at Odessa, Berlin, and Dorpat Universities. At Odessa leading member of Zionist students' society. Joined D.F., 1901. Settled in Palestine, 1911. During First World War medical officer in Turkish Army. One of founders, first Chairman, and, later, President of Palestine (Israel) Medical Association.

SHNEERSON (later, FEIWEL), Esther (?–1964). B. Liady, Byelorussia. M. 1906, Berthold Feiwel (q.v.). Geneva student of economics and active member of Geneva Zionist students' societies, c. 1900. Assisted W. in preparations for Z.Y.C. but in summer of 1901, before the Conference met, went home to Russia, and later in the year went for further study to Berlin, where she was in contact with Syrkin's Zionist-Socialist group.

SHRIRO, Samuel (1862–1928). B. Oshmiana, Lithuania. Baku oil magnate. The first substantial contributor to fund for preparatory work on Jewish University project, 1902. Seceded from Z.O. on 'Uganda' issue (1905) and became a Territorialist. Left Russia after the October 1917 Revolution and died in Paris.

SLOUSCH, Nahum (1872–1966). Orientalist. B. Odessa. *Hovev Zion* from his youth. As student in Geneva (1898–9) and Paris (1899–1904) member of Zionist students societies and correspondent of Hebrew periodicals in Russia. Delegate to II Z.C., 1898 and all succeeding Congresses up to and including Seventh, 1905. Took part in Z.Y.C., 1901, but became active opponent of D.F. On 'Uganda' issue a pro-Ugandist and, later, joined Territorialist secession from Z.O. Returned to Zionism after the Balfour Declaration and settled in Palestine in 1919.

SOKOLOW, Nahum (1861–1936). One of the most prolific and most widely read Jewish writers of his age and one of the foremost figures in the post-Herzlian development of the Zionist Movement. B. Vishogrod, Russian Poland. Educated with view to becoming a Rabbi but, after settling in Warsaw towards end of 1870s, drifted into journalism and in 1881 became editor of Hebrew daily *Hazefirah*. Not a *Hovev Zion*, but after attending I Z.C., 1897, converted to Zionism and took active part, especially as advocate of cultural work, in early Zionist Congresses and in Minsk Conference, 1902. Assisted in campaign for Jewish University project in Warsaw and Lodz, 1903. General Secretary of Z.O., at its Cologne Central Office, 1907–9. Visited London, 1906, on mission on behalf of Russian Jewry. In 1907 founded Hebrew weekly organ of Z.O., *Ha'olam*. Elected to S.A.C. at X Z.C., 1911 and re-elected at XI Z.C., 1913. Came to London at end of 1914 and closely associated with W. in discussions leading to, and following on, Balfour Declaration, in connexion with which undertook missions to French and Italian Governments and to the Holy See. President of Committee of Jewish Delegations at Paris Peace Conference, 1919. Presided at all Zionist Congresses from Twelfth (1921) to Sixteenth (1929). Elected President of Z.E. at XII Z.C., 1921 and held that office until 1931. President of Zionist Organization, 1931–5. Appointed President of K.H., 1935.

SOSKIN, EVGENY (SELIG) (1873–1959). Agronomist. B. Crimea. As Berlin student among first to join Russian-Jewish Academic Society. Worked in Palestine as agronomist, 1896–1903. Member of Zionist exploratory mission to El Arish, 1902. D.F. delegate to VII Z.C., 1903. Directed German plantation companies in Africa, 1903–15. A leading member of Zionist Revisionist Organization (as to which see below, s.n. Tyomkin), 1927–33. Helped to establish Jewish State party, 1933. Settled in Palestine, 1933. One of the founders of Nahariya and author of plans for cultivation by hydroponic methods in Palestine.

STIFF, NAHUM (1879–1933). B. Rovno, Ukraine. In early 1900s member of Kiev Zionist students society, *Kadimah*. Delegate to Minsk Conference, 1902. Active member of Jewish Self-Defence Organization after Kishinev pogrom, 1903. Later, among leaders of the Socialist Jewish Workers' Party ('Seymists'), and of Dubnow's 'Popular Party', as to which see above, s.n. Perelman. After Russian Revolution of Oct. 1917 lived for a time in Berlin but later returned to Russia, where he became a leading authority on Yiddish language and literature.

STUPNITSZKY, SAUL ISAAC (1876–1942). Publicist. B. Bielsk, Lithuania. As Berne student in later 1890s helped to found Berne Zionist Academic Society. Secretary of Jewish University Bureau in Geneva, 1903. D.F. delegate to VI Z.C., 1903. On 'Uganda' issue joined Territorialist secession (1905) from Z.O. Perished during Second World War in Warsaw Ghetto.

SYRKIN, NAHMAN (1868–1924). B. Mohilev. *Hovev Zion* from his youth. As Berlin student among first to join Russian-Jewish Academic Society. Delegate to I Z.C., 1897 and to all succeeding Congresses up to and including the Seventh (1905). At II Z.C., 1898, appeared as a Zionist Socialist. In 1901 published 'Manifesto to Jewish Youth' setting out Z.-S. ideas and founded in Berlin the Z.-S. Hessiana Society. During V Z.C., 1901, initiated discussions leading to the formation of *Cheirus* group, founded with object of forcing I.C.A. to co-operate with Z.O., but later turned into Zionist-Socialist organization. On 'Uganda' issue joined Territorialist secession (1905) from Z.O. Headed Zionist-Socialist Workers' Party in Russia, 1905–7. Settled in U.S.A., 1907 and became a leading figure in the American branch of the *Poale Zion*. Member of Committee of Jewish Delegations at Paris Peace Conference, 1919.

TRIETSCH, DAVIS (DAVID) (1870–1935). B. Dresden. Joined Z.O. at its inception but, contrary to the then accepted policy of the Movement, pressed for immediate colonizing activity. Promoted formation of Society for Jewish Settlement in the East, 1903. On editorial board of the Berlin German-language Jewish periodicals, *Ost und West*, 1901–2, and *Palästina* (published by the *Jüdischer Verlag*, of which he was managing director), 1902–3. Prolific writer on Jewish statistics, emigration, and colonization. Member of D.F. On the 'Uganda' issue an anti-Ugandist. Elected to G.A.C. at VI Z.C., 1903. During First World War advocated Zionist co-operation with Germany. Settled in Palestine, 1932; one of the founders of Ramat Hashavim.

TSCHERNIKOVSKY, SAUL (SHAUL) (1875–1943). One of the founders of the modern school of Hebrew poetry. B. Crimea. Associated with *Hovevei Zion* movement from his early years in Odessa and member of Zionist societies in his student days at Heidelberg and Lausanne. Settled in Palestine, 1931.

TSCHLENOW, YEHIEL (1863–1918). Physician. B. Kremenchug, Ukraine. In early 1880s one of the founders of *Bilu* and *Bnei Zion* societies in Moscow and an active *Hovev Zion*. At II Z.C., 1898, elected to G.A.C., and served as Zionist regional leader for Moscow area. Chairman of Russian Zionist Conferences at Minsk, 1902, and Helsingfors, 1906. Member of Council (*Aufsichtsrat*) of J.C.T. and of directorate of J.N.F. On 'Uganda' issue (1903–5) one of the leaders of the anti-Ugandists. Elected to S.A.C. at XI Z.C., 1913, and, abandoning a large medical practice, moved to the Zionist Central Office in Berlin. In London, as representative together with Sokolow, of S.A.C. during first half of 1915, after which returned to Russia, where in 1917, between the March and October revolutions, he came forward as the representative spokesman of the Russian Zionists. Came to London in October 1917, shortly before the Balfour Declaration and died there early in 1918.

TYOMKIN, VLADIMIR (ZEEV) (1861–1927). B. Yelizavetgrad, Ukraine. In early 1880s, while student in St. Petersburg, went over from Russian revolutionary movement to *Hovevei Zion*. Appointed head of Jaffa Bureau of *Hovevei Zion* Odessa Committee, 1891. Crown Rabbi, Yelizavetgrad, 1894–1914. At II Z.C., 1898, at which he spoke in favour of cultural work, elected to G.A.C., and served as Zionist regional leader for Yelizavetgrad area. On 'Uganda' issue, 1904–5, an anti-Ugandist. After First World War, joined Revisionist Party founded by Jabotinsky in 1925 in opposition to the then Zionist leadership, and was for a time President of the Union of Zionist Revisionists.

USSISHKIN, MENAHEM MENDEL (1863–1941). B. Dubrovna, Byelorussia. A *Hovev Zion* from his youth. One of the founders of Moscow *Bilu* Society (1882) and *Bnei Zion* Society (1884). Member of *Bnei Moshe*. Attended I Z.C., 1897. Elected to G.A.C., II Z.C., 1898, and served as Zionist regional leader for the Yekaterinoslav area. Took a leading part in Minsk Conference, 1902. Visited Palestine, 1903. In 'Uganda' controversy leading figure in anti-Ugandist group (*Zione Zion*), and promoter of Kharkov Conference of Russian Zionist regional leaders, 1903, from which delegation sent to Herzl to demand abandonment of 'Uganda' project. Member of S.A.C., 1905–7. Chairman from 1906 of *Hovevei Zion* Odessa Committee. At XI Z.C., 1913, supported project for Jewish University in Palestine. Member of Committee of Jewish Delegations at Paris Peace Conference, 1919. Settled in Palestine, 1919, and served as head of Zionist Commission until its replacement in 1921 by Palestine section of Z.E., of which he became Chairman. Appointed President of directorate of J.N.F., 1923, and thenceforth concentrated his activities on acquisition and development of land for Jewish settlement. Chairman of S.A.C. from 1935. At XX Z.C., 1937, a leading opponent of the partition proposals of the Peel Commission.

VEIT, SIGMUND (1863–1945). B. Sandhausen, Baden, but lived from childhood at Basle. Active in Zionism from late 1890s and elected to G.A.C. at II Z.C., 1898, but in later life took no part in Zionist affairs.

VOEGTLIN, CARL. Pharmacologist. B. Basle, 1879. Ph.D. Fribourg, 1903. Studied under W. at Manchester University, 1904–5. In 1905 settled in U.S.A., where, after holding various other appointments, he became, in 1938, director of the National Cancer Institute.

WEISSMAN, DAVID (1880–1966). Lawyer. B. Novozlatopol, Ukraine. Specialist in credit financing and housing schemes, on which submitted various projects to Z.O. Member, Municipal Housing Commission of All-Russian Union of Cities, 1917. Settled in Palestine, 1921.

WEIZMANN, ANNA (HANA) (? 1886–1963). Chemist. Sister of W. Studied at Zurich, 1905–12 and at Manchester University, 1913–14. During First World War employed in Moscow machine-tool factory. After the war joined Moscow Institute of Biochemistry. Settled in Palestine, 1933; member of scientific staff of Daniel Sieff Research Institute (later, Weizmann Institute of Science), Rehovoth.

WEIZMANN, FEIVEL (? 1872–1941). Brother of W. M. 1900, Fanya, sister of Chaim Lubzhinsky, husband of W.'s sister Miriam, (q.v.). Engaged in the timber business of his father, Ozer W. (q.v.). After father's death, 1911, accompanied his mother to Warsaw (where his brother-in-law, Lubzhinsky, was a prosperous timber-merchant), then to Pinsk, then to Warsaw, and finally to Moscow, where they lived until both settled in Palestine in 1920. Employed at Haifa on clerical staff of Palestine Electric Corporation Industries and, later, of Imperial Chemical Industries.

WEIZMANN (later DOUNIE), GITA. Music teacher. Sister of W. B. ? 1884. M. 1918, Tuvia Dounie, engineer (killed in Arab riots, 1938). Studied at Warsaw Institute of Music, 1901–5. Settled in Palestine, at Haifa, 1911. One of the founders, 1924, of Haifa School of Music, later known as the Dounie-Weizmann Conservatoire.

WEIZMANN (later LICHTENSTEIN), HAYA (1878–1959). Teacher. Sister of W. M. 1901, Abraham Lichtenstein (q.v.). In early years active Zionist in Pinsk and, after 1905, in Warsaw. Moved in 1909 to Vilna and in 1915 to Yekaterinoslav. Settled in Palestine, 1921; teacher at Herzlia High School, Tel Aviv, and later at Levinsky Women Teachers' Academy, Tel Aviv. President, 1946–56, of *Bnot Brith* Society. Published two volumes of memoirs, Tel Aviv, 5708 (1947/48) and 5713 (1952/53).

WEIZMANN, MIKHAIL (YEHIEL MIKHAL) (1892–1957). Agronomist. Brother of W. M. 1920, Yehudit Krishevsky, of Rishon-le-Zion. Studied agriculture at Kaiser Wilhelm Institute, Berlin. Settled in Palestine, 1914. Assistant Director, Palestine Government Department of Agriculture and Fisheries, 1920–8. Manager, Imperial Chemical Industries, Middle Eastern Zone, 1928–35. Later engaged on own account in industry and in development of Tel-Mond (founded 1929).

WEIZMANN (later LUBZHINSKY), MIRIAM (MARIYA) (1871–1950). Sister of W. M. 1888, Chaim Lubzhinsky (q.v.). Moved with her husband to Warsaw, c. 1896, and, at outbreak of First World War, from Warsaw to Russia. After his death in Petrograd in 1917, lived in Poland until 1938, when she settled in London.

WEIZMANN, MOSES (MOSHE) (1879–1957). Chemist. Brother of W. M. (1) Zinaida, daughter of Samuel Rivlin of Baku, and (2) Helena Levin. Entered Kiev Polytechnic as student of agriculture, 1900. Later, went over to chemistry, studying at Geneva and Grenoble. Settled in Palestine, 1924; became head of Organic Chemistry Laboratory at Hebrew University, and given rank of Professor, 1947.

WEIZMANN, Ozer (?1850–1911). Timber-transporter. Father of W. B. Syerniki, near Pinsk. M. 1867, Rachel-Leah Tchmerinsky, of Motol, near Pinsk. After living for some years at Motol, where he was the first and only Jew to be appointed *starosta* (head of the village), moved, *c.* 1894, to Pinsk. In later years, achieved a measure of prosperity through business association with his son-in-law, Lubzhinsky (q.v.). A devout Jew, of the enlightened type known as *Maskilim*, well versed in Jewish learning, and with Zionist sympathies; delegate to VI Z.C., 1903.

WEIZMANN (formerly TCHMERINSKY), Rachel-Leah (?1852–1939). Mother of W. Settled in Palestine, 1920; founded at Haifa the first Old Age Home for Palestinian Jews. For other biographical data, see s.n. Feivel W. and Ozer W.

WEIZMANN, Samuel (Shmuil) (1882–?). Engineer. Brother of W. M., 1905, Bazia Rubin, a Zurich medical student. Student at Kiev and Zurich, *c.* 1906 joined Zionist-Socialist Workers' Party (Territorialist). In 1909 worked for about a year in Manchester. Returned to Russia and engaged in engineering work in Kiev and, during the First World War, at the Moscow machine-tool factory at which his sister Anna (q.v.) was also employed. After Russian Revolution, directed industrial plants in U.S.S.R. Died after Second World War in Russian penal camp.

WEIZMANN, Vera—*see* s.n. KHATZMAN, Vera.

WERTHEIMER, Joseph (1833–1908). Appointed Chief Rabbi of Geneva, 1859. Professor of Philology at University of Geneva, 1874–1906. Supported Jewish University project, 1902–3.

WINTZ, Leo (Judah Leib) (?1876–1952). Journalist. B. Glukhov, Ukraine. Moved to Berlin in early 1890s. Member of Berlin 'Young Israel' Society. Delegate to IV Z.C., 1900. Contributor to Russian Jewish press, founder (1901) of 'Phoenix' Art Press, and of German-language Jewish periodical, *Ost und West*. During First World War operated Jewish news-agency in Copenhagen. Editor for many years of journal of Berlin Jewish community until settlement in Palestine, 1935.

WOLFFSOHN, David (1855–1914). B. Dorbyany, Lithuania. Lived from 1885 in Cologne. Prosperous timber-merchant, with international connexions. One of first *Hovevei Zion* in Germany. Meeting with Herzl in 1896 was the start of a close association and personal friendship. Attended I Z.C., 1897. Among the founders, and first Treasurer, of German Zionist Federation, 1897. First President of J.C.T., 1899. Accompanied Herzl to Constantinople, 1902. Chairman of S.A.C. and, in effect, President, Z.O., 1905–11. In face of mounting opposition from Russian and other 'Practical Zionists', first evidenced at IX Z.C., 1909, withdrew from leadership of Z.O. at X Z.C., 1911, and thereafter played no part in the direction of the Movement, though given the honour of presiding at the Eleventh Congress, 1913.

YASINOVSKY, Isidore (Israel) (1842–1917). Lawyer. B. Grodno Province. An early *Hovev Zion*, one of the organizers of Kattowitz H.Z. Conference (1884), an original member of the H.Z. Odessa Committee and head of H.Z. Warsaw Office. Delegate to I Z.C., 1897, at which elected to G.A.C., and to all succeeding Congresses up to the Seventh (1905). From 1898 Zionist regional leader for Warsaw area. On 'Uganda' issue joined Territorialist secession from Z.O. (1905) and became one of the leaders of the Jewish Territorial Organization (I.T.O.).

ZHITLOVSKY, Chaim (1865–1943). B. Ushatch, Byelorussia. Student at Universities of Berlin, Zurich, and Berne, 1888–1904. Closely associated with the Russian Social-Revolutionaries and one of their leading theoreticians. Strongly opposed to Zionism, but a Jewish nationalist and the earliest advocate in Russia of a combination of Jewish nationalism with socialism. After Kishinev pogrom (1903) joined movement for Jewish 'national autonomy' and became leading figure in Socialist Jewish Workers' Party ('Seymists'). Settled in U.S.A., 1908. During First World War joined American branch of *Poale Zion*, but severed connexion with Zionism after the War, becoming an ardent supporter of the Biro-Bidjan project.

ZOLOTAREV, A. (? 1880–?). B. Ukraine. Journalist. As a student at Kiev and a member of Kiev Zionist students' society inclined towards Zionist-Socialist ideology. From 1902 an active Bundist and from 1919 a member of the Communist Party.

ZWEIG, Egon (1877–1944). Lawyer. B. Moravia. Delegate to II Z.C., 1898 and to all succeeding Congresses up to and including the Nineteenth (1935). Director of Vienna J.N.F. Office, 1903–20, and of Vienna Palestine Office, 1918–20. Member of J.N.F. directorate at The Hague, 1920, and in Jerusalem, 1922–3.

INDEX

Abdul Hamid, Sultan of Turkey, Herzl's audience of, 24, 28, 145, 148; Herzl's complimentary telegram to, 219, 224–8; Herzl's negotiations, 232; and Jewish University, 260, 266.

Aberson, Rosa: in this volume, *see* Grinblatt, Rosa.

Aberson, Zvi, (Biog. Index 408), and Youth Conference, 117, 134, 140, 209, 212; attitude to Zionism, 201–2, 209; Congress delegate, 204; and Democratic Fraction, 216, 233–5, 262–3, 266; W.'s relations with, 286, 352, 357, 362; proposed book, 286, 350; mentioned, 183, 210, 257, 272.

Abrahami, Zvi, *see* Abramovich, Gregory.

Abramovich, Gregory, (Biog. Index 408), and Youth Conference, 87, 102, 104, 109, 139; in Odessa, 171–3; and Democratic Fraction, 216, 239; mentioned, 161, 239–40.

Academic Zionist Youth, Conference of, *see* Zionist Youth Conference.

'Action' as against talk, 351.

Actions Committee, xxviii, 118, 145, 149, 204, 210–11, 299, 301.

  Greater (*later* General Council), xxviii, **xxxii–xxxv**, 66, 70–71, 73, 76, 125, 176, 188–90, 195, 197, 396.

  Smaller (*later* Executive), xxviii, **xxxii–xxxv**, 71, 73, 148, 190, 199, 261, 269, 287, 295, 334, 357–8, 362.

  University project, and, 229, 261, 269, 287, 290, 295, 304, 306, 310, 316–17, 334, 406.

  Youth Conference, position regarding, 157–8, 162, 176, 190, 195.

Africa, North, Jews in, 37.

Ahad Ha'am (Asher Zvi Ginzberg), (Biog. Index 408).

  Bnei Moshe founded by, 55.

  Cultural Commission, member of, 25, 230, 241–2, 255, 362, 395.

  Democratic Fraction, and, 25–26, 256, 259.

  Hashahar's message to, 228.

  Hashiloah founded by, 62.

  Herzl, and, 19.

  impression of his teachings on W., 17–20, 85, 193.

  letters from W., 26, 28, 112–13, 123, 132, 194, 227, 256.

  meetings with W., 61–62, 115–16, 124–5, 163.

  Minsk Conference, attends, 394–5, 398.

  Odessa Committee's delegation to Paris, disappointment with, 114–15, 148, 150.

  photograph, request for, 125.

  University project, attitude to, 242.

  withdraws from public activities, 148, 150, 153.

  Youth Conference, and, 112–13, 125, 134, 148, 150, 196.

'Ahiasaf Yearbook', 220, 255.

Aid Funds for Jewish students, 199, 208; non-party fund, 199, 202, 210.

Aigle, 367.

Aix-les-Bains, 141.

Akiva, Rabbi, 42.

Alazarin, 237.

Aleinikov, Michael, 264, 404.

Aleksandrovo, 333.

Alexander II, Czar, 16.

Algiers, Dey of, 46.

Alien Immigration, Royal Commission on, *see* Immigration into Britain.

Alliance Israélite Universelle, **208**, 382.

Altschul, Dr. Michael, 376.

America, *see* United States.

American Zionist Federation, 206.

Anglo-Palestine Company (*later* Anglo-Palestine Bank), **xxxv**.

Annual Conference (Jahreskonferenz) ('Small Congress'), *see under* Zionist Congresses.

Anti-semitism, 92, 193, 226–7, 264, 312.

Anti-Zionists, 20–21, 86–88, 91–92, 231–2, 385–9, 392, 398.

Argentina, 167.

Ariana, Jewish party at the, 122, 128.

Aristo-crat, 36.

Aristotle, 36, 42.

Arkhiniantz, 111.

Armenians, 80, 140, 389.

Arndt, Arendt, *see* Brandt, Boris (Barukh).

Aronchik, *see* Eliasberg, Aaron.

Artels (artisans' co-operatives), **193**.

Assimilationists, 180, 227, 230, 232, 351, 382, 386–7, 389.

Auerbach (? Berne student), 74.

Augean stables, reference to, 80.

Austria, Cultural Commission and, 358; Jews in, 56, 151, 167, 296; and Youth

Austria (*cont.*):
Conference, 200, 209; Zionism in, 78, 151.
Avinovitzky, Feibush, **189**, 192, 397.
Axelrod, Luibov and Ida, 123.
Azayts, 352–3.

Baden, universities, 262.
Bahar, Jacques, 70.
Baku, 321, 326–7, 333–4, 339, 356, 366, 400; W.'s visit to (1902), 402–3.
Balfour Declaration (1917), 312; W.'s two thousand interviews, xi–xii.
'Bank, the', *see* Jewish Colonial Trust.
'Baron, The', 270.
Basle, 74, 80–81, 103, 215, 217–18, 221, 225–6, 251, 253; Congress Office, 68, 78; Congresses held at, *see* Zionist Congresses; Youth Conference at (1901), *see* Zionist Youth Conference.
Basle Programme, **xxxi**, 18, 22, 25, 109, 136, 138, 200, 203, 312, 381.
Batschevanov, M. (*Chéri*), **141**, 144, 188.
Bayer works, Elberfeld, *see* Elberfeld.
Beham (Boehm), Arieh Leib, Biog. Index **409**.
Bein, Alex, cited, 55, 75, 80, 105, 145, 229, 388.
Belkovsky, Gregory (Moses Zvi), (Biog. Index **409**), 407.
Bendersky, Dr. Solomon, (Biog. Index **409**), 134.
Berdyansk, 126.
Berger, Isaac, (Biog. Index **409**), 199–200, 346, 381–2, 384.
Berger, Juda Leib, (Biog. Index **409**), 51–52.
Berlin, W. a student at Berlin (Charlottenburg) Polytechnic (q.v.) (1893), 14, 16–17, 47; W. leaves (1895), 48; return delayed, 50, 52–53; returns to Berlin and resumes studies (1896), 50, 61–65; W.'s final departure (1897), 63, 65; W. visits (1899), 77, (1901), 141, 155, 160–1, (1902), 241, 243–50, 348, 356, 373–8.
Democratic Fraction, Berlin Group, *see under* Democratic Fraction; proposed periodical in, 256, 259; programme printed in, 380–1.
Jewish students, 58, 63, 70, 116, 133, 202, 376, 389.
Kadimah society, 86–88, 90–91, 117, 119, 129, 163, 194, 212, 220, 223, 235.
student colony, 16–17, 47–49, 102, 196.
University, 117, 376–7; restrictions on entry of Russian girls, 300, 302.

Youth Conference, and, 104–6, 128.
Zionism in, 70, 161.
Berlin, Mme, 321.
Berlin (Charlottenburg) Polytechnic, W. a student at, 14, 17–18, 28, 46–49, 61.
Bernard-Lazare, *see* Lazare, Bernard.
Berne, W. lives for a short time in (1899), 67–69; visits (1900), 81, (1901), 85, 90, 100, 102, 109, 160, 198, 202, (1902), 237–9, 369–71.
Kadimah society, 278.
lecture by W. in (1901), 85.
mentioned, 15, 71, 74, 106, 118, 123, 204, 299, 309–10, 315.
station burnt down, 303.
Swiss Zionist Conference, 272, 278.
Yeshiva students, 190.
Youth Conference, and, 88, 102, 104.
Berne Academic Zionist Society, 68, 90, 102, 158, 195, 199, 278.
Berne Zionist Students' Society, 133, 199, 203, 211.
Bernstein, Edward, 389.
Bernstein, Leon (Leib), (Biog. Index **410**), 111.
Bernstein-Kohan, Jacob, (Biog. Index **410**).
circulars distributed to study-groups, 78, 140, 146, 157.
Cultural Commission member, 230, 255, 269, 362.
Democratic Fraction programme committee member, 233, 262.
financial difficulties, 364.
Herzl, and, 24, 145, 176, 190.
Kishinev Correspondence Centre, Director of, 66, 78, 140, 190, 206, 363–4.
meetings with W., 112, 115–16, 171–2, 175, 189, 407.
mentioned, 182, 216, 219, 242–3, 272, 284.
Minsk conference, illness prevents attendance at, 383, 394.
Paris delegation to meet Rothschild, member of, 115.
Youth Conference, and, 109, 116–18, 134, 140, 146, 176, 190, 203–4, 209.
Bible studies, V.K. and, 280, 307.
Bickerman, Joseph, (Biog. Index **410**); critical analysis of Zionism, 386–9, 392, 398.
Bildung Society for dissemination of Yiddish literature, 58–60, 84, 91, 111.
Bilit (chemist, friend of W.), **95**, 111, 238–9.
Bioux, 365, 367–9, 371, 376.
Birnbaum, Nathan, (Biog. Index **410**), 62, 78.

Biske, M., 97.

Black Forest, Germany, 126.

Blank, Reuben, (Biog. Index **410**), 202, 210.

Bnei Moshe (Sons of Moses), 18, 51, 55; W. admitted to membership, 18, 55.

Bodenheimer, Dr. Max Isidore, (Biog. Index **410**); letter from W., 69.

Boehm, *see* Beham.

Bogolepov (Russian Minister of Education), 92, 166.

Boileau, Nicolas, quoted, 42.

Books, W. on, 46.

Borukhov, Aaron, (Biog. Index **411**), 102, 104.

'Boy, the', arrangements made for at Geneva, 254–5, 258–60.

Boys' circle in Rostov, 143.

Braff, Mme, 378, 388.

Brailovsky, Agnes (Zina), **98**, 122, 307, 316, 339–40, 365, 381, 389, 407.

Brandt, Boris (Barukh), (Biog. Index **411**), 92.

Breslau, 249.

Breslav, Dr. Israel, 404.

Brest-Litovsk, 82; W.'s meeting with Motzkin in, 53–55, 57.

British Royal Commission on Alien Immigration, *see* Immigration.

British Zionist Federation, 206.

Britschgi, Regina (Ina), *see* Schimmer.

Brno, 138.

Brodsky, Lazar and Leo, 404.

Bromberg (town), 339, 372.

Bromberg (*earlier* Dorfman), Anastasya, 175, 187, 299.

Bromberg, Fyodor (Feivel), (Biog. Index **411**), 175, 177, 181, 183, 187, 277, 299, 367, 385, 395.

Bromberg, Samson, 187.

Brovari, near Kiev, 53, 58, 61, 105.

Bruck, Dr. Gregory (Zvi), (Biog. Index **411**), 74, 76–77, 391, 396, 407.

Bruderkrieg, 73.

Buber, Martin (Mordecai Zeev), (Biog. Index **411**).

    Cultural Commission member, 255, 269, 358, 362.

    Democratic Fraction, and, 256.

    editor of *Die Welt*, 183.

    Eine Jüdische Hochschule, named as an author of, 167, 230, 303, 347, 383.

    Herzl, and, 23, 189, 232.

    Jüdischer Verlag, and, 27, 259, 299, 406.

    mentioned, 272, 287, 289, 298, 301, 303.

    University project, and, 29, 229, 331, 406–7.

Zionist Congress, and, 125, 229.

Buchs, V.K.'s 'letters from', 120.

Bukhmil, Joshua Heshel, (Biog. Index **412**), 117, 151, 153–4, 201, 216–17, 233.

Bulgaria, Communist movement in, 186.

Bund, and Bundists, The, 20–21, **86–88**, 91–92, 111, 187, 193, 200–1, 210, 232, 236; National programme, 87, 210, 231; W.'s correspondence with, 120–2; his attitude to, 208, 231; Syrkin and, 220–1.

Calendar, Gregorian and Julian, xxiv–xxv, 34.

Cambridge University, 319, 330.

Canada, Zionist records sent to for safe keeping, x; returned, xiii.

Caucasus, 131.

Censorship at Russian frontier, 354, 380, 382.

Central Office of Zionist Organization, **xxxiii–xxxiv**; in Vienna, xxxiii, 78, 139, 189, 204–5, 232, 260–1, 269.

'Cercle Israélite', 98, 99.

Chailly, 391.

Chamonix, 141–2, 144–5.

Charlottenburg (*see also* Berlin), 47, 82–83, 110, 116.

Charlottenburg Polytechnic, *see* Berlin (Charlottenburg) Polytechnic.

Cheirus group, 222.

Chemical literature, W. passes oral exam on, 73.

Chemistry, W.'s specialization in, 14–15, 30; studies in Germany, 47; teaching and research at University of Geneva (*see also* Laboratory), 13–14, 80, 140–1, 262, 284–5, 289, 302, 304, 306–7, 313–14, 334, 342; possible sacrifice of career in chemistry in Zionist cause, 15, 30, 284–5, 332, 363–4; disappointing evaluation of joint Weizmann–Deichler discovery, *see under* Elberfeld.

Chéri, *see* Batschevanov, M.

Chernin, Lydia and Deborah, 403, 405.

Chernyshevsky, N. G., 40.

Chillon, Castle of, 97–98.

Clarens-Baugy (Lake Geneva), 249–50, 274; W. at, 67, 69, 100, 215, 371; V.K. staying at, 93 ff., 144, 371.

Clericals, the, 24, 180.

Colline (pension at Clarens-Baugy), 371.

Cologne, 69, 101, 104, 243, 251, 253–4, 281.

Colonies, student, *see* Student colonies.

Colonization Commission, 396.

Congresses, Zionist, *see* Zionist Congresses.

Constantinople, Herzl's visits to, 23, 45, 232, 333, 350, 388.

Co-operatives, artisans', *see* Artels.

Correspondence Bureau, Munich, *see under* Zionist Youth Conference.

Correspondence Centre, Kishinev, **xxxiv**, 66, 78, 130, 140, 183, 187, 190, 206, 363–4; closed down and replaced (1901) by Information Bureau, Simferopol (q.v.), 206.

Cracow, 61–62.

Crimea, 370.

Cultural Commission, 25, 214, 229–30, 242, 255, 269, 357–8, 362, 396, 406; two Commissions elected at Minsk conference, 395.

Cultural work as part of Zionist programme, advocacy of, 25, 72, 87, 91–92, 104, 109, 189, 209, 214, 346, 382; Congress and, 24, 25, 76, 83, 125, 180, 214; Democratic Fraction and, 25, 27, 214, 221, 229; Minsk conference and, 390–1, 394–8.

Cycling, W. and, 96–97, 123, 131, 154.

Cyclists' Council, 96, 97.

Dacha, 50.

Daniel Sieff Research Institute, Rehovoth, xii–xiii.

Dante, 42.

Danzig, 38, 185, 339, 365, 370, 372; Technical College, 383.

Darmstadt, 72, 100, 234, 295.

Darmstadt Polytechnic, W. a student at (1892–3), 14, 47.

Darmstadt University, 262.

Darwinism, 95.

Davidson, Eliahu, (Biog. Index **412**), 47–50, 62–63, 89, 204, 209–10, 389; aligns himself with Bundists, 87, 91–92, 210.

Day of Atonement, Jewish, 50, 182.

Deborochka, *see* Chernin, Deborah.

Deichler, Dr. Christian, (Biog. Index **412**), 243, 245, 249–50, 271–2, 278, 284, 325, 340, 348, 369, 371–2; W.'s association with in research, 71, 88, 135, 141, 224, 237–41, 247, 291, 293–4, 309, 353; difficulties with 'quasi-fiancée', 253–4, 281.

Demnat, Morocco, 37.

Democratic elements in Zionism, 200–1, 206.

Democratic Fraction, formation (1901), **xxxii**, 25–27, **214**; disintegration (by 1904), 26, 214.

Berlin group of members, 255, 359–60; protest against Fraction members participation in Syrkin discussions, 215–24, 233–7, 239, 242, 245–7, 286; letter from W., 234.

Berlin Information Office, temporary, 381, 399.

Conference, projected, 223, 282–3, 285–6, 294, 308, 329, 334, 337, 359–60, 362.

constitution, 233, 282, 381.

cultural work, *see that title*.

Information Bureau, Geneva, 25–26, 86, 214–17, 219, 223, 233–6, 239, 242, 254, 282–4, 359.

leadership in Russia, 394.

membership, 394.

Minsk conference and, 345, 350, 361, 380, 386, 391, 394.

Moscow Centre, 380, 390, 394.

Motzkin's promised writings on, 220–1, 233, 255, 258, 360.

news-letters, 215, 219, 234–6, 254–5, 308, 359.

opposition to, 228, 326–7, 391.

periodical, proposed, 256, 259, 299–300.

programme, Youth Conference agrees on principles, 214; conference elects committee to draft, 25, 233, 258, 261–2, 265–6; Motzkin entrusted with final revision, 26, 272, 282, 286, 298, 305; delays in publication, 229, 234, 258, 272, 277, 281–3, 301, 305, 307–8, 322, 327; committee's Heidelberg meeting, 262, 265–6, 272, 275, 308, 359; unfinished text sent to Berne for copying, 310, 314–15; final revision and printing of, 295, 329, 333–4, 337, 339, 345, 349–50, 352, 357, 360, 362, 369, 376, 380, 384, 392, 399, 402; salient points, **380–2**.

propaganda tour of Russia, *see under* Propaganda.

subscriptions to, 233–5, 360.

W.'s attitude to, 25–26, 281, 299, 351, 359–60, 393.

Dengin (chemist), 280.

Descartes, René, 42.

Diablerets, 320–1, 325–6.

Diaspora, The, 79–80, 351, 379, 382.

Die Welt, see *Welt*.

Doar Hayom (Hebrew journal), 85.

Doktor, Miss, 98.

Donchin, Dr. Georgette, note on transliteration of Russian, **xxx**.

Dorfman, Anastasya, *see* Bromberg.

Dorfman, Catherine (Gittel), (Biog. Index **412**), 89, 127, 139, 156, 188, 199, 204, 271, 284, 299; family, 298, 322–3, 335; father, 181; letters from W., 85, 142 ff. (*see* List of Letters, p. 5 ff.); mother's illness and death, 298, 306, 322–3, 333; photograph of W. for, 187–8; relations with W., 23–24, 28, 187, 231, 257.

Dorshei Zion, Rostov, 129, 146.

Dostoevsky, F. M., 40, 43.

Dounie, Gita: in this volume, *see* Weizmann, Gita.

Dounie, Tuvia, 185.

Dresden, 106.

Dreyfus, Captain Alfred (Dreyfus affair), 66.

Dreyfus, Jacob, **67–68**.

Druskienniki, 75, 276, 296, 348.

Dubosarsky, Joseph, (Biog. Index **412**), 212.

Duelling, student, 278.

Dyestuffs chemistry, 14, 71, 73, 88, 134–5, 141, 237.

Economic organization of Jewry, 104, 114, 116, 138, 160, 163, 207, 213.

Education, Congress and, 125; higher, 229; nationalization of Jewish education, 398; Russian restrictions on Jews, 14, 28, **166–7**, 168–70, 182, 185, 229, 255, 268; Youth Conference and, 113, 207.

Edward VII, King, illness, 299, 301.

Eine Jüdische Hochschule (brochure), *see under* Jewish University project.

Elberfeld, W.'s association with Bayer chemical works, 14, 88, 127, 185, 224, 239, 243, 284; disappointing evaluation of discovery made jointly by W. and Deichler, 141, 237, 241, 247–53, 271–2, 291–4, 296, 298, 309, 311, 316, 331, 353.

Eliasberg, Aaron, (Biog. Index **412**), 161–2, 204, 238–40; bibliography of university question, 290, 298, 301, 317–18, 336; 'the child', 286; 'the baby', 340; letters from W., 126, 210, 257, 259–60, 290, 316.

Eliashev, Isidore (Israel), (Biog. Index **412**), 49, 53, 57, 61–63, 134, 140, 142, 200, 300.

England, boys' groups, 143; and Jewish University, 29, 303, 332; and the Jews, 37.

English language, W.'s knowledge of, xi, xxii, 330.

Esfir Grigoryevna, *see* Weinberg, Esther.

Espionage methods within Zionism, 190.

Esterman, Leo (Yehuda Leib), (Biog. Index **413**), 62, 65.

Esther, Book of, allusion to, 46.

'Eternal Jew', *see* Wandering Jew.

Ettinger, Yevgeny, 92.

Europe, and Jews, 37, 92; Kings of, 36–37.

'European, as a', 62.

Evans-Gordon, Major (*later* Sir) William, **401**.

Executive of Zionist Organization: in this volume, *see* Actions Committee: Smaller.

Factory project, 56.

Farbman, Michael or Zvi, *see* Abramovich, Gregory.

Farbstein, David Zvi, (Biog. Index **413**), 163, 201, 213, 406.

Feiwel, Berthold ('Toldy'), (Biog. Index **413**), Berlin address, 240–1; in Geneva, 245, 247–9, 252, 271, 299; at Leysin, 273–5, 277–9, 281–2, 285–7, 299, 318–21, 323, 340; moving to Bioux, 367–9, 371, 376; at Glion, 374, 376; at Chailly, 391; in Zurich, 364, 407.

Cultural Commission member, 362.

Democratic Fraction, and, 233, 261–2, 266, 274, 359; journal, 256, 259, 300.

editor of *Die Welt*, 151, 183.

health, 249, 270, 274, 284, 286, 291–2, 298, 301–2, 307–8, 310–11, 327, 330, 335, 351.

Jewish University project, and, 27–28, 255, 260, 263–4, 268–9, 286, 305–6, 310, 331–2, 361, 399, 407; named as an author of *Eine Jüdische Hochschule*, 28–29, 167, 230, 303, 347, 361, 383.

Jüdischer Verlag, a founder of, 27, 259, 298, 301.

mentioned, 125, 270, 272–3, 280, 283, 291, 294, 296, 328, 338, 349, 357–8, 366, 377, 383–5.

Shneerson, Esther, and, 298, 304, 314, 319–21.

translation of Rosenfeld's poems, 299, 301, 335.

W.'s tributes to, 292, 324, 369.

Youth Conference, and, 134, 150–1, 209, 213.

Feiwel, Esther: in this volume, *see* Shneerson, Esther.

Financial difficulties, W.'s, *see under* Weizmann, Chaim.

Finkelstein (Kherson Zionist), **175**, 177, 181, 183, 187.

Fira, Firochka, *see* Weinberg, Esther.

Flambeau (Paris monthly), 70.

Fluxman, Apolinaria, 403, 405.

'Fraktion' (word), 214.

Fraktion (proposed Radical group), 116, 118–19.

France, Dreyfus affair, 66.

Frankfurt, 99, 160, 164, 244, 340, 364, 369–70, 373.

Frauenkongress (Berlin, 1896), 62.

Freiburg, Germany, 164 ; University, 262.
French language, W.'s knowledge of, xi, xxii, xxiii.
Fribourg, Switzerland, 198.
Fribourg University, W. a student at, 14, 65, 67 ; awarded Ph. D. (1899), 14, 65.
Friedenau (Brandenburg), 50.
Friedlander, P., cited, 88.
Friedman, Shmarya, 50.
Fuchs, Sylvia, 98.
Futran, Dr. Michael, 404.

Galileo, 42.
Galuth ('Golus'), 52, 85, 180, 379.
Gaster, Moses, (Biog. Index 413), 92 ; letters from W., 75, 89.
Geiger, Abraham, 56.
General Confederation of Jewish Workers in Lithuania, Poland, and Russia, see Bund, The.
General Council of Zionist Organization: in this volume, see Actions Committee, Greater.
Geneva, W. in, 67, 69–159, 189–227, 254–96, 340–2, 368–70, 407 ; W.'s address, 188 ; W.'s hint of leaving, 246 ; V.K. and, 184, 406.
    anti-Czarist demonstrations (1901), 111, 143, 186.
    arrangements made for boy at, 254–5, 258–260.
    Chief Rabbi, see Wertheimer, Joseph.
    Congress delegate, 204.
    Democratic Fraction Information Bureau, see under Democratic Fraction.
    Jewish students, 20, 186, 219, 224–8, 298.
    library, 290, 339–42.
    Socialist-Zionists' conference, 196, 200.
    student colony, 20, 226.
    Youth Conference Organization Bureau, see under Zionist Youth Conference.
    Zionist Society, 69, 71, 199.
    Zionist students, 104: society, see Hashahar.
Geneva, Lake, 67, 69, 330.
Geneva University, W.'s post at, 13–14, 16, 20, 67, 73, 88, 142, 190 (see also laboratory work); V.K.'s examinations, 241–2, 247, 249; inquiries for admission of V.K.'s sister, 342, 377.
Genevois, Le, 95, 225–6.
Gentiles, W. on, 51–52, 85, 194, 229, 387.
German Chemical Society, 141, 224.
German language, W.'s knowledge of, xi,

xxii, xxiii, 40 ; V.K. and, 294, 296–7, 326, 328, 357.
Germany, anti-Jewish propaganda, 167, 230 ; Cultural Commission regional section, 358 ; foreign students, 255 ; Jews in, 28, 56 ; Social Democrats, 389 ; technical school, 167 ; universities, 230, 268, 290 ; W. in, 13–14, 47, 234, 377 ; Zionists, 69, 78, 226, 259, 261, 263.
Getsova, Rebecca (Rivochka), 68, 72, 74, 81, 119, 202, 204 ; letter from W., 74 ; fatal illness, 237–8.
Getsova, Sophia (or Sonia), (Biog. Index 414), W.'s first fiancée, 15, 65–66, 68, 72–74, 77, 81, 90, 119 ; letter from W., 82 (other letters from W. are in private hands and unavoidably omitted from this volume, xx, 13, 65); W. breaks off engagement (1901), 15, 155, 159, 168, 219, 272, 355; later references, 202, 204, 239, 309, 371.
Ginzberg, Asher Zvi, see Ahad Ha'am.
Ginzburg, Simon, (Biog. Index 414), 397.
Glickman, David, 359.
Glikin, Moshe, (Biog. Index 414), 236, 282, 381, 384, 407 ; letters from W., 381, 389, 399.
Glion-sur-Territet, 374, 376.
Goethe, Nietzsche's characterization of, 85.
Goettingen, 101, 116.
Gogol, N. V., 40, 46 ; characters in Inspector-General mentioned, 39–40.
'Golus' (exile), see Galuth.
Gordon, Yehudah-Leib, 37.
Gourland, Aaron, (Biog. Index 414), 86, 117–18, 134, 139, 201, 209, 216.
Goy, see Gentiles.
Graebe, Professor Karl, 67, 73, 142–3, 281, 284.
Granovsky, 128, 140.
Greater Actions Committee, see under Actions Committee.
Greek language, W. and, 36.
Greeks, 226.
Gregorian Calendar, xxiv–xxv, 34.
Griedenberg, Dr. B., 404.
Grigorovich, D. V., 40.
Grinblatt (later Aberson), Rosa, (Biog. Index 414), 127, 154, 160, 183, 186, 209.
Grodno, 117, 126, 200, 205.
Gunzburg, Baron Horace de, 182.
Gurevich, Boris (Chaim Dov), (Biog. Index 414), 105, 110, 114, 117, 119, 129, 139.
Guriel, Boris, xiii, xvi, 38.
Guten Yudin, 161.

Guterman, Hillel (Ilya), **129**, 131–2, 143, 146, 171.
Gymnasium, The, *see* Pinsk: Secondary School.

Hacohen, Mordecai Ben-Hillel, 163.
Haifa, 388.
Halle, 116.
Haman, allusion to, 46.
Hamelitz (Hebrew journal), 190, 197, 199, 228, 278, 395.
Hapoel-Hazair (Tel Aviv weekly), 35.
Hashahar (Geneva Zionist Students' Society), 98, **224**, 225, 228, 253, 319.
Hashiloah (Hebrew monthly), 19, 62, 228.
Hasudovsky, Benjamin (Yema), 121.
Hatzefirah (Hebrew journal), 58, 394–5, 397.
Hatzofe (Hebrew daily), 98.
Hazman (Hebrew journal), 395.
Health, W.'s, *see under* Weizmann, Chaim.
Hebrew language, 91, 113, 379, 382; W. and, xi, xxii, xxiii; transliteration, xxiii; W.'s teacher, 35; V.K. and, 280, 307, 326.
Heder (Jewish elementary school), 56–57.
Heidelberg, 74, 100, 139, 234, 253–4, 259–60, 286, 290–1, 307, 328; W. visits, 238–40, 290; Congress delegate, 204, 210; *Kadimah* society, 101; Programme (D.F.) committee's meeting, 262, 265–6, 272, 275, 308, 359; Russian Jewish students, 116; University, 260–2, 316–17; Youth Conference, and, 88, 117; Zionism in, 240.
Heine, Heinrich, allusions to, 25, 252; quoted, 388.
'Help', see *Hilfe*.
Heringsdorf, 72–73.
Hermoni, A., cited, 210.
Herzfeld, Benjamin, 94, 279, **281**, 293, 342, 383.
Herzfeld, Esther: in this volume, *see* Weinberg, Esther.
Herzl, Theodor (Benjamin Zeev), (Biog. Index **415**); death (1904), 30–31.
anti-I.C.A. demonstrations, and proposal for, 217–20.
cultural work, and, 24–25, 125.
Der Judenstaat, 19, 36.
diaries, W. never mentioned in, 31.
letters from W., 67–68, 74, 148–9, 156, 197, 225, 261, 263, 265–8, 304, 399.
London speech (1898), 76.
Memorandum for Herzl on Zionism in Russia, W.'s mention of composition of, 182, 185.

Palestine settlement, and, 76, 84.
Royal Commission on Alien Immigration, evidence before, 295, 299, 301, 306, **312–13**, 388, 401.
'Small Congress', attends (1902), 406.
Turkey, audience of Sultan (1901), 24, 28, 145, 148; complimentary telegram to Sultan, 219, 224–8; visits Constantinople for talks with government (1902), 232, 333, 350, 388, 406.
University project, and, 28, 229, 260–8, 287, 290, 294–5, 303–5, 316–17, 319, 334, 396, 399–400, 406.
'war on Herzlism', W. and, 23, 152, 170.
Weizmann, relations with, 19–25, 192, 276, 281, 283, 286; meeting with (Vienna, 1901), 183, 189–92, 197; letters from W., *see above*.
Youth Conference, attitude to, 23–24, 148, 151–3, 157, 159, 161–2, 165, 170, 176, 189–90, 197, 199; offer of financial assistance declined, 189.
Zionist Movement, founder of, 16, 36, 51; leadership of, 19–24, 70, 76, 80, 189–91, 206.
Hess, Moses, **84**, 196.
Hessiana society, 161, **196**, 200–4, 211, 223, 314.
Hibbath Zion ('Love of Zion') movement (Palestinians), 16, 18, **36**, 51–52, 55, 57, 61, 76, 376.
Hickel, Max, (Biog. Index **415**), 134, 138.
Hilfe ('Help') (mutual aid society), 49.
Hillel, Rabbi, 42, 356.
Hiller, Hirsch (Tsvi), **51**.
'Hirsch' (Tsvi), 38.
Hirsch, Baron Maurice de, 167.
History, W. on, 43.
Hitahdut ('Union'), **xxxiv**.
Hochschule, *see* Jewish University project.
Hol Hamoed, 77.
Holy Cross Day, 55.
Holy Days and Festivals, Jewish, 50, 66–67, 76, 171, 179, 182–3, 185, 187, 289, 311, 318 (*see also* New Year, etc.).
Homel, 75, 77, 117, 163, 180.
Homer, 42.
'Homogeneous elements', 99, 101, 114.
Hovevei Zion ('Lovers of Zion') societies, 16, 18–19, **36**, 37, 51, 72, 76, 114, 150, 206.

Idelevich, 98–99.
Idelson, Abraham, (Biog. Index **415**), 134, 183, 213, 344, 388, 390.
Idelson, Vladimir, 404–5.

Immigration into Britain, Herzl's evidence before Royal Commission, 295, 299, 301, 306, **312–13**, 388, 401; false report of Bill to exclude Jews, 301.

Information Bureau, Geneva, *see under* Democratic Fraction.

Information Bureau, Simferopol, **xxxiv**, 206, 299, 396.

Ingelheim, *see* Nieder-Ingelheim.

Inner Actions Committee, *see* Actions Committee: Smaller.

Intellectual development, W. on, 42, 44.

Intelligentsia in Zionist ranks, 150, 194, 200, 207, 255, 380.

Ismail (town), 150.

Israel, salvation of, 19; W. on, 31, 146, 179–80.

Israelitische Rundschau, 259.

Iza (Geneva student), 112.

Izzet Pasha, 260.

Jacobson, Victor (Avigdor), (Biog. Index **415**), 49, 134, 206, 299, 310, 350, 361, 370.

Jacubovsky, Ludwig, *Werther der Jude*, 137, 143.

Jaffe, Leib, (Biog. Index **415**), 163, 233, 235, 266, 329, 359, 388.

Jargon, synonymous for Yiddish (q.v.), 84.

Jargon Committee, 84, 91.

Jerusalem, 16, 36, 37; proposed Jewish University in, 27, 30, 260, 266.

Jewish Agency for Palestine, xxxi.

Jewish Colonial Trust (J.C.T.), **xxxiv–xxxv**, 70, 72, 76, 80–81, 192, 201, 206, **207**, 382; 'the Bank', 92, 201, 206–7.

Jewish Colonization Association (I.C.A.), 114–15, **167**, 208; proposed anti-I.C.A. campaign, 215–23, 233–6; Zionists antagonistic to, 312–13, 382.

Jewish history, W.'s lectures on, 166, 170.

Jewish Institution of Higher Learning, *see* Jewish University project.

Jewish language and literature, 194.

Jewish National Fund, **xxxv**, 206, 228.

Jewish people, regeneration of the, 16, 18, 20, 36–37, 122–3, 143–4, 231.

Jewish Reading-Room, **49**.

Jewish-Socialist Society, see *Hessiana*.

Jewish Statistical Bureau, *see* Statistical Bureau.

Jewish Students' Corporation, see *Kadimah*.

Jewish Tannaim, 42.

Jewish University project (*Jüdische Hochschule*, 27–30, 166–9, 255, 258, 260–9, 290–1, 301–6, 319, 372, 376–8, 382, 384, 391, 394, 396–407.

bibliography compilation, 264, 290–1, 298, 301, 317–18, 336.

brochure, see *Eine Jüdische Hochschule*, below.

Bureau in Geneva, 328, 331, 347, 363, 402, 404, 406–7.

collection of data from other universities, *see under* Universities.

direction by W. proposed, 331–2; V.K.'s attitude, 363–4.

Eine Jüdische Hochschule (brochure by Buber, Feiwel, and Weizmann), 28–29, 167, 230, 302, **303**, 305–6, 319–20, 333–6, 339, 347–8, 357, 361, 367, 369, 374–6, 382–5, 388, 390, 392–3, 398–9, 406; money for printing costs, 315–16, 321, 327, 333, 339, 344; proposed translations, 327, 334, 344, 351, 380.

Enquête, 264, 266, 282–3, 291, 360–1.

estimated budget, 260–3, 268, 290, 317.

funds for preparatory work, 269, 287, 305, 310, 321, 326–8, 331, 334, 356–7, 361–2, 366–7, 376, 383, 400, 402, 404, 406.

Jerusalem proposal, 27, 30, 260, 266.

Kharkov committee, 181, 404–5.

lectures, syllabus called for, 264–5, 290, 317.

Palestine or Europe?, 27–29, 195, 208, 229–30, 242, 263, 303, 406–7.

propaganda for, 167, 267–8, 331, 400.

Small Congress, proposed discussion by, 287, 290–1, 304, 334; held, 400, 406–7.

society, proposed founding of, 400.

W.'s career, possible effect on, 15, 30, 284, 331–2, 363–4.

W.'s preliminary 'Plan for a Jewish University', 28, **263**, 266, 269, 290, 294, 299, 301–3, 305, 316–17, 320, 327.

Jews (*see also* subject headings throughout the index), 'all Jews are responsible for one another', 352; conventional picture of, 79; servile inhibitions, 52, 85; traveller molested in train, 296.

Journal de Genève, 111, 140.

Journalists, W. on, 312, 388; International Congress (Berne, 1902), 315.

Judaism, 24, 36, 79, 346.

Jüdische Hochschule, Eine (brochure), *see under* Jewish University project.

Jüdischer Almanach ('Miscellany'), 298–9, 301, 335.

Jüdischer Verlag (Berlin publishing house), 27, **259**, 298–301, 320, 326, 357, 382, 406.

Juedische Volkszeitung, 48, 49.
Julian Calendar, xxiv–xxv, 34.
'Junker and Jew . . .' (quotation), 94.

Kadimah societies (*earlier* Russian-Jewish Academic Society, q.v.), 49, **87**, 102, 134, 139, 161, 202; Berlin, 86–88, 90–91, 117, 119, 129, 163, 194, 212, 220, 223, 235; Berne, 278; Cologne, 101; Heidelberg, 101; Kiev, 92, 99, 150, 383; Munich, 232.
Kahanovich, Yehuda, cited, 77.
Kahn, Leopold, 125.
Kanevsky (dentist), 150.
Karlsruhe, 104, 224, 234, 260, 262.
Karmin, 111.
Karolik, 200.
Karpovich, Peter, 92, 166.
Kasteliansky, Abraham, (Biog. Index **415**), 116, 298, 301, 336, 389.
Kattowitz (Katowice) conference (Upper Silesia) (1884), 16, 36, 37.
Katyushka, *see* Dorfman, Catherine.
Kaufman, Mr., 140.
Kazan, 163.
Khanevskaya (Geneva student), 94.
Kharkov, W.'s visits, 174, 178–83, 192–3, 325, 402–5; impressions of, 180–2, 403; interest in Jewish University project, 181, 356, 403–5; and Youth Conference, 117, 126, 200; University, 404; mentioned, 172–7, 326, 333, 339, 348, 396, 400.
Khatzman, Anna (Nyunechka) (sister of Vera), **121**, 366, 380, 388, 393, 403.
Khatzman, Issay (Isaiah) (Vera's father), 178.
Khatzman, Lev (Levchik, Lyolya) (brother), **121**, 295, 388.
Khatzman, Liubov (Liuba) (sister), **121**, 129, 131, 140.
Khatzman, Michael (Misha) (brother), **121**, 339–40, 388, 392, 402.
Khatzman, Rachel (Raya, Rayka, Rayechka) (sister), **121**; special greetings from W. in letters to V.K., 143, 274, 278, 287, 300, 304, 307, 328, 331, 339, 343, 366, 392 (and *passim*); W.'s request for photograph, 280, 330; and relationship between V.K. and W., 318–20, 327; W.'s gift, 340–1, 348–9, 365; knife found, 405.
Khatzman, Sophia (Sofochka) (sister), **121**, 295; her formal name, 292; special greetings from W. in letters to V.K., 186, 272–3, 279–80, 316, 339, 353, 357, 369, 403 (and *passim*); W.'s request for photograph, 280, 330; and

University project, 294, 380; correspondence with W., 303–4, 307, 325, 328, 333, 336, 343, 353, 358, 365, 368, 374, 378, 395; and relationship between V.K. and W., 318–20, 325, 327; W.'s gift, 340–1, 348–9, 365; inquiries about admission to Geneva University, 342, 377.
Khatzman, Sophia (sister-in-law of Vera), 388.
Khatzman, Theodosia (Vera's mother), 378.
Khatzman, Vera (later wife of Weizmann), (Biog. Index **416**), 14, 15, **84**; W.'s meeting with at Geneva (late 1900), 15, 84; his devotion apparent in the letters, 15–16; at Clarens-Baugy, 93; in Geneva, 115; at Rostov for summer vacation (1901), 119 ff., (1902), 269 ff.; difficulties of hastening return to Switzerland, 311, 332; return to Geneva (October 1902), 406.
Bible studies, 280, 307.
borrows money on W.'s behalf, 311, 314.
brothers, 121.
death (1966), xvi.
Democratic Fraction, copy of programme for, 399.
Eliasberg, signs letter to, 257.
German language and dialect, studies, 294, 296, 326, 328, 357.
health, 99, 241, 247, 329–30, 333, 351, 364–5, 380, 382.
Hebrew studies, 280, 307, 326.
Jewish traveller molested in train, witnesses, 296.
letters from W., preservation, xi, xxi; intimate form of address used, 84, 100, 102; text of letters, 84 ff. (*see* List of Letters p. 4 ff.).
medical student at Geneva, 84, 98, 332; examinations, 238–9, 241–2, 246–7, 249.
memoirs, *The Impossible Takes Longer*, cited, 84.
names, 'V.I.' (Vera Issayevna), 178; 'Revekka, Rivochka', 369.
new hat, 378.
photographs mentioned, 137, 141, 143, 280, 288, 303–4, 316, 330–1, 349, 353.
punishment by W., mentions of, 326, 364, 374.
relationship with W., question of telling the families, 311, 318–20, 325, 327, 332, 355; her sisters told, 327, 355; W. to meet her family, 333, 339–40, 354; W. visits her home, 403, 405.

Khatzman, Vera (*cont.*):
sisters, 121, 141, 143, 318–19, 325, 327, 355; W.'s requests for photographs, 280, 330.
University project, W.'s proposed direction of, 331–2; her attitude declared, 363–4.
'You have made me a Jewess', 318.
Zionism, and, 324, 326, 332, 352.
Kherson, Catherine Dorfman's home, 142, 159, 164, 273, 277, 298, 306, 322; W. visits, 173–4, 176, 187, 192, 298; Zionists, 159, 164, 175–6, 384; and University project, 299.
Khissin, Chaim, (Biog. Index **416**), 68, 77, 91, 102, 104, 195.
Kiev, 89, 92, 161, 163–4, 168, 172, 174, 177, 333, 389; Finance Office, xxxiv, 157; Jewish students, 116–18, 185; Motzkin in, 105–6, 110, 114–15; W.'s visit to, 400, 402, 404–5; and Youth Conference, 126, 128, 150, 200–1; Zionists, 61, 157.
Kiev *Kadimah* society, 92, 99, 150, 383.
Kiev Polytechnic, W.'s brother Samuel's efforts to gain admission, 147, 169, 171, 185, 344–5, 379, 383, 391, 393, 401.
Kilichek, *see* Weizmann, Mikhail.
Kishinev, 193, 201; pogroms (1903), 30; W. visits, 170–6, 192; Zionist Correspondence Centre, *see* Correspondence Centre.
Kissingen, 340, 348, 370.
Klausner, Fanya, 240.
Klausner, Joseph Gedaliahu, (Biog. Index **416**), 228, 233, 240, 261, 266, 396.
Kleinman, Moses, (Biog. Index **416**), 228.
Klugman, Dr., 130.
Koenigsberg, Anne, **85**, 89, 142, 154, 183, 188, 204, 219, 231, 253, 384; assistant to W., 117, 122, 139, 151, 199, 284, 299; at home in Russia during vacation, 139, 156, 173–4, 177, 271; W.'s letters handwritten by, 194, 198, 203, 210, 233; letters from W., 249–50, 282–3.
Kohan-Bernstein, Jacob, *see* Bernstein-Kohan.
Kokesch, Ozer, 148, 197, 287.
Kovno, 140, 200.
Krilov, allusion to, 352.
Krinkin, Dr. Boris (Meir), (Biog. Index **417**), 163, 187.
Kroll, Mikhail, 344.
Kunin, Lazare, (Biog. Index **417**), 49, 53, 62, 81, 194, 211–13, 219, 221, 237, 247, 378.
Kunin, Zina, 214.

Kursky, Franz, cited, 92.

Laboratory work, W.'s (see also Chemistry), 63, 70, 73, 134–5, 140, 146, 191, 227, 275–6, 281, 284, 332; joint discovery with Deichler, *see* Elberfeld.
Landau, Leopold, (Biog. Index **417**), 376.
Landsmannschaften, **xxxii**.
Languages, W.'s knowledge of, xi; W.'s native language, xxii.
Lausanne, 81, 97, 108–9, 197, 257, 287–8, 296, 330, 343, 365, 368–9.
Lavoisier, A. L., 42.
Lazare, Bernard (Bernard-Lazare), (Biog. Index **417**), 70, 115–17, 130–1, 136, 138, 140, 160, 225–7.
Laziness, W. on, 41–42.
Left-wingers, Jewish (*see also* Bund), 20, 104.
Leipzig, 91, 104, 106–7, 163, 293.
Leipzig Ziona Society, 101.
Letter-writing, W. on, 45–46; Motzkin on, 99.
Levin (unidentified), 384.
Levin (? Lewin) (Geneva student), 319.
Levin, Louis, 376.
Levin, N., **56**.
Levin, Shmarya, 49, 125.
Levinsky, 111.
Levinsohn, G. S., 404.
Levinson, Samuel, (Biog. Index **417**), 111, 294, 407.
Levitzky, N. V., **193**.
Leysin, W. at, 270–1, 273–5, 286–91, 294–320, 322–40, 343–69, 375, 384; described, 289, 330; picture sent, 330, 340.
Libau, 38.
Lichtenberger, Henri, **95**, 96–97.
Lichtenstein, Dr. Abraham (Biog. Index **417**), 67–68, 211, 391–2, 399; marriage to W.'s sister Haya, 68, 121, 139, 159, 161–2, 164, 171.
Lichtenstein, Haya (*earlier* Weizmann) (Biog. Index **426**), 68, 107, 171, 392; marriage, 68, 121, 139, 159, 161–2, 164, 171.
Lidochka, *see* Chernin, Lydia.
Lieberman, Meir, 399.
Lilien, Ephraim Moses, (Biog. Index **417**), 298–9, 316, 374, 378, 380, 382, 388.
Lithuania, 192, 194, 200, 276.
Litvaks, 192, 194.
Livshina (not identified), 98.
Locke, John, 42.
Lodz, 192.
Loewe, Heinrich (Elyakim), (Biog. Index **417**), 48; letter from W., 47–48.

London, 89; Fourth Congress held in (1900), 80–81 (*see* Zionist Congresses); W. in, 82–83; proposed demonstrations against I.C.A., 215; Herzl in, 295, 299, 301.

London University, 319.

Lorelei, 252.

'Love of Zion' movement, see *Hibbath Zion*.

'Lovers of Zion', see *Hovevei Zion*.

Luah Ahiasaf, 220, 255.

Lubzhinsky, Chaim (Biog. Index **418**), 50, 136, 140, 147, 165, 314, 378, 389.

Lubzhinsky, Fanya, *see* Weizmann, Fanya.

Lubzhinsky, Miriam (Mariya) (W.'s sister), (Biog. Index **426**), 136, 140, 179, 185, 276, 296, 314, 348, 378.

Lucerne, 234.

Lurie (family), **38**, 43.

Lurie, Bella, 44–45.

Lurie, Gregory, (Biog. Index **418**), 49, 51, 75, 393.

Lurie, Idel (Samuel), **38**, 43.

Lurie, Joseph (Biog. Index **418**), 53, 74, 134, 183, 209, 299–300, 344, 380.

Lurie, Ovsey (Hosea), (Biog. Index **418**), letters from W., 38–46.

Lurie, Saul (Sheyka, Sheychik), (Biog. Index **418**), 44, 100, 242, 276, 295, 298, 301, 327, 330, 340, 348, 369–70, 383; coached by W., 38, 40, 43, 45.

Machtet, G. O., **40**.

Mahorka (shag), 63.

Maimonides, W.'s father a student of, 36.

Mainz, 238, 240, 253–4, 364, 371, 373.

Makhlin, David, (Biog. Index **418**), 49, 58–59.

Malomian, 140.

Mamurovskaya, Maria, 339, 403, 405.

Mandelstamm, Max (Emanuel), (Biog. Index **419**), 404.

Mannheim, 261, 263.

Marmorek, Oskar, 148, 287.

Martigny, 144.

Marxism, Marxists, 180, 200.

Maryapol, 195.

Materialists, 80.

Mathematical science, 43, 53.

Matriculation examinations, 41, 47.

Maximov, Nicolai, **186**.

Mazkeret Moshé, 37.

Melamdim (teachers), 57.

Melitopol, 126.

Melnik, Joseph, **137**, 143.

Mesopotamia, 388.

Meyer and Company, 51.

Meyer-Cohen, Heinrich, **376**.

Mikveh Israel Agricultural School, near Jaffa, 208.

Military service, W. exempted from call-up, 50, 52–53, 55, 57; 'do military service' used as an expression, 171, 383.

Minkovich Yaakov Avigdor (of Pinsk), 55.

Minsk, 15, 76, 156, 333, 348, 382–3, 388, 393–400.

Minsk Conference (Russian Zionist) (1902), 308, 322, 339, 344–7, 350, 361, 367, 379–86, 390–8, 400–1; Democratic Fraction and, 394–8; organization report, 397–8; *Permanenz Ausschuss* (Standing Committee), 392, 395, 398; Praesidium, 396–7; W.'s five mandates, 384, 391.

Minsk *Poale Zion* group, **199–200**, 205–6.

Mir Bozhyi (Russian monthly), 92, 386.

Mirkin, Nahum, **61**, 92, 113, 200.

Miscellanies, Kiev project for, 92, 99, 101, 116, 118.

'Miscellany', see *Jüdischer Almanach*.

Mishnah (Oral Law), 42.

Mitava (Mitau), 38, 40–41, 43–45.

Mittweide, Saxony, 167.

Mizrahi movement (Rabbinical Party), **xxxii–xxxiv**, 345–6, 379, 384, 390, 395.

Mohilev, 76.

Moisey, *see* Weizmann, Moses (Moshe).

Monash, Berthold, **293**.

'Monograph' mentioned by W., 135, 140–2.

'Monomakh's cap' (expression), 245.

Montefiore, Sir Moses, 35, **37**.

Montpellier, 153.

Montreux, 94, 100, 247, 250, 271, 274, 330.

Morocco, Jews in, 37.

'Mortal little Jews', 31, 144.

Moscow, 117, 126, 128, 134, 200, 333, 380; secret police, 190.

Motol (Motole), Weizmann family's home, 13, 16, 35, **38**, 39, 45, 345; family moves to Pinsk, 48.

Motzkin family, home at Brovari, near Kiev, 53, 58, 61, 105.

Motzkin, Israel, **56**, 58, 83, 172; letter from W., 61–63.

Motzkin, Leo, (Biog. Index **419**), in Warsaw (1895), 53–55; moves from Berlin proper to Charlottenburg (1900), 47; leaves Berlin (March 1901), 99; visit to Russia, 101, 103, 105–6, 110, 114; returns to Berlin (May 1901), 101, 116.

'Collection of Writings' project, 62.

Motzkin, Leo (*cont.*):
  Democratic Fraction, and, 215–16, 222–3, 233–6, 247, 274, 300, 395; member of programme committee, 233, 266; entrusted with final revision of programme, 26, 272, 282, 286, 298, 305, 360; delay in production, 234, 272–4, 307–8, 310, 315, 327; final revised version of programme, 329, 334, 337, 345, 349, 352, 376; invitations and promises to write on, 220–1, 233, 255, 258, 360.
  examinations, 116, 135, 191.
  financial dealings with W., 47, 51, 53–55, 63–65.
  health, 62, 278, 322, 328.
  letters from W., 47 ff. (*see* List of Letters, p. 3); M. first addressed as Leo, 70.
  letters to W., none before 1901, 51.
  letter-writing, on, 99.
  meetings with W., in Brest-Litovsk (1895), 53–55, 57; Berlin (1901), 160, (1902), 245–6; Basle (1901), 214, 221; Minsk (1902), 393–5, 397–8.
  Minsk conference, attends, 380–1, 394–5, 397.
  Miscellanies project, 92, 99, 101, 116.
  relationship with W., 17, 19, 26, 99, 215–19, 221–4, 237, 245–7, 281, 358–62, 393–4, 398; first contact, 47; W. gives lessons to, 47; W. complains of letters not answered, 57–61, 63–65, 68, 70, 90, 93, 198; W.'s reference to 'persecution', 65.
  University project, and, 271, 282–3, 291, 336, 360, 393, 400.
  Verein, founder of, 49.
  Youth Conference, attitude to, 90, 92, 99, 101, 116, 118–19, 134, 138, 140, 160, 163, 212–14, 221; member of Bureau, 109, 114.
  Zionist Congresses, attends (1899), 74, 76; (1900), 83; (1901), 214.
Motzkin, Paula (Polya) (*earlier* Rosenblum), 22, **65**, 70–71, 75, 78–82, 90, 92–93, 101–2, 116, 194, 210, 237; letters from W., 65–68, 72, 82–83.
Mozyr, 77.
Munich, 91, 121, 139, 147, 156–7, 159, 204, 224, 272, 275, 297; Jewish students, 22, 87, 106–8, 232; W. visits, 99–110, 231–2; *Kadimah* society, 232; University, 262.
Munich conference (in preparation Zionist Youth Conference) (April 1901), 22–23, 88, 102, 104–8, **109**, 110, 112–15, 117–18, 126, 149, 157, 160, 195, 199, 248.

Mutual aid funds for students, *see* Aid funds.

Naphthazarin dyes, *see* Dyestuffs.
Narodniki, *see* Populists.
'National programme', *see under* Bund.
Nationalism, Jewish, 16, 18, 48–49, 56, 86–87, 92, 109, 312, 376.
Nauka i zhizn ('Science and Life'), 55.
Nemirovsky, Alexander, (Biog. Index **419**), 174, 404.
Nemser, Alexander, (Biog. Index **419**), 87, 102, 104, 109, 120, 147, 156, 159, 204, 216.
Neuberg, Mme, 46.
Neue Zeit (journal), 389.
New Year, Jewish, 50, 53, 75–76, 171, 177–9, 181–3, 289; liturgy quoted, 79, 138, 215–16.
Newton, Sir Isaac, 42.
Nicholas II, Czar, Coronation, 57.
Nieder-Ingelheim-on-Rhine, 71, 238, 241, 243, 245, 248–52, 348, 369, 372–3.
Nietzsche, Friedrich W., 85, 95, 123, 298, 323, 328, 340–1, 348, 365.
Nikolayev, 85–86, 154, 172–4, 177, 192–3, 282.
Nonsense, W. on, 95.
Nordau, Max, (Biog. Index **419**), 115.
Nossig, Alfred, (Biog. Index **420**), 125.
Nurock, Mordekhay, 397.
Nyon, 94.
Nyunechka, *see* Khatzman, Anna.
Nyusechka, *see* Ratnovskaya, Anna.

Odessa, 136, 140, 147, 230, 242, 256, 400; Ahad Ha'am's home, 18, 62, 112–13, 123, 132, 148, 150, 227, 256; *Hibbath Zion* Committee, 52; *Hovevei Zion* delegation in Paris, 114–15, 148, 150; technical school, 167; W.'s visit, 165, 170–6, 192–4; and Youth Conference, 117, 126, 134, 150, 200–1; Zionism in, 189, 192–4.
Okhrana (Moscow secret police), 190.
Olmütz, 134.
Oral Law, 42.
Order of Ancient Maccabaeans, xxxiv.
Ost und West (Jewish monthly), 387.
Ottoman Public Debt, 145, 388.
Oxner, 314.

Pale of Settlement, 28, 94, 127, 167, 184–5, 384.
Palestine:
  conditions in, proposed investigation for report to Youth Conference, 104, 109, 159–60, 163.
  cultural work in, 382.

Democratic Fraction and, 25.
Jewish Colonial Trust ('the Bank') and, 207.
Jewish colonization, xxxi, 16, 18–19, 27, 36, 61–62, 72, 76, 112, 114–15, 167, 208; on collectivist lines, 196, 203, 382 (see also Jewish Colonization Association).
Jewish Labour movement, 389.
Jewish national home, xxxi, 37, 84, 86, 91, 312, 382.
Jewish University in, proposed, 27–29, 195, 229, 242, 263, 303, 406–7 (see also Jewish University project).
land acquisition in, xxxv, 27, 382.
Socialist state, proposed, 133, 201.
theoretical study of, 207.
Turkey and, 29, 72, 76, 388.
Palestine Committee, 150.
Palestine Foundation Fund, xxxv.
'Palestinians', see Hibbath Zion movement.
'Pan', 40.
Paris, 255, 314; Odessa Committee delegation meets Rothschild in, 114–15, 148, 150; Peace Conference (1919), 17; W.'s visits, 67, 82, 113–16, 118, 124–5; and Youth Conference, 128–31, 140; Zionist students, 104, 140.
Party-system, xxxii, 26, 346.
Pasmanik, Dr. Daniel, (Biog. Index 420), 101, 109, 176, 189–90, 209, 270.
Passover, 98, 107–8, 256–7.
Patents, in names of W. and Deichler, 88, 135.
Paulsen, F., cited, 291.
Pawnbrokers, 64, 111.
Peace Conference (Paris, 1919), 17.
Perelman, Aaron, (Biog. Index 420), 104, 173, 216, 239–40.
Peretz, J. L., 52.
Periodical, creation by Youth Organization proposed, 207, 229; proposed Democratic Fraction publication, 256, 259, 299–300.
Permanenz Ausschuss (Standing Committee, xxxii, 392, 395, 398.
Personality cult, 381.
Peter the Great, 44.
Pevsner, Samuel Joseph, (Biog. Index 420), 220, 235, 255, 357, 360.
Philosophers, 42.
Photographs mentioned, of V.K., 137, 141, 143, 280, 288, 303–4, 316, 330–1, 349, 353; of her sisters, 280, 330; Berlin group, 140; of W. and others, 187–8, 304, 313, 316, 319, 330, 335, 337–8, 344, 367, 378, 380, 385, 388.

Pick, Herman (Chaim), (Biog. Index 420), 349.
Pictet, Raoul, (Biog. Index 421), 372, 376.
Pines, Meyer, 190, 199.
Pinkus, Felix Lazar, (Biog. Index 421), 248–52, 271, 273, 278, 284, 298, 301, 310–11, 314–15, 354, 365, 368–9; W. letter handwritten by, 268; and 'Bioux affair', 368, 376; postscripts by and greetings from, 248, 250–2, 257, 270, 368, 391.
Pinsk, W.'s schooldays in, 13–14, 38–47; his family move to, 19, 48; W. returns for year (1895–6), 49–61; factory work, 49, 51; W. visits (1897 and 1898), 65–66, (1899), 75, (1901), 156, 160, 162 ff., (1902) plans, 311, 318–19, 325–6, arrives, 379 ff.; Sophia Getsova in (1899), 72–73, 77.
fires affecting Jews (1901), 119, 127–8, 140, 162, 169.
Heder established in, 56–57.
intelligentsia, 48–49, 51, 166.
Jewish settlements, member of British Royal Commission visits, 401.
Jews in, 51–52, 59.
literary circle, 52, 58.
Secondary School (High School), W. attends, 13–14, 16, 35, 38, 47, 391.
University, 117.
wedding of W.'s sister, see Lichtenstein, Haya.
W.'s unpleasant impressions of, 39, 48, 51–52, 67, 383, 390–1.
Pinsker, Dr. Leo, 36, 78.
Pisemsky, A. F., 40, 43.
Plato, 42.
Plekhanov, George, 20–21, 79, 111, 209–10.
Plotsk, 150.
Poale Zion movement, xxxii, xxxiv, 199–200, 205–6.
Poets and poetry, 42.
Poland, 80, 358; Jews, 94, 401; students in Geneva, 225–6.
Polesie Railways, W. on, 39.
Political training, students and, 186.
Political Zionists, 19, 22–23, 27, 72–73, 75–76, 125.
Pollak, Adolf, 189.
Poltava, 173–4, 178, 326.
Poltava, Battle of (1709), 44.
Polya, see Motzkin, Paula.
Populists movement, 194.
Portugalov, Gregory, (Biog. Index 421), 134, 151, 204.
Postcards, W.'s dislike of, 293, 297, 300, 302, 307.

Pozner, C. V., cited, 167.
President of Zionist Organization, **xxxiii**; W. relinquishes presidency (1931), xii; again president (1935), xii.
Press, and Democratic Fraction, 220; Jewish, 142, 226–7; W. and non-Jewish press, 387–8; Zionist, 104.
Privat-docent, W.'s qualification as, 67, 73.
'Pro-Armenia', 226.
Propaganda, meetings, 67, 69; use of synagogues for, 76, 165–6, 170, 173, 180; role of Youth Organization, 104, 206–8; W.'s campaigns in Russia, (1901), 172–86, 192; (1902) plans, 237, 297, 299, 308, 310, 326, 329, 332–3, 335, 358, 361, in Russia, 379, 395, 400–6; Democratic Fraction and, 229.
Purim (Festival), 46, 240.
Pushkin, allusion to, 245.

'R' (form of address), **35**, 96.
Rabbinical Party, see *Mizrahi*.
Rabinovich, Jacob, **98**, 199.
Rabinowitz, Michael, 403.
Radical group (*Fraktion*), proposed, 116, 118–19.
Ratner, Mark, 389.
Ratnovskaya, Anna (Nyusechka), at Geneva, **95**, 97; at Clarens-Baugy, 100, 105, 107–12; at Geneva, 121, 135; in Rostov, 144, 171; at Geneva, 238, 248; in Rostov (1902), 273, 288, 293, 301–2, 339, 402; at Geneva, 407; father's name Zelik-Solomon, 100; letters from W., 104, 251; photograph with V.K. mentioned, 288; W.'s special greetings to, 100, 107, 121, 132, 273, 293, 325, 328, 366, 407 (other greetings, *passim*).
Raya, Rayka, Rayechka, see Khatzman, Rachel.
Reading, importance of, 40–41, 43–44.
'Reb', **35**, 96.
Regional leaders, conference advocated by W., 66; circulars distributed by, 383; and Praesidium, 396; reports to Minsk conference, 396–7.
Registration-fee for members of Zionist Organization, see Shekel, The.
Rehovoth, W.'s home in, xiii.
Reich, Arieh, **68**, 71, 78; letters from W., 68–69, 83–84.
Reines, Rabbi Isaac Jacob, 345–6, 395.
Religion, and cultural activities, 395; Democratic Fraction and, 381; 'practical religion', 133; 'Religious' Zionists, 24, 72, 125, 180, 190, 199, 346; Youth Conference and, 23–24, 190, 199.

Renan, Ernest, 356.
R.E.N.F., *see* Russian-Jewish Academic Society.
Rhine, river, 252.
Rhône, river, 303, 330.
Rivochka, *see* Getsova, Rebecca.
Rosenbaum, Simon (Shimshon), (Biog. Index **421**), 125, 346, 396–7.
Rosenblum, Paula (Polya), *see* Motzkin, Paula.
Rosenfeld, Morris, 299, 301, 335.
Rosenfeld, Samuel, 204.
Rostov-on-Don, Vera Khatzman's home town, 15–16; V.K. home for vacation (1901), 119 ff.; W. promises to visit (1901), 128, 130, 141; plans changed, 178–9, 183–4, 325; V.K. home for vacation (1902), 269–70 ff.; W. plans visit to (1902), 325–7, 333, 339–41, 354, 363, 380; W. visits and meets V.K.'s family, 403, 405.
  Geneva students from, 94, 95, 98.
  Youth Conference, and, 129, 171.
  Zionists, 129, 131, 143, 145–6, 171, 295, 302, 326, 387–9.
Rothschild, Baron Edmond (Abraham Benjamin) de (Biog. Index **421**), 37, 114–15.
Rothschild, 1st Lord (Nathaniel Mayer), (Biog. Index **422**), 312–13.
Rothschild, 2nd Lord, 312.
Rothschild agricultural colonies, 114–15, 167.
Rothstein, Isaac, (Biog. Index **422**), 387–8, 396–7, 402.
Rumania, 83, 167, 226, 301.
Russia:
  assassinations, of Czar (1881), 16; of Minister of Education (1901), 92, 166.
  British study of Jewish problem in, 401.
  Czarist régime, xxxiv, 111, 143, 186.
  Democratic Fraction conference, proposed holding in, 308.
  educational facilities, restrictions on Jews, 14, 28, **166–7**, 168–70, 182, 185, 229, 255, 268.
  Hovevei Zion societies, *see that title*.
  Jewish students, 151, 168, 182, 185, 268; in Geneva, 186, 225–6.
  Jews, 37, 91, 94, 146, 312; proposed memorial at Czar's Coronation, 57; Bund and, 86–87.
  'King' of, 36.
  Pogroms, 16, 30.
  Propaganda campaigns in, W.'s,

(1899), 75–77 ; (1901), 172–86, 192 ; (1902), 297, 299, 308, 310, 329, 332–5, 358, 361, 395, 400–4, 406.
revolution, possible, 112.
revolutionary movement, 20, 79, 95, 193, 208.
Social Democrats, 20–21, 86, 88, 95, 208, 210.
Universities, 168, 360 ; restriction on Jews, 14, 28, **166–7**, 169, 229, 255, 264, 268.
Weizmann's visits (1901), 139, 145, 154–6, 159–69, 192, 325 ; (1902), plans, 297, 310–11, 318–19, 327, 329, 332–9, 343–5, 356, 358, 360–1, 364–70, in Russia, 378 ff. (*see also* Propaganda campaigns, above).
Zionists, **xxxiv**, 31, 66, 78–79, 186, 192, 206, 335, 346 ; conferences (1898), 113, (1902), *see* Minsk conference ; societies, 242 ; 'theoretical groups', 140, 146, 151, 157 ; W.'s mention of memorandum on, 182, 185 ; youth groups, 140.
Russian-Jewish Academic Society (*Verein*, R.E.N.F.), 17, **48–49**, 55–56, 58, 60–61, 87 (later *Kadimah* societies, q.v.).
Russian language, 200, 209, 379 ; W. and, xi, xxii, xxiii ; transliteration, xxiii, **xxx** ; W.'s tutor, 35.
Russkoye Bogatstvo, 385–7.
Ruthstein, 111, 143.
Ryezhitsa, 163.

Sahli, Professor Hermann, 106.
St. Bernard Pass, 144.
St. Blasien, 126.
St. Petersburg, 204, 333, 400–1 ; referred to as 'Peter', 302 ; Russian Minister shot by student (1901), 92, 166 ; and Youth Conference, 126, 128, 131, 134, 151, 200.
Salisbury, Lord, 303.
Salkind, Jacob Meir, (Biog. Index **422**), 190, 199.
Salomon (unidentified), 98.
Salzmann, A., 197, 199.
Sarah (unidentified), 82.
Schachtel, Hugo, 336.
Schapiro (Munich student), 106.
Schapiro, Professor L. B., 167.
Schimmer (*later* Britschgi), Regina (Ina), (Biog. Index **422**) ; letter from W., 376.
Schmidt, M., 134, 183, 188.
Science, W.'s interests and work (*see also* Chemistry), 13–14, 30 ; and Zionist activities, 14–16 ; his aptitude for, 14 ; W.'s scientific writings, xix, xxi.

'Science and Life', *see Nauka i zhizn*.
Scientific basis for Zionism, 389.
Scientists, work for mankind, 42.
Scientists' meeting (1902), 322.
Seder service, 107.
Senator, Hermann, 376.
Separate Unions, **xxxiv**.
Sepey, 320.
Sforim, Mendele Mokher, 37.
'*Shabes*-Zionist', 131.
Shakespeare, William, 42.
Shapira, Professor, 27.
Sheinkin, Menahem, (Biog. Index **422**), 216, 233, 262, 359.
Shekalim, 206.
Shekel, The, **xxxi**, 66.
Shel'menko (invented name), 39–40.
Shereshevskaya (student), 111.
Sherman, Isaac (Biog. Index **422**), 104, 231.
Sherman, Moses (Biog. Index **423**), 173, 177.
Sheychik, Sheyka, *see* Lurie, Saul.
Shivat Zion (Return to Zion), 16, 36.
Shmarya, *see* Friedman.
Shneerson (*later* Feiwel), Esther, (Biog. Index **423**), in Geneva, 85, 142, 154, 160 ; taking examinations, 132, 145, 151 ; leaves Geneva for Russia, 85, 139, 163, 166, 188 ; continues studies in Berlin, 139, 188, 201, 245, 314, 376 ; at Leysin, 287, 289, 298, 301, 303–4, 306–7, 319–21, 330 ; at Lausanne, 368–9 ; moves to Bioux, 367–8, 376.
  assistant to W., 112, 117, 127, 132, 139, 156, 163.
  Democratic Fraction, and, 284.
  Feiwel, and, 298, 304, 314, 319–21.
  greetings and postscripts to W.'s letters, 142, 252, 220, 384 *passim*.
  Herzl signs letter to, 156, 158, 159.
  mentioned, 183, 186, 358.
  Nietzsche, W.'s copy of, 85–86.
  photograph mentioned, 338, 385.
  Pinkus and, 314, 354, 376.
  Syrkin's *Hessiana*, and, 201–2, 314.
  W.'s exchange of politics with, 354, 357.
  W.'s letters handwritten by, 112, 366.
'Shpak, Pan', 40.
Shriro, Samuel (Biog. Index **423**), 321, 326, 334, 339, 356–7, 366–7, 383, 400, 402, 407.
Simferopol, **xxxiv**, 206, 299, 370.
Simon, Leon, cited, 18–19, 62.
Skorchev, 111.
Slonim, 77.

Slousch, Nahum, (Biog. Index **423**), 228.
'Small Congress', *see* Zionist Congresses: Annual conference.
Smoking, W. and, 63, 137, 307, 324.
Social-Democrats, 20–21, 86, 88, 95, 111, 123, 133, 193, 201, 208, 210.
Social revolution, 231.
Socialism, 79-80, 88, 109, 176; Nietzsche and, 123; scientific, 389; Zionist Socialists, *see that title*.
Socialist Congress, International (1900), 88.
Socialist state (Jewish), proposed, 133, 201.
Société Helvétique des Sciences Naturelles, 322.
Socrates, 42.
Sofochka, *see* Khatzman, Sophia.
Sokolovsky, Shlomo Tsvi, 16, **35**, 36–38; letters from W., 35, 38.
Sokolow, Florian, 314.
Sokolow, Nahum, (Biog. Index **423**), xxxiii, 314, 358, 394, 407.
Sonechka, Sonia, *see* Getsova, Sophia.
'Sons of Moses', see *Bnei Moshe*.
Soskin, Evgeny (Selig), (Biog. Index **424**), 48.
South America, 167.
Standing Committee, see *Permanenz Ausschuss*.
Stapelmohr's (bookshop), 142–3.
Statistical Bureau, Jewish, 229, **264**, 334, 336, 360–1, 406.
Stiff, Nahum, Biog. Index **424**.
Strick, Mordekhai, **51**.
Student colonies, 209, 224, 230.
Students' Zionist societies, proposed formation of Association, 158.
Stupnitzky, Saul Isaac, (Biog. Index **424**), 68, 74, 407.
Swedes, 44.
Switzerland:
Cultural Commission, W. as Swiss representative on, 229, 358, 406.
electoral districts, 71.
Jewish University in, proposed, 28–29, 263, 303.
Radical Party, 226.
Social-Democratic Party, 201.
Technikum, 167.
universities, 230, 255, 262, 290.
W. in, 13–14, 16 (*see also under* Geneva, etc.).
Zionism, 67–68, 78, 234, 272, 278.
Symbolist literature, 257.
Synagogues, use for Zionist propaganda, 76, 165–6, 170, 173, 180; 'armchair politicians', 299, 301.

Syria, xxxv.
Syrkin, Nahman, (Biog. Index **424**), 49, 62, 158; lecture and pamphlet on Zionist Socialists, 133, 161, 193, 200, 203, 211; founds Zionist-Socialist Society *Hessiana* (q.v.), 21, 161, **196**, 197, 201, 203–4, 314; and Youth Conference, 197, 200, 204, 211; initiates discussions leading to formation of *Cheirus* group and to Democratic Fraction controversy, 215–23, 233–6, 239, 242.

Tabernacles, Festival of, 50, 66, 76–77, 179.
Taganrog, 402.
Talmud, 42, 352.
Talmud Torah, 57.
Tannaim, Jewish, 42.
Tarle, M., **154**, 159, 161, 173.
Tatare's Club, 86.
Tchmerinsky, Rachel-Leah, *see* Weizmann.
Technical schools and colleges, proposed, 28, 166–7, 263.
Technical *Verein*, 49, 56.
Tepper, Kalman, 193.
'Theoretical groups' (study-groups), 140, 146, 151, 157.
Thorn, 339, 365, 370, 377.
Tiflis, 333, 400.
Timber trade, 314, 339.
'Tirumoprutkevich, Mr.' (invented name), 39.
Tobacco smoking, *see* Smoking.
Tog, Der (New York Yiddish newspaper), 35.
Toldy, *see* Feiwel, Berthold.
Trachtenbergs, the, 122, 128.
Trade unions, 138, 221.
Trial and Error (Weizmann's Autobiography), xxix; cited *passim*.
Tribune de Genève, 226.
Trietsch, Davis (David), (Biog. Index **424**), 298, 374, 392, 407.
Troost, L., 143.
Tschernikovsky, Saul (Shaul), (Biog. Index **424**), 240.
Tschlenow, Yehiel, (Biog. Index **425**),115.
Tulin, Abraham, 35.
Turgenev, I. S., 40, 43.
Turkey:
finance, 145, 388.
Herzl, audience of Sultan (1901), 24, 28, 145, 148; complimentary telegram to Sultan, 219, 224–8; visits for discussions, 232, 333, 350, 388, 406.

Palestine, and, 29, 72, 76, 388.
Sultan, *see* Abdul Hamid.
Tyomkin, Vladimir (Zeev), (Biog. Index **425**), 150, 159, 161, 164, 172, 235, 315, 370.

'Uganda' scheme, 30.
United States, 37, 167, 208, 237, 313, 332.
Universities, collection of data regarding, 260–6, 282–3, 290–1, 298, 301, 319, 360; establishing of new, 229–30; Russian restrictions on admission of Jews to, 14, 28, **166–7**, 169, 229, 255, 264, 268; Jewish University project, *see that title*.
Upper Silesia, 16, 36.
Ussishkin, Menahem Mendel, (Biog. Index **425**), 115, 299, 327, 345–6, 387, 397, 403, 406–7; letter from W., 398.

Vannovsky, General, 166.
Vassilevsky, L., 181.
Veit, Sigmund, (Biog. Index **425**), 69, 71; letter from W., 71.
Verein, the, *see* Russian-Jewish Academic Society.
Verochka, Veronchik, Verusya, *see* Khatzman, Vera.
Vevey, 97, 144.
Vienna, 134, 272, 317, 374; letters addressed to Herzl in, 67 *passim*; W.'s plans for visits, 139, 179, 183, 185, 188–90, 337, 339, 363, 399–400; W. visits (1901), 24, 189–90, 197, (1902), 333, 406–7; Actions Committee meeting, 189–90; Small Congress meeting, 406–7; Zionist Central Office in, *see* Central Office.
Vilna, 111, 126, 167, 201, 345, 401.
Virgil, 42.
Visiting-cards, used by W. for communications, xxiii.
Vitebsk, 76.
Vitya, 82.
Voegtlin, Carl, (Biog. Index **425**), 280.
Volga region, 163.
Volodka, *see* Idelson, Vladimir.
Voskhod (Russian-Jewish weekly), 83, 117–18, 136–7, 143, 146, 152, 170, 190, 396.

Wandering Jew, 31, 144, 179.
Warburg, Otto, xxxiii.
Warsaw, 220, 255, 299–300, 314, 401; Motzkin in (1895), 53–55; W.'s plans for visits, 179, 183, 185, 188, 311, 333, 339, 364, 369, 377; W. visits, 113, 164, 192, 344, 378–80, 384; and Youth

Conference, 126, 134, 200; proposed technical school, 167.
Wasserman, Jacob, 85.
Weber, Georg, **40**.
Weinberg (*later* Herzfeld), Esther (Esfir, Fira), **94**, 257; student at Geneva, 94, 98, 111–12, 122; at Clarens-Baugy, 94, 105; at Rostov (1901), 132, 141; returns to Geneva, 238; examinations, 241; travelling to Rostov (1902), 339–44, 353–4, 357–8, 365, 373–4; arrives, 375.
death of brother, 185.
greetings and postscripts, 94, 96, 100, 240, 248, 402 *passim*.
Herzfeld, relations with, 94, 281, 383.
letters from W., 241–2, 251.
W. tells her of his relationship with V.K., 340.
Weinstein, Sonia, **253**, 298, 305, 385.
Weintraub, A., 158.
Weisgal, Meyer W., Foreword by, ix–xvii.
Weissman, David, (Biog. Index **426**), 195.
Weizmann, Anna (Hana) (sister), (Biog. Index **426**), 147, 379.
WEIZMANN, CHAIM (*see also* subject headings throughout the index):
birth date, xxx, xxxvi.
career, tug-of-war between scientific and Zionist interests, 14–15; possible sacrifices in cause of Jewish University project, 15, 30, 284–5, 331–2, 363–4.
concise table of dates, **xxxvi–xxxvii**.
dowry mentioned, 391.
education, 13–14, 35, **47**.
engagement to Sophia Getsova (q.v.) broken off (1901), 15, 155, 159, 168, 219, 272, 355.
financial circumstances, in Berlin, 47, 61–65; dealings with Motzkin, 47, 51, 53–55, 63–65; difficulties, 111, 122, 128, 131, 147, 275, 284–9, 325; money from V.K., 302, 311, 314.
health, 'very unwell' (1897), 63; sister's letter quoted (1900), 107; to see doctor (1901), 106–7; lung haemorrhage (many years later) traced to privations of his first months in Germany, 107; eyes hurting (1901), 187, 189; strain on (1901–2), 15–16, 199; 'my nerves are completely shattered', 201; mentioned in letters, 205, 224, 244, 265, 290, 351, 356, 358, 401; visit to doctor: 'general weakness and exhaustion' (1902), 403.

Weizmann, Chaim (*cont.*):
    joint author of *Eine Jüdische Hoch-schule*, see *under* Jewish University project.
    photographs of, *see* Photographs.
    self-analysis, 120.
Weizmann (*earlier* Lubzhinsky), Fanya (sister-in-law), 165.
Weizmann, Feivel (brother), (Biog. Index **426**), 36, 165.
Weizmann (*later* Dounie), Gita (sister), (Biog. Index **426**), 185.
Weizmann, Haya (sister), *see* Lichten-stein.
Weizmann, Masha (sister), 379.
Weizmann, Mikhail (Yehiel Mikhal) (brother), (Biog. Index **426**), 318, 379, 391.
Weizmann, Minna (sister), 379.
Weizmann, Miriam (Mariya) (sister), *see* Lubzhinsky.
Weizmann, Moses (Moshe) (brother), (Biog. Index **426**), 35, 147, 162, 164, 171, 345, 383, 390–1.
Weizmann, Ozer (father), (Biog. Index **427**), 98, 169, 183–5, 276, 316, 322, 339, 344, 348, 365, 370–2, 377–9, 391; timber-transportation business, 35, 38, 171, 185, 314, 339, 348.
Weizmann (*earlier* Tchmerinsky), Rachel-Leah (mother), (Biog. Index **427**), 35, 170–1, 185, 318, 372, 378–9, 391.
Weizmann, Samuel (Shmuil) (brother), (Biog. Index. **427**); efforts to gain admission to Kiev Polytechnic, 147, 169, 171, 185, 344–5, 379, 383, 391, 393, 401.
Weizmann, Vera (wife): in this volume, *see* Khatzman, Vera.
Weizmann Institute of Science, Reho-voth, xiv.
Welt, Die, official organ of Zionist Organ-ization, 72, 151, 157, 211, 213, 306, 312, 401; yellow cover, 151; edited by Feiwel, 151; taken over by Buber, 183; cited, 67, 88 *passim*; letters from W., 77–78.
Weltanschauung, Jewish, 80.
Wertheimer, Joseph, Chief Rabbi of Geneva, (Biog. Index **427**), 255.
White Russia, 192, 200, 276.
Wiesbaden, 348.
Winterthur, 167.
Wintz, Leo (Juda Leib), (Biog. Index **427**), 58.
Wissenschaftlich, one of W.'s favourite words, 30, 264.
Wolffsohn, David, (Biog. Index **427**), xxxiii, 333, 350.

Women, International Congress of (Ber-lin, 1896), 62.
Workers' League proposal, 118.

Yad Chaim Weizmann (Chaim Weizmann National Memorial), xiii, xvii, xxi.
Yasinovsky, Dr. Isidore (Israel), (Biog. Index **428**), 36.
Yavneh, 28, 230.
Yekaterinoslav, 126, 172, 184, 326–7, 333, 387, 398.
Yelizavetgrad, 150, 172, 177–8, 182, 192–3, 370.
Yema, *see* Hasudovsky, Benjamin.
Yeshiva students, **190**.
Yevrei, *see* Brandt, Boris.
Yiddish language and literature, 180, 194; W. and, xi, xxii, xxiii, 91; W.'s native language, xxii; 'jargon', 84, 91; society for dissemination of Yiddish literature, see *Bildung* Society.
Yiddisher Arbeiter (Bund organ), 87.
'Young Zionists', 200, 228; restriction on freedom to criticize leadership, 197, 199.
Youth, manifesto to Jewish (1901), 133, 137.
Youth Conference (1901), *see* Zionist Youth Conference.
Yud, Der (Yiddish weekly), 299–300, 404.
Yukhnovichi, 39.

Zakkai, Johanan b., 230.
Zelik-Solomon, 100.
Zermatt, 327.
Zhitlovsky, Chaim (Biog. Index **428**), 92.
Zhitomir University, 117.
Zina, *see* Brailovsky, Agnes (Zina).
Zion (monthly journal), 56, 62.
Zionism and Zionist activities of W., 13–20 *passim*; W.'s place in Move-ment, 30–31; 'Zionism does now exist', 178.
Zionist Congresses, **xxxi–xxxii**, 17, 129, 382; change to two-year intervals, **xxxii**, 269.
    Annual Conference, in non-Congress year (*Jahreskonferenz*) ('Small Con-gress'), **xxxii–xxxiii**, 269, 283, 287, 290–1, 304, 334, 350, 358, 400; held in Vienna (1902), 29, 350, **406–7**.
    Basle Office, 68, 78.
    Vorkonferenzen, 74.
    First Congress (Basle, 1897), **xxxi**, 19, 21, 27, 65, 78, 143; statement of aims, *see* Basle Programme.
    Second Congress (Basle, 1898), 21, 65–67, 73, 75, 78, 92, 158, 201; Syrkin's criticism of, 133, 203, 211.

Third Congress (Basle, 1899), 19, 21–22, 71–78, 92, 229.

Fourth Congress (London, 1900), 22, 24, 80–84, 125, 206, 229 ; W.'s article on, 101, 117–18.

Fifth Congress (Basle, 1901), plans, 125, 135, 138, 145–6, 162, 170, 176, 178–9, 189, 195–6, 206–7, 219–20 ; delegates, 204–5, 210–11 ; held, 25–27, 214–15, 225–6, 228–9 ; letter from W. to Bureau, 204–5 ; Cultural Commission set up by, *see* Cultural Commission.

Sixth Congress (Basle, 1903), 313.

Twelfth Congress (Carlsbad, 1921), xxxiii.

Seventeenth Congress (Basle, 1931), xii.

Zionist Correspondence Centre, Kishinev, *see* Correspondence Centre.

Zionist Democratic Fraction, *see* Democratic Fraction.

Zionist Federations, **xxxiv**, 206.

'Zionist Jews', 355, 364.

Zionist Organization :
Ahad Ha'am and, 19.
Central Office, *see* that title.
controversies within Movement (1899), 72–73, 75, 92.
Democratic Fraction and, 228–9, 382.
Herzl's leadership, *see under* Herzl.
Jüdischer Verlag taken over by, 298.
official organ, see *Welt, Die.*
parties within, formation of, 116, 200, 263, 327, 346, 391.
precursor of, 16–17, 36.
President, *see* that title.
structure and constitutional machinery, **xxxi–xxxv.**
Syrkin's criticism of, 133, 203, 211, 220–2.
Youth Conference and Organization and, 23–24, 112, 124, 129, 203, 206–8.

Zionist Socialists (see also *Hessiana*), 21, 153, 161, 193, 196–7, 200–1, 203–4, 314 ; 'Manifesto to Jewish Youth', 133, 137.

Zionist Students' Conference, *see* Zionist Youth Conference.

Zionist Youth Conference (Basle, December 1901), original idea for students' conference, 21, 86–87, 90–92, 158 ; organization of (preparatory conference, *see* Munich, below), 21–23, 99–102, 126–7, 160–3, 171, 187 ; agenda and arrangements discussed, 112–31, 134–40, 142, 150–1, 153, 189–90, 195–7, 200–6, 209, 211–13 ; agenda circulated, 209, 212–14 ; conference held, 23–24, 86, 117, 138, 163, 178, 183, **214** ; results, 23–27, 214, 216, 228.
campaign against, 131, 136, 189–90, 196–7, 199, 200.
Circular letter on, 94, 102, 209.
Correspondence Bureau, Munich, 109, 120, 139.
Democratic Fraction, *see that title.*
financial assistance declined from Herzl, 189.
Herzl, urges cancellation, 23–24, 148, 151–3, 157–9, 161 ; his more favourable attitude towards, 162, 165, 170, 176, 189–90, 199.
minutes, question of printing, 234, 350–1.
Motzkin's attitude to, 90, 92, 99, 101, 116, 118–19, 134, 138, 140, 160, 163, 212–14, 221.
Munich Preparatory Conference (April 1901), 23, 102, 104–8, **109**, 110–18, 126, 149, 157, 160, 195, 199, 248.
Organization Bureau, Geneva, 23, 108–9, 112–14, 120, 125–30, 148–9, 151, 153, 162–3, 190, 194–5, 198–200, 203–4, 209, 211–12 ; W. elected head, 23, 109, 126 ; assistants at, 112, 117, 127, 132, 139, 156, 163.
pre-Conference pamphlet, proposed, 150, 159, 161, 164, 166.
Protocol, 25–27, **214**.
Russian main language, 200, 209.
venue and time, choosing of, 126–7, 170, 178, 195.
W. and its organization, 21–27, 101, 109, 126–7, 160–3, 179, 185.

Zionist Youth Organization, proposed establishment, 24–25, 104, 109, 113, 116–18, 123–4, 130, 132, 134, 138–9, 190, 206–9 ; not agreed by Youth Conference, 24–25.

Zlocisti, Theodore, 358.

Zolotarev, A., (Biog. Index **428**), 150.

Zubatov, S. V., 190.

Zurich, 81, 100–1, 103, 158, 201, 351, 364, 407.

Zweig, Egon, (Biog. Index **428**), 134.

PRINTED IN GREAT BRITAIN
AT THE UNIVERSITY PRESS, OXFORD
BY VIVIAN RIDLER
PRINTER TO THE UNIVERSITY